The Essential Cook Book

First published in 1980 as *The Cook Book* by
Mitchell Beazley Publishers
This new edition first published in 1997 by Conran Octopus Limited,
37 Shelton Street, London WC2H 9HN

Published in 1997 and distributed by
Stewart, Tabori & Chang,
a division of U.S. Media Holdings, Inc.
575 Broadway, New York, NY 10012

Distributed in Canada by
General Publishing Company Ltd., 30 Lesmill Road
Don Mills, Ontario, M3B 2T6, Canada

Distributed in open market territories by
Grantham Book Services Ltd.
Issac Newton Way, Alma Park Industrial Estate
Grantham, Lincolnshire, NG31 9SD, England

COMMISSIONING EDITOR: Suzannah Gough
PROJECT EDITOR: Kate Bell
GENERAL EDITOR: Norma MacMillan
ART DIRECTION: Helen Lewis, assisted by Sue Storey
ART EDITOR: Alistair Plumb
PRODUCTION: Jill Beed, Suzanne Bayliss

Library of Congress Catalog Card Number: 97-66191

ISBN 1-55670-602-2

Printed and bound by Mohndruck Graphische Betriebe GmBh
Origination by Mandarin Offset, Singapore

10 9 8 7 6 5 4 3 2 1

Page 2: Rhubarb and Raisin Pie   *Page 6:* Salade Niçoise

The Essential Cook Book

The Back-to-Basics Guide to Selecting, Preparing,
Cooking, and Serving the Very Best of Food

Caroline Conran

Terence Conran

and

Simon Hopkinson

Recipe Photography by James Murphy

Additional Recipes: Rick Rodgers

Editorial Consultant: Judith Sutton

Stewart, Tabori & Chang
New York

Contents

HOW THE BOOK WORKS

The three main sections chart the progress of food from the market to the kitchen to the table. All sections are cross-referenced—for example, when reading about scallops in Part One, the reader will find, at the side of the page, cross-references to the preparation of scallops (also in Part One), the recommended specialist equipment for dealing with scallops (Part Two), and recipes including scallops (Part Three). This system allows the book to be used on many different levels. Novices can explore any subject in depth, while experienced cooks can easily find whatever information they require.

Introduction

This book is about food, and is intended as a reference book for cooks. It is significantly different from the many recent cookbooks by restaurant chefs, in that it concentrates solely on the terms and practices of home cooking. This is *the* book for home cooks who want practical information and a straightforward approach, and who like food cooked beautifully but without pretension.

It is concerned with food in all aspects—it is about raw ingredients and their preparation, and about the cooking and presentation of food. Fortunately, where food is concerned, the material is always fascinating. Food has a marvelous sensuality about it; even the simplest raw vegetable has a vitality and beauty of its own. The colors, texture, and smells of food are all stimulating to the cook, inspiring a desire to cook in the same way that a writer wants to write or a painter to paint. And, like a painter or writer, the cook never knows exactly what will emerge at the end. Good ingredients are so individual—one tomato varying from the next according to the sun, the soil, the season—that there are constant surprises to keep up interest.

Many variations can be made on each theme too. Every time a dish is cooked, there is a feeling that it can be improved upon, that it can be done a little differently from the time before. But to add this dimension to cooking, the cook's response must be both intuitive and well informed; the more one understands the subject, the more one's feeling for ingredients will develop, and the surer one's instincts will become. Therefore the wider the knowledge, the more interesting and successful will be the experiments. This book sets out to provide a knowledge of a vast range of different foods, so that the cook—like someone with an extensive vocabulary—can be fluent and confident. Take, for example, olive oil: you may go to the supermarket and buy an olive oil that has been refined, treated, and blended in order to keep the price to a minimum, and which therefore cannot afford to have much character. But, if you first find out about olive oil and then try different qualities and pressings with their strong individual flavors, you will be in a much better position to judge what the true olive oil taste is like, and which particular oil would be best suited to your purpose. Whether it is oils or cheeses, this book will encourage you to learn to hunt for and try individual products sold in specialty shops or markets, and to recognize the quality of foods not manufactured for mass appeal, but produced individually by people who are passionate about maintaining their high standards, and whose products have a unique character of their own.

As a matter of fact, all good food starts with the shopping—certainly living out of the freezer is convenient, but it does away with a good deal of enjoyment. The seasons and their differences are part of the experience of life. If you eat frozen green peas throughout the winter, where is the pleasure when the first young peas appear in the spring?

Obviously it is foolish not to freeze or preserve food when it is in abundance, and would go to waste otherwise, but does it make sense to ship or fly food many thousands of miles so that we can eat it all the year through? And surely shopping for fresh food in the market is a much more inspiring and entertaining activity than burrowing in the freezer for anonymous-looking frosty packages.

The recipes we have chosen for this book will provide a basis for everyday cooking. With these recipes, which for the most part are very simple, you can cook throughout the year. There are flights of culinary fantasy—stuffed breast of veal for example, and Mussels with Coconut Milk and Chiles—but we have, for the most part, tried to give recipes at a level that the busy cook can live with. Nowadays, with life getting more and more complicated, it is good to be both quick and simple whenever possible—simple surroundings and simple food, with the occasional elaborate dish for days when you want to glory in the whole process.

Simplicity does not mean dullness. There are countless enjoyable tastes, flavors, and experiences available to people who take the trouble to find and try them. This book is intended to help you to do so.

The purchase and preparation of food

Fish

Fish is a food of tremendous character and charm. To a cook who has true feeling for raw materials, there is great satisfaction to be found in the beauty of form, the shimmering colors of scale and skin, and the distinctive flavors and textures of fish of all kinds.

It pays to look beyond the inevitable cod, haddock, and sole—although these are no less good for their predictability. But the seas, rivers, and lakes are filled with an extravagant variety of fish, each with its own character. It is comparatively easy to obtain a thick slice of swordfish or a fresh trout, but more of a triumph to find a beautiful sea bass, a colorful red drum, or a fresh halibut steak. Cooking becomes more of a pleasure if one can make an occasional experiment or discovery, and among fish there are endless discoveries to be made.

Choosing fish

There is no excuse for bad fish being offered for sale any more, now that modern transportation practices make it easy to ship fish for long distances in a freshly caught state. What we are more likely to see in fish shops these days are fresh fish that have been in the shop too long, or fish that have been in and out of the freezer several times, thawed out and sold as "fresh." Unfortunately, the telltale signs of a poorly thawed-out fish are less easy to detect than those of a spoiled fish. If you are an expert, and are lucky enough to live near a large fish market, the best fish to buy are those you see in a crate, packed in ice and obviously straight from the docks or wholesale market. These will have been chilled—not flash-frozen—immediately after they were caught.

However, with frequent visits to the fish market, it soon becomes easy to

recognize the differences between good fresh fish that have simply been chilled, old fish, and thawed-out frozen fish. Don't be afraid to sniff the fish if you are suspicious, or to ask pertinent questions. Here are the signs to look for.

Fresh fish A really fresh whole fish looks almost alive and ready to swim away. It gleams, its color is bright, its flesh is firm yet elastic to the touch, and the skin shines with a viscous slime that is clear and evenly distributed. Bright, bulging eyes indicate freshness; dull and sunken eyes with red rims mean the fish is old. The gills should be clean and bright red. And fresh fish smells fresh and pleasant; the more offensive the odor, the older the fish.

It's easier to determine the freshness of a whole fish than of fillets and steaks, but there are still some signs to look for when purchasing these. As with whole fish, fillets and steaks should smell only pleasantly of the sea. The flesh should glisten and look almost translucent, and it should look firm, not mushy, without any gaping. Fillets and steaks from white fish should be pure white; those from dark-fleshed fish like tuna should not have shimmery "rainbows," which are a sign of age.

Frozen fish Commercially frozen fish, usually in fillets, are sold from freezers in shops and supermarkets. But there are other fish that have been frozen less efficiently and thawed out, and these are sometimes sold with no sign to indicate the previously frozen state. This is an unfortunate deception. Whole fish that have been flash-frozen at sea as soon as they are caught can be quite good, but these less well treated thawed-out fish are usually imported and/or have traveled

some distance. As long as you are aware of this, they need not be shunned—often they are the only chance you will have of tasting unusual fish from far away.

To detect a badly thawed-out fish, look for a sad appearance and flabby, dull skin that has lost its natural slime and shininess. If a fish has suffered badly from freezing and thawing, it will be unpleasantly watery and will have a soft, cottony texture.

Storing fish

There is only one essential piece of advice on storing fresh fish—don't. If you must keep it overnight, put it, well wrapped in several layers of newspaper, in the coldest part of the refrigerator. If you have the chance to buy fresh mackerel or sardines, or other fresh small oily fish, eat them on the day of purchase; if this is not possible, put them in the freezer overnight.

Freezing fish Most home freezers do not act fast enough to prevent large ice crystals from forming in the flesh of a fish. These destroy the delicate tissues, resulting in the loss of texture, juices, and flavor. So if you want a freezerload of fish as a standby, you would be advised to buy commercially frozen fish, which should keep for 2 to 3 months.

There is a way to preserve a degree of texture and flavor using a home freezer, and this procedure is called glazing. Place the cleaned and gutted whole fish, unwrapped, in the freezer set to the lowest temperature. When the fish is reasonably solid, dip it into cold fresh water. A thin film of ice should instantly form. Return the fish to the freezer immediately and, when the ice has frozen solid, repeat the process two or three times, until the fish is completely encased in a good coating of ice. Then store the fish in a freezer bag in the usual way.

Fish that best withstand the freezing process are those with fine-grained flesh, such as the sole and its flatfish relations. Salmon, and other fish with flesh that falls into flakes, can be frozen but are decidedly nicer fresh; the flesh becomes a little soft with the freezing and thawing process. The shorter the time any fish remains frozen, the better it will be.

Frozen fish should be defrosted before cooking. If it is cooked still-frozen, the outside may be overcooked before the inside has had time to thaw out.

A fresh fish will have bright, bulging eyes and skin that shines with a clear, natural slime (RIGHT).
A fish that has dull, discolored, sunken eyes and lifeless skin is well past its best (FAR RIGHT).

SALTWATER FISH

Fish from the sea can be roughly divided into those that have white flesh and those that are oily. Within these broad categories exist several natural culinary groups, such as the flatfish, the cod and its relatives, the sea basses and breams, and the oily salmon, mackerel, and herring. The great ocean fish, such as tuna and swordfish, have a category of their own, and there is a section for the multitude of fish, such as red snapper and skate, that do not fall easily into categories.

Flatfish

All flatfish are fine-fleshed, white, delicate, and lean, and two members of this group—turbot and Dover sole— rank in the top echelon of all sea fish.

Dover sole The true Dover, or Channel sole is perhaps the cook's perfect fish, a fact that is reflected by its prominence on restaurant menus in Europe and in a few select restaurants in America. The flesh is firm, white, and delicate and keeps well (in fact, sole tastes better if it is 24 hours old). It lends itself to almost any cooking method, and is excellent with many sauces, but is at its finest simply cooked on the bone and served with butter, parsley, and lemon. Only poor-quality fish needs dressing up. *Buying guide:* there is no true sole in American waters—although a number of other flatfish, such as Pacific flounder, may be labeled sole—but imported Dover sole is sometimes available in larger cities. Dover sole is available fresh all year in Europe. Buy whole if serving plainly broiled or panfried, or in fillets if serving in a sauce (it is hard to see and deal with bones in a fish covered with sauce). Each fish provides four good fillets. The price of Dover sole has become inordinately high; however, a 7- to 8-ounce sole is enough for one person, although vegetables will be needed if it is served plain. If you order filleted Dover sole from the fish market, take the head and bones with you—they are the basis of an excellent fish stock. *Best cooking methods:* broiled, sautéed in butter, or filleted and poached in sauce.

Flounder In America, the flounder family includes the excellent fluke (also known as summer flounder), the winter and yellowtail flounders, the gray sole, and the fine-textured petrale sole. (Gray sole, also called witch flounder, may be called witch or Torbay sole, or pole

filleting and skinning flatfish 26
trimming flatfish 26

Court-Bouillon 246
Fillet of Sole Meunière 274
Fish Stock 246

Brill

Plaice

Dover sole

Dab

European flounder

Yellowtail flounder

Turbot

Petrale sole

Gray sole

Halibut

Fluke

flounder in Britain.) These are all quite good eating when freshly caught, and are often used in recipes that call for Dover sole or turbot, since they respond to the same methods of cooking. The European flounder, or fluke, is a fish of poor reputation. It has a dark brown, distinctly rough skin and a pale belly, and little of the other flatfishes' delicacy of flavor. A better choice in England might be the fish labeled lemon sole, which is the American yellowtail flounder. A soft-textured but pleasant fish, it is considered to be slightly superior to plaice.
Buying guide: year-round for American flounder, except fresh summer flounder; winter months for European flounder. Sold whole and in fillets.
Best cooking methods: a good-quality thick flounder can be poached like turbot; a thin one should be sautéed gently in butter, broiled, or filleted and poached in sauce.

Turbot Turbot is one of the finest of sea foods. Its flesh is the firmest and most delicate in flavor of all the white fish, and this has to be paid for dearly these days. Despite this, any opportunity to buy it should not be missed. Unfortunately, "real" (European) turbot is almost never found in American markets at any price. The fish usually sold as turbot is in fact Greenland turbot, which has a much softer flesh; it can be substituted in recipes calling for turbot, but the result will not be the same. Recognize European turbot by its knobbly brown skin and awesome size: a fully grown specimen can weigh up to 28 pounds. In the heyday of the turbot, in the nineteenth century, a huge fish could be poached whole in a special pan, a *turbotière*, designed for the purpose. These days, most of us can only manage to cook chicken turbot (a young turbot weighing 2 to 6 pounds) in this way, substituting a large pan for the turbot kettle. If you can't manage a whole turbot, you can buy fillets or steaks.
Buying guide: imported turbot can on rare occasions be found in large American cities; in Europe, it is available all year, sold whole, in fillets, and in steaks. The flesh should be creamy white; a bluish tinge means that it is old.
Best cooking methods: turbot suits any cooking method, but is best simply poached or broiled and served with a parsley-and-butter sauce, or hollandaise. It is also very good in a salad.

Halibut A giant among flatfish, the halibut can grow up to 6 feet long and is not, in fact, particularly flat. It is a medium to darkish brown on top and pearly white underneath. It has almost as good a flavor as turbot. Atlantic halibut is usually considered finer than Pacific halibut because its flesh is firmer and its flavor somewhat more delicate, but the Pacific is also very good.
Buying guide: available all year. Halibut is almost always sold as steaks, but it is sometimes seen as fillets. Small halibut (weighing less than 3 pounds) may sometimes be sold whole and make a very good-looking lunch or dinner for four to six people. Avoid frozen halibut, which is dull and dry.
Best cooking methods: panfry, poach, or bake, and serve with a good sauce—lobster, parsley, or hollandaise. Halibut is also good when it is eaten very fresh, as in *seviche*.

Plaice Dark brown with russet spots on its upper side and white on its underside, plaice is a mainstay of every British fish-and-chip shop, its mild, soft flesh heavily encased in batter and deep-fried. It is certainly a perfectly palatable fish when served in this way, particularly when it is quite fresh. European plaice, not to be confused with the American dab, and often labeled plaice, turns up in some fish markets in the United States; it can be substituted in most recipes that call for sole or other flatfish fillets.
Buying guide: available all year, sold whole or, more usually, in fillets.
Best cooking methods: deep-fry in a good batter, or coated in beaten egg and bread crumbs, and serve with tartar sauce; or poach and cover with a cheese or parsley-and-butter sauce.

Dab, sand dab The American dab, or sand dab, which is sometimes labeled American or Canadian plaice, has reddish-brown skin and can grow up to 2 feet in length. Its fillets have reddish lines running through them. The European dab is not the most exciting of fish to eat, although its flesh is soft, fragile, and easily digested. It can grow up to 12 inches long, but is usually somewhat smaller than this.
Buying guide: available all year; European dab is best in autumn and winter. Dab is sold whole or in fillets.

Best cooking methods: grilled whole; fillets are very good sautéed in butter or coated in beaten egg and bread crumbs and then panfried.

Brill A very good European fish akin to turbot, the handsome brill has a mixed tweed coloring and is smaller than its cousin. Its flesh is a little softer and not so gelatinous, but it is sweet and delicate to eat. Brill is available in some larger U.S. fish markets.
Buying guide: available all year, sold whole or in fillets.
Best cooking methods: recipes for turbot, halibut, and sole suit brill, and it is one of the fish of choice for the French seafood stew called *matelote*.

Megrim A small, yellowish-gray, rather transparent fish, megrim is common in Britain, where it is also known as whiff, sail-fluke, West Coast sole, white sole, and lantern flounder. Not a particularly tasty fish, it has the advantage of being cheap, and makes a reasonably good contribution to fish soup.
Buying guide: rarely, if ever, seen in U.S. markets; in Europe, available autumn and winter, sold whole or in fillets.
Best cooking methods: as for sole or plaice, but probably best filleted and panfried.

The cod family
The members of this large family of white-fleshed fish—which includes such cornerstones of the fishing industry as cod, haddock, and pollack—keep their succulence best when they are lightly poached or steamed, panfried in batter, or bathed in a good, light homemade sauce. However, cod in particular is quite a versatile fish and will stand up well to most cooking processes, as long as it is treated delicately.

Cod and scrod The cod is a handsome fish and has a dappled skin of brown, greenish-gray, or gray. Once taken for granted as the fisherman's bread and butter, it is becoming more scarce due to overfishing in northern European and American waters. Too often it has been overcooked until dry and gray, and hidden under a blanket of sauce. When treated with care, cod proves to be very fine, but it must be very fresh to be first class. The flesh is succulent and breaks into large flakes—a really fresh fish will produce a cheeselike curd between the flakes, as salmon does. The cod has an excellent roe—used taramasalata—and its liver produces a disagreeable-tasting but effective vitamin supplement. Scrod is not, as many think, the name of a fish but rather a term that is used for young cod and other smaller members of the cod family. An adult cod can weigh as much as 80 pounds; small cod (also known as codling in Britain) are about 1 ½ to 2 ½ pounds.

Buying guide: available all year. Fresh cod is sold mainly as steaks and fillets. If you are able to choose a cut, pick the middle, which combines the tenderness of the tail with the flavor of the shoulder. Never buy fillets or steaks if you can see either yellow or pinkish patches on the flesh. Frozen cod, although reliable, lacks the flavor of really fresh cod, but is certainly a better buy than cod of dubious quality.

Best cooking methods: the flesh of cod falls naturally into large, firm flakes and keeps its texture well. It is splendid poached, and excellent in fish soups or chowders and in fish cakes. Also bake, broil, or panfry or deep-fry and serve with good homemade sauces such as fresh tomato salsa or tartar sauce. In addition to the traditional slices of lemon, *aïoli* (mayonnaise heavily flavored with garlic) is a particularly delicious accompaniment to a whole poached cod (cod is robust enough to take strong Mediterranean flavors). In order to whiten and tenderize the flesh of this fish, it is a good idea to rub it with a cut lemon half an hour or so before cooking.

Haddock Fresh haddock is sometimes preferred to cod by those who declare its texture and flavor finer, but it is really no better a fish. Haddock has a fresh marine flavor and a light, firm texture, and it is blessed with fairly good keeping qualities. It looks similar to cod in appearance, but has a grayer skin, larger eyes, and a marked black lateral line. Haddock is also smoked to make finnan haddie; in Britain it is often used for fish and chips.

Buying guide: available all year, but best in winter and early spring; generally sold in fillets.

Best cooking methods: any of the cooking methods described for cod can also be used for haddock.

Hake An elongated, deep-water member of the cod family, hake appears on some French menus as white salmon (*saumon blanc*), and is familiar all over the United States under a variety of names, including ling and white or red hake. Silver hake, from the East Coast, is a particularly fine fish that also goes under the name of Atlantic or American whiting (not to be confused with the European whiting, a lesser fish). Hake is popular in Spain, fried in a coating of beaten egg or served in an *escabeche*—a cold hors d'oeuvre of fried fish in an herb marinade—but it is sadly becoming an increasingly rare sight in the fish shops of northern Europe. No opportunity should be missed to buy it, though it does tend to be expensive. It has tender, soft, pinkish flesh, somewhat lighter than that of cod, with a delicate flavor, and the advantage of possessing few bones, which are fairly easy to remove.

Buying guide: fresh hake must be very fresh, or it may have an unpleasantly soft texture. It is sold whole, in fillets, and in steaks. It is also available frozen.

Best cooking methods: deep-fried in batter; panfried; baked with pine nuts, bread crumbs, and cheese; or poached and served on a bed of spinach or sorrel mixed with fresh cream.

European whiting This is a common but unexciting European fish not found in American waters (in the United States whiting is another name for the much finer silver hake, above). It is gray and white with a pointed head and backward-slanting teeth. A really fresh whiting is quite good, light, and easily digestible, but a tired and traveled specimen will be dry, dull, and tasteless. In France, whiting is known as *merlan*; in Spain, it is called *merluzzo*.

Buying guide: in Europe, available all year round but best in winter. Sold whole, or in fillets.

Best cooking methods: flaked and used in fish cakes; puréed for mousses and mousselines; poached and served with a julienne of vegetables; or coated with beaten egg and bread crumbs—which will improve the texture—and panfried.

Arbroath smokie 30
finnan haddie 29
salt cod, stockfish 31

Garlic Mayonnaise 259

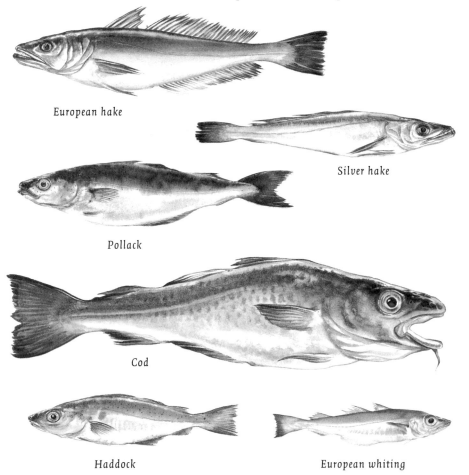

European hake

Silver hake

Pollack

Cod

Haddock

European whiting

Pollack Although pollack does not have quite the firmness and succulence of cod or haddock, it is a well-flavored fish with good texture, and one of its best features is its price. Atlantic pollack has been underappreciated until recently, no doubt in part because of its somewhat off-putting grayish flesh—which, happily, whitens considerably during cooking, even more so if rubbed generously with lemon juice. Pollack is one of the mainstays of the American market; one reason for this is that the heavily fished Alaskan pollack is a major source of Japanese surimi, or imitation seafood, as well as of frozen fish patties and fish sticks. It is also known as coley, saithe, and coalfish, both in the United States and in Britain; in France, it is called *lieu*.
Buying guide: available all year. Pollack is usually sold in fillets or, less often, as steaks; it is rarely sold whole.
Best cooking methods: in fish cakes and fish soups, or as for cod.

Some less-sought-after members of the cod family

Ling When this is dried, it is known as *lutefisk* or *lutfisk* and is popular in Sweden boiled and eaten with great quantities of butter, where it is also a traditional Christmas dish. (Do not confuse the European ling with the North American lingcod, which is not a cod at all but is in fact a member of the greenling family.) Ling has firm white flesh and can be used in any cod dish.

Cusk is almost always sold in fillets, usually labeled as scrod.

Pouting is a fish found in Britain. It should be eaten very fresh indeed as its main claim to fame is that it spoils very quickly—for this reason it is sometimes known as "stinkalive."

Bass, porgy, and grouper

Firm and white-fleshed, these fish go well with strong Mediterranean flavors—saffron, fennel, olive oil, tomatoes, white wine, and garlic. They are delicious when grilled whole or baked together with olive oil and fresh herbs.

Sea bass Whether one of the North American varieties—striped bass, black sea bass—or the beautiful silver bass of the Mediterranean and warmer northern European waters, sea bass is the ideal fish for a splendid meal at home. It is just the right size for a small family and has delicately flavored milky flesh.
Buying guide: available all year. Sold whole or in steaks and fillets.
Best cooking methods: bass up to 2 pounds can be grilled whole—in France they are cooked over charcoal with herbs and a handful of fennel twigs is put on the fire. Bake larger fish, and bake or poach steaks and fillets. Bass is also excellent in salads or *seviche*, or steamed on a bed of seaweed. Serve with mayonnaise or a butter sauce; with *salsa verde*, the piquant Italian sauce of parsley, lemon, and anchovy; or with a fresh tomato sauce.

Porgy and other bream American porgies are members of the large bream family that has dozens of species throughout the world. Some species are distinctly better than others: the finest of these is the Mediterranean gilt-head, with its gold spot on each cheek and its compact body. Most of the porgies in the United States, which are generally smaller than the European bream, come from the East Coast or the Caribbean. Red porgy is one of the tastier varieties; sheepshead porgy and scup are common types. Red porgy, called sea bream in Britain, is also found in the Mediterranean. The red bream is the bream found in northern European waters, a large fish usually sold in fillets and recognizable by its rosy-gray skin. All bream have rather coarse but juicy flesh and a pleasant taste that suits fairly strong accompanying flavors. They must be scaled—ask your fishmonger to do this for you, or cook the fish with its scales intact and carefully remove them with the skin just before serving.
Buying guide: available all year but best in autumn. Sold whole or in fillets.
Best cooking methods: season well and grill or broil, or bake in foil, or roll in cornmeal or flour and panfry briskly in oil. Make two or three slashes on each side if cooking porgy whole, so that the heat can quickly penetrate the thicker parts, ensuring that the fish cooks evenly.

Grouper A delicacy in Mediterranean countries, grouper is not widely available in northern Europe, which is a pity because its flesh is particularly firm and well flavored. The United States enjoys a number of varieties—red grouper is found from Virginia down to Florida, and the Gulf of Mexico has black grouper and the Nassau. Yellowmouth is also common along the East Coast.
Buying guide: sold whole, weighing up to 10 pounds, and in steaks and fillets.
Best cooking methods: panfrying or broiling, or otherwise as for sea bass.

Porgy

Striped bass

Mediterranean gilt-head bream

European silver bass

Red grouper

Mediterranean grouper

Oily fish and small fry

Absolute freshness is essential—all oily fish are inedible when anything less. The traditional accompaniments of mustard for bluefish and for herring and, in England, the tart green gooseberry for mackerel, help to counteract their natural oiliness.

Bluefish Familiar along America's East Coast in summer and in the warm waters around Bermuda, the bluefish can be identified by the blue-green sheen along its back. Although popular in New England, bluefish suffers from a reputation as a strong-tasting, oily fish. Part of its ill repute stems from poor handling; because of its high fat content, bluefish does not keep well. When you see very fresh bluefish, it's well worth buying. The delicate flesh is rather soft in texture and goes best with sharp accompanying flavors—lemon juice, capers, or mustard.
Buying guide: best in spring, summer, and autumn. Sold whole—2 to 3 pounds is a manageable size, but it can be up to 10 pounds—or as fillets.
Best cooking methods: brush the fish with melted butter before broiling or grilling, bake with a little white wine and butter, or poach whole and serve accompanied by melted butter.

Mackerel The mackerel is one of the easiest of all fish to recognize—the taut, steel-blue skin, mottled with blues and greens and a pattern of blackish bands, is so smooth it looks almost enameled. The belly is pearly-white, the inside of the mouth black. If the natural markings have lost their brilliance and the fish does not positively shine up at you, do not buy it. The pink-tinted flesh is firm, richly flavored, oily, and rich in vitamins. In Europe, mackerel roe is considered to be a delicacy, and can be served along with the fish or mixed into a stuffing.
Buying guide: at its best in April, May, and June. Mackerel is sold whole, usually weighing up to about 2 pounds, which will serve two people as a main course or four as a first course, or in fillets.
Best cooking methods: whole mackerel can be broiled, grilled over a charcoal or wood fire, or poached in white wine; broil or panfry fillets. Mackerel is also good stuffed. Sauces for mackerel include mustard and horseradish.

Horse mackerel This somewhat off-putting name, and others such as jack mackerel or, in Britain, scad or round robin, belongs to a group of fish regarded as poor man's mackerel—rather unfairly to the mackerel, since although the horse mackerel has much in common with the true mackerel, it is not related. (In fact, it is a member of the jack family.) The horse mackerel lacks the fine markings of the true mackerel and is not considered a quality fish, being rather coarse and bony.
Buying guide: sold whole—a large fish will feed two people, and a small one, one person; also canned.
Best cooking methods: treat as mackerel, or braise.

Herring Once plentiful, popular, and cheap, herring is rapidly becoming less available because of overfishing. This is a pity because it is a tasty fish and rich in protein, fat, iodine, and vitamins A and D. Fresh herring is popular and common in Europe, but in the United States, it is usually sold pickled or smoked.
Buying guide: in the United States, fresh herring is occasionally available at large fish markets; in Europe, it is available all year but best from spring to autumn. Choose large, firm, slippery herring.
Best cooking methods: panfry or score, brush with fat, and grill or broil. Never discard the roe, which is very good.

Smelt These silvery, semitransparent little fish (about 7 inches long) are anadromous, spawning in fresh water, and so are found not only along both the Atlantic and Pacific coasts, and in

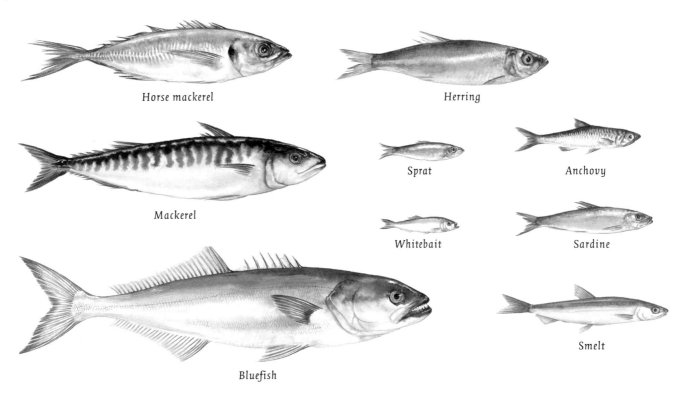

Horse mackerel

Herring

Mackerel

Sprat

Anchovy

Whitebait

Sardine

Bluefish

Smelt

European waters, but also in the Great Lakes, and other freshwater bodies. Smelt have a delicious scent when very fresh—some say of cucumber, others of violets—but this disappears very rapidly, so if they seem scentless when you buy them, it doesn't mean that they are old. They need delicate handling—leave the head and tail on and clean them through the gills.

Buying guide: best in winter and spring, but there are good and bad years, so buy smelt whenever you see them—it may be a long time before you see them again.

Best cooking method: dipped in milk and flour and deep-fried.

Sardine Fresh sardines are a delight, but they must be fresh. They travel badly, and so are usually only found close to where they are caught, such as the Mediterranean coasts of France and North Africa (the true Mediterranean sardine is named after the island of Sardinia); but they are appearing more often in East Coast markets. (The Atlantic sardine is actually a herring.) When you do find them fresh, they are simplicity itself to prepare. Cut the head almost through from the backbone and pull; as the head comes off, the intestines will come with it.

Buying guide: at their best in spring. Fresh sardines are sold whole; sizes vary, so judge by eye how many you need.

Best cooking methods: panfry in olive oil, or coat lightly with salt and olive oil and grill or broil. Eat them with halved lemons, chilled rough wine, and crusty bread.

Anchovy Seeing fresh anchovies for the first time, with their slim bodies and sparkling silvery greenish-blue skin, comes as something of a surprise when one's only previous acquaintance with this useful fish has been as canned fillets. Fresh, they can be distinguished from sardines by their narrower bodies and protruding upper jaws. To enjoy their delicate flavor at its best, they should be straight from the sea, which ideally means the Mediterranean, although varieties appear in northern European and North American waters.

Buying guide: sold whole.

Best cooking methods: panfry or broil as for sardines. Anchovies are also delicious marinated in olive oil and lemon juice with garlic, or boned and panfried with garlic and parsley.

Sprat Although unfamiliar in America, these are worth attention if only for their superabundance in European waters, which means that they are very cheap. Tiny silvery fish, they look rather like small herring but are shorter and stouter.

Buying guide: a winter fish, said to be best when the weather is frosty.

Best cooking methods: sprats are very oily, so are best when broiled; or they can be dusted with flour and panfried in a dry pan sprinkled with salt.

Whitebait The small fry or young of herring and sardines—or in fact almost any tiny, almost translucent specimens, including silversides—whitebait are the most delicious little fish. Bright, silvery, and slender, they are scarcely more than $1\frac{1}{2}$ inches long, and have for a long time been one of the summer treats of the British. In the United States, they can be found on both coasts. Whitebait are eaten whole, so there is no need to clean them—simply rinse them gently.

Buying guide: traditionally available from February to August. Allow about 4 ounces per person.

Best cooking method: the best and only way to cook whitebait is to dip them in milk, shake them in a bag of flour, and then deep-fry them. They should be so crisp that they rustle as they are put on the plates. Serve with lemon wedges and fresh bread and butter.

The great fish

The great ocean fish make firm, meaty eating. Their flesh is inclined to be dry, so it is a good idea to marinate it in olive oil and lemon juice or white wine with herbs before cooking.

Tuna and bonito Found in all the world's warmer waters, the powerful and beautifully shaped tuna family is related to the mackerel, and includes the bluefin, albacore, yellowfin, and skipjack. Bonito is another close relative. When you see fresh tuna, don't be put off by a reddish color—it improves during cooking. Tuna needs plenty of oil and seasoning, and care must be taken not to overcook it, or it will be dry. Bonito can be treated as either tuna or mackerel.

Buying guide: available all year. Sold in steaks; occasionally very small fish are filleted. Avoid tuna steaks with very dark marks, as these indicate bruising.

Best cooking methods: grill, broil, panfry, or bake in steaks, basting often with seasoned oil; or slice very thin into small scallops, dust with flour, and sauté gently in butter and oil for 2 to 3 minutes on each side. Serve with fresh tomato salsa or Italian herb sauce.

Swordfish Familiar in Mediterranean waters and popular in North America as "the steak of the sea," the swordfish is only a very occasional visitor to northern European waters. It makes delicious eating, but the flesh is close-grained and tends to be dry, so it is often marinated in wine, oil, and herbs before cooking.

Buying guide: available all year round. Sold in steaks.

Best cooking methods: grill or broil and serve with plain or herb butter or tomato sauce; or sear in butter and then bake in a sauce. Swordfish is also excellent when used to make kebabs.

Sailfish and marlin Well-known to American sport fishermen, these majestic fish are spectacular fighters and prized trophies. But if you don't want to put them on the wall, they make very good eating.

Buying guide: marlin is commercially fished in Hawaii, but not elsewhere; in other parts of the world, both fish are occasionally sold as steaks in ports near the fishing grounds.

Best cooking methods: as for swordfish.

Opah Whatever you call this splendid fish—moonfish or sunfish (not to be confused with the freshwater sunfish), mariposa, or kingfish—you should never miss a chance to sample it. It lives deep in the Atlantic, Pacific, and Indian oceans; most of the opah seen in the United States comes from Hawaii or California. The skin reflects blue, rose, silver, and gold, and the texture of the flesh may have a markedly different taste—and color—depending on which part of the fish it comes from.

Buying guide: should you ever see opah for sale at a fish market, ask for steaks or scallops.

Best cooking methods: bake, panfry, broil, or poach, but take care not to overcook. Serve with hollandaise sauce.

Shark The shark family includes the mako—or, in Britain, mackerel shark—and its close relative the porbeagle, the dogfish, and the hammerhead and blacktip sharks, as well as angel and thresher sharks. All sharks have very firm flesh, scaleless skin, and a cartilaginous skeleton (like skate). Not attractive fish, they tend to have an ammoniac smell that disappears in cooking. The flavor and texture are good.

Shark is usually presented for sale in steaks. The small dogfish may be euphemistically called grayfish, rock cod, and even—quite shamefully—rock salmon. The flesh is white or slightly pink and firm-textured, and deserves more attention than it gets.
Buying guide: available all year round; sold in steaks.
Best cooking methods: dust with well-seasoned flour and then panfry over gentle heat; or coat with batter and deep-fry; or marinate in an oil-based mixture and grill or broil.

Barracuda A large game fish with vicious teeth, the barracuda can reach 150 pounds. Although found in warmer Atlantic waters, it is also caught mainly on the Pacific coast of North America.

The meaty, firm flesh is rich in oil. Small barracuda (such as the Pacific or California barracuda, or scoot, which normally weighs 4 to 8 pounds) are the best ones to eat.

The Atlantic barracuda, which is fished in the Caribbean as well, can cause a type of poisoning from *ciguatera* toxins, and is best avoided.
Buying guide: sold whole or in steaks and fillets.
Best cooking methods: small fish can be broiled or baked whole; steaks can be marinated and then grilled or broiled.

Assorted fish
Many fish do not fall naturally into a culinary category except that they are good to eat. For many of them, their looks are not their greatest asset, but it is a pity that they should be so often passed by in favor of their better-known and more attractive cousins.

Monkfish Monkfish is also known as angler fish or goosefish; its French name is *lotte*. This unusual-looking fish has a huge head—and mouth—but it is usually sold

headless. Despite its rather endearing ugliness, it is one of the best fish you can buy. The smooth skin is easy to remove, as is the translucent membrane beneath. The flesh is firm, boneless, and white, and has the succulence of lobster—its taste is more associated with shellfish than with fish.
Buying guide: available all year. Ask for a good tail piece—3 pounds for six people. It can then be sliced or cooked whole.
Best cooking methods: can be treated almost as meat—in France it is roasted as *gigot de mer* (lamb of the sea). It can also be poached; or split the tail in half, brush with oil, and grill or broil. Best of all are scallops marinated in lemon and garlic, dusted with flour, and sautéed in butter.

Skate Only the wings of skate, also called ray, are eaten—they contain strips of gelatinous cartilage from which the flesh comes off in long, succulent shreds. Fresh skate is covered with a clear slime, which reappears when wiped dry, and the flesh should be pearly-white, resilient and not flabby. Large skate are generally kept chilled for a day or two before sale as they are inclined to be tough when very fresh.

Bouillabaisse 251–2
Normandy Fish Stew 281, 280
Skate with Brown Butter Sauce 281

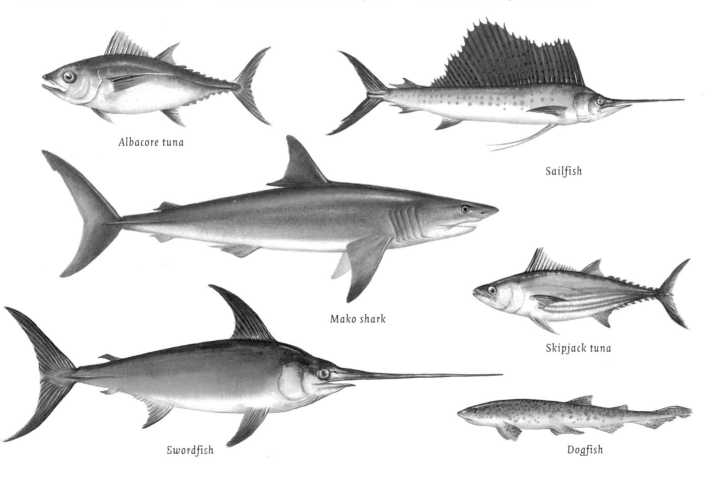

Albacore tuna

Sailfish

Mako shark

Skipjack tuna

Swordfish

Dogfish

Buying guide: best in autumn and winter. Small skate are, rarely, sold whole; usually only the wings are marketed. A very faint smell of ammonia is normal, and will disappear in cooking.

Best cooking methods: The classic French skate dish is *raie au beurre noir*—skate poached in court-bouillon and served with browned butter to which a handful of capers and their vinegar is added. It can also be broiled, deep-fried, or poached. The skin is easy to remove after cooking: simply scrape it carefully, working from the thicker part toward the edge. Because of its gelatinous quality, skate makes a good fish stock.

Red mullet The mullet families can be somewhat confusing. There are two species of fish—not related—called mullet in European waters. One is the gray mullet and the other the red mullet, which is by far the finer of the two species. In America, the term mullet applies to fish of the gray mullet family; fish belonging to the red mullet family that inhabit American waters are known as goatfish.

The Mediterranean red mullet (varying from 2 to 3 inches to 7 to 12 inches) is a superb fish, a shimmering deep silvery-rose with faint golden stripes along each side. The flavor is quite distinctive, something between shrimp and sole. This is the ideal fish to cook together with strong Mediterranean flavors—garlic, saffron, rosemary, and fennel. The liver is often left in the fish during cooking and provides an added richness of flavor, giving red mullet its English nickname of sea woodcock.

Buying guide: sometimes available in ethnic markets or fish markets in larger cities; it may be called by its French name, *rouget*. Look for bright color and transparent, shining eyes. (If the fish seem to be bent sideways, it means that they have been frozen and have just thawed out.) The fish will be sold whole (always ask for the liver to be left in). Large fish are less bony than tiny ones.

Best cooking methods: excellent broiled, baked, or *en papillote*—red mullet is seldom cooked with water—and also ideal for making fish terrines, pâtés, and mousses.

Gray mullet There are several varieties of gray mullet, known variously as striped mullet, black mullet, silver or white mullet, and lisa. In Europe, they are too frequently neglected in favor of the more highly prized red mullet, which is in fact no relation. Gray mullet has large, thick scales and a heavy head with thick, delicate lips. The flesh is coarse and slightly soft, but the flavor is very good, particularly if heightened with fennel or Pernod. The roe is excellent and, used salted, is the proper roe for making the Greek specialty taramasalata.

Buying guide: available all year; sold whole or in fillets. Look for firm fish caught at sea rather than flabby fish caught in estuaries, whose flavor will be muddy.

Best cooking methods: slash the sides and grill, or broil; or if more than 2 pounds, stuff with herbs and garlic, coat with olive oil, and bake. Do not cook gray mullet in water, unless using it as an ingredient for a rich fish soup.

Pompano One of the finest fish in the sea, with firm, white, meaty flesh, pompano is found fresh in Florida and

Mediterranean red mullet

Needlefish

Mahi mahi

Skate

Red snapper

Pompano

Monkfish

Gray mullet

appears on the menus of expensive restaurants elsewhere— notably in New Orleans, where Antoine's pompano *en papillote* is a specialty. The California pompano is related not to the Florida pompano but to the butterfish. Pompano are now exported to northern Europe from the Mediterranean.
Buying guide: available all year. Sold whole, or in fillets. Whole fish are usually about 1 ½ to 2 pounds, but may weigh as much as 3 pounds; avoid larger ones, which may in fact be permit, a similar fish that is not as nice.
Best cooking methods: brush with melted butter and broil, or poach in white wine. Pompano can also be stuffed and baked. Crabmeat or shrimp sauces make an excellent accompaniment.

Mahi mahi Nothing at all to do with the true dolphin, which is a mammal, mahi mahi—also known as dolphinfish or dorado—is a Caribbean native. It is also found in the Mediterranean, where it is often called *lampuga*. Easily recognized by its high ridge of fin, its flesh has a strong, excellent flavor.
Buying guide: sold in steaks or fillets. Steaks are better.
Best cooking methods: bake, grill, broil, or sauté with lemon and garlic. Serve with fresh tomato salsa.

Red snapper You will need to live close to the southern Atlantic or Gulf coasts of America to enjoy this blushing, large-eyed fish fresh from the sea, but red snapper is shipped all over the country— which is fortunate, because it is a fish much in demand, and understandably so. It is weighty, pleasantly textured and well flavored—a 2- to 5-pound specimen, stuffed and baked, makes a delicious meal.
Buying guide: sold whole or in steaks and fillets. Buy carefully, because other snappers, not always as good, may be labeled as red snapper in some markets.
Best cooking methods: bake, broil, or poach.

Needlefish The green and silver needlefish, or garfish—no relation to the freshwater species of fish more correctly called gars—is a pleasant fish to eat although not perhaps of the first order. The flesh is a rather poor grayish-purple in its raw state, but it whitens during cooking. The bones have a rather

startling advantage —they are bright green (this is quite harmless; the color is caused by a phosphate of iron) and easily picked out on the plate. The saury is a similar European fish with colorless bones.
Buying guide: worth trying whenever you see it. Sold whole.
Best cooking methods: cut the fish into segments, then panfry or bake with garlic, or poach and serve with dill or fresh tomato sauce.

Gurnard, sea robin A large family of sweet-tasting fish, despite their armor-plated appearance, the gurnards have several uses and are relatively cheap. In the United States, the best-known member is the sea robin, an often-overlooked fish found along the Atlantic coast. In Europe, the red gurnard—called *grondin* in France—is the best.
Buying guide: usually sold whole; have the fish market do the skinning if possible, as these fish are spiny and tough.
Best cooking methods: excellent in fish soups, sea robins and other gurnards can also be baked with white wine, or coated in beaten egg and bread crumbs, whole or in fillets, sautéed, and served with a Provençal-style or tomato sauce.

John Dory This grandly ugly fish belies its appearance and is, in fact, one of the most delicious of fish—firm, delicate, and excellently flavored. The dark circles on its sides are said to be the marks of St. Peter's fingers, hence its other name, St. Peter's fish. Although there is an American dory, it is not commercially fished and so is rarely seen; John Dory is on occasion available in fish markets in larger cities.
Buying guide: buy whenever you can find it. Remember that almost two-thirds of its weight is taken up by its excessively large, bony head and its intestines.
Best cooking methods: larger fish can be cooked whole or in succulent fillets, as for sole. Small ones are excellent in bouillabaisse.

Butterfish Butterfish, also known as dollarfish, harvest fish, and pomfret, the usual name in Europe, is a small, silvery, coin-shaped fish. The pomfret found in the Mediterranean does not make good eating. However, the pomfret of the Indo-Pacific is excellent, as is the butterfish, found all along the Atlantic

coast. The off-white flesh is rich, tender, and sweet to eat.
Buying guide: available all year round, but best in spring and summer.
Best cooking methods: usually sold whole, butterfish can be baked, broiled or grilled, panfried, poached, or steamed. A piquant sauce will complement the rich, fatty flesh.

Red drum The red drum, also known as redfish and channel bass or red sea bass, is part of a diverse family named for the distinctive drumming sounds the fish make—so loud they can be heard on land. Smaller members of the family are called croakers, for the particular sound they make. The moist, flaky flesh of the red drum is more flavorful than that of its close relative, the black drum. The two fish can easily be distinguished by the fact that only the black drum has barbels, or small whiskers, along its chin; the red drum also has a black spot on either side of its tail.
Found off the Atlantic and Gulf coasts of the United States, red drums can be as heavy as 30 pounds or more, but are usually marketed at about 2 to 5 pounds. Red drum is the fish that is used for blackened redfish, the Cajun dish that became so popular ten years ago or so; the result was overfishing so that red drum became a rarity. Now, however, it is being farmed in Texas, among other places, and so should become more readily available.
Buying guide: available year-round, whole or in fillets.
Best cooking methods: whole fish can be baked, grilled, poached, or braised; fillets can be broiled, poached, and panfried—with "blackening" spices or not. Red drum is also good when used in fish stews and soups.

Weakfish Another member of the drum/croaker family, the weakfish is found along the Atlantic and Gulf coasts. It is sometimes called sea trout or gray trout, but it is not in fact a relative. The weakfish is usually silvery-gray in color but may be multicolored, and some specimens have spots on the flesh, while others look striped. The delicious flesh is delicate in texture and sometimes has a pinkish hue. Whole fish are usually marketed at about 2-5 pounds.
Buying guide: available year-round, whole or in fillets.

freshwater eel and elver 25

Best cooking methods: whole fish are good panfried (weakfish have no pin bones, making it easy to deal with the whole fish) or baked. Fillets can be cooked in various ways: broiled, sautéed or shallow-fried, or baked.

Orange roughy This increasingly popular fish was only discovered about 20 years ago in the deep waters off the coasts of New Zealand. It is normally sold frozen, but some is air-freighted to American and British markets to be sold "fresh" (the fish is always cleaned and frozen at sea, and then partially thawed later on shore for skinning and filleting). The firm white flesh of the orange roughy is moist and tender, and has a sweet, mild, and almost crab-like flavor.
Buying guide: available all year round, most often in fillets weighing about 8 ounces each.
Best cooking methods: a very versatile fish, the orange roughy can be baked, grilled, panfried, coated with batter and then deep-fried, steamed, or poached. It can also be used in a range of fish soups and fish stews.

Tilapia, telapia This small African fish, usually only 1 to 1½ pounds in weight, can live in both salt and fresh water. New hybrids are being developed and farmed all over the world, with skin color ranging from dark gray-black to bright red. The white flesh of tilapia is moist, fine-textured, and tender with a mild, sweet flavor.
Buying guide: available year-round, whole and in fillets.
Best cooking methods: whole fish can be baked, with or without a stuffing, or grilled. Fillets are best coated with beaten egg and bread crumbs, or a batter, before broiling or panfrying, as this will help to keep them moist; alternatively, fillets can be either poached or steamed, notably with Chinese flavorings.

Sea lamprey A legendary fish that resembles a thick eel in appearance, the sea lamprey is distinguishable by the seven holes that lie behind its eyes and have given rise to its nicknames of flute and *sept-yeux* (French for "seven eyes"). It has a thick body, which is dark gray with mottled markings, and no scales.

The flesh is richly flavored, firm, and fatty. The sea lamprey is not seen in America, but is found on French tables and in Portugal and Spain.
Buying guide: sold whole.
Best cooking methods: prepare and cook as for eel, although you will need to scald the fish before skinning and marinate it before cooking. Sea lamprey can also be pickled in vinegar, or stewed with either port or red wine.

Conger eel The conger eel, or American conger, is one of two edible saltwater eels—the other is the moray, which is really only suitable for bouillabaisse. If you can contemplate eating conger eel, it makes a good meal, in spite of its long, sharp bones.
Buying guide: conger eels are available in some ethnic fish markets. When you buy, ask for a thick cut taken from the head end of the eel.
Best cooking methods: use in fish soups, and also in fish terrines. A good-sized, thick cut of conger eel can be roasted, basted with cider and butter, or simply poached in cider.

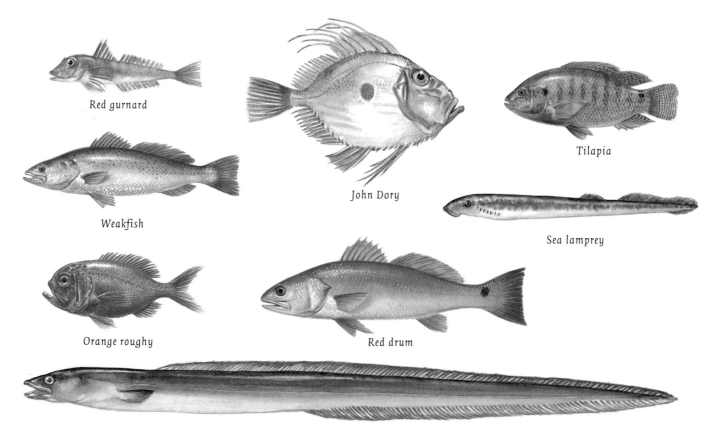

Red gurnard

Weakfish

Orange roughy

John Dory

Red drum

Tilapia

Sea lamprey

Conger eel

FRESHWATER FISH

Lake and river fish are often more frail than sea fish. Their tissues and organs take up a larger proportion of their bodies, and their skin, once scaled, is easily torn. The flesh is much lighter, tends to be dry, and is often riddled with a structure of hairlike forked bones of amazing intricacy. Because of the vulnerable nature of freshwater fish, it is imperative that they should be eaten in the freshest-possible state.

It has been said that freshwater fish should never touch another drop of water once they have left it, so when they are cleaned and scaled, they should be wiped down without washing whenever possible, and baked, grilled or broiled, or panfried in preference to being boiled or poached. If liquids are used, they should be wine, cider, or melted butter or cream rather than water.

The exceptions to the no-water rule are the members of the salmon family—these are exquisite poached in court-bouillon and eaten warm or at room temperature; do not chill.

When cleaning a freshwater fish, be sure to remove the gills, and see that no weed is left in its throat, because this can give a sour and reedy taste. Take particular care to remove the blood that lies along the backbone—this is bitter and must be cleaned away until there is not a trace left.

If you can choose your fish, take those with a silvery or green rather than a brownish hue—brown fish are more likely to have come from slow-moving, muddy haunts. (Various remedies have been suggested—keep the fish alive in a tank of clear water for a day or so, or pour a cup or so of vinegar or a couple of handfuls of salt into its mouth as soon as it is caught and killed, or bake it unscaled in clay, which means that the mud-flavored skin and scales can be removed all at once. But, in fact, there seems little point in trying to rid fish of their inherent taste, so if you dislike the flavor of one, choose some other fish that has a different character.)

Most freshwater fish need quite a lot of salt and other seasoning—in Spain, river fish are gutted, rubbed with salt, and left for several hours, or even buried in salt overnight, to make the flesh firmer and tastier. If you catch your own

fish and there are herbs growing near the pool or river, such as watercress or mint, it is a good idea to gather these and take them home for flavoring the fish—it may have been feeding on them and have a hint of their aroma in its flesh.

Small river fish have such a plethora of tiny bones that they are best pickled, so that the bones are softened by the vinegar, or used in a fish soup or a stew. If the fish are very small, they make an excellent "mixed fry" (a dish of deep-fried tiny fish) of the sort often served in the Dordogne region of France as a *friture de la Dordogne*; then the bones can be happily crunched along with the crisp golden-brown skin.

Salmon Known as the king of fish, the salmon is a majestic creature whose life is mysterious and exhausting. Spawned in fresh water, it spends most of its life in the sea, only returning to fresh water—usually to the river where it was born—to spawn. In fresh water, salmon take no sustenance, so on their way back to the sea after spawning, they are miserably thin and worn, and certainly not fit to eat.

A Scotch or Irish wild salmon in good condition, in May, June, or July, is considered by many to be the best in the world. It is a glossy, steely-blue fish shading to bright silver underneath, with black spots on the head and upper part of the body; the flesh is fine and pink.

Of the Pacific salmon, from the Northwest, Canada, and Alaska, the tastiest are the red-fleshed chinook, or king salmon, and the sockeye. Atlantic salmon is widely available; it is a somewhat richer fish than Pacific salmon. Salmon from Norwegian waters is also excellent, and so is that from Greenland.

Today, farmed salmon is readily available and a very good buy. Most of the salmon we see in the marketplace is farmed; almost all Atlantic salmon is farm-raised.

The author of *The Sportsman's Cookery Book*, written in 1926, said: "Salmon, which has a particular virtue of its own, is best plain, so do not attempt to better it." It should be cooked simply and served unadorned, except for an appropriate sauce or herbed mayonnaise and boiled new potatoes. If you are presented with a salmon straight from the river, you will need to clean it, but leave on the head and tail. It is better to cook it a day after it is

caught, when it is more succulent, unless you intend to prepare sashimi or sushi and eat it raw. After cooking, skin the salmon very carefully, removing the skin from each side in one piece.

Buying guide: good all year round, but wild salmon is at its best in spring and summer. It is sold whole or in steaks. When salmon is really fresh, there is a creamy substance between the flakes of flesh that sets to a cheeselike curd when cooked. Avoid steaks that look soft, grayish, oily, or watery. You will need to allow 6 to 8 ounces per person.

Best cooking methods: unless you have a truly enormous fish poacher, the best way to cook a salmon whole is to bake it in foil. If you do have a large fish poacher, or can borrow one, poach the salmon in court bouillon at the lowest possible simmer for a really succulent result. Hot, salmon is best with hollandaise or other creamy sauces, or with beurre blanc, a lobster sauce, or plain melted butter, with or without herbs such as chervil, tarragon, or parsley. Salmon steaks can be brushed with butter or oil, grilled or broiled, and served with the same kinds of sauces. Panseared salmon fillets are delicious. Cold, salmon is best eaten with plain or herbed mayonnaise or with a horseradish cream, and served with thinly sliced cucumbers and boiled potatoes.

Salmon trout, sea trout The European salmon trout—closely related to the brown trout found in rivers and lakes in both the United States and Europe—is perhaps the perfect fish. As the name suggests, it combines the best of both the salmon and the trout: it has the superior texture of trout, being less dense and more succulent than salmon, but has salmon's excellent flavor and pale pink-colored flesh. Salmon trout is also a much more useful size than salmon for cooking whole because it usually weighs less than 5 pounds, although it can grow to 10 pounds or even more.

The correct name for salmon trout is sea trout and that, too, is apt since the fish is really a trout that has taken it into its head to wander down to the sea to feed, returning to fresh water to spawn. It is a beautiful silver fish with a small head, not as pointed as that of the salmon, and with dark X-shaped spots on the gill cover.

In America, the steelhead trout, an anadromous rainbow trout, is the most similar to salmon trout, but other brown trout may be called salmon or sea trout. Steelhead may be as small as 1 pound or as large as 10 pounds, or more.
Buying guide: spring and summer. Sold whole or in fillets. Allow about 8 ounces per person.
Best cooking methods: salmon trout can be dealt with in the same ways as salmon and is particularly good baked in foil. Poached, it makes a delicious summer lunch. Allow the same cooking time as for salmon, or a few minutes less, and use the same sauces as you would for salmon.

Trout Of the many members of the trout family, wild brook trout may be the most delicious of all. Farmed fish cannot match it—it is sometimes so mild as to be almost tasteless—but occasionally does come close. Brook trout, native to the northeastern United States and Canada, may also be found in other parts of North America and in parts of Europe. Although the wild trout can be quite large, farmed brook trout is usually about 1 pound in weight.

The rainbow trout, which is native to California, is a familiar and delicious fish—it appears almost unfailingly on restaurant menus, and a very neat parcel of food it makes, just the right size for one person, pretty to look at, and sweet to eat. The farm-reared rainbow trout is

most familiar: white-fleshed and delicate and deserving better treatment than it often receives in restaurants. A hardy fish, it responds well to freezing, and frozen rainbow trout is quite a good buy. Farmed rainbow trout usually weigh 12 to 16 ounces. Wild rainbow trout, which has pink to deep-red flesh—and more flavor than the farmed fish—may be as large as 10 pounds.

Brown trout, the wild native trout of British rivers and streams, is a beautiful brown with red and dark gray spots. In Britain, it is usually only available to fly fishermen's families—a great pity, for it is quite delicious. In North America, however, the brown trout has thrived since its introduction at the end of last century, and is a hardy and popular fish.

Take care when cleaning trout to wipe rather than wash it. Remove the gills but leave the head on—the eyes will turn quite white as the fish is cooking. The skin can be removed after cooking, if desired, in one whole piece.
Buying guide: available all year, fresh (farmed) or frozen. Sold whole or in fillets. Allow one trout per person, unless the trout are particularly large.
Best cooking methods: trout can be poached in court-bouillon, sautéed and served *à la meunière* (in browned butter with parsley and lemon), baked, broiled, or simply panfried, preferably outdoors over a fire, or smoked in a home smoker. It can also be cooked in beer with horseradish and

served with horseradish sauce. Whole trout can be grilled; it's best to use a grilling basket so the skin doesn't stick or tear. If the trout is still alive or is extremely fresh, it can be cooked "au bleu," in water with vinegar in it; served with hollandaise, it is worth the trouble. In Sweden, trout is boiled in salt water and served with butter.

Char The Arctic char of Canada and northern Europe, the Dolly Varden, alpine trout, and lake trout of North America (also chars), and the *omble chevalier* (char) of the deep lakes of the French and Swiss Alps all belong to the enormous and excellent salmon family.

The Arctic char is a silver, salmon-like fish with a pink underside, which flushes deep red during spawning. It has firm, delicate flesh and makes a delicious meal. Most of the Arctic char in the marketplace is farm-raised in Canada or the northern United States, but wild char from Canada can sometimes be found. The Dolly Varden, alpine trout, and lake trout are very good table fish and deservedly popular. In France, the *omble chevalier*, which resembles trout, is eaten throughout the summer, and is definitely worth ordering if you see it on a menu.
Buying guide: the wild Arctic char is best in early autumn; farm-raised Arctic char and American chars are available all year. The small trout and sometimes small farmed Arctic char are sold whole; larger trout and Arctic char are sold in steaks or fillets.

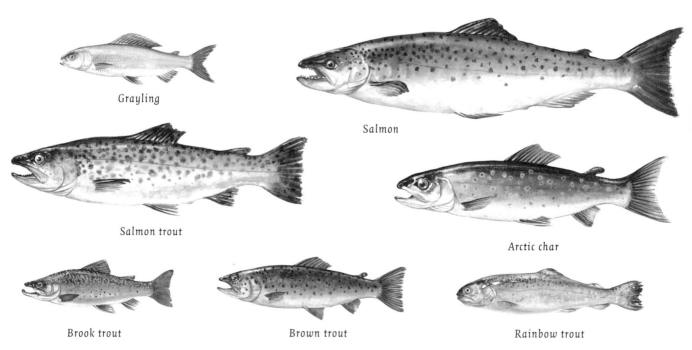

Grayling

Salmon

Salmon trout

Arctic char

Brook trout

Brown trout

Rainbow trout

Best cooking methods: as for trout or salmon. Steaks can be poached, perhaps with bay leaves, and eaten cold.

Grayling A delicious, thyme-scented fish, called by St. Ambrose the flower fish or flower of fishes, grayling should ideally be eaten as soon as it is caught because the delicate flavor is fleeting. It is a graceful fish, silver with finely marked geometric scales and a long spotted backfin. It cannot survive in even slightly polluted water and thrives only in cold, crystal-clear, turbulent rivers, often living alongside trout and eating the same food. A very fresh grayling has much in common, in both taste and texture, with trout, and bears up well in comparison.

You will probably have to catch your own grayling to try one. Scale it before cooking—scald with boiling water and use a knife or a fish scaler, or pick the scales off with your fingernails. Grayling never weigh more than 4 pounds, and are usually less than 2 pounds.

Best cooking methods: brush with butter, flavor with thyme—especially if you find thyme near where the fish was caught—and broil; or sauté gently in butter.

Carp One of the hardiest of all fish, the carp is known to have existed in Asia thousands of years ago and is reputed to live to a grand old age. A somewhat lumbering fish, in its natural state it lives in slow and muddy rivers or lakes, but it can survive well in domestic ponds and is extensively farmed. In Poland, carp is traditionally eaten on Christmas Eve.

Although variants have been bred with just a few large scales that can be picked off with your fingernails, or with no scales at all, the common carp is covered with large scales that are difficult to remove. To scale a common carp, pour some boiling water over it first—better still, ask the fish seller to scale it for you. A compact and meaty fish, carp needs to be cooked with plenty of interesting flavors.

Buying guide: almost always sold whole, and usually a good size for four people.

Best cooking methods: stuffed and baked, or poached and served with horseradish or sorrel sauce.

Catfish So called because of the long barbels that hang about its mouth like drooping cat's whiskers, the catfish is a particularly hardy creature. It is easily transplanted from one region to another, and is a candidate for intensive farming. It should be skinned before cooking.

Buying guide: almost always sold in fillets. The fillets should be white in color and sweet-smelling.

Best cooking methods: fillets are often deep-fried and served with tartar sauce. They can be panfried or baked; they also make a good basis for a fish soup that should include plenty of tomatoes, garlic, herbs, and white wine.

Pike, pickerel, and muskellunge

The predatory pike is quite handsome in its way, especially the younger fish, which has bold markings on a golden-brown or greenish-silver background. An adult pike can weigh up to 40 pounds or more, although those at the market are usually 5 to 10 pounds, and the flesh is white and firm. The muskellunge of northeastern and north-central North America can grow even larger, but the pickerel, or chain pickerel, of the eastern and southern United States is much smaller, usually around 3 pounds. In France, pike is much admired, and *quenelles de brochet*, the lightest of fish dumplings, served with a white wine sauce, is a classic dish.

The theories about cooking pike are many: it should be bled to remove the sharp, reedy taste; it should have quantities of salt forced down its throat and be left to stand overnight to dissolve the bones; it should not be washed because its natural slime keeps it tender. However, a medium-sized pike is perfectly good cooked without any of these refinements. Simply scale it before cooking—pour a little boiling water over it first. Watch out for the bones when you eat it, for they are vicious and plentiful; and don't ever eat the roe, which in some cases can be poisonous.

Buying guide: best in autumn and early winter. If you do see pike for sale, a small whole one is best. Large pike are usually cut into fillets or steaks. Pickerel and muskellunge are both sport fish, not seen in the market.

Best cooking methods: pike tends to be dry, and a very large one may also be tough, so a whole fish should be stuffed before baking and steaks should be marinated before being panfried or broiled. Small pike can be poached and served with beurre blanc, melted butter, or a parsley-butter or caper sauce. Pike is also traditionally used for gefilte fish. In Scandinavia, pike is boiled and eaten with horseradish.

Perch and pike perch The perch is a beautiful little fish, pale greenish-gold with a white or yellowish belly and superb coral-colored fins. The back has dangerously sharp spines and the scales are stubborn, but the fish is well worth the trouble of preparing: it is firm-fleshed, delicate, and light, and has a very good flavor. It is a fish that should only be eaten when it is gleamingly fresh.

The pike perch is also known as the walleye, wall-eyed pike, or yellow pike. Looking somewhat like a cross between pike and perch, with a bony head, thick skin, and spiny dorsal fin, it is a most delicious fish, with firm, white, well-flavored flesh, more interesting than trout and well worth purchasing whenever you see it. The European pike perch, or sander (*sandre* in France), is farmed, like trout, in special conditions for fast growth.

The yellow perch, which is abundant in the Great Lakes and throughout the Midwest, is also found in the eastern part of the country and in eastern Canada. A popular sport fish, it is closely related to the common perch and can be cooked in the same ways.

To prepare perch and pike perch for cooking, first carefully cut off the spines and fins with strong scissors, then bend the fish over and scrape off the scales, which will be raised a little from their usual flat position. The procedure is slightly easier if you hold the fish firmly by the tail with a cloth or paper towel; or you can sprinkle your hands with salt. A pair of strong scissors is also useful for opening the fish to gut it.

Buying guide: these fish are generally sold whole, although large pike perch are sometimes filleted. Smaller fish are more delicate in flavor than the large ones.

Best cooking methods: perch and pike perch are probably best panfried very slowly in butter, about 10 minutes on each side for a 1½-pound fish. They can also be baked, boiled, or broiled. Small perch are good when split to butterfly them, seasoned, and grilled, and then served with plenty of melted butter and chopped parsley. Crisply fried sage leaves can be substituted for the parsley.

scaling round fish 26

Beurre Blanc 257
Oven-Fried Catfish with Remoulade Sauce 281–2
Tartar Sauce 259

Shad The shad is a large migratory member of the herring family that spawns in fresh water. White-fleshed and nutritious, it has a good flavor, but also, unfortunately, a multitude of fine, wirelike bones. The roe is particularly good to eat—it is even classed as an aphrodisiac by more hopeful gourmets.

The American shad has been successfully transplanted from the Atlantic to the Pacific, and in the spring can be found in the St. Lawrence River in the East and the Columbia River on the West Coast. In Europe, the allis shad, which can grow up to 2 feet long, and the smaller twaite shad are caught in the Loire and Garonne rivers of France in the springtime, when they are spawning.

Remove as many of the bones as possible before cooking shad, using tweezers if necessary. When the fish is cooked, cut deep lengthwise parallel slits about 4 inches apart in the flesh, and remove any accessible bones before serving, moving your finger over the flesh to detect the hidden ones.

Buying guide: best in spring in spawning season. Sold whole, or in fillets (sometimes boned). A 3-pound shad will feed six. Ask the fish dealer to scale and possibly bone the fish when he cleans it. Shad roe is sold frozen and canned as well as fresh.

Best cooking methods: stuff whole shad with sorrel and then bake, or bake and serve on a bed of sorrel. Shad can also be filleted, with the skin left on, and gently broiled. Serve with fresh tomato sauce, beurre blanc, or a sorrel purée mixed with fresh cream. The delicate roe can be quickly sautéed in butter or gently baked in butter.

Perch

Pike

Largemouth black bass

Lake whitefish

Shad

Catfish

Eel

Mirror carp

Sturgeon

Sturgeon A huge and somewhat prehistoric-looking creature, the sturgeon spends most of its life in the sea, but is most sought after when it comes into rivers to spawn. It can grow up to 20 feet or more, and the beluga sturgeon—usually a more modest size and the source of the most expensive caviar—can live to the ripe age of 100. Sturgeon are still caught today in some American and European rivers, but they are most plentiful in the Caspian Sea, using its southern rivers for spawning. Recently, sturgeon has begun to be farm-raised in California.

The flesh of sturgeon is white, very firm, rich, and firm-textured, and it is frequently likened to veal. It is inclined to be dry and is improved by being smoked or steeped in a white wine marinade before it is cooked.

Buying guide: best in spring. Sold as steaks or fillets.

Best cooking methods: broil or sauté in butter, like veal; or poach in white wine and serve with a creamy sauce. In France, a luxurious dish is sturgeon poached in Champagne. It is also very good smoked and cut into thick slices, eaten with lemon, horseradish, and brown bread and butter.

Bass This is the collective name for a large family of bony fish equipped with spiny fins, which includes the magnificent sea bass. All make good eating. There are numerous freshwater bass, but the most well-known are the largemouth and smallmouth black bass; other bass include the white, yellow, and spotted bass. Farmed striped bass are actually a cross between wild white bass and sea bass. Cook small ones whole, panfried, baked and stuffed, or grilled over fennel twigs. Larger fish are best filleted and skinned, or the flesh may taste muddy; the fillets can be poached, served à la meunière, or fried.

Eel and elver Eels have a life cycle as strange as that of any fish. The American and European eel is spawned in the Sargasso Sea and promptly travels up to 4000 miles to find the fresh waters of its ancestors, where it will spend most of its life, only returning to the Sargasso to spawn and then die. (Australian and Japanese eels have spawning grounds closer to land, but still have a very long

way to travel.) By the time they reach the river mouths, the tiny baby eels have grown into elvers 2 to 3 inches long. These little creatures, looking like transparent spaghetti, are good to eat, deep-fried (they must be soaked for some hours in salt water with a dash of vinegar before cooking). In Spain they are a seasonal delicacy. By their second winter in fresh water the elvers have become small yellow eels, which are not so good to eat. These then mature into the familiar silver eels, velvety-brown on their backs and silver below, and are excellent to eat—meaty, even-textured, succulent, and very rich.

Buying guide: elvers appear in the spring; eels are in season all year but are best in autumn to winter. Try to buy live eels—they become tough and spoil almost instantly once killed. If you flinch at the prospect of having to deal with a live eel yourself, have the fish dealer kill and skin it for you and chop it into pieces. Ask for 3-inch pieces, which look better and are better able to keep their moisture during cooking than smaller lengths; for deep-frying, have it cut into ½-inch slices. Skinned eel is also available frozen.

Best cooking methods: An eel dish is always part of the traditional Italian Christmas Eve dinner; jellied eels are an English seaside treat. You may prefer to stew your eel in red wine, wrap it in bacon and sage leaves and broil it, or sauté it with a few bay leaves and serve it with Italian herb sauce. Elvers should be rinsed and patted dry, then dipped in flour and cooked immediately in hot oil with chile peppers and garlic. In Spain they are served in a fried tangle with a fiery tomato sauce.

Other freshwater fish

Most of the following fish are not commercially fished or farmed, and are unlikely to be in a fish shop. These are mainly fished for sport, and are trophies for the angler rather than the cook.

Bleak A small, slim, silvery fish found in the rivers of northern Europe, which can be cooked just like whitebait.

Bream Freshwater bream needs interesting seasonings and ingredients because the flesh is somewhat dry and tasteless. The European bream can be cooked like carp.

Buffalofish A popular freshwater fish from the Great Lakes and the Mississippi Valley, which makes good eating. It is often

smoked, but can be prepared like carp when fresh. Buffalofish are actually several different species of the fish known as suckers. The three types are the bigmouth, or redmouth; the black buffalo; and the smallmouth, or razorback.

Burbot This handsome golden fish, also called ling fish, is the only member of the cod family to inhabit fresh water, and it is found in North America, the British Isles, and throughout Europe. Burbot has good, firm, fatty flesh and a richly flavored liver that can be sliced to release its oils and then baked or poached with the fish; the roe is poisonous. The fish may be cooked in red wine, or served with a tomato, cheese, and cream sauce.

Chub A fish that precisely fits the description "cotton wool stuffed with needles," chub is watery-fleshed, full of small forked bones, and not really worth eating. If, however, you do catch one and don't want to waste it, try stewing it, panfrying it, or baking it in foil with herbs. It should be cooked as soon as possible after being caught as the flavor deteriorates in a very short time. The chub available in the American marketplace, often smoked, is actually cisco, a member of the whitefish family.

Crappie Known to anglers as white or black crappie, this is an excellent Mississippi Valley and New England freshwater fish. Members of the sunfish family, crappies are also known as calico bass, speckled perch, and strawberry bass. They are usually panfried.

Sheepshead Not to be confused with the saltwater porgy of the same name, this is the only freshwater drum, found in Canada, the Midwest, and the southern states. It can be either poached or panfried when very fresh.

Whitefish This large group of fish, related to salmon and trout, is found in deep-water lakes and rivers throughout the northern United States and Canada. American whitefish, which include the ciscoes and lake whitefish, are fished by anglers and commercially, and are sold fresh and frozen as well as smoked. Lake whitefish, found in plentiful supply in the Great Lakes and Canada, is good to eat and can be used in trout or salmon recipes. Vendace, the European cisco, and powan, or lavaret, are fished in the clear lakes of northern Europe, including the lochs of Scotland and Ireland. The whitefish roe is much prized.

à la meunière 422

caviar 31

conger eel 20

jellied eel 32

porgy 14

saltwater bream 14

sea bass 14

smoked eel 30

smoked sturgeon 30

whitefish caviar 32

Italian Herb Sauce 260

PREPARING FISH

flatfish II

filleting knife
224
**kitchen
scissors** 225

Trimming flatfish
1 Snip off the tough upper pectoral fin.

2 Trim the tail, and cut away the dorsal
and anal fins.

1

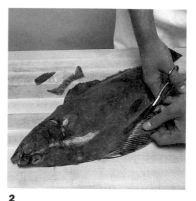

2

3 Cut off the head just behind the gills.
If you are planning to serve the fish
whole, gently press on it to release the
viscera (intestines), and rinse the fish
thoroughly under cold running water.

3

1

2

3

Filleting and skinning flatfish
(above and above right)
1 With a sharp knife, make a slit down
the backbone from head to tail.

2 Slice down one side of the fish from
head to tail, sliding the knife between
the flesh and the bones. For the second
fillet, slice away the flesh from the
opposite side of the fish. For the third
and fourth fillets, turn the fish over
and repeat the process.

3 To skin the fillets, hold each firmly by
the tail end and work the knife down the
length of the fillet, keeping the blade as
close to the skin as possible.

Scaling round fish *(left)*
Holding the fish by the tail, scrape
away the scales with the back of a knife,
working toward the head.

Cleaning round fish

1 Before cooking a fish whole, it is important to remove the bitter-tasting gills. To do this, lay the fish on its back and ease open the gill flaps. Carefully push the fan of gills (they can be sharp) out from between the gill flaps; sever and discard them.

1

round fish 12–16, 18–25

filleting knife 224

2 Cut off all the fins.

3 Slit open the fish's belly and ease out the viscera (intestines). Rinse the fish thoroughly, inside and out, under cold running water.

2

3

1

2

Filleting round fish

1 Starting just behind the head, cut into the back of the fish and slide the knife along one side of the backbone to release the fillet, keeping the knife close to the bone.

2 Continue slicing down the length of the fish, severing the fillet just behind the gills and at the tail.

3 Cut the second fillet from the other side of the fish. Skin the fillets in the same way as for flatfish.

3

round fish 12–16, 18–25
salmon 21

knives 222–4
meat pounder 226

Boning round fish

1 Cut off the head behind the gills, without cutting quite through the bottom part of the fish; ease the head away from the body, taking most of the viscera (intestines) with it. Remove the rest with the help of the knife.

2 Carefully slice down the back of the fish between the flesh and backbone, keeping the knife against the backbone; do not puncture the belly. Open the fish out like a book.

3 Turn the fish flesh side down, and cut away the backbone and small adjoining bones.

4 This method of boning is particularly suitable when the fish is to be stuffed, or it is to be opened out flat for grilling, sautéing, or frying.

1

2

3

4

1

2

Cutting salmon scallops

1 Take a tailend section of fresh salmon.

2 Slice off the top fillet, starting at the tail and holding the knife as close to the backbone as possible. Turn the fish over and repeat the process to remove the second fillet. Discard the backbone, and skin each fillet as for flatfish.

3

4

3 Cut each fillet horizontally into two thin slices, using a long, sharp, and flexible knife.

4 Place each slice of salmon between two pieces of dampened parchment paper or between two sheets of plastic wrap. Gently but firmly flatten the fish into scallops, using a rolling pin or a meat pounder.

Preserved Fish

Fresh fish deteriorates fast and has always been a natural subject for traditional preserving methods. Indeed, the smoking, pickling, salting, and drying of fish used to be a matter of simple necessity—when fishing boats relied on the wind, and overland transport on the horse and cart, fresh sea fish was practically unknown inland. Moreover, as fish was the prescribed food for the numerous meatless days in the Christian calendar (as many as twelve a month), to preserve it, and to preserve it palatably, was a matter of great importance.

Smoked fish

Fish must be salted before smoking. This process, which entails either soaking the fish in a brine strong enough to keep a potato afloat, or rubbing into it a generous amount of dry salt, improves both the flavor and the keeping qualities. After salting, the fish is dried and then cold- or hot-smoked. The protein content remains unchanged, but calories are diminished.

To find smoked fish you like, try different varieties, because they vary enormously, and regional specialties still find their way into the marketplace. Some are pale and oak-smoked, while others are oversalted and artificially dyed in fierce hues of red or yellow.

There are several ways of improvising a smoker in your backyard—all you need is a large container/chimney for the smoke with a few airholes for the fire. Although you can convert your barbecue grill to a smoker, if you intend to smoke a great deal it will be worth rigging up a real smoker. For the less ambitious, a small stove-top smoker is much less of a production. It is used indoors, and will quickly hot-smoke a gutted, salted fish. These smokers use sawdust, to which you could add thyme, rosemary, or juniper berries; this will make your fish smell and taste much more interesting.

Store-bought smoked fish will keep for about 3 days, or up to 20 days in the freezer. Home-smoked fish should be eaten at once. Only dried and salted fish keeps indefinitely.

Cold-smoked fish Cold-smoking takes place at temperatures of around 75°F, which smoke the fish but do not cook it. Products of the cold-smoking process are either eaten raw, like smoked salmon, or may require further cooking, like finnan haddie.

Smoked salmon The British think that salmon is best when caught in Scottish waters; Norwegians say that those caught in Norwegian waters are better still; and others argue for the salmon from the Pacific Northwest or Canada. All agree that farmed salmon come fourth, but can still be excellent when smoked. Smoked salmon should be fresh and succulent, melting away under the knife as it is sliced. The best of all is the pale pink-gold, rather undersalted salmon. A darker red or a deep orange color usually means dyed or overcured fish, and is not a good sign.

The traditional Scottish way of kippering salmon, as the process used to be called (kippers—kippered herring—having merely borrowed the word), involves brining boned sides of salmon, wiping them, drying them, oiling them, and then covering them in brown sugar. Another wipe with a cloth, often soaked in whisky, another anointing with oil, and another whisky wipe, and then the sides are smoked over a fire of peat and oak chips.

Fresh cold-smoked salmon is usually sliced for you in the market, but if you can afford it, buying a whole side often works out to be more economical. A side runs the whole length of the fish from shoulder to tail. Buying a whole side has the advantage of giving you both the richer, fattier cuts toward the tail and the fine-grained center. To slice the salmon, go across the grain of the flesh—that is, cut from the shoulder toward the tail. You need an extremely sharp, long, flexible knife—a slicer with a scalloped edge is best. Or you can buy a side of salmon presliced and reassembled.

Smoked salmon is eaten sliced transparently thin, with lemon and thin brown bread and butter. Lox (from the Yiddish word for smoked salmon) tends to be more heavily cured than other smoked salmon; it is most often served with cream cheese and bagels. *Royktlaks*—Norwegian smoked salmon—is used for *smørbrød*, the Scandinavian open-faced sandwiches.

Frozen and canned smoked salmon are available, but both are no more than vividly pink shadows of the fresh variety. However, sliced vacuum-packed and chilled smoked salmon can be perfectly acceptable. And what can be a good buy at the delicatessen are "trimmings"— untidy scraps of fresh smoked salmon with bits of skin attached. Provided they are moist and soft, they are ideal for smoked salmon mousse or for any dish requiring chopped smoked salmon.

Finnan haddie Finnan haddie, or smoked haddock, is so called because it was in the village of Findon, in Scotland, that the method of curing this fish, giving it its distinctive pale appearance, was invented. Originally the beheaded fish were dried and cold-smoked in the smoke of seaweed. By a modernized process, finnan haddie is now produced far beyond Scotland, in New England, among other places. So too are its imitations—fillets of white fish that are artificially dyed a bright, bright yellow and may be chemically treated to taste of smoke. It is easy to tell the true from the false: the color is a complete giveaway.

Finnan haddie is eaten hot. Broil it, or poach it for a few minutes in milk or water, then simply serve it with butter, or with a poached egg on top and a piece of hot buttered toast. Or use it to make dishes such as the creamed finnan haddie that is a favorite in New England; the Anglo-Indian kedgeree, a rice and lentil dish; or the poached smoked haddock of Scandinavia, served with carrots, eggs, and butter. Scotland eats "ham and haddie," frying the fish in fat rendered from slices of smoked ham.

Kipper Kippers, or kippered herring, are split washed herring that are briefly brined, hung on "tenterhooks" to dry, and then smoked for 4 to 6 hours. Kippers are a mainstay of the British table—grilled with a lump of butter for breakfast or high tea, or served cold in salads and pâtés for lunch.

Many kippers are dyed during brining, emerging mahogany-colored after smoking. There are, however, undyed kippers to be had, and these are worth finding. Buy a fat kipper—lean kippers tend to be dry. And buy kippers fresh— frozen kippers, although they keep their texture fairly well, do not taste as good.

Smoked halibut Young halibut is sometimes lightly smoked. Its taste is delicate and its texture firm. It is served in the same way as finnan haddie.

Bloater Bloaters are herring that are lightly salted and then smoked without the intestine being removed. The slight fermentation of the enzymes occurring during this process causes the fish to get bloated and develop a somewhat gamy flavor. Bloaters are silvery in appearance, and the flesh is soft and moist. They do not keep as long as kippers, and must be gutted before they are served. They may be broiled, or simply mashed to make a sandwich filling. The famous *harengs saur* of Boulogne, on France's northern coast, are even more plumped up than the ordinary bloater, and the Swedish *surströmming* is so bloated that it seems on the point of explosion. This last is not much exported, but is deeply loved at home, where it is eaten with thin crispbread or potatoes.

Smoked sturgeon If fresh sturgeon, with its fine-grained white flesh, tastes rather like veal, smoked sturgeon resembles nothing so much as smoked turkey both in color and taste. It is, however, more delicious still, more buttery and melting in the mouth, and of course a great deal more expensive. Eat it like smoked salmon.

Smoked roes Fish eggs from any number of species are smoked and enjoyed. Note that what are called hard roes alone are eggs—soft roes are not roes at all but "milt," or sperm, from the male of the species. Smoked roes should be firm and moist with no signs of skin breakage. Smoked cod roe is deliciously grainy and glutinous. This or smoked carp roe can be used to make taramasalata, the creamy Greek spread, or dip.

Hot-smoked fish Hot-smoking takes place at temperatures of about 180°F, and is the method used for eel, trout, and mackerel, which are smoked and lightly cooked at one and the same time. They are bought ready to eat and can also be served hot.

Smoked trout The best smoked trout has gone into brine as soon as it left the water. It is gutted only after it has been drained, and is then ready for smoking. In England, silver birchwood is said to give it the best and sweetest flavor, and a little peat and a few pine cones make it taste even better. The fish turns golden and then, if left longer, to bronze. Look for springiness in a smoked trout: the flesh should be neither mushy nor dry— the fine, firm texture of a nice plump smoked trout is as much of a pleasure as its delicate flavor. Serve smoked trout for a summer lunch or supper with lemon wedges, thin brown bread and butter, and a dash of horseradish mixed with lightly whipped cream; or serve it in a salad.

Smoked mackerel Silvery-gold smoked mackerel can be very good indeed. As this is not a very subtly flavored fish, it emerges from smoking tasting straightforwardly of itself and is, usually, rich and juicy. Best bought whole, it is also available filleted. Avoid any smoked mackerel in a package that oozes with oil: this indicates that the fish has been stored for too long or at the wrong temperature, and the flesh will be dry.

Eat smoked mackerel cold accompanied by horseradish sauce or lemon.

Bucklings are popular in Europe, and allegedly get their name from a fourteenth-century Dutchman, William Beukels, who invented this method of preserving ungutted herring. A nice fat buckling is tasty eaten with brown bread and butter and lemon wedges, and also good mashed to a paste. In Germany, buckling is sometimes lightly broiled or gently panfried, with the roe, and served with sauerkraut or scrambled eggs.

Sprat, sild, and brisling are all small European herring that, when smoked, are simply served with brown bread, butter, lemon, and a glass of beer. (Sild, or sill, is the Scandinavian term for herring.) As well as being candidates for smoking, they also sometimes find themselves canned as sardines.

Arbroath smokie A British delicacy, these are small smoked haddock that have been beheaded and gutted but not split, and hot-smoked. After brining, they are placed over birch and oak smoke until pale golden. A favorite way of serving them is to put butter in the cavity of the fish, season with black pepper, and heat gently under a broiler or in the oven. The dark skin is then peeled off to reveal a golden outer crust and gradually paling flesh.

Smoked eel Some say that the densely textured smoked eel is even more delicious than smoked salmon. Smoked

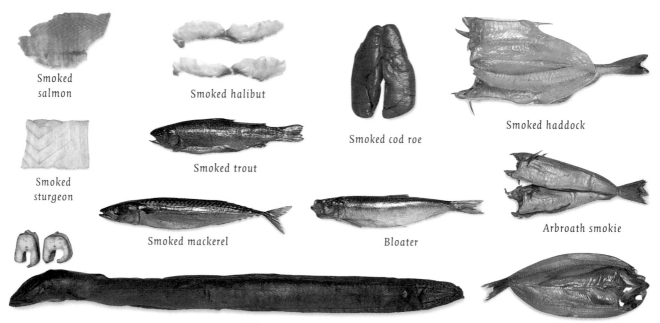

Smoked
salmon

Smoked halibut

Smoked cod roe

Smoked haddock

Smoked
sturgeon

Smoked trout

Smoked mackerel

Bloater

Arbroath smokie

Smoked eel

Kipper

eel is very rich and filling, and is usually served with pepper, lemon juice, and brown bread and butter. Pinky-beige smoked eel fillets laid over a plateful of golden scrambled eggs make a first course that is especially delicious. Or buy it whole, skin on, if you want larger, more succulent fillets. It is easy to skin and then serve with horseradish sauce.

Cured, pickled, and salted fish

The curing process is particularly suited to oily fish, such as herring. They are steeped in a vinegar or brine solution, which halts enzyme action in the same way that cooking does.

Gravlax is a most delicious Swedish specialty—it is raw salmon cured with dill, sugar, salt, and white peppercorns. It is traditionally eaten with a rather sweet mustard and dill sauce. Gravlax is quite popular in the United States, and it and other variations on the theme—such as tequila-and-cilantro-cured salmon—appear on trendy restaurant menus.

Salted herring are sold whole in many European markets. They must be soaked for up to 12 hours, and then filleted and chopped for salads or bathed in sour cream for an hors d'oeuvre.

Matjes herring are considered to be the best salted herring. They are lightly salted fat female fish with translucent, slippery flesh of a beautiful old-rose color. They need no soaking.

Pickled herring, marinated herring These are marinated in spices and vinegar, then bottled in a sour cream or wine sauce.

Schmaltz herring These are larger herring (schmaltz is the German word for fat) that are skinned, filleted, and preserved in brine.

Bismarck herring These herring, blue of skin and white of flesh, are first steeped in white wine vinegar. Then, after they are gutted and boned, their heads and tails removed, and split, they are cured for 24 hours layered in a dish, well seasoned and interspersed with onion rings and sometimes with raw carrot. Eat them with new potatoes, or bathed in sour cream or a mayonnaise dressing.

Rollmop These are Bismarck herring—halved lengthwise—that have been rolled up tightly around peppercorns and slices of onion and fastened with toothpicks before being put into jars with hot spiced white wine vinegar.

Soused herring, potted herring These are a favorite in Britain, where many people like to souse herring at home by steeping them in a vinegary marinade to which herbs and spices are added. Soused herring can be found in specialty shops.

Anchovy Preserved salted anchovy fillets usually come canned in oil, those in olive oil being the best. Plain salted anchovies, sold direct from a barrel or a large can, need a brief soaking in fresh water to make them less harsh.

An anchovy is the most versatile of piquant ingredients, seasoning a great many dishes without imparting the least hint of fishiness. Anchovies are good for *salsa verde*, the Italian herb sauce, or for braised veal, stews, and pizzas, and in potato salad and salade Niçoise. Melted in butter with garlic, they make the Italian *bagna cauda*, a sauce served with raw vegetables as an antipasto.

Dried fish

Fish hung up to dry in the sun and wind provided an almost indestructible food supply for our ancestors. This earliest method of preserving fish is the precursor of modern freeze-drying. Salting is another way to extract moisture from fish, thus discouraging spoilage.

Salt cod, stockfish Dried to a flatness and hardness resembling hide, cod and other members of its family—haddock, pollack, ling—spring back to life when they are soaked. Salt cod has been salted and dried, while what is called stockfish has just been air-dried. In Scandinavia, where stockfish is much eaten, it appears in a fish pudding, light as a soufflé, which is served with hollandaise sauce. In Holland, Belgium, and Germany, stockfish is often soaked in lime water before being cooked.

In Portugal, where *bacalhau*—salt cod—is almost a staple food, they boast that they have more than a thousand different ways of cooking it. Some of the best recipes for dried cod are from the Basque region of Spain, and variously involve the fish—*bacalao*—with garlic, oil, tomatoes, peppers, onions, and potatoes. The French make a rich garlicky purée of salt cod that is called *brandade de morue*.

Bombay duck Made from a cured dried fish found in the Indian Ocean, Bombay duck has a pungent aroma. It can be obtained from Indian and specialty

markets and is used to season rice that is eaten with curry.

Dried shark's fin This is delicately flavored cartilage of the fin, which, when you buy it whole, looks like the tousled beard of Santa Claus. It requires soaking overnight, or even longer, in many changes of water, until it softens. In China, shark's fin is banquet food: it goes into party soups, into rather liquid stews and braises, and, shredded finely, into omelets. Its gelatinous properties have been likened to those of calf's foot. Found in Asian markets, dried shark's fin is also sold in strands. In some shops, frozen shark's fin is available; even more expensive than the dried, it is prepared and ready to use.

Salted roes

Into this category fall the costly caviar and its less exotic alternatives.

Caviar The fish that are used for commercial caviar production are the sevruga, the large osetra, and the giant beluga, which has a huge roe to match. All are members of the *Acipenser* tribe, and are collectively known as sturgeon. The roes are passed through fine-meshed sieves to separate the eggs, which are then salted. The brining of caviar is a delicate business. The condition of the fish and the size of the eggs both have a bearing on it, and the finest grade emerges from the care of the master tasters as *malassol*, a Russian term meaning "slightly salted."

Caviars come in a variety of sizes and colors. Sevruga is small-grained and greenish-black. Osetra, larger-grained, may be golden-brown, deep-green, or slate-gray; it can also be pale—almost bluish-white. Beluga, the largest and the most rare, is gray or, very rarely, golden. The closer to spawning the fish is caught, the paler the roe—and all of these, depending on their quality, make what is called "first-grade" caviar.

First-grade caviar is sometimes pasteurized, which lengthens its shelf life. Nonpasteurized caviar is kept refrigerated at 32°F: warmer, and it loses its texture and becomes oily; colder, and its flavor is ruined. The contents of an open container may be kept, covered, in the refrigerator, but should certainly be eaten within a week.

This also applies to pressed caviar—which is slightly less expensive than the *malassol* but is, in fact, the first choice of some caviar experts. It is caviar that has been drained of some of its liquid. The eggs, of course, are squashed in the process, and what emerges is a fairly solid mass, saltier than *malassol*, but tasting more intensely of sturgeon, since 2 pounds of fresh caviar are reduced to make 1 pound of pressed. Second-grade caviar may be saltier caviar of a single variety, or a mixture of different caviars, some of them highly superior.

To educate the palate, one really needs to eat a lot of caviar, not with tiny special caviar spoons but by the mouthful. In Russia, where large helpings of second-grade caviar are fairly unceremoniously served, it is often eaten with blinis—fat little buckwheat pancakes—and sour cream. But as a rule it is best with a little lemon, some fresh Melba toast and unsalted butter.

Gray mullet roe Known as *tarama* in Greece, the salted, dried, pressed roe of the mullet is considered a great delicacy, ranking only slightly lower than caviar and above salmon roe. As the name suggests, it makes taramasalata—the creamy Greek fish spread served as an appetizer. For this purpose, the roe is pounded with oil, lemon juice, and crushed garlic, and bound with soft white bread crumbs or mashed potato, and sometimes with an egg yolk. Smoked carp or cod roe makes a good substitute.

Salmon caviar The roe of the salmon, this is bright orange and large-grained, not so much an imitation caviar but a fresh-tasting product in its own right. Sometimes called red caviar, it too can be eaten with sour cream, or just with toast, butter, and a squeeze of lemon.

Lumpfish caviar The pink eggs of the lumpfish are salted, colored black, or sometimes red, and pressed. Lumpfish caviar is used on cocktail party canapés. Alone, it is less interesting than true caviar but is pleasant with sour cream and raw onion, and is fairly inexpensive.

Whitefish caviar Sometimes called American golden caviar, whitefish caviar is composed of small yellowish eggs. It can be served like lumpfish caviar.

Canned fish

Fish is one of the few foods that stand up well to canning. Canned tuna and sardines are foods worth eating in their own right—quite different from their fresh counterparts, but still good.

Salmon Canned salmon comes in many grades, from the not-so-good bright red to a more acceptable pink (the darker it is, the oilier). It can be good and is useful in fish cakes and sandwich fillings.

Sardines Good brands of sardines have been gently brined, correctly dried, and lightly cooked in olive oil, then stored for about a year, so that the flavors of fish and oil are mingled. Sardine is actually more a general term for a number of soft-boned saltwater fish, including pilchards, sprat, and some herring. The sardines caught off the western coast of France are the best and most expensive. Portuguese and Spanish sardines are less fine but much cheaper. Eat sardines bones and all, with brown bread and butter and a squeeze of lemon.

Tuna The best canned tuna is taken from the albacore, king of the tunas, which alone is permitted to be described as "white meat." Other tuna varieties—skipjack, yellowfin, bluefin—are a little darker, but all make good salads. Use canned tuna for the classic Italian *vitello tonnato* (cold veal with a creamy tuna sauce). Buy good-quality tuna, which comes in solid pieces, packed in olive oil.

Jellied eel A traditional Cockney delicacy, jellied eel is sold in cans, and makes a good appetizer; serve it with little bunches of watercress.

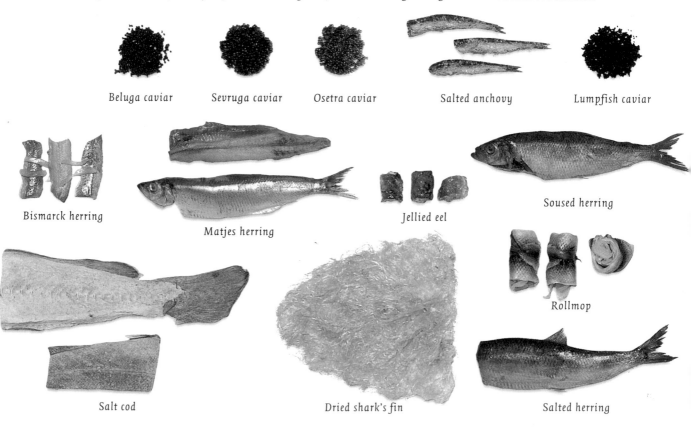

Beluga caviar   Sevruga caviar   Osetra caviar   Salted anchovy   Lumpfish caviar

Bismarck herring   Matjes herring   Jellied eel   Soused herring   Rollmop

Salt cod   Dried shark's fin   Salted herring

Shellfish

Although overfishing and pollution have taken their toll of shellfish, there are signs that things are improving. Waters that were a hazard to the health of both shellfish and consumers have been radically cleaned up, and new farming methods are making it possible to harvest fast-growing shrimp, for example, in large quantities.

True, the shrimp most readily available may not be the high-quality Gulf of Mexico ones, or we may find oysters on the market the size of tennis balls that can only be eaten chopped like large clams and cooked. But we should be able to enjoy more abundant and possibly less costly supplies; and the delicious local varieties of shellfish are still available. Buy them from a dealer who specializes in them and can be trusted to sell them only when they are sweet and fresh.

If you are buying cooked shellfish, a quick sniff should distinguish the freshly cooked from the fading. Shrimp lose the color in their shells and become lighter as they dry up. Lobsters and crabs also lose weight—choose heavy specimens with tension in the tail or claws. If they are floppy and unresisting, they are less than fresh. If you want to cook them live, plunge them into rapidly boiling salted water, seawater, or court-bouillon. Take care not to overcook them—all shellfish toughens and becomes rubbery if it is cooked for too long.

Crab To pick the meat out of a crab is a labor of love but always worth the effort—the flavor and texture are almost equal to that of lobster, and certainly less expensive. The sweet spider crabs beloved of the French, the soft green-backed shore crabs that are a Venetian specialty, and the large crabs with fearsome claws that are found around the British coast are all delicious. But in America, the crab really comes into its own, with an abundance of blue crabs from the Atlantic and Gulf coasts; the superbly flavored Pacific Coast crab, the Dungeness; the Florida stone crabs; the Alaska king crab and snow crab; and the rock crabs and Jonah crabs found all along the Atlantic coast.

Soft shell crabs are actually blue crabs that have just shed their hard shells and so can be eaten shell and all. They are available from May to September.
Buying guide: whether they are alive or cooked, choose crabs that feel heavy for their size and smell fresh and sweet, with no hint of ammonia. Soft shell crabs should always be purchased alive. About 1 pound of crab in the shell, or 4 ounces of crabmeat, is usually sufficient for each person, depending on how it is prepared. Fresh crabmeat, which may have been pasteurized, is most often from blue crabs; lump or jumbo, then backfin, are the best.
Best cooking methods: the best crab is the one you boil and pick yourself, eaten cold with mayonnaise. Hard-shelled crabs are also good steamed and eaten hot, and can be used to make a very delicious bisque. Soft shell crabs can be eaten sautéed in butter, or broiled, grilled, or deep-fried.

Lobster "There is nothing more delicious in life," said Byron, "than the fireside, a lobster salad, and good conversation." With or without the embellishments, lobster is a treat for both the eye and the palate. The colors—creamy-pink flesh, and a shell speckled cream and coral underneath and deep, old brick-red on the back; the texture—firm, delicate, and luscious; and the flavor—an appetizing, elusive marine taste—are all highly desirable. And, alas, expensive.

Lobsters from colder waters are generally the finest. The best are the northern lobsters from Maine to Nova Scotia, on the American side of the Atlantic, and the smaller Irish and Scottish lobsters and those from Brittany, on the European side. The male lobster is firmer-fleshed than the female and has larger, meatier claws, but the female has a more delicate flavor, a broader tail, and the delicious coral, or roe, which turns scarlet when it is cooked.
Buying guide: fresh lobsters are available all year, but are at their best and most abundant during the summer. Choose a lobster that is heavy for its size and has both its claws—sometimes a claw is lost in a fight, and some of the best meat is in the claws. Alive, by far the best way to buy lobsters, the shell is dark red to black; if already boiled, the shell should be bright red. If the lobster is precooked, check that its tail springs back into a tight curl when pulled out straight. This shows that it was cooked when alive. If you are brave enough, give it a sniff underneath, too, to make sure it is quite fresh.

If you are intending to cook the lobster yourself, make sure that you get a lively specimen and, again, that it is a heavy one—sometimes lobsters get quite thin in captivity waiting for someone to come along and buy them. To keep a live lobster in the refrigerator—although you should not keep it like this for more than a day or two—roll it loosely in damp newspaper to prevent it crawling about, enclose it in a paper bag pierced with air holes, and put it in the vegetable crisper.

removing the meat from a cooked crab 40–1

European crab

Blue crab

Dungeness crab

33

If you are called upon to face cutting a live lobster in half or in pieces before cooking it, lay it on a cutting board, stomach down, and cover the tail with a wet cloth (the claws should be secured with rubber bands). Hold the lobster down firmly and, with a strong, sharp, pointed knife, make a swift incision into the cross mark in the head and push the knife down. This severs the spinal cord and kills the lobster instantly. Leave for a few minutes for the reflexes to cease, then cut the lobster into pieces, or split it in half lengthwise through the stomach shell and open it out flat, or cut it completely in half right through the hard back shell. Clean it, removing the grain sac from the head and reserving any coral and the delicious creamy tomalley, or liver, to use in lobster sauce if you like. Cook the lobster immediately.

Small lobsters are usually the most tender: a 1 ¼-pound lobster will feed one person. Large lobsters are excellent — and work out to be less expensive—for salads and sauces. Fresh cooked lobster meat is sometimes available; frozen and canned lobster meat is really best forgotten or used as an ingredient in a shellfish salad. Never have anything to do with a dead uncooked lobster—the meat spoils very quickly.

Best cooking methods: the simplest are the best: plain boiled, steamed, or broiled, served hot or cold with melted butter and either a little lemon juice or a good mayonnaise. Keep the shells to put into fish soup, or use them as a basis for lobster bisque or lobster stock.

Spiny lobster Depending on where you find it, this comparatively clawless cousin of the lobster is also known as rock lobster, crawfish, or crayfish—but do not confuse it with the little freshwater crayfish which, in turn, is sometimes known as a crawfish. Depending, too, on where it comes from—it thrives in the warm waters of the Pacific, the Caribbean, and the Mediterranean—it ranges in color from brownish-green to reddish-brown with yellow and white markings. Slightly paler than regular lobster when cooked, it has dense white flesh, which is well flavored but inclined to be coarse. The choicest meat is in the tail, and there is a lively market for frozen tails.

Buying guide: fresh is best, in late spring or early autumn, but fresh spiny lobsters are usually found only locally. The frozen tails are far more widely available. If you see fresh spiny lobsters for sale, choose specimens without eggs, as those that have eggs are not considered to be wholesome. Otherwise, follow the same guidelines as for ordinary lobsters.

Best cooking methods: when fresh, they are best eaten simply boiled with melted butter. Anything leftover makes a fine salad, with mayonnaise, or a very good bisque together with some shrimp in their shells, and plenty of cream and Madeira or brandy. Otherwise, use the same recipes for spiny lobster as for lobster.

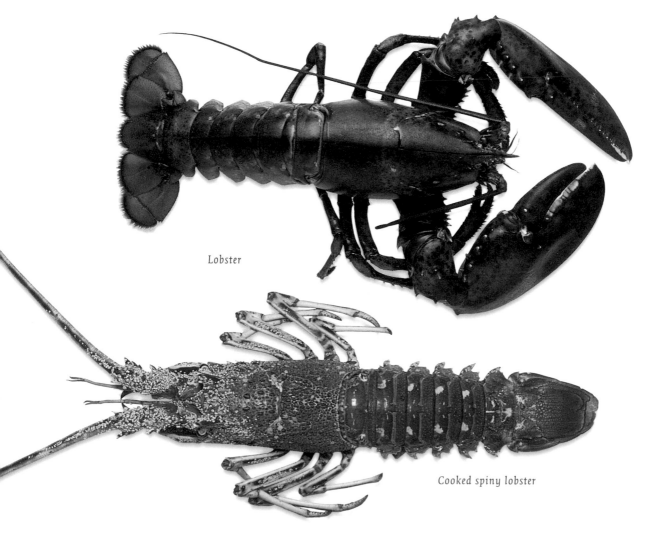

Lobster

Cooked spiny lobster

Crayfish A sweet-fleshed miniature of the lobster, the crayfish (alias crawfish, crawdad, and freshwater lobster) is the only edible freshwater shellfish. Almost an institution in Louisiana, crayfish are also relished in France, where they are called *ecrevisses*; in Spain, where they are known as *astaco* or *cangrejo de rio*; and in Scandinavia. They were once a great feature of country-house tables in Britain, but there the native wild crayfish is now scarce. Although fresh crayfish were at one time limited to Louisiana and the West Coast, they are now farmed and fresh crayfish are often available in larger markets throughout the United States. They may also be found frozen, or cooked whole. Keep fresh crayfish in a bowl in the refrigerator, covered with a damp towel, for no longer than 24 hours. Before cooking them, remove the dark intestine by twisting off the middle tail fin, which will bring the intestine with it (or do this after cooking).
Buying guide: If you buy crayfish fresh, make sure they are lively—they spoil very quickly once dead. Allow at least ten to twelve crayfish per person.
Best cooking methods: boiling is best. In New Orleans, where a crayfish boil is an event, they are boiled in large pots of court-bouillon or water flavored with Creole spices. For simple boiled crayfish, put some smooth stones in the bottom of a large pot of water—this will keep the heat up so that the crayfish don't suffer when they are dropped in. Bring the water, into which you have put plenty of salt and fresh dill, to a rapid boil. Drop each crayfish in separately so that the water keeps boiling all the time and cook for about 5 minutes, until they turn bright scarlet. Remove from the heat and let them cool in the cooking liquid; serve cool or chilled. The French cook them *à la nage*—in a well-flavored court-bouillon—and serve them hot in an appetizing scarlet mound with hot melted butter, or cold with mayonnaise. Crayfish are also used to make a beautiful creamy bisque, and for *sauce Nantua*, the most delicate of sauces, frequently served with *quenelles de brochet* (pike dumplings).

Dublin Bay prawn Whether you meet them as *langoustines*, their French name, lobsterettes, Norway lobster (their Latin name is *Nephrops norvegicus*), Italian

scampi, or Dublin Bay prawns, these pretty pinky-orange-shelled creatures with their pale claws can be treated as exceedingly large shrimp or very small lobsters, depending on which way you like to look at them. The predictability of finding them in their frozen shelled form on the menus of bad, expensive, and pretentious European restaurants has led to their being passed over by many people interested in food, but cooked with care, and not surrounded by soggy batter, they make many delicate dishes.
Buying guide: at present, Dublin Bay prawns are a rarity in U.S. markets, and are most likely to be frozen. If you are lucky enough to find them fresh, they may be preboiled. Sometimes only the tails are sold. To feed four people, buy 2 pounds in their shells, or half that amount if they are already shelled.
Best cooking methods: if raw, cook them in their shells in gently boiling, well-salted water for not more than 10 minutes and then serve them with melted butter.

Overcooking makes them soggy and tasteless. Preboiled, reheat them gently for a hot dish; never recook them, as they easily toughen. Cold, they make a very good salad with oil and vinegar dressing or mayonnaise. In Venice they are dipped into a very light eggless batter, with a few other kinds of small fish and shellfish, then deep-fried and served with lemon wedges. They are also excellent grilled with oil and garlic—even frozen ones are good cooked in this way.

Shrimp and prawn There are so many species in the shrimp family that distinguishing them is often difficult, particularly because in different parts of the world—and in different regions of the United States—the names shrimp and prawn often do not refer to the same variety. In the United States, where more shrimp is consumed than anywhere else, classification is usually by size, from the largest of the luscious Gulf shrimp (ten to twelve make 1 pound) to the tiny cold-

Court-Bouillon 246
Italian Seafood Salad 361, 360
Mayonnaise 259

Peeled rock shrimp

Cooked shrimp

Cooked European brown shrimp

Cooked Dublin Bay prawn

Tiger shrimp

Cooked crayfish

water specimens that need 100 or more to tip the scales at that weight. Shrimp is the preferred term in much of the country, but prawn may also be used, usually but not always to refer to the larger varieties. In Europe, any member of the family that is more than about 2 inches long is often called a prawn, and it is the discerning French and Italians who award them the distinction of separate names. The *crevette rouge*, or *gambero rosso*, for example, is the large, expensive shrimp, very strong-flavored, and greatly enjoyed by the Italians, who often eat a whole pyramid of them with a bowl of mayonnaise and a bottle of white wine. A clear, deep-coral color with a violet splotch showing through the transparent shell of the head, it turns a bright pink-red when cooked. The delicious *crevette rose*, or *gamberello*, is the common large pink shrimp seen throughout Europe, best eaten cold with brown bread and butter and lemon juice, or with mayonnaise or in a salad. The *crevette rose du large*, or *gambero rosa*, with pretty red markings on its crested head, is one of the best, very delicate and much appreciated in northern France, where it is simply boiled, laid on a bed of brown seaweed with ice and halved lemons, and served with brown bread and butter.

Also delicious are the cold-water shrimp of Scandinavia, with their firm meat and fresh taste. They are usually boiled in seawater on board the trawler as soon as they are caught, which gives them a mild, sweetish flavor. These are often found frozen or canned throughout Europe.

Freshly caught and freshly boiled, little brown shrimp (in France *grises*) are difficult to shell because they are so small, but perhaps it is this job that makes the reward so worthwhile. Much more delicate than their larger cousins, these are delicious. Brown shrimp will turn browner when cooked; pink shrimp are grayish-brown when caught and turn pink when they are cooked.

Large warm-water shrimp or prawns, farmed by aquaculture methods all odver the world, are now widely available raw, in the shell, with or without heads. These include the famed black tiger shrimp from the Indo-Pacific region, the East Asian king prawn, and the Hawaiian blue prawn, or giant river prawn, a freshwater prawn with a brilliant blue tail.
Buying guide: almost all the shrimp sold in the U.S. marketplace is frozen (not necessarily a bad thing, if it was flash-frozen at sea as soon as it was caught)—or was once. Among the more common

types are the delicious Gulf white and Gulf pink, along with the less-exciting Gulf brown shrimp. Others you are likely to see are the black tiger shrimp, usually quite flavorful, and the Chinese white, which varies in quality but may be quite good. Rock shrimp, cold-water shrimp found off the southern Atlantic Coast, are usually sold peeled because they're so difficult to shell, and often cooked. If you do come across fresh raw shrimp or prawns, they should be springy, with bright, crisp shells—avoid any that are soft or limp or have a smell of ammonia about them. Frozen shrimp really should be bought frozen—those thawed-out specimens in packages at the fish market may have been around for some time, and defrosted food spoils much more quickly than fresh food. If you must buy them thawed, make sure they smell fresh, and avoid any with black spots on the shell, which are a sign of deterioration.
Best cooking methods: simply drop them into a large pan of boiling seawater or salted water and simmer them for a minute or two, depending on their size—don't overcook them, as they will lose their delicate texture and turn tough. Recooking shrimp toughens them, so those bought already boiled should be

Belon oyster

Blue mussel

Green-lipped mussel

Pacific oyster

Atlantic oyster

heated gently and for as short a time as possible when being used in a hot dish. Shrimp can be shelled and deveined before or after cooking. The larger the species, the better it lends itself to grilling, panfrying, or broiling.

Oyster Oysters are a luxury you either love or loathe. To some people they are the height of ecstasy, to others a cause of revulsion. Aldous Huxley once said, "I suppose that when the sapid and slippery morsel—which is gone like a flash of gustatory summer lightning—glides along the palate, few people imagine that they are swallowing a piece of machinery (and going machinery too) greatly more complicated than a watch." Perhaps oyster lovers prefer not to think about it. It is certainly hard to believe that oysters were once the food of the poor: they only became fashionable and expensive as they became scarce, and in Europe might have disappeared altogether if a French marine biologist had not discovered the ancient oyster beds at Lake Fusaro, near Naples, and learned how oysters could be artificially reared.

Most American oysters, in contrast to those in Europe, are harvested in the wild. The Atlantic, or Eastern, oyster,

Crassostrea virginica, goes under a variety of names, usually denoting the area where it was caught—Blue Point, Wellfleet, Chincoteague, and Apalachicola are some of the best-known. On the West Coast, the Pacific (*C. gigas*), or Japanese, oyster is the most common type. The Olympia, *Ostrea lurida*, another Pacific oyster, is the only one native to the West Coast.

There are three species of European oyster, all of which are farmed by aquaculture. The best British oysters, *Ostrea edulis*, known as natives or flats, include the Whitstable, the Colchester, and the Helford. These have rounded shells and a subtle flavor. In France, this type is known as *belon*; the American Olympia oyster is a relative. The second type, known as the rock oyster, is *Crassostrea gigas*, the Pacific oyster when it's in America. In France, these are *huîtres creuses*. They have elongated shells and a sharper, more oceanic flavor. The third species, *Crassostrea angulata* or the Portuguese oyster, is being supplanted by *C. gigas*, which is thought to be finer.

Oysters come in many sizes, and not everyone prefers the largest ones. There are stringent regulations to keep oysters safe from pollution, but if you do have one that tastes bad, spit it out.

Oysters are best eaten raw, on the half-shell. Serve them in the deep halves of their shells, on a bed of crushed ice, and take care not to spill the liquid they contain—it has an exquisite salty, marine flavor with a hint of iodine. Accompany them with halved lemons and, if you like, Tabasco sauce or cayenne pepper, or with red wine vinegar with a few chopped shallots afloat in it, and brown bread and butter. Drink a chilled Chablis or an Alsatian wine. *Buying guide*: oysters are at their best from about the end of October to the end of February, when the sea is coldest. In summer, as the sea warms up, they may start breeding and can be milky, fat, and soft. Canned smoked oysters make a good hors d'oeuvre.

Best cooking methods: oysters are delicious in a creamy oyster stew or chowder, or with a dry white wine and cheese sauce spooned over them, sprinkled with bread crumbs and placed under the broiler until the crumbs are golden-brown.

Scallop These are a particular favorite among shellfish lovers, partly because they are such a delight to eat and partly because they are beautiful and symbolic. Often represented in painting (notably Botticelli's *Venus*), the scallop shell is a

Queen scallop

Littleneck clam

Cherrystone clam

Chowder clam

Sea scallop

Manila clam

Cockle

symbol of Christianity and a badge of the religious pilgrim.

The most common American scallops are the large sea scallop and the small, tender bay scallop—a third type is the calico, smaller than bays and with less flavor. Europe can boast some of the best of the many species of scallop that abound, including the most common great scallop, the pilgrim scallop, and the queen scallop, or queenie. These latter are much smaller than ordinary scallops, with two slightly hollow shells rather than one convex and one flat. Small and delicate, they have the texture of butter. Unlike American scallops, European scallops are always sold with their scarlet coral, or roe, which is considered by some to be the best part. *Buying guide:* at their best in late fall and winter, scallops are becoming expensive, but fortunately you do not need many— three or four large ones per person is usually sufficient. If using smaller scallops, allow between ten and fifteen per person. Look for "diver scallops"— especially from Maine—which are prime handpicked specimens. In America they are always sold already shelled and cleaned, whereas in Europe you can often buy them still in the shell (and then use the shells as serving dishes). In America, scallop shells are more likely to be found in gourmet shops.
Best cooking methods: be careful not to overcook scallops, or they will be tough—small ones take only a few seconds, large ones a minute or two at the most. They can be pan-seared with garlic and parsley or baked in the oven in butter with parsley, garlic, and lemon juice. Or, sauté and serve perhaps with a little port and cream stirred in to make a sauce. They can be broiled with bacon on skewers, made into a chowder, or lightly poached or steamed and served in a white wine sauce, sprinkled with bread crumbs and browned under the broiler. Served in Mornay sauce, the rich cheese sauce, they have become known simply by their French name, *coquilles St. Jacques.*

Clam America is the place to appreciate clams: aficionados can take delight in steamers, or long-necks, and littlenecks, cherrystones, Manila clams and razors, surf clams, butter clams, and the enormous geoduck. The familiar Atlantic clams called littleneck (which should

not be confused with Pacific littleneck), cherrystone, and chowder clams are not in fact separate species, as many people think, but merely different sizes of the hard-shell quahog. Clam chowder is almost a national dish, and a clam bake is a serious and favorite pastime, while expressions like "happy as a clam" are frequently heard along the shorelines— and inland as well. At clam bakes, the shellfish, and usually lobsters too, along with fresh corn, is steamed on a bed of seaweed over heated stones on the beach. Clam bakes are most popular on the East Coast, especially in Massachusetts and Maine, and here too you can find roadside stands where clams, gathered from the shore, are sold, deep-fried in batter and served with tartar sauce.

In France you may be offered *tellines, clovisses, palourdes, olives,* or *praires* (the best, called Warty Venus in England!); in Italy, *vongoli* or *tartufi di mare;* in Spain, *almejas, margaritas,* or *amayuelas.* In England, clams are not as impossible to find as they once were, and the large quahogs are sometimes available. *Buying guide:* available all year. Since clams vary so much in size from one variety to another, ask the clam seller how many to allow for each person. Canned clams are also widely available. *Best cooking methods:* the soft-shell or long-neck varieties such as razor and Ipswich clams can be eaten raw, just like oysters, and so can small hard-shell clams such as cherrystones. Larger ones like quahogs can be steamed open and chopped for chowder; sautéed in olive oil with lemon juice and parsley; broiled with butter, bread crumbs, and garlic; or chopped and made into the excellent sauce for spaghetti *alla vongole,* which is also delicious made with tiny cherrystone clams.

Mussel Clumped in blue-black masses on rocks and piers or attached singly to shingle stones in estuaries, mussels have in the past quite unfairly been considered the poor man's shellfish. Their status, however, has been improving rapidly. In America, where they are to be found on both coasts and are widely farmed, they have grown steadily in popularity, and in Europe, where they are extremely popular, there are mussel farms around Mediterranean coasts, where the mussels are bred on long stakes in clean seawater. If you are collecting your own mussels,

make sure that they are living in unpolluted water and known to be safe. Discard any that are even remotely damaged.

Mussels are usually sold cleaned, but wash them in several changes of water to rid them of grit, then scrape the shells clean with the back of a knife if necessary and rinse thoroughly in cold water. If the stringy "beard" is attached, pull it out (cut it off if necessary) and rinse the mussels again in a bowl of clean water. Discard any that float to the surface or whose shells are damaged or open.

The French are enthusiastic about raw shellfish and will eat whole platefuls of raw mussels with lemon juice as if they were oysters. The smooth, thin-shelled French species are the best to eat in this way, and they should be from a very pure source.

A more recent arrival is the green-lipped mussel from New Zealand. It is larger and meatier than the blue mussel and has a more pronounced flavor. *Buying guide:* mussels are inexpensive. Medium-sized or smaller ones are best; large mussels are not so appetizing. Always buy slightly more than you need, to allow for any you must discard. For two people, buy a quart (2 pounds). *Best cooking methods:* one of the best-known recipes for mussels is the excellent *moules à la marinière,* mussels steamed in white wine with shallots, herbs, and butter. They can also be, once opened, broiled with bread crumbs, garlic, parsley, and butter, or used in a garlicky tomato sauce, pasta sauce, or seafood salad, or deep-fried.

Cockle Although these can be found along the Atlantic coast, cockles are more favored in Britain than in America, traditionally sold with periwinkles and whelks at the seaside, accompanied by vinegar and brown bread and butter, and outside London pubs. Cockles are a traditional ingredient in *char kway teow,* a Southeast Asian fried noodle dish. Here, cockles are also steamed and served with a piquant chile dipping sauce. *Buying guide:* cockles are at their best in the summer. *Best cooking methods:* eat them raw, or steam them in court-bouillon until their shells open. They also make a splendid soup, with mussels, garlic, potato, bacon, and milk, and are a good addition to risottos; or they can be stewed in a tomato sauce and served with pasta.

PREPARING SHELLFISH

Killing a live lobster

In some recipes a lobster is cut up before cooking. First, cover the tail with a cloth and hold it firmly. Insert the point of a sharp, heavy knife into the center of the cross mark in the head, and quickly push it down to the board; this will kill the lobster immediately.

lobster 33–4

knives 222–4
lobster crackers, pick, and pincers 229

1

2

Preparing a cooked lobster

1 If you wish to remove the claws and legs, simply twist them off.

2 To extract the meat from the claws and legs, crack them open, using the back of a knife, lobster crackers or nutcrackers, or a small hammer.

3

4

3 Splitting a lobster in half is easiest to do in two stages (you can prepare an uncooked lobster in the same way). First, draw a sharp knife through the head from the tail section toward the eyes.

4 Reinsert the knife and move it in the opposite direction, cutting down to the tip of the tail and splitting the lobster completely in two.

5

6

5 Pull the halves apart to expose the flesh. This fine female lobster has an excellent red coral, and also some darker external roe, which is unusual. Both are edible and should be reserved.

6 Discard the grain sac from the top of the head, and the intestinal tract, which runs down the middle of the tail. As well as the coral, the creamy green tomalley, or liver, of the lobster should be reserved to make a sauce.

Removing the meat from a cooked crab

1 Pull off and discard the narrow triangular "apron" from the underside of the crab (this is a Dungeness crab).

2 Turn the crab over and carefully pull off the top shell.

1

2

3 Pull out and discard the gills (known as "dead man's fingers") and the intestines from each side of the crab.

4 Twist off the claws and legs.

3

4

5

6

5 Crack the claws and legs with lobster crackers, nutcrackers, small hammer, or with the back of a large, heavy knife.

6 Pull out the meat from the claws, removing it in large pieces; use a lobster pick if necessary to remove the meat from the tips of the claws.

7

8

7 Remove the meat from the legs, using a lobster pick if necessary.

8 Cut the body into several large pieces with a large, heavy knife.

9 Use a lobster pick to remove the meat from the body.

10 The crabmeat from the body, legs, and claws is now ready to be eaten or used in a recipe.

9

10

1

2

Peeling, deveining, and butterflying shrimp

1 Pull off the legs with your fingers, and then peel the shell away from the body. If you like, leave the last section of tail on the shrimp.

2 To devein, use a small, sharp knife and carefully cut a shallow slit down the back of each shrimp.

3

4

3 If the intestinal vein is black or brown, pull it out with the tip of the knife or with your fingers and discard it. (The vein is removed only because of its appearance.)

4 To butterfly, slice the shrimp down the back but without cutting quite all the way through, and then open the shrimp out like a book.

Shucking clams

1 Hold the clam over a bowl, with the hinge in your palm. Insert the blade of a clam knife between the top and bottom shells, and work it around the shell until you reach the hinge. (You may want to protect your hand with a towel.) Be careful not to pierce the clam meat.

2 Cut through the hinge muscle and carefully open the shell. Cut the clam free from the top and bottom of the shell, and drop it into the bowl along with all its liquor.

1

2

oyster 37
scallop 37–8

oyster knife 225

Shucking oysters

1 Hold the oyster steady, and carefully insert an oyster knife between the top and bottom shells, next to the hinge. (Unless you are very proficient, you may want to hold the oyster in a towel to protect your hand.)

2 Keep a firm grip on the oyster and, pushing against the hinge, carefully work the knife in, twisting it slightly until the hinge breaks.

3 Open the oyster and sever the muscle that adheres to the flatter upper shell.

4 Run the knife underneath the oyster to free it from the rounded lower shell. Remove the oyster, or serve it with its own juices in the rounded bottom shell.

1

2

3

4

1

2

Preparing scallops

1 Using a strong, sharp, wide knife, pry the shells apart and detach the scallop from the rounded shell by carefully sliding the knife underneath the muscle.

2 Rinse the scallop under cold running water. Pull away the film of membrane and discard it.

3

4

3 With the scallop still under cold running water, and holding back the white flesh and coral with your thumb, push away and sever the black intestine.

4 The scallop and the delicious orange coral are now ready to cook.

Other Seafood, Snails, and Frog's Legs

Many creatures are so strange to look at and are so unlike anything else that they are usually, for want of a better label, called "miscellaneous." But unappetizing though they may look to some people, with their spiny, shell-y, jelly-like, or leathery exteriors, many of us really like to eat them. Indeed, some of these creatures, such as squid, snails, sea urchins, and octopus, rank among the most delicious of foods, and all of them provide a challenge to the adventurous cook.

Some seafood—such as limpets—although it is perfectly edible, is not worth marketing commercially and so you will have to rely on gathering it yourself, always remembering that any living thing gathered from the sea and its shores is potentially dangerous if it comes from a polluted area, and that many varieties are simply inedible. If in any doubt about the safety of your haul, check with the local office of the E.P.A. (Environmental Protection Agency) or the state or local health department.

Squid, octopus, and cuttlefish
The Mediterranean countries understand best how to deal with these extraordinary creatures, having long eaten them in great quantities. They also play an important role in the cuisine of China and Japan. All are at their sweetest and most tender when they are small in size; however, larger specimens can be improved by soaking for several hours in a marinade of wine vinegar, sliced onion, and salt and pepper.

Squid Familiar in Mediterranean dishes as *calamari, calmar or encornet, calamaro,* or *calamar,* squid is delicious to eat if you understand the principle that the cooking must be either very brief or very long—anything in between and your squid will be as tough as rubber. Once cleaned, the squid can be rapidly broiled, or stuffed with chopped meat and the chopped tentacles, and then baked in a tomato- and garlic-flavored sauce. Sliced into rings, it can be deep-fried plain or dipped first into a light batter. Larger specimens can be stewed gently with olive oil, wine, and tomatoes.

It is a pleasure, in Spain, to be served two little dishes at the same time, one holding a fragrant stew of the tentacles, with onions and garlic, and the other the sliced, crisply fried rings of the body. Squid can also be cut into rings and boiled very briefly—no more than a minute or two, until the rings lose their pearly, translucent look—and then put into a seafood salad. The squid ink found in a sac inside can be used in risotto, pasta, and sauces. The tiniest squid, with fragile bodies no more than 3 inches long, can be very quickly deep-fried in a coating of beaten egg and flour.

Octopus can be very tough, and the larger it grows, the tougher it gets, so it is a wise precaution, having removed the beak and head (if the fish dealer has not already done so) and turned out the contents of the body, to pound the legs and body with a meat mallet until they are soft. The octopus contains its ink within its liver, and this is sometimes used to make a very strong and heavily scented gravy. The ink can also be used as a pasta sauce. Frozen cleaned octopus

preparing squid
47

meat tenderizer
226

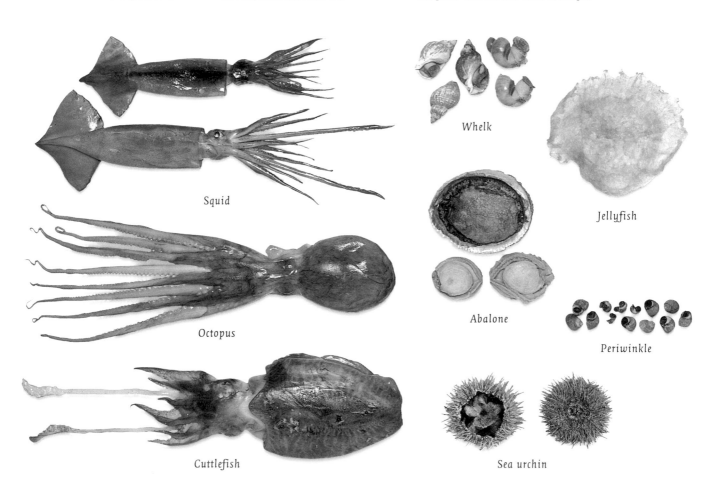

Squid

Octopus

Cuttlefish

Whelk

Jellyfish

Abalone

Periwinkle

Sea urchin

seviche 423

meat tenderizer 226

has recently become available in many supermarkets and good fish shops.

Octopus can be stewed, or stuffed and baked like squid, but a large specimen will need up to 2 hours or more to become tender. Little ones can also be panfried gently in olive oil and make a delicious salad, often eaten warm, with lemon juice, olive oil, garlic, and chopped parsley.

Cuttlefish Often rather gracefully camouflaged by striped markings, the cuttlefish has a larger head than the squid and a much wider, dumpier body. Inside lies the white shell, or cuttlebone, found washed up on Mediterranean beaches and given to pet birds to peck at (ground, it was once used as tooth powder, jewel polish, and as face powder by Roman ladies who wanted to look delicate). More tender than octopus or squid, cuttlefish, only rarely available in the United States—imported and expensive—can be cooked in the same ways, and very small ones are delicious deep-fried. They are prepared in the same way as squid. The ink, or *sepia*, can be used to make a sauce in which the cuttlefish can be stewed, and goes into the Italian dish *risotto nero* (black rice).

Single-shelled creatures

These all belong to the same family that includes the familiar garden snail, and all move around on a muscular "foot." They can go into fish soups, sauces, and stews as well as being tasty snacks on their own, served with plenty of vinegar, pepper, and brown bread and butter.

Abalone "Delicious ambrosia," an enthusiast wrote in the 1600s about these white-fleshed shellfish. With their curiously ear-shaped shells, the inside gleaming with pearly colors, abalone, also called ormer in Britain, can be found fresh in the warm waters off California and around the Channel Islands and the Breton coast at certain times of the year.

Fresh abalone, even little ones, need to be well beaten with a mallet to make them tender. Very small abalones can then be eaten raw with a squeeze of lemon juice; larger ones are usually thinly sliced and marinated in white wine, oil, herbs, and chopped shallots, then sautéed very briefly in butter— overcooking only toughens them. They can also be used like clams in soup or chowder. Canned abalone is a good substitute for fresh. Frozen abalone,

sold in Asian markets, is ready to use and often quite good; should you come across dried abalone, it is hardly worth the effort of making it edible—it needs to be soaked for 4 days before anything can be done with it.

Periwinkle, winkle There is something homely and comfortable about periwinkles, and their little dark shells are small enough to make them completely acceptable in a way that many large snails are not. In France, you are likely to be given a plate of *bigorneaux* with a glass of kir—cassis and white wine— in an Alsatian brasserie while waiting for your *choucroute garnie* or your slice of foie gras. In England, winkles are eaten with bread and butter and a pot of tea, and make a tasty snack on seaside piers, accompanied by vinegar. Whatever the circumstance, a long pin is indispensable for wheedling the little shellfish out of their shells. To cook periwinkles, which may be found fresh in Asian markets along the East Coast, boil them in their shells in salted water for 10 minutes. Eat only the first part of the body—the second part is easily separated.

Whelk These handsome but decidedly unaristocratic shellfish, with their ribbed, deeply whorled shells, are sold already boiled, fresh or frozen. In the United States, they can be found in Italian markets, where they are called *scungilli*, and in other ethnic markets. Whelks look something like periwinkles, but are a much more substantial mouthful and easier to remove from their shells. The large "foot" is the part that is usually eaten. Whelks can also be used in fish soups and stews. On the Scottish island of Iona, where whelks are a traditional part of the islanders' diet, whelk soup is made by thickening seasoned whelk stock with oatmeal and finely chopped onion.

Conch The term conch—pronounced "konk"—is often used to include the periwinkle and whelk, but what is usually thought of as being the best of the family is the large Caribbean conch with the graceful spiral-shaped shell in which one seems to hear the sound of the sea. Fresh conch meat needs to be tenderized by vigorous beating and can then be stewed in a wine sauce with herbs and spices, or thinly sliced and deep-fried. It also goes into chowders and in parts of the Caribbean it is used for *seviche*.

Limpet Limpets are exceptionally tough—you can tell they are going to be tough by the strength of the muscle that clamps them to the rocks as soon as they are touched and makes them almost impossible to pry off, unless you can take them by surprise. With persistence they can be gathered at low tide (they are rarely marketed, except in some fish stores in coastal areas) and eaten raw or used to flavor a soup. They can also be panfried in butter with chopped parsley, pepper, and vinegar, or baked for a few minutes with a little butter in each shell. The smaller ones are better boiled and eaten with vinegar, pepper, and bread and butter. Slipper limpets, native to North America, prey on oysters, which makes them very unpopular with oyster lovers, but they too are good to eat either cooked or raw.

"Fruits" of the sea

Some of the most astonishing candidates for any sort of cuisine are nonetheless considered delicacies by their devotees.

Sea urchin A menace to the bather but a pleasure to the gourmet, the sharp-spined sea urchin is plentiful in many parts of the world, and its pretty lacy-patterned shell—minus the spines— is often brought home as a memento of seaside vacations. Best for eating are the green sea urchin and the black sea urchin. These can be lightly boiled and are sometimes pickled, but are best eaten fresh, raw and straight from the shell. To accomplish this, the sea urchin is cut in half using a sharp knife (in France, sea urchin is called *oursin* and is cut with a *coupe-oursin*, designed for this task). This exposes the rose-colored or orange ovaries, or roe, which are simply given a drop of lemon juice and scooped out with pieces of fresh crusty bread. The crushed roe can also be used in omelets and as a garnish for fish.

Sea anemone These inhabitants of rocky pools, enticingly waving their multitude of soft arms, are sometimes eaten in Japan, Samoa, and France. The snake-locks anemones, known as *orties de mer*, are carefully gathered in France, then marinated, dipped into a light batter, and fried. They also go, together with a few red *tomates de mer* and a lot of shellfish, into a Mediterranean soup.

Figue de mer, violet This very odd, leathery-skinned creature is particularly relished in France's Provence, where it has the proper accompaniment of hot sun and a plentiful supply of white wine. Found anchored to rocks or the sea floor, syphoning water in through one spout and out of the other, it is cut in half and the yellow part inside eaten raw.

Bêche de mer Also known as sea cucumber, because of its shape, and as sea slug, *trepang*, and *balatin*, this warm-water creature is sliced and eaten raw in Japan with soy sauce, vinegar, or mustard. Several species are smoke-dried and used in soup. In China it has a reputation as an aphrodisiac. One recipe using dried sea cucumber involves 4 days of preparation and yields twelve Chinese servings or ninety-five Western servings, which is either a miscalculation or says a great deal about the sea slug's lack of appeal to the Western palate.

Jellyfish The Chinese are great users of dried jellyfish, primarily to add texture to a meal, and slabs of dried jellyfish can usually be found in Chinese markets. If the jellyfish has been salted, it will need to be washed and allowed to soak for some hours in several changes of water. Once soaked, it should be briefly blanched in boiling water, then refreshed in cold water. It can be cut into slivers and stir-fried with chicken, or scalded, which produces crunchy curls that are served with a sauce of sesame oil, soy sauce, vinegar, and sugar. In Japan, jellyfish is cooked into crisp-textured strips and eaten with vinegar as a side dish.

Samphire and seaweeds

Apart from being such a pleasure to gather, in the early months of summer when most of them are at their most luxuriant, seaweeds are a rich source of minerals as well as of intriguing textures and flavors. If you gather your own, cut the plant well above its base so that it can grow again, and always be sure to wash it thoroughly in fresh water before cooking. Most of the better-known seaweeds can be found in dried form in health food stores or Asian markets, and can be restored by soaking. Samphire is occasionally sold in specialty produce markets, when in season.

Samphire, marsh samphire This succulent green plant, also known as glasswort or pickle plant, or, in French, *pousse-pierre* or *saint-pierre* can be found growing in seaside marshes. It is best at midsummer. The flavor of fresh marsh samphire is salty and iodiney—like seawater but green; it is the crisp texture that is interesting.

Samphire can go fresh into salads and is often steeped in vinegar to make a delicate pickle. In many regions, it is greatly appreciated as a vegetable served

Carragheen

Dulse

Samphire

Hijiki

Kelp

Nori

Kombu

Snail

Frog's legs

Wakame

with fish, or on its own simply boiled and dipped in melted butter, then drawn through the teeth like asparagus to strip the succulent part from the central core.

Nori With its delicate taste of the sea, this reddish-purple seaweed, also known as laver, was very popular in England in the eighteenth century. When fresh, nori is seldom appreciated in the West today, except in Wales, where it is enthusiastically boiled until it turns into the spinach-like pulp called laverbread—although why it should be called bread is a mystery. But dried, it is well-known to aficionados of Chinese and Japanese cuisine, and to any sushi lover. In Japan, where nori is cultivated, it is pressed and dried in thin sheets. Nori is toasted lightly before being wrapped around vinegared rice to make sushi; or it may be crumbled over rice as a salty garnish. In China, nori is dried and then simmered to produce a nutritious jelly.

Carragheen, Irish moss Although Ireland and the village of Carragheen have given it its most commonly used names, this pretty red-tinged, frond-like plant is found along most northerly Atlantic shorelines growing on rocks and stones. It can be used fresh or dried, when it bleaches to a creamy white, and is an important source of agar-agar, a vegetable gelatin much used in the food industry. In Britain a carragheen gelatin dessert is made by simmering the moss in milk or water until most of it dissolves, then straining it and allowing it to set. The result is very nourishing. For those who don't like its faint taste of the sea, it can be flavored with vanilla, honey, or fruit.

Kelp A number of large seaweeds are popularly known as kelp and have long been used as a source of food and of medicine, being particularly rich in iodine. Much liked in Japan, where it is called kombu, kelp, also called sea tangle, finds its way to the table as a delicate salad vegetable, a seasoning for root vegetables, or a garnish for rice, or fashioned into miniature baskets, deep-fried, and stuffed with vegetables. It is also used for making soups and stocks, such as *dashi*, or can simply be cooked as a vegetable to accompany fish.

To make the all-purpose Japanese stock called *dashi*, cut a piece of kombu into quarters using scissors and place it in a pan with 4 cups water. Bring to a boil, then remove the pan from the heat at once and cool the boiling liquid by adding ¼ cup cold water. Add 1 cup dried bonito flakes (*katsuo bushi*), bring the liquid back to a boil, and immediately remove from the heat. Strain the liquid through cheesecloth or a fine sieve. For a vegetarian version of the stock, omit the *katsuo bushi*.

Dulse Another of the familiar purplish-red seaweeds, with fan-shaped fronds up to 10 inches long, dulse is to be found growing plentifully on rocks and on larger weeds throughout the British Isles and the Mediterranean. Known in Ireland as *dillisk*, dulse can be eaten raw as a salad, and around the Mediterranean it sometimes goes into ragouts, but it is a very tough, rubbery plant and needs to be cooked for up to 5 hours. Dried, it can be chewed as a rather unconventional appetizer, without any further preparation, or used as a relish. It has a salty, fish-like flavor, and is said to be "principally eaten by sailors and children."

Wakame A rich source of minerals, this dark green seaweed is much used in Japan. The soft leaves go into salads or are cooked with other vegetables, and both leaves and stems are used in soups. In the United States, wakame is sold dried and must be soaked in lukewarm water before using.

Snail

The French, of course, are the major eaters of snails, and the snails the French prize most are the hefty specimens from the vineyards of Burgundy, where they are fed—like the snails of ancient Rome—on grape leaves until they have grown fat and luscious. The classic method of preparing snails is the Burgundian way, in which case they become *escargots à la bourguignonne*, served sizzling in their shells with great quantities of rich garlic butter and fresh crusty bread for mopping. However, as there are never enough Burgundian snails to meet the demand in France, the alternative is a smaller striped snail, the *petit gris*, which makes up for its lack of size by being sweet, tasty, and tender. (A drawback is that the *petit gris* shells, unlike those of the Burgundian snail, may be too fragile to be used once their occupants have been removed, but this is solved by using special little ceramic pots, easily washed and always ready to be used again. Other essentials for the enjoyment of snails are the dimpled plates called *escargotières*, which hold six or twelve snail shells, tongs for picking up the piping hot shells, and special forks with two prongs for twisting the snails out of their shells.)

The business of preparing live snails means that it is much simpler to buy snails canned, or fresh already cleaned and ready to cook. As a change from garlic butter, snails are very good simmered in olive oil with garlic, tomatoes, and fresh rosemary or mint—the traditional dish to serve on Midsummer's Eve in Rome.

Frog's legs

Like snails, frog's legs as a delicacy have long been associated with the French. Escoffier, the "king of chefs," is credited with making them acceptable to the English: in the 1890s, for a party held by the Prince of Wales at the Savoy Hotel, London, he prepared what he called *nymphes à l'aurore*, frog's legs poached in white wine and served cold in aspic with a little paprika to evoke the rose-gold glow of dawn. Presumably he called his frog's legs "nymphs" out of delicacy of feeling for the English diners. When he wasn't preparing them for the Prince of Wales, Escoffier simply seasoned them with salt and pepper, dusted them with flour, and sautéed them in butter, serving them with a squeeze of lemon juice and a sprinkling of parsley.

Today, in the Dombes region of eastern France, those who know their frogs still go frogging in the ponds and lakes; however, not all frogs are edible and what appears fresh or frozen in the market and on restaurant menus will have come from special frog farms. Frog's legs are light and easily digestible, rather like chicken in flavor—in China, where frogs thrive in the paddy fields and frog's legs are much enjoyed at banquets, they are known as "field chickens." In America, frog's legs are often big enough to be fried like chicken legs, but the smaller legs are usually more tender and have subtler flavors. In any case, Escoffier's way with them is still the best: cooked in oil or butter for 5 minutes until they are golden-brown, and served with lemon and a sprinkling of parsley; or they can be poached in a little white wine and served hot with a creamy sauce. They can also be prepared *à la provençale*, with garlic and tomato.

PREPARING SEAFOOD

1

Preparing squid

1 Grasp the squid with one hand and, with the other, reach inside the body and pull out the head and tentacles.

squid 43

knives 222–4

2 Pull off and then discard the body's mottled skin.

3 Feel inside the body for the long piece of transparent cartilage, or "quill." Pull this out and discard it.

2

3

4

5

4 Wash the body thoroughly, inside and out, under cold running water and then pull off the two flaps from the body. You will find that they separate quite easily, as if held in place only by suction.

5 Cut the tentacles from the head. If the long, narrow ink sac is present and still intact, you will find it attached to the head; remove it carefully and put it aside to use in an accompanying sauce. The head itself, which contains the viscera, can be discarded.

6 Leave the body whole for stuffing or cut it into thick rings. Slice the flaps into strips, and cut the tentacles to a manageable size. The squid is now ready to cook.

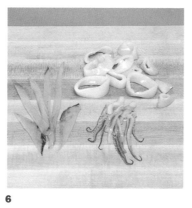

6

Meat

Meat is such an important and delicious part of our diet that it makes sense to buy it as intelligently as possible. If you go to a high-class specialty butcher (possibly one who sells organic meat), who buys meat by the carcass and then hangs it until it has reached the peak of juiciness and flavor, and who butchers it with finesse, you will seldom have a disappointing piece of meat.

You will also be able to buy meat in greater variety, as the butcher will be able to offer you the lesser-known cuts that can go a long way toward making your food more interesting. Because there will be little waste by way of unwanted fat, gristle, and awkward bones, his prices will be high, but cooking will be a joy.

Choosing meat

Failing such a paragon, it pays to develop your own expertise when it comes to shopping. Most butchers will give friendly and sometimes disinterested advice when asked. However, at the supermarket there often is no one to turn to, and the packages of meat can look distressingly similar. Some stores do label their meat as suitable for "roasting," "broiling," and "stewing," for example, but many others will simply give you the name of the cut, and leave it at that.

Although all meat must be inspected by the United States Department of Agriculture before sale, grading meat for quality is only voluntary. Some packing plants follow U.S.D.A. grading, but others use their own systems. The U.S.D.A. system is based on the amount of marbling—the flecks of fat in the meat—and on the age of the animal. Marbling gives meat its tenderness, flavor and juiciness. Beef and lamb are the most commonly graded; veal sometimes is. Beef and lamb may be labeled prime, choice, or standard; veal is usually labeled either prime or choice. Prime meat is the best and most expensive; prime beef is not usually found in the average supermarket. Choice beef is the most common grade found in the supermarket; although choice meat is less marbled than prime, it can still be tender and juicy to eat. Standard beef is the leanest and least expensive; it is also tougher and less flavorful than choice.

Today, with fat definitely off the menu, special attention is paid to the ratio of fat to lean when the herd is still on the hoof, while organic farms, where the animals' diet is carefully supervised, offer the healthiest meat.

The look of meat At a really good store all the cuts, even the cheapest, will look appetizing. They should look silky, not wet. All boned and rolled roasts should be neatly tied. Where there are bones, these should be sawn smoothly, not jaggedly chopped, and smaller cuts of meat, particularly chops and cutlets, should be neatly and thoroughly trimmed, with excess fat removed.

The cut surface of meat exposes the grain, or muscle fibers, which are potentially coarser and tougher in an older animal, or in parts of the anatomy, such as the leg or the neck, that have had more active use. However, the fineness or otherwise of grain is not really a reliable indicator of either the meat's flavor or its tenderness.

Tenderness When all pieces of meat look equally good, it can be hard to distinguish between the tender and the not so tender, and many factors, apart from anatomy, contribute to this: the age and breed of the animal, the way it was handled before slaughter, the way the meat is cut, and so on.

There are many schools of butchery, producing different cuts of meat not only in different countries but in different regions; in fact, there are as many regional variations and names for the different cuts as there are regional recipes. However, no matter where and how a carcass is divided, most of the best meat of each animal comes from the hindquarter and loin, and the tenderest meat of all comes from the parts that have had the least exercise. Exercise means the development of muscle fiber and of the connective tissue that holds the muscles together in bundles, and it is connective tissue that is primarily responsible for toughness.

The tender cuts with little connective tissue respond to dry heat (roasting, panfrying, and broiling/grilling), but the others will need slow cooking in moist heat (braising, stewing, or boiling), which breaks down the connective tissue into gelatin. Although commercial

tenderizers are sometimes used on beef, this is not, fortunately, general practice. Based on papain (from papayas), with its tenderizing enzymes that "digest" proteins, they may be applied to the tougher pieces by the wholesaler. Although the meat will be more tender, it will also become duller to eat. As the enzymes work on all the flesh, the tender parts as well as the tougher ones, the advantage of the breaking down of connective tissues is often balanced by a general loss in character and flavor— a decided disadvantage. Tenderized meat does not become any less fibrous—the fiber merely becomes soft as it is "digested" in this process.

There are ways of preparing tough meat in the kitchen so that it arrives at table full of flavor and juice, fit to be cut with a spoon. Try marinating the meat in a marinade including wine, lemon juice, vinegar, yogurt, or even chopped tomatoes. The acids present in all these ingredients will help to break down connective tissue. Oil, too, is used in many marinades to add succulence, especially in the cooking of Greece and the Middle East. Of course, lengthy cooking in moist heat must follow to complete the process, but this is no disadvantage since the tougher cuts need time, above all, to develop their flavor to the fullest.

Pounding or scoring is another way to break up connective tissue, thus making tough meat more tender, but then quite a lot of flavoring—chopped onions, garlic, herbs both fresh and dried, spices, seasoning, assertive sauces or relishes— is needed to make it taste good. Cube steak is beef top or bottom round that has been commercially tenderized with a cutting machine that chops the meat first one way and then the other. You can perform the tenderizing operation on meats yourself with a sharp, heavy knife or by pounding with a rolling pin.

Aging Aging improves the taste and tenderness of meat; unfortunately, aging meat is no longer a matter of course in this country. Carcasses to be aged are hung in a refrigerated storage space for a certain period of the time so that their moisture evaporates, and enzymes in the meat break down tendons and tough tissues. Beef should be aged for up to 3 weeks, or even longer. Lamb can be aged for a shorter period of time, but the stronger flavor of aged lamb does not appeal to most American tastes; it is more popular in Europe. Pork may be cured, but it is not aged, nor is veal. Kosher meat is never aged.

Since aging leads inevitably to weight loss, properly aged meat costs more to buy than fresh meat. However, it is well worth the difference in price, and a butcher who can supply you with meat that has been correctly aged is certainly worth cultivating.

Storing in the refrigerator Always unwrap and then rewrap meat as soon as you get it home, and put it in the coldest part of the refrigerator. All cuts keep best when they are loosely covered, not so tightly wrapped as to rule out the circulation of air. Waxed paper serves this purpose well. Despite advice to the contrary, never put meat away wrapped in plastic wrap, as this will cause it to deteriorate rapidly, developing a sticky and bad-smelling film over the outside.

Cooking processes

Obviously, it is wisest to use the correct cooking process for each cut: dry heat for the tender ones, moist for those not so tender. Broiling and grilling, panfrying, and roasting come into the first category; braising or pot-roasting, stewing, and boiling into the second. Of course, delicious results can be achieved by using a superior cut for the humbler processes, but the reverse is not the case.

Broiling and grilling Broiling is suitable for small, reasonably thick pieces of good-quality meat from the most tender parts of the animal. The meat, sometimes first brushed with butter or oil to prevent it from drying out, is seared on both sides close to the source of heat to produce color and flavor. Generally speaking, the thinner the piece of meat, the closer it should be to the heat source to sear it. It should then be moved a little way from the heat so that it can finish cooking more slowly. Salt should not be added until halfway through the process, as its moisture-retaining properties would inhibit searing and browning. Always allow broiled meat to rest for a few minutes after cooking so that the juices

APPROXIMATE MAXIMUM STORAGE TIMES FOR MEAT

Uncooked meat	In the refrigerator	In the freezer
BEEF		
roasts, steaks	3–5 days	6–12 months
ground, cut up	1–2 days	3 months
VEAL		
roasts	1–2 days	4–8 months
steaks, chops, ground	1–2 days	3–4 months
LAMB		
roasts, chops	3–5 days	6–9 months
ground, cut up	1–2 days	3–4 months
PORK		
roasts, chops	3–5 days	4–6 months
ground	1–2 days	3–4 months
sausage	1–2 days	1–2 months
VARIETY MEATS	1–2 days	3–4 months
Cooked/processed meat		
HAM	3–5 days	1–2 months
BACON		
unopened package	2 weeks	1 month
opened package	1 week	1 month
CORNED BEEF	1 week	2–3 months
ROASTED MEAT		
sliced in sauce	2–3 days	3 months
whole	3–4 days	2 months
CASSEROLES	2 days	3–6 months
PÂTÉ	1 week	3 months

INTERNAL TEMPERATURES FOR MEAT

The following temperatures are a guide to doneness when roasting meat. Cuts of meat will continue to cook after being removed from the oven, so take the meat out when the thermometer registers 5 to 10°F below the final desired internal temperature. During the 10- or 15-minute period of resting before carving and serving, the internal temperature will rise to the correct temperature.

Meat	Rare	Medium-rare	Medium	Well-done
Beef*	125°F	130°F	140–145°F	160°F
Veal			140–145°F	160°F
Lamb*		130°F	140–145°F	160°F
Pork			155–160°F	170°F

* Because of concern over bacteria in rare meat, the U.S. Department of Agriculture currently recommends cooking beef and lamb to a higher internal temperature. The recommendations for beef are: 145°F for medium-rare, 160°F for medium, and 170°F for well-done. The recommendations for lamb are 145°F for medium-rare, 160°F for medium, and 170°F for well-done.

will be evenly redistributed. Since with this process there is no pan gravy, or cooking juices, broiled meat is often served accompanied by a sauce or a pat of herb butter.

Much of the same applies to grilling meat outdoors: the meat may be lightly brushed with oil, though more often this is merely to keep it from sticking to the grill. It is seared on both sides, as for broiling, and then the grill rack may be raised or the meat moved away from the hottest part of the fire to finish cooking. Allow grilled meat to rest for at least a few minutes, and serve it with a sauce or salsa if desired. Although steaks, chops, and other smaller tender cuts are most often used for grilling, larger cuts can also be grilled, sometimes with the grill covered for part of the cooking time. Or cuts such as leg of lamb may be butterflied for grilling.

Panfrying Thinner, good-quality cuts are needed for this process. They are cooked in a very little hot oil or butter, or a mixture of the two, in a shallow preheated pan so that the meat browns rapidly. The meat is usually turned once as it cooks to sear it on both sides. Do not pierce it while it cooks, and keep a fairly high heat going under the pan, or the juices will escape too fast (if they do, the meat will boil in its own juices and toughen). Do not overheat the fat, as it will burn, and burnt fat imparts an unpleasant, bitter flavor. Panfried meat, like broiled meat, should be allowed to rest for a few minutes after cooking, before it is served.

Choose a frying pan with a good, heavy bottom, and make sure it is the right size. Meat has a tendency to stew in its own juice and steam in an overcrowded pan; in contrast, if the pan is too big, the cooking juices may evaporate too quickly and the meat may all too easily burn. A very good reason for not allowing this to happen is that the pan juices, deglazed with a little wine, water, or stock, make the best possible accompaniment to panfried steaks or chops.

Roasting Top-quality meat goes into a hot oven in an open pan so that it is browned on all sides as the outside is seared. The meat can go straight into a dry pan, fat side down, or into a little hot oil, or it can be cooked on a rack in a dry

pan or in a pan with a little water or wine in it. Some people like to put all meat on a rack in a pan, so that the fat collects beneath it as it roasts, but this is only essential for really fatty cuts. Frequent basting with the pan juices helps to prevent the meat from drying out.

Roasting times and temperatures vary according to the type of meat, the cut, and its quality, but after the initial searing it is a good idea to lower the oven temperature so that the interior of the meat is able to cook more slowly. However, top-quality cuts of meat will always be tender, no matter how briefly or how fast they may have been cooked. A regular meat thermometer or an instant-read thermometer is a foolproof gadget for determining the exact moment when the meat is cooked to the required degree.

There are two golden rules for all cuts of meat: do not season with salt until after roasting, and let the meat sit in a warm place for at least 20 minutes after it comes out of the oven to allow the juices time to settle, making the texture and color more even and the meat easier to carve.

Braising or pot-roasting Large pieces of medium-quality meat respond well to this process, which can be carried out either in the oven or on the stove top.

Braising means slow cooking in a small amount of liquid in a covered pot. The term pot-roasting means essentially the same thing. Braising needs a tightly covered pan so the steam from the cooking meat can condense on the bottom of the lid, falling back onto the meat and basting it as it cooks. The meat is browned first. Then it may be placed on a bed of chopped vegetables, which can be tossed in hot oil or butter first, or sliced onions and other aromatic vegetables may be scattered around the meat. Bacon or salt pork that has also been sautéed beforehand is a possible addition. Usually, stock, tomatoes, water, wine, cider, or beer is added—just enough to cover the vegetables. The meat is then slowly cooked in the casserole at a very moderate temperature (325°F) until meltingly tender. This usually takes about 30 minutes per pound, plus an extra 30 minutes, but the times will vary according to quality. The meat is turned and basted once or twice during cooking, and seasoned halfway through. If the

meat is salted at the outset, there is a danger the salt may draw out too much moisture too quickly.

If you plan to serve the braising vegetables, you may find it better to replace them with a fresh batch towards the end of the cooking time, as the hours they have spent in the pot may well have rendered them lifeless and tasteless.

Stewing A tougher cut of meat does best when cut into smaller pieces and cooked long and slowly in a little liquid—not too much, or the meat will be boiled rather than stewed. The liquid is provided by the meat juices as well as whatever is specified in the recipe. Many recipes call for an initial browning of the meat to give both color and flavor—usually in fat in which a few vegetables have been gently sautéed until they are golden; cooking liquid, flavorings, and seasonings are then added. When the meat is tender (which may take from 1½ to 3½ hours, depending on the type of meat), the gravy may be thickened. Sometimes the thickener, usually flour, is added early in the cooking process; the meat is usually coated with it before or while being browned, and care must be taken not to burn it. Stews cooked on the top of the stove will need stirring occasionally to prevent the meat from sticking to the pan.

Boiling Simmering in liquid, rather than actually boiling, is the best way to render large pieces of meat tender. Such good things as New England boiled beef dinner and all the other dishes served in the rich broth characteristic of the process really need at least a medium-quality meat. If you want to keep most of the flavor in the meat, plunge it into unsalted boiling water or, better still, into boiling stock. If, on the other hand, you want to create a rich, well-flavored broth at the expense of the meat, put the meat into a pan of cold water and then bring it slowly to the boil.

Once the liquid has reached the boiling point, turn it down to the gentlest of simmers. If meat is subjected to the intense heat of rapidly boiling water, the gelatinous connective tissue will dissolve and the meat will become tough and dry, while at a gentle simmer the connective tissues melt gradually, keeping the meat succulently moist and tender.

After the scum has been skimmed off, and foam has ceased to appear on top of the broth, salt, vegetables, and herbs are added for flavoring both the meat and broth, and the meat is simmered to tenderness. The slower the simmer, the less cloudy the broth will be. Allow 20 minutes per pound plus 20 minutes extra for pieces more than 6 pounds in weight; 30 minutes per pound plus 30 minutes extra for smaller pieces. The meat can be served with the cooking liquid as is, or it may be thickened for gravy. Or the liquid can be served separately as a first-course broth, or reserved for another dish. To serve the broth as consommé, it must be clarified to render it crystal-clear.

Meat for the freezer

When freezing meat, it makes the most sense to freeze it in the quantities you will be serving, whether as individual steaks or larger roasts. Smaller cuts or individual portions are best because they will freeze more quickly, preserving more of their texture and juiciness, but larger cuts such as pot roasts can be successfully frozen as well. It's nice to have cut-up stewing meat and ground meat on hand, as well as beef steaks and other cuts. Cooked meat can also be frozen, but usually for no longer than a month or two.

Always place meat that is to be frozen in the coldest part of the freezer (the temperature should be 0°F or lower).

Storing meat in the freezer Limits are placed on the storage times for meat not because the meat will become unsafe to eat, but because the quality deteriorates. Meat storage times are determined largely by the fat content, as fat eventually turns rancid even in the freezer. Pork fat turns rancid more quickly than lamb or beef fat, and salted meats (such as bacon or ham) become tough and can retain water; these are best frozen at the lowest possible temperature setting.

Meat that has been inadequately wrapped for the freezer will develop so-called freezer burn, which manifests itself as grayish-white or brownish patches on the meat. These patches are caused by dehydration at the surface, which results in changes in color, texture, and flavor. The meat will be perfectly safe to eat but will taste dry and unpleasant, so be sure to wrap all meat securely in heavy-duty freezer bags, and then to expel all the air before sealing the bags.

Cooking frozen meat All meat is infinitely better if thoroughly thawed before cooking. Bone-in roasts and small cuts of beef or lamb may be cooked still-frozen without any risk to health, but inevitably the outside will be overdone before the inside is cooked. For frozen roasts, you will need a meat thermometer to check on the internal temperature. For frozen steaks, chops, cutlets, and so on, it will be necessary to start the cooking at a lower temperature and to cook for almost twice as long as usual. Boneless rolled roasts, however, must never be cooked still-frozen, as the inside and outside surfaces of the meat will have been handled when the roast was boned and tied, and it is therefore important to destroy any bacteria that may be present by thorough cooking. Nor should pork be cooked still-frozen; although today's pork is quite safe and can be cooked to medium rather than well-done, it should be completely thawed out first.

To thaw large cuts, allow 6 to 7 hours per pound in the refrigerator, leaving the meat still wrapped. This is much the best way, as the slower the thaw, the more the juices get reabsorbed. Only about 2 to 3 hours per pound are needed at room temperature. Start to cook the meat as soon as it has thawed—while still cold to the touch. If it is left to thaw longer than necessary, the juices will have further opportunity to escape.

Steaks and chops need about 5 hours in the refrigerator in order to thaw out properly, or 2 to 4 hours in the warmth of the kitchen. If you are in a hurry, thawing the meat in cold water will help, as long as the package is watertight.

Another means of thawing frozen meat is to use the microwave, but this must be done carefully to ensure that some parts do not start to cook before others have finished thawing. Use the Defrost power level, and follow the manufacturer's instructions.

BEEF

The best beef of all is aged, by being hung, usually for around 3 weeks, sometimes longer, to reach its peak of flavor and tenderness. However, this process results in considerable weight loss, which is reflected in the price, so expect aged beef to be expensive.

Choosing beef

The color of lean beef varies from coral pink to a deep burgundy-red. The color variations of the lean meat indicate the age, sex, and breed of the animal, not the quality. Freshly cut surfaces of any piece of beef will be bright red, deepening to a brownish-red on exposure to air—thus a well-aged piece of beef will have a dark, plum-colored crust. The color of the fat will vary according to the animal's diet. Something positive to look for is the marbling—the meat of good roasting beef should be well endowed with flecks and streaks of fat that melt during cooking, basting the roast from within and guaranteeing tenderness.

The quality of ground beef is fairly simple to judge—it should look red. If it is pink, the proportion of fat will be too high.

As a provider of beef, the steer, or bullock (a young castrated male), is the undoubted king. Different countries consider him to be at his peak at different ages—from ten months to six years old—but all agree that a steer, and perhaps a heifer (a cow that has not calved), produce the most succulent meat. In the British Isles, the Scotch beef is considered the best, with Aberdeen Angus the most highly prized of all. In the United States, the Black Angus are the descendants of the Scotch Angus cattle imported into the country in the late 1800s, and Black Angus beef is much valued.

Cooking with beef

When beef is good and succulent, little is needed in the way of added flavors. Horseradish sauce or mustard makes a good accompaniment to roast beef, while the gravy of roast beef is nicest when the pan juices are simply reduced together with a little water and perhaps some red wine, and plainly seasoned with salt and pepper. Most vegetables go well with beef—from green beans to carrots—but potatoes are the traditional and favorite vegetable, whether mashed, oven-roasted or french-fried. In England, the Sunday roast beef always comes to the table accompanied by a golden Yorkshire pudding.

Tastes in beef eating have changed over the years. There was a time when beef was considered at its best when roasted to a crisp. Today more and more people are enjoying their roasts and steaks rare or on the "blue" side of rare—or even raw. The Italians introduced beef *carpaccio*—raw fillet steak cut very thin and served with olive oil and lemon juice or a mustardy dressing—which appears on fashionable menus.

Broiling, grilling, and panfrying
The timing depends so much on the thickness of the steak that you can only be sure whether it is done to your liking by pressing it with your finger as it cooks. If the steak feels soft and wobbly, it is rare; a little give, and it will be medium-rare; firm, and it will be well-done; hard, and it will be quite ruined.

Roasting
The finest cuts of prime beef respond best when roasted at a high temperature, which makes them crisp on the outside and leaves them a tender rosy-pink within. Overcooked beef turns leathery, even when it is meat of the very best quality. For larger, choice cuts such as beef tenderloin, allow 12 minutes per pound at 450°F for rare meat; 15 minutes for each pound for medium-rare, and 18 minutes per pound for medium. The coarser cuts, such as the thick ribs, make juicier eating when roasted more slowly—allow 20 minutes per pound at 375°F for thinner pieces or for bone-in cuts; allow 30 minutes per pound for thicker cuts or roasts that are boned and rolled. Roast beef should be allowed to rest for at least 20 minutes after it is removed from the oven before carving.

Braising or pot-roasting In general, you should allow 30 to 40 minutes per pound over medium heat on the stove top, and 40 minutes per pound in the oven at 325°F for pot roasts, but a great deal depends on the quality of the meat chosen for this cooking process.

Boiling The tougher boiling cuts may need up to 1 hour per pound of beef at a gentle simmer.

The cuts
Since butchering techniques vary from country to country, and indeed from region to region, the various cuts used for roasting, braising or pot-roasting, stewing, and boiling differ slightly all over the world. It remains true, of course, that in the case of beef (as well as the other animals raised for the table), the very best and most expensive cuts come from the back half of the animal, and most of the very best of those from the fleshy hindquarters; but the actual names of the cuts and their shapes differ considerably, as do the direction of the grain and the way the bones are dealt with.

Cuts for panfrying, broiling, grilling, and roasting These are the top-quality cuts that respond best to cooking in dry heat.

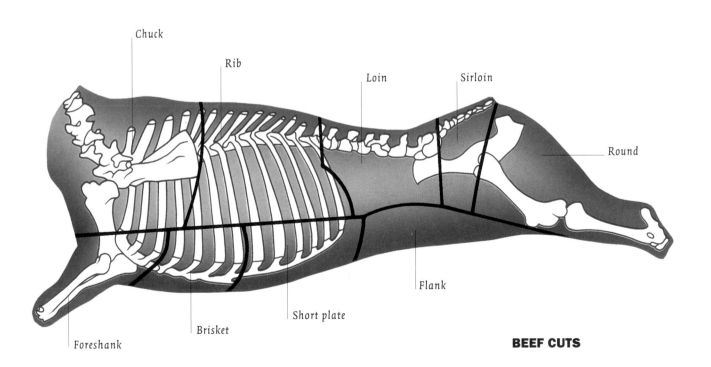

Chuck
Rib
Loin
Sirloin
Round
Flank
Short plate
Brisket
Foreshank

BEEF CUTS

Loin provides the most tender meat that beef or any other animal has to offer. The most luxurious piece of all is the tenderloin or fillet—a tapering strip of practically grainless flesh running inside the rib cage, parallel with the spine. Some butchers offer the tenderloin in its entirety: it can be roasted, sometimes brushed with butter or oil to keep it moist. The tenderloin is also used for the once-classic dinner party dish Beef Wellington, where the meat is enclosed in pastry, with a stuffing between the pastry and the meat to add moisture. The tenderloin is often cut into steaks—the thinnest part makes filets mignons; the wide end can be used for Châteaubriand, a steak so hefty that it is considered a meal for two hungry people.

Finely chopped raw beef tenderloin, spiced to taste with cayenne, Tabasco, Worcestershire sauce, and capers and bound with a raw beaten egg, makes the classic steak tartar. Cut into thin strips, tenderloin is the meat to use for beef Stroganoff, though many unfortunate versions are made with lesser cuts.

There are many people who consider any part of the tenderloin too bland, soft, and almost cottony, much preferring for texture and flavor shell (or New York) steaks, porterhouse steaks, sirloin steaks, and T-bone steaks (which include the end of the sirloin and a piece of tenderloin).

The various national schools cut their steaks differently, some leaving the tenderloin in place to form part of larger steaks, but this does not really affect the cook, since the principle of cooking steak remains constant, and the various forms of serving it differ only in the presentation. As steaks that are grilled are seared so fast that they do not make their own gravy, they may be sent to the table with a separate sauce or an herb or other compound butter. Steaks may also be panfried—filets mignons are usually cooked by this process. Classically they were served on large croutons to absorb the juices; today they are more likely to appear simply, perhaps with a light pan sauce. Panfried, broiled, or grilled, steaks are much enhanced by lighter sauces such as a simple shallot sauce, the classic béarnaise, or even an uncooked sauce of shallots, lemon juice, and oil, similar to a vinaigrette. Crisp french fries and a green salad are the best accompaniments.

The top loin lies above the tenderloin; with the tenderloin, it is called the short loin. The sirloin, which is behind the short loin, may be sold in a single piece for roasting, either on or off the bone, with or without the tenderloin.

In America and in France, the sirloin is often cut into large steaks, which are cooked on the bone and carved into slices at the table. In Britain, steaks are usually cooked in individual portions. Porterhouse, T-bones, and shell or strip steaks come from the top loin.

Rump This is part of the round, and yields rump roasts and beautiful juicy steaks for broiling, grilling, and panfrying. There will be a few tough sinews running through the meat, and these should be lifted out with a sharp knife. Rump roasts are often cooked using moist heat.

Rib When Americans say roast beef, what first come to mind are the great standing roasts from the rib section. Such roasts may be referred to as prime rib roasts, but in fact, with most beef graded prime going to restaurants, these roasts are almost always choice beef. Rolled rib roasts are not quite as flavorful when cooked as rib roasts on the bone, but the boneless rib-eye roast from the middle of the rib section is tender and a luxury. The French rib roast is boned and rolled, and served *au jus* (with its pan juices), accompanied by *pommes frites* and a simple green salad. The traditional English Sunday joint (roast) is the rib or forerib—served with Yorkshire pudding, roast potatoes, and lightly cooked vegetables, not forgetting the horseradish sauce.

Cuts from farther down the rib cage, toward the chuck, fare best braised or pot-roasted, rather than roasted by dry heat. They are juicier when left on the bone but can be tricky to carve. Below lie the short ribs, with a lot of fat and bone, which can be precooked, or marinated, and then barbecued.

For stewing, pot-roasting, and boiling The cuts used for these processes are the tougher pieces that benefit from slow cooking in moist heat. **The round** is the meat from the hind leg, which is divided into top round, eye of round, and bottom round; it is called topside or silverside in Britain. Although part of the round may be cut into steaks,

it is usually used for boneless roasts. From the round comes the very best *boeuf bouilli*, France's classic boiled beef dish, which is eaten in its bouillon with boiled potatoes and the vegetables that were cooked alongside it; little gherkins called cornichons are often served separately. Top round is good pot-roasting meat—being very lean, it often gets a wrapping of fat. Top round can also be roasted, although it may well be rather on the dry and tough side; it remains much juicier when it is kept very rare, in which case it is also excellent cold.

Salted and spiced, top round makes the traditional English boiled salt beef, eaten with carrots and dumplings. As well as nice pot roasts, the round makes good stews, and ground round makes tasty lean hamburgers.

Boneless sirloin tip Called top rump, or thick flank in Britain, this comes from the underside of the hind leg, where leg meets flank. Whole, it can be roasted or pot-roasted, and cut into cubes it makes excellent stews of all sorts, including France's *boeuf bourguignonne*. Ground, it makes good hamburgers.

Shoulder The shoulder area of the carcass is juicy and well flavored. It is known as chuck in the United States and chuck or blade in Britain. Blade steak is cut from the flat of the shoulder blade. When scored across with a heavy knife to cut through all the fine connective tissues, it can be panfried like any steak. Chuck is excellent for pot roast, stews, and other slow-cooked dishes. Ground chuck can be used to make good meat loaves, meatballs, and of course, hamburgers.

Brisket is the flesh of the breast, running from between the forelegs to the front end of the flank. It is fatty meat but is very versatile. It is the favored cut for traditional New England boiled dinner; in Texas, real barbecue always means beef brisket. Corned beef (called salted beef in Britain) is usually brisket, though beef round is sometimes corned; it is boiled and often eaten cold, cut into very thin slices.

Flank meat is coarse, and there can be plenty of fat. The flank may be braised or used for making stews, but the fattier part of the flank is more often ground for patties and the like. Flank steak is a lean boneless muscle that most often appears as London broil. It benefits from marinating before cooking, and, after grilling or broiling, must be sliced thinly across the grain.

Skirt is another muscle from the same region. Like hanger steak, or *onglet*, skirt steak is what is sometimes referred to as a "butcher's cut." Although such cuts are overlooked by the average consumer, butchers know them as some of the most flavorful parts of the animal. Along with flank, this is the cut of choice for fajitas, the Southwestern/Tex-Mex dish.

Foreshank The foreleg is known as the shank or shin. It gives gelatinous stewing meat with a lovely flavor, but takes several hours to cook. The shank—or meat from the flank—is used in the Indonesian dish *rendang*, slowly simmered in spiced coconut milk.

Leg This is the hind leg; it has more gristle and sinew than the foreleg, but it can be slowly cooked to make a well-flavored stew.

Marrow

This is the soft, fatty substance found inside the large bones of beef and veal. Although marrow is not particularly

fancied for eating in the United States, it is regarded as a delicacy throughout much of Europe. It is an integral part of Italy's famous *osso bucco*, made from veal shanks, with their rich supply of marrow, and it is a favorite of restaurant chefs and other gourmands in this country. Beef leg bones are fairly widely available, cut into pieces, although they may have to be special-ordered at the supermarket or butcher.

Marrow makes a wonderful addition to stocks, in which case the split bones are boiled along with the other ingredients to give up their goodness. If you want to use the marrow for sauces or for spreading on toast, the bones should be soaked overnight in cold water, then wrapped in aluminum foil and cooked in a fairly hot oven for 45 minutes. The marrow can then be scooped out from the center of the bones. (In Victorian times, marrow spread on toast was very popular; the bones were served wrapped in starched white napkins and the goodness was scooped from inside with long, narrow marrow spoons.)

VEAL

Veal is a light, delicate, and versatile meat—it is the perfect vehicle for a range of flavors, from subtle and creamy to strong and piquant.

Choosing veal

There are two types of veal: the first and more delicate type comes from milk-fed calves that were slaughtered between 8 and 12 weeks of age, and the second from grass-fed calves, which are usually slaughtered at between 3 and 6 months old.

Milk-fed veal should be the palest pearly-pink in color. It should look firm and moist, but never wet, and have bright, pinky-white, translucent bones. Grass-fed veal is a little darker in color, but never red. Redness is a sure sign that the animal was too old before slaughter. If veal has a brown or gray tinge, it is old and should be avoided. Veal has a little marbling, which should be hard to spot because the fat is practically the same color as the meat. If there is too much marbling and too much covering fat, it means the calf was

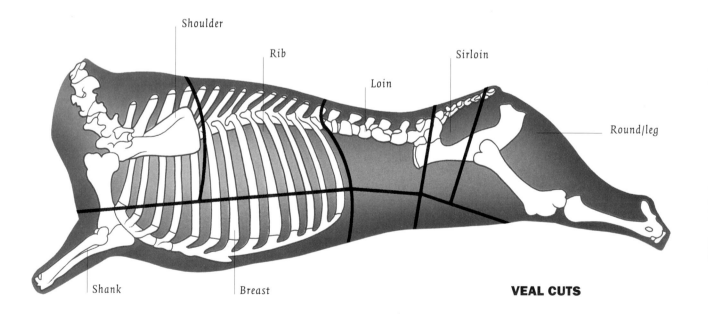

VEAL CUTS

overfed. What fat there is should look like white satin, and there shouldn't be much of it.

Cooking with veal

Because it hasn't much marbling, there is little interior lubrication while the meat is cooking, and veal can be dry unless other fat is added by way of basting (or, sometimes, larding or barding) for roasting, or by using plenty of butter, good olive oil, or even bacon in sautéed, pot-roasted, and stewed dishes.

The flavor of veal is unassertive, so a strongly flavored garnish is often welcome: the combination of veal and anchovies dates from the earliest times. Lemon and orange often feature in the best sauces, as does white wine and, particularly, Marsala. In Italy, a veal roast may be studded with strips of anchovies; in Parma, they slit a leg of veal and insert strips of paper-thin prosciutto. Scallops and cutlets of veal may also appear under a slice of mildly cured ham on which a generous slice of cheese is gently melting.

Onions have a special affinity with veal, not only because of their taste but also because of their texture—they are often put into the pan with a roast. As for accompaniments: any really fresh-looking vegetable is good, as is salad. Veal is pale in color, so both dark-green spinach or beans will provide a beautiful background. Potatoes, of course, go with veal in almost any form, and so do rice and noodles. Golden saffron rice is the traditional side dish for *osso bucco*, and a ring of snow-white rice often surrounds a pale-golden creamy *fricassée* of veal or a *blanquette*. Tagliatelle is often served with veal in Italy, the texture of the delicate pasta compensating for any possible dryness in the meat.

All veal bones are extremely gelatinous and give an excellent texture and flavor to sauces and stocks: if the butcher has trimmed the meat for you, be sure to carry a few of the bones home with you and add them to the pot when braising a piece of veal, removing them before you serve it.

Broiling and frying Because of the lack of interior fat, the smaller cuts of veal—chops, cutlets, scallopine, or scallops, medallions, and the like—are more often panfried or sautéed than broiled. Thin scallops or cutlets should be sautéed quickly over medium heat;

chops should be first seared over high heat and then allowed to finish cooking slowly, or they will become tough and dry. Because of the high temperature of the initial cooking, chops will need to be panfried in oil or in an oil-and-butter mixture, as butter alone would burn, but scallops can be successfully sautéed in butter. Serve them with wedges of lemon.

Roasting Baste veal frequently if you do decide to try roasting it—braising is often more successful with this dry meat. Roast for 25 minutes per pound plus 20 minutes in a moderate oven (375°F) for cuts that are thinner or on the bone; 30 minutes per pound at 325°F, for those that are thicker, boned and rolled, or stuffed.

A hefty cut, like a leg, will preserve its succulence better if covered with strips of bacon before it goes into the oven. The lean little roasts, such as a boneless loin, are best threaded with strips of fatback (larded) or covered with a layer of pork fat (barded). This extra fat will ensure that the meat remains moist.

Braising This is the best method of cooking a large piece of veal. Add some little onions, shallots, or carrots to the pot to help produce the moisture that will prevent the veal from drying out. In Italy, a carrot is sometimes inserted in the center of the meat for the same purpose. Allow 40 to 50 minutes per pound at 325°F, basting frequently with wine and butter.

Stewing This should be carried out very gently, for well over an hour. Veal is good in the traditional *blanquette*, stewed in a flavorful broth that is thickened and enriched at the end of the cooking time with egg yolks and cream.

Boiling This is, more strictly speaking, poaching, and should only involve a mere simmering.

The cuts

Like beef, cuts of veal vary according to the various butchering techniques. However, since calves are smaller than full-grown beef cattle, there is not quite so much scope for variations and not as much difference among the cuts. In fact, most countries follow the economical French style of butchering for veal— and that involves trimming away all

gristle and sinew most meticulously and dividing the meat neatly along the natural seams in the muscles.

Cuts for panfrying, broiling, and roasting Veal needs plenty of additional fat to stop it drying out completely in the dry heat of these processes.

Leg/Round Only the hind leg of veal is referred to as the leg, as the foreleg is called the shank. The cuts from this large and fleshy joint can be roasted under a layer of sliced bacon; alternatively, and better still, braise them with vegetables in order to keep them moist and juicy.

The roast from the leg is called round roast, the top slices of which go by the name of round steak. Round steak is often boned and tied; it is good stuffed with a mixture of fatback, anchovy fillets, and currants and then braised.

The most delicate leg meat is from the muscle that runs vertically along the thigh bone. In France, this cut may be sold separately as the *rouelle*, but, in general, leg of veal cuts tend to be sliced crosswise, containing some of each of the three muscles, which are very similar in taste. So, whether on or off the bone, a cut from the center part of the leg makes good eating. It is this bit that is used for the famous Italian dish *vitello tonnato*— always eaten cool and coated with a sauce of tuna fish pounded to an emulsion with olive oil, lemon juice, and capers.

Rump Situated at the point where leg meets loin, this is usually boned and rolled for slow roasting and braising.

Scallops It is from the leg that the best veal scallops are cut, across the grain and on the bias. Of course, many shops sell thin pink slices of fatless, trimmed veal under the name of escalopes, *scallopine*, or medallions from other parts of a calf's anatomy, but high-class butchers only recognize those from the leg as the real thing. Ask the butcher to pound them flat for you for extra tenderness. When you dip these diaphanous slices in egg and a Parmesan-bread crumb mixture and quickly panfry them, you get the perfect Veal Parmigiana.

If you have to pound the scallops yourself, do take care not to beat the life out of them—a well-cut scallop will require only a gentle flattening. If you don't possess a meat mallet, then use a rolling pin, or ease the meat into shape with the heel of your hand.

There are many, many ways to serve veal scallops. This rich diversity is in part due to the fact that the scallop is one of the mainstays of Italian cooking, and it features often in the varied cuisines of France, Germany, and Austria. In Italy, for example, a great favorite is *saltimbocca*—which means, literally, to "jump into the mouth." This is a dish consisting of small scallops, each one rolled up around a stuffing of prosciutto and fresh sage. *Piccate* are tiny scallops; traditionally, these are dipped in flour and panfried. They are usually sautéed in butter and served with a good lemony sauce.

In France, veal scallops are often simply browned in butter, with the last-minute addition of a handful of finely chopped shallots or scallions and a slice of lemon. The Germans and Austrians are, of course, famed for their *Weinerschnitzel*—traditionally dipped first into flour, then into beaten egg and in bread crumbs, and briefly deep-fried in hot oil.

Loin A lean cut, the loin contains the tenderloin, which is the equivalent of a beef tenderloin. In Europe, it often contains the kidneys, but these, as well as the tenderloin, are often removed to be sold separately. The tenderloin makes nice little medallions. The loin can be sold as chops or whole for roasting.

When roasting a loin, keep it very well basted with butter or olive oil, or cook it in a covered casserole to keep it moist.

Rib This is sold whole, bone in or boneless, for roasting, or it is divided into delicious chops, which should not be cut too thin. Chops should be cooked very gently after browning, or they may become dry. Veal chops are often served with their garnish sitting on top. Fontina cheese, prosciutto, white mushrooms, and, of course, anchovies may all feature. When rib chops are not quite severed at the base of the veal rack, and are curved around to form a crown roast of veal, an onion and mushroom stuffing may go into the center before roasting.

Shoulder This can be roasted, but is better braised. It provides shoulder chops or steaks, also called blade steaks. They can be prepared in much the same way as loin or rib chops, though they are sometimes seared in butter and then enclosed in foil together with shallots, mushrooms, onion and parsley and baked, to be served *en papillote*. Off the bone, the shoulder meat is good for stews and goulash.

For braising or pot-roasting and boiling

Veal adapts particularly well to moist heat, absorbing both moisture and any flavorings added to the pot.

Shoulder A fairly lean cut, this is suitable for slow-roasting or pot-roasting. It is almost always sold boned and rolled, sometimes with stuffing, although it is vastly preferable to make your own. For this purpose, good butchers may leave an empty pocket in the center. Boned and cubed shoulder is a prime candidate for stews and ragouts—especially when mixed with the meat from the breast region. Particularly good is a simple braise made with plenty of oil, garlic, tomatoes, and mushrooms.

Ground shoulder meat, flavored with marjoram and rosemary and bound with egg, makes delicious meatballs—made more so with the addition of a sauce of white wine, cream, shallots, and dill.

Breast This is often seen boned, and provides a vehicle for some very good stuffings. Traditionally, something green is included in these: spinach, perhaps, or peas, or pistachio nuts. Served cold, a stuffed breast of veal, simmered, then gently weighted down and allowed to cool in its own cooking broth, makes a beautiful summer lunch. A breast is also very good hot—braised with a chunk of slab bacon and some large, juicy onions.

Shank This is a gelatinous, sinewy, but well-flavored piece of meat consisting mainly of bone. Sawn into thick slices and long-cooked, it makes one of the most delicious veal dishes of all—*osso bucco*.

Neck This is actually a versatile cut; in Britain, it may be used for stewed dishes, as it provides meat that is suitable for long simmering. Ground, it makes meat loaves, meatballs, and stuffings, and can be used in pâtés. Veal neck bones make an excellent stock.

LAMB

The choicest lamb has rosy flesh. Its bones are slender, and the fat is white, silky, and resilient. The very best lamb, meltingly tender but expensive and difficult to find, is baby lamb, with flesh of the palest pink that turns almost white when cooked. It is especially good when cooked in the ancient way, grilled over an herb-strewn glowing wood fire.

Next comes spring lamb, which once referred to "lamb season," when most lambs were born in the fall and sold in the spring. Now spring lamb, which is available all year long, simply means lamb that was butchered at between 3 and 5 months of age. Regular lamb has darker flesh than spring lamb. Lamb only qualifies for the name when it has been slaughtered before its first birthday. After that, it becomes yearling, and then mutton.

Although they do not appeal to most American tastes, mutton and yearling remain popular in Britain. Yearling meat is a little darker and a little stronger-tasting than lamb. The more strongly flavored mutton is dark red, not at all pink. Fans of mutton find it just the right sort of meat for heftier regional dishes. Ironically, however, even in Britain, because good lamb is now so readily available (not least because this meat freezes particularly well), people who actually want to buy good old-fashioned mutton often experience considerable difficulty in finding it.

Choosing lamb

When buying lamb, go for the leanest piece you can see—even the fatty cuts vary greatly in their proportions of fat to lean. Avoid those with fat that looks brittle and crumbly or discolored—the most appetizing-looking pieces will make the best eating and will have the most flavor.

Where sheep are raised can affect the flavor of the meat. Some of the most delicious lamb in the world comes from sheep that have grazed on salt marshes: the *pré-salé* ("pre-salted") lamb of France's Atlantic coast is justifiably famous. Mountain, or hillside lamb, small and slender-boned, is a regional specialty in many countries, from Wales to Greece. Mountain lamb is a touch gamier in flavor than other lamb, and this is the reason that there are many recipes for cooking lamb like venison, using the traditional marinades and the same accompaniments: red-currant jelly or a compote of cranberries.

Cooking with lamb

Lamb is basically a tender, succulent meat, so take care not to overcook it—generally, lamb should be pink and juicy inside.

Broiling and panfrying Chops and cutlets of lamb, nicely trimmed, are equally good broiled or panfried. The timing depends on the thickness of the pieces. Test them by pressing them with your finger during cooking: when they are becoming firmer but are still supple, they are done.

Roasting Much depends on the age of the animal and the quality of the meat. The timing varies according to whether you like your roast rosy-pink or well-done.

A leg of lamb should be pink within, most gourmets would agree, although not everyone shares the taste of the French, who like it rose-red in the center. The rib and loin are best fairly rare—cook these cuts at 375°F, allowing about 20 minutes per pound and maybe 15 minutes more for larger cuts, but test by piercing: when the juice runs red, the meat is rare; rosy, it is fairly rare; when it runs clear, the meat is well-done.

The shoulder and all boned, rolled cuts, including stuffed breast, are better when they are well-done: cook them at 325°F, allowing about 30 minutes per pound.

Pot-roasting or braising This is done at an even lower temperature: 300°F, allowing approximately 2 hours for a whole leg or shoulder, and 1¼ hours for smaller cuts. A lamb stew should be ready for eating after 1¼ hours of cooking. Because lamb fat congeals so quickly, it is important to take your stew to the table in a preheated dish and to serve it as soon as possible on very hot plates.

The cuts

Most large cuts of lamb can be roasted successfully; even the fattier ones will taste very good.

Leg This succulent piece, simply roasted on the bone, is one of the greatest cuts of meat there is. It may be subdivided into the shank half and the sirloin half. The sirloin half, in turn, makes sirloin chops. Divested of all membranes, this meat, cut into cubes, makes lovely little kebabs. Leg of lamb is much easier to carve if it is partially boned. The butcher can remove the hip and tail bones.

The leg is also sold completely boned. It is usually rolled, but is sometimes butterflied—cut so that it can be opened out flat. Butterflied leg of lamb is delicious grilled outdoors; marinating it beforehand in olive oil and fresh herbs will produce delicious results. In whatever form, this cut makes a lovely roast. Roast lamb should be left to rest for at least 15 minutes after it is removed from the oven and before carving.

Serve young spring lamb with freshly made mint sauce if possible, rather than the ubiquitous green jelly, and spring vegetables, and older lamb with root vegetables. Rosemary or thyme and garlic are favorite flavorings for lamb in France; or if half a leg of lamb is braised on a bed of vegetables, with cream and tarragon used in the sauce, it becomes *agneau jardinière*. But what is particularly delicious and all too rarely encountered, even in Britain, is a noble, very English, boiled leg of lamb—the shank end—served with caper or onion sauce.

Sirloin The upper part of the sirloin half of the leg, lying next to the loin, is sometimes sold as a separate cut for roasting, on or off the bone. In some types of butchering, it simply forms part of the leg itself.

Loin The two unseparated loins make a saddle roast, an elegant but extravagant roast for a dinner party. A regular single-loin roast may be bought on the bone, but it also comes boned and rolled.

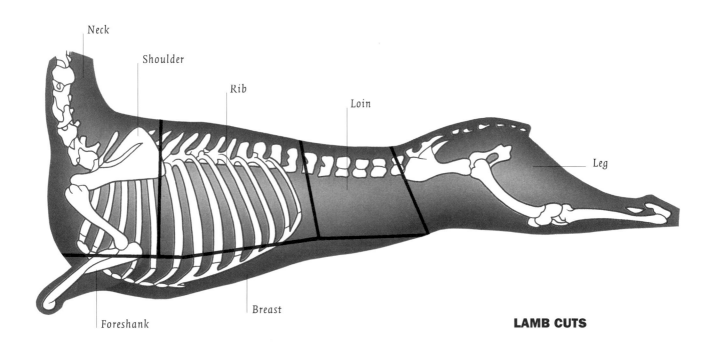

Neck
Shoulder
Rib
Loin
Leg
Foreshank
Breast

LAMB CUTS

The loin is divided into delicious chops—each with a small T-shaped bone dividing the two pieces of lean meat, double lamb chops are cut from the saddle. There are a hundred ways of garnishing chops; when they are simply panfried or broiled, serve them pink inside with watercress and mashed potatoes. Loin chops may also be boned and trimmed of any excess fat.

Rib Rack of lamb, or the rib roast, lies next to the loin. If you mean to roast or braise it, ask the butcher to remove the chine bone for you, to enable you to carve neat chops after cooking. Two racks of lamb, placed opposite each other, fat side out, bones in the air, and interlinked like swords at a military wedding, make a good dinner-party indulgence, called guard of honor. A good, moist stuffing goes in between the two racks, the same type that you would put into the center of a crown roast of lamb, which is made from the identical two cuts, joined at both ends. The rack can also be boned and sliced into noisettes.

The rack gives chops that are a fraction less juicy than loin chops, but these are still very good. When they are "Frenched" (a reference to the elegance and care the best French butchers bestow on all the meat they handle, in this case meaning that the bones extending from the chops are thoroughly trimmed of fat and meat), they are sometimes eaten with the fingers. The farther back the rib chops lie, the leaner they are; toward the front, they tend to become quite fatty.

Rib chops are probably best of all when sprinkled with olive oil and lemon juice and broiled; boneless chops, or cutlets, from the rib, or the loin or leg, may be coated in egg and bread crumbs before panfrying.

Shoulder Easy to cook, this makes a sweet and juicy roast. It is fattier than the leg, and harder to carve, especially when it is on the bone, but is often a more succulent roast. Boned and tied, it may be stuffed. The shoulder also provides the blade and arm chops, which are good for braising.

Shoulder, trimmed of all fat and membrane, is the cut that is often ground, perhaps together with meat from the foreshank, for use in moussaka, stuffed peppers, dolmades (stuffed grape leaves), and the like. In the Middle East, this cut of lamb is sometimes pounded to the consistency of an ointment: this smooth paste, which also includes bulgur, is called kibbeh and may be eaten raw or cooked.

Neck The neck is a decidedly bony and fatty cut, but it is useful for broth and lamb stew, including the famous British dish that is known as Lancashire hotpot. This is also the cut used for Moroccan tagines, made with apricots or prunes, almonds, and spices; or use neck to make a good Irish stew—a dish that once used to be made with kid.

Because neck is fatty, add plenty of starchy ingredients to soak up the juices. In Lancashire hotpot, a top layer of thickly cut slices of potato benefits from the rich aromatic fat that rises as the meat cooks. Shepherd's pie, with its covering of mashed potatoes over ground lamb, works on the same principle, as do French haricots of lamb or mutton, where dried beans act as the blotting paper. Pilafs, too, use stewing lamb, but this time with rice.

Breast This thin, fatty cut tastes better when it has been slowly cooked. The breast cage makes riblets for barbecuing; the less bony parts can be boned, stuffed, and rolled, or tied flat, like a sandwich, with the stuffing in the middle. In Britain, boneless breast is simmered, cooled, cut into squares, then coated with egg and bread crumbs and panfried; these morsels are called epigrams, a charming name and a good dish.

Shank is from the foreleg. It is full of flavor, but needs long, slow cooking to make it tender.

Kid

Athletic lamb from craggy hillsides with no pasture to speak of produces meat that is notable for flavor, but it can be tough or dry. This is where kid, better adapted to such regions, is much preferred to lamb.

Cooked in oil and wine with garlic, wreathed in rosemary or myrtle, young kid, creamy-white and tender, makes the festive dishes in Corsica and Sardinia, while lamb is for everyday. Saudi Arabia, too, feasts on kid: rubbed with coriander and ginger and onion juices, stuffed with rice, dried fruits, and nuts, and served with clouds of rice and hard-boiled eggs. Lamb can be substituted—as far as recipes go, the two meats are interchangeable. But as kid is mild in taste, it needs plenty of flavoring.

PORK

Prime fresh pork should be a lovely pearly-pink and fine-textured; the fat should be dense and milk-white. The pork that we buy today is very different from that available 20, or even 10, years ago. Pork used to be a very rich, fatty meat; even a suckling pig, slaughtered at about 3 weeks, would make a rich, filling meal, although it had hardly had time to grow stout. Now pigs are much leaner, the meat offering more protein and much less fat.

Choosing pork

The term pork refers to any pig under 1 year old, but most of the pork in the market comes from animals slaughtered at between 6 and 9 months. In older swine, the meat has darkened to rose-pink and the bones, pinkish in young animals, are white. Deep rose-colored meat and white, brittle bones are signs of advanced age. Although pork that is not well trimmed or is fatty-looking is to be avoided, with some cuts—chops particularly—you should choose those that have some marbling (the small flecks of fat that are a sign of good beefsteak as well), or the meat will be dry. If the meat looks wet and slippery rather than moist, it will be of poor quality. If there is any kind of smell, the meat is spoiled or close to it.

Cooking with pork

Today's pork usually benefits from cooking at lower temperatures than those recommended in earlier times. The leg, for example, does not have much in the way of intramuscular fat, so meat from this part of the animal may appear to be on the dry side: to remain as juicy as possible, it should be cooked slowly.

All cuts of pork, without exception, need to be cooked through—this is both because raw pork may contain microscopic parasites that are killed only when the meat reaches an internal temperature of about 140°F and because underdone pork tastes less good, but it is no longer necessary to overcook it. However, to be on the safe side, most pork should be cooked until it reaches an internal temperature of 155 to 160°F— a far cry from the 185°F recommended in cookbooks of just a decade or so ago— which will still leave it juicy and tender.

The humbler cuts of pork tend to be cooked and served with more fat on the meat, and so the best accompaniments are those such as mashed potatoes, beans, dried peas, and lentils, which will absorb some of the fat. Chestnuts have the same effect. In Spain and Portugal, potatoes are added to braised or stewed fatty pork dishes about half an hour before serving to soak up the fat that has risen to the top of the pot.

The more expensive, less fatty cuts of pork—leg and loin—are often served with fruit or vegetables to provide a contrast to the rich, dense meat. Apples are probably the best-known such accompaniment, while in France's Loire Valley, *noisettes* or medallions of pork are cooked with prunes. In Denmark, prunes are used to stuff a loin roast, and a mixture of soaked dried fruit is used in Poland. In Germany, the starchy and fruity elements are combined in a dish called "heaven and earth"—a mixture of puréed potatoes and apples.

For moistening purposes, beer, wine, and stock are all used, but cider is the liquid that is most traditionally associated with pork.

By way of herbs, pork takes kindly to the warm flavor of fennel and caraway seeds, as well as to the pungent flavor of sage. Sage and onion is a classic stuffing

for roast pork or stuffed pork chops. In Italy, pork is often cooked with rosemary or bay leaves; it is good also with juniper berries or whole peppercorns and with thyme. And, of course, a loin of pork is wonderful with truffles.

As for side dishes, all the cruciferous vegetables, led by sweet-and-sour red cabbage, are naturals for pork. The more delicate roasts, such as leg or loin, look most appetizing with something fresh, such as little carrots or turnips, leeks, bright-green cabbage, or spinach. Young peas and artichoke hearts bathed in melted butter make one of the best combinations. A simple lettuce salad, served on the same plate with a broiled or fried chop, and eaten bathed in the meat juices, is extremely delicious.

Broiling and panfrying A medium chop should take about 15 minutes at medium heat. Turn it from time to time as it cooks, and test it by piercing—when the juices run clear, it is ready to serve.

Roasting This must be thorough. For smaller, thinner cuts allow a full 25 minutes per pound, plus 25 minutes extra, at 350°F; and 30 minutes per pound, plus 30 minutes extra, for thicker pieces like leg or shoulder roasts. Fresh pork is not seen with the skin on in our

markets, but in some regions, and in many countries, the skin is regarded as a treat. Many Englishmen, at least, think the crisp "crackling" that results from rubbing the skin with oil or salt (but not both) before cooking the pork is the best part of the roast.

Braising or pot-roasting On top of the stove, simmer pork over medium heat. Or place it in a casserole with a little vinegar, whole black peppercorns, and bay leaves and cook slowly in the oven at 325°F.

Boiling It is not usual to boil fresh pork, except for the pig's feet (trotters to the British), but any of the pickled or salted and smoked cuts make perfect candidates for boiling, or, rather, simmering. These may need soaking beforehand: if necessary, ask the butcher how long to soak.

The cuts

There is no cut of pork that cannot be satisfactorily roasted—the pig is too lethargic a beast to develop much by way of tough muscle and connective tissue. The coarser cuts with little in the way of visible fat may be better braised or slowly stewed. A coarse, fatty cut will still make a lovely braise or stew,

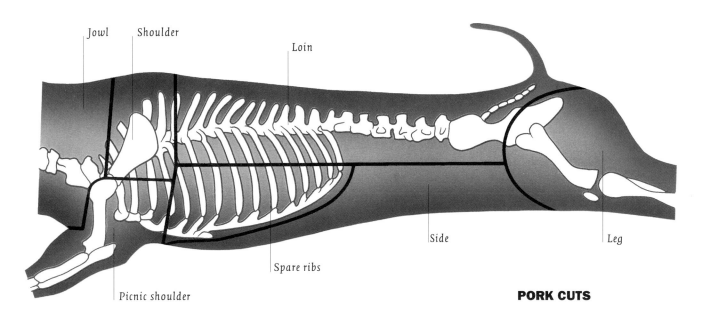

Jowl Shoulder Loin

Picnic shoulder

Spare ribs

Side Leg

PORK CUTS

provided it is trimmed of most of the fat, which would make the sauce too rich and indigestible.

Leg A whole leg of pork, or fresh ham, makes a really imposing dish. But even a small one—larger ones may weigh up to 15 pounds—can be rather daunting, so it is often divided into the shank or leg end and the butt end or top leg (called, somewhat more elegantly, fillet end in Britain). Leg of pork is more often sold boned than not.

The shank end is easier to cook evenly when it is boned and rolled, but it will then look less handsome on the serving platter. When cooking shank on the bone, it is a good idea to protect the thinner bony part by wrapping it in aluminum foil halfway through the cooking time, leaving the meatier end exposed to the full heat.

The butt end of the leg can be cooked as a roast, boneless or not. It may also be sliced into lean cutlets about ½- to 1-inch thick—and cooked as you would a steak. The butt end of leg may be cut into cubes to be cooked as kebabs.

A fresh leg of pork is sometimes, especially in Italy, first simmered in milk and then finished off in the oven, surrounded by quantities of garlic (the milk ends up as a light, golden gravy). Some countries pickle the leg, which can then be boiled. This is eaten with the coarse purée of green split peas that is known and loved as pease pudding in the north of England.

Loin The sirloin, the fleshy part of the loin, is usually cut into delicious large chops, called sirloin or butterfly chops, or into thick sirloin cutlets, but this is another cut that may be roasted either on or off the bone, seasoned with sage, rosemary, or thyme.

Delicate and very tender, the loin itself makes a wonderful meal if it is boned, stuffed with chopped garlic, a few prunes or herbs, and mushrooms, or even truffles, then rolled, and roasted. On the bone, a loin cut is sometimes served sitting on a bed of unsweetened apples and sweet chestnuts.

It is the loin that provides most pork chops: rib or loin chops to be panfried, broiled, after being lightly brushed with oil; or braised, moistened with beer, white wine, or cider. Pounded thin, dipped in beaten egg and seasoned bread crumbs, and panfried, they become pork

chops *alla milanese*. Chops taken from the hind end of the loin may bring with them a portion of the tenderloin.

Tenderloin Pork tenderloins are now sold in most supermarkets, usually vacuum-packed in plastic. They generally come two to a package, weighing ¾ to 1¼ pounds each. Lean and tender, pork tenderloin is a versatile cut. Tenderloin is good roasted—perhaps slit down the middle and stuffed, or wrapped in bacon and roasted whole like a miniature pork roast. Whole tenderloins can be grilled for a change-of-pace summer meal. The tenderloin may also be cut into medallions or scallops, but their taste, like that of veal, is delicate, so some interesting flavoring is needed to give them character. In France, apples or prunes are used as a garnish for tenderloin cutlets or medallions, which are lovely cooked with crushed allspice berries or fennel seeds. In Germany, they are cooked with caraway seeds or with a rich sauce made with sour cream and the delicious pan juices.

Shoulder Pork shoulder, or butt, is often referred to as Boston butt. Blade roasts and steaks come from the shoulder too, as does the picnic roast (and picnic ham). In addition to being roasted, this rather rich cut can be ground for sausages, meatballs, or patties and for the famous Pennsylvania Dutch scrapple—a cooked mixture of pork and cornmeal, sliced and fried in butter or bacon drippings. Pork shoulder is a favorite for traditional barbecues, and the steaks sliced from the shoulder are particularly good cooked over charcoal.

Ribs Spareribs come from the lower part of the rib cage and the breast, and are either sold in slabs or separated into single or double bones, each with its cartilage. The sheets of ribs are sometimes cooked sandwiched together with a stuffing in between them—the Pennsylvania Dutch like to spread this sandwich with apples, the Germans with cabbage and caraway. But the favorite way to prepare spareribs, and other pork ribs, is to barbecue them—and each region has its own special variations of barbecue sauces, marinades, and rubs.

Spareribs are always eaten with the fingers. Because they are so bony, allow at least 3 pounds for two people.

Back ribs come from the loin, above the spareribs; baby back ribs are from

younger animals and so are smaller than ordinary back ribs. Country-style ribs come from the blade, or shoulder, end of the loin. These are big, thick, meaty ribs.

Side The side, or belly, provides bacon and the rather fatty meat that is cured to become salt pork. It is good for enriching dishes of beans, lentils, and cabbage. It is useful for making pâtés, and, if you don't mind the fat, it can be roasted, sliced, and then broiled, sautéed (allowed to render its fat, it makes delicious cracklings), or braised Chinese-style with star anise.

Suckling pig

These young pigs, which have been slaughtered between the ages of 3 to 8 weeks, contain proportionally little meat; however, what there is, is perhaps the sweetest and richest of all pork.

In northern Spain, suckling pigs are a specialty. These pigs start their short lives on a diet of mother's milk and wild herbs. They are traditionally roasted in a slow-burning wood oven, and served simply with boiled potatoes and apple sauce.

Choosing suckling pig You will need to order a suckling pig specially from your butcher. They range from about 10 to 20 pounds, and a medium-sized one is a good buy because it will have developed enough meaty parts without sacrificing the tender succulence of the smaller pigs. As a rough guide, a 12-pound suckling pig should feed ten people.

Roasting a suckling pig Suckling pig, which should have been prepared for you by the butcher, can be stuffed with any stuffing suitable for pork (a combination of bread crumbs, parsley, onions, sausage, chestnuts, and brandy is good), or simply brushed with oil or rubbed with salt and lemon juice and sprinkled with herbs. Place the suckling pig on a rack and prick the skin before and during roasting to allow the fat to drip out into the roasting pan. It won't need basting, and the skin will turn a shiny, crisp brown. A medium-sized stuffed pig will take 2½ to 3 hours to cook; an unstuffed one will be ready in 2 hours. Allow 20 minutes per pound at 350°F.

Suckling pigs are usually reserved for festive occasions, such as colorful Hawaiian luaus, where the central feature is a spit-roasted suckling pig, liberally basted with barbecue sauce and presented on a tray with a red apple in its mouth.

VARIETY MEATS

Some of the best dishes in the world are made with humble pieces of meat that are collectively known as variety meats, or offal. While, unfortunately, Americans tend to shy away from these, they are treated with special respect in France and the Mediterranean countries, where their distinctive flavors and textures are preserved by careful cooking.

Luckily, many of these meats are among the most economical buys. While some of them, particularly those from veal, may command a high price, only small amounts need to be purchased because of their rich flavor and lack of bones; those from less expensive animals are full of wholesome flavor. Whichever type you buy, make sure it is fresh, and cook it as soon as possible.

Sweetbreads A fine delicacy, sweetbreads are sold in pairs, being two parts of the thymus gland, which sits in the throat and chest of young animals. The rounder, fatter one is the better of the two. (The sweetbreads that come from the pancreas gland, and that are sometimes referred to as belly or stomach sweetbreads, are coarser than true sweetbreads.) Calf's sweetbreads are the best, especially the very large ones from milk-fed veal. They are whiter and larger than beef or lamb sweetbreads and less tedious to prepare, and they have a finer flavor. Pork sweetbreads are small and not particularly good.

No matter how they are to be cooked, all sweetbreads need to be prepared first to make them white and firm. To prepare them, soak them in salted water for 2 hours, changing the water from time to time, until they lose all trace of pinkness and turn white. Put them in a pan of cold salted water, bring to a boil, and simmer for 2 minutes. Drain and rinse them under cold running water. This process firms up the sweetbreads and makes them easier to handle. Peel away the skin, connective tissues, and gristle—some sweetbreads will fall naturally into smaller portions. Finally, flatten the sweetbreads between two plates for an hour before cooking. One of the best ways of cooking them after the initial preparation is to coat them in beaten egg and bread crumbs and to sauté them gently in butter until brown.

Liver Fresh liver is the most nutritious and widely eaten of all organ meats. It is sold either whole or in slices and is often already trimmed, but if it still has a thin covering of membrane, this needs to be removed or the liver will curl up in the pan. Less delicate livers, such as pork or beef liver, will become more tender if soaked in milk before cooking.

Calf's liver Pale and plump, liver from milk-fed veal is the most delicious, but is expensive. Liver from grass-fed veal will be thinner, darker, and not as mild. Panfried liver is delicious if it is cooked very lightly and rapidly and is still rosy inside—overcooking makes liver unappetizingly tough, dry, and leathery. In the famous *fegato alla veneziana*, calf's liver is cut into the thinnest slices, fried for mere seconds, and served on a bed of golden fried onions. Liver is also good when served with fried bacon and watercress.

Beef liver is often the only liver available in the supermarket, and is usually a darker red than calf's liver. Its flavor is stronger and it is not at all as delicate. It should be prepared in the same ways as calf's liver.

Lamb's liver is a deeper color than calf's liver and doesn't have as good a flavor, but it is as tender. It is served in the same ways as calf's liver.

Pork liver is not ideal for frying, as its texture is granular and its taste rather powerful. It is best used in pâtés, or braised in one large piece with wine and vegetables.

Kidneys All kidneys should be firm and smell sweet. Once prepared, they can be broiled or sautéed briefly or simmered slowly and for a long time—anything in between and they will be tough.

Veal kidneys are multilobed and will be very large and pale when they come from milk-fed veal, darker and much smaller from grass-fed veal. They are best when broiled and served with bacon, or briskly browned in butter to seal in their juices. The piquancy of a mustard and cream sauce is the perfect complement. In Europe, kidneys may be sold still in their fresh white surrounding fat, and they can be roasted in this fat; this takes about an hour, and the resulting kidneys will be pink and succulent.

Lamb kidneys have a mild but delicious flavor, and are excellent fried in butter. With the two halves not quite severed, they form an essential part of the dish called a mixed grill.

Pork kidneys are larger than lamb kidneys and are thought by some people to be strong flavored, but they are tender enough to be broiled or panfried, and are a favorite dish on the menu in French brasseries. They are also good cooked slowly in wine and served with boiled potatoes and watercress to offset their richness.

Beef kidneys are dark and quite strongly flavored, and are best suited to braising. They also provide just the right flavor and plenty of rich gravy in Britain's famous steak and kidney pie.

Beef tongue

Honeycomb tripe

Caul fat

Veal sweetbreads

Veal kidneys

Oxtail

Calf's liver

Tongue While tongue can be purchased fresh, it is more usual to find it cured, smoked, or pickled. It is a very smooth meat. Beef tongue is best; calf's tongue, although good, has less flavor; and lamb's tongue is rather dull. Pork tongue is not very often seen.

Whether it is fresh or cured, choose a tongue that feels soft to the touch. Soak cured tongue overnight if necessary to remove the salt, and then simmer it with vegetables and herbs until tender (this can take 3 hours or more, so allow plenty of time). Skin it carefully and serve it hot with Italian herb sauce, or walnut or raisin sauce, and with mashed or boiled new potatoes. Cold, tongue is usually eaten with pickles, horseradish or mustard, and green salad.

Tripe Usually from beef, tripe is the lining of the animal's first and second stomachs. It comes in a variety of textures, some honeycombed, which are considered to be the best, some just slightly rough (called pocket tripe, this is less common), and some smooth. Tripe has to be cleaned and blanched meticulously before cooking, and would take hours to cook if bought truly fresh—an authentic *tripe à la mode de Caen*, the Normandy dish flavored with vegetables and Calvados, needs about 12 hours of simmering before it will reach its gelatinous best.

Thankfully, tripe is usually sold already prepared and partly cooked; always buy tripe that looks white and fresh. In Provence, lamb's tripe is folded into little parcels enclosing garlic, herbs, and salt pork, and simmered with sheep's feet, to make the famous dish called *pieds et pacquets*. Menudo is a much-loved hearty Mexican tripe stew.

Caul fat After the fat has been removed to make fine-quality leaf lard, a very thin membrane of fat that lines the abdominal cavity of the pig is separated to become the delicious and delicate caul fat. This fat, with its lace-like appearance, may need to be special-ordered from the butcher. The sheets usually have to be soaked in warm water until they soften and become pliable for cutting into squares with scissors and wrapping around sausages and chopped meats, as in French charcuterie. In Chinese cooking, caul fat is used to envelop poultry before it is deep-fried or baked. The fat provides a basting layer, melting into nothing and leaving behind a delicate, delicious, golden-brown crust.

Heart A heart is a hard-working muscle and, as a result, is never especially tender to eat. Beef heart is particularly tough, and is best prepared by slicing and braising it with plenty of onions to give it a good flavor. Lamb, pork, and calf's hearts, being more tender, can be blanched, stuffed, wrapped in bacon, and roasted.

Brains Calf's brains are decidedly the best, although lamb brains are also quite good. Pork and beef brains are less favored. Like sweetbreads, brains need preparation before they are used, and thorough cooking. They can be gently fried or poached. *Beurre noir* (butter cooked to a rich dark brown), with a few capers added, is the classic sauce. Brains are also good *à la meunière*—sautéed and served with brown butter, lemon, and parsley—or made into a salad with chopped garlic, chiles, and coriander.

Head, tail, and feet

Although not always available, heads, tails, and feet are often well worth the trouble and the long, slow cooking needed to make them tender and to bring out their velvety, gelatinous qualities.

Head Daunting to look at, the head of a calf, pig, or sheep can be a lengthy business to prepare, but an obliging butcher will do this for you and split it into manageable pieces.
Pig's head makes head cheese (called *fromage de tête* in France, and brawn in Britain), the chopped meat suspended in a translucent jelly flavored with herbs, spices, and vinegar (heads are very gelatinous). This is eaten cold with mustard and a green salad.
Calf's head can be cooked, boned and sliced, and covered with a vinaigrette containing capers and onions, to make the *tête de veau vinaigrette* sold in French charcuteries. It is sometimes used to make head cheese.
Sheep's head makes a broth much liked in Scotland but thought depressing elsewhere. Sheep's head is, however, a great favorite much on view in Morocco's street food markets.
Calf's and pig's ears are cartilaginous, and considered a delicacy by the Chinese.

Braised pig's ears sometimes appear in the beloved *choucroute garnie* of Alsace, and in some of the pork dishes of Portugal.

Oxtail Oxtail stew, in winter, is one of the very best and most warming dishes. Choose an oxtail with a high proportion of lean, and with fresh, creamy fat. Allow a whole oxtail for two to three people. It will usually be sold cut up and needs only to be trimmed of any large lumps of fat. Generally only the meatier upper joints need trimming.

Oxtail needs long, slow cooking to develop its excellent gelatinous texture. The large amounts of fat that rise to the surface will be easier to remove if the stew is made the day before serving and allowed to get completely cold. Oxtail stew reheats particularly well.

Feet Calf's foot is not much seen today, but pig's feet are quite readily available. **Pig's feet**—trotters in the British Isles—are sold fresh, pickled, or smoked. They are usually split in half, and can be quite plump and meaty. Often they are just simmered and then served either hot with sauerkraut or cold in their own jelly. They are also very good cooked and then coated in bread crumbs and broiled, served with mustard.
Calf's foot can be stewed, and it goes into the making of rich stocks and glazes. Traditionally, calf's foot jelly was given to invalids, being both nutritious and easy to eat and digest.

Gelatin Extracted from calf's feet, pig's knuckles, and the like, gelatin is sold either in powdered form in individual packets, or in shiny sheets. The sheets are the preferred form in Europe; in the United States, sheets may be found in pastry supply shops or through specialty mail-order sources. Gelatin has virtually no taste and dissolves into a clear liquid. Sheet or leaf gelatin is less likely than powdered to turn lumpy. Do not boil gelatin. Powdered gelatin should be softened in cold water before dissolving it; sheet gelatin can simply be dissolved in a little hot liquid in a cup standing in a shallow pan of hot water. Gelatin does not take kindly to freezing.

An alternative to animal gelatin is agar-agar, the jellying agent extracted from seaweed. It can be found in health food stores and Asian markets.

PREPARING MEAT

Preparing a beef tenderloin

1 With the rounded, neater side of the tenderloin uppermost, start cutting and pulling away the fat from the wide end.

2 Cut away all the fat that lies along one side of the tenderloin.

3 Cut off the large lump of fat that is attached to the wide end.

4 Turn the tenderloin over, and pull and cut away the fatty strip, or chain muscle.

1

2

beef cuts for panfrying, broiling, grilling, and roasting 52–3

knives 222–4
meat pounder 226

Filets Mignons with Shallot Sauce 292

3

4

5

5 Return the tenderloin to its original position. Using a sharp knife, remove the shiny layer of membrane, or silverskin. This should leave the meat completely free of fat and membrane.

6 Prepare the tenderloin for roasting whole by securing any loose pieces neatly with kitchen string. Fold the thin end of the tenderloin under itself and secure it, if you like, for more even cooking.

7 Alternatively, cut small filet mignon steaks from the thin end of the tenderloin, and medium-size tournedos from the center. The wide end can be used as a small roast as is, or prepared for Châteaubriand: wrap it in a clean cloth, turn it on its side, and, using the side of a cleaver or a meat mallet, flatten it to half its original thickness.

8 In this way, the tenderloin has been divided into a Châteaubriand (bottom), three tournedos (top), and three filets mignons. Use the trimmings to make beef Stroganoff or another dish, or for steak tartar.

6

7

8

Preparing veal scallops

1 Using a sharp knife, cut even slices from a boneless cut from leg of veal, such as top or bottom round.

2 Place each slice between two pieces of dampened parchment paper or two sheets of plastic wrap, and flatten it gently but firmly, using a rolling pin or a meat pounder. Here, a prepared scallop is compared with a freshly cut slice.

1

2

1

Preparing a large pork scallop

1 Pork tenderloin is normally cooked whole or cut into slices or chunks, but a large tenderloin can also be flattened and then rolled around a stuffing. Slit the tenderloin open down the middle, being careful not to cut all the way through it.

2

2 Open the meat out like a book and then place it on a dampened piece of parchment paper or on a sheet of plastic wrap.

3

3 Cover the meat with a second piece of parchment paper or plastic wrap, and flatten it gently but firmly with a rolling pin or a meat pounder.

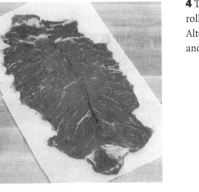

4

4 The scallop can now be stuffed, rolled, and secured with kitchen string. Alternatively, cut it into smaller pieces and use as pork scallopine.

Boning a shoulder of lamb

1 Lay the shoulder fat side down and grasp the exposed end of the shank bone. Cut around the bone with a sharp knife, pushing the meat back as you work toward the joint.

shoulder of
lamb 58

knives 222–4

**Lamb with
Indian Spices**
302, 303

1

2 Cut into the joint between the shank and the center (arm) bone, then bend the shank bone back until the joint breaks. Remove the shank bone.

3 Grasp the exposed end of the center bone and cut back the meat in the same way as with the shank bone, cutting as close to the bone as possible. Avoid cutting through the meat. Pull the center bone away from the blade bone to which it is attached and pull it out.

2

3

4 Turn the meat around so that the triangular blade bone is facing you. Insert the knife into the meat against the bone, and cut the meat away from either side of the flat bone. Pull the bone out, and trim any excess fat from the meat.

4

5 Roll up the boned meat, with the fat on the outside, and secure it with kitchen string. The three bones that have been removed are, from left to right, the blade bone, the center (arm) bone, and the shank.

5

Boning a leg of lamb

1 Grasp the broad, curved hip bone, which protrudes at the wider end of the leg, and carefully run a sharp knife around it, releasing it from the meat and the tendons that attach it to the leg bone. Pull out the bone.

1

2 Grasp the shank bone at the other end of the leg, cut it away from the meat, severing the tendons that attach it, and then pull it out.

3 Set the leg with the wide end up, and, using the knife, tunnel into the cavity left by the hip bone, cutting as close to the leg bone as possible.

2

3

4 When all the meat has been separated from the bone, pull the bone out of the hip cavity. Trim away the excess fat from the meat.

5 The three bones that have been removed here are, from left to right, the shank bone, the main leg bone, and the hip bone.

4

5

6 Tuck the shank end of the meat into the cavity left by the bones, and roll up the boned meat to make a neat roast. Tie with kitchen string.

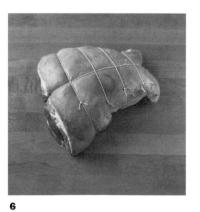

6

Butterflying a leg of lamb

1 Lay a boned leg of lamb fat side down. Cut down to the cavity left by the leg bone and slit open the leg, without cutting it all the way through. Trim off all the excess fat and the sinews.

2 Open the leg out flat, then slash it lengthwise in the thickest parts so that it will be reasonably even in thickness; do not cut all the way through the meat.

1

2

leg of lamb 57
rack of lamb 58

Grilled Butterflied Leg of Lamb with Dijon and Herbs

304

Preparing a rack of lamb

1 If the butcher has not already done so, cut away the backbone, or chine, from the meaty end of the rack, using a strong, sharp knife or a cleaver.

1

2 Trim off most of the fat from the rack, leaving only a thin layer.

3 Cut through the fat across the rib bones, about 2 inches from the meaty part of the rack, and then cut off the layer of fat and meat over the ends of the rib bones.

2

3

4 Strip the meat and fat from between the exposed rib bones, and scrape the bones clean.

4

Ham, Bacon, and Salted Pork

Theoretically, and indeed in practice, every kind of meat can be cured, but pork has long been the prime candidate—not only because of pork's doubtful keeping qualities in the days before refrigeration, but also because this fine-grained and well-lubricated meat emerges from the cure in a succulent and delicious state, and remains so juicy and tender when it is boiled, fried, or roasted.

Dry air, salt, and smoke are the age-old curing agents. Nitrates and nitrites, added in minute quantities to reinforce the preservative powers of salt, are comparative newcomers, and it is these additives that cause the pinkness in cured pork products.

Ham

Pigs used for ham tend to be older and heavier than those that yield fresh pork for our tables. Before the cure, their meat is deep pink or clear red, and the fat is firm and white rather than ivory-colored. After the cure, the outside skin may be creamy-gray to mahogany, depending on whether it has been smoked or not.

Most but not all hams are smoked: some of the finest are simply salted, either in a bath of brine or by the dry-cure method, which involves massaging salt into the ham and storing it for a certain period of time to allow the salt

to permeate the meat, then rinsing and drying the ham. Sometimes, but not always, the cure is repeated several times. This is a slow process, but it ensures that the minimum of salt that is necessary for preservation penetrates the meat; the brine treatment is faster but tends to introduce more salt into the flesh. Some brine-cured hams are injected with brine before they go into their salty bath to speed up the process. In both brine-curing and dry-curing, certain flavoring agents—herbs, spices, and sweeteners—may be added. When sugar is added, the ham may be labeled "sugar-cured."

After they are cured, almost all hams are smoked. "Supermarket"-type canned hams may be smoked lightly, for a short time, while "gourmet" hams are smoked for a longer time, ensuring a stronger flavor. (Some excellent American country hams, however, are not smoked.)

Once cured, and perhaps smoked, most hams are matured. The time and methods for this process vary from place to place (some are buried in wood ash, some hung up in an airy place for months on end) and it is to these differences, as well as to the type and diet of the pigs, that we owe our immense variety of hams. There are also differences in the cuts. Strictly speaking, hams are the hind legs of pigs, but there are other parts of the anatomy, such as the loin, hock, and shoulder, that are cured in similar ways.

Whole hams may be bought cooked, partially cooked, or uncooked.

Cooked ham Baked or boiled ham is an extremely versatile meat: it can be served whole as a hot main course with

a parsley sauce and young vegetables, or plain with velvety spinach. It may also be eaten with heartier vegetables, such as root vegetables or cabbage, or dried peas and beans, which may themselves be cooked together with a ham bone or a piece of bacon. Sliced reasonably thick, ham often comes in a mustard, cream, or tomato sauce, although gourmets insist that a spoonful of Champagne is all the moistening a first-class boiled ham really needs. Cold, in thinner slices, ham can make a first course, or, with a salad, a nice lunch. Chopped, it adds flavor and character to a vast number of dishes. Ham with red-eye gravy, a traditional dish from the American South, is made with a slice of regular or country ham.

Specialty hams When buying one of these hams to cook at home, do not be put off by a little bloom on its rind, since this indicates that the ham is cured to perfection. This must, however, be scraped off before the ham is immersed in the cooking liquid for boiling or simmering, or is baked, as country hams occasionally are. Do note that many of these hams must be soaked, often for as long as 2 to 3 days, before cooking. Some of these hams are sold at specialty butchers; others, like Smithfield ham, can be mail-ordered.

Virginia ham is among the more well-known "country-cured" hams. Pigs destined to become Virginia hams were originally fattened on peanuts and acorns, but today they are grain-fed; the meat is usually smoked over scented hickory and applewood.

Smithfield ham is cured and smoked in Smithfield, Virginia. This is probably the

Coppa

Kaiserfleisch

Kasseler

Cooked ham

Westphalian ham

Prosciutto

York ham

Bayonne ham

Black Forest ham

most famous country ham. It is spiced with pepper and heavily smoked.

Kentucky ham is another country ham, and is perhaps a little drier than the Virginia hams. It owes its flavor to a large proportion of clover in the young pigs' food and a diet of grain toward the end of their lives.

York ham is firm and tender and is the best known of the British "boiling hams." It is delicately pink, with fat that is white and translucent. It is cured by the dry-cure method, and smoked over oak sawdust until it develops its fine, mild flavor.

Suffolk ham is traditionally cured in brine with spices and honey. This British ham is then smoked and hung to mature. During this process it develops its characteristic blue mold and a full, delicate flavor.

Bradenham ham has coal-black skin and deep red flesh, and is another famous English ham. It is cured with molasses and so has a sweet but robust flavor.

Gammon or Wiltshire ham is unlike true hams, which are first cut and then cured; it is cured instead as part of the whole pig, which is then divided into various cuts. English gammon is mild and does not keep as well as most other hams. It is sold smoked or unsmoked, and comes in a variety of cuts. It is best boiled and served with root vegetables or dried peas or beans.

Prague ham is perhaps the most admired central European ham. It is traditionally salted and mildly brined before being lightly smoked over beechwood embers, from which it emerges as perhaps the sweetest of all smoked hams.

Jambon de Paris In France, ham ready to be cooked is sold as *jambon de Paris*, and cooked ham as *jambon glacé*.

Other hams Buying a whole hams is a substantial investment usually reserved for festive occasions, and so ham is usually sold in portions as well. Half-hams (called *jambonneau* in France) come from either the meaty, more expensive butt end of the leg or from the bonier, cheaper shank portion. Hams are also sold boned, or partially boned, and cut into either steaks or slices. Hams can be bought with the fat and rind left on, or partly skinned with the fat trimmed. Skinless hams, although popular, tend to lack the flavor of hams with their skin and fat still intact.

Hams may also be bought canned, the better among them being the Dutch, Danish, and Polish. Lean and flavorful,

they are boneless and ready to eat, but taste better baked with cider, brown sugar, mustard, and cloves. Other canned hams may have little flavor.

Kaiserfleisch and Kasseler Other cured pork products include the delicate smoked Austrian *Kaiserfleisch*, and the *Kasseler* so popular in Germany, Denmark, and Poland. Taken from the loin of the pig, these cuts look like a row of pork chops, but they may also be sold by the chop, boned or unboned, or sliced. In Germany, *Kasseler* is so popular that pigs have been bred with an extra set of ribs to yield more of this cut. Austria eats its *Kaiserfleisch* with bread-based dumplings and red cabbage. German *Kasseler* is sold uncooked in its native country, but is usually sold cooked and sliced elsewhere.

Raw ham Local differences in the traditional cures show most clearly in the hams that are not meant to be cooked but are eaten raw.

Prosciutto When you go into a shop in Italy to buy prosciutto, you will be asked if you want it *cotto* (cooked) or *crudo* (raw), because the word simply means "ham." But outside Italy, prosciutto means raw ham, and the best comes from Parma.

Prosciutto is lightly salted and air-cured for many months. A crown stamped upon its golden hide tells you that it is the genuine article produced from local pigs. The thousands of hams sent to Parma for the cure from all over Italy are less delicate and do not bear this hallmark.

Eat prosciutto in paper-thin slices, with melon, fresh figs, or butter.

Culatello Looking like a half-size Parma ham, culatello comes from the choice butt end of the leg. It is less fatty and more spicy than prosciutto.

Coppa When Italian recipes specify raw ham, most Italian housewives tend to use coppa. This is the cured shoulder and neck portion of a pig, pressed into a skin, and is fattier and less expensive than prosciutto. It can also be thinly sliced and served as an antipasto.

Bayonne This most celebrated of French hams comes from the Pyrenees. Wine plays an important part in the curing process and accounts for its special taste. Locally, Bayonne ham is eaten with eggs or added at the last moment to stews; however, it is most delicious eaten raw like prosciutto, but sliced thicker.

Westphalian ham is the best-known of the German hams and the star of a German *schinkenplatte*, a plate of assorted cold hams. Traditionally, it is cured and then smoked over ash or beech with a bit of juniper. It is a deep golden-pink. Eat it thinly sliced on dark bread such as pumpernickel.

Black Forest ham Strongly brined and strongly smoked, this German ham has well-flavored flesh and milk-white fat. Its robust taste goes well with sourdough bread.

Jambons de campagne and other European country hams The Dordogne area of France is well known for its splendid farm-cured hams. These are often rather salty and chewy because the cure is very heavy, but are delicious when thickly sliced and served with unsalted butter and French bread. Spanish and Italian country hams are also excellent.

Jambon de Grisons This Swiss ham comes from a region with a climate that is ideal for the curing of meats. It is first lightly salted and then dried in the cold, clear air of the Alps.

Lachsschinken comes from Germany. It is smoked pork loin, wrapped in snow-white pork fat and bound with string; it should be pink and moist inside. It can be bought sliced or in its entirety, but should be eaten thinly sliced or minutely diced, with crusty buttered rolls.

Jamón serrano This highly esteemed but chewy delicacy is always eaten raw. Cured and air-dried in the Sierra Morena mountains in southwestern Spain, it is delicious on rough peasant bread. It is reputed to be the sweetest ham in the world. The variety from the province of Huelva is thought to be the best.

Bacon, pork belly

Whether you buy *pancetta*, *lard de poitrine*, *poitrine fumé*, *speck*, *paprikaschinken*, or *tocino*, what you carry home is cured belly of pork, which, when sliced, is known as bacon. Cures, and fattiness, vary.

Pancetta is pink and white in even proportions, and may be smoked or unsmoked. *Pancetta stesa* is left flat; it is used mainly in cooking, in such Italian dishes as *spaghetti alla carbonara*, and in other pasta sauces and bean casseroles. *Pancetta arrotolata* is rolled, flavored with cloves and peppercorns, and used for cooking, or, if smoked, eaten as it is.

Lard de poitrine France's version of bacon can be extremely fatty and generally has less lean meat than its pickled *petit salé*. *Lard de poitrine* is given a bacon cure and comes smoked, when it is called *poitrine fumé*, or unsmoked. It is used to enrich stews and stuffings, and is an essential part of *coq au vin* and many beef stews. It is also used to bard roasting birds or dry cuts of meat. Cut into strips, it becomes lardons. *Poitrine fumé* is splendid fried like bacon, or added to omelets.

Speck is basically fat with a thin layer of lean. When it is more meaty, it becomes *schinkenspeck*. In Germany, Holland, Scandinavia, and other European countries, speck, which can be smoked or unsmoked, appears as a garnish on dishes that need the taste of bacon fat. Speck yields such a large quantity of rendered fat that part of it is often poured off and eaten on bread. The drippings are also used for frying potatoes or mushrooms, and for browning beef or veal before roasting.

Paprika speck is translucent white and rindless, and dusted on the outside with bright red paprika. It is not used so much in cooking, but may turn up in various European countries on a platter of cold cuts.

Tocino is the Spanish version of speck; it is strong-flavored and packed in salt. It goes into *fabadas*—bean stews slowly simmered with vegetables and sausages.

Bacon Although most American bacon is smoked, in other countries, bacon can be bought smoked and unsmoked—or "green" in Britain. Smoking makes the rind look golden-orange and turns the flesh a nice deep pink. Unsmoked flesh is pale pink, and the rind looks anything from off-white to dark cream. As far as the taste is concerned, smoking adds depth and interest to the flavor.

Americans tend to like their bacon crisp, and the diet our pigs are fed causes their fat to be on the soft side, so that it melts easily and our bacon curls and crinkles as it cooks, becoming crisp and crumbly. In other parts of the world, crispness is only possible if the bacon is sliced almost paper-thin.

Center-cut bacon is the leanest. Sliced bacon comes thin, regular, and thick cut. Unsliced bacon is called slab bacon; its rind may need to be removed.

In those countries, especially England, where entire carcasses of pigs are cured in brine, a number of ham-like cuts appear on the market. The leaner cuts are good hot or cold, boiled with onions and root vegetables, or first boiled and then liberally basted with fruit juice or cider and roasted. Bacon chops and steaks can be broiled or fried, and served with applesauce.

British sliced bacon comes not only from the belly (streaky bacon), but also from the back of the pig and from the meaty part of the leg.

Canadian bacon comes from the loin. Called back bacon in Canada and top back in Britain, this smoked pork is quite lean and needs to be fried in a little fat. It comes in rough cylindrical cuts.

Salted pork

The salt pork of the United States, the *petit salé* of France, and the pickled pork belly of Great Britain fall into a category all of their own, being not fully cured but lightly salted in brine.

Salt pork Not to be confused with fatback, salt pork comes from the belly, and may be well streaked with lean or virtually all fat. Salt pork from the leaner end of the belly is what goes into Boston baked beans. Salt pork is also known as corned belly and is chiefly used as a flavoring agent. As such, it is an essential part of a New England clam chowder.

Petit salé is lightly brined, and can be either the leg end of pork belly or the fatty parts of the neck. It is eaten in the traditional French *potée*, a rich cabbage soup containing other cured meats and vegetables. It may also sit in pink-and-white slices on top of puréed peas and beans, or on a dish of cabbage, when it is called *petit salé aux choux*, and it is a vital ingredient in the cooking of sauerkraut.

Pickled pork The English contribution tends to be slightly more heavily cured in brine, with sugar added. It usually consists of belly, although shank is sometimes also prepared in the same way. This meat may need soaking before it is simmered with carrots, turnips, and other root vegetables. Pease pudding is a traditional accompaniment.

Sylte is pickled belly of pork, rolled around crushed peppercorns and mustard seed. It is delicious thinly sliced and often appears on Scandinavian cold tables.

Jowls Pork jowls are cured and usually smoked, and are good when not too fatty. They turn up in Southern regional cooking, in boiled dishes or with black-eyed peas. England calls pork jowls bath chaps, and serves them bread-crumbed.

Lard de poitrine

Smoked speck

British unsmoked streaky bacon

British smoked back bacon

Pancetta

Canadian bacon

Bacon

Cured Meat and Poultry

By far the greatest number of preserved meats, whether brined, air-dried, smoked, or canned, contain pork and pork mixtures. But other meats, game, and poultry also lend themselves to the curing process, producing interesting and luxurious alternatives to ham.

Salted beef There are many ways to treat a corned or salted cut of beef, a number of them a welcome legacy from kosher Jewish cuisine.

Corned beef Corning is an old term for salting, and in the United States corned beef means the salted and well-spiced briskets that go whole into a New England boiled dinner and chopped into corned-beef hash. To most Europeans, however, corned beef means what is called bully beef, canned, pressed, salted beef, pink in color and speckled with fat, that is eaten with salad or in fritters or hash.

Salt beef The British alternative to corned beef, this is simply beef soaked in brine. The addition of saltpeter makes it red—in its natural state it is grayish-brown. Some types of salt beef are so heavily brined that some soaking will be necessary before the meat goes into the pot, while others may be ready for cooking just as they are. Salt beef—beef round is the traditional cut—is often boiled with plenty of carrots and served with potatoes and dumplings.

Pastrami In the Balkans, the word pastrami is used to describe any kind of preserved meat, from beef, pork, and lamb to goose. Elsewhere, it has come to mean salt beef that has been highly seasoned, usually with whole black peppercorns, dry-cured, and then smoked. Since Rumania, above all other Balkan countries, excels in making pastrami, its methods are the model for the rest of the world. Sold fully cooked in slabs or slices, pastrami is delicious with rye bread or hot potato salad.

Dried beef This is beef spiced and salted and then air-dried to the very essence of beefiness.

Bündnerfleisch Grisons in Switzerland is the home of this mountain air-cured beef. As it tends to be rather dry, slivers of it, scraped rather than cut, are eaten with an oil and vinegar dressing.

Bresaola is the Italian counterpart. It is a specialty of Lombardy and is eaten thinly sliced. The usual dressing is made with olive oil, chopped parsley, and lemon; or bresaola may be served with olive oil and slivers of Parmesan or white truffle.

Chipped beef is a rather poor American relation sold in jars. It is sometimes served on toast, or can be mixed with scrambled eggs.

Biltong comes from South Africa, and it is strips of cured, air-dried beef or game, or, more recently, meat such as ostrich. Biltong can be very good indeed, and will keep indefinitely.

Jerky is the American version of biltong, and is strips of beef, traditionally dried in the sun. It is chewy, but full of flavor.

Smoked poultry and game Unlike hams, smoked poultry and game are always hot-smoked, or first cooked and then smoked. The birds can be bought either whole or sliced and resemble ham in flavor, but are as perishable as fresh-roasted birds. Smoked chicken and smoked turkey breast offer plenty of delicate meat; smoked duck is excellent, and smoked quail extravagant. In Europe, smoked guinea fowl is common, but the most prized of all is smoked goose breast obtained from the Baltic coast of Germany, where the geese tend to be the most deep-breasted. Also excellent is smoked reindeer meat from Scandinavia.

Confit d'oie and confit de canard
An everyday food in southwestern France, where vast numbers of geese and ducks are fattened for foie gras, confits are simply salted or salted and spiced pieces of goose (oie) or duck (canard) preserved in fat. Confit can be bought in a jar and will keep for several months, but all that is needed to make it at home is the bird, its rendered fat, coarse salt, and patience. The wings and legs are heavily salted and refrigerated for 12 hours, then wiped dry and gently cooked in their own fat, plus extra pork fat if necessary. After this, they are placed in jars, where they must be completely covered with their own fat. They will keep well in the refrigerator for several months.

A portion of confit is an essential ingredient in a cassoulet, but confit can also be eaten on its own, gently sautéed in a little of its preserving fat, and served crisp on the outside, succulent inside, with a green salad dressed with walnut oil.

Smoked mutton "No sort of meat," say the Scots, "is more improved by smoking with aromatic woods than mutton." The people of Norway are in perfect agreement. Norwegian fenalar is smoked and air-dried until it develops a highly concentrated flavor, to be enjoyed with crisp Norwegian flatbrød and butter. The Scottish mutton ham has a rich, interesting flavor, and is good sliced and eaten raw, or braised with vegetables.

Pastrami

Smoked turkey breast

Beef jerky

Confit d'oie

Bresaola

Smoked quail

Bündnerfleisch

Salt beef

Biltong

Smoked duck breast

Sausages

When country people killed their own animals, particularly pigs, to provide themselves with meat, there was always a tremendous amount of work to be done to make sure that every part of the animal could be either eaten at once or, for the most part, stored for later use.

The liver, heart, kidneys, and so forth were eaten at once, and the legs, bellies, shoulders, feet, and heads salted for the winter, while certain cuts and all the scraps were gathered together and turned into sausages, with the animals' own intestines serving as casings. These sausages were either spiced, to help prolong their life by a few days, and eaten fresh, or dried and preserved by various means, often by salting and smoking, for eating later.

The type of meat, the proportion of fat to lean, and the endless variations of seasonings and cures account for the myriad different sausages we enjoy today. What makes the ideal sausage is largely a matter of regional taste. Some people like sausages so coarse that the meat seems to be chopped, not ground; others prefer the stuffing ground to a paste. But all agree that the meatiest sausages are the best. The seasonings used also vary tremendously from country to country and from region to region.

Most interested sausage eaters prefer their sausages in natural casings, true intestines being marginally more digestible than the artificial kind, less liable to burst during cooking, and producing a more attractive, rustic, natural-looking result. Natural casing can be recognized by the fine, slim knots between the links; artificial casings tend to be less elastic and to untwist, leaving air spaces between the individual sausages.

Fresh sausages

While fresh homemade sausages are fairly simple to make and easily rival the best store-bought ones, farmers' markets, some butchers, and specialty shops now offer some very good fresh sausages. These should be treated like fresh meat and eaten within a few days of purchase. They need really slow cooking—too much heat and they burst their skins, because the contents swell at a faster rate than the casings. Prick them in one or two places before frying in a little oil, and make sure they are thoroughly cooked. In England, fresh sausages and sausage meat go into sausage rolls, pies, and toad-in-the-hole. In Italy and France, sausages are poached and boiled and used in soups, *choucroute garnie*, and *cassoulet*. Also in

France, cervelas sausages are sometimes wrapped in brioche dough and then baked. Algerian merguez, heavily spiced lamb sausages, are the favorite for barbecues in the South of France. In Spain, blood sausages and chorizo are essential components of bean stews.

American and British sausages
Usually bought by weight, these can be made from fresh pork or, usually less good, from fresh beef, veal, or venison. Smoked and unsmoked chicken and turkey sausages are also becoming increasingly popular. Sage is the traditional sausage seasoning, but new types are introduced all the time— one excellent combination is pork and leeks, while pork and fresh chile peppers is another. The best are made of pure, coarsely chopped pork. Broiled and served with fried eggs, fat sausages make a filling and delicious breakfast. Accompanied by mashed potatoes, when they are called bangers and mash in England, they are lovely for lunch or supper. Slender, half-sized sausages, filled with pork or beef, are known as chipolatas in England and France, although the term is in fact Italian.

Unless they are labeled 100 percent meat, sausages are likely to contain a filler: this filler was once fresh bread crumbs, but cereals and other additives are now generally used. Sausages often contain a good deal of moisture, since crushed ice may be introduced into the sausage machine to prevent overheating of the meat as it is ground.

Bratwurst and weisswurst These fine-grained, pale, almost white sausages—the best known are those from Germany and Switzerland—are usually made of veal, though bratwurst sometimes contain pork as well. Literally "frying sausages," bratwurst, and weisswurst, can indeed be fried, or they can be grilled so that they are branded with golden stripes. These sausages are of a fine consistency and have a delicate taste. Bratwurst is particularly popular in the Midwest, where it's sold precooked as well as fresh.

Saucisse Small fresh sausages in France generally go under the name of *saucisses*, while larger ones are *saucissons*. Regional recipes make for difference of

Saucisse d'Auvergne

Bratwurst

Kielbasa

Luganega

Merguez

Saucisson de Toulouse

Fresh pork sausage

Natural sausage casing

texture and taste, but whether coarse or fine, highly seasoned or not, all are made of pure meat, which is so important when making the *saucisses en brioche* (sausages in brioche) encountered throughout France, if the result is to be light and delicate. There are any number of excellent locally made French country sausages—called *saucisses de campagne*—that go into cabbage soups and stuffings as well as being broiled. A wide variety of seasonings is used for these sausages, ranging from pistachio nuts, chard, truffles, or Champagne to sage, sweet and hot peppers, or fresh parsley. **Saucisse d'Auvergne** These are *saucisses fumées*, or smoked sausages. They are eaten either broiled or fried, and their rich flavor combines beautifully with a hot potato salad.

Cumberland sausage This meatiest of all British pork sausages is made in a continuous spiral, rather than being twisted into links. The filling is coarsely chopped and spiced with peppercorns. It is sold by length and is usually fried.

Kielbasa In Poland any number of fresh sausages, called kielbasa, are added to hearty *bigos*—cabbage and meat stews—but in the United States and elsewhere kielbasa refers to a particular garlicky and spicy sausage sold either smoked or fresh, sometimes already fully cooked. It is good broiled and served with sauerkraut and a mild mustard.

Luganega This sausage from northern Italy, which consists of pure pork shoulder, often seasoned with Parmesan cheese, is made in enormous lengths; it is narrow, unlinked, and cut to the customer's order. Italian housewives fry it in oil, adding tomatoes or sage, and serve it with polenta; or they may simply scrape all the meat out of the casings and use it as a basis for a thick pasta sauce.

Salsicce Seen hanging in Italian shops, *salsicces* have a rustic flavor and may either be highly spiced with chile peppers or may be very mild, especially if they are made simply with ground pork and pancetta. The common Italian link sausages (and bulk Italian sausage meat) are seasoned with fennel seeds and garlic and may be hot, with red chile peppers, or sweet.

Homemade sausages

While it may be a tedious job to stuff the sausage meat into its casings, nothing can be more rewarding than to see links of fresh homemade sausages emerging in your own kitchen. Using a basic chopped or ground pork mixture, any number of delicious varieties of sausages can be made by simply adding various herbs and spices, and if you have your own smoking equipment in which to smoke the sausages, the possibilities become even greater. Seasonings can range from sage, oregano, marjoram, onions, or garlic to sliced truffles and pistachio nuts. Chopped pancetta or bits of ham or smoked tongue can also be added, and the mixture can be enriched with eggs. If you don't want to bother with sausage casings, form fresh sausage meat into little patties and panfry them.

Sausage meat A basic sausage mixture consists of about half lean meat to half fat, although some may use less fat to meat. For pure pork sausages, use lean meat from the shoulder, or loin, and an equal amount of fatback. For other sausages, veal and game such as venison can be used. Fatback is the best fat to use for any type of sausage. Cut it into cubes along with the meat, and put them both through a grinder. Alternatively, you can chop them briefly in a food processor, which works particularly well, especially for the coarser-textured sausages. Take care to remove gristle and sinew from the chopped meat. The ground ingredients should be mixed together well before the seasonings are added. The best way to determine how the sausages will finally taste is to panfry a little patty of the mixture and, after tasting it, to adjust the seasonings accordingly.

Casings Some sausages, such as *crépinettes*—the flat little sausages made in vast varieties in France—are merely encased in caul fat. Others can be skinless, in which case they are bound with eggs or dipped in beaten egg and bread crumbs or simply floured. Sausage meat can also be poached wrapped in cheesecloth or foil, but natural casings are best for neatly bound sausages.

Casings can be bought in specialty butchers and from butchers' suppliers, or through mail-order sources. These 1¼-inch hog casings usually come in

approximately 20-foot lengths and can then be cut and used as required. Store the casings, layered in salt, in a screwtop jar in the refrigerator.

Stuffing sausages It is not difficult to force the freshly ground, seasoned meat into the casings, and although there is a certain amount of domestic machinery available that will help you to turn out professional-looking specimens, you really only need a funnel and a pastry bag, some string, a pusher, such as the handle of a wooden spoon, and a faucet.

After disentangling the casing and soaking it in warm water until it is soft (1 to 2 hours), slip it over the faucet and run cold water through it, cutting out and discarding any sections with holes. Then cut lengths for convenient handling and wrinkle each one up over the funnel, leaving a good bit dangling at the end. Knot the end and start to feed in your mixture; force out any air bubbles, and then tie or twist the casing at intervals. Dry your handiwork for about 24 hours—in an airy, cool place if you are sure the temperature is below 40°F, on a rack in the refrigerator if not—and then cook in the usual way.

Other cooking sausages

Apart from fresh raw sausages, there are those that have been treated in some way to preserve them. Some, such as the frankfurter, have been fully cooked, but are reheated and served hot. Others have been salted and smoked and then left to mature but still require further cooking.

Saucisson de Toulouse These large, delicately seasoned sausages are made from coarsely chopped pork. They are an essential ingredient of *cassoulets*, but are also fried or broiled and served with sautéed apples and mashed potatoes.

Frankfurter It is the light smoking that gives the skins of frankfurters their familiar color. Unless marked kosher, in which case they are made of pure beef, authentic European frankfurters contain a mixture of finely ground beef and pork, and are usually quite highly spiced and salted. Genuine frankfurters are always sold in pairs. The classic accompaniments are potato salad, or sauerkraut and mustard; they are also sometimes added to potato soup.

In the United States, hot dogs—from miniature cocktail franks to "foot-longs"—may be made of pork, beef, chicken, or turkey, and are always precooked. Those labeled "beef" or "all-beef"—or "kosher"—by law contain only beef, without added fillers. Those labeled "meat" may be a combination of beef and pork, but cannot contain fillers; "frankfurters" can contain added fillers and are usually a combination of meats.

In Austria a piece of lean roast beef becomes a *wurstelbraten* when small frankfurter-type sausages called *wurstel* are inserted into it before braising.

When heating frankfurters, it is best to put them into a saucepan filled with water that is just below the boil, not actually boiling; too much heat and their thin skins will split.

Knackwurst, knockwurst This short, stumpy, precooked sausage is made of finely ground pork, beef, and fresh pork fat, flavored with salt, cumin, and garlic. Knackwurst are usually sold in pairs or in long links. They are often served with an accompaniment of sauerkraut.

Bockwurst These fresh sausages are prepared in the same way as frankfurters. In Germany they are traditionally made in the spring, when the winter-made bock beer is ready to drink. The *Berliner bockwurst* is a smoky red cooked sausage, while a Düsseldorf favorite is bockwurst wrapped in bacon with mustard.

Cervelas The best version of this pure pork sausage, which is a type of *saucisson*, also called saveloy in the United States, comes from Lyons. It is a large, fine-grained sausage and is sometimes delicately flavored with pistachio nuts or with truffles and truffled brandy. It is best poached, or wrapped in foil, together with a few spoonfuls of red wine, and baked. It is served hot, sliced, with warm potato salad or *choucroute garnie*. It may also be wrapped in brioche dough before being baked. The English version of the cervelas, the saveloy, is a very poor substitute.

Cotechino From northern Italy, this fresh sausage is made of pork moistened with white wine and subtly seasoned with spices. It comes in various sizes and is usually salted for a few days. Cotechino is simmered with dried white beans, lentils, or other legumes, or is sometimes served simply alongside helpings of rather soupy mashed potatoes. It is one of the essential ingredients of *bollito misto*—an Italian dish of mixed boiled meats.

Zampone and stuffed goose neck Besides intestines, stomachs, and bladders, which medieval jesters used to flaunt indecently, other parts of a range of animals can be turned into interesting sausages.

Zampone—a specialty from Modena, Italy—is one such example, and is really a cotechino stuffed into a boned pig's foot. Fresh, zampone is sometimes available in Italian markets. It usually needs soaking and then simmering for about an hour, but some of these sausages are precooked and only need heating through.

Stuffed goose neck In Europe, the fat skin of a goose neck is used in a similar way. The filling consists of meat and innards—liver, stomach, heart—perhaps morels or truffles, air-cured bacon, bread crumbs, and an egg for binding it all together. It is sewn up or tied at both ends and may then be fried to a golden-brown; poached, weighted, and then eaten in slices; or simply poached in stock fortified with a little white wine.

Loukanika Sliced and then served as a Greek *mezze*—hors d'oeuvre—a loukanika usually means coarsely ground pork seasoned with coriander, marinated in red wine, stuffed into casings, and, sometimes, left to air-dry. A loukanika in Greek communities in North America, however, is a combination of ground lamb and pork seasoned with orange rind, and is usually grilled and served at barbecues or for breakfast.

Chinese sausage These narrow sausages are dark red in color with white bits of fat. They are cured and air-dried. Chinese sausages flavor a number of chicken and vegetable dishes and are sometimes mixed with rice.

Andouillette and andouille French andouillettes can contain beef, pork, or veal tripe and chitterlings (large intestines), cooked to a gelatinous tenderness. The skins are made from pig's intestines. Veal andouillettes are the most sought after. They often come covered in lard, and are broiled or sautéed and eaten with mashed potatoes or sautéed apples. The larger andouilles, which may be black-skinned, are hung to dry, and are sliced and eaten cold.

Frankfurter

Cajun andouille

Cotechino

Knackwurst

French andouillette

Chinese sausage

Loukanika

Mexican chorizo

Bockwurst

Zampone

Cajun andouille This large, rich sausage, from Louisiana, is made with lean pork and pork fat, generously spiced with cayenne or chile peppers and flavored with herbs and lots of garlic. Like the French andouille sausage, Cajun-style andouille was traditionally made with chitterlings, but this is not always the case today. It is often heavily smoked, and is the traditional sausage to use in Cajun dishes such as jambalaya and gumbo.

Blood pudding and other cooked sausages

These are the ancestors of all the fresh sausages, and contain cereal additives as well as meat.

Blood pudding These get their color from pig's blood, their richness from cubes of pork fat, and their body from oatmeal—at least it is this cereal that is always used in Scotland and northern England. Elsewhere, other cereals, even bread crumbs, may be used. In Ireland, lamb's blood goes into the local version, which is called drisheen. The French boudins noirs may, variously, also contain onions, apples, chestnuts, eggs, garlic, and the leaves of chard. They are simmered by their makers, but may afterwards be poached, baked, or fried. In France, they are sometimes served with thinly sliced, fried onions, but are at their best when broiled and served with fried apples.

Blood sausage These are also known as black sausages, but differ from blood puddings in that they have fewer cereal additives and less seasoning. They always contain pig's blood, and come in a great variety.
Blutwurst There are many varieties of German blood sausages, but perhaps the blutwurst is the best known. It is made of diced bacon and calf's or pig's lungs, and is seasoned with cloves, mace, and marjoram. It is often served with boiled potatoes and cooked apples. Other German blood sausages include *rotwurst*, which is usually sliced and eaten on bread, and *schwarzwurst*, which is smoked and air-dried, and seasoned with garlic, cloves, and pepper and salt.
Morcilla Made and smoked in Asturias, Spain, this blood sausage is made of pig's blood, fat, spices, and onions,

and is an essential ingredient of *fabada asturiana*, or bean stew. There are two varieties—ordinary morcilla, which is the most popular and has a strong smoky flavor, and *morcilla dulce*, which has a sweet, spicy flavor.

Boudin blanc Made of white meat such as chicken, veal, rabbit, or pale pork, with bread crumbs or ground rice, cream, and perhaps eggs, these sausages are precooked, and may be slowly sautéed, grilled, broiled, or baked. Called white puddings in Britain, they are delicate and should be cooked slowly and at a gentle temperature, or they will burst and brown, losing their succulent softness. As with boudin noirs, these can be served accompanied by succulent fried apples.

Haggis Although called a glorified sausage, a haggis is really in a class of its own. In Scotland it is regarded with reverence and treated with ceremony, and is often the centerpiece of special occasions. Haggis is made of roughly chopped, freshly cooked sheep's innards (liver, lungs, and heart), toasted oatmeal, onions, suet, and herbs, all loosely packed into a sheep's stomach, which is then sewn up. The filling swells as the haggis is boiled, and makes it look like a grayish baseball.

Faggot These British sausages are little round parcels that contain pig's liver and lungs, cereal, and salt pork, or bacon. They are wrapped in caul fat (the lacy, fatty membrane that lines the abdominal cavity of a pig), and are then cooked slowly in the oven. Faggots are also known as poor man's goose or savory duck.

Cayette, caillette These flat sausages from the Ardèche, in France, contain chopped Swiss chard leaves, along with a mixture of ground pork, liver, garlic, herbs, and other seasonings, wrapped in caul fat. The sausages are cooked in the oven, like the aforementioned British faggots, but are usually far more appetizing in appearance.

Slicing sausages

These are usually available either cooked or smoked. The sausages in the following list are eaten cold, often in

sandwiches or as part of a simple lunch, accompanied by bread, olives, and plenty of red wine. They are best bought uncut or freshly sliced, although it is important to remember that once they are sliced they don't last very well. The varieties that are sold presliced in vacuum-packed packets are usually mass-produced and of inferior quality.

Mortadella Made of finely ground pure pork, this is the best and most famous of all Italian sausages, patterned perhaps with green flecks of pistachio nuts and white cubes of fat. The best mortadellas, which are made in enormous sizes, come from Bologna, where only the finest ingredients are used in their production, and where the flavorings include wine and coriander.

There are, however, other varieties— some good, some very pale imitations. Although these have never been anywhere near Bologna, they are still called bologna, or Bologna sausages, or, rather contemptuously, baloney. As well as the ubiquitous bologna sandwich meat, there is an American mortadella sausage, flavored with garlic and studded with pork fat. Canned cooked versions of Italian mortadella are available in the United States, but they are vastly inferior to the real thing, which, unfortunately, cannot be imported.

Eat mortadella with a plate of mixed antipasto or in sandwiches.

Jagdwurst This German sausage owes its character to quite sizeable pieces of pork fat and rosy pork meat embedded

Blood pudding

Blood sausage

Haggis

Boudin blanc

in the pale-pink pâté base, which is slightly porous due to the fact that it is made by a process that involves the use of moist heat.

Bierwurst Although much larger in circumference than jagdwurst, this sausage has a similar taste and texture. Ham bierwurst, or *bierschinken*, shows bits of ham in each of its large slices. It is also known as beerwurst (*bier* being German for beer), and is often flavored with garlic.

Mettwurst The word *mett* is the medieval German description for lean pounded pork. There is *grosse mettwurst*, which is coarse in texture and red, and *feine mettwurst*, which is pink and smooth enough to spread.

Zungenwurst When a blutwurst is interlarded with bits of tongue, it becomes a zungenwurst. Bits of pork fat and a lot of pig's blood are used to make this dried black German sausage, which, unlike blood sausages, does not usually contain cereal additives.

Presswurst Reminiscent of a head cheese, Hungarian presswurst consists of meat from the pig's head, neck, and feet, blood, and seasonings. Cased or uncased, it is cooked, lightly pressed, and cooled until the mixture jells. Sage is the most usual flavoring.

Sulzwurst Similar to presswurst, this sausage is made of large pork pieces. It can be spread on bread, or eaten with sliced onions and accompanied by an oil and vinegar dressing.

Cervelat sausages

Almost always smoked, cervelats (not to be confused with cervelas) are far less firm than salami sausages because their maturing time is half as long. There is, however, a slight resemblance between the two. They are always moist, and, being made of finely pounded meat and fat, they have, when cut, a velvety surface and a color of mottled pink. Fat or thin, cervelats are always pliable and look rather like large frankfurters.

German cervelat Made of finely ground beef and pork, these are very popular in Germany. They are delicate, mild in taste, and easy to slice.

Holsteinerwurst Elastic enough to be sold in rings as well as straight lengths of sausages, the Holsteinerwurst

originated in Holstein on the German-Danish border. Although counted among the cervelat-type sausages, the Holsteinerwurst is so heavily smoked that it could also be categorized among the German country sausages—the sort that used to hang above heather, beech, or peat smoke in northern chimneys.

Plockwurst With its smoke-darkened skin and dark meat, which contains a high proportion of beef, this tasty sausage often comes studded with whole peppercorns.

Katenrauchwurst This cottage-smoked German sausage is produced in some quantity and is eaten throughout much of northern Europe. It is made of coarse pieces of pork, and is dark in color and firm in texture. For serving, it should be cut diagonally into thick, oval slices.

Thuringer Among the American cervelats—also sometimes called summer sausages because they keep well, not requiring refrigeration—is the coriander-spiced variety called Thuringer. It is named after a sausage-producing area in central Germany. In the Midwest, where many German immigrants settled, dozens of different cervelats are still made today.

Danish cervelat Air-dried and hot-smoked, this is rather a bouncy cervelat. Its skin is a glossy red.

Salami sausages

Among the thousands of traditional sausages, it is the salami, or *salame*, that is perhaps the most celebrated. The Italian salamis—and there are almost as many regional variations as there are villages in Italy—may be considered by purists to be the only authentic salamis, but it is worth noting that most of central Europe has made this type of tightly stuffed sausage for a number of centuries, so that German and Hungarian salamis, for example, are not pale imitations of the Italian original but indigenous sausages; only the Italian name is borrowed.

Most salamis, wherever they are made, consist of a mixture of lean pork and pork fat and sometimes beef. Occasionally veal takes the place of beef,

German cervelat

Plockwurst

Ham bierwurst

Presswurst

Zungenwurst

Bierwurst

Mettwurst

Mortadella

and sometimes donkey or wild boar is used. They can be flavored with red or white wine, with rum, with peppercorns, fennel or other herbs or spices, garlic, paprika, or chiles, and perhaps a few teaspoons of sugar.

Only a few types of salami are smoked, but all are matured for periods that may vary from a few weeks to a few months. During this time they lose a good deal of weight in the form of moisture, while the flavor of the meats and the seasonings added to them— wine, spices, garlic—in turn becomes more concentrated.

Buy salami that is a fine fresh red or pink in color, not brown or greasy, on its outside surface. If you squeeze the salami in your hand and it gives a little, you can be sure that it will be fresh and fragrant. The harder the salami sausage, the more thinly it should be sliced. Cut it at an angle, whether you serve it as an hors d'oeuvre, as they do in Italy (where the Genoese eat their local salami with raw young fava beans), or whether you mean to serve it as a meal in its own right with bread and butter.

Genoa salami This is one of the salamis that traditionally contains a high proportion of veal. To make up for the possible dryness of this meat, a little more pork fat than usual goes into the mixture; as a result, this type of salami is quite fatty.

Cotto salami Almost as well known as Genoa in the United States, this salami is garlicky and comes studded with whole black peppercorns.

Salame di Felino Made near Parma, this pure pork sausage is among the best of all the Italian salamis. Since it is made by hand, it is less perfectly geometrical in shape than most of the other sausages. Containing white wine, garlic, and whole peppercorns, it is subtle in flavor and succulent in texture. It does not keep well, but when sent abroad is encased in wax for a longer life.

Salame napolitano Seasoned with chile peppers, this salami is made with pork and beef. It is usually garlicky and extremely peppery and hot.

Salame finocchiona This pure pork salami has the unusual but very good flavor of fennel seeds. A similar salami, known as *frizzes*, is flavored with aniseed and comes in both spicy and mild or sweet varieties.

German salami Because this is not usually cured for long, it is fairly moist. It is mild with a hint of garlic and usually has a medium-fine texture.

Danish salami This is bright pink or red because it usually contains a coloring agent. Made since the fifteenth century, this is one of the types that is salted and then sometimes hung over smoke that is just cool enough to make the flavor more interesting and to brown the casing, but not warm enough to cook the meat. Danish salami tends to be fine-textured and rather fatty and to have a bland, rather predictable flavor.

Hungarian salami One of the densest of salamis, this is not necessarily made in Hungary, despite its name. Other countries, especially Italy, also produce this type of salami, which contains paprika as well as other peppers. It is surprisingly mild and is often smoked. Since it is matured for about 6 months, it is one of the really hard salamis and is ideal for slicing.

Genoa salami

Salame napolitano

Saucisson de Lyon

Hungarian salami

Salame di Felino

Saucisson de l'ail

Rosette

Chorizo de Lomo

Pepperoni

Landjäger

Cacciatore

Kabanos

Saucisson de Lyon In France, salami is known as *saucisson sec*. Perhaps the most famous of the French salami-type sausages is the saucisson de Lyon, which is made of pure pork or of pork and beef flavored with spices and garlic. Cotton twine is used to keep the salami straight while it dries. It has a medium-fine texture with large cubes of fat, a good rose-pink color, and an excellent flavor.

Rosette Perhaps the finest of the Lyonnaise sausages is the rosette, which is ridged, large, and tapering. It is slowly matured and, due to its extra fat and strong casing, made from the lower end of the pig's intestine, is more moist than other salamis.

Saucisson de l'ail Many of the salamis of France, no less than those of Italy, are flavored with garlic. However, the one that is known as garlic sausage ("*de l'ail*") is different insofar as it is only lightly spiced, so that the strong, distinct taste of garlic predominates.

Chorizo Widely used in Spanish and Mexican cooking, chorizos are coarsely textured, strongly flavored with paprika and garlic, and either mild or hot. In Spain they are normally cured or smoked, while the Mexican version is a fresh pork sausage, which may be air-dried. Chorizos imported from Spain are usually air-dried and are suitable for

Leberkäse

Teewurst

Liver sausage with herbs

slicing or cutting into chunks to be eaten raw or used in a dish; fresh Mexican chorizo is usually removed from the casing and crumbled before cooking. Chorizo de Lomo is one of the finest Spanish chorizos for slicing and eating.

Salsicha This salami-type Spanish sausage is usually served as a snack. It is made of a combination of finely chopped pork, pork fat, and whole white peppercorns.

Small salamis

These are usually bought whole rather than by the slice, and can be short or long.

Pepperoni A Sardinian salami, pepperoni can be mild or spicy. It is usually eaten hot. Sliced, it's a familiar pizza topping.

Kabanos These slim, garlic-flavored sausages of Polish origin are smoked until they show wrinkles. Too thin to slice, they are bought whole and then eaten in chunks.

Landjäger, gendarmes, and cacciatore

Landjäger and gendarmes presumably owe their names to the uniformed officials who used to patrol and administrate the German and French Alpine regions, carrying a good supply of these hard, salami-type sausages in the pockets of their tunics. The sausages are usually smoked in little frames, which accounts for their strap-like shape. They are normally eaten in chunks.

The Italian version, called cacciatore, or "hunter's sausage," is somewhat thicker than the others. It is not usually smoked but instead is briefly cured and matured, and is just about large enough to slice. Chunks of these sausages are sometimes added to Italian stews, which they enrich and flavor.

Linguiça A slim and very garlicky Portuguese sausage, this is used in *caldo verde*, the traditional Portuguese kale and potato soup.

Pâté-type sausages

Some pâté-type sausages, such as liver sausages and teewurst, can be soft in consistency and are meant for spreading, while others, such as leberkäse, are firm enough to be sliced.

Liver sausage, liverwurst These may be large or small, curved or straight, or fine- or coarse-textured. They may contain chunks of fat, bits of liver (which is especially good in the case of goose-liver sausage), truffles, garlic, and any number of finely chopped herbs. Some liver sausages are soft and smooth and are intended for spreading, while others, such as France's Strasbourg liver sausage, which also includes pork meat and is smoked, are meant to be thickly sliced.

All liver sausages can be eaten just as they are, but they are occasionally an essential ingredient of cooked dishes: the Swedish black soup, for example, needs the Swedish *gåsleverkorv*. Flavorings, besides herbs and truffles, may include nutmeg, cinnamon, browned onions, or anchovies; where anchovies predominate, liver sausage is known as a *sardellenwurst*.

Most liver sausages are made of pig's liver mixed with pork or veal—some may contain other innards as well as liver—but there are also pure liver sausages. Calf's liver sausages are particularly good, and there are also the sausages made of goose and other poultry livers.

German liver sausage The authentic German liver sausage is almost always smoked. It is prepared by a blanching process, which tends to lead to the formation of a harmless whitish film on the natural casings. Braunschweiger is the most well known German liverwurst.

French liver sausage These have more in common with blood puddings than with the creamy German liver sausages. They are eaten hot, often with lightly sautéed apple rings.

Danish liver sausage These are made of pig's or calf's livers to which anchovy is often added. They are excellent spread on dark Danish rye bread, garnished with slices of cucumber.

Leberkäse A mixture of pork and liver baked in an oblong tin, this German sausage/pâté has no skin. Sliced, it can be eaten as it is, or it can be sautéed.

Teewurst This is the name given to small liver sausages of the spreadable type. They are usually made of a spiced, finely pounded mixture of pork and beef.

Game

In the city, most game is a luxury, and the best restaurants feature it on their menus. It is usually served carefully carved or boned on a dainty bed of exquisite vegetables. The situation is somewhat different in the countryside where, during the open season, you might be given some as a present. Fortunately, however, farm-raised—or ranch-raised—game is increasingly available, and the price should become more reasonable as game becomes more familiar on American tables again. You will find that this meat above any other is worth your time, skill, and attention. Apart from the subtlety of flavor and texture, game is considered to be one of the healthiest of meats.

To tenderize the more athletic and older creatures, particularly wild game, a marinade is useful. This, as a rule, contains vinegar to break down tough fibers, oil to add succulence, and wine, herbs, and spices to permeate the meat with flavor. There are cooked and uncooked marinades, the cooked ones being more powerful. The marinade should completely cover the meat, which should be turned periodically during the time it is steeped.

All wild game is protected by laws, which vary from country to country. These laws are intended to prevent the shooting of creatures that are too young and to allow mating and the rearing of young to take place; they are also important because the game population of any given area will vary from year to year. As a further safeguard, the numbers of any species allowed to be shot by each sportsman are limited in many parts of the world. Some species of game have been hunted almost to extinction—the American buffalo is an example of this, but fortunately it has been reintroduced and is now being successfully raised on game ranches.

Venison

Once bagged, deer becomes venison. It does not matter whether it started life in the wild as red deer, roe deer, fallow deer, white-tailed Virginia deer, axis deer, or the black-tailed variety called mule deer. The term can even be used for antelope, reindeer, caribou, elk, and moose. Nor does it matter if these animals have been bred especially for the table, have lived in the wild, or, as in the case of European roe and fallow deer, have been raised in parks; wild or semi-tame, they all become venison.

With the advent of farm-raised venison, this meat has become relatively easy to obtain. In the United States, venison is farmed in Texas, Wisconsin, and Upstate New York; many of these farms raise the axis deer, which has a fairly mild flavor. New Zealand venison, relatively mild but flavorful, has become rather popular; the collective name for the venison from the many small farms there is Cervena venison. Venison is available from game purveyors and also at many specialty butchers; the meat freezes well, so don't hesitate to try venison if frozen is your only choice.

Buying venison When buying venison, make sure that the flesh is bright red and close-grained and that the fat is clear and bright. Among the cuts game purveyors are likely to offer are the saddle and loin, both on the bone and boneless, the rack, and the leg (sometimes boneless), along with cutlets from the leg, chops or steaks, and meat for stewing. Trim off the fat before cooking venison; however, the farm-raised meat will usually have been well trimmed already.

Cooking with venison Venison is by nature a dry meat, and the fat is often replaced by pork fat or bacon before cooking—the venison having been placed first in a marinade of oil, vinegar, spices, and plenty of red wine, to which juniper berries may have been added. In Italy, venison is sometimes soaked in olive oil with excellent results.

When it is time to cook a venison roast, lift it out of the marinade and wipe it dry. Brown it in butter in a large frying pan. Then, if you like, cover the roast with a jacket of sliced fatback or strips of bacon. (Some cooks find it best to lard the meat with thick strips of fatback, then to cover it with foil.) When cooking venison, it is usual to allow 20 to 25 minutes per pound, in a fairly hot oven (375 to 400°F). The meat will be cooked when, on piercing the skin with a metal skewer or the tip of a sharp knife, the juices run out clear. Any sign of blood in the juices indicates that the meat needs more time, unless you wish to eat it rare or medium-rare.

Prepared with devotion, venison makes a memorable meal. The tenderloin, saddle, loin, and the leg make the best roasting cuts. The loin can also be eaten as chops or steaks, while the rest of the animal is usually used for sausages, stews, ragouts, and pâtés. Spicy venison chili is a favorite in Texas and on the menus of Southwestern restaurants. Smoked reindeer tongue is a delicacy in Scandinavia, as is smoked and salted reindeer meat, and moose.

Serving venison Wild venison has a strong but muted flavor, sometimes described as old lamb that tastes of beef. Farm-raised venison, however, has less of a gamy taste. In either case, it generally needs the encouragement of some sharp, sweet, spicy, or piquant accompaniment to taste its best, so serve it with red-currant jelly, cranberry sauce, a sauce of spiced cherries, or a classic Cumberland sauce. Other flavors that marry particularly well with venison include those of thyme, rosemary, lemon or orange juice (if possible from the bitter Seville orange), and spices such as cloves, cinnamon, mace, allspice, and nutmeg.

Among the many dishes that have an affinity with venison are wild rice, which is traditional—but expensive—with game in America, and the noodles or dumplings, made of pasta dough, eaten in southern Germany, Switzerland, and Austria. There venison is also sometimes served with a sauce made of sour cream blended with the pan juices. This sauce also accompanies venison in northern Germany and in Scandinavia, where it is mopped up with mashed potatoes or potato dumplings. Spiced red cabbage often appears with venison, and chestnut purée is invariably served with it in France, while both celery and celeriac complement its taste and smooth texture beautifully.

Rabbit

The rabbit is both the ancient enemy and old friend of the countryman: ancient enemy because it eats crops, and old friend because it can, in turn, be eaten.

Buying rabbit Wild rabbits are stronger-tasting than domestic ones; they are also less plump and tender. Perhaps the best is a fat, farmed rabbit that is not too young, when it will be tasteless, nor too old, when it becomes dry and tough. Rabbit meat is very lean, almost fat-free, and has a slightly sweet taste. It is also high in protein, as well as low in calories. (In short, rabbit would certainly be a great deal more popular in the United States if Americans could just get over the idea of "bunnies.") Avoid any rabbit meat that does not seem fresh (e.g., that looks discolored and has lost its resilient quality and glossiness).

Frozen rabbit is available in many supermarkets, but fresh rabbit can often be ordered by the market or at the butcher's shop. Try to find rabbit that is not frozen, as freezing tends to make it dry and fibrous. Look for pink meat, and do not be put off by a pearly sheen. Allow half a young rabbit per person.

Tenderloin of venison

Rack of venison

Leg of venison

Cooking with rabbit Although it has a definite flavor of its own, rabbit also makes a good vehicle for other flavors. This works to the lucky cook's advantage in the case of cooking the wild rabbits of Provence, which feed on the tender shoots of wild rosemary and thyme and come with an added herby flavor. Farmed rabbits, however, no longer brought up on lettuce leaves and dandelions, are unlikely to offer unexpected flavors, so it is worth adding a variety of herbs and spices to make them more interesting. Rabbits do not have to be marinated, although a large rabbit, especially a wild one, will develop a good flavor if it is marinated in white wine, olive oil, garlic, and herbs.

Rabbit stew and braised rabbit have long been favorite country dishes. The pioneers used to enjoy rabbit in a delicate *fricassée*. Once eaten as an everyday food throughout the South, rabbit featured in the traditional Cajun and Creole cooking of New Orleans, where, cooked in red wine with tomatoes and hot pepper, it was served as *lapin en matelote*.

Apart from the famous French rabbit dishes, such as *lapin à la moutarde* (rabbit with mustard), there are some splendid traditional British recipes, such as rabbit pie, flavored with salt pork or bacon, grated lemon zest, and nutmeg, or rabbit stew with bay leaves, carrots, and onions. In some parts of England, the stew is moistened with cider, which gives a delicious flavor.

In Spain, rabbit is practically a staple food. When it is not roasted, covered in olive oil and sprinkled with sprigs of rosemary or chopped garlic and parsley, it is stewed in wine or served in a light potato pastry shell. In Italy, it is cooked with tomatoes, eggplant, ham, or bacon; and Sicilians, true to their early Arab heritage, eat it with pine nuts and an *agrodolce* (sweet-and-sour) sauce made with raisins, herbs, stock, and vinegar. Scandinavians roast rabbit like hare and serve it with red cabbage.

Hare

The flesh of the hare is always a dark mahogany-brown regardless of the color of its coat, which varies from species to species. The blue Scotch hare is a first cousin of the Arctic hare of North America, called the snowshoe rabbit; this name is an example of the linguistic confusion that has overtaken the hare, which is not helped by the fact that the highly palatable, domestically bred Belgian hare is, in fact, a rabbit. American jackrabbits are actually hares too, which becomes clear when it comes to eating them, because there can be no confusion between the strong, gamy flavor of hare and the mild and more delicate taste of rabbit.

Unless you have a sportsman to provide you with hare, it may be almost impossible to find. Specialty purveyors occasionally offer wild blue hare, and brown hare imported from Scotland.

Hare is best eaten when young, under one year of age. The meaty hind legs and the fleshy saddle are particularly esteemed in haute cuisine. The other classic cuts are the saddle or the saddle with the hind legs included, but a tender, less muscular foreleg can be more succulent than either.

Cooking with hare Hare may be marinated and then larded or wrapped in pork fatback to counteract its tendency to be dry. It can then be roasted slowly and served quite rosy if young and tender. The larger the hare, the longer it should be cooked—give it 15 to 20 minutes per pound in a medium oven (350°F).

The flavor of hare, which should never be too pronounced, is improved by the addition of cloves in moderation and red wine in abundance, and also by port, red-currant jelly, bacon, mushrooms, shallots, juniper berries, and cream or sour cream. In France noodles, in Italy polenta, and in Switzerland celeriac purée are served with roast or braised hare. In Italy, hare makes a superb pasta dish, *pappardelle alla lepre*.

Jugged hare is a famous English dish. The original method was to place the hare in a jug with herbs, vegetables, spices, and port and then to put the covered jug in a pot of boiling water; nowadays, however, the hare is often simply stewed or braised.

Wild boar

Any wild pig, whether it is male or female, once killed becomes wild boar. Although wild boar still roam the woods of the world, especially in the wilder districts of southern France, much of the wild boar found in the butcher's shop has been reared on preserves—

environments that are as similar as possible to the wild woods, but where the animals can be fed and are able to raise their young successfully.

Despite the fact that there are wild pigs to be found throughout Texas and the American Southwest, wild boar generally needs to be ordered from a specialty game purveyor.

Wild boar meat should be dark, with little fat. It tastes of pork with strong gamy overtones and, like pork, has a certain natural succulence. Younger animals, under one year, make the best eating. Very young boar may not need it, but meat from larger animals is usually tougher and requires marinating. The top part of the leg and the saddle make noble roasts; the smaller cuts, such as steaks and chops, are often broiled or braised. But no matter how you cook wild boar, it is a lengthy operation, and the meat must be thoroughly cooked, with no trace of pinkness.

In elegant French country restaurants the mounted mask of a ferocious boar with its tusks at a war-like angle may look down on you as you are served, in the autumn, *marcassin* accompanied by chestnut purée and a *poivrade* sauce, which owes its flavor to wine, spices, and Cognac. In America, where boar was introduced from Germany in the early twentieth century, steaks of wild boar may be broiled and eaten with a pepper and mushroom sauce, flavored with plenty of garlic and onion. It is also often marinated in cider and served with applesauce or sautéed apples. In German country inns, wild boar is served with a sour cream sauce, boiled potatoes, and a side dish of golden chanterelles. As with venison, a spicy accompaniment is required, such as cranberry sauce, or sour cherries poached in red wine and cinnamon.

Since boar is eaten wherever it is found, and the method of preparing it follows national traditions, it is no surprise that it is made into curry in India. And in Italy, it is used to make a prosciutto, as well as salami and other sausages (although some of these come from farm-raised animals that are a cross between a wild boar and a pig).

Other game
As Americans' tastes become more adventurous, some types of game, such as buffalo, are now being rediscovered.

Upscale restaurants have also been known to feature such items as antelope chops. But other game, such as squirrel and bear, seem somewhat less likely to become trendy. And alligator and rattlesnake—despite recipes for alligator steaks or grilled rattlesnake—surely will remain in the category of exotic game.

Buffalo is now being raised on ranches throughout the American West and Canada. The meat tastes much like beef, not at all gamy, but it is leaner and higher in protein. It may be found at some specialty butchers, but usually must be mail-ordered. The cuts are similar to those for beef, and buffalo can be cooked following any beef recipe. Buffalo chili, grilled buffalo steaks, and even buffalo rib roast can be delicious.

A decade or so ago, there was much talk about beefalo, a cross between buffalo and beef, as "the new meat"—like buffalo, the meat is lean, but with a somewhat stronger taste. However, little has been heard recently about this "pseudo" buffalo, while interest in ranch-raised buffalo is growing.

Squirrel The squirrel was once highly sought after. A sixteenth-century cook's manual ends its recipe for rabbit pie with the words: "If you cook for a lord, use squirrel instead of coney [rabbit]— it is the fitter meat for the table." The squirrel is no longer regarded as a delicacy in Europe; indeed, it is now not eaten at all and as a result has become a destructive pest.

In the American South, Brunswick stew was traditionally made with squirrel. Today chicken, or perhaps rabbit, is used. Kentucky burgoo was once a squirrel—or rabbit—dish too, but various other meats are used today. A Louisianan Creole recipe from earlier this century suggests stewing squirrel (or opossum) with garlic, herbs, red wine, and the zest of a lemon.

Bear is now so rare that few of us will be faced with the problem of having to prepare it for the pot. Those who are should know that the paw is reckoned to be the best bit, and that every part of the animal needs to be thoroughly cooked, because bear, like pork, can be dangerous if it is eaten underdone.

1

2

3

Cutting up a rabbit or hare
1 Cut off the hind legs by inserting a strong, pointed knife into the ball joint just above each thigh.

2 Cut off the forelegs in one piece, slicing cleanly through the rib cage.

3 Split the forelegs down the middle. The forelegs, saddle, and hind legs of this rabbit have been divided into five pieces. If you do not want to keep the saddle whole for roasting, cut it into serving-sized pieces.

Game Birds

For many cooks, one of the traditional pleasures of autumn is the arrival of game on our tables. Today, however, many of the game birds once found only in the wild are being raised on game farms, so the season is, in many cases, no longer limited to the fall. While farm-raised game birds are often milder-tasting than those in the wild, they can still be quite good.

It is the general rule that the natural foods of the bird provide the best and most appropriate company with which to send it to the table. So cranberries, juniper berries, and chestnuts, as well as watercress and celery, play their part in game bird recipes.

Wild goose

This migratory bird flies vast distances and as a result is usually more muscular and has none of the fat of the domestic goose. Like the duck, the wild goose should be eaten within a day or two of being shot. It is best well barded with fatback and roasted with a moist stuffing of apples or prunes. An older bird is best stuffed and braised in red wine or cider. Serve wild goose with red cabbage, a sour cream sauce, and perhaps a tart orange and Belgian endive salad.

Wild duck

The **mallard** is the most common variety of wild duck and also the largest—a fat mallard will feed from two to three people. The **canvasback** obligingly feeds on wild celery and the aquatic plant tape grass, which make its flavor interesting and delicate, lacking any fishy overtones. The **widgeon** is considered superior to the mallard in flavor. One bird will feed one hungry person, or two at a pinch. The **teal** is an ornamental duck, tender of flesh, and looks almost too pretty to eat. It will feed one.

Other varieties include the excellent pintail, the Nantais, the black duck, and the gadwall.

Most species of wild duck enjoy a diet of plants growing below the water and so the flavor is, according to their particular biochemical processes, more or less strong, distinctly aquatic, and, not to put too fine a point on it, fishy. This can be countered by placing a raw onion inside the bird for an hour or two (remove it before cooking) or by rubbing the bird inside and out with half a lemon dipped in salt; or you may find that it is enough just to spike the gravy with lemon juice and cayenne or Tabasco.

No matter what the species, wild duck should be cooked within 24 hours of killing. The two small nodules by the tail, which exude a fluid that helps to waterproof the bird, should be removed, as they can give the flesh a musky taste. Leaner and dryer than domestic ducks, all species of wild duck should be roasted at a high temperature on a rack, alternately basted with butter and whisky, red wine, or port; most benefit from barding before roasting. They must be served juicy and slightly pink—the longer they cook, the tougher they get. The juices that run out when the bird is carved make the best gravy, mixed with orange or lemon juice, red wine, port, and Tabasco. Skim the drippings in the roasting pan and taste—if the juices are not bitter, they too can be added to the gravy. Serve very hot, with homemade potato chips, and a tangy salad of orange, celery, and watercress, or Belgian endive and oranges. Braised wild duck is good with red cabbage.

Pigeon and squab

All varieties of pigeon—including wood pigeon, mourning dove, and other wild doves—and squabs (commercially raised young pigeons) have an agreeable beefy flavor and produce a most appetizing brown gravy. If wild pigeons have fallen from favor, it is because older birds especially can be so tough that preparing and cooking them can be difficult. Today, however, squabs, the farm-raised birds, are increasingly available both fresh and frozen in specialty markets and even in some supermarkets. Although no longer served under glass, as both squab and pheasant once were, squab appears in many upscale restaurants and makes a good special-occasion dish at home.

A Malaysian recipe recommends that pigeons be given a swig of alcohol before their thus-intoxicated and unsuspected demise. This is thought both to be kinder and to improve their taste. They are then rubbed with aniseed inside and honey outside and sautéed in sesame oil. In the Western world, it is usual to serve squab with baby peas, braised onions and mushrooms, cabbage, and bacon, or, for a homier dish, with braised red cabbage.

Partridge

Partridges are a more common sight in Europe than in the United States. In England, these round little birds explode from the stubble in small groups during autumnal country walks. The most common types are the red-legged and the gray partridge. The chuka partridge, which is related to the wild Scottish red-legged bird, is likely to be the partridge found in the marketplace. Confusingly enough, other small birds such as ruffled grouse and quail are referred to as partridge in some parts of the country. Partridges are available frozen, or sometimes fresh, at specialty butchers; a few purveyors offer partridge imported from Scotland. Partridges make the best eating when they are young—about 3 months old, weighing about 1 pound, most of which is supplied by the plump breast. Allow one bird per person.

Roast partridge is a great delicacy. In Europe, *partridge en chartreuse*—a pie of partridge, cabbage, sausage, carrots, onions, and cloves covered with pastry—is a welcome dish on a cold winter's day.

Young wild partridges and farm-raised partridges have a delicate taste that should not be overpowered by strong flavors. Place a lump of butter and two to three sage leaves inside the cavity before roasting. The more tender farmed birds can be grilled or sautéed, as well as braised or roasted. A simple gravy, sautéed potatoes or homemade potato chips, and watercress are really all that is needed with roast partridge. Cold roast partridge with a green salad is a delicious lunch.

Quail

The American quail is the bobwhite, also called blue quail, or partridge in the South. Unlike the American quail, the European quail is a migratory bird, and in Egypt and around the Mediterranean, particularly in southern Italy and Sicily, these birds are easily caught on their journey to or from North Africa. Now, however, since wild quail are scarce and are protected all the year round in many parts of the world, most birds that find their way into kitchens come from quail farms. Quail can be found frozen, and sometimes ordered fresh, at specialty butchers and high-end supermarkets. Some game purveyors offer free-range quail, which has a slightly stronger flavor than the farm-raised birds.

Quail are so small that unless you have run out of appetite, you are likely to eat at least two. They are best roasted in butter, first on one side, then the other, and finally breastside up. This keeps the meat moist—what there is of it. Make a sauce with the pan juices and a little Madeira or vermouth, and, if you like, add a few tablespoons of cream and some raisins soaked in Madeira. The birds can also be rubbed with crushed juniper, allspice, and fennel seeds or wrapped in grape leaves and then roasted. Or cook them in a casserole with shallots and garlic, softened in butter. Quail are a nice indulgence, even though more delicate in flavor than other game birds.

Most farm-raised quail weigh only about 4 ounces, but some producers are now raising "jumbo" quail, which may be as large as ½ pound. These plumper, meatier birds are suitable for broiling and grilling—marinating first is best—and braising, as well as any of the methods used for the tinier quail.

The grouse family

Grouse are neither as popular nor as common in the United States as in the British Isles, where they are deemed one of the greatest treats of late summer and early autumn, and in the rest of Europe. This is no doubt in part because grouse has a gamier taste than other small birds, which is a flavor much prized by gourmands in England and Scotland, but not always by Americans. The question of which makes better eating, partridge or grouse, is a subject of debate among serious game lovers; in England, the northern British red grouse is thought to be the best. Smaller than any of its relations, it has a delicious gamy taste.

To enjoy wild grouse, you will have to rely on a hunter friend—or perhaps on a specialty game purveyor who may import this favorite bird from Scotland in season, at a price to be sure.

Grouse are quite easy to cook to perfection. Young birds, less than 1 year old, need simply a vest of slices of bacon; roast in a hot oven for 20 minutes, until they are just pink and slightly rare. The classic way to serve them is to sit them on a piece of toast with a few straw potatoes and a little watercress. Older birds, while very delicious, take more time to prepare. They are good braised in red wine and stock with plenty of celery, onions, and carrots, and tiny pearl onions added just before the end of their cooking.

The **wood grouse** is also known as the capercaillie, and is the largest of the grouse tribe. It is a northern European bird, and owing to its habit of feeding off the tops of young pine trees, it tastes distinctly of turpentine, which is not agreeable, to say the least. Old English recipes suggest that to remove the pungent tang the bird should be soaked in milk or vinegar; another good method is to stuff the bird with raw potatoes, which are discarded after cooking.

In Scandinavia, cream plays an important part in the cooking process. In Denmark, this might take place in a covered oven dish. Toward the end of the lengthy cooking time, the bird is allowed to brown, and it is served in its sauce with a tart cranberry sauce, little gherkins, and potatoes. In Norway, a creamy, cheesy sauce is poured over the carved roasted bird.

The **ptarmigan** is a northern game bird also called the rock partridge, and is becoming scarcer. Its size is similar to that of the British red grouse, as is its taste, which makes it excellent eating. It is cooked in much the same way as grouse, but in northern Europe slices of bacon may be inserted under the skin as well as tied over the top. Sour cream goes into the sauce, or there might be a cold sauce of apples cooked in wine, blended with mayonnaise.

Pheasant

Pheasant makes delicious eating. The wild cock (male) pheasant is the more handsome, but the hen, although slighter and less gloriously plumaged, is often the plumper, juicier bird. A hen makes a superlative meal for two; a large cock can just feed four.

celeriac 149
Seville orange 165

Pheasant with Chestnuts 311–12

Quail

Squab

Partridge

Today pheasants are being farmed throughout the United States. Their flavor is not really the same as that of the wild bird; the free-range birds, however, are more succulent than the ordinary farmed pheasants. Pheasants are available from various game purveyors and, occasionally, at butcher shops.

In Europe, the bird is traditionally hung to improve its succulence and flavor; Americans prefer the less gamy taste of birds that are not aged this way. Since pheasant tends toward dryness—it can sometimes taste rather like a dry version of the chicken (to which it is closely related)—it usually needs a jacket of bacon (very young farm-raised birds may not need this treatment). It also needs basting with butter and/or bacon fat, partly to keep it moist, partly to make the skin crisp. Traditionally a young pheasant is served roasted, with Brussels sprouts and braised celeriac, creamed celery or braised Belgian endive, watercress, and a simple pan gravy.

Pheasant is also good braised and, cut into serving pieces and marinated, grilled over a hot fire. Older birds may need to be stewed or boiled, like older hens. A plump pheasant boiled and served on a bed of celery, accompanied by a celery sauce with the merest dash of lemon juice, has been described as a dish for the gods. Roast pheasant with bitter orange is also good: the juice of a Seville orange is used to baste the bird toward the end of the cooking. Spiced cabbage, even mild sauerkraut, accompanies pheasant in parts of Europe.

Wild turkey

This is almost a different bird from the plump Thanksgiving turkey, with darker flesh and a stronger, more gamy taste. Wild turkey is not easy to find, although it is being farm-raised today in some parts of the country. It can be ordered from a few specialty purveyors. It is more likely to be available frozen, but fresh wild turkey can sometimes be found in the holiday season.

Woodcock and other small game birds

A few small game birds are farm-raised and may be available from specialty purveyors, but most are only found in the wild. Among these are the woodcock, the coot, the thrush, and the snipe. Ortolans, one of the tiniest, have long been considered a delicacy in France; in the United States, however, it is illegal to hunt these birds.

The **woodcock** is gently dappled and speckled with a brown-leaf light-and-shade pattern, and has a long and very distinctive beak. It eats greedily of almost anything it comes across, and as a result of its omnivorous diet it should be a fat little bird with a fair amount of meat for its size. One bird will provide just the right amount to feed one person. Traditionally, woodcock is plainly roasted and is then served on toast together with the cooked mashed entrails, which are considered to be a delicacy by connoisseurs.

The **snipe** is a smaller bird than the woodcock, with a similar long beak. It may be cooked in the same way as the woodcock, but in Britain its more diminutive size has given it a cooking method of its own: it is encased in a hollowed-out baking potato that has been cut in half and is then carefully tied together again. When the potato is done, so is the bird.

Mallard

Pheasant

Poultry

When France's King Henry IV summed up his plans for making his people happy, he wished that all his subjects should be prosperous enough to enjoy a succulent chicken in a pot every Sunday. He was not the last ruler, or politician, to offer such a promise (think Herbert Hoover), but in spite of his best intentions, it is only relatively recently that poultry has moved out of the luxury class.

Chicken

In the days before factory-raised poultry became available, when chicken was a rare Sunday treat, young farmyard fowls had to be specially fattened for the table. In France, a young fowl would be roasted; an older bird, nicely stuffed and boiled with plenty of vegetables, would become *poule au pot*; and a large, heavy cockerel would go into a *coq au vin* with its heady smell of wine, onions, mushrooms, and herbs. The *backhähndl* of Austria (a young roasted rooster) was accompanied by a paprika-sprinkled salad of cucumber cut transparently thin. In America, the Sunday roast chicken would be served with fresh garden peas and possibly other vegetables, but always accompanied by mashed potatoes for dousing with flavorful gravy. With its crisp skin and juicy flesh, roast chicken is still always a success. And then, of course, there is the Jewish mother's panacea for any kind of debilitation, from flu to stress—chicken soup made from a fully matured hen, which is by far the best provider of sustaining broth.

Today we eat chicken often and in a thousand and one ways. Unlike its ancestors, the factory-raised chicken is fattened so fast and killed so young that it does not have time to develop its full flavor. Sad though this is, a modern chicken responds to being enhanced and improved and makes a good vehicle for any number of different flavors. Even so, it pays to begin with the best chicken you can find. Free-range birds undoubtedly have the best flavor because of the variety of their diet as they scratch happily for their living, and the fact that they have been able to run about in the sunshine gives them altogether more character. But even among the pale, battery-reared supermarket poultry, there are varying degrees of taste.

The diet on which the chicken has been fed will determine the color of its skin. There are, for example, the yellow corn-fed chickens, that often have richer flesh and an old-fashioned chicken flavor. But be aware that other chickens may be yellow—sometimes unnaturally so—because of additives in their diets. And a bird that has a pale skin is not necessarily lacking in flavor—despite advertising to the contrary. Kosher chickens, which are available in many supermarkets, often have more flavor than the battery-raised birds.

Chicken, whole and cut up, is sold either fresh or frozen. However, some chickens sold as fresh have actually been chilled to below the freezing point during packaging and transport; there are currently efforts by consumer advocates to prohibit producers from marketing these partially frozen chickens as fresh.

In any case, birds bought from a butcher or market will not be free-range unless specifically advertised as such. The majority will be intensively reared birds. These chickens, cut up or whole, and wrapped in plastic, are usually the cheapest variety. Frozen mass-produced chicken may be even cheaper because, provided the bird is stored at the correct temperature, it will not deteriorate. Also, for both fresh and frozen birds, the plastic wrap substantially retards the weight loss through evaporation that the unwrapped birds presented for sale in the display case undergo.

The quality of free-range chickens can vary, and they are more expensive, so if you decide to purchase these birds, you may want to try a selection from several different farms. Some of these will be more tender and flavorful than others. Needless to say, mass-produced chickens, fresh or frozen, can be rather characterless, needing quite a lot of flavoring and enhancement to make them taste of anything.

When buying frozen chicken—or the so-called fresh chicken that has been deeply chilled—avoid any with freezer burn (they will be dry and tasteless) and also those with noticeable chunks of ice between them and the bottom of their wrappings—these have at some time been partially thawed and refrozen, which is not good for the quality of the flesh. All chickens, fresh or frozen, are immersed in a bath of water as soon as they have been plucked and drawn. In the case of the fresh bird, the water has evaporated before it reaches your kitchen. In the case of the frozen bird, however, the water drains off only when the chicken is defrosted at home, and the bird ends up in a pool of pink liquid.

Thaw your frozen bird thoroughly and cook it soon afterwards. Not to do so is dangerous, since bacteria develop as the bird is exposed to the warmer temperature, and these must be killed by thorough cooking. Salmonella is always a concern when dealing with chicken, whether it has been frozen or not.

Thawing is best done slowly in the refrigerator. The second-best method is to plunge the bird into cold water. Change the water every 30 minutes or so as the bird thaws, to keep it cold. Never give a stiffly frozen chicken a bath of warm water: not only does rapid defrosting spoil the texture of the meat beyond redemption, it also promotes bacterial growth and is dangerous.

As soon as you can while it is thawing, remove the wrapped giblets from the chicken so that air can get to the cavity. Never forget to remove the giblet package from any bird before it goes into the oven. This may sound a little basic, but there have been too many surprise stuffings for the advice not to bear repetition.

Poussin, squab (baby) chicken

These are small immature birds and are, generally speaking, rather dull. They do not have a great deal of flavor, but can be good split, butterflied, and grilled over charcoal or broiled under fierce heat. Marinate in olive oil, lemon juice, and herbs before grilling or broiling. Poussin can also be tasty when roasted at high temperatures. Poussin weigh about 1½ pounds; the smaller ones almost have to be eaten with the fingers. Allow one poussin per person.

Do not confuse these small chickens with the true squab, which is a farm-raised young pigeon.

Cornish game hen Game hens, or
Rock Cornish hens, are not game birds at all but a type of small chicken that is a cross between the Cornish and White Rock breeds. They usually weigh about 1½ pounds. The smaller ones make an elegant main course at a dinner party—one for each guest—and the larger ones are just the right size to serve two.

Cornish hens are at their best roasted or butterflied and grilled or broiled. They benefit from marinating, as for poussin.

Broiler-fryer These tender young chickens, found in every supermarket, range from 2½ to 4 pounds in weight. They can be used in most recipes and are often sold cut into serving pieces.

Capon These are young neutered roosters fattened on corn or a similar diet, sometimes to an immense girth. Often considered the best chicken available, they are especially succulent because their flesh is marbled with fat, which melts during the cooking process. Capons are best roasted.

In France, fat, neutered young hens, firm and tender and as prized as capons, are called *poulardes*. The most famous come from Bresse, a district so jealous of its superiority that a true *poularde de Bresse*

proclaims its provenance by a metal disk clipped to its wing and is displayed with great pride at the poultry shop (or touted on a restaurant menu).

Stewing hen, boiling fowl Once abundant, these are now hard to find, but any of the older recipes that specify boiling fowl can be made at a pinch with a young roasting chicken. The stewing hen is an older bird and therefore a good deal tougher as well as stronger in flavor—and cheaper. But treated to long, gentle simmering, it can be made tender. Like that of a turkey, the light and the dark meat has a pronounced flavor of its own. Useful in pot pies and salads, a stewing chicken also provides a very good broth.

Roasting chicken Roasting chickens may be as small as 3 pounds or as large as 7 to 8 pounds, but they are usually

around 4 to 5 pounds. These flavorful chickens can be used in most recipes, as well as simply roasted. You should allow a 3½- to 4-pound roaster to feed four people.

Chicken parts Of course, you can also buy cut-up chicken, chicken quarters, legs, thighs (both boneless and on the bone), and whole or boneless, skinless chicken breast halves. Chicken parts are particularly convenient if you are short of time. Fried with a lovely crisp golden coating—seasoned flour, a delicate batter, or even crumbs, depending on regional allegiances—a cut-up chicken becomes wonderful Southern fried chicken. Boneless chicken breasts wrapped around a piece of chilled herbed butter, dipped in egg and bread crumbs, and then deep-fried, make the aromatic and delicious chicken Kiev that spurts hot butter when the eater's fork is inserted; it is

Cornish game hen

Poussin

Roasting chicken

Capon

Stewing hen

Broiler-fryer

a gastronomic indulgence to be sure these days, but a delicious one.

Chicken breasts and legs are staple grilling items, with barbecued chicken a classic. Chicken wings can be marinated in Asian seasonings and served as an hors d'oeuvre, while "buffalo wings," deep-fried and served with a spicy sauce and a blue cheese dressing, are an ever-popular snack. Boneless chicken thighs, a relative newcomer to the supermarket, cook much more quickly than bone-in thighs, and their dark meat offers more flavor than the ubiquitous boned breasts.

Cooking with chicken Since chicken is such a good vehicle for flavors, there are as many ways of preparing it as there are regional tastes. In Morocco, it is rubbed with honey and stuffed with ground almonds and sweet basil or with dried apricots and raisins. It is served with peanuts in the West Indies and with almonds in China, and in West Africa it is cooked inside a scooped-out melon. It is poached with truffle slivers inserted under its skin *en demi-deuil* (in half-mourning) in the higher reaches of French gastronomy, and, as one might expect, it comes with tomatoes and garlic in Italy, where, simply roasted, it is also eaten with a *salsa de fegatini*—a sauce made of chicken livers, diced ham, mushrooms, chicken stock, and Marsala.

If chicken can be said to have a special affinity with any herb, it is with tarragon. Marjoram or oregano, thyme, and, of course, parsley are good too. The best additions and flavorings for cooking a chicken are bacon, garlic, cream, yogurt, olive oil, white wine, sherry, saffron, and ginger; the best accompaniments are mushrooms, shallots, potatoes, and rice. The best fruits and nuts are raisins, walnuts, lemons, apricots, pine nuts, and almonds.

Turkey

An American Thanksgiving and an English Christmas would be incomplete without a fine, plump, roasted turkey, served with all the ceremonial trappings. You will need to calculate 1 pound per person—thus a 20-pound bird will provide twenty helpings as well as seemingly endless sandwiches, stock, and soup.

Turkeys usually weigh between 12 and 18 pounds; smaller birds, sometimes called fryer-roasters, weighing about 5 to 9 pounds, are becoming more widely available. Turkey is sold both fresh and frozen year-round. If you are buying a fresh bird, choose one with fresh-looking but not moist skin and a pearly-white, rather than purple or blue, tint to the flesh. Although frozen birds can, of course, be quite good, the taste may be rather dull. Free-range turkeys are occasionally seen at specialty markets in the holiday season, but despite their expense they are not always much more flavorful than an ordinary fresh bird.

A frozen turkey usually takes at least 48 hours to thaw. Put it in the refrigerator 2 days before you want it (or 3 days before if it is really large) and leave it there to thaw gradually. If turkey isn't completely thawed, it won't be cooked in the middle, and poultry that is not cooked through is dangerous. Once it has thawed, it should be cooked soon. Resist the temptation to prestuff the turkey in order to save time on the day of the dinner, even though there will be so many other traditional bits and pieces to see to. Get the stuffing ready the night before by all means, but refrigerate it separately and put it inside the bird just before it goes into the oven. If the stuffing sits around inside the bird, it may spoil, even if the stuffed bird is kept in the refrigerator.

Although most Americans expect their Thanksgiving turkey to be stuffed, many people find it preferable to cook the stuffing separately, for reasons of both taste and health. An unstuffed bird cooks more evenly and quickly—and because it takes longer to cook the stuffing through in a stuffed bird, the meat, especially breast meat, dries out long before the stuffing is done. Although some people insist that stuffing cooked in the bird is more flavorful because of the juices it absorbs, often it just gets soggy. Stuffing cooked separately in a casserole, added to the oven during the last hour or so as the turkey roasts, is lighter and turns golden-brown and crisp around the edges as it bakes.

Cooking with turkey Everybody has a favorite stuffing for turkey—some cooks even make a special one for the neck cavity, to make a nicely plumped-out shape under the skin, and a different one to go inside the bird. Bread cubes or crumbs combined with sautéed onions and celery, sage, and melted butter make one of the classic stuffings. Cornbread stuffing is particularly popular in the South; sausage is often featured, and many people like chestnuts in the mixture. You can also add truffles, mushrooms, celery, oysters, or prunes. A plain marjoram and onion stuffing flavored with lemon zest is good but can be rather dry in texture unless it has enough butter in it.

Some people like to cook a turkey simply, basting it only with butter, and starting it off, like a chicken, breastside down. This is an excellent way of keeping what is by nature rather a dry-fleshed bird succulent. Some like to wrap the breast with a few strips of bacon; and others to roast it wrapped in foil, which must, however, be folded back toward the end of the cooking time to give the breast a chance to become brown and crisp. In very slow cooking, which gives good results, a cup or two of white wine can be added to the juices in the roasting pan halfway through the cooking.

One noted wine and food expert compares big birds like the turkey to the cygnets (young swans) and peacocks that once upon a time counted among the greatest delicacies. "One should be content to meet them occasionally at some friend's dinner table," he says, "without troubling to order them when one is the host." It is easy to agree with him, except on traditional occasions.

For the Thanksgiving turkey the traditional accompaniments are both mashed potatoes and sweet potatoes, creamed onions or creamed celery, succotash, particularly in New England, or green peas or string beans, giblet gravy, and cranberry sauce. For an English Christmas dinner, the turkey comes with roasted potatoes, Brussels sprouts and chestnuts, gravy, bread sauce, bacon, and perhaps, if there is no sausage stuffing, a chain of crisp little sausages draped about its breast. On national holidays in Mexico—the home of the ancestral turkey, from which the domestic variety descends—the bird is eaten with *mole*, a velvety, not-at-all-sweet chocolate sauce, spiced with chiles. The Spanish, in a festive mood, stuff their turkey with sweetbreads and truffles.

All these rich meals are best enjoyed once a year and then forgotten until next time. However, we meet turkey with increasing frequency on nonfeast days.

Supermarkets now sell it in all sorts of forms, from boneless roasts to drumsticks and thighs to breasts, bone-in breast halves, and boneless cutlets and tenderloins. Because turkey is a lean meat, ground turkey and turkey sausages, spicy or sweet, are becoming ever more popular. And, more and more, the smaller fryer-roasters may appear on the barbecue grill in the summer (or even throughout the year).

Duck

A duck is an odd-shaped bird: it is a bony, flat-breasted creature covered in fat. When you carve it—and here you may come to blows with the bird before you have finished—you will find that there is not enough breast meat to go around. But hot or cold, duck has such an excellent flavor, richness, and succulence that it is well worth the occasional extravagance.

The most popular American variety of duck is the Long Island duckling. This, like the best French ducks, the small Nantais and the larger Rouen, and the English Aylesbury, is a descendant of the Imperial Peking duck, a Chinese snow-white breed of special excellence, which was once reserved for the Emperor alone.

Long Island duck is also called Pekin duck. The other most common breed in the United States is the Muscovy, or Barbary, duck, which has a stronger flavor than the Pekin. The Barbary duck is also a favorite of the French. The Moulard is the duck raised for foie gras, both in France and, increasingly, in the United States. The exceptionally plump, meaty breasts of these ducks are called magrets, and they are more likely to be available, at specialty butcher shops, than the whole birds are.

"Duckling" was once, strictly, the term for birds under 2 months old, but because our farmed ducks are usually slaughtered at a young age, it is now used more or less interchangeably with the word duck. Very young birds do not have enough meat on their bones to be worth eating; older ones can be tough. However, the best eating age and weight vary with the breed. When buying fresh duck, make sure that the duck's breast, when pinched, feels meaty.

As for how many persons a duck will feed, it is hard to say. A wit once observed that the duck was a difficult bird—too much for one, too little for two. However, two people can dine more than well even on a Long Island duckling, and three or even four, if helpings are modest, on a large Muscovy.

Ducks take quite kindly to freezing—their greater fat content, compared with that of the chicken, assures that when defrosted they retain their succulence, and the stronger flavor is not so easily frozen out. However, fresh is still better than frozen. Like chicken or turkey, frozen duck should be properly thawed in the refrigerator, and the process may take 2 or 3 days. Unlike the intensively reared chickens, which may never have set foot to ground throughout their lives, battery ducklings may have been allowed to waddle about the yard in their youth, before the fattening-up process puts an end to exercise. Frozen duck is available year-round; fresh duck may be found from early summer through the fall.

Cooking with duck Before roasting a duck, it is best to prick its skin in all the fatty places; this will allow some of the subcutaneous fat, which insulates the duck against cold water (even though a farmed duck may never have had a swim in its life), to run out during cooking. This makes a wonderful fat to use for frying potatoes. To help crisp the skin, the bird should be roasted on a rack.

Moulard duck breast (magret)

Barbary duck

Long Island duck

Like chicken, duck is cooked and eaten in countless ways. The Chinese, especially, who domesticated ducks more than two thousand years ago, have a multitude of delicious dishes composed of crisp duck morsels with steamed pancakes. They also have tea-smoked ducks, and deep-fried ducks that are first steamed to remove the fat; sometimes called lacquered ducks, these are a glistening reddish-mahogany color and so soft that the flesh comes away at a touch. The Chinese even like to chew the brittle bones, saying that the crunchiness is the chief attraction of these vividly glazed ducks, which are often seen hanging in the windows of Chinese markets and restaurants.

The Danes and the Swedes boil their ducks with herbs. The Danes serve theirs with mustard and dark rye bread; the Swedes dish up boiled duck with a creamy horseradish sauce.

The classic flavors for duck include oranges, both bitter and sweet, turnips, and onions—all designed to offset the somewhat richly flavored meat. Other classic accompaniments are crisp sautéed potatoes, young peas, sour Morello cherries, green olives, red wine, and vermouth. Newer "inventions" include duck with eggplant and ginger, and duck with apples, walnuts, and prunes.

Goose

The raucous cry of geese was responsible for saving the ancient Romans from barbarian invasion—but that has not stopped the Italians from eating goose, richly stuffed with sausage meat, olives, and truffles. In northern Europe, St. Martin's Day, November 11, is the traditional day for eating goose. This is, presumably, an extended annual punishment meted out to these birds, whose cackling once gave away the farmyard hiding place of the modest St. Martin as he was attempting to evade admiring followers who wanted him to become Pope.

When you are buying a goose for the table, choose a young bird with a pliable lower beak and breastbone. A well-filled plump breast denotes succulence—and also good value for money. Look too for creamy skin with a warm tinge to it, almost pale apricot, without a trace of blue or brown.

A gosling, or young goose, weighs up to about 5 pounds and can hardly help being tender and delicate. At 8 to 9 months old it becomes a goose (in culinary terms it is never a gander), and, weighing 8 to 12 pounds, is in its prime. With advancing age it becomes fatter and tougher, needing longer and longer periods of braising or stewing—very delicious, but perhaps not quite the rare treat that goose is usually expected to be.

Most geese, available at specialty markets and butchers, are sold frozen. Fresh geese are more likely to be found during the holiday season.

Cooking with goose Roast goose is generally reserved for a special occasion. Goose is eaten on religious and other holidays, especially in northern Europe, where it is the traditional Christmas bird. It comes to the feast magnificently brown, with crackling skin, copious gravy, and a stuffing of tart apples, which may be layered with boiled chestnuts or raisins, or, in Scandinavia, with prunes. (A stuffing of sausage meat, it is rightly agreed, makes this bird far too rich.) In the United States, a wild rice stuffing is the classic one to use for goose, but fruit—particularly dried fruit—stuffings and those with chestnuts are also traditional. In Ireland, geese are stuffed with boiled potatoes, which successfully sop up the fat.

Goose

Turkey

The skin of a roasting goose needs to be well pricked, like that of a duck. Pour a pot of boiling water over the skin before placing the bird on a tall rack in a roasting pan so that it stands clear of the fat that will pour out as it cooks. (Although it is a hot and messy job, it is a good idea to pour off some of the fat halfway through the cooking.) Shortly before the end of the roasting time, some people like to sprinkle the bird with a little flour, which forms dark, crusty speckles. But the best finishing touch is to increase the heat for a few minutes just before the goose comes out of the oven and to splash the bird with drops of cold water. These hiss and evaporate as they would on a hot iron, leaving the skin delicately crisp.

Rendered goose fat makes a wonderful cooking medium, particularly good for frying potatoes. It is more highly flavored than duck fat, and each bird yields so much that in days gone by it was used not only in the kitchen but also on the farm: cows' udders were rubbed with it to prevent chapping, as were the hands of dairymaids; harnesses and leather were kept supple by its liberal application; and cold plasters made with brown paper coated with goose grease were a common household remedy for colds.

Guinea fowl

This elegantly spotted fowl, of West African ancestry, is an endearing but stupid bird. Looking somewhat like a walking sofa cushion, its feathers are a marvel of pattern—white-spotted on black, rather like old ladies' dresses— or sometimes a delicate lavender.

The domesticated breeds are delicious to eat, and are plumper than their wild counterparts, but both have a tendency to be dry and thus require regular basting during cooking with seasoned butter, or barding with strips of bacon. It is nice to put a sprig of marjoram under the bacon if you do not plan to stuff the bird. The meat of the hen is more tender than that of the male. The smaller birds are called guinea squab.

Guinea fowl taste like slightly gamy chicken. Recipes for pheasant, partridge, or smaller roasting chicken will do justice to their delicate flavor, and they make a worthwhile alternative to these. The demand for guinea fowl is not enormous, but they are on the market all year round, fresh and frozen.

Cooking with guinea fowl The prime concern when cooking this bird is to keep the flesh moist, so recipes that call for a stuffing of vegetables or butter under the skin will certainly enhance the texture. In Poland, guinea fowl is rubbed inside and out with ground ginger an hour before roasting, and it is served with chestnut purée. The traditional way to cook guinea fowl is to stuff it, roast it, and serve it with giblet gravy, just like turkey. In the west of England, it is sometimes braised in hard cider.

Older birds are good either stewed or braised in stock and cream. Breasts of guinea fowl can be sautéed in butter and served with a sauce of chestnuts, garlic, and sweet wine such as a Sauternes. A spit-roasted bird, stuffed with a bread crumb, shallot, and marjoram stuffing, sprinkled with Cognac, and served with a well-seasoned "jus," is French bourgeois cooking at its best.

Ostrich

Although still a rarity, the meat of this bird is appearing more and more frequently on restaurant menus and is occasionally available from some specialty purveyors.

Ostrich, which is being farmed in California, is rather like slightly sweet beef, with an agreeable texture similar to tender steak. Because there is very little fat, it is best to cook it like a very lean meat, such as a filet mignon, and to serve it with a sauce—for example, shallot sauce or something a little sharp and fruity, such as a rich red wine sauce enhanced with tomato.

Giblets

The giblets—the neck, heart, gizzard, and liver—of most poultry other than chicken are now removed before packing. However, the giblets of almost any bird make a wonderful stock for gravy and soups. To prepare these for cooking, remove the yellowish gallbladder sac from the liver and trim away all yellowish patches, which will give it a bitter taste. Trim the fat, blood vessels, and membrane from the heart, and discard the outer skin and inner sac containing stones and grit from the gizzard. When making a giblet stock, it seems wasteful to boil the liver too, when it is so good panfried or used in a stuffing or sauce.

Chicken and other poultry livers Chopped chicken livers are a well-known feature of Jewish cooking, and these and other poultry livers are also an essential part of a wide range of pâtés, terrines, and stuffings. Left whole, chicken livers are delicious when wrapped in slices of bacon, skewered, and grilled, or lightly seasoned and sautéed in butter with a dash of dry vermouth.

Chicken livers, especially, appear in almost every national cuisine: in sauces for spaghetti, in risottos and pilafs, in fancy mousses and simple spreads. Much better fresh than frozen, the fine-grained pale livers are considered to be the best for eating.

Foie gras and goose liver The eighteenth-century English essayist and wit Sydney Smith memorably defined his idea of heaven as "eating foie gras to the sound of trumpets." Indeed, there can be nothing to compare with the exquisite, pale, fattened liver of the goose or duck, for which the birds are expressly bred, particularly in southwestern France.

To make foie gras, geese are force-fed until their livers weigh around 4 pounds. The best type of foie gras comes from a breed that was known even to the ancient Romans. These geese have an extra pleat of skin under the breast, which neatly accommodates the enlarged liver.

Ducks are also increasingly being bred for foie gras. Duck foie gras has been produced in the United States for the last decade or so, with the result that fresh foie gras is now available here for the first time (it is not legal to import fresh foie gras into this country). The breed preferred for foie gras is a cross of the Muscovy and the Pekin duck.

The liver of a goose on a normal diet weighs about 4 ounces. Soaked in milk it will swell a little and become even more tender when cooked. It is good sliced, fried, and added to a risotto or eaten with scrambled eggs. Pounded together with fresh bread crumbs, marjoram, chopped mushrooms, and diced bacon and bound with egg, it is sometimes used to stuff the fatty skin of the neck, to make a sort of sausage, which is then poached in giblet broth and white wine, or panfried in goose fat. In France, no part of a goose is wasted, and in some country areas even the blood is used in little patties flavored with garlic and poached.

PREPARING POULTRY

1

2

Trussing a chicken

1 Place the chicken breast side up with the tail toward you. Take a piece of kitchen string about 3 feet long, and place the center of the string under the tail. Cross the string over the top of the tail, then bring the string up over the ends of the drumsticks and cross it over tightly to tie them together.

2 Bring the ends of the string toward the neck end, passing them under the pointed end of the breastbone and over the thighs.

3 Turn the chicken over. Bring the string over the wings, pressing them close to the body, and tie the string over the neck flap of skin.

chicken 85–7
game birds 82–4

knives 222–4
poultry shears 225
skewers 240
trussing equipment 230

3

Butterflying poultry and game birds

1 Place the bird breast side down. With poultry shears or a sharp, heavy knife, cut down along both sides of the backbone, cutting through the skin and bone. Discard the backbone, or reserve it for making stock.

2 Turn the bird over. Press firmly on the breastbone with the heel of your hand to crack the bone and flatten the breast.

3 Make a small slit in the skin on either side of the pointed end of the breast, and then insert the ends of the drumsticks into the slits.

4 Tuck the wing tips under the breast. If you like, insert two metal skewers crosswise through the bird, one at the breast and one at the thigh, to keep the bird flat during cooking.

1

2

3

4

1

2

Cutting up a chicken

1 Using a sharp knife, cut off each of the legs at the point where they join the carcass, forcing the knife blade through the ball joint and slicing down on either side of the tail.

2 Slide a large, heavy knife inside the bird and make two cuts, one on either side of the backbone and as close to the bone as possible.

3 The backbone can now be withdrawn from the body and reserved for making soup or stock.

3

4 Turn the bird over and cut along either side of the breastbone.

5 Discard the breastbone, and cut each breast half crosswise.

4

5

6 The resulting portions are two legs, two wings with a portion of breast, and two breasts. The legs can be cut in half to give two drumsticks and two thighs.

6

Stuffing chicken breasts

1 Take a boneless breast with wing bone attached, and cut off the wing tip at the second joint. Lay the breast skin side down, and push a spoonful of stuffing (a roll of chilled Garlic and Herb Butter is shown here) under the flap of skin.

2 Seal the flap closed by pressing the edges together, then roll the breast up from the pointed tip toward the wing bone. Tie with kitchen string to make a neat parcel.

1

2

1

2

3

4

Stuffing and trussing a turkey

1 Using a small, sharp knife, cut out the wishbone, which is just under the skin at the neck end. (This will make the breast easier to carve.)

2 Spoon some of the stuffing into the neck end, putting in only as much as can be covered by the flap of neck skin. (If you like, loosen the skin over the breast by easing in your fingers, then press a thin layer of stuffing over part of the breast meat.)

3 Turn the bird over. Pull the neck skin over the stuffing and secure the flap of neck skin to the back by inserting a small skewer.

4 Turn the bird breastside up again. Loosely fill the body cavity with the remaining stuffing (the stuffing will expand as it cooks, so do not pack it).

5

5 Using kitchen string, tie the ends of the drumsticks to the tail, looping the string under the tail and crossing it as when trussing a chicken. If you like, tuck the wing tips under the turkey, as when butterflying a bird.

butterflying poultry and game birds 91
chicken 85–7
trussing a chicken 91
turkey 87–8

trussing equipment 230

Garlic and Herb Butter 258
Roast Turkey with Herb and Apple Bread Stuffing 323, 324–5
stuffings for turkey 418

1

2

3

4

5

Boning and stuffing a duck

1 Lay the duck breastside down. Cut off the wings at the second joint (if you like, reserve the wing tips for making stock). With a strong, sharp, short knife, split the skin down the center of the back from neck to tail.

2 Cut down along each side of the backbone, starting a little behind the neck cavity, and ease back the skin and meat until you encounter the ball joint of the thigh bone.

3 Place the knife in the thigh joint on one side of the duck, and then twist the knife to sever the thigh bone. Do the same on the other side.

4 Slide the knife in the other direction toward the neck until the upper part of the wing bone is well exposed. Free the other wing bone in the same way.

5 Cut through the wing joints, and continue to cut, keeping the knife as close to the bones as possible, until you reach the breastbone.

6

6 Lift up the bones, cutting away the remaining flesh. Take care not to puncture the breast.

7

8

7 Sever the carcass at the neck, so that you separate it completely from the flesh. Discard the carcass, or reserve it for making stock.

8 Free the leg bones from the body, starting from the inside of the duck and pushing down on the meat, keeping the skin as intact as possible. Once you have reached the "knob" at the end of each drumstick, cut off the leg bone with a cleaver, leaving the "knob" in the duck.

9 Slip out each wing bone in exactly the same way as the leg bones, and leave the "knobs" at the end of the wing joints in the duck.

10 Stuff the bird with a stuffing of your choice; do not to pack the stuffing too tightly, or the duck will split during cooking. Using a trussing needle and kitchen string, sew up the slit.

9

10

11 Press and push the duck into a long oval shape. Prick the bird all over, just piercing the skin, to allow the fat to run out freely as it roasts.

11

Eggs, Milk, Cream, and Butter

EGGS

For primitive man, with a mind far less tortuous than ours, there was no such thing as a chicken-and-egg dilemma: he recognized the egg as the beginning of life and celebrated it as such. It was in this context that people began to decorate eggs, as a symbol of springtime and fertility. In the kitchen, the hen's egg is celebrated still. Indispensable to the cook and rich in vitamins and minerals, it is one of the most versatile and valuable of foods.

There is a popular misconception that brown eggs are somehow better than white (indeed, the Turks simmer their eggs in coffee to give both flavor and a healthy tan). But shell color reflects neither flavor nor nutritional content, merely the breed of the laying bird. The best egg, brown or white, large or small, is one that has been freshly laid by a free-range or organically raised hen. You can determine freshness by checking the pack date on the box, which will run from 1, for January 1, up through 365, for December 31.

From the time when an egg is laid, the membranes weaken and the flavor changes. The white of a fresh egg is thick (making wonderful fried and poached eggs), getting runnier and thinner as time goes by. The yolk of a fresh egg is round and tight when the egg is cracked and dropped into a bowl or pan, while in an older egg the yolk is flatter and more fragile. It is easy enough to tell if an egg is fresh or not once you get it home. At the rounded end of the egg, between the shell and the membrane, there is a small air chamber, all but invisible when the egg is fresh, increasingly large as the egg gets older and loses moisture through its pores. So one way of assessing freshness is to hold the egg upright against a strong light and examine the size of the air space. Another is to weigh it in your hand: the heavier for its size, the better it will be. Yet another method is to lay it down in cold water: a perfectly fresh egg will stay put. An older egg will tilt; if more than 3 weeks old, it will rise to a vertical position. If an egg floats in the water, it is really getting old.

When cookbooks specify eggs they generally mean large ones. Eggs are classified by both size and quality. The best are Grade AA or A; Grade B eggs are more often used for commercial purposes. Sizes, which are determined by weight per dozen eggs, include jumbo, extra-large, large, medium, small, and peewee. Eighteenth- and nineteenth-century recipes instructing the cook to "take three dozen eggs" should cause less amusement than they do, since the average egg used to be a great deal smaller than it is today and was probably laid by a small bantam hen.

"Factory" eggs are no less nutritious than organic ones, and their flavor is standard and good, if rather slight, but they are paler and less rich-tasting than eggs from contented hens scratching about for their food in the farmyard. If you come across genuine farm-fresh eggs, perhaps at a farmers' market, you should eat them as soon as possible, especially if they have been cleaned, because washing removes the natural protective film from the shell.

It has recently been discovered that there is some risk of food poisoning, caused by salmonella bacteria, associated with eating raw or only lightly cooked eggs (the yolks are more likely to carry the bacteria than the whites). For this reason, it is recommended that pregnant women, the elderly, infants, and those whose immune systems are compromised do not eat raw or less-than-completely-cooked eggs. However, the risk is in fact quite minimal, so for most people it makes sense just to be cautious, avoiding any eggs that are cracked or dirty.

Because egg shells are porous, they are highly susceptible to neighboring smells, which is fine if they are intended for truffle omelets and stored in an egg basket together with a truffle, as they are in parts of Périgord. But it is not such a good thing if their near neighbors are strong-smelling foods such as onions or particularly ripe cheese.

Eggs should always be kept in the refrigerator—with the rounded end up to allow the air space to "breathe." For soft-boiling, some cooking, and baking, they should be at room temperature—eggs straight from the refrigerator will crack if plunged into boiling water; a cold yolk will not emulsify reliably in mayonnaise and sauces, for example; and cold whites will not whisk well.

Cooking with eggs A beaten egg will thicken soups, stews, and sauces because heat causes the egg to coagulate, thus holding the liquid in suspension. The raw yolk will emulsify with oil or melted butter, holding it in suspension, and to this happy fact we owe such good things as mayonnaise and hollandaise

Quail egg

White hen egg

Brown hen egg

Duck egg

Goose egg

sauce. An egg is sticky and sets when cooked, and so will bind mixtures for stuffings or meat loaf. As for food that is to be deep-fried, not only will a dip into beaten egg keep the bread crumbs or other coating in place, but the film of egg will protect the food from absorbing the oil and therefore becoming greasy. A light brushing of beaten egg gives a handsome sheen to pastry, and whisked whole eggs, with their millions of tiny trapped air bubbles, give a rise to cakes and other batters.

The volume of beaten egg white—so essential for light soufflés and mousses—depends on the eggs being at room temperature before you start, and on the way you whisk them—electric mixers are very fast and produce a dense texture, whereas "balloon" wire whisks, while taking a little more time and energy, do produce a desirable airy froth.

Apart from omelets and batters, such as those for crêpes or pancakes, which are cooked briefly over high heat, eggs respond best to gentle warmth—too high a heat and too long a cooking time makes them leathery.

Other eggs No other bird has proved anywhere near so obliging as the domestic hen, which lays up to 250 eggs a year, but hens' eggs are by no means the whole story.

Quails' eggs are miniature in size and beautifully speckled, and come both fresh and preserved. When fresh, they make a good first course served hard-boiled with celery salt. Poached, they look charming on salads.

Duck eggs are sold in some parts of the country. These are extremely rich with somewhat gelatinous whites—so, although they taste quite good on their own, they are best in custards, mousses, and other desserts.

Goose eggs are available in some areas. These are also rich and make very good omelets, custards, and mousses.

Ostrich eggs (one ostrich egg is equal to two dozen hens' eggs) are rarely sold these days—but Queen Victoria once tasted one made into a giant omelet and declared it to be very good.

Gull eggs are eaten in England and other parts of Europe, where they are in season briefly in the spring. They are usually eaten hard-boiled, together with celery salt for dipping.

MILK, CREAM, AND BUTTER
The cow is a good friend to mankind, providing us with one of our most complete foods. Milk contains most of the nutrients required by the human body—proteins, vitamins, and minerals, especially calcium—and, since cows are so generous with their supply, milk and other dairy products are still economical.

Milk
Most children and quite a number of adults enjoy drinking milk, and it is also used in a variety of ways, including for cooking. In Italy and Germany, it is even used for roasting pork, the meat bubbling away under a golden skin that eventually caramelizes with the pan juices into a delicious gravy. In Saudi Arabia, lamb cooked with rice in milk is the descendant of an ancient dish. There are also many other sauces and dishes cooked all over the world, as well as cheeses, yogurts, and fermented drinks, that are based on using milk that wouldn't have kept for long in the days before refrigeration.

According to the U.S. Department of Agriculture's Food Pyramid, adults should have two to three servings every day from the milk and milk products food group. Children and teenagers need more than that, and pregnant women and nursing mothers even more.

The vast majority of milk sold today is pasteurized. Pasteurization was one of the successes of Louis Pasteur, whose work in the field of microbiology led to the eradication of many animal-borne diseases. It involves heating the milk to a point where any potentially dangerous bacteria are killed, but without affecting the flavor of the milk. Ultrapasteurized milk is heated to higher temperatures than ordinary pasteurized milk, thus extending its shelf life. However, its flavor is not as good. Unpasteurized milk is now the exception and is sold as raw or untreated milk; it is usually only available at health food stores. It must always be certified—that is, stringently tested at the farm to make sure that no harmful bacteria are present.

Milk should always be heated slowly and cooked at low temperatures. A skin forms on the top when it reaches high temperatures, helping it to boil over the sides of the pan—with the resulting characteristic smell that gives the impression things are getting out of

hand in the kitchen. This skin consists of solidified proteins and milk fat. To avoid it, do not boil, but instead scald the milk: that is, remove it from the heat just as it shows a wreath of tiny bubbles around the edge. Nonstick surfaces have made it much easier to clean pans used for heating milk, but milk tends to scorch on the bottom of the pot if overheated.

If the recipe calls for the addition of flour or sugar, these, too, help prevent a skin from forming. To prevent the skin that appears on the top of a milk-based sauce such as white sauce as it sits rub a small piece of butter over the surface using the point of a knife. This makes a protective film and then can be stirred in at the last minute. Alternatively, place a sheet of plastic wrap directly on the surface of the sauce.

Fresh milk There are two main types of fresh milk, both of which need to be kept cold.
Whole milk This is milk with its natural cream intact, and has one of the best flavors of all milk sold. In days gone by the cream would rise to the top of the milk in a golden layer. Today, however, almost all milk is homogenized, which means that the milk is treated so the cream, or milk fat, is evenly suspended instead of being allowed to float to the top. Milk that has not been homogenized may be found at some small dairy farms.
Low-fat and nonfat, or skim, milk Low-fat and nonfat milk has been divested of some or all of its rich, delicious cream. Our ancestors went to great pains to avoid their milk being skimmed, even to the extent of making the urban dairyman bring his cow to the city streets to be milked on the spot so that the customers could see the cream going into the jug.

Today, the cream is removed by centrifugal force and the result is low-fat milk—called either 2 percent (meaning that it is 98 percent fat-free) or 1 percent (99 percent fat-free) milk—or nonfat, or skim, milk. Skim milk contains less than 0.5 percent milk fat. These milks are sometimes given extra milk solids and vitamins to restore something of the nutrients they have lost.

Long-life milk Heavily sterilized, these milks will keep, unopened, for much longer than ordinary pasteurized milks and are therefore extremely useful for people who are frequently away from home or without refrigeration available. Pasteurized, homogenized, and then held at a high temperature until all the bacteria have been destroyed, they will keep unopened for long periods but have a slightly peculiar taste due to the caramelization of the sugar present in milk, known as lactose. Once opened, however, or reconstituted, they must be refrigerated and will keep only as long as fresh milk.

UHT (Ultra Heat Treated) milk First pasteurized, this milk is then heated to a much higher temperature only briefly, which means that the lactose does not caramelize to such an extent that the flavor is impaired. It will keep unopened for several months and is an invaluable standby in case one runs out of fresh milk.

Evaporated and condensed milk Evaporated milk is the less sweet and sticky of the two, as it is simply regular milk from which 60 percent of the water has been removed. Whole, low-fat, and skimmed evaporated milk are all available, the reduced-fat versions increasingly so. The extra sugar in condensed milk, which is sweetened evaporated milk, helps it to keep better once opened. Condensed milk tends, however, to taste more like caramel than milk. Both can be used in cooking and can even be whipped. Before whipping, chill the milk in the freezer until soft crystals have formed around the edge.

The quality of these milks in cooking is open to controversy; some hold that they enrich foods, while others feel that they impart a strange, oversweet taste.

Dry milk Also called powdered milk, this is milk that has had almost all the water removed; powdered whole milk, nonfat milk, and buttermilk are available. Dry milk has a flat but unobjectionable flavor

that bears little resemblance to real milk. It can be used in cooking either in reconstituted or dried form and can also be used to make yogurt: a few tablespoons of powdered whole milk stirred into the measured quantity of regular milk before heating makes a thicker and slightly richer yogurt.

Soy milk and other milk substitutes Soy milk, made from soybeans, is a nondairy alternative for those allergic to cow's milk. Although high in protein, it is low in calcium; however, many soy milks are enriched with calcium. Nondairy creamers are merely whiteners, used in tea or coffee by those who are allergic to or want to avoid real milk. They are usually made with vegetable, palm, or coconut oil. Other additives such as color, emulsifiers, and sugar are also often present.

Other milk Although Western society drinks mainly cow's milk, there are many other kinds, such as sheep's, goat's, and water buffalo's milk. These latter animals, huge, black, curly-horned beasts, stand up to hot weather better than cows and are found in India and in the hottest parts of southern Italy. Desert dwellers drink camel's milk, and Tibetans drink yak's and donkey's milk, while the Kurds like mare's milk.

Both sheep and goats give milk for cheese such as pecorino, Roquefort, and Spanish Manchego, while buffalo's milk is a fine basis for mozzarella.

Goat's milk has the special quality of being highly digestible and is excellent for babies and people who have poor digestions and for those who are allergic to cow's milk. It should, however, be avoided by those who are unable to cope with a full cream content: since the

cream does not separate as easily from goat's milk as it does from cow's milk, only the whole milk is available.

Soured milk products Milk that has been soured is often looked upon as a food. It also makes a drink that is enjoyed in various parts of the world under different names and soured by various methods. *Kefir* is from the Caucasus and is slightly fermented. The Russian *koumiss* is made from mare's milk that turns sour as it hangs in leather bags on the mare's own warm sides. *Villi* is a Finnish sour milk drink. Yogurt has long been a daily food in the Balkans, parts of India, Russia, Turkey, Greece, and the Middle East, and is now widely available throughout America and Europe.

It is the presence of living lactic acid bacteria in milk that makes it go sour. This used to be a real problem before pasteurization, and it was the need to use milk before it became too sour that led to the making of yogurt and cheese. Pasteurization, however, kills the lactic acid bacteria and now milk, if left, will often not sour but just go bad. Therefore, a souring culture, such as a tablespoon of buttermilk, must be added to make soured milk products.

Acidophilus milk The bacterium *Lactobacillus acidophilus*, killed during pasteurization, is reintroduced in a dormant state to pasteurized milk to produce acidophilus milk. This milk has been found to be easily digestible even by those who cannot manage ordinary milk and is called "the milk of the future" by some nutritionists. It looks and tastes like fresh pasteurized milk. The bacterium is said to be extremely beneficial, as it helps to achieve a better bacterial balance in the digestive tract.

Buttermilk This used to be a favorite drink of farmers' children. It had a fresh, slightly acid flavor, and was made from the liquid left over when butter was made on the farm. It was also used in cooking to activate the bicarbonate of soda that was used as a leavening agent in baking to give a soft, tender quality to cakes and some biscuits. The buttermilk sold today is still delicious, but far less rich; it is made by adding a culture to nonfat or low-fat milk. Powdered buttermilk is also available.

Yogurt Credited with powers of increasing health and prolonging life, yogurt is made daily in those countries where it has a

Buttermilk

Crème fraîche

Heavy cream

Clotted cream

long history. It is eaten as a dessert and is used extensively as a marinade for meat, in soups and salads, and in cooked dishes. For cooking, yogurt can be stabilized to prevent it from separating.

Good yogurt can be easily made at home in a special yogurt maker or simply in an earthenware or ceramic bowl. Commercial yogurts are produced by injecting whole, low-fat, or skim milk with a culture of *Lactobacillus bulgaricus*, *Lactobacillus acidophilus*, or *Streptococcus thermophilus*. A combination of these strains produces the most acidic yogurts, often considered to have the best flavor. Some, especially the varieties with fruit in them, have had milk solids, sugar, cream, edible gums, and/or gelatin added, but none of these contributes to the acid flavor of yogurt, which is particularly desirable in cooking. Although some yogurts are labeled "live," the only ones that are in fact not live are those that have been sterilized.

Heavily sweetened frozen yogurts are now a popular alternative to ice cream.

Cream

Creams vary in thickness and richness according to the amount of butterfat present—the thicker the cream, the more butterfat it contains, and the richer it will be.

The thickest cream—heavy cream, or heavy whipping cream—is for spooning over strawberries, and is whipped for filling cakes and éclairs, and decorating cakes and other desserts. Whipping cream, or light whipping cream, is slightly less rich but can be used for the same purposes. Light cream, also called coffee or table cream, is ideal for soups and sauces, for pouring over puddings, and for putting into coffee.

The richer creams are usually used in soufflés, ice creams, and mousses. Light cream will not whip no matter how long you work at it, because there is not enough butterfat to trap the air bubbles—nor will half-and-half, a combination of milk and cream—so buy heavy cream or whipping cream.

Whipped cream should be light, airy, and about doubled in volume. A balloon or spiral whisk will achieve the best result. An electric mixer can be too fast and even a rotary beater too fierce. To achieve the right texture, the cream, bowl, and whisk should all be cold. A spoonful of cold milk or a crushed ice cube added to each ¼ cup of cream as it thickens gives a lighter result. If you add a little sugar to the cream, the whipped result will not separate so easily, although it will not be so "pure" in flavor.

As well as varying in texture, cream can be pasteurized, which is the best for all purposes, or ultrapasteurized, when it has a long life but is not the best choice when flavor is important. Nor does it whip as well as regular pasteurized cream. Pasteurized cream is obviously the first choice and this should keep, refrigerated, for up to a week or even longer. Some farms still offer untreated cream, which may be found at local stores or farmers' markets, and this is the cream with the best flavor of all.

Sour cream Light cream is treated with a souring culture to make sour cream. Light sour cream is made from half-and-half. Nonfat sour cream has none of the taste of the real thing. In Russia, sour cream is called *smetana*, and in that country it is served on borscht and salads and is used in marinades. Germany, Austria, and Scandinavia include sour cream in sauces, which it makes glossy

and slightly acid. A plain grilled pork chop eaten from the same plate as a cucumber salad dressed with sour cream produces the most delicious mixture as the meat juices mingle with the dressing. To make your own version of sour cream, simply add a few drops of lemon juice to heavy cream (don't use ultrapasteurized).

Crème fraîche This thick cream is quite rich and has a lively, nutty taste. Real French crème fraîche is made from unpasteurized cream and so thickens naturally; in the United States, a culture or souring agent must be added to pasteurized cream to thicken it.

Clotted cream This is a specialty of the west of England, where great pans filled with milk are heated, cooled, and then skimmed of their thick, wrinkled, creamy crust. This cream is usually eaten in Devon and Cornwall piled onto scones with strawberry jam. The commercial variety, occasionally available in gourmet markets, is not nearly so good.

Butter

Experts can tell where a particular butter comes from by its color, texture, smell, and taste. There are some superb French butters—ivory-colored and rich—such as *beurre des Charentes* and *Isigny*. Melted, these resemble cream; spread on bread, their taste is sweet and nutty, and their texture firm and smooth. There are no visible beads of water on the surface (if butter has a water content of more than 12 percent, it will not cream well). The aroma of these French butters is delicate and mild. They are all that butter could hope to be and so are really worth buying for a treat, if you see them, expensive though they are.

French butters are available in gourmet markets, and some premium European-style butters are now being produced in the United States. But for normal everyday use we tend to buy butter by brand name or by price. Both for eating and cooking it is always better to buy a good-quality butter, since a low-grade butter can have an off taste that spoils the flavor of fresh vegetables and delicate sauces such as hollandaise. If possible, take your butter out of the refrigerator some time before you intend to use it. Always be sure to keep it well away from strong-smelling foods in the refrigerator, particularly anything flavored with garlic, and soft fruits such as strawberries—butter readily absorbs

Unsalted butter

Salted butter

Ghee

these flavors and, once tainted, no amount of airing will make it recover. Butter does freeze well.

Butter can either be salted or unsalted. Salting used to make all the difference between butter that stayed fresh and butter that quickly turned rancid, and it still improves the keeping qualities of our butter today. Unsalted, or sweet, butter has a sweeter taste. It makes an excellent table butter and is preferred to salted butter (sometimes labeled sweet cream butter) in cooking. Its delicate flavor lends itself particularly well to cakes, and it is better than salted butter for frying or sautéing—salted butter contains deposits that burn at a fairly low temperature. Unsalted butter has fewer of these deposits and is therefore able to withstand higher temperatures. Whipped butter has had air beaten into it to make it softer and more spreadable than regular butter. It may be either salted or unsalted. Do not substitute whipped butter for ordinary butter in recipes because the measurement will not be accurate. Butter-margarine blends, a combination of the two, tend to be cheaper than real butter.

Butter can be blended with a number of ingredients to make delicious garnishes and fillings for sandwiches. Mix it with herbs, especially parsley, to serve with fish or meat. Mixed with garlic, it makes the classic accompaniment for snails. Blended with Roquefort cheese, it is delicious with steak, and with mashed anchovies or mustard (or with lobster coral, should you have any on hand), it makes an excellent garnish for fish.

There are many superb butter sauces, including beurre blanc—velvety-smooth butter flavored with white wine, vinegar, and shallots; *sauce meunière*, a combination

of foaming butter and lemon juice; and beurre noir, which, despite its French name, should on no account be black, but rather golden-brown.

The addition of a little oil will prevent butter from burning when cooking, but perhaps the best butter for frying very delicate foods is clarified butter, from which all the milk solids have been removed. This is the ghee used in India, but only for special occasions—less expensive vegetable ghee is used for everyday cooking. Clarified butter, however, is nowhere near as appetizing on vegetables—particularly on new or baked potatoes—as fresh butter.

Fresh cream butter American butters, and most British butters, are made from fresh cream. The cream is pasteurized, deodorized, cooled, and placed in aging tanks for at least 12 hours before being turned into butter.

Ripened butter This is traditionally made in the Netherlands and Denmark, and like fresh cream butter can be either salted or unsalted. A pure culture of lactic bacteria is added to the cream, which is then allowed to ripen to develop a delicious, slightly acidic flavor before the butter is made. This butter has a slightly more pronounced taste than fresh cream butter and is also softer.

Making your own dairy foods

Many milk-based products can be made quite easily at home. Starter packets for cultured products such as yogurt can be bought from health food stores, or a little of the unflavored ready-made product can be used. All you need then are very clean, well-covered jars or bowls (not metal), an undisturbed environment, and a constant temperature to allow the culture to grow.

Store the culture in the refrigerator and always keep a little aside as a starter for your next batch.

Buttermilk To make buttermilk, add approximately 2 tablespoons of cultured buttermilk to 1 pint skim milk; cover and leave to stand in a warm place for about 12 hours. The buttermilk can be served as a drink or used to make biscuits and soda bread.

Yogurt Any kind of milk (except for evaporated or condensed milk) can be used to make yogurt. The milk should be brought almost to a boil and then kept at a temperature of 170 to 180°F for 15 minutes, before being cooled to about 110°F. The milk then needs to be kept at this temperature throughout the rest of the process so that the bacteria can grow. Stir 1 teaspoon of live yogurt or a packet of culture into each scant quart of milk and leave to stand overnight in a warm place. Alternatively, and much more reliably, buy a yogurt-making kit. When the yogurt has reached the consistency of thick custard, fruit, nuts, and so forth can be added if you like. The yogurt should then go straight into the refrigerator.

When heated, yogurt has a tendency to curdle, so if you intend to cook with it you should stabilize it first to prevent this. Make a little paste with cornstarch and water. Heat the yogurt, stir in the cornstarch paste, and simmer for about 10 minutes, until it thickens. Then proceed with the recipe.

A delicious fresh cheese can be made very easily by putting some yogurt in a cheesecloth bag and then suspending it overnight to drip (attaching it to the taps over the sink is a good method when the weather is not too hot; alternatively, place the bag in a strainer over a bowl and refrigerate it).

Cheeses

There are no rules about serving cheese at home, but if you want to enjoy this most splendid and noble of foods in all its variations, the first thing to do is to find a good cheese shop or cheese department run by someone who really cares, where the cheeses are kept in good condition and allowed to ripen to perfection quite naturally. (If cheeses are stored in an overrefrigerated storeroom, they will not mature properly.)

Having found your source, buy only one or two types of cheese at a time, taking one generous cheese or piece of cheese in perfect condition rather than all sorts of bits and pieces. Keep the cheese, if at all possible, in a cool pantry rather than in a refrigerator, with the cut surfaces covered. If no such cool place is available, keep it loosely wrapped (preferably in plastic-coated paper rather than plastic wrap, and then in aluminum foil, allowing the passage of air) in the lower part of the refrigerator. Take the cheese out a good hour before you intend to serve it, to give it time to recover from the chill, and do not leave it too long before you eat it.

The serving of cheese varies from country to country. In France, it is generally served after the salad, which has then done its job of refreshing the palate. Accompaniments are crusty French bread and good unsalted butter, which sets off the subtlest cheese flavor and will not spoil the most delicate. (Some of the richer Normandy cheeses, obviously, don't need any butter at all.) The burgundy or claret served with the main course is finished off and appreciated with the cheese.

In America, cheese is often served as an hors d'oeuvre with drinks, a practice that horrifies the French because it dulls the appetite for the meal to follow. In Britain, as in America, a cheese or cheese plate may be brought to the table at the end of an elegant dinner, after the dessert. There is usually fresh bread or plain crackers on the table for those who want them, and, again, unsalted butter. A strong cheese may be served with crisp apples or perhaps with walnuts or celery.

When cooking with cheese, it is unwise just to use up any old scraps or ends of on-the-verge-of-moldy cheese. The best results are obtained by using the best cheese. A piece of good, mature farmhouse Cheddar will be worth any amount of cheap mass-produced block cheese in cooking—and, whatever the manufacturers may say, it is possible to tell the difference. Another thing to notice is the difference between cheeses that are made from pasteurized and unpasteurized milk. The unpasteurized cheese, such as some French Bries and Camemberts, for example, will go on developing and maturing because the milk that the cheese was made from was "alive"; cheese made from pasteurized milk does not have the ability to develop the same subtle flavors and textures.

FRESH CHEESES

Also called unripened cheeses, these are the simplest of all . They are made from the curds of soured milk or from milk that has been coagulated with the help of rennet—a curdling substance obtained from the stomachs of unweaned calves or sometimes, in the case of vegetarian rennet, from artichokes. They can also be made from whey, the thin liquid left over from cheese making. The milk used for making fresh cheese has often been skimmed of its fat content, but some fresh "cream" cheeses have a high fat content and are used to make some of the world's most fattening desserts—cheesecake for one.

These cheeses used to be made on country or mountain farms from surplus milk or milk and cream, but are now usually mass-produced in factories from pasteurized milk and, sadly, in the process have become rather bland. Some fresh cheeses, however, are left to ripen and ferment for weeks or months, during which time they develop a characteristic bloom and an agreeable sharpness.

Cottage cheese Made from the curds of low-fat or skim milk and therefore having a low fat content, this cheese is eternally popular with people who are trying to lose weight. The curds are broken into different sizes, resulting in small-curd, medium-curd, and large-curd cottage cheese. Cream is sometimes added, in which case it is known as creamed cottage cheese. Its slightly acid taste makes cottage cheese a refreshing accompaniment to a summer fruit salad. In Germany, where a version known as quark is popular, it is often mixed with fruit purées; in Provence, a similar homemade white cheese, called *fromage frais*, is traditionally eaten with tiny new potatoes cooked in their skins. Pot cheese is cottage cheese allowed to drain longer than usual, so that it is drier; farmer's cheese is cottage cheese that has been drained even longer and is quite firm in texture. Scottish crowdie, a cottage cheese, is made from fresh sweet milk and butter.

Cream cheese Rich and creamy, soft and mild, cream cheese can be made from whole milk or from a combination of whole milk and cream. It is delicious when mixed with scallions, chopped raw vegetables or herbs, or nuts and raisins, and is an essential ingredient of cheesecakes. American neufchâtel is a lower-fat cream cheese. In France, a vast number of fresh cream cheeses are sold, with varying fat contents (*double crème*, *triple crème*), such as Explorateur and Brillat Savarin; when fresh cream cheese is put into heart-shaped molds and drained, it becomes the dessert *coeur à la crème*, eaten with wild strawberries.

Liptauer, Liptoi Originally from Hungary, this ripened fresh cheese is usually made from goat's or sheep's milk. It has a piquant taste and is delicious when blended with butter, seasoned with salt, paprika, and caraway seeds, and spread on rye bread.

Mysost and Gjetost In Norway, any cheese made from thickening the whey after it has been separated from the prepared curd is known as Mysost. There are several varieties, but the most popular is Gjetost. It is cooked until it looks like fudge, and has a sweet flavor.

Gomost This Norwegian fresh cheese is made from soured unsalted milk, and is similar to the French cheese known as Caillebotte. White and creamy, it is sometimes eaten with sugar or mixed with stewed or fresh ripe fruit.

Pultost This is also a Norwegian curd cheese but is stiffer and stronger than Gomost. It is made from buttermilk or whey, and caraway seeds are often added.

Ricotta Traditionally made from the whey left over from making the Italian sheep's-milk pecorino cheese, this can also be made from the whey of other cheeses, or from a combination of whey and milk, or even just milk. Its bland taste makes it ideal for mixing with fruit and raisins, or it can be eaten—as it is in Rome—with salt, or with cinnamon and sugar. It features in numerous Italian dishes—including Italian cheesecake—but it is especially good mixed with Parmesan, spinach, and Swiss chard and used to stuff ravioli.

Fromage blanc A favorite of dieters, this popular creamy French cheese is made from skim milk soured with a culture. It is excellent eaten with fresh raspberries or other berries.

Fontainebleau Rarely available outside its native France, this cream cheese is made from a mixture of curd and whipped cream and is usually eaten with sugar. It can be made at home by blending Petit Suisse with whipped cream, although this method is unlikely to produce the super-aerated result that is achieved by the commercial manufacturers.

Petit Suisse French in origin, but called Swiss because a French-employed Swiss cowman is credited with its invention, this mild, light little cream cheese is delicious with fruit and is excellent in any recipe where cream cheese is required.

Demi-sel Small and square, soft and white, this French cheese is sold under a number of brand names, but it is especially good when it has been made in Normandy, where it originated. It has a high fat content and, as its name implies, is slightly salted.

Neufchâtel This whole cow's-milk cheese (which should not be confused with American neufchâtel) comes from Normandy. It is either eaten fresh, when it is covered with the first growth of a soft white down and has a delicate taste, or is allowed to ripen until it is firm and pungent with a warm-colored, bloomy rind. It comes in a variety of shapes.

Mascarpone Originally made in Lombardy and Tuscany, this rich creamy cheese is now being produced by some American cheese makers. It is used in the popular dessert tiramisù and in other cooking; it is also eaten with fruit or sugar and cinnamon, or spread on slices of sweet bread.

Mozzarella This fresh white cheese was originally made from water buffalo's milk, but now cow's milk is often used; it is sold swimming in water to keep it fresh, and should be soft and springy.

Two popular forms are *bocconcini*, or little balls, and a smoked version. Mozzarella is served as an hors d'oeuvre in southern Italy, with olive oil and freshly ground pepper, and is often part of a simple salad with just sliced ripe tomatoes, fresh basil, and a drizzle of olive oil. It is ideal for cooking, being a traditional ingredient of pizza. Once opened, always keep fresh mozzarella in a bowl of water in the lower part of the refrigerator. Commercially produced mozzarella has a less-delicate flavor and texture, but it melts better than the fresh.

Feta Crumbly and salty, this is the best known of the white cheeses ripened in brine or salt and known as "pickled cheeses." It was originally made from sheep's milk by shepherds in the mountain regions near Athens, and is popular in Greek cooking, especially crumbled into the well-known salads of tomatoes, cucumbers, and black olives, with olive oil. It's also made from goat's milk and even from cow's milk. Feta can be made less salty by soaking it in water with a touch of milk.

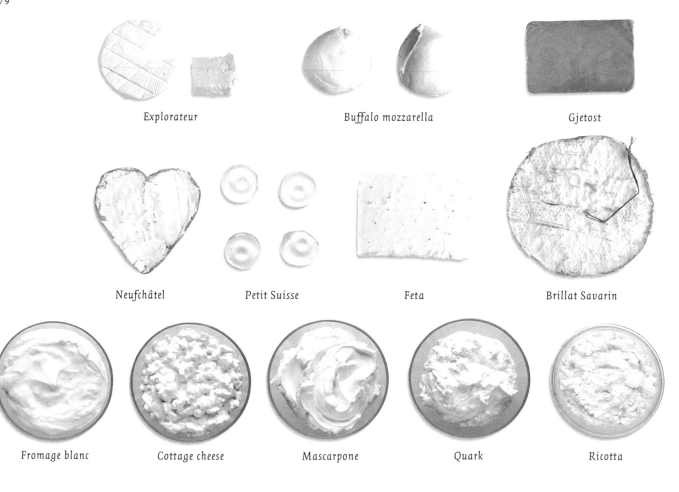

Explorateur

Buffalo mozzarella

Gjetost

Neufchâtel

Petit Suisse

Feta

Brillat Savarin

Fromage blanc

Cottage cheese

Mascarpone

Quark

Ricotta

HARD CHEESES

The word hard, when applied to cheeses, means that they have been subjected to pressure to make them dense. They will be softer or firmer according to their age.

Hard cheeses develop their various characteristics according to the milk used and the methods by which they are made. The speed of coagulation, the way the curd is cut, and whether the curd is then left to ripen or is cut again all affect the taste and texture, as does the treatment the cheese receives during the ripening process.

Some of the cheeses we have today are derivations of more famous originals; while some of them remain only copies, others have developed a character of their own and deserve to be considered as cheeses in their own right.

Grana cheeses

The hard, grainy cheeses that are collectively called *grana* are the well-known Italian grating cheeses, familiar to anyone who has ever eaten a plate of pasta or a bowl of minestrone soup. Their slow aging process and low moisture content give them their long-keeping qualities and their crumbly texture. The younger *grana* cheeses are more delicate, and they are delicious when broken into chunks and eaten accompanied with white wine.

Parmigiano-Reggiano, or simply Parmesan, the most famous and expensive of all the *granas*, is sweet and fragrant. It keeps for years, growing harder and fuller as it ages. When young, it can be served at the end of a meal. It is an essential ingredient of many of the best and most characteristic northern Italian dishes, and it is grated and then scattered on top of soups and pasta.

Of course, there are other Parmesan cheeses made in the United States, of varying quality, but none compares to the real thing. When buying Parmesan, look for the name Parmigiano-Reggiano burned in dots on the rind as proof of authenticity. The cheese should be straw-colored and brittle, with pinprick holes that are scarcely visible but give it a rocky surface. It should never be gray, sweaty, or waxy-looking, and it should always smell fresh. Ground Parmesan cheese is an extremely poor substitute for fresh.

Pecorino is the name given to *grana* cheeses made from sheep's milk, which are used in much the same way as Parmesan. A pecorino is round, hard, and white, with a yellow crust when mature (except for that made in Siena, which is red). The taste is strong, pungent, and salty. There are many varieties, which often go by the names of the districts in which they are made. Pecorino Romano is the original variety and is still considered to be the best.

Grana Padano This is made in the Po valley. Since it is cheaper than true Parmesan, it is often used in cooking.

Asiago is an ancient Italian cheese from the Veneto region, in the northeastern part of the country. Young Asiago can be served as a table cheese, but it is more familiar aged and grated for use in cooking.

Sbrinz This ancient and splendid Swiss cheese is equal in virtue to (although distinct from) Parmesan. Its texture is granular and brittle, and it has an uneven surface with pinprick holes. In central Switzerland, it is often shaved in thin slivers and served with a glass of wine. It is also ideal for cooking.

Sapsago Also known as Schabzieger or simply as green cheese, this cheese from Switzerland is a hard, truncated little green cone. Made from skimmed cow's milk, it ferments naturally, and is mixed with pulverized blue melilot, a sweet clover, which gives it its green color and characteristic pungent flavor. It smells of coriander or cumin, and is grated and used as a condiment for a variety of dishes.

Cheddar-type cheeses

These are the real grass-roots cheeses, made and eaten all over the world and used in all recipes that call for cheese.

Cheddar No hard cheese has been more widely imitated than English Cheddar, which originated in the small town of Cheddar, in Somerset, and was well established by the sixteenth century. It is a splendid all-purpose cheese, good to eat and to cook with. It has a sweet, full flavor when young and mild, and a sharp nutty flavor when mature.

Mature English farmhouse Cheddars, still made on some farms and ripened for months or years, are among the world's greatest cheeses. They compress more than ten times their weight of creamy milk when pressed into a cylindrical form and wrapped in a cloth, which may then be waxed. A traditional Cheddar weighs about 50 to 60 pounds, while small, whole Cheddars, known as truckles, usually weigh about 14 pounds. English Cheddar is also made in large blocks, but these do not develop and mature like the traditional aged cheeses.

Smaller Cheddars of various shapes are made outside England, but may vary widely from the true Cheddar flavor. In New York State, the home of the first Cheddar-cheese factory in America, a number of Cheddars are still made in varying sizes—some even come rindless. Wisconsin is also known for the quality of its Cheddars, but most of these, and most other Cheddars, like the Australian and New Zealand varieties, are made from pasteurized milk and lack the authentic taste of the English farmhouse variety. Tillamook cheese, however, from Oregon, is a delicious raw-milk Cheddar, and other smaller cheese makers are also now using unpasteurized milk for their Cheddars. Canadian Cheddars, which are still sometimes made from unpasteurized milk, have a characteristic tangy, nutty flavor. Look for Black Diamond (with a black waxed surface) or Belleville-Brockville Cheddar (in a plain waxed cloth).

Cantal Sometimes called the French Cheddar, Cantal has a smooth texture and, if the truth be told, a duller flavor than Cheddar. It is large, hard, and yellow and is made in cylindrical forms. Cantal can be good if it is allowed to mature—it takes as long to ripen as farmhouse Cheddars.

Cheshire Known as "Chester" in France and Italy, this is the oldest of the British cheeses. It is crumbly, nutty, and salty, and can be red, white, or blue. The red, which is dyed with annatto and is a marigold-orange, makes excellent eating as well as first-class soufflés. It is fat and rich, with a special piquancy that is also to be found in the white and blue varieties. The white variety, which is in fact a pale cream, is sharper than the red. It ripens faster but does not keep as well. The blue Cheshire is farmhouse-made, and is not often seen outside England.

Gloucester This is a hard and robust English cheese. Single Gloucester is made partly from skim milk and is ready for eating in 6 to 8 weeks; double Gloucester is made from whole milk and is eaten after about 4 to 6 months. In taste, Gloucester lies between Cheddar and Cheshire, although there is none of Cheshire's

Gruyère

English farmhouse Cheddar

New York Cheddar

Cantal

Appenzeller

Leicester

Parmigiano-Reggiano

Cheshire

Gloucester   Pecorino Romano

crumble about it. Farmhouse Gloucester has a natural hard crust. Gloucester is a good cooking cheese and makes delicious cheese crackers.

Caerphilly One of the mildest, softest, crumbliest, and fastest-ripening of the British hard cheeses, this was once known as the Welsh miners' cheese because it was the favorite packed lunch at the mine. The best Caerphilly today, however, is produced on farms in Somerset, England. Made from skim milk, it has a slightly sour taste and is eaten rather immature. It is suitable for dishes calling for a mild cheese flavor.

Wensleydale This English cheese is white, moist, and flaky, with a delicately sour buttermilk flavor.

Leicester The largest English cheese in circumference, Leicester is a rich orange color and shaped like an old millstone, with a hole in the center. It is mild and nutty, moist and flaky, and very different from Cheddar in texture, as the curd is shredded, making it crumbly. It melts easily and is ideal for cheese sauce.

Cotswold is an orange, somewhat crumbly cheese that is often flavored with chives and onions.

Sage Derby Once made for eating at harvest suppers, this English farmhouse cheese is a sage-flavored version of plain Derby, which is similar to Cheddar but with a denser texture and more distinct flavor. It should be aged for at least 9 months and be mottled with natural-looking sage-green streaks; at its worst, however, it is heavily marbled with a vivid green, artificial in taste, and too waxy in texture to even recall the real thing. Sage cheese is a similar cheese, tangy and succulent, made in Vermont.

Gouda-type cheeses

Firm and fat, these familiar round cheeses become drier and sharper with age. Those that are flavored with cumin or caraway seeds are particularly good with rye bread and wine.

Gouda Made in the town of Gouda, outside Amsterdam, this is the archetypal Dutch cheese. It is creamy, golden, and flattish, with a yellow, or sometimes a red, paraffin-waxed protective skin. A mature Gouda will be more pungent than a youthful one and can be very worthwhile. A black coating indicates that the cheese is 7 or more

years old, when it becomes known as an Alt Gouda. Gouda is a simple eating cheese, which in its native Holland appears for breakfast, and in the kitchen it is fried together with potatoes, grated into sauces, and melted to make a type of fondue.

Edam Made from partially skimmed milk, Edam, which is encased in a bright red or yellow coating for the export market, has a lower fat content than Gouda and is less smooth and round-flavored. When young, this cheese tends to have a somewhat boring flavor, but once aged and ripened, it acquires a rather pleasant mellowness.

Mimolette This Dutch cheese, the size and shape of a cannonball, is similar to Edam but bright orange inside, turning a rich red with age. The best Mimolettes are aged for up to 2 years and have a glorious rich flavor; however, most are young and flabby.

Leyden Resembling Gouda, this cheese has a sharp, tangy taste. It is usually flavored with caraway seeds, but varieties with cloves and cumin are also available. It is branded with the crossed keys of the arms of the Dutch city of Leyden.

Emmentaler

Mature Gouda

Derby

Wensleydale

Havarti

Edam

Fontina

Jarlsberg

Comté

Caerphilly

Gruyère-type cheeses

Reminiscent of alpine meadows, these cheeses range from mild-flavored to a rich, full nuttiness. Straw-yellow in color, they are characterized by holes caused by gas forming during ripening. These are the cheeses most popular with French cooks, who appreciate their melting qualities, so well suited to the making of gratins and sauces.

Gruyère This Swiss cheese is made of cow's milk and has a fairly smooth rind. Ivory-yellow with tiny pinprick holes spaced far apart, it should have a waxy rather than a velvety surface. It is a main ingredient of the classic cheese fondue because of its fine melting qualities, and is also often served after a meal.

Comté This French cheese is a first cousin to Gruyère. The best, "fruitiest" cheeses are made in one-man village dairies, or *fruitières*, to which the village farmers bring their milk, and they can be identified by a green oval plaque on the outside of the whole cheese. These cheeses often have almost no holes at all.

Emmentaler, Emmental This is the famous Swiss cheese with the large holes. It comes in huge, shiny golden wheels.

Its ivory-colored interior is riddled with bubbles, which form during its fermentation and cooling period. It has a sweet flavor that grows fuller with age, and is excellent for eating and cooking.

Jarlsberg This Norwegian cheese is similar to Emmentaler but milder and more rubbery. Its taste is slightly nutty.

Fontina Made in the Piedmont area of Italy and also in Switzerland, Denmark, and the United States, this is a fat, rich, semi-firm cheese. Experts recommend the Swiss version for the table and the Italian for cooking. It melts beautifully and is used for Piedmontese *fonduta*, a fondue served with sliced white truffles.

Appenzeller, Appenzell A Swiss relation of Emmentaler, washed in a mixture of white wine and brine, this makes a tasty fondue when young. When mature, it is firm but buttery with a rich and sweet flavor.

OTHER SEMI-FIRM CHEESES

These cheeses, some of which resemble Cheddar, are characterized by their firm but elastic feel. They are sometimes soft and tender, but, unlike truly soft cheeses, do not become runny as they mature.

Caciocavallo Made from cow's milk, this Italian cheese is often smoked. An ivory-white cheese with a golden-yellow to gray rind, it is often displayed in pairs joined by a string and is usually eaten at the end of a meal. It is one of the *pasta filata*, or drawn-curd cheeses, so named because they are stretched into strands in hot water during their making.

Provolone There are two main types of provolone, another *pasta filata*, or drawn-curd cow's-milk cheese: *dolce*, which is young and usually dull; and *piccante*, which is strong and often very salty, but a good cheese. The *piccante* is sometimes available from good Italian delicatessens. It may be smoked, and is molded by hand into various shapes. Provolone is also produced in the United States.

Monterey Jack This pale California cheese, with small holes, comes in various shapes and degrees of softness. When it has a high moisture content and is quite soft, it is often simply called Jack. The harder grating varieties are called aged or dry Jack. The softer versions are often flavored with chile peppers.

Colby This cheese of Wisconsin origin is similar to Cheddar but has a more

Provolone

Danbo with caraway

Manchego

Tilsit

Colby

Monterey Jack

These cheeses are considered ready for eating when soft, so they will bulge in the middle of the cut surface, although some people prefer them runny. Any smell of ammonia indicates that the cheese is past its prime. Soft cheeses are delicious on French bread. The most famous varieties come from Normandy, which has some of the best pastures and produces the richest, creamiest milk in the world (although Normandy farmers say that artificial fertilizers are changing the quality of this wonderful milk).

Brie Some decent Bries are now being produced in the United States and in other countries, including England, but French Bries are widely acknowledged to be the best. A whole round, flat Brie usually measures 14 inches across and is most commonly sold in wedges. The unliquefied part in the center of a ripe Brie is called "the soul of the Brie." Farmhouse Brie, known as Brie de Meaux *fermier*, is the creamiest variety and has a bouquet that is full and mild. Nowadays, French Bries are mainly produced in factories and there are many imitations, but do buy unpasteurized farmhouse Brie from Normandy whenever you get the chance. The Brie de Melun *affiné*, a smaller cheese, is one of the finest of all.

Camembert A farmhouse Camembert is made from raw milk, while the more common factory-produced Camembert is always made from pasteurized milk. The best Camemberts are from Normandy, and are made in rounds weighing 8 to 9 ounces. Camembert is also available in half-moons and in wedges, but unfortunately it is only reliable if ripened as a whole cheese: proportion and thickness of the crust and consistency of the interior are all affected by cutting the cheese before it is fully ripe. A well-made and properly ripened Camembert is smooth and buttery, even runny; it should not be eaten if smelling of ammonia.

Pont-l'Evêque This cheese is square, soft, and fat, with a shiny golden or reddish salty rind and a warm, ripe taste. It should always have "Pays d'Auge" and *lait cru* or *nonpasteurisé* stamped on the wrapping paper or box, proving that it comes from unpasteurized milk.

Livarot This strong, pungent cheese, still made at its village of origin and elsewhere in Normandy's Pays d'Auge, is round, weighs about 1 pound, and is

open texture. It is a soft, mild cheese, and does not keep as well as Cheddar.

Tilsit German in origin, this yellow cheese is pungent, with a slight smear to its surface. It is sometimes made with caraway seeds.

Havarti A cheese of the Tilsit type, this is named after the farm of one of Denmark's great cheese makers. Havarti is made in round loaf shapes and in blocks, and has a strong individual taste, somewhat sharp when mature.

Danbo and Samsoe These firm, nutty, Swiss-style cheeses are the national standbys of Denmark. (Samsoe is named after the island where it is made.)

Manchego This Spanish cheese has a high fat content, and can be made from cow's or sheep's milk. Young Manchego is called *curado*; aged (*viejo*) Manchego may be left to mature for up to 3 years, sometimes spending a year ripening in olive oil. It may be either white or yellow in color, and with or without holes, and it varies widely in taste.

Brick is an American original that was made in Wisconsin as early as 1875. It has a dry reddish-brown crust and a softish, ivory-colored interior. The flavor should be mellow, stimulating, and somewhat sweet. Depending on its age and its ripeness, it is compared to both Cheddar and limburger.

SOFT CHEESES

The characteristic flavor of the creamy-white soft cheeses comes from bacterial growths, which begin at the outer edges of the cheese and move into the center. A ripe cheese will be soft at the center and can be tested by pressing at the "waist" with the fingers. The bloomy white rinds are also a result of bacterial growth. They are natural in farm or artisan production, where the mold is present in the ripening premises themselves, and are induced in many factory-made cheeses by spraying penicillin or other bacteria onto the crust. (The same applies to cheeses with a russet-brown washed crust.)

about twice as tall as a Pont-l'Evêque. It has a thicker crust and, although it is obviously of the same family, has quite a distinct flavor.

Vacherin Usually banded with spruce bark, which saves it from collapse and gives it a faint aroma of resin, Vacherin is a seasonal cheese, made in winter by the French and Swiss Comté-producing farms when there isn't enough milk, or when transport is too difficult, to produce the Comté that they make in summer. When truly ripe, Vacherin is served with a spoon for digging into the buttery, runny center. It has a sweet, flowery, nutty flavor.

Maroilles Square and strong-smelling, this comes from northwestern France and is ripened for up to 4 months, with much crust-washing as it ages. It is delicious with a full-bodied wine, and is used to make *goyère* and *flamiche*, the cheese pies traditional in the region where it is produced.

Reblochon This fine cheese from the Savoy region in southeast France is smooth and creamy, with a pinkish-gold crust and a strong, ripe flavor.

Port-Salut Also called Port du Salut—"haven of rest"—after the Trappist abbey where it was first made, this is a velvety-smooth whole-milk cheese, semi-soft

or semi-firm, and mildly pungent. One variety, Fermiers-Réunis, is still made by the monks at their Champagne dairy from the unpasteurized milk of their cows. Commercial Port-Salut, made by a farmers' co-operative in the nearby village, is a more rubbery and less tasty affair, as is the Bricquebec—a similar cheese made in the monastic dairy.

Taleggio Made from whole cow's milk, this comes from Lombardy in Italy. It has a smooth pink skin with a straw-colored interior, and is fruity in flavor.

Munster, Muenster Originating in the Vosges, this is the national cheese of France's Alsace. Its interior is firm, and

Port-Salut

Limburger

Maroilles

Chaource

Camembert

Livarot

Taleggio

Bel Paese

Soumaintrain

Tomme de Savoie

Saint Nectaire

Pont-l'Evêque

Brie

Munster

Reblochon

Epoisses

*Crottin de
Chavignol*

Chèvre with herbs

*Chèvre with herbs
and garlic*

Selles sur Cher

Pouligny St. Pierre

its rind red and smooth. It has a pungent smell and flavor. American Munster cheese is, unfortunately, only a pale imitation of the original, with an orange rind and a much duller flavor.

Limburger This cheese may take the form of a log, a horizontally corrugated roll, or a little disc or blob, and has a moist, pale rind and an overpowering smell. It is an acquired taste and should be eaten with robust country bread. An American cousin known as Leiderkranz is actually more like a pleasant Pont-l'Evêque than an aged Limburger.

Bel Paese is the trade name for a soft, cream-colored cheese of which there are many local and factory-made variations throughout Italy. Today it is also made in the United States. It is tender and mild.

Tommes This is the family name of a large number of rustic cheeses, made of sheep's, goat's, or cow's milk and in almost any shape. The Tommes were originally from Savoy, the southern mountain ranges of France and the eastern part of Switzerland. Tomme au Marc is coated in fermented grape *marc*—made from the pressed skins and seeds of grapes left over from wine making, which gives it its taste, while Tomme de Savoie has a nutty flavor. At least one artisan cheese maker is now producing a Tomme in the United States.

Saint Nectaire This French mountain cheese is a round, flat cheese with a dark rind and a soft, supple but not creamy, straw-colored inside. It has a nice light flavor.

Epoisses A smelly cow's-milk cheese from Burgundy, this is cylindrical and reddish on the outside, and oozy and rich inside, with a strong earthy taste.

Soumaintrain Like Epoisses, this flat, round cheese comes from Burgundy. It is semi-soft, with a sticky red-brown crust, a strong smell, and an earthy taste.

Chaource is one of those small, white, downy, luxurious-looking cheeses that give a fresh note to an otherwise heavy meal. From the Champagne district, it has a faintly acid, fruity flavor and a velvety rather than a creamy texture.

GOAT CHEESES

In Europe, there are infinite varieties of goat cheeses; most are simply described as *chèvre* (the French for goat) and have no distinguishing names. They are made on farms and dairies all over France and the Mediterranean, and are usually known as *frais* or *mi-frais*, which means fresh; *affiné*, which has been matured and should be velvety, occasionally creamy, and fairly soft; and *vieux*, which is well aged and varies from soft and creamy to rock-hard. They should not be chalky or soapy—often a sign that they have been refrigerated. Over the last decade or so, a number of artisan cheese makers have been producing goat cheese in the United States, most notably in New York and New England and in California.

The flavors of goat cheeses vary according to the ripening period, the locality and altitude (which have a bearing on the taste and quality of the goat's

milk), and on the different mold cultures used. But in general all goat cheeses, whether strong (like Pouligny St. Pierre) or mild (like Selles sur Cher), should taste nutty and sweet with a slight piquancy. Crottin de Chavignol, from the Berry region, has a reddish or gray crust and a white, piquant, and full-flavored interior.

Some goat cheeses are flavored with chives or garlic and other herbs, while others are rolled in wood ashes. Some goat cheeses are sold wrapped in leaves; they may be coated with herbs or pepper, or preserved in oil.

BLUE CHEESES

Blue cheeses first turned blue by a happy accident. Roquefort, the ancestral blue cheese, was once just a humble fresh curd cheese made of sheep's milk. Had it not been for a lovelorn shepherd, who, as legend has it, set off in pursuit of a country girl, leaving his lunchtime cheese in a limestone cave, the blue mold might never have happened. However, returning after a week or so of dalliance, the shepherd found that his lunch had changed in texture, color, and taste and become "blue." Since that time, the penicillin molds that turn cheese blue have been identified, and blue cheeses have multiplied. The cheese may be firm or creamy, buttery or brittle, and any color from chalk-white to golden-yellow.

Roquefort The veining of Roquefort, a sheep's-milk cheese, is due to *Penicillium glaucum*—now better known as *Penicillium roquefortii*—which thrives in the caves high upon the Cambalou plateau in the Aveyron region of southern France. These ancient caves, cool and damp owing to underground springs, are still used for maturing Roquefort. The blue veining is now accelerated by layering the curd with crumbled bread molds, but even so, the ripening process still takes 3 months, and the cheese will not be at its best until at least 6 months old.

A Roquefort in its prime is creamy, with green-blue marbling. *Persillé*—"parsleyed"—is the French term. It is smooth, firm, and buttery, but crumbly owing to the mold. It is strong, with the fine grain and extra pungency that sheep's milk produces. It should not be salty—although cheeses for export tend to be oversalted to prevent spoilage.

Bleu des Causses is a cheese of high quality, somewhat similar to Roquefort.

It is from the same region and has the same mold, but is made from cow's milk.

Gorgonzola Once exclusive to the Italian village of that name, this cheese is now produced all over the lush plain of Lombardy. The squat, cylindrical cheeses, made of cow's milk, are no longer matured in the local caves but rather in the great maturing houses in the district. *Penicillium mycelium* accounts for the streaking. Gorgonzola is often described as an early copy of Roquefort, but it is softer, milder, creamier, and less salty. It should have little rind, being wrapped in foil, and should be rather smooth and cream-colored, marbled with blue-gray or blue-green. The cheese should feel springy. It may smell a little musty, but not overpowering. Other Italian blues include the creamy, mild, factory-made Dolcelatte, also called Gorgonzola latte, and a smaller Mountain Gorgonzola.

Pipo Crème is a round French cheese. It was first produced as a competitor of Gorgonzola, but has its own character.

Danish Blue is similar to Roquefort but is made with cow's milk. It can be round, rectangular, or square, and is white with blue veins. It is high in fat and has the saltiness inevitable in this type of cheese. Danablu is a well-known variety.

Bresse Bleu A French cheese similar to Gorgonzola, this soft blue cheese comes from the Bresse region, which also produces a heavier blue called Bleu de Bresse, another heavy one called France Bresse, and, most recently, Belle Bressane, with a hole in the middle.

Maytag Blue is a tangy and smooth-textured blue-veined white cheese made in Iowa, is one of the best American cheeses. Maytag Dairy Farms is a family operation that has been making its cheese since the early 1940s.

Torta di Gordenza Also marketed as Gorgonzola con mascarpone, this is a cheese made from layers of piquant Gorgonzola and fresh mascarpone—a delicious combination.

Fourme d'Ambert A naturally blued cow's-milk cheese, this is from the Auvergne region of France. It is exceptional in being almost the only non-English blue cheese to have a hard crust, which is gray flecked with yellow and red. The cheese comes in cylinders weighing about 3 pounds, and is sharp and strong in flavor.

Stilton One of the few English foods to be admired by the French, this cheese is made only in Derbyshire, Leicestershire, and parts of Nottinghamshire. Although a noble cheese, Stilton is a comparative latecomer and, in fact, was never made at Stilton. But it was in that small village, in the eighteenth century, that it was first served. Stilton should be a creamy color with greenish-blue veining throughout. It should be open-textured and velvety, never dry, or salty.

Blue Wensleydale Among the other English blue cheeses, Blue Wensleydale is claimed by its admirers to be even better than Stilton. It should be creamier, sweeter, and nuttier, but is nowadays not as soft as it should be.

Dorset Blue Vinny is a hard white cheese with bright-blue veining. It is made using vegetarian rennet and skim milk, which make it agreeably sharp.

Other blues There are a number of lesser-known blue cheeses made in France and elsewhere, including a rather good blue Brie from Germany.

mascarpone 102

Gratinéed Onions in Gorgonzola Sauce 372–3

Danish Blue

Torta di Gordenza

Bresse Bleu

Maytag Blue

Dolcelatte

Roquefort

Bleu des Causses

Fourme d'Ambert

Blue Wensleydale

Dorset Blue Vinny

Stilton

Gorgonzola

Cooking Fats and Oils

Every cook in the world uses fat or oil of some kind as a cooking medium. In the cool northern regions, the fats from grass- and grain-fed animals are traditionally used, while in the hot Mediterranean countries, where the blessed olive tree grows, olive oil is the essential ingredient for a whole range of recipes. Other regions may use goose fat or mustard seed oil, grapeseed oil, or sesame oil, each of which lends its own distinctive flavor to the local dishes.

Today, the limitations of climate count for far less than they used to, and we can obtain and cook with almost any medium we choose. But the flavor of food depends very much on what fat or oil is used, and a good cook will always try to use the right medium for the right dish in order to keep the flavor as authentic as possible.

Unfortunately, the amount of fat, whether animal or vegetable, in our Western diets has come under major criticism from doctors and nutritionists. Not only do we get our chief source of energy from fats that are an "invisible" part of most foods, but we are all too likely to load up on rich fats in the form of butter and other saturated fats. Vegetable fats, unlike the traditionally suspect animal fats, do not contain any cholesterol. Olive oil, canola oil, and sunflower and safflower oil are all recommended as particularly healthy, and suitable in low-cholesterol diets.

Fats

Fats—and oils—are either saturated or unsaturated. Most saturated fats are of animal origin, and they are usually solid at room temperature. Tropical oils, including palm and coconut, are an exception, as they are saturated fats that are liquid at room temperature. Margarine and vegetable shortening are also saturated fats. Animal fats are a source of cholesterol, and all saturated fats are associated with increased cholesterol levels.

Unsaturated fats are mostly plant products and are liquid at room temperature. Monounsaturated fats, such as olive oil and canola oil, are considered somewhat more healthful than polyunsaturated fats, such as corn and soybean oil.

Margarines Margarines are based on vegetable and/or plant oils, such as corn, soybean, or canola. Some contain a small percentage of cream or milk. To make margarine, the oils are "hydrogenated," or converted from their normal liquid form into a solid one. The process of hydrogenation also turns some of the oils' unsaturated fatty acids into what are called trans-fatty acids, which some experts believe have the same—or more—harmful effects on the body as saturated fats.

With the exception of the all-important flavor, the characteristics of margarine in the kitchen are somewhat similar to those of butter. Reduced-fat, or diet, margarine is not particularly suitable for frying since it contains more water and less fat than regular margarine and splutters and burns easily; nor can it be used for baking. Soft margarines are too soft to be rubbed into flour when making pastry; to make a dough with this type of margarine, mix together the margarine, water, and only one third of the flour at the start, then gradually add the rest of the flour until you have a smooth dough that can be rolled out as usual. Whipped margarine, which, like whipped butter, has air beaten into it to make it more easily spreadable, cannot be substituted for regular margarine in baking.

Vegetable oil spreads, which usually appear alongside margarines, cannot be satisfactorily used for cooking and baking purposes.

Lard Lard is rendered pork fat; before technology took a hand, lard had to be used fresh, and it had a strong taste and no creaming properties. The lard we see now is usually light and clean-tasting. Lard is the fat of choice throughout much of South America and is preferred in many European countries as well. In the United States, lard fell out of favor a few decades ago, but recently some cooks have championed it, pointing out that it's no less healthful than many other cooking fats—and more so than some. Lard is used mainly for frying—it was once the traditional medium for English fish and chips—and for baking, where its creaming properties are appreciated. Old-fashioned Southern cooks and many European bakers find lard the essential ingredient in making a good pie crust (when making pastry,

a mixture of butter and lard produces a crisp, light, crumbly texture).

The best lard is rendered from the belly fat of the pig; leaf lard, which comes from the fat around the kidneys, is considered the finest and most delicate. Lard made from other parts of the pig has a stronger taste; it is the lard most widely sold.

Suet Suet is the white fat surrounding the kidneys of cows, lambs, and other animals. In England, beef suet is widely used. It goes into sweet dishes such as Christmas pudding and into pastry for savory ones like steak and kidney pie.

Fatback This is the fat that runs along the back of the pig, over the loin. When cut into long, thin sheets, it is used primarily for barding dry meats, such as veal and game birds. The pieces are tied over the birds like a vest, and the fat bastes the flesh during cooking. Cut into strips called lardons, the fat can be inserted with a special needle into the flesh of dry meat to keep it succulent while it cooks.

Fatback is also used for lining terrines for pâtés, and for rendering lard at home. Rendering is done by cutting the fatback into very small cubes and then gently melting the cubes with a little water in a very low oven or over very low heat. When the water has evaporated, the clear liquid fat is poured off into a jar. What is left in the pan are the crisp brown cracklings—used in "cracklin' bread" and other Southern recipes. (In New Orleans, pork cracklings are sometimes called *grattons*, their French name.)

Drippings and poultry fat A good old-fashioned way of acquiring a delicious cooking fat is to strain and reserve the fat that has dripped from poultry or meat as it cooks. Once these drippings have cooled and solidified, the juice or jellied liquid underneath is removed (it is excellent when added to a gravy or stock) and any sediment from the bottom of the cake of drippings is scraped away and disposed of. Drippings from different kinds of meat and poultry should not be mixed.

Chicken fat, when rendered, is fine and delicate and is much used in Jewish cooking. Use the fat from goose or duck for bean dishes, roast vegetables, poultry, and, particularly, fried potatoes. European cooks may use beef drippings to sauté the meat for beef stews, or pork drippings for other savory dishes. (Of course, classic English Yorkshire pudding is made using the drippings from the roast beef it accompanies.) Lamb drippings smell and taste rather unpleasant and are not used very much, except in the Middle East, where lamb's tail fat is much liked.

Shortening Any hard fat, such as butter or lard, is shortening, meaning that it is capable of producing a crumbly "short" pastry crust (the greater the amount of fat in the mixture, the greater the shortening effect). However, it is the solid white vegetable fat that has claimed the name.

Vegetable shortening is made of vegetable oils or plant oils that, like the oils used for margarine, have been hydrogenated to make them solid. Its texture is light and fluffy. Although vegetable shortening makes a flaky pie crust, it is totally flavorless and will not contribute one iota toward the flavor of a pie or tart.

Oils

Oils perform the same function as fats in shallow- and deep-frying, but oils have the advantage of being reusable once or twice, as long as they are not overheated and are carefully strained after each use. (But beware of the taint of overused or overheated oil, which spoils the flavor of so much of the fried food in restaurants.)

When frying, oils should be heated slowly to the correct temperature. If the oil is not hot enough, too much will be absorbed by the food; overheating is dangerous. Overheated oil decomposes and will start to smoke; eventually, if heated further, it develops harmful toxins, and will finally catch fire. Any oil overheated by accident should be thrown away. A simple rule is to wait for a blue haze to rise from the oil but never to allow it to smoke. Test the temperature with a thermometer: the oil should be around 325°F for meat and 375°F for french fries and other vegetables. Poultry and fish come in between. If you do not have a thermometer, add a cube of day-old bread to the heated oil: if the bread turns golden and crisp in 1 minute, the temperature is roughly right.

The object of deep-frying is to seal the surface of the food. The crisp outside crust encloses a food whose inside is cooked in the heat of its own steam. The pieces to be fried should be of uniform size as much as possible so that they cook evenly. If you dip the food in batter, let the excess drain off before you put the food into the oil; if you coat it in bread crumbs, press the crumbs on well so the oil can remain as free as possible of small dark brown—and finally burned—crumbs (these will give the oil a bitter flavor).

You should be able to use good oil up to three times. Strain it well after each use. When reused, it should neither foam nor smoke excessively—the smoking point gradually decreases with age. It should not smell or look dark or thick": these are definite signs that the oil has reached the end of its useful life.

There are a great many oils in the world. Even without going into such exotics as Brazil nut oil, used as hair oil by the inhabitants of the Amazon rain forests, or juniper oil for gin, or even clove oil for toothache, the subject of oils is a complex one. To start with—and this goes a long way to help one make a sensible choice— there is the distinction between oils that are unrefined and refined.

Unrefined oils are those that have simply been cold-pressed and then left to clear and mellow for a few months before being bottled. They tend to be cloudy but come to the customer in full possession of their natural flavor and color. Often called cold-pressed oils, they are—not surprisingly—more expensive than their refined counterparts.

Refined oils have been extracted by pressure under heat. They may then be "degummed," neutralized, heated and blanched, "winterized" to keep them

à la grecque 422
coating with egg and crumbs 423

deep-fryer 239
deep-fry thermometer 233

Margarine

Shortening

Lard

Goose fat

Suet

from turning cloudy, deodorized by an injection of steam, and finally given artificial preservatives to make up for those lost in the processing.

Olive oil Indispensable for pasta dishes, salads, and many Mediterranean recipes, olive oil, the finest of all oils, varies in character from country to country. Choice is often a matter of personal preference. Generally speaking, Spanish olive oil has a strong flavor, Greek a heavy texture, Provençal a fruity taste, and Italian a nutty one.

There are two distinct means of pressing olives: the artisanal olive mill, where the olives are crushed and the oil is extracted by pressure in the traditional manner, and the modern mill where the oil is extracted mechanically. ("Cold-pressed" and "first-pressing" are terms less frequently used today because with hydraulic presses in modern mills the olive pulp is now pressed once only, and requires no heat to facilitate the extraction of the oil.)

The very best and most expensive olive oil, from whatever country it originates, is virgin oil, which is pure enough not to need refining. Virgin olive oils are separated into two grades: "extra virgin" (with 1 percent acidity) and "virgin" (2 percent acidity). Virgin oil is usually a greenish color—often helped by putting a few leaves into the press—but may also be golden-yellow. The best virgin oils come from green Provençal or Tuscan olives (the town of Lucca is reputed to

produce the best Tuscan olive oil). Use virgin olive oil in salads and in cold fish dishes, where its beautiful, fruity flavor can be most appreciated.

Cheaper oils, labeled simply "olive oil" or "pure olive oil," have been refined to remove naturally occurring impurities, and are usually blended with one another; they might then be mixed with a small proportion of virgin olive oil to improve the taste. Olive oil has a blander and less characterful flavor and a paler color than extra virgin and virgin olive oils, but is excellent for cooking. It is unsuitable for deep-frying as it cannot tolerate high frying temperatures.

Peanut oil Known also as groundnut oil in Britain and as *huile d'arachides* in France, this is the favorite cooking oil of those French chefs who do not cling to olive oil. It is also often considered to be a good replacement for olive oil, particularly when used for frying, as it has very little smell and no flavor.

Peanut oil is used for salads and mayonnaise when a delicate flavor is desired, although extra seasoning, lemon juice, or vinegar may be required. Less refined oil can impart a slight peanut flavor to food such as fried chicken. The Chinese, who use this oil a great deal in their cooking, like to flavor it by frying a few slices of fresh ginger, garlic, or scallions in it before use. Chinese oils are generally less processed than Western peanut oils and have more peanut flavor.

Corn oil This is one of the most economical oils for both shallow- and deep-frying, having one of the highest smoking points. Corn oil can also be used for salad dressings, although its detractors find it lifeless, weak, and flabby. Unrefined corn oil, sold in health food stores, has a distinct flavor of corn. Refined corn oil is practically tasteless when cold, but, surprisingly, it produces a strong and not particularly agreeable smell during frying.

Sesame oil There are various types of sesame oil. The thicker and browner the oil, the more aromatic it is. Light sesame oil has only a delicate nutty taste. It can be used for cooking and in salads and other cold dishes. Asian cooks use the dark oil, made from toasted sesame seeds, more for seasoning than for frying, as it burns easily. The Chinese believe that sesame oil added to seafood before cooking will remove fishy odors, but if it is added after cooking, to lamb, vegetables, and sauces, it imparts a pleasant, aromatic flavor.

Ali Baba's efficacious formula "Open sesame" was based on the fact that sesame pods burst open with a sharp sound to release their seeds. The jars in which the thieves hid were no doubt waiting for that year's sesame oil.

Sunflower oil Sunflower oil is light, mild, and thin. Excellent for cooking (although it has a relatively low smoke point), it is also good for using in

Almond oil

Corn oil

Olive oil

Extra virgin olive oil

Grapeseed oil

Walnut oil

combination with more expensive oils when making delicate salad dressings. It is the best oil for recipes where a fairly neutral oil is required.

Safflower oil This oil, so often confused with sunflower oil, is made from the safflower, a pretty thistle-like plant with orange, red, or yellow flowers. Usually a deep golden color, safflower oil is found refined in supermarkets and unrefined in health food stores. It is very light and can be used in the same way as sunflower oil.

Canola oil This bland oil, which is also known as rapeseed oil, is widely used in Mediterranean countries and in Asia for frying and salads. It has become quite popular in the United States in the last few years because it's the lowest in saturated fats of all oils, and only olive oil has more monounsaturated fat. Consequently, it is the oil that is most recommended for use in the diets of heart patients, and has been seized upon by other cholesterol-conscious cooks.

Canola oil is also often blended with other oils to make margarine.

Mustard seed oil Although mustard seed oil has a distinctive smell and taste when cold, most of this dissipates when the oil is heated. This oil is used in parts of India as an alternative to ghee, and in northern Indian curries. It is also used as a preservative in pickles and relishes, including Italy's colorful *mostarda di frutta*.

Soybean oil More oil is produced from the soybean than from any other plant, and most of that oil goes into blended vegetable oils, shortening, and margarines. A good brand, marked 100 percent soybean oil, is quite pleasant in salads, although it tends to have a heavy texture.

Grapeseed oil This light, aromatic oil is a by-product of the wine industry and is popular in France and Italy. The seeds yield a golden oil. Used in salads and for gentle sautéing, this oil comes into its own as the best cooking medium for *fondue bourguignonne* (beef fondue).

Walnut oil Cold-pressed from the new season's walnuts, strong, and with a deliciously nutty flavor, this is an unusual salad oil. Best mixed with a lighter oil, or used a little at a time, as a flavoring, it is especially good on a spinach salad, with a few walnuts added.

Walnut oil does not keep well, so it should be bought in small quantities as needed and kept in the refrigerator. This oil is also very expensive, and is not suitable for frying.

Almond oil When almond kernels are simply pressed, they produce a clear, pale-yellow oil. In European countries, the oil obtained from the bitter almond is used to make a fatty oil that can be used for candy making. When further processed, this oil becomes oil of bitter almonds, a flavoring now often produced synthetically.

Wheat germ oil Extracted by cold-pressing, this strong, nutty-tasting oil is mainly taken by the spoonful as a vitamin E supplement. It is also used in salad dressings, either by itself or, since it is expensive, blended with other oils.

Vegetable oils The most economical oils are the highly refined, pale-golden oils that are a blend of vegetable products—soybean, cottonseed, rapeseed, palm, and coconut oils. They have little taste, but their high smoking point makes them good for frying. Unlike other vegetable oils, palm and coconut oils are high in saturated fat and not suitable for low-cholesterol diets.

Flavored oils Many flavored oils are available in supermarkets and gourmet shops, usually based on olive oil to which flavorings such as herbs, garlic, and sun-dried tomatoes have been added. These are good in dressings, mayonnaise, and other cold preparations—heating can greatly reduce their flavor and aroma. Chile oil—sesame oil tinted red by the hot chiles that have steeped in it—is much used in Chinese cooking.

You can make your own flavored oil by dropping herbs, spices, or aromatics—for example, chiles, sprigs of rosemary or fennel, or lemon zest—into a jar or bottle of good olive oil and leaving it to steep for about a month so that the flavoring can permeate the natural olive oil flavor. A good mixture to use for Provençal cooking would be tiny dried chiles, thyme, and peppercorns.

Peanut oil	*Safflower oil*	*Asian sesame oil*	*Sunflower oil*	*Soybean oil*	*Canola oil*

Grains, Thickeners, and Breads

GRAINS

Besides yielding flour for our daily bread, grains are the staple foods of many countries. The polenta of Italy, the couscous of North Africa, the kasha of Russia, the porridge of Scotland, and countless other grain dishes are all basically the same thing: a local grain, in one form or another, cooked in steam or boiling water until swollen and tender, and then eaten either on its own or with whatever else makes up the local diet.

Wheat

One of the first cereals to be cultivated, wheat has become the most valuable of all food grains, widely used in all its stages, from whole and unadulterated to finely milled and sifted. When "flour" is called for in modern recipes, it is wheat flour that is meant. Broadly speaking, the wheat flours can be divided into those made from the high-gluten hard wheats grown in hot, dry areas and used for bread and pasta and the soft wheat varieties grown in temperate places, suitable for cakes, cookies, and general use. The terms spring wheat and winter wheat refer to the time of year the wheat is planted, not to any specific variety.

Wheat berries or whole wheat grains are available in health food stores. To eat them as a grain, soak them overnight before cooking and then boil in plenty of water for about 1 hour. Eat them in the same way as rice with meat, fish, or vegetables, or mixed into a salad.

Cracked wheat is simply the whole wheat berries cracked between rollers. It is eaten in the same way as wheat berries, but takes only about 20 minutes to cook. It is also good cooked like porridge as a hot breakfast cereal.

Bulgur (sometimes called burghul) is wheat that has been parboiled or steamed; it is then dried and some of the bran removed before the wheat is cracked. This process makes the grain easier to cook and gives it a less pronounced flavor and a lighter texture. Eat it in place of rice, or in the Lebanese salad called tabbouleh, for which bulgur is mixed with chopped onions, parsley and mint, olive oil, and lemon juice.

Bran consists of the thin, papery outer covering of the wheat grain. It is a by-product of the refining processes of wheat and can be bought in health food stores and many supermarkets. For extra fiber,

sprinkle it on breakfast cereals, eat it plain with milk and sugar, or add it to bread, cake, and cookie doughs and batters.

Wheat germ is the heart of the wheat grain, and is often extracted or destroyed during wheat-refining processes. It can be bought toasted and raw from supermarkets and from health food stores. Wheat germ should be kept in the refrigerator, since the oil in the germ quickly turns rancid (it is often extracted from wheat flour to improve the flour's keeping qualities). Sprinkle it on breakfast cereals or mix it with yogurt. When baking bread, sprinkle wheat germ on the sides of the greased bread pan for a nice finish to the loaf.

Semolina When wheat grain is first milled, it is separated into bran, wheat germ, and endosperm—the floury part of the grain. It is the first millings of the creamy-yellow endosperm that are known as semolina.

Semolina is quite widely used in making desserts, ranging from milk and fruit puddings in England to sweet, round Indian cakes, for which the semolina is first fried and then mixed with raisins, nuts, and honey. The finest ground semolina, called semolina flour, is used to make one kind of Italian gnocchi. Semolina milled from hard durum wheat (Triticum durum) is used to make most commercial Italian dried pasta. Flour-coated semolina grains make couscous, part of the excellent North African dish of the same name. Couscous semolina can be purchased precooked; choose the quick-cooking type rather than instant couscous.

Whole wheat flour This is flour from the whole wheat grain. Stoneground flour has a better flavor than the roller-milled supermarket types, since the slow grinding of the stones doesn't overheat and destroy the vitamins in the wheat germ. However, the stoneground flour does not keep as well, so do not buy more than a month's supply and keep it in the refrigerator. Whole wheat flour makes a dense loaf with the warm, earthy taste of the wheat. Using all whole wheat flour would result in a very heavy loaf, so a good compromise is to mix whole wheat flour with bread or all-purpose flour, either in equal amounts or with a higher proportion of the white flour. To make pastry dough with whole wheat flour, sift the flour first and use the fine

part in the dough. When the dough is kneaded and ready for shaping, roll it in the remaining coarse particles of bran.

Graham flour was developed by the Reverend Sylvester Graham, inventor of the graham cracker. It is a whole wheat flour that is somewhat coarser and flakier than regular whole wheat flour.

Whole wheat pastry flour is lighter in texture than whole wheat flour and so produces a less dense dough. Baked goods made with whole wheat pastry flour retain some of the sweet, nutty taste of the wheat. Ground from soft wheat, whole wheat pastry flour makes good cookies, pancakes, and waffles and can be used for pastry dough.

All-purpose flour is a blend of soft and hard wheats, and contains virtually none of the grain's bran or germ. However, any flour that doesn't contain the wheat germ is required by law to be fortified, so some of the lost nutrients are restored during processing. Unbleached all-purpose flour, which has been allowed to whiten and mature naturally, has a creamy color and a better flavor than the bleached variety, which, as its name suggests, has been whitened artificially. All-purpose flour is suitable for all types of baking, from bread to light sponge cakes to pie dough, and in cooking, for coating and thickening.

Bread flour is ground from hard flour and is unbleached. It is suitable for all yeast baking, as its high gluten content gives a stronger crumb structure, and it makes excellent loaves and pizza dough.

Cake or pastry flour is the refined and bleached product of soft wheat. Soft wheat flours produce only a small amount of gluten and so give a light, short texture in baking. They are very good for cakes, biscuits, and pastry doughs but are not recommended for yeast baking. All-purpose flour can be substituted for cake or pastry flour, but use 2 tablespoons less all-purpose flour per each cup of cake or pastry flour called for in the recipe.

Self-rising flour is all-purpose flour mixed with baking powder and salt. The baking powder will gradually lose its potency, so use up a box of self-rising flour within 2 or 3 months.

Instant flour is a granular flour that blends well with hot or cold liquids, without lumping. It is used mostly for thickening gravy or sauces.

Corn

Corn (the word was once the generic term for all grains) is second in importance only to wheat. There are countless varieties—some hard, some soft, some golden or white, some red, even some purple. Corn is a New World plant, and Europeans call corn maize, from the Native American word for it.

Cornmeal is ground from white, yellow, or blue corn, is available in coarse and medium grinds. The best cornmeal is ground by the old millstone method, but stoneground cornmeal does not keep as well as cornmeal ground by more modern processes. It should be bought in smaller quantities and kept in a cool place or in the refrigerator.

Throughout the United States there are various traditional cornmeal dishes, such as griddled johnny cakes (or jonny cakes), deep-fried hush puppies, and spoonbreads, lightened with egg whites. Cornbread is often served with chili, and in the South it usually accompanies fried chicken. Fried cornmeal mush is served with syrup for breakfast.

In the south of France, cornmeal is mixed with wheat flour to make rough, flattish loaves. The northern Italian dish of polenta, essentially cornmeal mush, is eaten both soft and, after it has set, sliced and fried. Cornmeal imported from Italy and labeled polenta is sold in gourmet markets; other coarser-ground cornmeals may be used as well.

Hominy is an old Native American name for hulled and dried white or yellow corn. It can be bought either dried or cooked, in cans. The dried grains must be soaked overnight before use. Hominy is also available ground and is then known as hominy grits. The whole grains are cooked and eaten as a side dish, as well as being added to stews. Coarse-ground hominy grits cooked in milk and served with butter and syrup or with gravy is a traditional Southern breakfast dish. Medium- or fine-ground grits are used in cakes and puddings, and to give body to casseroles and stews.

Masa harina is the flour used to make tortillas, and is a hominy relative. It is ground from white corn that is soaked in

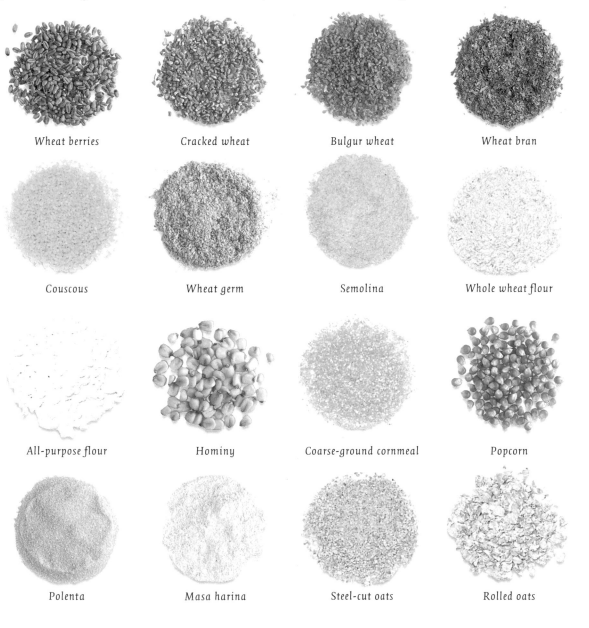

Wheat berries · Cracked wheat · Bulgur wheat · Wheat bran

Couscous · Wheat germ · Semolina · Whole wheat flour

All-purpose flour · Hominy · Coarse-ground cornmeal · Popcorn

Polenta · Masa harina · Steel-cut oats · Rolled oats

limewater. Masa harina can be bought as a wet dough, in Latin American markets, or dried in many supermarkets.

Cornstarch is the white heart of the corn kernel, ground to a silken powder. In England it is known as cornflour. Used primarily as a thickening agent, cornstarch can also be added to cakes, shortbread, and biscuits to give a fine-textured result. A little cornstarch added to an egg custard will stop it from curdling.

Corn flour is finer than cornmeal. It is used for breading foods, as well as for pancakes or waffles and some baked goods. It may be yellow or white.

Oats

These are among the most nutritious of all cereal grains. Being rich in oils, oats soon become rancid, so do not buy more oats or oat products than you can use in about 3 weeks, and keep in a cool place.

Whole oat groats are the whole grain with just the tough outer hull removed.

Steel-cut oats are also called Irish or Scottish oats, and are groats that have been cut into several smaller pieces. Steel-cut oats are good in thick soups and stews. In the British Isles, medium oatmeal, which is cut finer, is also available. It is traditionally used in the north of England and in Scotland to make oatcakes; it is also used for porridge, and to give bulk to sausages.

Rolled oats are oats that have been steamed and flattened between rollers, a process that makes them quicker to cook. Oatmeal takes only 10 minutes to make when using rolled oats. They are a popular ingredient for cookies and muffins, and in Britain they are used to make "flapjacks"—sticky, chewy cookies. Uncooked or toasted rolled oats are the main ingredient of granola and of its cousin, the Swiss breakfast cereal called muesli.

Oatmeal flour is ground from whole oat groats. It can be used in breads and other baked goods; in Britain, it is used for scones and oatcakes.

Rye

This strong-flavored and hardy grain is particularly popular in Scandinavia, Russia, and Germany.

Rye berries are the whole kernels with only the tough outer hulls removed. Boiled until tender, they can be added to stews or mixed with rice.

Rye flour is widely used in bread making in many parts of Europe, and makes a rather heavy and distinctive loaf. Coarse-ground dark rye flour goes into pumpernickel bread; the flour is often called pumpernickel as well. The more finely ground dark rye flour is used for European and Russian black breads. Light rye flour contains less bran than the dark. Light-colored rye breads are made with a combination of rye flour and wheat flour. European rye breads are traditionally made with a sourdough starter. Rye flour is also used to make Scandinavian crispbreads.

Barley

Although more widely used for brewing beer or making whiskey than for eating, barley has a pleasant nutty taste and can be cooked in a variety of ways.

Hulled or whole-grain barley is the whole grain minus the outer hull. Steep it overnight and cook for several hours, then eat it like rice or add it to stews.

Pearl barley is the polished grain. It comes coarse, medium, or fine and will cook to tenderness in 1½ hours or less. It is traditionally used in Scotch broth, to which it adds body and a smooth taste.

Barley flour Ground from pearl barley, barley flour can be added to wheat flour when making bread.

Rice

At least one third of mankind eats rice as its staple food. There is an enormous number of varieties, each with its own special properties, and it is important to choose the right variety for the right dish.

Brown rice is any rice that has been hulled but has not lost its bran. To the regret of dieticians, polished white rice is usually preferred to brown rice, which contains more nutrients, particularly vitamin B (a deficiency of which causes beriberi). It takes rather longer to cook than the white variety. Brown rice is available in short, medium, and long grains. Long and medium grains are best eaten as a vegetable, or as a basis for a pilaf. Short grains are delicious when used to make rice puddings.

Long-grain white rice   Short-grain white rice   Brown rice   Wild rice

Arborio rice   Basmati rice   White glutinous rice

Long-grain white or polished rice has a long, milk-white grain. It can be simmered in twice its volume of water, cooked in plenty of salted boiling water for about 15 minutes, until just tender, or steamed. The center of each grain, when cooked, should have a slight resistance but no hint of chalkiness. Well-cooked white rice produces a lovely mound of separate grains, good for pilafs, salads, stuffings, and most dishes.

Converted rice This is steam-treated long-grain white rice. It is actually more nutritious than one might think, because it is processed before it is hulled and so has the chance to absorb the bran's nutrients before the bran is discarded.

Basmati rice is available in Asian markets and now in many supermarkets, and is a superior long-grain rice. It is slightly more expensive than regular white rice, but its better flavor and consistency are well worth the extra cost. Before cooking, it sometimes needs to be carefully picked over for any bits of grit and husk, and should then be rinsed thoroughly under cold water. Basmati is ideal for pilafs and as a soothing foil for highly spiced Indian dishes.

Jasmine is an aromatic long-grain Thai rice that is similar to basmati. It is available in many supermarkets as well as Asian and specialty markets.

Short-grain rice is, in fact, a shortish version of long-grain species. When cooked, the grains swell enormously without disintegrating. Popular in Europe, it is very suitable for puddings, whether baked in the oven until caramel-colored within and brown on top, as in England, or cooked on the stovetop and served with sugar and cinnamon as in Germany. This rice is also suitable for making rice rings and for stuffings.

Italian risotto rice These rices have medium-short, roundish grains that are either white or creamy in color. The best varieties include Arborio, which is widely available, and Carnaroli and Vialone Nano. Their grains can absorb a great deal of liquid over a long period without becoming soft or mushy. This, and their distinctive flavor, make them ideal for risottos as well as for any dish such as paella or jambalaya that needs long cooking. Italian rice is often paired with strong-flavored foods such as squid, white truffles, and wild mushrooms, for which it is an excellent vehicle.

White glutinous rice Much used in Asian cooking, this short-grain rice has fat, round, pearly white grains that cook into a sticky mass; it is also called sticky or sweet rice. It must be soaked overnight before steaming or cooking in water. Glutinous rice is also ground into flour, to be used for sweet dumplings, cakes, and pastries, and it is fermented to make low-alcohol wines, such as the Japanese sake and mirin and Chinese Shaoxing, as well as rice vinegar.

Black glutinous rice This rice has a nutty flavor and is used in Southeast-Asian desserts.

Wild rice grows in North America, and is actually the seed of an aquatic grass related to the rice family. Wild rice is expensive, but it has a distinctive, nutty flavor not to be missed. To cook wild rice, add it to a large pot of salted water and bring it to a boil, then reduce the heat, cover, and simmer for 45 to 60 minutes, or until the grains begin to open. Serve plain or in salads, or mix into stuffings for poultry and game birds.

Rice bran is particularly high in dietary fiber. It can be added to cookie or bread doughs for extra texture.

Rice flour is polished white rice finely ground to a silky consistency. Health food stores also sell a coarser, off-white rice flour ground from brown rice. A little rice flour can go into a walnut or hazelnut torte of the type that uses no flour, only grated nuts. It is a useful thickener for dishes to be frozen (wheat flour-thickened sauces are prone to separating when reheated after freezing).

Buckwheat

Buckwheat, a plant related to sorrel and rhubarb, grows in great quantities in northeastern Europe. Buckwheat is available toasted or untoasted. When it is toasted, it is usually called kasha. The toasted grain has a nutty flavor and is a staple in Russian and Eastern European cooking. Kasha comes whole and ground fine, medium, or coarse. Cooked whole-grain kasha is the perfect foil for goose and a comforting dish in cold

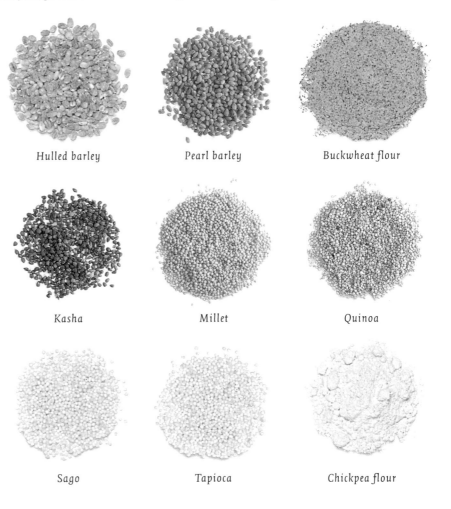

Hulled barley · Pearl barley · Buckwheat flour

Kasha · Millet · Quinoa

Sago · Tapioca · Chickpea flour

weather. Buckwheat is the correct flour to use for Russian blini—small, speckled, yeast-risen pancakes that are eaten with caviar. It is also used to make crêpes and can be added to other, lighter flours when making bread.

Millet and sorghum

Millet is invariably sold hulled because the husk is extremely hard. Its greatest characteristic is that the grains swell enormously—at least five parts water are needed to one part millet. Millet has a blandish, slightly nutty taste. It is best cooked and eaten like rice, but bear in mind that a small handful produces a large helping. To reduce the cooking time, toast the grains a little in a dry heavy pan on the stovetop before putting them in the pot to boil. Millet can be toasted, like buckwheat, and cooked like kasha. The cooked toasted whole grain is excellent with sour cream as an accompaniment to chicken. Millet flour produces flattish breads and is best combined with wheat flour.

Sorghum is a close relative of millet and can be eaten in the same way, but in the United States, it is more commonly used as animal feed. A sweet syrup is processed from the sorghum plant.

Quinoa

This tiny South American grain is a healthy addition to the diet, being higher in unsaturated fats and lower in cholesterol than most other grains and very rich in nutrients. Rinse it well, then cook it like rice and use in dishes where its subtle, delicate flavor can provide the background for more assertive flavors, just as rice and couscous do.

Tapioca and sago

Tapioca, prepared from the tuberous roots of the tropical cassava plant, or manioc, is tasteless and starchy. Pearl tapioca is made into the creamy pudding. Tapioca flour is used as a thickener.

The starch obtained from the stem of the Southeast-Asian sago palm, sago is usually exported in pearl form. It comes in varying sizes and consists purely of starch. In Asia and Europe, it is most commonly made into sweet puddings, which are thought to be easily digestible and so are fed to children and the elderly. In Norway, sago is made into a soup with sugar, egg, and sherry. It is sometimes used as a thickener in the United States.

THICKENERS

All starchy meals and flours will, in the presence of heat and moisture, act as thickeners. They cannot simply be used indiscriminately, but the cook can experiment with the two broad categories. Finer flours, before being added to the pan, must first be blended to a lump-free paste with a little of the cooking liquid or with some butter, to make a beurre manié.

As an alternative to all-purpose flour for thickening soups, stews, gravies, and other such dishes, try using something a little more robust, such as fine-ground cornmeal or whole wheat, barley, or chickpea flour. These will add flavor and color as well as body. If you have none of these at hand, a crustless slice of bread or a boiled potato, mashed and blended with a little of the liquid, will work too. Chickpea flour, also known as gram flour or besan, is much used in Indian cookery. It makes a very good batter and is used for *pakoras* (spicy Indian fritters).

Fécule is the general French name for starchy powders used in cooking. It is usually associated with potato flour, which is the thickening agent used by cooks in many European countries when making soups and gravies. The other very fine, quick-thickening flours, such as cornstarch, arrowroot, tapioca flour, and rice flour, are all virtually tasteless. They have double the thickening power of wheat flour, turn translucent when cooked, and are suitable for thickening delicate chicken or game dishes and sauces. Arrowroot and potato flour are particularly suitable for thickening fruit sauces because they turn completely clear when cooked. Arrowroot is also ideal for cooking at low temperatures— an advantage when making such things as sauces that contain eggs. Take care not to overcook these fine flours, as they tend to lose their thickening power.

Yeast and baking powders

When buying flour for baking, you will probably also need a leavening agent, such as yeast for bread, pizza dough, and rolls, and baking powder for biscuits and cakes.
Fresh yeast or compressed yeast is a pale beige, pasty substance that should be solid but crumble easily; it should have a clean, sweet, fruity smell. It will keep for a couple of weeks in the

refrigerator and for several months if stored in the freezer; if frozen, it will need to be thawed thoroughly and brought back to room temperature before use. Look for fresh yeast in health food stores and the refrigerated section of some supermarkets; sometimes a bakery will also sell you fresh yeast.
Active dry yeast has now virtually replaced fresh yeast. It will keep for several months if stored in a cool, dry place, and needs to be dissolved in warm liquid to be reactivated. Never use more of this yeast than the recipe calls for, or you will have a coarse, sour-tasting loaf that quickly becomes stale. Quick-rising dry yeast makes doughs rise in about half the time of regular yeast.
Brewer's yeast Old cookbooks called for brewer's yeast, which was bought at breweries or skimmed off homemade beer and was very temperamental. The brewer's yeast sold these days for home brewing is not suitable for baking.

The brewer's yeast found in health-food stores has no leavening properties but is high in vitamin B. It should be treated as a nutritional additive to mix into drinks and sprinkle over foods.
Baking powder combines acid (such as cream of tartar) and alkaline substances (baking soda) that act together when they come in contact with moisture to create carbon dioxide bubbles; these expand during baking to give a fine and delicate-textured result. Baking powder also contains a small proportion of cornstarch to absorb the moisture in the air. It is sold in airtight containers, and great care should be taken to keep it dry, because any hint of moisture will set the chemicals working. Double-acting baking powder is the most common type today, sold in every supermarket. It reacts in two stages, first when it is combined with a liquid and then later when it is exposed to the heat of the oven. Single-acting baking powder, not often seen, releases all its carbon dioxide when mixed with a liquid; if you use the single-acting type in a recipe, you must work quickly once the liquid and dry ingredients have been combined so that the resulting carbon dioxide cannot escape. You can make your own baking powder: use two parts cream of tartar to one part baking soda.
Baking soda is alkaline, and will work alone as a leavener, without baking powder, in a recipe in which there is

an acid ingredient present, such as buttermilk, orange juice, or molasses.

Cream of tartar is a fine white powder crystallized from grape acid. It is an ingredient of some baking powders. A pinch or so helps increase the volume and stability of beaten egg whites.

Ammonium carbonate (sometimes called hartshorn because it was once derived from that deer's horns) is used in Scandinavia as a baking powder to produce light, crisp cookies.

BREADS

The qualities of the plain white loaf are, of course, proper for such things as breakfast toast and croutons, but there is a host of other breads, of completely different tastes and textures. Small artisan bakers are producing a great variety of specialty breads in different parts of the United States today, often inspired by classic European breads.

French bread is most often seen in long sticks, or *baguettes*, and has a hard, crisp crust and a wide-holed crumb. When made in the authentic French manner, it will keep only a few hours, but it is bread at its very best. A thick slice, either plain or toasted, is often floated in soups and consommés.

Light rye bread has a satisfying sour flavor and is popular for sandwiches, particularly those of roast beef, pastrami, or ham and cheese. And of course it's essential in a Reuben sandwich. Light rye bread is also good with smoked fish.

Dark rye bread and pumpernickel A dark rye loaf, with its hard, thick crust, will keep fresh for a week or more, while pumpernickel, which often contains molasses, loses its moisture quickly— it is best wrapped in foil and then stored in a cool place. Both these dark breads should be sliced very thin and are good in open-faced sandwiches, with smoked ham, cheese, or smoked fish.

Bagel These are the ring-shaped rolls that are boiled before baking, and are a well-known Jewish specialty. Cream cheese or cream cheese and lox (smoked salmon) are classic accompaniments. There are endless varieties of these shiny, chewy rolls, including onion, poppy seed, garlic, and egg.

Croissant The soft, doughy crescents that are such an essential part of the French breakfast, these are made from a rich dough of milk and flour layered with butter. Eat hot with butter and jam, or on their own with a cup of good coffee.

Brioche These are rich, feather-light rolls with a crisp golden crust, made from a dough of milk, water, eggs, and butter; they also come as large loaves. Eat warm with butter and jam, sliced and toasted, or hollowed out and stuffed with perhaps sautéed mushrooms or pâté de foie gras.

English muffin These are very popular for breakfast or brunch, when pulled or "forked" in half and toasted. Top with almost anything, sweet or savory.

Crumpet These well-known British breads, about the size of an English muffin, are toasted first on the underside and then on the holey top, then eaten piping hot and dripping with butter.

Bap These are soft, floury rolls from Scotland. They are eaten straight from the oven, split and spread with butter.

Pita bread is originally from the Middle East. It is only slightly leavened and forms flat, hollow rounds. Eaten hot, the breads

Brioche

English muffin

Crumpet

Bagel

Croissant

Scandinavian crispbread

Pumpernickel

Pretzel

Naan

Rye bread

are sometimes cut in half and filled with grilled lamb and salad. They are always eaten plain with Greek meals, at which it is customary to tear off a bit at a time to use as a scoop for hummus.

Focaccia is thought to be Italy's oldest bread, is usually shaped into a flattened round or slab. It was traditionally baked on a hot stone in a wood-fired oven. The bread can be simply flavored with salt and herbs, or other toppings—such as sautéed vegetables, garlic, olives, chopped tomatoes, and cheese—can be added before baking.

Ciabatta is an Italian slipper-shaped bread with a soft, chewy crust. Freshly baked, it is excellent with salads, soups, and pasta dishes. It can also be used for sandwiches, particularly those with Italian-inspired fillings.

Tortilla This unleavened Mexican bread is made with either masa harina or with white or whole wheat flour. Corn tortillas are fried and filled to make tacos or enchiladas, or are simply fried until they are crisp to make tostadas. Plain wheat tortillas are eaten hot to accompany a main course, or they are filled and

rolled or folded to make burritos, fajitas, quesadillas, and so on.

Chapati Unleavened Indian breads made from *atta*—fine-ground whole wheat flour—chapatis are eaten hot with curries and many Indian dishes. They are torn into pieces and used to pick up the food.

Puri This is a deep-fried, puffy, air-filled Indian flat bread.

Paratha is a shallow-fried, butter-enriched, unleavened Indian bread.

Naan, nan Naan is a teardrop-shaped, rich, leavened Indian bread. It is traditionally slapped onto the side of a charcoal tandoori oven to cook. Other versions of naan, made in different sizes and shapes, are eaten throughout Central Asia.

Crackers and crispbreads

There is a huge array of crackers and crispbreads—and their relatives—on the market today. A few varieties, however, deserve special mention.

Scandinavian crispbreads or flatbreads (*flatbrød*) are generally made from rye flour. They are popular with some dieters, as rye is the most filling cereal

and so gives one a feeling of satisfaction with relatively fewer calories. These can be eaten spread with almost anything—sweet or savory. Available in light and dark varieties, they are sometimes sprinkled with sesame seeds.

Matzo This crisp unleavened Jewish flatbread, similar to a plain cracker, is traditionally made with only flour and water. Matzos are good when eaten with butter or cheese.

Poppadom, pappadom These wafer-thin, crisp Indian breads are available plain or spiced, and only need to be grilled or deep-fried for a few seconds. Eat them immediately, with curries or drinks.

Pretzel These are often studded with salt crystals, and are available twisted into many shapes and sizes. They are usually crisp but some varieties are soft inside. They are best served with drinks or cheese or simply as a snack; the soft ones are good with spicy mustard.

Breadsticks are also known by the Italian name, *grissini*, and are long, thin sticks of bread with a fine texture, baked until crisp. Eat with drinks, or to accompany an Italian meal instead of bread.

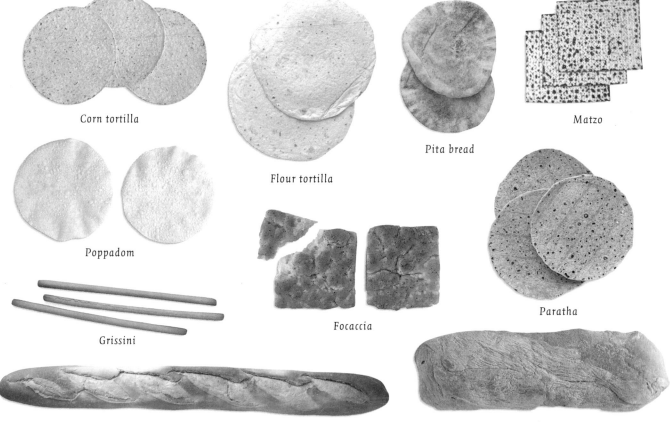

Corn tortilla

Flour tortilla

Pita bread

Matzo

Poppadom

Focaccia

Paratha

Grissini

French bread

Ciabatta

Pasta, Noodles, and Dumplings

Six hundred or so pasta shapes are made in Italy—most Italians rely on a daily supply of pasta in one form or another to keep up their spirits. Many other types of pasta come from China and Japan, where noodles and stuffed dumplings are an important and ancient part of the classic cuisine.

Pasta

Records show that the Chinese were eating pasta as long ago as the Shang dynasty, some 3500 years ago, and it was long believed, rather romantically, that Marco Polo brought pasta to Italy from the court of Kubla Khan. But Etruscan murals in Tuscany show all the kitchen equipment needed for pasta making, from the kind of wooden table still used to roll it out on (so far Formica has not replaced it in Italian households) to the fluted wheel with which to cut pappardelle, lasagne, and ravioli. Even without the murals, the story had been put in doubt by the estate of a military man who died in the thirteenth century, leaving among his effects a precious chest of *maccheroni*.

Whatever its origins, the Neapolitans have always been Italy's most serious pasta eaters, and Naples and the surrounding area have long been regarded as the center of the dried pasta industry. Certainly the best flour for pasta making, milled from the extra-hard wheat *Triticum durum*, comes from the hot, dry south. This flour absorbs a minimum of water as it cooks. The warm, dry, windy climate means, too, that fettuccine, for example, can be dried in the open air, swathed like curtains over long canes that are supported on tall stands—although with industrialization, modern factories have taken the place of the old traditional family enterprises.

Although dried pasta made in the United States can be good, most experts agree that Italian pasta is superior; some assert that the pasta made in southern Italy, especially the Abruzzi, is the best. When buying dried pasta, make sure it is a clear yellow color without any chalky grayish tinge. Thinner pastas should be translucent when held up to the light, with the exception of dried egg pastas, which should be a sunny bright yellow.

Pastas can generally be described as long or short; round, tubular, or flat; smooth or ridged; solid or hollow. An attempt to classify their shapes by name, however, is a problem, since one shape can have several different names and sizes. The north of Italy insists on one appellation, the south another, and even different regions quite close together cannot reach agreement. Miniature pastas, or *pastine*, which come in every shape you can think of, from stars to cars to apple seeds, are in a category of their own. They can be made from egg pasta or plain pasta (without eggs), and are generally cooked and served in *brodo*— in chicken or beef broth and in soups.

The long, round, solid pastas that are coiled around the fork, such as spaghetti, vermicelli, and spaghettini, are generally eaten dry (*asciutta*)—as opposed to in broth—with oil or butter, a tomato-based sauce, or a seafood sauce. Meat sauces, with the exception of Bolognese sauce, are not generally eaten with these, as they do not cling to the pasta well. Short, hollow pastas, such as conchigliette and penne, are the ones to serve with meat sauces as the pieces catch easily in the pasta's hollows and curves.

The larger short, hollow pastas, such as cannelloni and manicotti, are usually boiled and then stuffed with cheese or meat before baking. Macaroni, ziti, and rigatoni are sometimes boiled and then baked in a sauce in the oven—perhaps as part of a molded shape called a timballo, which is among the oldest of all pasta dishes. Lasagne and tagliatelle can also be baked in this way, as can farfalle, conchiglie, ruote, and lumachine.

Serve short, ridged, hollow pastas with cream sauces, since they will catch the cream and do not slip off the fork. Tagliatelle and other flat fresh pastas are generally eaten with rich meat or vegetable sauces, and the same dough is used to make stuffed pastas such as ravioli, anolini, tortelloni, and tortellini.

Spaghetti This is the best-known of all pastas. It is marketed in a number of widths that go under such names as cappellini, spaghettini, vermicelli, and thin or thick spaghetti. Fusilli is a spiral spaghetti, available in long and short lengths. The thicker ones are better with rich sauces, while the thinner ones are better with plainer sauces.

Spaghetti has long been the traditional pasta of Naples, and the traditional way of eating it is still *alla napoletana*—first tossed with oil and then topped with a ladleful of tomato sauce. Naples also eats its spaghetti *all'aglio e olio*—pasta bathed in olive oil with sautéed garlic. Grated *grana* cheese such as Parmesan or pecorino is served with all spaghetti dishes except those with seafood, such as *spaghetti alla vongole*. This is made with tiny clams and is another Neapolitan specialty, although it is, of course, much enjoyed all over Italy.

Macaroni It is not known how the idea of making the tubular pasta called macaroni, or *maccheroni*, started. But the most likely theory is that someone wrapped a piece of rolled-out pasta around a filling, leaving the ends open.

Macaroni comes in an even greater range of sizes than spaghetti. Apart from the long variety, such as bucatini, with center holes that can be measured in fractions of an inch, there are also those that can be measured in inches, or half-inches, such as cannelloni—but these are despised by purists as too modern, invented solely to make filling our pasta easier. However, we ought to be grateful that we are not obliged, as was the composer Rossini, to fill our macaroni with the aid of a silver syringe. He is said to have used this for filling pasta with foie gras, for which he had a passion.

Apart from bucatini and cannelloni, there are ribbed rigatoni, ziti, short or long, penne—cut to resemble quills— and elbow macaroni—the curved, short lengths of macaroni that are used in baked pasta dishes.

Macaroni used to be virtually the only pasta known and loved by English-speaking countries. Called macrow, it was eaten at the court of Richard II of England, in the late fourteenth century. It fell into decline, but was rediscovered by eighteenth-century Englishmen on the Italian part of their "grand tours" and taken back to Britain. Soon macaroni and cheese became an important high-tea dish, and it is now an American classic (in fact, it has even been "rediscovered" by some upscale restaurants).

Egg pasta In northern Italy, until recently, housewives made egg pasta, or *pasta all'uovo*, daily, with eggs and flour. Emilia-Romagna, the area with the richest farming land in Italy, was renowned for its beautiful handmade pasta, and young women from that region were keenly courted by young men—and their mothers—for their pasta-making skills. Egg pastas are richer and lighter than ordinary pastas.

Pasta making is a craft, and to see an expert rolling out a golden circle of dough, as thin as fine suede, to the size of a small tablecloth is a wonderful experience. In Bologna, the gastronomic center of Emilia-Romagna, you can watch it being made in a shop window. It is then turned into tortellini—little stuffed, folded-over pasta triangles—at lightning speed in front of your eyes.

Fresh pasta can be made at home (when, in Italy, it becomes known as *pasta casalinga*), either by hand or with a pasta machine. Perfectionists say the former is better as the machine squeezes the pasta and tends to give it a slippery surface that does not hold sauces as well.

In fact, a great deal of the *pasta all'uovo* now eaten in Italy and elsewhere is made in factories. By law, dried Italian pasta must contain five eggs to each kilo (2.2 pounds) of flour.

The best-known of the egg pastas is fettuccine, or—as it is called in northern Italy—tagliatelle: those golden strands that were supposed to have been inspired by the long blonde hair of Lucretia Borgia. In Bologna and Parma and all the other places of gastronomic pilgrimage with which northern Italy abounds, the tagliarini (thin tagliatelle) is still normally freshly rolled out every day. Malfatte (which means badly made) are irregular shapes of fresh pasta.

Tagliatelle is, of course, even in Bologna, eaten not only *alla bolognese*, but also *in bianco*, mixed with plenty of melted butter, grated Parmesan, and cream; or *al burro*, with just butter and cheese. Bologna also eats its tagliatelle mixed with delicious strips of sautéed pancetta and grated Parmesan.

Lasagne Dried lasagne can be bought in long, wide, flat strips or in curly-edged pieces that will not stick together as readily as flat pieces do when boiling. Fresh lasagne can also be bought as larger sheets or squares, which are easier to fit into a baking dish. In Bologna, strips of green lasagne, or the narrower lasagnette (also called malfadine or trenette), are layered alternately with plain strips, and with Bolognese sauce and rich creamy béchamel sauce. This dish is baked in the oven and emerges, glazed here and there with deep golden flecks, as *lasagne al forno*.

Colored and flavored pasta Lasagne verdi (green) and fettuccine verdi prove that spinach has a special affinity with pasta. Both are widely available, colored by a small amount of spinach purée worked into the dough. Other colorings and flavorings for pasta doughs include tomato paste, saffron, squid ink, herbs, and coarsely ground black pepper.

Tuscany and Umbria serve a pretty mixture of yellow and green tagliatelle or tagliolini, which is called *paglia e fieno*, meaning "straw and hay." It is eaten with melted butter and cream and sprinkled, as usual, with Parmesan.

Whole wheat elbow macaroni

Conchigliette

Farfalle

Tomato fusilli

Gnocchi

Rigatoni

Tagliatelle

Spinach gnocchi

Ditalini

Ravioli

Spinach tagliatelle

Bucatini

Lasagnette

Spinach tagliarini

Whole wheat and buckwheat pasta Although Venice has always had its thick whole wheat spaghetti called *bigoli*, it is not common throughout Italy. There are, however, some relative newcomers, such as buckwheat and other whole wheat pastas, which are to be found in health food stores and some supermarkets.

Pastas such as whole wheat lasagne and macaroni and buckwheat spaghetti have a nutty flavor and are richer in vitamins and minerals than the more traditional pale pastas. They take longer to cook, as they contain far more fiber than pale pasta. The Italian whole wheat pastas are, on the whole, lighter than those made elsewhere.

Whole wheat and buckwheat noodles also feature in Japanese cooking. They are often eaten cold as a light snack in the late afternoon.

Stuffed pasta Pasta stuffed with a large variety of finely ground or chopped fillings is eaten throughout Italy. Parmesan cheese and mortadella sausage with pork and veal, diced or pounded and mixed with ground turkey breast, provide the traditional stuffing for tortellini and tortelloni. These are the curved half-moons that are the famous Bolognese version of ravioli; they are by custom eaten on Christmas Eve and for big celebrations. On these same occasions, Perugia, in Tuscany, eats cappelletti, or little hats, whose stuffing includes ground veal and sweetbreads or brains. The shells called conchiglie or the larger conchigloni and even lumache (the largest shells, whose name means "snails") can also be stuffed.

Throughout Italy, ravioli with delicious spinach, beet greens, or Swiss chard fillings are to be found. The chopped

Penne

Ziti

Ruote

Anellini

Tortellini

Vermicelli

Whole wheat lasagne

Cannelloni

Stelline

Lasagne

Plain spaghetti

Buckwheat spaghetti

leaves are mixed with soft white cheese such as ricotta, or with Parmesan or pecorino, bound with egg, and flavored with a touch of nutmeg or garlic, depending on the local preference. They can also be stuffed with pumpkin or squash, wild mushrooms, or even lobster.

Soup pasta If the dough and the basic shape of *pasta asciutta* are fairly consistent—allowing for a thousand and one small regional variations—the same cannot be said of soup pastas. The range of these is vast and includes both anellini and stelline, which are used for serving in clear broth, and larger varieties, such as farfalline, conchigliette, and ditalini, used for making hearty soups such as minestrone or *pasta e fagioli*.

Italy garnishes its soups with tiny car radiators, wheels, flying saucers, hats, boots, and letters and numerals, all made of pasta. The more traditional shapes include grains of rice and melon seeds, twisted bow ties or butterflies, stars, crescent moons, seashells of every description, rings, hoops, elbow macaroni, and noodles that are thinner than matchsticks.

These garnishes are sometimes cooked separately and added to the soup just before serving, as they tend to shed a bit of their starch and so may make a clear broth cloudy.

Pasta sauces Pasta of one kind or another is the main part of most Italians' daily diet, and there are almost as many pasta sauces to be found as there are types of pasta.

All the classic pasta sauces have their origins in regional cookery. They are made from what is readily at hand. Piedmont, with its famous white truffles, makes a delicious sauce of truffled chicken livers. Tuscany makes a richly flavored sauce with hare. Pounded anchovies, truffles, garlic, tomatoes, and onions go into the sauce that, in Spoleto, makes *pasta alla spoletina*. In Sorrento, there is a sauce made of zucchini. Pesto, the mixture of fresh basil, pine nuts, olive oil, garlic, and Parmesan or pecorino cheese, is served with linguine in Genoa. When Tuscany offers a cream sauce to accompany its tagliarini, it saves the sauce from blandness by adding a rich meat glaze (this is made from reduced stock).

Spaghetti alla carbonara, despite the story that it was created during World War II to please the Allied armies, with their vast appetites for eggs and bacon, is a specialty of Rome. The sauce consists of pancetta stirred into spaghetti with some Parmesan and beaten raw egg, which partly sets in the heat of the pasta. The secret is not to drain the spaghetti too enthusiastically, or the result will be dry.

In the Abruzzi and Molise regions of central Italy, one favorite sauce is made with lamb and green peppers, another with smoked pork and tomatoes. The pasta eaten there is *maccheroni alla chitarra*—long strands cut on a frame strung with wires like a guitar. In the Marches, the region between the Abruzzi and Emilia-Romagna, black olives preserved in a special brine are incorporated into the sauces, not only for pasta made with the conventional dough but also for a local variation that is made with a yeast-like bread dough. Chickpeas also appear, in a pasta dish that goes by the name of *tuono e lampo* (thunder and lightning).

Toward the south, sauces include red and green bell peppers and a fiery pinch of ground hot chiles. Since the sea is not far from any spot in Italy, there are often marine accompaniments, such as cockles and clams, and, in the Veneto, the region around Venice, a delicious black sauce is made with squid ink.

Gnocchi

In Italy, the dumplings known as gnocchi are eaten in the same way as pasta and at the same point in the meal, but they are not strictly speaking pasta. There are several local variations, made from ricotta cheese and spinach, or semolina, or mashed potatoes or potato flour. They are usually simmered gently in boiling salted water until cooked, when they rise to the surface. They are then served with a variety of sauces. Gnocchi are generally made fresh, the semolina variety being particularly easy and quick to make.

Nudels, nouilles, and dumplings

In the German-speaking countries, which are supposed to have introduced *nudels* into Italy in the Middle Ages, flat *nudels* have been eaten for centuries. They are often baked with golden raisins and sweetened lemon-flavored fresh cheese and served as a dessert; noodle *kugel*, or pudding, sweet or savory, is a traditional Jewish-American dish. In Alsace, in northeastern France, noodles are known as *nouilles* and are prepared in countless savory and delicious ways. Coq au vin, for example, is often accompanied by *nouilles*—which are always better fresh. In Alsace, we also find the ancestral dumpling known as *noque*, while farther south, in Austria, Germany, and Switzerland, it appears under the name of *nockerln*. By whatever name, it is a pasta dumpling and can be eaten with a number of different sauces.

Chinese noodles

Wheat flour, rice flour, arrowroot, and bean starch are the main ingredients of Chinese noodles. These come in a variety of thicknesses and shapes, some of which can be used interchangeably, and are often tied in bundles or coiled into square packages. The majority, however, are long, as these are thought to symbolize and encourage long life.

Although most Chinese buy their noodles, some do make their own. Fresh noodles are obtainable from Chinese markets and taste best when they are first parboiled and then steamed in a colander over boiling water. Once boiled or steamed, Chinese noodles become part of more elaborate preparations that often involve several cooking methods for one dish.

Soup noodles These are traditionally served in broth with a topping of finely cut meat or seafood and bright, fresh-looking vegetables. The cooked noodles are put into the bottom of the bowl, the hot broth is poured over them, and then the stir-fried meat or seafood and vegetables are added as the garnish.

In northern China, where wheat is the primary grain, wheat noodles, with or without egg, are used. Egg noodles are often sold in little nests, while pure wheat noodles may be packaged in bundles as well as in square-shaped nests. In the southern districts of China, where rice paddies abound, translucent white rice noodles are used. These range from coiled rice sticks in square packets to the thin thread-like rice vermicelli that comes tied in bundles. White arrowroot vermicelli is also available.

Cellophane noodles—also known as transparent or bean thread noodles, bean threads, or vermicelli—are made from ground mung beans. They are never served alone but are used in soups and in stir-fried or braised dishes, to which they add a distinctive slippery texture.

Fried noodles Crispy fried noodles, known as *chow mein*, are a Cantonese specialty. Since many Chinese restaurants in the West are Cantonese, these are among the best-known of all noodle dishes. They can either be flattened in a frying pan with plenty of seasoned oil and then turned like pancakes, or they can be fried gently with leftover vegetables and meat from a noodle and soup dish. Cellophane noodles can also be fried if a crisp garnish is all that is required.

Sauced noodles In the West, where Chinese thickeners such as lotus root flour are not readily available, sauced noodles, or *lo mein*, are usually served in sauces thickened with cornstarch. Since to the Chinese texture is just as important as taste, a crunchy element is often introduced into these sauces with matchstick slivers of bamboo shoots or crisp sticks of scallions and leeks. Protein is provided by meat or chicken, shrimp, or oysters.

Dumplings and spring rolls

Chinese dumplings, or wontons, are similar to the Italian ravioli. The delicate ingredients, finely minced and variously flavored, are wrapped in squares of fine noodle dough. They can be made at home in the same way as fresh pasta. Paper-thin wonton dough, cut into squares or rounds, can also be purchased at Asian markets. Boiled or steamed, wontons are often served floating in a clear broth.

One of the prettiest meals available during the day in a Cantonese Chinese restaurant is *dim sum*, which is often presented in a towering pagoda of baskets. Each one fits into the other and contains bite-sized morsels, such as steamed buns, savory pastries, and dumplings containing pork, shrimp, or other meat or fish fillings. *Dim sum* are ideal for a brunch or light lunch.

Paper-thin wrappers are also used to make spring and egg rolls, which are filled with a savory mixture of shredded vegetables and sometimes meat or fish and are then deep-fried.

Very thin, semitransparent rice paper wrappers, or *bánh tráng*, are used to make Vietnamese and Thai spring rolls. The wrappers, which are dried on bamboo mats in the sun, need to be soaked briefly in warm water to soften them before rolling them up around the filling mixture.

Japanese noodles

There are four main types of Japanese noodle, all of which play an important part in the national cuisine. *Soba* are thin, brownish noodles made from buckwheat flour. They are used in soups and sometimes served cold with a garnish. *Harusame* are equivalent to Chinese cellophane noodles and can be deep-fried, or soaked and then cooked in various dishes. *Somen* are very fine white noodles—you can substitute Italian *vermicelli* if *somen* are not available. *Udon* are made from white flour and are more substantial.

bamboo shoot
140
buckwheat flour
117–18
mung beans 128
rice flour 117
wheat flours 114
whole wheat and buckwheat pasta 123

Chinese Egg Noodles with Browned Garlic, Chiles, and Cilantro 346
Vegetable Stir-Fry on a Noodle Pillow 347, 347

Chow mein noodles

Somen

Soup vermicelli

Rice paper wrapper

Rice vermicelli

Cellophane noodles

Fresh egg noodles

Fresh wheat noodles

Wonton wrapper

Rice sticks

Fresh rice noodles

Wheat noodles

Arrowroot vermicelli

Udon

Egg noodles

Wheat noodles

Spring roll wrapper

Soba

125

Dried Beans

The dried seeds of podded plants were first popular many thousands of years ago. In Egypt, the Pyramids have been found to contain little mounds of dried beans—not only to sustain departed pharaohs on their journey to the next world, but also because Egyptians believed beans to be of particular help in conveying the soul to heaven.

Unfortunately, apart from the fact that they are an excellent and sustaining food, and very suitable for those about to embark on long journeys, beans have the annoying property of engendering flatulence. Perhaps this characteristic helped lead to their gradual banishment, after medieval times, from Europe's more elegant tables. Another probable reason for their steady decline in general appeal was the greater availability of fresh vegetables at that time.

It was not until this century, when the Western world found a new taste for simple, sturdy, regional foods, that dried beans and peas were seriously rediscovered. A growing interest in Indian and Middle Eastern cooking brought Eastern species to Western shelves, and with them the Indian word *gram*, which is one of the collective names for dried beans and peas, particularly the chickpea. In the United States, the term dried beans usually includes peas as well; in England, the collective name is pulse, originating from the ancient Roman word *puls*, meaning pottage, a thick stew.

Although thousands of species of beans and peas, botanically known as Leguminosae, now exist, they have many common characteristics. Flavor and mealiness may vary, but all have a straightforward earthy taste and satisfying sturdy quality. All are a rich source of protein and, being a healthy and body-building form of food, make a very sound substitute for meat, especially when combined with cereals.

A popular misconception is that dried beans have an indefinite shelf life. In fact, they should not be stored longer than a year, for they toughen with age and become difficult to cook. There are two methods of preparing them for cooking, both of which help to tenderize them. The most common method is overnight soaking, preferably in soft water, to which all dried peas and beans respond. The dried peas and beans sold

in the supermarket are usually quite clean, but it's still best to pick through them for stones or debris. The alternative to overnight soaking, useful when you are short of time, is the quick-soak method: put them into a pan of cold, unsalted water, bring to a boil, and simmer for 5 minutes. Cover the pan, remove it from the heat, and allow the beans or peas to cool. Then drain them and cook them as called for by the recipe.

All these vegetables should be cooked in soft water—a pinch of baking soda will soften hard water—and simmered rather than rapidly boiled. Unless very fresh, they require lengthy cooking. They should be salted toward the end of cooking—if salted at the start, the skins will split and the insides will toughen. A little fat added to the cooking water— salt pork, bacon, or oil—improves the texture of all dried beans and peas. When they are bought canned rather than loose or packaged, they are already cooked, and therefore only need rinsing and draining before heating.

Haricot bean, white bean The word haricot covers the botanical species of beans Phaseolus. It derives from medieval times, when dried beans were used chiefly to go into a pot containing a *haricot*, or *halicot*, of meat—meaning simply that the meat was cut in chunks for stewing. When English and French cookbooks specify dried haricots, what is meant are white beans, smooth and oval rather than kidney-shaped. In the United States, they are known, sensibly enough, as white beans.

Soissons are large and white, and are generally considered to be the finest white beans. They are used in the famous French dish *cassoulet*, from Toulouse, which is cooked with preserved goose, mutton, and sausage.

Flageolets are an important ingredient in another classic French dish, *gigot d'agneau*. They are a delicate pale green in color with a subtle flavor.

Cannellini are also called white kidney beans, and are much used in Italian cooking. They are popular in Tuscany in soups and in dishes such as *tonno e fagioli*—served cold with tuna fish in a garlicky vinaigrette.

Navy beans are also known as Yankee beans. Small and white, they are used in a variety of dishes, particularly for

Boston baked beans. At one time, these small round beans were served by the U.S. Navy—hence their name.

Great Northern beans are grown in the Midwest, and are larger than navy beans. They can be used in the same ways as navy or other white beans.

Pea beans are sought out by discerning New Englanders for authentic Boston baked beans, but, although they are smaller, they are used interchangeably with navy beans in canning.

Lima bean Also known as butter beans, these can be large or small. Although they are highly prized when fresh, the large dried bean easily becomes mushy when cooked and so is best used in soups and purées. When a recipe calls for either white or lima beans, it is the smaller lima beans that should be used.

Red kidney bean Probably best known for their part in chili con carne—although Texans, among others, think that beans have no place in real chili—red kidney beans are a staple in Central America. These are the beans that, with black beans, were cooked by the Central American Indians in their earthenware pots (still the best receptacle for baked beans, which should be served from the pot). After the introduction of lard from Spain, beans were often mashed, formed into a stiff paste, and fried to become *frijoles refritos* (refried beans)—still a very popular way of eating beans in Mexico. In this form they may be used to accompany a main dish, or as a filling for tacos or tostadas. Red kidney beans also appear in many dishes in New Orleans, particularly in red beans and rice. A smaller red bean, also called red Mexican bean or red chili bean, is used in many of the same dishes as the red kidney bean, particularly chili.

Black bean As well as being used interchangeably with red kidney and pinto beans to make *frijoles refritos*, black beans, also called turtle beans, with their glistening black skins and creamy flesh, are the staple of many soups and stews in South and Central America. There they are often baked with ham or other cured pork and flavored with garlic, cumin, and liberal amounts of chiles, and they are an essential ingredient in *feijoada*, the Brazilian national dish. In the South and other parts of the United States, black bean soup is a great favorite. The beans are cooked with a ham bone or hock, blended to the consistency of a heavy sauce, and served with chopped hard-boiled eggs and with slices of lemon floating on top.

Pinto bean Often mottled in color, the pink-splotched pinto bean grows all over Latin America and throughout the American Southwest. It is an ingredient in many regional stews and is often mixed with rice. Appaloosa beans are a recent hybrid of the pinto bean.

Cranberry bean The cranberry bean is often mottled like the pinto bean, but it is rounder and a darker red in color. It is popular in Italy, where it is known as the borlotti bean; mixed with pasta, it makes the soup called *pasta e fagioli*.

Black-eyed pea These white beans with their characteristic black splotch came to America and Europe from Africa, brought over in the late seventeenth century by the slave traders. The black-eyed pea thrives in warm climates and is a favorite food crop in the southern United States, where it is eaten fresh

as well as dried. It is often served with pork and corn bread, and is the essential ingredient in the dish called Hoppin' John—a mixture of black-eyed peas, white rice, and salt pork or bacon—which is traditionally eaten on New Year's Day to bring good luck.

Fava bean Also known as broad beans, these are the strongly flavored beans that form the basis of the Egyptian *ta'amia*, or falafel: deep-fried little patties made with soaked and pounded dried beans and flavored with garlic, onions, cumin, coriander, and parsley. Most often used in their fresh green state, as in the rib-sticking *fabada* from northern Spain—a mixture of beans, cured meats, sausage, and plenty of garlic—they become brown in color when dried.

Ful medame, Egyptian brown bean These small, brown, knobbly beans, actually a type of fava bean, are grown in Southeast Asia and in Egypt, where they are a staple food. In Egypt the cooked beans are usually sprinkled with garlic and parsley, with oil and seasonings passed separately. They also make a filling

for an Arabian bread to become a sort of meatless hamburger, eaten with tomato and onion salad, and they are good when served in a tomato sauce. These beans require lengthy soaking and cooking.

Chickpea, garbanzo bean The botanical name for this bean is *Cicer arietinum*—this is because of its alleged resemblance to the skull of a ram, although to those of us with a less-discerning eye it looks more like a small hazelnut. The flavor of chickpeas vaguely recalls that of roasted nuts, and indeed they are eaten with drinks in Greece. Like other dried beans, they should be soaked overnight before cooking. Once cooked, *ceci*, as they are called in Italy, are very good dressed simply with oil and eaten as a salad. The Italians also make chickpea soup, and mix them with pasta—a dish known as *tuono e lampo* (thunder and lightning). In France, where chickpeas are called *pois chiches*, they are stewed in good stock with herbs and also used in soups and as a garnish. In Spain, *garbanzos* form the basis of *olla podrida* ("rotten pot"; traditionally this contains chickpeas, chunks of meat,

Adzuki bean

Black-eyed pea

Black bean

Cranberry bean

Fava bean

Flageolet

Red kidney bean

Cannellini bean

Pinto bean

Lima bean

Mung bean

Navy bean

Soybean

Ful medame

Chickpea

pig's feet or ears, preserved pork, sausages, and vegetables, all simmered together slowly); in Portugal, they are combined with spinach and eaten with *bacalhau*—salt cod—and other dishes. In the Middle East, chickpeas are mashed with tahini, lemon, and garlic to make the delicious spread hummus, and Israel uses them for its version of falafel, which is so widely eaten that it has almost become the national dish. Chickpeas are a common ingredient of couscous, and they are also mixed with beef and vegetables to make a rich and filling Israeli dish called *deene*, or *daphna*. They are an important crop in India, where they are often cooked with garlic and chiles and tossed with aromatics before being fried with herbs and spices in the clarified butter known as ghee.

Split pea Although there are still some dingy-gray, whole dried peas to be had, most are now sold skinned and split, a bright green or golden yellow. Thick yellow pea soup—*ärter med flask*—is the traditional Thursday evening dish in Sweden, keeping alive the memory of the unpopular King Eric XIV—whose last

Yellow split pea

De Puy lentil

Brown lentils

supper eaten on earth, on a Thursday, consisted of this very dish. His brother had contrived to slip a dash of arsenic into this humble food, which would hardly have crossed royal lips had Eric not been imprisoned at the time by his eventual successor. Split pea soup made with green peas, or yellow ones, is popular throughout the United States and in many other European countries as well. Green split peas form the basis of a traditional English dish, pease pudding. Although an egg is sometimes beaten into the mushy pea mixture to make it creamier still, it is one of the characteristics of split peas, yellow or green, that they turn into a purée by themselves and do not have to be mashed. Nor do they have to be soaked before cooking.

Lentil Red, brown, and green lentils have all the virtues of dried peas and beans, and the additional one of needing less cooking time (particularly split lentils) and no presoaking. The small red split lentil, originally a native of India, becomes tender with about 20 minutes' cooking, quickly turning into a mush if overcooked. The brown lentil, the ordinary green lentil, and the green lentil of France, *lentille de Puy*, take a little longer to cook.

Lentils make excellent purées and soups. In Germany, they sometimes accompany roast duck, while in France, lentils cooked with garlic and flavored with a squeeze of lemon juice are eaten with a *petit salé*—hot salt pork.

Dal, Dhal This is not a particular type of bean but the Hindi word for dried beans and peas. Most packages labeled dal in the West will contain split varieties, such as chickpeas, lentils, and the pigeon pea, which is known as *tur dal*. They are not soaked but are cooked for 40 to 45 minutes and served spiced as a thick purée, or are mashed to make thick soups. Another of the dals, *urad dal*, is often ground and becomes the basis of the crisp Indian bread poppadom, without which no curry dish is complete.

Mung bean These beans, also called green gram or golden gram, can of course be cooked in the usual way, but they tend to become rather sticky. In India, they are ground into a flour, and the ground beans are the basis

Green split pea

Split red lentil

Green lentils

of some Chinese and Japanese noodles. In the West, mung beans are now chiefly used, like alfalfa seeds and soybeans, for sprouting.

Soybean The soybean is the most nutritious of all beans and the most easily digested. Better known for its products than for the bean itself, it is one of the few sources of complete protein. It has been periodically rediscovered by the West, but was first brought to Europe in the eighteenth century, when it confounded scientists with its amazing qualities. It is still the subject of considerable research.

But while the West has only recently started turning soybeans into steaks of tempeh and processing them into cheese, the Chinese have for thousands of years called soybeans "the meat of the earth." They use soybean curd—the bland cakes known as tofu, which readily soak up other flavors—as a substitute for meat, fish, and chicken. The extracted "milk" is used in cooking many vegetable dishes; soy sauce is used for flavoring; and a fermented paste made from the bean, called miso, is used as a basic seasoning in everything from sauces, soups, and salad dressings to casseroles and, when sweetened, in desserts and other sweets in the manner of jam.

Of the thousand or so known varieties, two soybeans are chiefly cultivated—one sort for commercial purposes, the other to be eaten both fresh (when young) and dried, in which case they are prepared and cooked just like other dried beans. Soy milk is a useful substitute for those allergic to dairy products.

Adzuki bean The adzuki, or azuki, bean is one of the most delicious of the dried beans, and also one of the more expensive. A native of Japan, it is small and red with a curiously shaped white-striped ridge. It is a fairly recent arrival in the West and is found mainly in health food stores and Asian markets.

The adzuki bean is cooked in the same ways as other dried beans, both in Japan and abroad, but since it is very much sweeter than most other beans, its flour is also much used for cakes and pastries in Japan, and the crushed bean is made into puddings and ice cream by the Chinese. It is one of the most easily digestible of all the dried beans.

Vegetables

SALAD GREENS

It was a scholarly seventeenth-century English diarist, John Evelyn, who said of a salad that it should be composed like a piece of music, with each ingredient playing its due part without being overpowered by anything of strong taste. Since his time, a salad has come to be widely regarded as an essential part of the everyday diet, so much so that in many countries it is served instead of a vegetable.

Exactly at what point of the meal to serve a green salad is a matter of taste. Ancient Romans, who regarded lettuce as a panacea for all ills, believed that its milky juices "lined the stomach," enabling people to drink more with their food. Accordingly, lettuce was served as a first course—as it is still sometimes eaten today, although hardly for the same reason, in the United States. It is becoming more usual, however, to eat it immediately following the main course, as in France and England, or at the same time, on a side plate or, not so agreeably, on the same plate (although this has something to recommend it in the case of such dishes as chops, steaks, or roast chicken because the meat juices mingle so delectably with the dressing).

Green salads should not meet their dressings until they are on the point of being served, since once dressed, they will rapidly become limp. A good compromise is to prepare the dressing in the bowl, put the crossed salad servers over it, and place the leaves lightly on top, without mixing them. Some people prefer to mix the dressing at the table, while Italians simply pour olive oil and then vinegar onto the salad—they say you need a generous person for the oil, a miser for the vinegar, a judge for the salt, and a madman to mix it.

To make sure that your salad greens are fresh and good, see that the leaves look vigorous and show no sign of brown. Inspect the trimmed parts: they should be sound, neither discolored nor soggy. The heavier the lettuce for its size, the more tightly packed it will be, giving you more leaves for your money.

A lettuce in good condition will stay fresh in the refrigerator if it is wrapped in a plastic bag to retard the evaporation of its moisture. Should it already have wilted, it can be refreshed by being plunged briefly into cold water, shaken dry, and then put into the refrigerator either in a plastic bag or wrapped in a damp dish towel.

Shortly before you use them, salad greens should be washed well and then thoroughly dried—either by absorbing the moisture by shaking the lettuce in a clean dish towel or by getting rid of it in a salad spinner or shaker. The leaves should be torn rather than cut, to avoid bruising.

Apart from being used in salads, lettuces and other leafy plants can be cooked. The less substantial the leaf, the faster it collapses, and while heavier leaves may retain a bit of body, lighter ones do not. For braising, choose small, plump lettuces and cut them in half or braise them whole.

Round and head lettuce

These vary greatly in size and crispness but have in common their general round shape. Although there are many varieties, ranging from soft to very crisp, there are three main types.

Butterhead or butter lettuce These are floppy, loosely packed, and delicate head lettuces. Bibb, a particularly melting variety, is prized in the United States; Boston is another favorite. Continuity, a variety grown in England, sports leaves with a reddish tinge to them. Butterheads tend to be rather floppy, a characteristic that is by no means a defect, as long as the loose leaves are fresh.

Iceberg Whereas there is not much joy in eating a tired and wilting butterhead, these hearty head lettuces, when fading on the outside, may still be full of vitality in the middle. (Despite the fact that all the head lettuces of this type are usually called icebergs, iceberg is actually just one type of crisphead lettuce.) Although not strong in flavor, icebergs are by far the crispest lettuces. They are usually sold without their aureole of outer leaves, looking like tightly wrapped heads of cabbage. Webb's Wonderful is a favorite British iceberg.

Leaf or looseleaf lettuce These lettuces have no heart at all. Instead of the leaves, which are often crinkled, becoming more tightly packed toward the center, they all splay outward from the middle. Some varieties have red-, bronze-, or ruby-tipped leaves. Lollo Rossa is a red-tipped, curly, and somewhat tough example of a looseleaf lettuce. It is a good salad lettuce but is often used indiscriminately as a garnish.

Romaine lettuce, cos lettuce

Far more elongated in shape than the round lettuces is the romaine or cos lettuce. Tall and large, with a nutty flavor to its vigorous leaves, it has a beautifully crisp and tender heart. Its two names—romaine in the United States and France and cos in England—testify to its origins: the Romans found it on the Greek island of Cos and brought it back to Rome, whence it was introduced to the rest of Europe. A lovely small variety, Little Gem, shares the same good qualities as ordinary romaine, and has a vivid young heart.

Celtuce

This tall Far Eastern specimen is among the less well-known salad plants. So called because it tastes just slightly of celery and looks rather like a head of lettuce with long, pale stalks and a head of leaves, it also used to be called asparagus lettuce. However, it tastes neither like asparagus nor much like celery, or even lettuce. The similarity to celery lies mostly in the crunch of the stalks, which, like celery, can be eaten raw, making a good salad when peeled and chopped. The similarity to lettuce is confined to the tender central leaves. The stalks can also be cooked like Swiss chard, and make a similar vegetable dish to be eaten with butter or a creamy sauce, while the tough outer leaves can be cooked like spinach.

Lamb's lettuce, corn salad

This is what you are served when you order a dish of *mâche* in France; the French name is increasingly being used in America as well by gourmet markets and trendy restaurants. The spoon-shaped leaves grow in dark-green rosettes, which are hard to wash as they harbor sand. It is more substantial than other lettuce and has a nutty taste that blends very well with the sweetness of beets for a winter salad.

Chicory, endive, and escarole

Wild chicory has pretty blue flowers, and is the ancestor of varieties now grown primarily for their roots. These are roasted and ground to make a coffee substitute. Its leaves are bitter and can be mixed with other salad greens.

Belgian endive First bred in Belgium, and sometimes called by its Flemish name, *witloof*, this is the best-known of the cultivated chicories. It is "blanched" by being grown in the dark or under sand or peat, and with its tightly furled leaves, it resembles a fat white cigar with a pale yellow (not green) tip. Sliced crosswise or with the leaves separated, it makes an interesting salad on its own, or it can be mixed with sliced orange or watercress and some oil and fresh lemon juice. In England, Belgian endive is called chicory.

What little bitterness there is in Belgian endive tends to come to the fore when it is cooked, so it is usually blanched in a little stock and a few drops of lemon juice before being braised. In this way it is particularly good with ham, veal, chicken, and pheasant.

Radicchio There are several types of this chicory introduced from Italy. Looking like miniature colored lettuces, the plants can be either deep ruby-red,

cream splashed with a fine wine red, or marbled pink. When they have not been carefully shaded, they look green or dark copper-colored and less pretty.

It is its beauty that recommends radicchio: it tastes much like a lettuce but with more bitterness, and has somewhat tougher ribs. It makes a very beautiful salad mixed with bright green lettuce and pale green escarole.

Curly endive and escarole The curly-leaved endive, often called chicory in the United States, and the broad-leaved escarole are more robust than the lettuce tribe. Although by nature they are bitter, they become less so when the jagged rosettes are shielded from the light and blanched to a succulent pale golden-green. Look for these in winter—they have much more character than most hothouse-reared winter lettuces.

Curly endive looks like a frizzy, pale greenish-white mop, and escarole has long, broad, crinkled leaves with a rather leathery texture and a pale yellow center. Prepare curly endive and escarole as you would any lettuce, but with a more highly flavored dressing; use them to give texture to a salad made of more delicate leaves, or on their own. A few walnuts and perhaps some small strips of bacon make good additions, and these are the greens to eat with a Roquefort dressing.

In Britain, escarole is often called by its variety name, Batavia, while the other names used for endive must stem from its Latin name, *Chicorium endiva*—in France it is known as *chicorée frisée*. French frisée, more delicate than regular curly-leaf endive but just as bitter, can be found in some gourmet produce markets, usually at exorbitant cost.

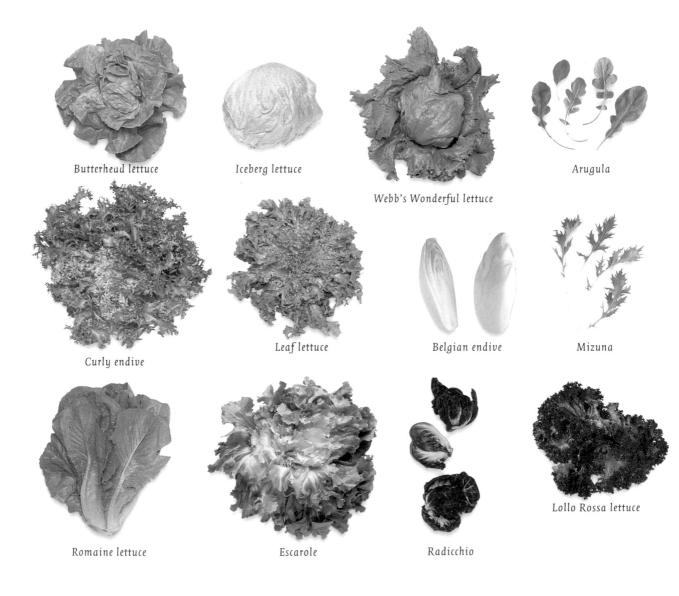

Butterhead lettuce

Iceberg lettuce

Webb's Wonderful lettuce

Arugula

Curly endive

Leaf lettuce

Belgian endive

Mizuna

Romaine lettuce

Escarole

Radicchio

Lollo Rossa lettuce

Cress

Watercress Dark-green, bunched sprigs of watercress make a beautiful garnish for grilled lamb chops or rack of lamb and game, and little sprigs enhance both the taste and look of a green salad or one containing sliced oranges. A watercress sauce is an excellent and pretty complement to fish, while nothing is fresher-tasting than a good watercress soup. When buying watercress, the rule is the darker and the larger the leaves, the better they are. Use watercress soon after purchase, keeping it meanwhile in the refrigerator in a plastic bag or in water, leaves down, like an upside-down bouquet, in a jelly jar—or even completely submerged in a bowl.

Other cress The tiny embryonic leaves of pepper cress, or curly cress, and garden cress are delicious in the thinnest and most delicate sandwiches—especially those containing hard-boiled egg or chicken, to which they bring a warm, sharp flavor—and as a garnish sprinkled over salads. Look for these and other cresses at farmers' and specialty markets; store them in the same way as watercress.

Arugula

This salad green, with its pale yellow flowers, looks something like a cross between mustard greens and radish leaves. The young leaves give a pungent, peppery taste to plain green salads, and in southern Italy wild arugula is used for extra flavor in the mixed salads eaten with pasta or veal. Arugula is also known as rocket, rugola, and rucola.

Mizuna

This feathery, delicate salad green has been cultivated in Japan since antiquity. Its flavor is mildly peppery, and it makes a good addition to *mesclun*, the mixture of young and tender salad leaves.

Radish

As a family, these roots belong to the mustard tribe, which, considering their hot pungency, is not surprising. In shape and color they range from little scarlet or white globes to long red and white types such as the Icicle radish. There is even a black radish, which has snow-white flesh.

Pungency varies not only according to type but also according to the soil in which the plants are grown. The elongated red-and-white type tends to be the mildest and goes by the name of French Breakfast radish, although one has yet to meet a Frenchman who actually eats them first thing in the morning. The most pungent of the pure white radishes is the type offered in Bavarian beer halls to encourage thirst. Except in Asia, where radishes are eaten as a full-fledged vegetable, they mostly provide an appetizer. As "they carry their pepper within," they can simply be dipped in salt and eaten with crusty French bread and butter, or may themselves be buttered and then sprinkled with sea salt. To serve them this way, wash them, trim off the roots and leaves, leaving a tuft about ½ inch long, and crisp them in the refrigerator with a few ice cubes on top. Radishes often appear on *crudités* platters, but they are more likely to be thought of as a garnish. In Italy, thin white slices of radish with their pretty red edges are scattered over green salads, perhaps with some equally thin slices of carrot.

Spring and winter radishes Radishes like the familiar globe, the French Breakfast, and the Icicle are

Lamb's lettuce

Watercress

Mustard sprouts and cress

Scarlet globe radish

French Breakfast radish

Icicle radish

Black radish

Daikon

all considered spring radishes. Their growing season may be as short as 4 weeks. Winter radishes, such as some black radishes, take much longer to mature; these large varieties, with flesh that is compact and firm, can be cooked or grated into salads.

Daikon This is the winter radish from Asia, the birthplace of radishes. Long, white, cylindrical, and enormous, with a less peppery flavor than ordinary radishes, it can be pickled, or grated and mixed with grated fresh ginger to make a sauce for stir-fried vegetables. It also features in tempura dishes.

OTHER GREENS

This group of green-leaved vegetables includes several that are now considered to be weeds. Once they were as well known as spinach, which, since its wide cultivation, has displaced them. But while spinach is now the most widely grown and popular of all our leaf vegetables, there should still be a place in the kitchen for its old-fashioned relations. All types of greens should be very fresh and need to be bought in generous quantities; this is because they will reduce significantly in volume when they are cooked.

Spinach

The long cultivation of spinach, since its first appearance in Persia many thousands of years ago, has resulted in succulent leaves of a beautiful green, which may be small and rounded—the best type to use for salads—or larger and more pointed, and either smooth or curly.

Since spinach greatly reduces in volume when cooked, you need to allow ½ pound for each person. If the stems are coarse, they should be removed, and the center ribs should be torn from larger leaves, by folding the leaf inward and pulling the stem toward the tip. The spinach should then be well washed in several changes of water to remove the grit it often contains. Cook over low heat, the pan uncovered, with only the water that clings to the leaves. As the lower layer softens, stir the spinach, and continue in this way until all the leaves have wilted. Spinach must be very thoroughly drained, because it tends to exude water after it is cooked.

Spinach can be used in a multitude of ways. As a side dish, it can be served simply with plenty of butter, or in a creamy cheese sauce, or as a purée with cream. Sweet spinach purée, although it sounds rather odd, is an ancient dish:

Queen Elizabeth I sat down to a bowl of boiled spinach mixed with rose water, raisins, vinegar, butter, and sugar. And a pastry shell filled with spinach and candied orange and lemon peel, bathed in a rich creamy custard, is a Christmas dish in southern France.

In Italy, there are dozens of lovely spinach recipes: spinach is eaten in soufflés, frittatas, and dumplings; mixed with ricotta, Parmesan, and nutmeg to make a filling for stuffed pasta; and used to make the fresh green pasta that looks so pretty when combined with a cream or tomato sauce. No wonder that on French menus a spinach garnish goes under the Italian name of *alla fiorentina*. Eggs Florentine are eggs arranged on a bed of cooked spinach under a covering of cream or cheese sauce; fish and sweetbreads *à la florentine* have spinach in the sauce.

Spinach can also be eaten raw: delicious salads can be made with small, young spinach leaves garnished with pieces of crisply fried bacon and hard-boiled eggs, tossed in a garlic-laden vinaigrette.

There are also some wild plants that are reminiscent of spinach in flavor, two of them so close to spinach in taste that they are sometimes cultivated.

Nettle

Purslane

Sorrel

Dandelion greens

Spinach

Chinese mustard cabbage

Collards

New Zealand spinach is a fleshy-leaved plant discovered by Sir Joseph Banks, botanist on Captain Cook's *Endeavour*, who brought it back to Europe. It is still grown outside its native land, flourishing where excessive heat and lack of water would make true spinach bolt. Somewhat tougher than true spinach, it may be sold in specialty markets, or at farmers' markets.

Malabar spinach This thrives in tropical Asia and in tropical parts of Latin America. The large, bright, shiny leaves have a distinctive but good taste and are treated in the same way as spinach. In China, it is cultivated for its fleshy berries, which yield a dye that has been used by women as a rouge and also by high-ranking officials for sealing documents.

Cabbage greens

Any member of the cabbage family that does not form a proper head becomes simply one of many "greens," sometimes called spring or winter greens. See that the center ribs are crisp and firm. Any woody stems, coarse center ribs, or damaged leaves must be ruthlessly discarded.

Collards are the Cinderellas of the vegetable world, but, like Cinderella,

Beet greens

Kale

they are good and can be quite splendid when properly dressed. The leaves are particularly tender and delicate when cooked. They are excellent for heartier side dishes such as the Southern "mess o' greens," which usually contains salt pork or bacon; the cooking juices are referred to as "pot likker." These braised greens are always eaten with corn bread to mop up the broth.

Kale or curly kale has crimped leaves, like frisée or chicory. It was known by the early Greeks and Romans, whose climate was too warm to grow cabbage. There are many varieties of kale; some are grown as ornamental plants, and there is even one type whose stems become so hard and woody that when dried they are made into walking sticks. The edible ones taste rather like spring greens but stronger, and can be used for all cabbage recipes.

Cavolo nero is an Italian kale with dark green, strong-flavored leaves. It is much used in vegetable soups or eaten sautéed in oil with chile pepper.

Beet greens

The first-century Roman gourmet Apicius included in his book recipes for beet greens with mustard, oil, and vinegar, and for barley soup with beet greens. Beet greens are still grown extensively in Italy and in eastern districts of France, where, together with Swiss chard, they are known as *blettes* and are used interchangeably with chard. They are often mixed with sorrel to counteract the latter's acidity, being themselves extremely mild but earthy. When cooked, beet greens are used like spinach, and in Italy they are very popular as a stuffing for ravioli or agnolotti, together with ricotta and Parmesan cheese.

Mustard greens

This dark green leafy vegetable is very popular in the South. The leaves have a hot taste and are delicious when lightly braised with garlic and chile flakes. The young leaves, far less pungent than the larger older ones, make a zesty addition to a green salad.

Chinese mustard cabbage or greens (*gai choy*) resemble collards in appearance. They are eaten fresh, as well as stir-fried, used in soups, and pickled in a sweet-sour sauce.

Sorrel, dandelion greens, and purslane

Sorrel Of all the different types of sorrel, it is the cultivated French variety that is best for eating, adding an acid, lemony note to salads, soups, purées, sauces, and omelets. The classic *potage Germiny* consists of sorrel cut into delicate ribbons—called a *chiffonade*—cooked in butter and then moistened with chicken stock and thickened with egg yolk. A purée of sorrel is the traditional accompaniment to grilled shad and is also an exceedingly good foil for salmon. Because sorrel, even more than spinach, is rich in oxalic acid, it should be eaten in moderation.

Dandelion greens In some countries, gardeners wage constant, if ineffectual, war against this golden flower, regarding it as a particularly troublesome weed. In other places, they carefully sow seeds and then take great trouble "blanching" the plants with soil or a cover to keep the leaves tender and white for use in salads. In France, where housewives buy dandelion greens from market stalls, they are called *pissenlits* (literally, "piss-in-bed," illustrating their diuretic properties—so those who are addicted to dandelions should be warned). Their other French name, which is the source of the English word, is *dent de lion*, meaning "lion's tooth," because of their jagged edges.

Weed though they may be, they are certainly useful. The roots can be used as a caffeine-free coffee substitute, and the leaves make excellent salads. Perhaps the best is the French *pissenlits au lard*, a bowl of small, fat, juicy, whole dandelion plants in vinaigrette, over which is thrown a panful of sizzling pieces of salt pork or bacon and bacon fat.

You can remove most of the bitterness from wild dandelion greens by placing a plate over a patch of young plants to blanch them. But the juiciest, least bitter dandelion greens are those grown from a packet of domestic seed. Blanch them before they start to produce flower buds, and pick them young.

Purslane A native of India, where it has grown wild for thousands of years, fleshy-leaved purslane spread to England in the Middle Ages and was popular pickled and as a salad. It was introduced to North America by the early colonists, but today most people discard it as a weed. In England, too, it was once cultivated in gardens, but it is now uncommon. The French are more astute and still consider purslane—which they know as *pourpier*—to be a salad plant worth cultivating. The succulent leaves can also be boiled, and are good when quickly fried in butter and then used to fill an omelet. In the Middle East, where it is also cultivated, purslane is an important ingredient in *fattoush*— a salad mixture including tomatoes and cucumber eaten with pita bread.

Wild greens

There are still many edible green-leaved plants growing wild and free which, if nothing else, can be regarded as survival food. However, much enjoyment can be had gathering these plants on country walks and experimenting with cooking and eating them at home. Make sure, though, that you know exactly what you are gathering. If you are uncertain of what the plants look like, take an illustrated field guide with you so that you can identify the plants you want to find.

Nettle Northern countries used to prize the nettle, but it is now something most people avoid because of its sting (which completely disappears when the nettle is cooked). In Scandinavia, the leaves were boiled like spinach, and the coarse fibers of the stalks used for cloth, in the manner of flax. (This explains, without making it any less sad, the task of the fairy-tale maiden set to stitching nettle garments for her seven brothers, to lift the spell that had transformed them into swans.) Ireland combined nettles and oats in a broth, but her nettle haggis— a purée of nettles, leeks, cabbage, bacon, and oatmeal boiled in a bag—would not, one imagines, pass muster with a Scot. Italians still eat nettle purée or soup in the spring, as it is supposed to be excellent for cleansing the blood.

Nettles should be picked when they are only about a finger-length high; later on, they become bitter and tough. Remember to wear gloves, and use scissors to snip off the leaves.

Goosefoot Goosefoot is better known in Europe than in the United States. In Britain, two of the more delightfully named members of the family are Good King Henry and Fat Hen, both of which were staples in antiquity but have now been superseded by spinach. Fat Hen is a tall, stiff-stemmed plant, which grows prodigiously wherever there are people— or weeds. It tastes much like spinach but is considerably milder. The leaves of Good King Henry are also treated like spinach, and some suggest that the shoots can be prepared and eaten like asparagus.

Amaranth The green leaves of this species, also known as pigweed, have a taste similar to spinach, although more tender and sweet. The celery-like stalks taste somewhat of artichokes.

Chickweed is so called because poultry has a particular yen for it. It grows in all temperate climates of the world. Probably the most common of all edible weeds, it is a tender vegetable that, cooked in butter with chopped onion, goes well with rich meats.

Brooklime This makes a perfectly acceptable, though slightly bitter, substitute for watercress. Brooklime is found by streams and in marshy places in North America and in northern Europe.

CRUCIFEROUS VEGETABLES

Cabbages that form a head are members of the vast Brassica family, which also includes cauliflower, broccoli, and Brussels sprouts (as well as turnips and kohlrabi, which are eaten, respectively, for their roots and their swollen stems). In America, brassicas are referred to as cruciferous vegetables, or crucifers; all the members of the family have gained more respect than they once had, for crucifers are believed to have cancer-fighting properties.

All crucifers are descendants of the wild cabbage, which still grows in coastal regions of Italy and France—a tough, tall plant, almost all trunk. They are rich in vitamin C and minerals, but half of the vitamin content is lost when they are cooked. They all contain sulfur compounds, which give them their characteristic "cabbagey" smell when they are overcooked.

Cabbage

There are three main types of cabbage that form a head, distinguished mainly by color and texture: green, Savoy, and red.

Green cabbage Early-season green cabbages are a deeper green and more loosely packed than the later ones, and often have pointed heads. Buy them in the spring, checking that the leaves— frequently curly at the edges—are fresh and crisp; if you're buying at the farmers' market, where they are likely to be sold with all their outer leaves intact, even the outer leaves should be tender. Do not worry about the lack of heart—they simply have not had time to develop the firmness associated with the later kind. The later-season green cabbages, the type we usually see in the supermarket, are altogether tougher, and have solid hearts.

Green cabbages that are the very palest of green, almost white, are called white cabbages, or sometimes Dutch cabbages, in Britain. They have smooth leaves and are quite hard and firm. These pale-white cabbages are used in the coleslaw mixes available in the supermarket produce department and in some commercial coleslaws.

Savoy cabbage The crimped-leaved Savoy cabbage is particularly tender and mild-flavored and needs less cooking than other cabbages. The Savoy's head

Bok choy

Napa cabbage

is quite firm, for all its crinkliness, and is a beautiful green with a touch of blue. It stands up well to frosty weather and is therefore readily available throughout late winter. This is the best variety for stuffing.

Red cabbage Although this cabbage has magenta or dark purple skin, the color fades during cooking unless a little vinegar is added (the flavor is also improved by this added sharpness). Red cabbage is at its most delicious when braised with oil or another fat, vinegar, sugar, and plenty of spices and flavorings, and it is also good eaten raw or pickled.

Buying and storing cabbage When buying cabbages, no matter what kind, look not only at the leaves, which should be sound and unblemished, but also at the core. This should be neither dry and split nor woody and slimy. Those heads that have wilted outer leaves or a puffy appearance should be avoided.

The firmer the cabbage, the longer it will keep—Savoys can be kept in the refrigerator for several days at least; green and red cabbages will keep for one week or longer.

Cooking with cabbage Red cabbage is cooked very differently from the green variety, with such ingredients as wine vinegar, red wine, apples, raisins, onions, brown sugar, and spices going into the pot after the cabbage has been sautéed in oil or butter (or goose fat).

A sweet-and-sour red cabbage dish is also much improved by the addition of some dried prunes during the cooking. Red cabbage is traditionally served with the Christmas goose in many northern European countries and is also excellent with pork or game.

The simplest way to cook green cabbage is to boil it, after removing the core and tough outer leaves, and

washing it well in a bowl of cold water with 1 tablespoon salt to deal with any creatures that might lurk between the leaves. Cut into quarters or shreds, it needs no more than a few minutes to cook—the moment it starts to sink to the bottom of the pot, it is ready—and it should be cooked uncovered.

The smell of overcooked cabbage is a dreary one, and the sodden leaves that mark overcooked cabbage have to take much of the blame for the ruin of Britain's culinary reputation. Yet cabbage that has been carefully cooked and gently but thoroughly drained, and then heated with a generous quantity of butter, makes a delicate, light vegetable dish. Long, slow cooking gives it a succulent texture quite different from cabbage cooked quickly and served quite green.

There are several good slow-cooked dishes in which the cabbage is started off with fat and onions and then cooked

rendered goose fat 110

Braised Red Cabbage 368

Cauliflower

Purple sprouting broccoli

Broccoli

Savoy cabbage

Red cabbage

Purple cauliflower

White cabbage

Brussels sprout

Green cabbage

with meat added to the pot, including the Irish-American dish of corned beef and cabbage. Then there are the filling, stock-based cabbage soups, poured over slices of bread for extra body, which make complete meals by themselves.

In northern Germany, there is the famous hunter's cabbage, with golden cubes of bacon bathed in a piquant sauce, which accompanies the equally famous bratwurst. In Bavaria, in the southeast, cabbage is braised with chopped bacon, caraway seeds, and white wine. The nineteenth-century Bavarian king of the dream castles, the eccentric Ludwig, liked to eat his cabbage braised with pike and served with a crayfish sauce.

Stuffed cabbages are a category of their own: stuffings of all descriptions are layered between the blanched and semi-unfurled leaves. Ingredients may include different kinds of meat, bacon, chicken livers, herbs, rice, onions, and chestnuts, all bound with eggs and possibly rice or bread crumbs. Cabbages can also be stuffed after being hollowed out, with their tops cut off but replaced before going into the oven; or the individual leaves can be stuffed and tied into little parcels.

Sweet-and-sour cabbage dishes are popular in Jewish cooking, and in Russia, cabbage baked with apples is eaten with smoked meats. From sweet-and-sour it is only a small step to sour; cabbage ferments and becomes sauerkraut when packed in a barrel with salt. Fresh sauerkraut, or that sold in plastic bags, is preferable to the canned or jarred versions. Raw green cabbage makes a good salad either as coleslaw, with its thick creamy dressing, or simply shredded into a bowl and dressed with oil and vinegar.

Chinese cabbage

A wide variety of cabbages is grown in China, and they frequently end up in large wooden barrels, coarsely chopped and pickled in brine. Pickled cabbage is often used for dishes that need a piquancy or bite to them.

The Chinese cabbage that we know best is a variety called, in Chinese, pe-tsai; we know it simply as Chinese cabbage, or Chinese celery cabbage, or as Napa cabbage. It somewhat resembles a large, pale head of romaine lettuce, and is crisp and delicate with a faint cabbage flavor. Its crinkly inner leaves are best used in salads, while the outer leaves, once divested of their tough ribs, can be braised, stir-fried, simmered, or treated like ordinary cabbages.

Another Chinese cabbage is bok choy, or pak choi. It has large dark-green leaves at the top of long white stalks. Bok choy is used in soups and stir-fried meat dishes as well as being prepared in the same ways as spinach or cabbage.

Broccoli

Like the cauliflower, broccoli started life in the Mediterranean region, where the warm, dry climate encouraged wild cabbages to shoot into buds rather than concentrate on making leaves. The earliest broccoli was the purple sprouting type, which has green stalks and loose green rudimentary flowers. Broccoli is a delicate vegetable, and the best broccoli can be said to combine the subtle, fresh texture of cauliflower with the succulence of asparagus.

Look for broccoli that is deeply colored a brilliant emerald green. Broccoli that is tinged with purple or bluish green is considered the best. The spears should look firm and fresh, and the florets should be tightly closed; avoid any that show the least sign of turning yellow.

Broccoli is best steamed or boiled briefly so that it still preserves some crispness. It is often eaten with hollandaise or a cheese sauce, or simply with butter and a squeeze of lemon juice. Bright green broccoli florets and pure white cauliflower make a lovely combination.

Sprouting broccoli The Romans ate purple sprouting broccoli either cooked in wine or dressed in oil and sharp garum—a sauce of fermented fish—and also added it as a garnish to a soup of chickpeas and lentils, peas, and barley. In Sicily, broccoli is still cooked in the oven with anchovies and onions. In the rest of Italy, it is often parboiled and finished off with oil, garlic, and chile flakes in the frying pan, perhaps eaten with pasta.

Although less succulent than regular broccoli, sprouting broccoli is a very fine vegetable. In addition to the purple sprouting broccoli, there are white and green varieties; the stalks of all types are usually cooked whole, with the small loose buds still attached, and served drenched in butter. Purple sprouting broccoli turns green when cooked; the others keep their original color. The flavor of all kinds is excellent, but sprouting broccoli must be picked young, or it becomes stringy and tough.

Cauliflower

Since early cauliflowers used to be no larger than tennis balls, one can justify the complaint made by six seventeenth-century travelers to Italy who rose from the table in a marble palazzo as hungry as they arrived, having shared among them one cauliflower, a dish of anchovies, and three hard-boiled eggs. Modern cauliflowers can be enormous, although ironically a strain no larger than golf balls is being grown once more. One type of cauliflower, originally from Sardinia and southern Italy, is purple but turns green when cooked and another is green with a pointed head. Another beautiful cauliflower, rather confusingly called broccoli Romanesco in the United States (but Romanesca or Roman cauliflower in the British Isles), is bright green all the way through— a more grassy green than broccoli. Its curds (these are so called because they resemble soured-milk curds) grow in whorls like a snail shell. And despite its name, the pale-green broccoflower is not a cross between broccoli and cauliflower, but simply a variety of cauliflower.

A fresh head of cauliflower will have a compact cluster of creamy white florets, or curds, and will feel heavy for its size. Loose or spreading florets mean the cauliflower is overmature.

When cooking cauliflower whole, test for tenderness after 8 to 10 minutes by carefully sticking a skewer into a side stalk; continue testing until there is little, but still some, resistance. Florets take 6 to 8 minutes and will cook more evenly.

Cauliflower needs sauce—a light creamy sauce flavored with cheese or mustard; or perhaps an Italian sauce incorporating chopped onion, capers, olives, and anchovies—or fried bread crumbs and chopped hard-boiled eggs. Cauliflower and cheese have a special affinity: cauliflower au gratin is a classic. Florets of raw cauliflower, as part of a plate of crudités, arranged around a bowl of mustardy mayonnaise, make a good cocktail party offering, and cold cooked florets in a mustard vinaigrette make a delicious salad.

Brussels sprout

At their best, Brussels sprouts look like tiny green buds, and at their worst, like miniature full-blown cabbages. Developed in Flanders, the vegetable garden of Europe, some time in the Middle Ages, Brussels sprouts grow at the intersection of leaf and stalk on a tall plant that much resembles the old wild cabbage. They have a delicate nutty taste, especially when they are small. Cooked until just tender but not too soft, they are an excellent vegetable.

The ideal size for Brussels sprouts is no bigger than about an inch in diameter; the smaller the sprout, the more tender. Do not waste much time before using them—they soon turn yellow. Look for compact green heads and uniform size so that they will cook evenly. Some people cut a cross in the stem, but this is really only necessary in large specimens cut from coarse, wide stalks; fresh small ones do not need such incisions. Prepare by washing and trimming off any yellowing leaves, then cook in rapidly boiling well-salted water without a lid so that they preserve their good green color.

Brussels sprouts are a traditional accompaniment to turkey, together with separately braised chestnuts, at many Christmas dinners. On less festive occasions, they appear simply tossed in butter, or with browned butter and toasted bread crumbs. If they are used to garnish a meat dish or game birds in France, the dish is called à la bruxelloise. Some people like Brussels sprouts with a white or cheese sauce, or with crisply fried and crumbled bacon.

SHOOTS AND STALKS

Although shoots and buds often look appetizing, there are in fact only a handful that make serious eating: the buds of the palm tree are familiar to us as hearts of palm, and asparagus and bamboo shoots are two of the best vegetables there are—particularly asparagus, one of nature's kindest gifts to man. Stalks are mainly enjoyed in the form of celery and sweet fennel, chard and cardoons, while the globe artichoke, a companion delicacy, is a flower bud.

Fennel

Looking like a short, bulbous celery plant, fennel is also called Florence or sweet fennel or finocchio, and it is sometimes incorrectly referred to as anise. Florence fennel is a close relation of common fennel, the herb, and the same feathery leaves can be seen emerging from its fat, overlapping stalks. Like the herb, it tastes of anise, and its leaves can be used to flavor a court-bouillon for a fish dish. Southern Italians eat it raw, very thinly sliced and simply dressed with a fruity olive oil or with garlicky aïoli; northern Italians slice and parboil it, then bake it with butter and grated Parmesan. It makes a very good addition to a green salad.

When braising fennel, allow one bulb per person. Trim away the base and, if the outer leaves are tough, string it as you would celery, then halve or quarter the bulbs. Choose rounded, fat bulbs in preference to long, thin ones, which tend to be less succulent. Buy fennel as fresh as possible; the bulb should be white in color and firm in texture—any yellowness is a sign of age. It will keep crisp in a plastic bag in the refrigerator.

Asparagus

Although there are many species of asparagus, ranging from the thorny ones of Spain to the shiny ones of the Far East, it is always something of a luxury because its season is so short. There are also many differences in the way it is raised: white French asparagus is cut below the sand that covers the crown once the tip has emerged above the soil; American and English asparagus is allowed to grow above the ground, which gives it its green color all the way down the stalk; Dutch and German ivory-tipped asparagus is always grown under mounds of soil, which help to blanch it, and it is cut as soon as the tips begin to show.

Whatever the color, the thick varieties of asparagus are usually the most

Sliced bamboo shoot

Globe artichoke

Cardoon

Fennel

Asparagus

Fiddlehead fern

137

expensive. The famed asparagus of Argenteuil, with their white stalks showing a purple tinge toward the top, and their pointed green and purple heads, are considered to be the very best, certainly in France, but this does not stop America from considering its more modest green asparagus to have a superior flavor. In fact, each of the great asparagus-growing areas, no matter the country, tends to prefer its own asparagus above all others, because although asparagus travels well, it starts to lose flavor from the moment it is cut. It is a revelation to eat asparagus fresh from the garden, cut and cooked within the hour or even sooner.

Thick or thin, the tips are the best part, and this is the part to inspect when buying asparagus. The tips should be tightly furled, with the scales close together, and none of them discolored or moist.

The difficulty encountered in cooking asparagus arises from the fact that the tips, being much more tender than the stalks, cook more quickly and may break off when you transfer the asparagus to the serving dish. The answer is to cook asparagus in an asparagus cooker or steamer, a special pot with a perforated insert. Failing this, cook them tied together in bundles in a wide shallow pan. With the second method, it is extremely important not to overcook the asparagus, or to boil it too fast, or the tips will become damaged.

To prepare the asparagus, wash it well, cut off the hard ends, and peel the lower part of the stalks with a knife or potato peeler. Then tie the asparagus into small bundles, if you are not using an asparagus cooker. Bring well-salted water to a boil in the cooker (or a wide pan). Lower the asparagus into the water (in the cooker just the stalks are in water; the tips will cook in the steam) and return to the boil as rapidly as possible. Cover and cook for 8 to 10 minutes, until the lower parts of the stalks are easily pierced with the tip of a knife. Don't overcook them—they should be just tender when pierced, and the tips will break up if boiled for too long. If you like, save the asparagus water as well as a few token stalks of asparagus for making soup. Serve the rest, carefully drained.

Asparagus can be served as a course on its own, at the beginning of the meal.

Swiss chard

Celery

It is best eaten with the fingers. Served warm, asparagus is best with melted butter, or with hollandaise or mousseline sauce (hollandaise with whipped cream added to it). In France, asparagus *à la flamande* has halved hard-boiled eggs and browned butter served separately. When it is served *à la polonaise*, the browned butter—butter that is heated in a pan until it is a pale hazelnut color—is poured over the tips, which have been sprinkled with finely chopped hard-boiled eggs. In Italy, asparagus is eaten with freshly grated Parmesan cheese and butter over the tips, melted just for a moment under a broiler.

If asparagus is to be served cold, either mayonnaise or a vinaigrette dressing is the usual accompaniment. As asparagus contains a certain amount of sulfur, it spoils the taste of wine, so save the wine for other courses when you are serving the asparagus separately.

Asparagus also makes a good vegetable dish, of course, and goes well with delicate, light meats: veal, sweetbreads, chicken breasts, slices of turkey, or rosy boiled ham, thinly sliced. And asparagus can also go into risottos or omelets.

Celery

Although this can be white or golden in color, which means that it has been blanched during cultivation or is the self-blanching kind, most of the celery in the market is the green Pascal variety. The ribs, or stalks, should be thick and crisp, the leaves green and full of vitality, and the base sound. Revive limp celery by wrapping it in moist paper towels and standing it in a jar of water. Celery should be thoroughly washed before use.

Raw celery is excellent served with cheese, standing in a tall jar with the decorative leaves intact; however, the coarse outer strings should be removed first. Do this by cutting partway through the rib bases and pulling off the attached strings down the length of the ribs.

Chopped, raw celery is often mixed with tuna or egg salad as a sandwich filling. Celery also goes into poultry stuffings and sauces, and can be stewed with bacon to accompany game and other meats. It is delicious parboiled and served *au gratin*, and it is equally good when braised in broth or water, or *à la grecque*—with olive oil and lemon juice—and eaten cold.

Swiss chard

Swiss chard is grown both for its pale, wide center ribs and for its leaves. Green chard, with its white ribs, is more familiar, but there is also red chard, with green leaves and red ribs, and ruby chard, which has reddish leaves and ribs. Although baby chard can be cooked whole, usually the stalks and leaves are cooked separately. The leaves can be prepared like spinach or beet greens, while the stalks have a delicate flavor and are extremely succulent when boiled or steamed. They can be served *au gratin* or simply with melted butter. In France, chard, or *blettes*, is served with béchamel sauce and sausages, while in Italy, it makes stuffings for tarts and ravioli or is chopped and cooked in risotto.

Globe artichoke

Although not strictly a shoot or stalk, but rather a bud, the globe artichoke is usually considered in the same group as delicacies such as asparagus. While some of its flavor lies in the fat base of each of its leaves, the best part—the *fond* (bottom)—lies deep within its center.

When you buy artichokes—they can be green or purplish—make sure they still have a good bloom on their leaves and that the centers are well closed, not looking almost ready to burst into great purple thistle-like flower heads. They don't keep well and should be used at once, but if you must keep them, place them in a plastic bag in the refrigerator.

To prepare artichokes for cooking, if the stalks are long enough, twist them off, which will also remove some of the tougher fibers from the base. Then, with a stainless steel knife, cut the base of each globe flush so that it won't wobble on the plate when it is served and rub the cut surface with lemon to prevent it from turning black. If the leaves are very spiky, cut them into a pretty V shape or simply trim off the tops. Wash the artichokes and then boil with a little lemon juice in a stainless steel or other nonreactive pan— perhaps with a slice of lemon tied to each base. Test for readiness by tugging at a leaf: when it comes away and is tender, the artichoke is done and ready to be drained upside down on a rack.

One of the best ways to eat globe artichokes is simply to pull off the leaves with your fingers, one at a time; dip the fleshy part in turn into melted butter, vinaigrette, or hollandaise, then draw it through your teeth, eating the fleshy part, and put the remains of the leaf on your plate. When you reach the tiny pale leaves in the center, which seem to be arranged in the form of a little pointed hat, grasp them tightly at the top and pull off the whole rosette. Then pull away and discard the prickly, straw-like choke, which may come away with one tug or

1

2

3

4

5

Preparing globe artichoke bottoms

As you work, rub all the cut surfaces with lemon halves to prevent discoloration.

1 Snap the stalk off at the base of the artichoke, pulling out the coarse fibers with it.

2 Bend a large lower leaf out and over toward the base until the leaf snaps, then pull it off. Continue snapping off all the large outer leaves in this way.

3 Cut off the cone of paler green, soft inner leaves, cutting straight across just above the hairy choke.

4 Using a small knife, trim off all the dark green parts from around the sides and base of the artichoke bottom, trimming it into a neat round shape.

5 Scoop out the hairy choke in the center using a teaspoon (or do this after cooking the artichoke bottom according to the recipe instructions). Cook the artichoke bottom immediately, or immerse it in water acidulated with lemon juice, to prevent discoloration.

need a bit of scraping. Finally, eat the bottom, which is slightly pitted, with a knife and fork.

It is possible to remove the chokes before cooking, to form little cups. The artichokes can also be trimmed and the artichoke bottoms then filled or stuffed, perhaps with a béchamel sauce and Parmesan, or with a purée of mushrooms. They are usually parboiled before they are stuffed, and then go into the oven, anointed with butter or oil, until the stuffing is cooked. For delicate dishes, or when artichoke bottoms are required as a garnish, all the leaves are removed and the bottom trimmed; this is often done in sophisticated restaurants, where artichoke bottoms, whole or trimmed, appear in various dishes.

Among the many ways of preparing artichokes, the Italians have produced the most inventive. They simmer artichoke bottoms in broth or wine, or in wine with oil, tomatoes, and garlic, and fry small, tender artichokes in oil. Sometimes they blanch the smaller ones and then dip them in batter before deep-frying them. As elsewhere, artichokes are also eaten cold in Italy.

Sliced sautéed artichoke bottoms may be mixed with peas and ham or scrambled eggs, and if in France you are given a soup called *Chatelaine*, you will find that it is made of puréed artichoke bottoms. In the south of France and some parts of Italy, tiny young artichokes are eaten raw, either whole with *aïoli* or *bagna cauda*—a hot anchovy-and-garlic-flavored dip—or thinly sliced and tossed with Parmesan in olive oil.

Seakale

Highly popular in earlier times, although less often seen now, this European plant is a member of the mustard family. A frail, pale vegetable, it grows wild in English coastal districts, forcing its stalks up through mounds of sand so that they emerge perfectly white. The juicy but delicate stems of cultivated seakale are sometimes found in the market.

Cardoon

A relative of the globe artichoke, the cardoon is cultivated for its young leaf stalks and has a flavor that faintly resembles that of the artichoke. Left to itself, it produces smaller, spikier heads than the artichoke, which in Greece are

picked and eaten stewed, but what you may find in markets in winter and early spring is the bottom part of the plant, looking like overgrown gray-green celery. Cardoons are grown covered with soil to blanch the stalks, which gives them their delicate texture and delicious flavor.

The finest cardoons are those from the region of Tours in the center of France, but since Italians enjoy their *cardoni* even more than do the French, you are likely to come across cardoons in Italian markets.

To prepare them, trim off the skin, which is fibrous and prickly at the ridges, blanch the cardoons in boiling water, and then cook them for about 30 minutes in a *blanc* (boiling water to which 1 tablespoon of flour has been added); this helps to keep the color, because, like artichokes, cardoons will discolor easily when cooked. Serve them with a béchamel or cheese sauce, or *alla piedmontese*—dipped into a sauce of anchovies, oil, and garlic—or simply eat them with melted butter. In North Africa, they are used to flavor meat stews.

Bamboo shoot and heart of palm

Edible young bamboo shoots—not all bamboos are edible—are bought fresh in the Far East and stripped of their tough brown outer skins before being eaten. Their texture is similar to celery and their taste to a globe artichoke.

The canned variety is the most readily available outside Asia. It needs no peeling, but it should be rinsed before use, whether packed in brine or water, because it otherwise has a pronounced tinny taste. Chopped bamboo shoots can be used in a number of stir-fried vegetable and meat dishes, and as a garnish for clear chicken broth. They can also be served with any of the sauces that are suitable for asparagus.

Hearts of palm are the buds of cabbage palm trees. Fresh hearts of palm are sometimes available in Florida, where they are grown, but in the rest of the country, only canned are available. The fresh ones need to be blanched before being cooked to get rid of their bitter flavor. Served hot, they are eaten with any of the sauces suitable for asparagus; cold, they need a vinaigrette dressing. They are also good in mixed salads. Hot or cold, they are usually served cut in half lengthwise.

Hop shoot

While the dried flowers of hops are used for brewing, the young blanched shoots, popular throughout Europe, can be cooked and eaten with melted butter, like asparagus. In France, where they are known as *jets de houblon*, they are considered to be a delicacy. Their delicate flavor goes especially well with creamy sauces. In Belgium, young hop shoots are served with eggs.

Fiddlehead fern

Found in the eastern part of the United States and Canada, fiddlehead ferns are not, in fact, a particular type of fern, but simply young ferns of any type, with their shoots still tightly coiled. The small, rich green shoots have a satisfying chewy texture and a flavor that has been described as a mixture of asparagus, green beans, and mushrooms. Eat them raw, in a salad, or sauté in butter with lemon juice and black pepper.

Bean sprout

Corn

PEA, BEAN, AND CORN

From the moment they are picked, peas, beans, and corn start converting their sugar into starch. Because this process subtly alters both their taste and texture, it is freshness just as much as youth that matters, and they should be chosen carefully and eaten the very day they are bought. Freezing, however, arrests these changes, which is why frozen peas, beans, and corn retain their sweetness and texture so well.

Pea

Once inordinately expensive and considered a great luxury, peas have become one of the best loved of all vegetables. Endless varieties have been developed, especially in England, where the climate suits them to perfection.

Garden pea The green garden pea is also known as the English pea. Although there are dozens of varieties of English pea, most have disappeared from the marketplace. The reason is, of course, the ubiquitous frozen pea—a great timesaver.

Green peas respond to all sorts of treatment: in the United States and England they are liked best of all plain, boiled and bathed in butter, although some cooks add a sprig of fresh mint. In Italy, peas are often mixed with fine shreds of raw ham, or with rice, in which case the dish becomes *risi e bisi*. In the countries, such as France, where vegetables are habitually served in a light coating of white sauce, peas, too, are given this treatment.

Contrary to popular belief, the small garden peas called petits pois are small not because they are immature but because they are a dwarf variety. These are the peas that are canned in vast quantities by the French and Belgians, and they are excellent: tiny, dull green, and very sweet, they are quite unlike most other types of canned peas, which are best avoided altogether.

Snow pea These are also called Chinese pea pods; as their French name, *mangetout* (literally, "eat-all") suggests, they are eaten pods and all. There are many varieties, all bred with the minimum of thin, tough membrane that lines the pod of the common green pea. Look for young snow peas, bright green and with scarcely visible seeds. If they have strings at the sides, these should be removed during topping and tailing.

Snow peas taste best when they are briefly boiled or steamed. When cooked, they should still have a little bite to them, and they are best served perfectly simply, with just enough butter to coat each pod. Very young snow peas are good in salads, and all snow peas are also excellent when stir-fried.

Sugar snap pea These are like snow peas in that they have an edible pod, but they are eaten after the peas inside have matured and swollen. As a result, the pod is lumpy rather than flat.

Béchamel Sauce 256
Fresh Peas with Lettuce Française 373
Peas in the Indian Fashion 373

Baby corn

Sugar snap pea

Okra

Fresh garden pea

Haricot vert

Fava bean

Snow pea

Green bean

Pole bean

Green bean

This is a general term that is used to describe beans with edible pods, but in fact they come in colors ranging from deep green and purple to pale yellow. The two main types, however, are the round green bean and the flatter pole, or runner, bean. Beans of either type may also be known as snap beans, because they should snap in half juicily if they are fresh.

Of the round green beans, there are dozens of varieties available. The highly prized haricot vert is slim and delicate and should be eaten very young, when it is no larger in size than the prong of a carving fork. The yellow wax bean is also a round bean and is somewhat mild in taste.

Pole beans have long, rough, and usually stringy pods, although stringless varieties are available. As their name suggests, they are a type of climbing bean, rather than a bush bean, like most other green beans. There is a delicious purple-podded pole bean that has stringless purple pods, but these turn the normal green when they are cooked.

Whatever the type, podded beans should always look both crisp and bright—avoid buying wilted ones or overly mature beans with tough-looking pods. They all need their ends trimmed, and some types still need de-stringing. Test for stringiness by keeping the top or tail end just attached to the pod and drawing it downward: if a portion of tough string comes away, careful de-stringing is indicated.

All podded beans are cooked in the same way. They should be briefly steamed or plunged into well-salted, rapidly boiling water and cooked until just *al dente*—too often they suffer from overcooking. Once drained, they can be tossed in butter until they glisten. Green beans especially can be served in a sauce containing shallots, or cream and butter with chives, or bathed in a tomato purée with a touch of onion.

Lima bean and fava bean

In their first youth, neither lima beans nor fava beans strictly require shelling, but the pods are nearly always discarded to reveal large, flattish seeds.

Lima bean These are named after the capital of Peru. They are most familiar in America in their shelled and frozen state, but are at their best when they can be bought fresh and in their pods. They appear in the American Indian dish succotash, which also includes corn. Lima beans are sometimes called butter beans in the South. There are two types of lima bean—the baby Sieva, pale in color, and the larger Fordhook.

Fava bean Also called broad beans, these are the original Old World bean, much appreciated in Italy and Spain. (*Fava* is the Italian name.) These large, lumpy beans with their furry lined pods should be shelled immediately before going into the pot, unless they are very young, in which case they need only to be trimmed and can then be cut up, cooked, and eaten pods and all. Older fava beans will need skinning after they are cooked.

For a plain dish of lima beans or fava beans, plunge the shelled beans into a large pan of rapidly boiling water and cook until they are just tender, but not a moment longer. These beans are also delicious with cooked ham or bacon.

Okra

These curved and pointed seed pods originally came from Africa. They traveled to America with the slaves and feature a great deal in Creole cooking. The flavor of this vegetable resembles that of eggplant, but the texture is mucilaginous, and this is what gives the body to the Creole stews and gumbos to which okra is added.

Crossbreeding has produced a range of colors and surfaces, but the slim, green, octagonal okra is the one that is usually sold in our markets. Look for small, crisp pods and avoid any that are shriveled or bruised.

To cook okra whole, trim off the tip and the cap, but be sure not to expose the seeds and sticky juices inside, or the okra will split and lose shape during cooking. Steamed or cooked in boiling salted water until tender, okra can be served with a tomato sauce or simply tossed in butter, or it can be used in vegetable ragouts and stews.

Corn

One of the delights of late summer is the appearance on the market of fresh, tender young corn. The husks should be clean and green; the silk tassels bright and golden-brown with no sign of dampness or matting; and the kernels plump, well filled, and milky, with no space between the rows. Avoid ears with dark yellow kernels or older large ones that look tough and dry.

When dealing with fresh corn, time is of the essence—the briefer the span between picking and eating, the sweeter and more tender the corn will be. There are now supersweet varieties being bred that will stay sweeter much longer than other types, but even with these, the fresher, the better. If you are not able to use corn immediately, then keep it stored in plastic bags in the refrigerator for no more than 2 or 3 days. Be sure to allow the corn plenty of space—if the ears are piled on top of one other, this will tend to generate warmth and "cook" the corn.

To cook corn on the cob, strip away the green packaging and silk tassel, then steam or plunge into briskly boiling water. A little sugar can be added for extra sweetness—especially for the corn sold in Europe, which is never quite as sweet and tender as American corn. Never salt the water used for boiling corn—salt will toughen it. Serve with plenty of butter, salt, and freshly ground pepper, and with large napkins. Fresh corn on the cob can also be grilled, either in the husk (don't soak the husks first, as many books advise—you'll just be steaming the corn) or out, and it can be roasted, husked, in a hot oven.

Baby corn, which is imported from Thailand, is a popular addition to stir-fry dishes. It has a crisp yet tender texture but not much flavor.

Bean sprout

The sprouts that can be bought in plastic bags, or sometimes in plastic boxes, and are an ingredient in many Asian dishes have usually been sprouted from mung beans or soybeans. Look for crisp, pale sprouts; even a hint of exuding brown juice means that they are past their prime.

Mild-flavored bean sprouts will add a crunchy texture to a range of salads, or they can be stir-fried briefly over high heat and seasoned with soy sauce, fresh ginger, garlic, and scallions. Always serve the sprouts immediately, or they will lose their crunch.

Keep bean sprouts in their plastic bag or box in the refrigerator while they are waiting to be used.

THE ONION FAMILY

The onion, or Allium, family, including garlic and leeks, has a great many members, both cultivated and wild. It is because the onion is such an ancient vegetable that it has been bred in so many forms. While many of these can be used interchangeably, each type has a particular use.

Onion

Being both flavoring agent and vegetable in its own right, the onion is something that no kitchen can ever be without. There are few savory dishes that don't start with a sliced or chopped onion, and few that would be good without it. Then there are onions in onion soup, creamy or clear, quiches like *zwiebelkuchen* from Austria or the French *tarte à l'oignon*, as well as all the garnishes that this versatile vegetable provides. Among these are the glazed, bronzed pearl onions, good with any plainly roasted meat, particularly veal; fried onions that go with steak and liver; little pickled onions; and the smaller, fresh green-tailed scallions that are sometimes part of a *crudités* platter and can be eaten with cheese.

Green or fresh onions

These are generally eaten raw in salads, but can also be cooked. There are two types of fresh green onions, which are so called because of the green leaves that form above the white part. These are scallions and Welsh onions, or Japanese bunching onions.

Scallion These may be tiny and thin, like miniature leeks, except that their leaves are tubular, or they may have been lifted from the soil after small silvery bulbs have formed just above the roots. On the West Coast and in some other parts of the United States, these are usually called green onions. They taste mild and quite delicate, and both the white bottoms and the green tops are used as lively additions to salads and salad dressings. When cooked, scallions are added to some savory dishes where other onions would add too strong a flavor. They are also good when finely chopped and mixed with mashed potatoes, in omelets, and as a fresh-looking garnish on pork dishes.

Welsh onion, Japanese bunching onion If you find scallions mentioned in Chinese or Japanese recipes, these are the onions you should use, if you can get hold of them—they are not widely known in the West and certainly not in Wales, despite their name. The names Japanese bunching onion and Chinese onion are more precise, since they are very popular in Asia. Welsh onions grow in clusters, and, if the young leaves are harvested early in the year, the bulbs will grow more leaves. Eat the small, young green leaves raw in salads, and the mature stems in any recipe that is suitable for leeks, or in onion soup.

Boiling onion

Torpedo onion

Garlic

Shallot

Red onion

Yellow onion

Leek

Spanish onion

Vidalia onion

Dry or storage onions It is a good idea to try to buy ordinary dry onions in assorted sizes, or to choose smaller rather than larger specimens, because once cut, they do not keep well. To keep back the tears when peeling an onion, try peeling it under running water.

Chopping an onion into dice can be quite a fast business if efficiently tackled. Peel the onion but do not cut off the root end. Halve the onion through the root and lay the half-onion cut side down. Slice down into narrow strips, cutting from tip end to root end, but do not let the strips fall apart. Now, holding the half-onion together, cut across the strips, at right angles to the first cuts. Remove the root end and the onion will fall into dice.

Once chopped, the onion is often "sweated" in hot fat—meaning that it is allowed to become soft and translucent without coloring—or is sautéed to a more or less deep gold in order to develop its characteristic flavor. It is then incorporated with the other ingredients for the dish in the making.

Storage onions come in all sizes, from small white pearl onions to coppery spheres as large as grapefruit, and in a variety of shapes: oval, round, slender, and flat. All come to a peak at the top, like the domes of the Kremlin, which owe their shape to the fact that the many-layered onion—"a sky within a sky"—was regarded as a symbol of eternity in its native Asia and beyond.

Yellow onion Known by this name although its outer skin is golden-brown rather than yellow, this is considered to be the most pungent of all onions. Look for sound, dry specimens, with no trace of moisture at the base or the neck, and no growth of light greenery at the top—a sign that they have begun to sprout again at the expense of the soundness of their core. The yellow globe onion is the basic all-purpose onion.

White onion This globe onion, which can be quite large in size, is not quite as pungent as the yellow. White globe onions are favored in Mexican cooking.

Spanish onion This large, flattened, pale copper-colored onion is generally inclined to be milder and sweeter in flavor than either the yellow or the white variety. Its size makes it particularly suitable for stuffing and baking, and its comparative gentleness makes it ideal as fried onions, in salads, and for use in dishes that need its additional substance, such as creamy soups and sauces.

Bermuda onion Large but rather more squat, this can be used in the same ways as Spanish onions and is ideal with hamburgers.

Red onion This is relatively mild and distinguished by its deep red skin and the red-tinged layers below the skin. Sweet in flavor, it can be used for the same purposes as Spanish onions, and is good raw in antipasto and in salads.

Boiling onion This is a small yellow or white globe onion, about 1½ inches in diameter. Despite the name, boiling onions are often added whole to braised dishes and stews.

Pearl onion This relatively mild little onion has a shimmery silver skin. It is about the size of a walnut, and is best either added to stews or served in a cream sauce. Small pearl onions are used for pickling, and in many French dishes such as coq au vin. They are delicious, too, made into a confit, by slow cooking in a caramelized, tart-flavored syrup. Very tiny white onions are called cocktail onions. Sold in jars, these are used as a garnish in various cocktails such as the Gibson—which is what a Martini becomes when an onion replaces the usual olive.

Vidalia onion This very juicy onion from Georgia is much sweeter than the Spanish or Bermuda onion, and is excellent both raw and cooked. Walla Walla onions, from Washington State, and Maui onions, from Hawaii, are similar large, sweet onions. New varieties are being developed all the time.

Rocambole Also known as Italian or serpent garlic, or in England as tree onion or garlic-onion, this is a curiosity for the gardener. It produces a cluster of little copper-colored bulbs at the top of the plant, where one normally expects to see only flowers. If these are planted in winter or spring, they will produce larger bulbs with a good flavor, somewhere between garlic and shallots.

Torpedo onion This is spindle-shaped and up to 6 inches long, with a sweet, mild flavor.

Scallion

Welsh onion

Rocambole

Shallot

This pear-shaped bulb with a long neck and skin that ranges from copper to pinkish to the gray of French shallots, is intense in taste without being unduly pungent. Shallots grow singly or in clusters. The crisp layers of their flesh are finely textured. Because shallots taste sweet and delicate, they are mostly used for flavoring. No other member of the onion family produces such an exquisite flavor in a sauce such as beurre blanc, the butter sauce that features them cooked in wine or in wine vinegar.

When recipes specify shallots, they should be used. And, although it would be extravagant, you can use shallots instead of onions if you want a lighter, more delicate taste. The exception comes when browning is involved, as this makes shallots taste a little bitter; shallots cook much faster than onions.

Shallots are an important ingredient in the cooking of northern France, featuring in *marchand de vin* sauces, made by reducing shallots to a purée with wine (red wine to go with steak and white wine for fish dishes).

Garlic

By far the most pungent member of the onion family, garlic grows in a cluster of pointed cloves from a single base. Many people are prejudiced against garlic because it lingers on the breath, but by way of compensation, when garlic is eaten in company, the nose develops a tolerance toward the garlic-laden breath of others. A slowly cooked dish using a great deal of garlic—say a chicken cooked on a bed of whole cloves of garlic—or even whole heads of garlic, which can be roasted unpeeled and eaten by picking up the cloves at the end and squeezing out the pulp within, taste much sweeter and far less garlicky than something like a salad with peeled and bruised raw garlic included in the dressing.

Garlic grown in a hot climate is considered to be the most pungent. But wherever it comes from, whether it is sold in little nets or loose, and whether it is snow-white, gray, purple, or pinkish, look for fat, round, hard bulbs.

Very fresh garlic, available in the spring, when garlic is harvested, has an especially subtle flavor and is favored by connoisseurs for their salads. However, most garlic is allowed to dry: it keeps well in cool, dry, airy storage conditions. Too much moisture in the air, and it will start sprouting in due course; too much warmth, and the interior cloves will eventually turn to black dust. In Provence, garlic is sometimes smoked to help it keep a little longer.

To prepare garlic, carefully peel as many cloves as you plan to use. Whether you chop them in the ordinary way, mash them with salt under the flat of a knife, or crush them in a garlic press is a matter of taste: the finer the result, the more of the pungent oil is released, and it is probably true that the garlic press produces the least subtle taste. If the garlic clove has a green shoot inside, remove it before chopping, as it has a bitter taste.

There are many dishes to which garlic gives its essential flavor. It bonds well with meat, particularly lamb, with chicken and fish and many vegetables, especially the Mediterranean ones such as tomatoes and eggplant, and with mushrooms, whose flavor it enhances. Without it there would be no *aïoli*, the garlic-laden mayonnaise served in France with fish soups, boiled chicken, and every sort of fresh vegetable. And garlic is an essential ingredient in the cooking of southern Europe, of India and Southeast Asia, and of China.

Leek

The leek that the Welsh adopted as their national symbol was, in fact, their native non-bulb-forming onion. Leeks were once used interchangeably with onions, but they are, with their flat leaves arranged in chevron formation, more delicate in taste than onions. A leek is certainly a more subtle flavoring for broth, earning it the title of "king of the soup onions." Scotland's cock-a-leekie is a justifiably renowned soup composed of chicken and leeks, and the leek's talents were taken to their logical end when the *chef des chefs* of New York's Ritz-Carlton Hotel invented his *crème vichyssoise*.

Sadly, many cooks quite ignore the leek's virtues as a vegetable on its own. It is excellent simmered in butter or stewed in red wine, lightly browned and then cooked in a tomato sauce, or eaten cold with a vinaigrette.

If leeks have a drawback, it is that they can be rather a bore to clean. There is no problem when recipes call for chopped leeks, when it is a case of chopping them first—after pulling off any outer membrane and trimming the wilted part of the greenery—and cleaning later. This is best done by placing the chopped leeks in a colander set in a bowl in the sink and running cold water over them until all the grit has settled at the bottom of the bowl. But when recipes call for whole or split leeks, it is necessary to loosen the leaves gently so that the water can run right into the furled vegetable. Most leeks on sale appear to be quite clean, but in fact it is only the outside dirt that has been removed by the growers; when you get it home and into the kitchen, it is usually a question of making little slits with the point of a knife in appropriate places and of rinsing until all the grit has gone, or cutting them almost in half down the middle if they are very gritty.

When you buy leeks, examine them at both ends. The white part should be firm and unblemished and the green part fresh and lively—the green is useful for soups or stock even if your dish only calls for the white part. When leeks are sold trimmed, without much greenery, you may suspect that they are not only elderly, but so mature as already to have formed a solid tubular flower stalk in the middle. This you will have to discard, being left with a disappointingly hollow stem as a result.

ROOTS AND TUBERS

The root vegetables and the tubers—turnips, parsnips, and rutabagas, carrots, beets, and potatoes—certainly make rather a humble-sounding list when they are all lumped together. It is true they are of the earth, rustic, robust, and ordinary, but it is because of this that they have always been so useful.

In hard times, when people couldn't afford to buy bread, or were forced to make it out of whatever roots they could find, including fern roots, it was root vegetables, particularly turnips, and herbs that kept them alive: herbs can be gathered wild, and roots, surviving the worst rains or droughts, can be stored through the winter. And in better times, roots were the vegetables liked best in most households, alongside a piece of boiled or roasted meat—hence boiled beef and carrots, roast duck with turnips, and everything with potatoes.

Potato

Potatoes, whose mysterious underground swellings make better use of their patch of ground than any cereal, are one of the world's most important food crops. They are a most obliging and good-natured vegetable. Easy to grow, cheap to buy, simple to cook, and tremendously filling, they also seem to be the one vegetable, apart perhaps from tomatoes, that nobody ever gets tired of.

There are endless varieties of potatoes. Popular varieties change rapidly, coming into favor with the growers because they keep well or are resistant to disease, and then being ousted by newer, even hardier kinds with higher yields or fewer eyes. This makes it extremely difficult to prepare a catalogue of varieties.

However, different types of potatoes, round, oval, or kidney-shaped, pink, red, white, or, more rarely, blue or purple, do have very different qualities. In Europe, potatoes can be differentiated by variety—at least if you have a well-informed supplier. In the United States, the wholesale marketers do not identify them this way, but, often, instead, by where they were grown. However, all potatoes can be classified by their starch content. There are floury or mealy high-starch potatoes, which are ideal for mashing and baking, but annoying if you want to boil them whole, as they tend to

fall apart in the water. Waxy low-starch potatoes, such as red-skin potatoes and fingerlings, are very firm-fleshed and not at all good for mashing because they become glutinous, but they make excellent potato salads, lovely boiled potatoes, and excellent potato gratins, when the potatoes are cooked in slices that are supposed to remain whole.

There are also medium-starch all-purpose potatoes, whose texture is quite firm. These can be used for almost anything, except perhaps potato salads. They don't disintegrate, can be made into good french fries, and are excellent for baking. Most of the all-purpose potatoes grown in America have white flesh, while many European varieties, including some of the best, are yellow-fleshed. However, the Yukon Gold is a delicious new medium-starch yellow-fleshed potato from Canada that is increasingly available throughout the United States.

As well as different types and varieties, there are also new—and not-so-new—potatoes. New potatoes are not a specific variety of potato, but any potato harvested when small and young. True new potatoes are dug in the spring and early summer. The small red- or white-skinned waxy potatoes available year-round can be treated like new potatoes, but they are not the real thing.

Buying and storing potatoes New potatoes should be small and faintly translucent; the skin should be taut, but if it is a little ragged and so tender that you can pull it off in strips, so much the better—this shows that the potatoes are fresh and will be easy to peel if so desired. New potatoes do not keep particularly well, as they lose flavor after a few days, so buy them in small quantities and keep them in a cool, dark place. New potatoes can be difficult to peel if not perfectly fresh, but the skins are thin and delicate, so many cooks just scrub them and cook them in their skins.

Older potatoes are more amenable and some can be stored in a cool, dark, dry place for months on end. Choose dry potatoes free of sprouts and without the green patches that appear when potatoes are exposed to light—these contain poisonous alkaloids. If your potatoes do have green parts, cut them off. Avoid potatoes that have scaly or soft patches. If buying potatoes in plastic bags, avoid those that look damp or show signs of condensation, as you may find that they have an unpleasant, moldy flavor.

Potatoes for boiling The very best dish in the world is probably new potatoes boiled and served with lots of melted butter and a sprinkling of coarse salt. For perfection, choose walnut-sized

All-purpose yellow potato

All-purpose white potato

*Red- and white-skinned
waxy potatoes*

Baking potato

Long white potato

Blue potato

Orange-fleshed sweet potato

Yellow-fleshed sweet potato

potatoes, peel or scrub them, and drop them into already boiling salted water. Bring them back to a boil, and after 8 to 10 minutes of gentle boiling, test frequently with a thin-bladed knife or skewer. Drain as soon as they are tender. A small sprig of fresh mint added to the water heightens the flavor.

When peeling potatoes, remove as thin a layer of flesh as possible, because many of the vitamins are concentrated just under the skin. If they are not to be cooked immediately, the peeled potatoes must be put straight into a bowl of water, or they will discolor on contact with the air. But don't soak them too long, as this can also lead to a loss of vitamins.

For a delicate but somewhat earthy flavor, older waxy and all-purpose potatoes can be scrubbed and boiled in their skins (this conserves the vitamins too), then peeled while still hot—unless you want to be rustic and serve them with skins on. But peeling the skin from hot potatoes can be tedious, so don't attempt it when you are preparing potatoes for more than two or three people.

To cook potatoes other than the little new ones, put them in a pan of salted cold water, bring it to a boil, and then cook them fairly gently—fast boiling causes them to bump against each other, which breaks them up. When they are just tender, drain them thoroughly and return them to the pan. Let them steam for a minute, then drop in a few chunks of butter and turn the potatoes over gently until they are well coated.

Boiled potatoes are very absorbent and good for all dishes with a lot of gravy to mop up. In some countries, raw potatoes are placed on the top of stews about 30 minutes before the end of cooking—the potatoes absorb any fat that has risen to the top of the stew and also help to stretch the dish a bit further.

Potatoes for sautéing The dry, firm texture of all-purpose potatoes makes them ideal for sautéing. Cut them up and drop them into a large pan of boiling, well-salted water to blanch for about 5 minutes before sautéing them, or fry them from their raw state, drying them with a kitchen towel before putting them into the hot fat.

Potatoes can also be grated before they are sautéed. *Rösti*, the Swiss national dish, is usually made with potatoes that have been boiled the previous day and kept overnight—traditionally in the snow but the refrigerator will do—to dry them out a little. They are then grated, formed into a pancake, and fried gently in butter; for serving, they are inverted onto a plate with the golden crust upward. *Pommes lyonnaise* are potatoes sautéed with fried onions.

Potatoes for deep-frying For french fries, choose firm, dry potatoes. Baking potatoes or a variety such as Yukon Gold are best, although all-purpose white potatoes can be used; in Europe, the yellow-fleshed varieties are preferred. These are also the potatoes to use for homemade potato chips, *gaufrettes* (waffle-cut potato chips), matchsticks, croquettes, potato puffs, and all the many other varieties of fried potatoes.

Sliced or cut-up raw potatoes for fries or chips should be soaked in cold water for at least half an hour to rid them of their surface starch, or the slices will stick together when deep-fried. Dry them well, since hot fat foams up over wet potatoes and could bubble over. Fried potatoes should be salted after cooking, and like other fried foods they will turn soft if covered to keep them warm.

Potatoes for roasting Most all-purpose potatoes are fine for roasting, but small potatoes should be avoided because roasting tends to dry them out. New potatoes do not roast well (sauté them instead). Potatoes roast better if they are first boiled in well-salted water for about 5 minutes, then drained well and returned to the pan to dry off over low heat, uncovered, for a minute or two, before they go into the oven.

Potatoes for mashing Baking potatoes are ideal for mashing. Peel and boil them until they are very tender, drain them well, and mash them thoroughly or purée with a potato ricer or a food mill— but not a food processor, as it will ruin the texture. Then add any liquid, which should be hot for best results. Add butter at the end, beat thoroughly, and taste for seasoning—potatoes always need extra salt. In France, meat juices are sometimes added to mashed potatoes instead of milk.

In the United States, mashed potatoes flavored with everything from roasted garlic to truffle oil have turned up on the menus of trendy restaurants, but these variations will never replace the simple and delicious original.

Potatoes for baking The large russet potatoes, such as Idahos, are the ideal ones for baking. Baked potatoes are extremely healthful, since there is no loss of goodness or flavor into water that is then thrown away. They are also a wonderful vehicle for fillings such as cheese, sour cream, bacon bits, and chopped fresh chives.

Prick the potatoes in a few places with a fork before baking—this allows the steam to escape, and the flesh will be light and fluffy. Never wrap potatoes in aluminum foil for baking—they will steam inside the foil and the skin will be soft rather than nice and crisp.

Potatoes for salads The classic potato salad is plainly boiled and sliced waxy potatoes mixed with a simple, sharpish vinaigrette while they are still hot. A little more dressing is added just before serving. Another version mixes the potatoes first with a little dressing while still warm, and then with some good, creamy homemade mayonnaise when cool. Celery, freshly cooked thin green beans, and dill are all good additions to fresh potato salad.

No summer picnic would be complete without potato salad to go along with the hamburgers and hot dogs. Serve potato salad, too, with sausages or salted fish— its mild flavor is an excellent foil to their assertiveness. For the same reason, potato salad is good with smoked fish, such as trout.

Sweet potato

The tuberous roots of a tropical vine, sweet potatoes have a taste of faintly scented artichoke. The small or medium-sized ones are best: they should be firm and well shaped. Avoid any with cracks and damp patches.

Sweet potatoes are one of the key ingredients used in Creole cookery. Throughout the American South, these potatoes are eaten fried, whipped up into soufflés, and with sugar-cured Virginia ham. (They were the traditional accompaniment to possum.) They are often boiled and mashed with nutmeg, as well, or made into a sweet potato pie.

Taro

Cassava

Yam

Candied, sweet potatoes are a traditional accompaniment for the Thanksgiving turkey. In Australia, they are parboiled and roasted with pork.

Yam, taro, and cassava

The yam belongs to a family of climbing plants that flourish in tropical climates. It comes in a large number of shapes and sizes, and the flesh is white or yellow, with a texture similar to potatoes. In the United States, where true yams are not cultivated, orange-fleshed sweet potatoes with brownish skins are often erroneously called yams. The true yam, however, is much sweeter and moister than the sweet potato, although both are usually prepared in much the same ways: boiled and served with butter, nutmeg, and other spices, as well as with apples, oranges, and nuts. Like sweet potatoes, they are delicious when fried.

Looking something like yams (and found in the same markets) are taro root, or dasheen, and cassava, also called yuca—the source of tapioca. They taste much like potatoes and can be prepared in the same ways, but the taro root will turn a grayish-green color when boiled. Try them sautéed, or mashed together with milk and butter, chopped scallions, and salt and pepper.

Carrot

These range from slim little slips, pale apricot in color and no longer than a little finger, to long, stout cylinders, light orange to the deep color of nectarines.

Young carrots, tender and melting, have a most delicate flavor. Washed and cooked in boiling water for no more than about 7 minutes, then simply tossed in butter and sprinkled with parsley, they are one of the celebratory dishes of early summer. Parboiled and then glazed with butter and possibly a little sugar to emphasize their natural sweetness, they become one of the essentials of *haute cuisine*. Young carrots are best if they are boiled unpeeled. They can then be drained and eaten with their skins on, or rubbed in a towel to slip off the skin.

Sturdier carrots are the great standby for winter, and accompany such hearty dishes as boiled beef and dumplings. And it is to carrots, together with onions, celery, and leeks, that good warming broths owe their flavor—but don't put in too many, or the broth will become so sweet that people will think there is sugar in it. Carrots are also used to make the excellent classic French carrot soup, *potage de Crécy*.

The bright orange, almost translucent carrots of uniform size usually found in supermarkets are bred more for the convenience of the seller than the buyer, because they travel well. Although their flavor is a little elusive, they are delicious raw, and they make a good dish on their own, either sliced and simmered in water and butter, then sprinkled with parsley, or simply served with butter and parsley.

Buying and storing carrots Avoid specimens that have a rubbery texture, are blemished or cracked with age, or are sprouting little roots. Store carrots in the vegetable compartment of the refrigerator after taking them out of their plastic wrapping.

Parsnip

Related to the carrot, the parsnip is almost as sweet but blander. It is delicious in soups and stews. Parsnips are more popular in Europe than in the United States, and there particularly many old-fashioned recipes exist for parsnip custards or flans and other desserts that make good use of the vegetable's sweetness. This is often emphasized by the addition of ginger, spices, and honey. Sweet parsnip dishes are part of the English country tradition, as is parsnip wine, a clear, pale gold, and delicious drink. In England as well, boiled parsnips mixed with mayonnaise were once served as mock lobster, but they are actually nicer without the pretentious title.

Parsnips are available year-round, but the peak season is from early fall until spring. They are at their best in midwinter, especially when their ivory skin has been touched by frost. They are usually sold already washed, but those with traces of soil still clinging to them will keep better. Those with brown patches or that look wizened or dry should be avoided.

Store parsnips in a cool place—the Dutch seventeenth-century paintings that show root vegetables spread around the housewife's feet do not signify untidiness but the fact that the tiled floor of the kitchen was the coolest place. The crisper compartment of the refrigerator is more convenient nowadays.

Salsify

Black-skinned salsify, which has snowy white flesh, is also known as scorzonera; white salsify is sometimes known as the oyster plant because its taste is supposedly reminiscent of oysters. In fact, the flavor of both black and white salsify has a nodding acquaintance with that of asparagus. It is just as delicate and therefore at its best when simply boiled or poached and served with a good chunk of butter, or perhaps with a creamy white sauce made from a roux

Carrot   Parsnip

and be no more than pale shadows of themselves when they are cooked. For the same reason, beets are never peeled before cooking.

When making borscht, the ruby-colored Russian soup, however, it is desirable to make use of the beet's tendency to bleed. For this reason, the beets are chopped before being cooked into a soup. The purple color can become almost brownish with long cooking, though, so it is generally a good idea to cook one or two beets whole and cut them into julienne strips to add shortly before serving, or to add some fresh beet stock, to bring the fine dark red color to the soup.

To serve sliced beets as a vegetable dish, sauté them gently, moistening them with red wine vinegar to set the brilliant color and give them a perfect flavor. The greenery attached to beets can be cooked separately and tastes like spinach.

You can also find golden and white beets, which taste the same as the red, but are rather disappointing to look at. Chioggia beets, however, are striped with red and white—thus their other name, candy cane beet.

Roasted beets are delicious, with a more intense flavor than when boiled. In France, beets are sometimes roasted in the ashes of a wood fire, which gives a charred skin and an earthy, smoky flavor.

Rutabaga and turnip
Both these roots are, in fact, members of the cabbage family, and are so closely related that it is not surprising to find their names sometimes used interchangeably, or the rutabaga referred to as yellow turnip. To add to the confusion, rutabagas are also called swedes or Swedish turnips. However, rutabagas, with their pale, dense flesh, grow to immense sizes without impairment to taste or texture, while white-fleshed turnips will coarsen if they become any larger than tennis balls.

Rutabagas and turnips should be heavy for their size, with no signs of spongy patches, worm holes, or large blemishes. Those with side roots should be avoided.

Rutabagas have a warm, strong flavor and make a delicious winter dish when mashed on their own or cooked in stews. They are the essential ingredient for "mashed neeps," a Scottish dish served with haggis, in which the rutabagas are mashed with potatoes and butter.

moistened with the cooking liquid and a dash of cream.

Salsify is not easy to peel or to clean, so it is best boiled in its skin and peeled afterward, or thinly peeled with a swivel-bladed potato peeler and plunged immediately into a saucepan containing a "*blanc*"—boiling water to which 1 tablespoon of flour has been added (vegetables cooked in a *blanc* will keep their color). It should then be cooked, drained, and finished with a little butter. As it is water-retaining, salsify will not easily burn, provided the pan is heavy and has a well-fitting lid.

Salsify is generally available from fall through late winter. When buying it, choose white salsify with a topknot of fresh-looking leaves; black salsify is usually already trimmed of its leaves. Avoid any, of either type, that look sad or shriveled.

Celeriac, celery root
The edible bulbous root of a member of the celery family, celeriac is not a neat-looking vegetable and needs to be peeled with a sharp knife. Under its brown exterior, the flesh is pale, but it discolors when exposed to the air so should be

plunged immediately into a bowl of acidulated (lemon) water. Cooked, its texture is similar to that of a potato, but less smooth and with more bite to it. Celeriac is a great standby, not only because soups and broth are often improved by a slight celery flavor, and it is milder and less overpowering than regular celery, but also because *céleri rémoulade*—grated raw celeriac coated in mustard mayonnaise, one of the delights of French cuisine—cannot, of course, be made without it. Boiled and diced, celeriac is delicious in potato salads, and in Germany it is served with diced apples, potatoes, and beets in a herring salad. Puréed with potatoes, it is also excellent with duck and game.

Beet
Globe-shaped or somewhat elongated, beets come in bunches with edible greenery at the top when young; older ones may be trimmed of their leaves and sold loose. When buying beets, make sure that their "whiskers" are intact and that they have at least 1 to 2 inches of stem at the top—if too closely trimmed, they will bleed, meaning that they will give up their color to the cooking water

acidulated water 422

Baby turnips, globe-shaped, conical, or flattened, with a sweet, mild radishy flavor but not the hot sting, are as different from older turnips as new potatoes are from more mature ones. They should not be peeled before cooking, but rubbed afterward: the skin comes off easily and beneath it lies their flavor and goodness. Although it seems a pity to do more to any young vegetable than to boil it for a few minutes, glazed baby turnips are delicious and a classic accompaniment to roast duck. Their fresh greenery can be cooked in the same way as other greens. Older, larger turnips may have a purplish tinge to their tops, and are peeled before roasting or boiling.

Kohlrabi

White, pale green, or purple, kohlrabi is a member of the cruciferous family that is bred for its bulbous stem. It looks like a horizontally ridged turnip, and is at its best when young and small, since it becomes coarse and fibrous as it grows larger. The leaves, which grow in stalks from the spaced-out ridges, can be used in the same way as young turnip tops, but are usually removed before the vegetable reaches the market. The skin can be peeled easily with a kitchen knife to expose the pale green flesh below. Tiny kohlrabi can be cooked whole, but the larger ones need to be sliced. They can then be boiled, eaten with fresh butter or a creamy sauce, served with any meat that responds to a delicate cabbagey taste.

Jerusalem artichoke

These knobbly tubers are not artichokes, and nor do they come from the Holy City—in fact, they are from the New World. Like the sunflower, to which they are related, they were christened *girasole* by the Italians—from whence "Jerusalem"—because their yellow flowers tend to turn toward the sun. They may also be called sunchokes.

Jerusalem artichokes are at their best from winter to spring. When buying them, look for neat specimens with the minimum of knobs. Their skin is brownish, like that of potatoes, but more delicate. The white flesh must not be exposed to the air, as it quickly turns a gray-purple color. When boiling Jerusalem artichokes, add a squeeze of lemon juice to the water. This will prevent them from discoloring, especially if you plan to make the delicious white soup, sometimes called Palestine soup, that owes its pearly color as much to the artichokes as it does to the milk or cream that goes into its making. Jerusalem artichokes are delicious roasted like potatoes.

Crosne Also known as Chinese or Japanese artichokes, these taste similar to Jerusalem artichokes but are nuttier and more delicate. These tiny, spindle-shaped vegetables dry out too quickly after being pulled to be widely available. The yellowish patches that tend to develop on fresh white crosnes in no way impair the flavor. Crosnes were once quite popular in France but are no longer common in Europe; you may come across them at a farmers' market here. They should be scrubbed—a tedious job as they are so tiny—and cooked very briefly in boiling salted water, then tossed in plenty of butter.

Jícama

A tropical tuber that looks somewhat like a turnip-shaped yam—and is sometimes called yam bean—jícama has crisp, sweet, juicy flesh. Popular in Mexican and Southwest dishes, it can be peeled and eaten raw or sliced and stir-fried with other vegetables; it can also be roasted like a potato.

Jerusalem artichoke

Jícama

Black salsify

Turnip

Beet

Celeriac

Kohlrabi

Rutabaga

VEGETABLE FRUIT

Glossy black olives, rich purple eggplants, bright scarlet tomatoes, red, green, yellow, and purple peppers, and green cucumbers need hot sun to ripen, and these vegetables bring Mediterranean color and warmth into the kitchen. Others in this group—avocados, tender squash, and huge pumpkins—provide exotic shapes, textures, and tastes.

Tomato

Ripened to a marvelous blazing red in the sun, tomatoes are one of the cook's most essential provisions. Ideally, one should have tomatoes in the kitchen at all times, both fresh and in cans (fortunately, tomatoes are one of the very few vegetables that take happily to being canned).

Belonging to the Solanum family (as does nightshade), the tomato used to be considered unhealthy and was not eaten raw for many centuries after it arrived in Europe from its native South America, via Central America. Spain was the first country to use tomatoes in cooked dishes, and the rest of Europe followed suit, but it was not until the middle of the nineteenth century that tomatoes were eaten raw. Even then they do not seem to have been highly regarded. And the tomato did not have much of a following in the United States before the turn of the century.

Today, however, there is no better salad than a tomato salad, preferably scattered with fresh basil leaves, which have a great affinity with tomatoes. The Italians often add slices of mozzarella, the fresh cheese that goes so well with tomatoes. As dressing, a good sun-ripened tomato needs only olive oil, since it provides its own astringency, but a duller one needs vinaigrette. Tomatoes should never be allowed to sit in their dressing, because this will turn them soggy.

The large beefsteak tomatoes, deep red and often quite misshapen, tend to be the best. The more ordinary globe tomatoes, grown to uniform medium size, often have very little flavor. Cherry tomatoes can be used whole in salads, while the richly flavored Italian plum tomatoes, with relatively small seed clusters and pulp that is inclined to be dry, are perfect for sauces and purées. Fleshy tomatoes are best for sandwiches as there is less liquid; slice them across rather than downward.

Golden-yellow tomatoes are like red tomatoes in every aspect except color, and make a pretty salad when mixed with the reds or on their own. Yellow pear tomatoes are the size of cherry tomatoes, but are, not surprisingly, the shape of a pear. Tiny currant tomatoes sometimes appear at specialty markets, and unusual heirloom varieties of many hues and shapes may be found at the farmers' market.

Buying and storing tomatoes The best tomatoes are those that have been allowed to ripen slowly on the vine, developing their flavor in the warm sun.

Buy bright red, ripe tomatoes for immediate use; for use in the near future, choose those of a paler red color—after a day or two in a cool spot, they will be a vivid red. If tomatoes have been picked when green but after reaching maturity, they will redden well if they are kept in a brown paper bag (they will ripen faster with a red tomato keeping them company, exuding its ethylene gas, which is responsible for the color change). Tomatoes picked when green and unripe will never turn red naturally and are best used for making pickles and chutneys, and, of course, fried green tomatoes. The cottony flavorless tomatoes found in the supermarket are picked green and "force-ripened"— to no more than a pale imitation of a true vine-ripened red tomato.

Cooking with tomatoes Traditional tomato dishes include tomato soup, which may be delicate and translucent or creamy and strong, perhaps flavored with basil or chives; tomatoes with stuffings of cooked seasoned rice mixed with lamb, currants, onion, and garlic, or with bread crumb-bound fillings of olives, herbs, or mushrooms; and fragrant tomatoes *provençale*, which are broiled with a sprinkling of herbs, garlic, and olive oil. A la *provençale* invariably means the presence of tomatoes in a dish, and just as Provençal cooking relies

Cherry tomato Sun-dried tomato

Tomatillo

Beefsteak tomato

Plum tomato

on tomatoes, so does Italian cooking, using them liberally for pastas and pizzas, in soups and vegetable stews.

Many recipes require tomatoes to be peeled, seeded, and roughly chopped (the French culinary term is concasséed). The skin of Italian plum tomatoes may come off easily, but most tomatoes need a quick dip in boiling water first.

Sun-dried tomato These are tomatoes that have been halved and dried—not always in the sun. The drying intensifies and sweetens the flavor and makes the texture leathery. It's much cheaper to buy the tomatoes loose, in bags, rather than packed in oil in jars. Then soak them for an hour before storing in good olive oil with herbs and chiles if you like. Sun-dried tomatoes are eaten as an antipasto or with prosciutto in sandwiches. They are also used in cooked dishes, such as stews and braised vegetables, in pasta sauces and on pizzas, and in salads.

Tomatillo

Related to the Cape gooseberry and belonging to the same family as the tomato, the tomatillo does in fact look very like a walnut-sized green tomato, except that it comes wrapped in a thin, papery husk. It is firm in texture, with a flavor like that of a tart apple. Tomatillos are much used in Mexican cooking, in meat stews and green *mole* sauces, and with onions and chiles to make *salsa verde*, served with tacos and enchiladas.

Pepper

Peppers may be mild and sweet, or hot and unbearably fiery, but they are all members of the Capsicum family. The large sweet peppers include the bell, the cubanelle, the frying or Italian frying pepper, and the sweet banana. Sweet peppers may be red, yellow, orange, purple, white, or green, and squarish or long in shape.

Chile peppers add heat as well as flavor to a dish, although some of them are quite mild. They can be green, red, yellow, or purple-black; in general, the smaller the chile, the hotter it is. When testing them for heat, simply touch a piece of the broken flesh to your tongue.

Most peppers are green to begin with, ripening to red and finally becoming red-brown when dried, although some peppers turn a pale yellow or bright orange, or a deep mahogany color, when ripe. Peppers that are sold half-ripe—part red and part green—may never ripen to a full red.

Paprika, cayenne pepper, and Tabasco sauce are all made from peppers.

Sweet pepper Bought fresh, large sweet peppers (which are a good source of vitamin C) are quite light in weight. Red peppers are sweeter than green, and the yellow and orange ones are closer in flavor to red peppers than to green.

Capsicum means box, and the fleshy walls of sweet peppers contain no more than a few ribs and a cluster of seeds. These should all be discarded to the last flat seed, which even in the mildest pepper can occasionally be bitingly hot. The empty "boxes" can then be filled with any number of stuffings—cooked rice mixed with ground meat and perhaps yogurt, or with a mixture of tomatoes, anchovies, and garlic, or olives and capers. They are then put in an oiled pan and baked slowly. Some people like to blanch the peppers in boiling water for a minute or two before stuffing them.

As well as being stuffed, sweet peppers can be cut into strips and used in a variety of dishes. Sicilians make lovely salads with grilled red or yellow peppers, mixing them with anchovy fillets, capers, garlic, and olive oil. Yugoslavians have a similar salad, which is made using peppers roasted until they

Jalapeño chile

Ancho chile

Bird chile

Dried hot chile

Anaheim chile

Yellow bell pepper

Green bell pepper

Red bell pepper

have blistered and then skinning them. In the South of France, there is the beautiful *pipérade*, a mixture of sweet peppers, tomatoes, onions, garlic, and, sometimes, bacon, to which beaten eggs are added at the last moment. Sweet peppers are also sometimes combined with chile peppers, as in rouille—the bright orange, fiery sauce that floats in a bowl of bouillabaisse, and is served with a number of other fish dishes that have their origins in the South of France.

Pimiento, the Spanish word for peppers, has come to mean the peeled and seeded cooked red peppers that are sold in jars. But you can roast or grill any bell peppers at home, and peel and seed them. Once prepared, they will keep in the refrigerator, covered, for up to a week.

Chile pepper When fresh, a chile pepper should look bright—dullness is a sure sign of overmaturity—with no brown patches or black spots. Chiles can vary in size from 12 inches in length down to just ¼ inch, and in taste they may be anywhere from mildly warm to blisteringly hot. As well as fresh, they are sold dried (whole, crushed into small flakes, or ground to a powder), canned, and bottled, often pickled.

In Central America, notably Mexico, chiles are second only to corn in their importance in cooking. They are widely used in the cuisines of other countries, including Africa, India, China (Hunan and Sichuan cooking), and Thailand. In North America and most of Europe, hot chiles are generally used sparingly.

Chile experts, of course, are able to distinguish between the dozens of varieties, but nonexperts tend to differentiate only between the mild, the hot, and the unbearable. Large chiles include the mild Anaheim or California (when fresh and green this is used for *chiles rellenos*—stuffed with cheese and deep-fried; the fresh red pepper is also called Colorado chile); the similar but slightly longer and hotter New Mexico; the poblano, which can range from slightly hot to hot (when ripened to red and dried this is called an ancho, which is sweet but can be quite pungent); and the pungent yellow Santa Fe Grande. Among the smaller chiles are the hot to very hot jalapeño (when smoked, this becomes a chipotle) and the cayenne, Thai, and bird—all three similar in size

and shape and all quite hot. Other small chiles include the extremely hot, slender green serrano, the fiery, lantern-shaped habanero and its cousin the Scotch bonnet, and the blistering, tiny tabasco, which is used to make Tabasco sauce.

With chiles, not only are the seeds hot, but the box itself is pungent. It is a volatile oil called capsaicin, found mainly in the seeds and ribs, that accounts for the heat. Capsaicin irritates the skin and especially the eyes, so keep your hands—even after washing—away from your eyes, lips, and other sensitive areas for a while after you have prepared chiles. Also, rinse the chiles in cold, not hot, water, or the irritating fumes may rise into your face. To prepare chiles, pull off their stems and cut each in half, all under cold running water. Chiles soaked in cold salted water will be less hot. They can also be blistered on the grill or under a broiler for a lovely smoky flavor.

Canned chiles should be washed to remove the brine in which they have been preserved. They may be already sliced or diced, or they may need to be seeded like fresh ones. Dried whole chiles, torn into small pieces, can be used as they are to season dishes, or they can be rehydrated in water first. For a much milder flavor, put dried hot chiles into a pan of cold water, bring slowly to a boil, and then drain. They can then be used, more or less discreetly, to heat up dishes such as chili con carne and other Tex-Mex favorites; for curries, especially Thai curries; for any number of Creole and Cajun dishes, especially those that include shrimp or pork; and in many of the dishes of the American Southwest.

Eggplant

This can be long and slim or as fat as a blimp, with a glossy purple or almost black skin, or it can be a plump ivory-white oval (to which version it owes its American name; in France and Britain, it is known as *aubergine*). All varieties have the same slightly acrid taste. The difference lies in consistency: the plump ones, marginally juicier, are the ones to use for such dishes as moussaka, with its golden layers; or the Balkan *okrochka*, also layered but without the white sauce or eggs; or in eggplant Parmesan. The long, slim ones, being drier, are best for frying.

When buying eggplants, chose those that feel heavy for their size—they are

likely to have the smallest seed channels because their flesh will have filled out. They should have smooth, unblemished skins with no rough, spongy patches or brown spots.

It is a good idea to salt eggplant before cooking to sweat out some of the moisture and possible bitterness, although some modern varieties do not really need this treatment. To salt them, cut them into thin slices, sprinkle with salt, and allow them to drain in a colander for half an hour, then rinse them and pat dry with paper towels.

It is not usually necessary to peel eggplant, because the skin contributes to their flavor and color, and in dishes such as stuffed eggplant, it prevents them from disintegrating. But in dishes that involve puréed eggplant, such as the dish sometimes known as "poor man's caviar," the traditional way of peeling them is to roast them in their skins over a charcoal fire or under a broiler until they are soft, and then to scoop out the flesh, which will have acquired a delicious smoky taste.

Although ratatouille—the delicious Provençal stew of eggplant, tomatoes, zucchini, onions, and sweet peppers—is one of the great Mediterranean dishes, the best eggplant recipes come from southern Italy and the Middle East. In the Middle East, eggplant purées are flavored with tahini and garlic and served as a salad.

The most famous eggplant dish is the Turkish *Imam Bayildi*, or "the Imam has fainted"; this is apparently what an *imam* (Turkish priest) did when presented with an incredibly rich dish of fried eggplant mixed with onions, tomatoes, spices, and golden raisins, all swimming in oil.

Eggplants may be halved and stuffed, or filled from the stem end after the seeds and a portion of the flesh have been removed to make room for the stuffing. They look very beautiful if they are first peeled in strips so that white flesh and purple skin make handsome stripes around the outside. Fill them with cooked ground lamb or beef, rice, tomatoes, garlic, onions and spices, and their own chopped pulp. Then sprinkle them with oil and bake until tender.

Whether eaten hot or cold, in batter, or in a garlicky marinade, eggplant is almost always first fried in hot olive oil. It absorbs vast quantities of oil, so should be fried quickly and drained well.

Avocado

The avocado was once called the alligator pear because its original Spanish name, *aguacate*, based on the Aztec word, was too difficult to pronounce; in Britain, it was also called the butter pear, because of its consistency. It is, strictly speaking, a fruit, but is used mainly as a salad vegetable because its flavor is bland, mild, and nutty.

Particularly rich in oils, proteins, and vitamins, the avocado was used by the ancient Mayans, Incas, and Aztecs both as a food and for skin care. Avocados were a luxury in northern countries until Floridians and then Californians began to cultivate them in the nineteenth century. Some people consider these comparatively northerly avocados to be only pale replicas of those grown in the tropics, but they are still very good, as are the Israeli avocados that supply many European markets in their season.

There are two main types of avocado: those varieties grown in California and those grown in Florida. The California avocados, of which the Hass is the most common variety, have rough, pebbly skin that is green when unripe and purple-black when ripe, and golden-yellow flesh. The Fuerte and other Florida varieties are usually larger, with smooth green skin and pale green to yellow flesh. In the case of Florida avocados, the skin color is no indication of ripeness; the test for this is to apply gentle pressure at the stem end—if there is some give, the avocado is ready.

In Mexico, where avocados are abundant, they are eaten in soups, salads, and stews. They are also the essential ingredient in guacamole—the coarse avocado purée with green chiles, chopped onions, and lime or lemon juice which may be eaten on its own or, as in Mexico, with tortillas. It is best to purée avocado shortly before it is to be eaten, because it turns brown when exposed to the air. So does the flesh of a cut avocado, so either halve or slice it just before serving, or rub or sprinkle the cut surfaces with lemon.

In the Caribbean, avocados baked in their skins are sometimes served with turkey and chicken. But there is no better way to serve them than halved, or sliced, with a good vinaigrette, or, even more simply, with a sprinkling of fresh lime juice and salt.

Olive

Groves of gnarled olive trees flourish in the Mediterranean countries and in California, producing a great variety of olives, large and small. Greek and Italian olives are reckoned to be the finest—in ancient Rome, olives were eaten both at the beginning and at the end of meals from sheer love of them.

Whether olives are green or black (they may actually be brown or purple) is not a matter of type but of timing: olives picked young are still hard and pale green; black olives have had time to ripen and darken on the tree and have developed more of their oil. In order to make them edible, black olives are soaked in an alkaline solution—traditionally rainwater and wood ash (lye), now more likely to be caustic soda—and exposed to the air to remove their excessive bitterness.

Green olives are treated rather differently, first soaked under running water or steeped in an alkaline solution, then put into tightly sealed barrels of brine and left for up to a year to develop their olive-green, smooth succulence. Olives destined for the

Small white eggplant

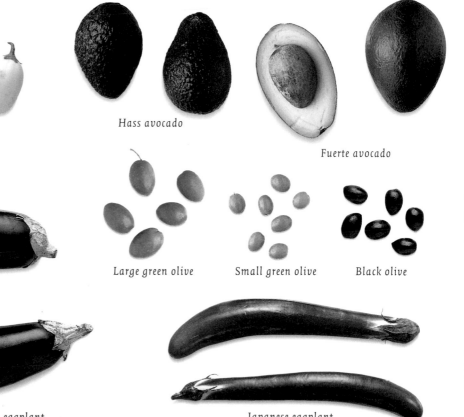

Hass avocado

Fuerte avocado

Large green olive   Small green olive   Black olive

Common purple eggplant

Japanese eggplant

oil presses are allowed to ripen fully; some of these, looking a little shriveled and quite small, are also cured in salt to be eaten, and can be the best of all.

Olives are preserved in a number of different ways. The black ones range from those that are marinated in oil with herbs to those in brine. There are also cracked green olives—which may be plain or flavored with garlic, spices, or herbs—and whole pitted black or green olives spiced with chiles.

Of the many olives on the market, among the most commercial and widely available are the big, green, solid Spanish olives, which are slightly acid—and which connoisseurs like to dip in olive oil before eating—and the small, succulent Spanish Manzanillas. These are often stuffed with strips of *pimiento* or, less frequently, with almonds, anchovies, lemon or orange peel, or pieces of black olive. Italian olives, such as the large green Cerignola, the black olives from Castellamare, and the tiny black wrinkled ones from around Rome, go on top of pizzas and focaccia. Plump Kalamatas and other olives from Greece go into a salad with tomatoes and sliced onions. And the black olives of Provence are used in rich *estouffades* and *daubes*, and in other braised dishes, as well as in an olive pâté or purée and stuffings with mushrooms, anchovies, herbs, and bread crumbs.

Besides the best-known green and black olives, there are also the pale or dark brown ones found in Italy and Cyprus, the tiny, delicate black Niçoise ones, and the straw-colored California olives, which some people prefer above all others.

If you buy olives and do not use them all at once, store them in the refrigerator, perhaps in some olive oil or in a mixture of water, oil, and vinegar. You can roll olives in fresh olive oil, perhaps with a few herbs, chiles, or crushed coriander seeds, to liven them up before eating. If you want black olives without pits for cooking, use an olive pitter, or simply split the flesh and remove the pits.

CUCUMBER, SQUASHES, AND PUMPKIN

These belong to the climbing or rambling family known as Cucurbitas, together with melons and the decorative autumn gourds.

Cucumber

English cucumber

Cucumber

Before cucumbers had the bitterness bred out of them, they were invariably peeled, salted, and drained. This is no longer necessary, unless you want to make a delicate Austrian or French cucumber salad, for which salting and draining are essential—this alters the texture to a soft crispness by extracting some of the water, and heightens the flavor. Otherwise, cucumber salads are likely to consist of slices cut paper-thin and dressed with sour cream or vinaigrette, or, in the Hungarian version, of little dice dressed with yogurt and chives and sprinkled with paprika. Cucumbers are also good peeled, cut into strips or cubes, and cooked briefly in butter, to be served hot.

Small kirby cucumbers have plentiful seeds and smooth, dark green skins. They are also called pickling cucumbers because they are the ones that are brined, or used to make sweet or dill pickles.

The long, clear green cucumber (known as the English or hothouse cucumber) has fewer seeds than regular cucumbers and an exceedingly thin skin. It is often sold in a tight plastic jacket to keep it fresh. Europe has the enormous Zeppelin cucumber, firm and juicy, that turns a pale yellow when fully ripe. Another unusual variety is the lemon cucumber, almost round and with crisp, juicy flesh and tough yellowish skin; this should always be peeled.

Cucumbers are best when they are young and tender and look as if they are bursting with juice. They can be stored in the refrigerator for about a week at most. Avoid waxed cucumbers if you can; peel them if you can't.

Tiny gherkin cucumbers are usually found pickled in vinegar (then often called cornichons), and are eaten with cold meats or with *pâté de campagne*, or chopped and used in sauces such as tartar sauce.

Squashes and pumpkin

Some squashes are soft-skinned and for eating when young and tender, which is why they are known as summer squashes; these should be cooked as soon as possible after being picked. Others are best when they have been allowed to mature slowly to develop firm, sweet flesh and tough, inedible skins; these are known as winter squashes.

Zucchini Smaller zucchini are infinitely superior to the larger overgrown ones, with a much more interesting and delicate taste. They may have green or yellow skins. There is hardly any work involved in their preparation: just give them a little wash, then leave tiny ones whole and cut larger ones into circles, or slice them lengthwise into halves or quarters. Give them a very few minutes' boiling, steaming, or sautéing, add some herbs such as basil or parsley and, perhaps, a dash of cream or some butter or olive oil, and an extremely good dish is ready to eat. But don't keep it waiting, because the vegetable continues to soften even after it has been taken off the heat.

Zucchini are excellent fried in oil, either plain or in batter, and their big golden flowers are also sometimes stuffed and deep-fried in a crisp batter or chopped and used in risotto. They form part of an Italian *fritto misto*, in which there may also be apples, artichoke hearts, eggplant, brains, tiny veal chops, croquettes, pumpkin, and peeled figs.

A parboiled or a blanched large zucchini, halved and hollowed out, makes a good vehicle for a ground beef and onion stuffing bound with an egg, or a rice and meat stuffing, but both will need lively flavoring because the squash itself is bland in taste.

Straightneck and crookneck yellow squash Much like zucchini in flavor and texture, these can be used in the same ways. The crookneck has somewhat bumpy yellow skin and curves at the neck; the straightnecks often have smooth skin.

Vegetable marrow The large vegetable marrow is the pride of many English gardens. The enormous prize-winning specimens, however, are not very delicate as a vegetable. Boiled into a watery mush, medium-sized marrows can be equally disappointing, but started off with a little butter and chopped onion and steamed in their own juice, and then sprinkled with a generous handful of chopped parsley, they can be fresh-looking and delicious, especially when tomatoes are added.

Spaghetti squash Sometimes known as vegetable spaghetti, this stubby yellow watermelon-shaped squash is grown with particular attention to its tendency to produce stringy flesh, and is eaten, with sauce, just like spaghetti. It is baked or boiled, the end pierced so that the heat reaches the interior. Then it is served cut in half lengthwise, or the flesh is scooped out; pass a tomato sauce separately. It is also quite good eaten simply with butter and grated cheese.

Pattypan squash Usually creamy in color, although it also comes in shades of yellow and pale green, this tastes rather like zucchini. It is best no bigger than 4 inches across, when the skin is soft and the interior tender, and the scalloped shape need not be spoiled by slicing. Boil it or bake it whole, then cut off the top, scoop out the seeds, and fill the hollow with melted butter; eat with a spoon. It also makes good fritters.

Chayote, mirliton, christophene This small, pear-shaped squash has a large seed, which in very young chayotes

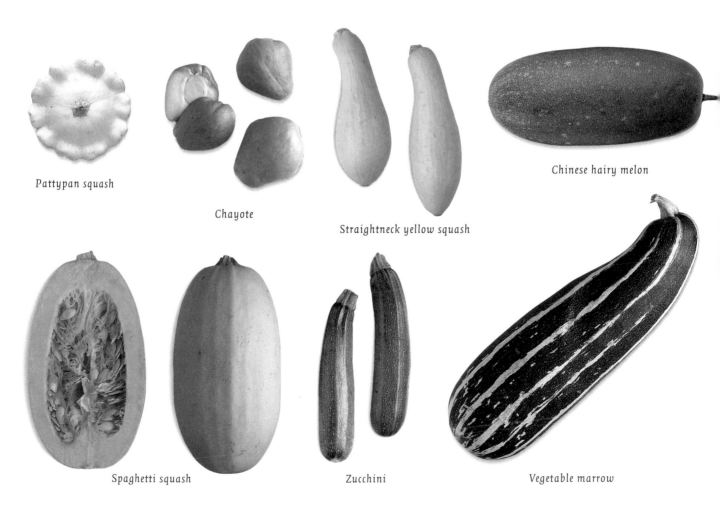

Pattypan squash

Chayote

Straightneck yellow squash

Chinese hairy melon

Spaghetti squash

Zucchini

Vegetable marrow

is edible. It features in Central and South American cooking, where besides being used like other soft-skinned squashes, it is candied, filled with nuts and raisins, and eaten as a dessert.

Chinese hairy melon, fuzzy melon Looking like a large green or bluish-green torpedo, this can be bought in Chinese markets. When young, the melon is covered with a silky fuzz, which is easily washed off by running your hand over its skin under cold running water. In maturity, it is usually coated with a white wax-like layer, and needs to be peeled.

This melon has a slight bitterness but is excellent stir-fried, braised, and used in soups. A half-ripe specimen makes the best eating. In Indonesia, it is candied to be eaten with tea, and is used in cakes and cookies.

Winter squashes A favorite winter vegetable in North America, winter squashes, or many of them at least, can now be found year-round. The most common varieties of winter squash include the acorn, which can be green or orange or a combination of the two; the smooth-skinned, long, pale butternut squash, which swells toward the blossom end; the colorful, bumpy-skinned turban squash, of which the dark green buttercup, with its lighter-colored turban, is one variety; and the large, warty Hubbard squash, often sold in chunks or wedges. Look for firm, unbruised specimens, or chunks that show no signs of softening around the edges.

Peeled, cut into pieces, and boiled or steamed for about 20 minutes, winter squash can be served mashed with butter and salt and pepper, or a little orange juice. The smaller squashes can be left unpeeled, halved, seeded, and baked in the oven for about 30 minutes with butter and brown sugar or maple syrup in their hollows.

Calabaza Often sold in wedges to display its golden-orange flesh, this squash, also called West Indian pumpkin, features in Caribbean soups. Otherwise, it can be used in any hard-skinned squash or pumpkin recipe.

Pumpkin Best-known of all are the handsome, golden field pumpkins that are carved into smiling, gap-toothed faces for Halloween. However, these are not really the ones for pumpkin pie, pumpkin soup, or pumpkin bread; instead, for cooking, choose smaller varieties like sugar pumpkins, also called pie pumpkins. Nowadays, of course, because of the business of baking, straining, seeding, scraping, and puréeing pumpkin, many people use canned purée—one of the few foods that can be better canned than fresh. For pies and for pumpkin soup, canned purée can also be used, but for baked and sautéed pumpkin, you need fresh ones.

Italians use pumpkins in soups and risotto, and also as a stuffing for ravioli. The English pumpkins are much softer fleshed, and because they cook so readily into a mush, they are best used for pumpkin soup. Alternatively, they may be combined with potatoes or root vegetables to give them a little extra body when used in vegetable soups.

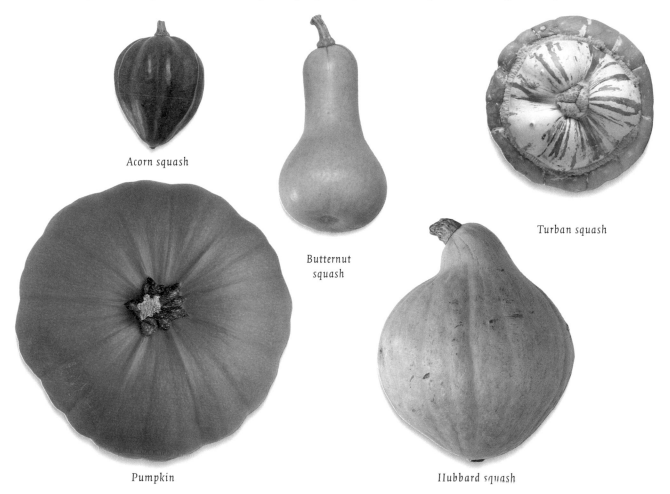

Acorn squash

Butternut squash

Turban squash

Pumpkin

Hubbard squash

Mushrooms and Other Fungi

In many countries, mushroom foraging is an autumn treat, with whole families combing the ground for the eighty or so edible species of fungi that are sold in the local markets, dried, or enjoyed fresh as a luxurious addition to the normal diet. It is important to remember, however, that for the amateur picker going out in the morning dew, the business of mushrooming is fraught with risk. Some mushrooms are indigestible; a few are lethal. In France and Germany, where mushroom gathering is particularly popular, pharmacists will check the morning's pick.

Plenty of wild mushrooms do find their way to the world's vegetable markets, harvested by people with a long tradition of mushroom gathering. As a change from the ubiquitous cultivated white mushroom, it is one of the greatest pleasures of autumn to see a selection of wild forms, including the fat brown cèpe and the golden-pleated chanterelle,

both worldwide in distribution and probably far and away the best of the woodland mushrooms. These, along with the morel, a springtime delicacy, are the truly great mushrooms of fine cooking. For those who can find an expert to tell them which varieties to choose, there are also many other pleasant treats to be had.

Gathering your own wild mushrooms

Fungi are plants that lack chlorophyll, and so cannot use direct sunlight to provide themselves with energy. Instead they get their energy by decomposing the life around them that contains energy in the forms of sugars and starches. The word fungi covers everything, including the mold that grows on your ceiling or on old jam, so the term mushroom has been used for those covered here.

Each species of mushroom inhabits a specific environment. There are three main types: the parasitic, which live on

a living organism without benefiting the host; the saprophytic, which live on dead material such as tree stumps; and the mycorrhizal, which associate with the root hairs of a tree—the mushrooms get nutrients from the tree and the tree gets nutrients from association with the mushroom (usually a very precise association—some types will only grow on pine trees or even on a particular pine, others only on an oak or birch).

What you see above ground is the fruit of an underground plant. The hidden *mycelium* is actually the plant; it grows well in a warm summer. When its season comes, and after a period of high humidity, the fruiting bodies emerge above the ground, fed by the rapid intake of water. The mushroom comes up in a matter of hours; it emerges to release spores when the *mycelium* stops growing, as the days shorten and it gets colder. Most mushrooms grow from autumn to the first frosts, September and October being the best months, but as it gets

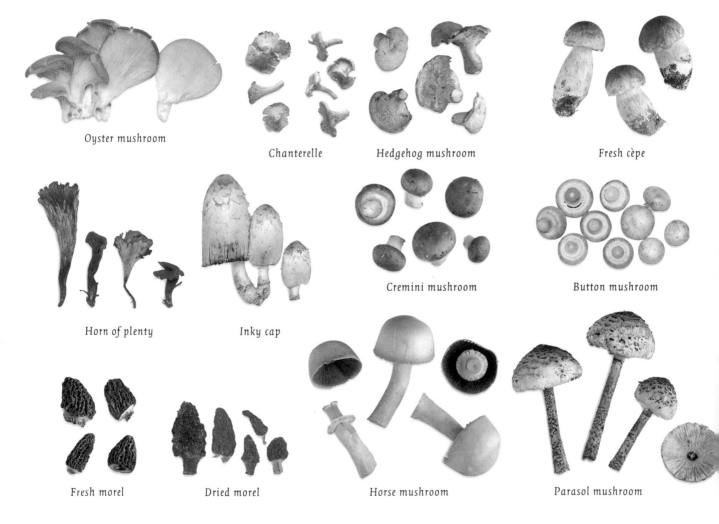

Oyster mushroom

Chanterelle

Hedgehog mushroom

Fresh cèpe

Horn of plenty

Inky cap

Cremini mushroom

Button mushroom

Fresh morel

Dried morel

Horse mushroom

Parasol mushroom

farther into autumn, the leaves cover the mushrooms, so they are harder to find. September rain is crucial to many species—it is more important than heat at this time of year. Because they lack chlorophyll, most mushrooms will grow regardless of whether it is light or dark, or the days long or short. Only the first frosts will end their growth.

(Essential advice for anyone who is considering taking up the hunt for the first time: LEARN YOUR SUBJECT. The means of identifying edible mushrooms and avoiding all poisonous or dubious species is of crucial importance. It is vital to use a guide that gives clear identification information.)

Some edible wild mushrooms

Cèpe or porcini (*Boletus edulis*) This is considered by the French and Italians to be the king of mushrooms, and in Austria it is called *Herrenpilz* (gentleman's fungus). While fresh cèpes are relatively abundant in much of Europe in autumn, they are

Dried cèpe (porcini)

Portobello mushroom

Giant puffball

unfortunately a rarity in the United States. The fresh mushrooms are sometimes offered, at a price, in specialty markets; otherwise, only the dried are available. The flesh of the fresh mushroom is almost white, firm and fleshy, tasting sweet and nutty with a pleasant smell. Firm, fresh cèpes will keep in the refrigerator for up to a week. The dried ones are usually labeled porcini, the Italian name; choose creamy-fawn ones (they blacken with age).

Do not wash fresh cèpes; just wipe with a damp cloth. Then, if young, they can be sliced to eat raw in a green salad, possibly dressed with walnut oil. They make the best risotto, and in France's Dordogne are eaten in omelets with garlic and parsley, or sautéed with potatoes and garlic. Dried porcini must be soaked in warm water for 20 to 30 minutes before use (use the soaking liquid in the recipe as stock).

Horn of plenty (*Craterellus cornucopioides*) Also known as *trompette des morts*, black trumpet, or black chanterelle, this mushroom is trumpet- or funnel-shaped and looks like old, dusty black leather. The cap is 1 to 3 inches long, and deep brown to black when the weather is damp, but paler grayish-brown in dry weather. It is hollow all the way down the center and paler inside. The gills are more like radiating folds or wrinkles. Horn of plenty grows in autumn in deciduous woods, sometimes in large colonies beneath beeches, but can be hard to see.

The taste is strong and earthy and the flesh remains black in cooking. Cut open down one side to clean them. They should be sautéed gently in butter with garlic and parsley and used in an omelet, or perhaps in a cream sauce with chicken instead of the more expensive morels, which have a short spring season.

Chanterelle (*Cantharellus cibarius*) In Germany, golden chanterelles are known as *pfefferling* or *eierschwamm*, on account of their egg-yellow color. The small ones in France are known as *girolles*. They are both beautiful and delicious, bright golden-yellow all over, 1 to 4 inches across, smooth, and funnel-shaped, with edges that are rolled at first and then wavy and irregular. The underside has blunt, gill-like waves and folds. The stem is short and thick, and the flesh smells of apricots and pepper. They are found in

autumn in little clumps in mixed woods, often under moss, and also on banks of ditches or paths or among leaves.

Chanterelles are hard to clean, but very good to cook with—any mushroom recipe will be even better made with chanterelles. They are particularly good with scrambled eggs or in an omelet, flavored with garlic and parsley, and they are wonderful with chicken or squab.

There are other good edible chanterelles in addition to the golden one, such as yellow leg (*Cantharellus infundibuliformis*), which has a small, funnel-shaped, dark brown cap and hollow, bright golden stem. The flesh is yellowish and thin, slightly bitter when raw, and it smells aromatic. It grows in autumn in acid soils, in woods, usually in clumps. The golden chanterelle grows particularly well in California; other varieties are more common in the East and other parts of the United States.

Morel (*Morchella esculenta, M. augusticeps, M. elata,* and *M. deliciosa*) These are spring mushrooms, very highly prized by serious mushroom hunters. Wild morels grow in parts of New England, in Michigan, and in the Northwest; morels are now being cultivated as well but are usually less flavorful. Fresh morels are quite expensive and limited in availability; dried morels are easier to come by. Characteristically sponge-like, with domed caps 2 to 5 inches tall and hollow stems, morels come in a range of colors—from white or pale buff to cream-colored to black. Fresh morels should be trimmed of their tough stems, then thoroughly washed before cooking. Dried morels are very good indeed, retaining the rich nutty flavor well; cook them, after soaking, in cream and serve with free-range chicken or with veal.

Horse mushroom (*Agaricus arvensis*) Called *boule de neige* in French, this does look somewhat like a snowball when young, but when fully opened, a horse mushroom found in a grassy field looks more like a dish on a green tablecloth. It is large and thick, 4 to 8 inches across, with a bright creamy-white cap that slowly turns yellowish with age. The cap is smooth and silky and can stain brownish-yellow when handled; the flesh is firm and white and smells of anise seeds. The closely packed gills are grayish-white, quickly turning to chocolate-brown and finally black. The stem is white shaded

Chicken with Potatoes and Mushrooms 315–16 **Tagliatelle with Tuscan Meat Sauce** 339 **Trattoria Beef Stew with Polenta Dumplings** 294–5

with rose and up to 1 inch thick; it has a double ring around it. Horse mushrooms can be found in unplowed fields and old grassy meadows from July onward. They can be seen from a long way off.

This mushroom is very fine. It has a much stronger flavor than its close relative the field mushroom and is less watery. Eat it young, as it gets tough and and dry with age.

Horse mushrooms can be cooked in all the best ways you might prepare ordinary mushrooms. A rather nice Swiss recipe suggests cooking them in butter and then setting them on a mound of spinach flavored with finely chopped onion cooked in butter, to look as if they were growing on a grassy bank.

Cauliflower fungus (*Sparassis crispa*) This wonderful cream-colored mushroom looks like a large sponge, up to 12 inches across. In Switzerland, it is called a broody hen; in Britain it is sometimes known as brain fungus. It has brittle, wax-like flesh and a pleasant smell; with age it becomes darker and tougher. It is not uncommon and can be found growing at the foot of old fir trees and around pine stumps. It is good to eat when young, but needs careful cleaning. Slice it and fry in butter with garlic and parsley. You can also pull it into pieces and, having washed and dried it, dredge it with flour and then sauté in butter with finely chopped onions or shallots.

Giant puffball (*Lycoperdon giganteum/Langermannia gigantea*) This lovely mushroom ranges in size from that of a large turnip to almost a full yard across, when it can be seen for miles. White at first, it has a kid-glove-like, smooth exterior, taut to the touch when it is young, becoming softer and somewhat dingier-looking with age. It is found between May and November in fields, pastures, and gardens; it often reappears in the same place year after year. Picked young, sliced, and sautéed, puffballs have a flavor like a mixture of bacon, mushrooms, eggplant, and fried pototoes all at once, especially if cooked in bacon fat. Some books say that the mushroom is exactly like sweetbreads in taste and flavor. You can sprinkle it with lemon juice before or after sautéing, but don't overcook it. Puffball with bacon is a good start to a day in the country.

Inky cap (*Coprinus comatus*) Known as lawyer's wig or shaggy inky cap in Britain, these tall, white, bell-shaped mushrooms liquefy as they age, and the resulting black fluid has been used as a substitute for ink.

Inky caps are a familiar sight on grassy roadsides and recently disturbed soil. The caps are shaggy, and gills are white at first, then pink and finally black. The best specimens are very young and firm: peel them, discard the stems, and sauté them in butter with salt, pepper, and a last-minute sprinkle of lemon juice, or bake them in cream for at least an hour, or possibly longer. They will taste like Dover sole.

Blewit (*Lepista nuda*) The blewit, or wood blewit, is a beauty—bluish-lilac or violet when young, with lilac gills. Usually found late in the season in woods, or in heaps of garden compost and leaves, it is good to eat if gathered when it is dry and sound; it's a useful mushroom at the end of the season. The larger caps have a particularly nice texture; slice them and sauté in butter, or grill them whole. Another blewit (*L. saeva*), called blue legs, is one of the few species that the English feel is safe to eat. Its flesh is fragile and tends to be watery, so it is best stewed in butter with softened onions, then coated with sour cream and chives, and a little flour, until bathed in a creamy sauce. In Switzerland, blewits are eaten in a sauce flavored with paprika, onion, and parsley.

Parasol mushroom (*Lepiota procera*) This handsome mushroom starts off as a tight brown dome that is quite hard to spot in the shortish grass it favors. It emerges as a glorious tall, shaggy-topped umbrella up to 12 inches across, which can be seen for miles.

With its characteristic shape, and creamy flesh and gills, goes a pungent, meaty smell, which makes it easy to identify. A larger version (*L. rachodes*) is called the shaggy parasol. However, not everybody is attracted by the strong flavor. The parasol mushroom should be eaten young. Discard the stems, and fry with eggs and bacon.

Hedgehog mushroom (*Hydnum repandum*) This is easily identified by the clustered spines beneath the cap, which gave it its name. It is golden-yellow, with an undulating top 1 to 4 inches across that sometimes becomes slightly funnel-shaped, and it has a slightly acrid smell. Found in deciduous woods from autumn to late winter, the hedgehog mushroom is not particularly special to eat. To cook it, scrape away the gills (some people leave them, but the texture is not good), wipe the caps clean, and sauté in butter; or use in soups and stews, risottos, and pasta sauces where a mixture of different mushrooms is called for.

Oyster mushroom (*Pleurotus ostreatus*) This mushroom is now cultivated widely, but is also found growing in the wild. It looks like an ear or a bracket, and grows in tiers on the stumps, logs, and branches of hardwood trees, especially beech trees. Colors vary from oyster-gray, pale buff, or white to yellowish-brown to almost black. The flesh is thick and soft with an almost waxy surface. The stems are short and tough, and the gills are white to pallid, often fused near the stalk.

There are dozens of varieties of oyster mushrooms and, as they tend to be in season at different times, oyster mushrooms now appear almost all year round. They are good to eat when young, but toughen as they age, becoming bitter. The wild ones need long, slow cooking as they can be hard to digest. Snip off the woody stems and either slice and fry until crisp or sauté in butter. They can also be used in stews or stir-fries, or pickled. The texture is good, slightly gelatinous and crunchy.

Shiitake mushroom (*Lentinus edodes*) These mushrooms also grow on trees. First cultivated by the Chinese, and then commercially developed by the Japanese, they were originally grown on teak, mahogany, or oak logs. Now they are often grown indoors on sterile wood sawdust.

Shiitake mushrooms, which have dark brown caps with inwardly rolling edges and a small, tough stem, do not grow in the wild in North America. They are, however, extensively cultivated for today's market, in Pennsylvania, California, and other states.

Fresh shiitakes have a firm and meaty texture; the stems are tough and should be removed. They are good in tempura, with shrimp and vegetables, and in stir-fries. They can be used together with dried shiitakes to make a good sauce for pasta, or in rice pilafs and risotto.

Dried shiitakes are also called Chinese black mushrooms. They can be used, soaked for at least 30 minutes, in any recipe where a small quantity of mushrooms is needed for flavoring.

Cultivated mushrooms

Although lacking the pleasing diversity of wild mushrooms gathered by season, cultivated forms have the merit of year-round availability. Moreover, they are consistent and utterly safe. Most common, of course, is the common white mushroom (*Agaricus bisporus*), cultivated relative of the field and horse mushrooms, and sold in several sizes.

Now that a wider range of mushrooms is becoming available, large mushroom farms, which formerly stuck to rearing our good old agaric species, are experimenting with other types: straw mushrooms, which have been grown in China for something like 2000 years, and enoki, as well as morels. Growers are also doing research on the requirements of mycorrhizal fungi, those species such as chanterelles and cèpes that can only grow in partnership with another plant.

Button mushrooms are small and succulent, and slightly weaker in flavor than the more mature grades. Remaining pale (although an aluminum saucepan may darken them slightly), they are useful for white, creamy sauces and also for salads. The larger white mushrooms, the kind where the membrane is just breaking to expose the gills, can be kept pale if rubbed with a cut lemon, or if a few drops of lemon juice or white wine are added to the cooking liquid. These mushrooms are ideal for stews and casseroles. The largest ones can be stuffed or, with the stems trimmed off level with the cap, can be filled with cream and cooked in the oven.

Cremini Also called common brown mushrooms or Italian mushrooms, these are actually a variety of the ordinary white mushroom. They are pale brown in color with a deeper flavor than the white mushroom. They can be used in any mushroom recipe.

Portobello These large mushrooms—from about 3 inches up to 8 inches across—are the mature version of the cultivated white mushroom, the grown-up cremini. They resemble wild field mushrooms and have a rich flavor and meaty texture. They can be grilled whole and served on a salad of arugula with olive oil. Or slice the caps and sauté with garlic and plenty of black pepper and chopped parsley.

It is best to buy mushrooms a few at a time and often. Mushrooms can lose moisture and dry out even in the refrigerator, and their flesh soon starts to shrivel. To limit evaporation, they can be kept in brown paper bags. All but the densely fleshed button mushrooms act like sponges when they are cooking, absorbing more than their own weight in liquid, so add them to stews or casseroles toward the end of the cooking time.

Japanese and Chinese mushrooms

Long before mushrooms were first cultivated in Europe, the Japanese were harvesting *take* specially grown in the water-softened bark of various tree trunks. In addition to shiitakes there are enoki, also called golden mushrooms or golden needles (*Flammulina velutipes*), and the meaty-tasting matsutake, grown on pine logs. Unlike the shiitake and the enoki, the matsutake has not been successfully cultivated.

As well as dried shiitakes, which are the black mushrooms served in Chinese restaurants, Chinese markets carry a stemless mushroom known as cloud ear, tree ear, or wood ear, used for texture rather than flavor. These dried mushrooms must be soaked for half an hour to revive their unusual texture.

Another Chinese mushroom is the tiny straw mushroom (*Volvariella volvaceae*), so called because it is grown on straw from paddy fields. It is normally sold canned.

Truffles

One of the rarest and certainly the most expensive of all fungi, the black Périgord truffle (*Tuber melanosporum*) grows on the roots of young oak trees. This is the most sought after of the truffle species, and is detected beneath the soil by pigs or specially trained truffle hounds.

With its rich, mold-like flavor, a little of the black truffle goes a long way—one of the good reasons it is used sparingly in such things as omelets, scrambled eggs, or stuffing for roast chicken. The classic dish *truffe sous cendre*—truffle wrapped in bacon fat or pastry and baked (traditionally under cinders)—is highly rated by gourmets. Sadly, truffles found in pâtés often have no flavor at all and were probably canned.

The white truffle of Italy's Piedmont is larger, stronger in flavor, and almost as expensive as its Périgord cousin. While the latter is invariably eaten cooked, the Italians use their white truffle raw, grating or slicing it over risottos and salads.

Dried cloud ear

Straw mushroom

Shiitake mushroom

Enoki

Black truffle

White truffle

Fruit

APPLE AND PEAR

Apples and pears, although frequently bracketed as if they were almost one and the same fruit, could scarcely be more different.

Apples are the most common, the most easy-going, and the most useful of all fruits, both to eat casually at any time of the day and to cook with—there are more apple desserts than any other sort. Pears, on the other hand, are a fragile luxury—large and aesthetically pleasing, they make a grand ending to a grand meal, and speak to the diner of sunny orchards and of careful harvesting and marketing.

Apple

Today, the choice of apples is getting smaller and smaller—although there are several thousand different apples cultivated in gardens and nurseries, very few find their way into commercial orchards, where the fruit must keep well and be tough, disease-resistant, and good at traveling. Of the seven thousand varieties known in the United States, only twenty or so are seriously marketed.

This is sad, since there are so many aromatic old-fashioned apples that are worth growing. But there has been a marked interest in some of the antique or heirloom varieties, and more of these are being cultivated now. So hunt through country markets and the more enlightened supermarkets, and you may come across some interesting varieties.

Apples sold as windfalls are also good buys and are perfect for cooking, since these unripe apples have plenty of acid, essential to the flavor of apple pies, tarts, and crisps. The best eating apples are those that retain some acidity even in their final sweetness, and have a mellow flavor and firm, juicy texture. The bright red apples known as Empires and the tart, green Granny Smith are especially good. The most popular American varieties are listed in the chart; others to look for are Baldwin, Northern Spy, Jonathan, Gravenstein, and Winesap.

Buying and storing apples While obviously one should avoid apples with bruises and soft spots, do not be put off by a few dull, rough, brown patches on sound apples. This is called russeting, and does not indicate spoilage. The term russet, in fact, refers to a whole category of winter apples with rough brownish

NAME	APPEARANCE	FLESH	TYPE
Red Delicious	large, elongated, thick-skinned, shiny red	juicy, very tender, no acidity	eating
Golden Delicious	large, conical, green ripening to yellow	tender, very sweet, no acidity when ripe	all-purpose
Granny Smith	medium to large, conical, green with whitish flecks	crisp, juicy, sweet-tart	all-purpose
McIntosh	medium, round, two-tone red and green to red	crisp, juicy, firm, slightly tart	all-purpose
Rome Beauty	large, round, thick-skinned, shiny red	crisp, juicy, firm, slightly tart	baking whole
Empire	medium, round, strong dark red	crisp, juicy, firm	all-purpose
Newtown Pippin	medium, round, greenish-yellow	crisp, juicy, firm, mildly tart	all-purpose
Cortland	medium, round, red tinged with green	crisp, firm, slightly tart	all-purpose
Gala	medium, round, yellow flushed and striped with orange and red	crisp, juicy, sweet-tart, aromatic	eating
Crispin (Mutsu)	medium to large, yellow-green	crisp, juicy, mild but slightly acid	eating
Cox's Orange Pippin	small, round, greenish-yellow tinged with red	crisp, juicy, firm, sweet, some acidity	all-purpose, best for eating
Orleans Reinette	small, flat, golden tinged with crimson	crisp, juicy, firm, some acidity	all-purpose
Egremont Russet	medium, round, with brown-orange russeting	soft, very sweet, some acidity	all-purpose
Laxton's Superb	medium, round, greenish-yellow, flushed with red	juicy, firm, sweet, some acidity	all-purpose
Bramley's Seedling	extra-large, irregular, green sometimes flushed with red	crisp, juicy, acid	cooking
Worcester Pearmain	medium, round, red, sometimes two-tone red and green	crisp, juicy, firm, sweet, slightly tart	all-purpose

skins; since Americans tend to like bright, shiny apples, russets are more popular in Europe. They are splendid with cheese, and cook well.

Those buying for the trade test for ripeness by grasping apples around the waist and applying gentle pressure: if the flesh is firm or the skin wrinkles only slightly, the apples are at the peak of perfection. Fragrance is also important, and the fruit should be firm.

Apples continue to ripen after they have been picked. If they are to be stored, they should be spread out so that they are not touching one other. If you want to buy apples in quantity, at one of the pick-your-own farms, for example, keep them on racks in a cool, dry, dark place.

Cooking with apples Selecting the right apples for cooking is important if you do not want your pies to end up watery or your baked apples to collapse in a frothy mess all over the oven. Some apples, such as America's favorite eating apple, the Red Delicious, are too tender for cooking and lack the acidity that gives apple dishes their delicious flavor.

The hard, crisp apples such as the popular Granny Smith or baking apples like the Rome Beauty will require longer cooking than the softer-fleshed ones.

Applesauce When making applesauce, choose crisp, juicy apples with plenty of acid—adding sugar toward the end of the cooking time—as these will quickly turn to a froth. Tart apples give a sweet-acid taste that is delicious with pork, pheasant, or goose.

Cooking sliced apples Many of the dishes involving apples, such as pies and tarts, turnovers, crisps, and fritters, depend on apples keeping their shape. Sugar and/or butter added at the start of cooking helps to prevent them from disintegrating. Among the best "pie apples" are Empires and Newtown Pippins. The Golden Delicious retains its shape well, but lacks flavor, so cook it with cinnamon and plenty of butter and sugar. Europe's favorite reinettes and russets, noted for their unique subtle flavor, are excellent for cooking: these are the apples that French cooks use when making *tartes aux pommes*.

Baking apples These are cored with an apple corer and the cavity filled with sugar, butter, and perhaps raisins, almonds, or blackberries. They are then baked, possibly basted or flamed with Calvados or brandy, and served with heavy cream. The best apples for baking are the large ones. Run your knife around the circumference of the apple (to prevent the skin from splitting) before you stuff them and put them in the baking dish. Thick-skinned varieties such as Rome Beauty are ideal, since their skins are less likely to burst. The harder the apple, the longer it will take to bake: it is done when the top is frothy and seeping with juice.

Fried apples A classic accompaniment to pork chops is peeled, sliced apples fried until golden in butter. Fried apples are good with sausages at breakfast, and they are also very good with pheasant.

Stewing apples When stewing apples, as for a compote, use the same varieties as you would use for pies and tarts. To vary the flavor, you can add cloves, cinnamon, or perhaps coriander seeds and grated lemon zest. Rum or Calvados and butter are also good with stewed apples. Some savory dishes, such as Iran's *khoresh*, involve apples with cinnamon and onions. In West Germany, apples are stewed, sprinkled with bread crumbs, and then fried, to be served with ham.

Raw apples Sliced or chopped apples give a crisp, crunchy texture to salad. The famous Waldorf salad of celery, apples, and walnuts tossed in mayonnaise is especially good if made right. A squeeze of lemon juice will prevent cut-up apples from turning brown. Any crisp, sharp eating apple will make a good salad.

Lady apple

Lady apples, usually found in specialty markets or farmers' markets, are miniature apples about the size of a crabapple. They may be red or yellow flushed with red. They can be eaten raw or cooked—there's no need to peel them—and are often used as a garnish.

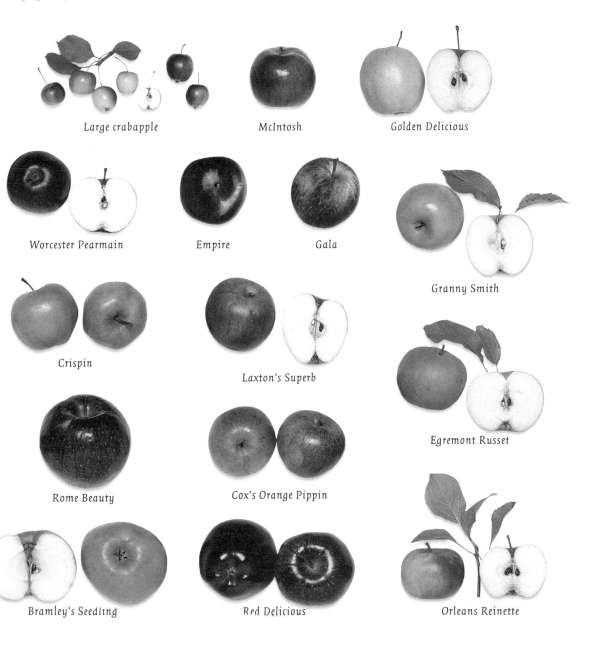

Large crabapple

McIntosh

Golden Delicious

Worcester Pearmain

Empire

Gala

Granny Smith

Crispin

Laxton's Superb

Egremont Russet

Rome Beauty

Cox's Orange Pippin

Bramley's Seedling

Red Delicious

Orleans Reinette

Crabapple, quince, and medlar

These three fruits, like the apple, are related to the rose family.

Crabapple Roasted and still hot, the crabapples that "hissed in the bowl" in the hot spiced ale punches of Shakespeare's day were most likely the small, sour apples that grow wild or in gardens and that are the ancestors of all our modern apples. These beautiful tiny fruits, which can be yellow, red, or green, are no longer eaten (except by birds), because they are generally not worth the bother, being mostly core and often very sour. They do, however, make a lovely clear, golden-pink jelly, which is excellent on buttered bread and with good cream cheese. Larger crabapples, which are slightly sweeter, grow from the seeds of cultivated apples that have become wild. They have a crisp, tart flavor.

Quinces came originally from Central Asia. Yellow-gold and aromatic, they are a pleasing sight in autumn and are usually used to make jellies or jams. The astringent fruit, always eaten cooked, is not as popular in America as in Europe, which is unfortunate. A slice or two added to an apple pie or tart gives these dishes a delicious scent and flavor. Quinces can also be boiled down with sugar to a thick paste—called *membrillo* in Spain, *cotignac* in southwestern France, and quince cheese in Britain—which is then dried and eaten as a sweet.

Medlar This unusual European fruit rarely comes to market, but is sometimes cultivated in gardens or seen growing wild in hedges. Medlars look like open cups of a warm golden-brown and resemble a large rose hip. Since they do not ripen on the tree, they need to be picked and kept until they turn soft before they are edible. The ripe state is easily recognizable, because the unripe fruit is rock-hard. Medlars are usually baked or made into jam or jelly, or the flesh is scraped out and eaten with sugar and cream. The taste and texture are slightly reminiscent of marzipan.

Pear

This fruit, which can be so delicious, is more temperamental than the apple. It has an unpleasant habit of becoming mealy from the core outward, a state that is described by English growers as "sleepiness," and it does not keep as well as the apple.

Pears come in almost as great a variety as apples. Europe has about five thousand named varieties and America about one thousand, but, as with apples, only a small proportion reach the market. Three shapes predominate: the ordinary pear shape, the long-necked shape, and the oval, almost round shape. Colors, too, vary a great deal, from a soft blurred brown to bright green with dark brown, gray-black, or green flecks, to golden with a handsome red-gold flush.

Comice pear This French variety, properly known as *Doyenné de Comice*, is considered to be one of the best pears. It has a perfect balance of sweetness and acidity and a certain spiciness. Its juicy, sweet flesh is buttery—meaning that it is melting and not grainy. Medium to large and greenish-yellow, it has a red blush where it has been exposed to the sun. Its thick, shiny skin is stippled with tiny gray spots and fawn patches.

Bartlett This popular pear is usually known as the Williams' pear in Europe, as it was propagated by an English grower named Williams. It was first introduced to North America by an American called Bartlett. It has a sweet, musky flavor and a smooth skin that turns from dark green to yellow as it ripens; eat it when its speckles are still surrounded by a tiny halo of green on an otherwise golden skin. These superb pears are unfortunately bad travelers and extremely perishable.

Anjou One of the most widely grown varieties of pear in the United States, the Anjou remains green even when fully ripe. It has sweet, spicy, juicy flesh speckled with tiny brown spots.

Packham's Triumph This descendant of the Bartlett or Williams' pear looks somewhat like its distinguished ancestor but is not nearly so delicate. It keeps well and is therefore exported in great numbers from Australia, where it is grown in profusion.

Medlar

Quince

Seckel pear

Anjou pear

Asian pear

Comice pear

Bosc pear

Conference pear

Bartlett pear

Conference pear A favorite English pear, this was so named when it won the top prize at a fruit growers' conference because of its fine, tender, melting flesh and delicious flavor. This pear is slim and long-necked, stippled with fawn and gray russeting, and turns pale yellow when it is ripe.

Bosc More properly known as the Beurré Bosc, this is one of a number of pear varieties that have the French word for butter in their names and are characterized by their creamy, melting quality. The Beurré Bosc is so named in honor of a former director of the Jardin des Plantes in Paris, who propagated it. It has a long neck and a fine brown russeting. Juicier and plumper than the Beurré Bosc, the Beurré Hardy, a popular European variety, takes its name from a nineteenth-century Belgian and is a plumper pear. Both pears in their youth have enough juice for delicious eating and are also excellent when poached.

Bonne Louise This French pear is now also known as Louise Bonne de Jersey, and in German-speaking countries as *gute Louise von Avranches*. Good it certainly is, and well known not only in its native country but wherever French pears are exported. Smooth-skinned, with the merest speckle of russeting, the Louise tends to be greenish on the shaded side and yellow washed with pink on the side ripened in the sun. It makes an excellent dessert pear.

Seckel, Seckle This was discovered growing wild in Pennsylvania by an eighteenth-century trapper. It is small and rather round, with a green to russet skin sometimes tinged with rose. It is sweet, juicy, and spicy.

Clapp's Favorite This medium pear has green skin that turns golden-yellow when fully ripe, with some russeting and, occasionally, faintly red cheeks. It is a popular variety for cooking.

Passe crassane This fat, juicy, rounded Italian pear has a lovely flavor and makes an excellent dessert pear. It keeps well.

Asian pear The many varieties of Asian pear range in size from tiny to huge, and may be round like an apple or elongated like a pear. Skin color is golden-brown or greenish-yellow. The flesh is firm and crunchy when ripe and extremely juicy.

Buying pears Pears for eating or cooking should always be sound. Test for ripeness near the stem end, where there should be more than a little give, and at the blossom end, where there should be no oozing softness, since this usually indicates trouble within. Pears are at their best for a very short time, and although they can be left to mature for a little while, they must be inspected frequently.

Cooking with pears Most large pears are eating pears, although some are juicier than others. All pears, however, can also be poached in wine or light syrup, and well-flavored eating pears such as Bartletts are, in fact, best for such dishes as pear sorbet.

The best pears for cooking are the harder, firmer varieties. Poached in vanilla-flavored syrup, they make good compotes and can also be cooked in spiced red wine, in the process of which they become dyed to "a fine Oriental red." In Italy, they are halved and baked in Marsala, the cavity of each half stuffed with a mixture of ground almonds and crystallized fruit. They can also be made into a relish or chutney with lemon juice and ginger or with horseradish, mustard seeds, and black pepper; or they can be preserved or pickled with sugar, cinnamon, and white wine vinegar. Cooked with butter and sugar, they used to be served hot with game in Germany. They are still served cold there, poached in lemon juice with cranberries.

Around the North Sea, pears also go into main dishes: in the Netherlands, they are boiled along with green beans, potatoes, and beef, while in Hamburg they are cooked with beans and bacon or with cured meats. Boiled potatoes mixed with pears and a dash of vinegar are also sometimes served in northern Europe; try pear and spinach purée with roast duck.

CITRUS FRUIT

The beautiful citrus fruits, probably East Asian in origin, all have one thing in common: they ripen while they are still on the tree. Once they have been picked, they stop developing and will not get sweeter or improve in flavor. But most of them travel well and remain in good condition for many weeks in the right environment, only gradually losing weight and pliancy as their juices and oils lose freshness.

Natural untreated citrus fruits are subject to what is called regreening. This does not necessarily mean that the fruits are unripe, but is simply a matter of temperature: the chlorophyll in ripe fruit fades as the thermometer drops and revives as it rises again; inside the skin, the fruit remains unaffected. However, since green patches are unattractive on citrus fruit that should by rights be orange or lemon-yellow, they are often treated with ethylene gas, which fades the chlorophyll, making the fruit more acceptable to the consumer.

When buying citrus fruits, choose those that feel heavy for their size, as this means plenty of juice. The fruit should be sound, with no signs of bruising, damp patches, or soft spots. If you want to use the peel in cooking or for making marmalade, try to find fruit that is unwaxed, and wash or scrub it well to remove any residues of pesticides or other treatments it may have had.

Citron

This fruit is the elder of the citrus tribe. It has a thick corrugated skin, and looks similar to a large, rough lemon. Since its pulp is too bitter to eat, the citron is now mostly grown to make the most beautiful translucently green candied peel, which is used in fruitcakes.

Orange

Oranges may be orange, but they can also be green, greenish-yellow, and even red. There are three main varieties of orange: the smooth, thin-skinned sweet oranges, such as the Valencias and blood oranges, which range from bright gold to blood red and are full of juice; the larger, rougher, thick-skinned seedless navel oranges, which have the best flavor and are easy to peel; and the bitter oranges, also known as Seville or Bigarade oranges, which are used for making the best marmalade. The bergamot, a small, acidic citrus fruit similar to an orange, yields an essential oil from its rind that is used in perfumes, confectionery, and Earl Grey tea.

Orange marmalade, which was invented in Scotland, owes its origins to a boatload of Portuguese oranges that arrived in Dundee in the eighteenth century and unexpectedly turned out to be extremely bitter. Bitter oranges occasionally come onto the market in their short New Year season, and marmalade making is about the only occasion on which we boil oranges to good purpose.

For the most part, however, we like our oranges fresh. In Trinidad, they are sold in the street, halved and sprinkled with salt. Orange juice, freshly squeezed and served with ice, used to be standard refreshment in all countries. In Sicily, a paradise for oranges, the juice is drunk not so much as an appetizer but as a final refreshment after a meal—especially the glorious tomato-red juice of blood oranges, which is particularly sweet and full of flavor.

When making orange juice, thin-skinned oranges such as the virtually seedless Valencias are the best choice. This is not so much because navel oranges lack juice, but because their imposing size makes them more expensive, and since their skins have a thick padding of pith, a lot of what we pay for is thrown away. The thin-skinned

oranges are, of course, in fact sometimes simply called juice oranges. The navel orange, which can be peeled neatly and is virtually seedless, is the best one to eat as a dessert or snack.

Mandarin and tangerine

These and their many cultivars such as clementines and satsumas are the smaller members of the citrus family and their names are sometimes used interchangeably. All are distinguished by having skin that does not cling to the fruit, and flesh that separates easily into segments.

These fruits are known as various mandarin cultivars to the botanist, but simply as different types of tangerines to the shopper. Those of North African descent, which are grown in and

exported from Tangiers, with loose skins and perfumed juice, are responsible for the name tangerine. Canned segments are sold under this name, although most are actually satsumas.

Clementine These are considered by some people to be mandarins crossed with the Algerian wild orange, but clementines are generally recognized as a variety of tangerine. They are usually tiny, with a very good flavor—children are particularly fond of them.

Satsuma These are the tangerines that are grown and exported from Japan and Cyprus. They can have quite a sour taste and are very refreshing.

Temple orange A cross between a tangerine and a sweet orange, temple oranges have loose, deep-orange skins and a sweet-tart flavor.

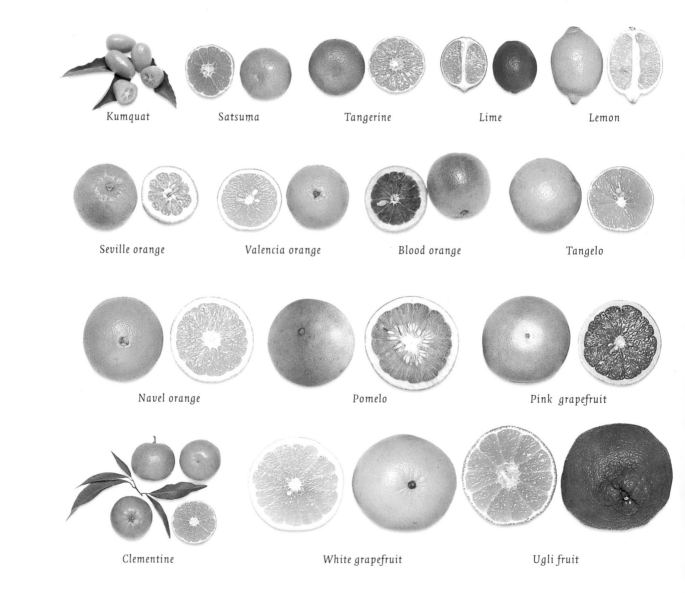

Kumquat   Satsuma   Tangerine   Lime   Lemon

Seville orange   Valencia orange   Blood orange   Tangelo

Navel orange   Pomelo   Pink grapefruit

Clementine   White grapefruit   Ugli fruit

Murcott (honey tangerine), ortanique, king, and tangor Along with many other small hybrids, these are related to both tangerines and oranges. They are often found growing together on the same tree, which shows how easily they cross with each other. All are sweet, spicy dessert fruits, and all are easy to peel.

Tangelo and ugli fruit

The tangelo is a cross between a tangerine and a grapefruit. It is loose-skinned and ranges from deep-red orange to orange-yellow. The Minneola, or Mineola, variety is particularly sweet and juicy and easy to peel.

The ugli fruit, larger than most tangelos, is another tangerine-grapefruit cross (or, possibly, a tangerine-pomelo hybrid). Its extraordinary bumpy, mottled skin is greenish-yellow, but the light orange flesh is sweet, juicy, and delicately flavored, with a flower-like perfume.

Grapefruit and pomelo

The large familiar globe of the grapefruit—either yellow, when it is called white; rosy, when it is called pink; or ruby-red fleshed inside a yellow or pinkish-yellow skin, when it is called ruby—is a descendant of the pomelo, a citrus plant brought from Polynesia to the West Indies in the seventeenth century by an English sea captain. The grapefruit is perhaps more popular in America than anywhere else. It is primarily a breakfast fruit, but it also ends meals in mousses and sorbets, and in between turns up in salads mixed with avocado, or with oranges and mint, and served on a bed of lettuce.

The pomelo, or pumelo, is also called shaddock, after that English sea captain. It may be found in Asian or specialty produce markets in winter, at least as large as a grapefruit and often larger, and ranging in color from greenish to yellow. The pink or pale-yellow flesh can be very juicy but is sometimes dry, and the taste may be either sweet or pleasantly tangy.

Kumquat

This originated in Japan and has recently been cast from the citrus family by botanists, although it continues to look and taste like a tiny orange. Tart in flavor, kumquats are usually eaten with their skin, and are often bottled in syrup.

Lemon

This most indispensable of fruits, which is rich in vitamin C, can be either large or small, with a smooth, thin skin or a thick and knobbly one. For culinary purposes, such as mousses and sorbets, lemon curd, lemon soups, and frothy sauces, and for the wedges served with fish for squeezing over, it is always better to use smooth-skinned lemons if possible, as they have more juice.

Choose specimens that are truly lemon-yellow in color. Butter-yellow lemons may have lost some of their acidity during the ripening process, and lemons that look dull and do not have a moist-looking sheen may be dry and "ricy," meaning that the almost invisible little sacs containing the juice have turned grainy through evaporation.

Lemons owe much of their flavor and aroma to the oil contained in the outer part of their skin, which is known as the zest. When serving lemon quarters, cut them lengthwise so that, when they are squeezed, the juice will be directed downward onto the food. Whenever possible, lemon juice should be added to dishes after they have been cooked, to avoid any loss of its valuable vitamin C, which disappears when heated.

In addition to its use as a flavoring, lemon juice has certain other qualities that are of value to the cook. When poaching or stewing fruit, 1 teaspoon lemon juice added to each ¼ cup water will help prevent the fruit from breaking up or losing its shape. A few squeezes of juice will help poached eggs set, and a few drops will acidulate water sufficiently to prevent the discoloration of vegetables such as Jerusalem artichokes or salsify. Lemon juice can be used instead of vinegar in salad dressings, and, since it helps to counteract the richness of foods, it can aid digestion when used with fried foods.

Lime

This can be pale or dark green and has a tart greenish pulp; if the skin is yellowish, it usually means that the tang has gone. The Mexican or West Indian lime, which features so much in Southwest and Creole cooking, is sharp and aromatic in flavor, as are the larger Tahitian limes, of which the Persian and the Bearss are two types. The Key limes of Florida have a delicious sharpness to them and are used to make Key lime pie.

Limes are the most perishable of all citrus fruits: unfortunately, they dry up and shrivel all too fast, and develop soft brown patches on their skins. They can be used for many of the same purposes as lemons, and their juice, which is pale when fresh but often has added green color when it's been commercially extracted, goes into daiquiris, margaritas, and other tequila drinks.

1

2

Peeling and sectioning citrus fruits

1 Using a serrated knife, cut a slice from the top and bottom of the fruit to expose the flesh. Peel the fruit in the same way as you would an apple, cutting just beneath the pith.

2 Hold the fruit in one hand and cut out each segment, freeing it from its membrane as you cut. The resulting sections should be completely free of membrane and pith.

STONE FRUIT

Although imported peaches can be found for much of the year, there is still something wonderfully seasonal about stone fruits. Their year begins with the first cherries and ends with the last of the plums, with local peaches, nectarines, and apricots in between. All are closely related members of the Prunus family and when talked about collectively are known as drupes.

Cherry

Firm-fleshed or melting, deepest lip-staining black, or the palest cream tinged with a rosy blush, the cherry comes in hundreds of varieties. They are generally classified by their growers as sweet or sour. There is also a third type, which is a mixture of sweet and sour; two of these hybrids are Dukes and Royales. Usually black or translucent red, these are all-purpose cherries and can be eaten and cooked in a variety of ways.

Sweet cherry Sweet cherries (*Prunus avium*) used to be neatly divided into the hard, crisp bigarreaus and the soft, sweet cherries known as hearts or heart cherries in America (or, sometimes, jeans), *guignes* in France, and geans in England. Now, however, with the appearance of many hybrids, the distinction has become blurred.

Among the most delicious of the bigarreaus is the Bing—large, heart-shaped, and deep red to almost black, with firm, sweet flesh. The Royal Anne is also a bigarreau—big, crisp, and golden with a red cheek.

Another red-black cherry that is tender and has an excellent flavor is the black Tartarian, a type of *guigne*. The Lambert is a large deep-red sweet cherry that is similar to the Bing but slightly smaller and not quite as good. The Ranier is a sweet golden cherry with a pink blush.

Bings are the first choice for a fresh sweet cherry pie. Sweet, juicy, black *guignes* are used to make the delicious dessert clafoutis, which comes from France's Dordogne; in Kent, England's cherry-orchard county, a similar dish goes by the name of battered cherries. The same juicy cherries also go into the exquisite Swiss black cherry jam, shiny, slippery, and full of whole cherries.

Sour cherry If the word sweet is sometimes used too optimistically as far as cherries are concerned, sour is almost an understatement. The dark, short-stemmed, juicy Morellos, or *griottes* as they are known in France, are so acidic that they are almost impossible to eat. They are small, round, and deep red to almost black. The famous Black Forest cherry cake called *schwarzwälder kirschtorte* is authentically made with Morellos grown in the Black Forest region, and with *kirschwasser*, the Black Forest version of cherry brandy. Cherries such as the Montmorency, brighter in color and with pale, clear juice, are so sour that they are not normally eaten uncooked. Early Richmond is another sour cherry.

Sour cherries (*Prunus cerasus*) go into translucent jams; into pickles to eat with game, pork, poultry, rich meat dishes, and pâtés; and into liqueurs and cherry brandies. Fresh sour cherries make the most delicious pie. Duck Montmorency, now something of a cliché, requires cherries for its fruity wine sauce, although they do not have to be the sour Montmorency cherries of France; any

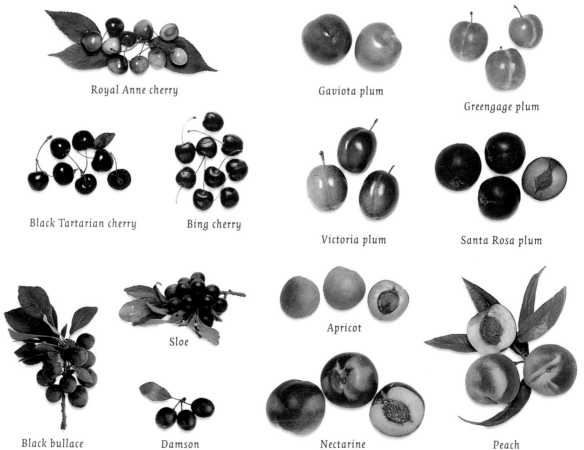

Royal Anne cherry

Gaviota plum

Greengage plum

Black Tartarian cherry

Bing cherry

Victoria plum

Santa Rosa plum

Sloe

Apricot

Black bullace

Damson

Nectarine

Peach

acidic red cherries will do. And cherries set alight in a brandy sauce and poured over vanilla ice cream make Cherries Jubilee. Morello cherries are often preserved and make good tarts and pies.

Maraschino cherry The sweet, sticky liqueur maraschino is made from a small, wild cherry from the Dalmatian region of Yugoslavia, the *damasca*, or *marasca*. Maraschino cherries, however, which were originally preserved by being steeped in the liqueur, are now more likely to be ordinary cherries that have been bleached and then steeped in syrup flavored with almond or mint.

Buying and storing cherries Look for brightly colored fruit; whether heart-shaped or spherical, the plump ones are always best. The fruit should be clean and glossy, with unbroken skins and stems that are fresh and green. Make sure the stems are attached on most of the fruit, or the fruit may have been spoiled by mold or rot in transit. Ripe cherries are perishable, but will keep for a few days in the refrigerator; wash them just before they are to be eaten.

Cooking with cherries Prepare cherries for cooking by pushing out the pits with a cherry pitter or hooking them out with the U-bend of a paper clip or hairpin. If you try to squeeze the pits out, too much juice will be lost.

Canned cherries lack firmness and flavor and are best used in sweet, rather than savory, dishes, although they still won't be very good.

Plum

"No other fruit," said Pliny, "has been so cleverly crossed"—and since he wrote this some 2000 years ago, the growers have not been idle. Some plums are grown primarily to be eaten fresh, although many, like the greengage, are equally delicious cooked.

Eating plums These are usually larger and juicier than cooking plums, with a higher sugar content.

Santa Rosa These pleasantly tart, bright red plums are grown largely in California, where the climate suits their warm temperament. Derivatives of the wild Asiatic plum, they are often referred to as Japanese plums, although they were grown originally in China. Others of this type are the Laroda, with reddish-yellow skin, Friar, Queen Anne, and the Kelsey, a dark-green to yellow plum.

Greengage Of all the European plums, none is more sweetly perfumed than the greengage, known in France as the Reine-Claude. In the United States, the Kelsey is sometimes marketed as a greengage plum, but it is not the real thing. In Europe, there are several other varieties in addition to the old greengage, round and firm-fleshed, with its rose-flushed cheek. There are also many golden descendants of the old French "transparent gage," large and translucent, with the delicious honeyed flesh characteristic of all the gages.

Italian or prune plum These small purple plums are quite good eaten out of the hand, but are usually at their best in the kitchen, stewed or used in baking.

Gaviota and Victoria The Gaviota is one of the newer European varieties, grown to giant proportions; it is sweet and juicy, and ruby-colored right down to the pit. Golden-red and pink-bloomed, the Victoria is one of the most prolific of plums. Oval-shaped with golden flesh, it is a favorite in the kitchen and is also excellent eaten out of hand.

Cooking plums These are usually the smaller, drier, sharp-flavored plums that retain enough acidity to make them delicious when cooked.

Damson These have a lovely acidity even when ripe, and are used for jams, pies, and other desserts. Damsons are not as common as they once were, but are well worth seeking out. In England, they may be turned into damson cheese, an old country confection made of puréed fruit and plenty of sugar, which is aged before it is ready to eat. Damson cheese is a close relation to the more pliable *mus*—made from the quetsch plum—which used to be very popular.

Beach plum These grow wild along the Atlantic Coast, especially on Cape Cod. The small, tart, dark purple fruits grow in large clusters and are avidly gathered to be made into beach plum jelly or jam.

Sloe and bullace Dark and mouth-drying, the sloe is a wild European plum that grows on spiky hedges and is used for making sloe gin. The wild bullace, larger than the sloe, is less acidic and can be stewed or made into jelly or preserves. These are rarely seen in U.S. markets.

Zwetschen, Quetsch plum Also known as *switzen*, or, in the Slavonic languages, *slivy*, these are small, dark blue plums with a heavy bloom. They thrive in central Europe, where they are made into the plum brandy *slivovitz*, and in Germany and in Alsace, where they are used to make a potent fruit brandy.

Mirabelles are also called myrobalans or, in Britain, cherry plums. They are very small, with red or yellow skins and golden flesh. These European plums are soft and juicy and are excellent stewed or made into jams. They are also used to make an *eau-de-vie* called mirabelle.

Buying and storing plums When buying plums, make sure that they are firm and free from damage. They should be stored in a cool place, but not for too long; ripened plums do not keep for more than 2 or 3 days.

Cooking with plums All dark plums, like the purple Empress and the almost black El Dorado, and some of the lighter varieties, such as the small golden-yellow Mirabelle, have bitter skins. This makes a delicious contrast to the sweetness of their flesh when cooked. They can be used to make jams and jellies that are transparently luminous when freshly cooked, but darken with aging. They also make a delicious sweet-sour sauce to serve with meat and with the pancakes that accompany Peking duck.

In Austria, plums, fresh or dried, go into the middle of lovely deep-fried little dumplings that are rolled in fine sugar mixed with grated chocolate, and go into strudels. Throughout Germany, the plum season means *Pflaumenkuchen*—plums riding on a yeast-based dough that absorbs the juice of the fruit. In Britain, many recipes such as plum pudding do not require plums at all, the word being used to mean raisins.

Peach

The flesh of peaches ranges from almost silvery-white to deep gold or deep red. White-fleshed peaches are tender and juicy, yellow ones slightly coarser but often very good; the little-known red-fleshed *pêches-de-vignes* of France can be the richest in flavor. With some peaches, the flesh clings to the stone, hence clingstone peaches, while with freestone varieties, the flesh comes away cleanly.

Known as *Prunus persica*, the peach reached Greece from its native China via Persia, and then Rome and the rest of Europe via Greece. It arrived in America by way of peach pits carried by Columbus, and the American soil and

cooking with wine and spirits 208–9
dried peach 184
prune 184
cherry pitter 225

Peach Melba Cobbler 398

climate suited the peach tree so well that it spread faster than the settlers. But it is Georgia, especially, that is known as the peach state. The freestone Belle of Georgia, crimson cheeked, its creamy flesh delicately marbled and its stone sitting in a carmine-tinted pit, comes from seed that was sent directly from China at the end of the nineteenth century. Elberta, another favorite Georgian, has juicy yellow flesh, firm but tender. It is equally popular fresh or canned, but while canned peaches in heavy syrup are nice enough, they differ almost more than any other fruit from their fresh counterparts.

Buying and storing peaches Large peaches command the highest price but are not always the most delicately flavored. In China, where peaches symbolize longevity, the highly venerated ancestor of all the peach trees in the world bears fruit that is relatively small, with large pits, and yet its flavor is said to be unsurpassed by any of our hybrids.

Peaches are a fragile fruit and should be handled very gently. They should feel firm with a little give; greenish fruit should be avoided, as it will never ripen at home. Store ripe peaches in the refrigerator, but keep those that are still a little too firm at room temperature.

Cooking with peaches Some people eat peaches in salads, and spiced or pickled peaches are excellent with ham, but it is in desserts that peaches come into real use. Peach sorbets and ice creams are both delicate and subtle, and there are scores of sundaes and *coûpes* made with peaches, the most famous of which must undoubtedly be Peach Melba. Invented by Escoffier for a late dinner for Dame Nellie Melba, the opera singer, this involves a ripe fresh peach gently poached in syrup, with vanilla ice cream, whipped fresh cream, and crushed fresh raspberries for the sauce. In France, peaches and raspberries are combined in an exquisite fruit salad.

Nectarine

One of the most beautiful of all fruits, with rosy cheeks like those of a blushing girl, the nectarine is smooth-skinned like a plum. It is like a ripe plum in texture, but tastes of peach, although it is a little sharper and more scented. Nectarines can be used in all the same ways as peaches, but are usually devoured, messily, as a dessert fruit or snack—much juicier than peaches, they are rarely peeled, because their skin is much thinner. Called *brugnons* in France, they are eaten there in vast quantities in July and August, the white-fleshed varieties fetching higher prices than the yellow ones. Nectarines can be purchased underripe, as they will ripen at room temperature.

Apricot

Even in the days when fresh fruit was regarded with suspicion, apricots were generally accepted as wholesome food. Known as *Prunus armeniaca* because the Romans obtained them from the Far East via Armenia, they span the spectrum of gentle orangey tones, from the very pale to the very rich. Depth of color, however, is not necessarily an indication of flavor; it merely means that some varieties have more carotene than others and are richer in vitamin A. The deep-orange apricot called Moorpark is always sweet and delicious to eat.

The flesh of apricots is much firmer and drier than that of peaches and nectarines, which makes them ideal for eating fresh as well as for cooking—they will not turn into a mush, thereby ruining your tart or whatever else.

Buying and storing apricots An apricot picked before its time does not sweeten, it only matures a little, so test for ripeness by pressing the fruit gently between two fingers; it should feel soft. Ripe fruits will keep in the refrigerator for a few days. Unripe, they will keep for longer, and if they are too hard and sour to be eaten fresh, they can be cooked in tarts, and a compote, or pickled in vinegar with cloves; this treatment makes an excellent relish that is delicious when eaten with cold pork or ham.

Cooking with apricots In France, large, fresh apricots, arranged on light flaky pastry, make mouthwatering tarts, and a compote of apricots, sometimes flavored with Madeira, is served hot on crisp, golden croutons. Austria's *knoedels*, or apricot dumplings, are made from fresh peeled apricots individually wrapped in thin pastry, and then poached and eaten with hot melted butter, sugar, and cinnamon. And brandied apricots are delicious, the fruit poached with sugar and put up with brandy in equal quantity to the syrup.

BERRIES AND RHUBARB

The arrival of berries heralds the coming of summer, but they will not be so fully flavored and sweet as later on in the season, and they are also likely to be expensive. In the case of most berries, however, it is a pleasure to buy at least a few early ones for decorating creamy mousses or other desserts, to which they give an allure that is quite disproportionate to their numbers.

The real feasting begins in the high season, and it is then that most berries taste best, simply sprinkled with sugar and eaten with milk or cream or possibly sprinkled with wine. When the first flush of excitement has worn off somewhat, they can be combined with other fruit or made into ice creams and sorbets.

There are usually at least 2 weeks each summer when a great number of berries are available simultaneously. This is the time to make fresh berry desserts or to offer great bowls of mixed berries, sugared well beforehand so that they yield some of their juice. Later in the season, when berries are more abundant, and cheaper, it is time to think about making jams, jellies, and syrups.

When buying berries, it is important to look not only at the top of the box in which they are likely to be packed, but also at the underside. Bad staining or wetness suggests squashed fruit, which will soon turn moldy. Some packers still call to mind the Elizabethan "strawberry wives," who, according to their monarch, were given to "laying two or three great ones at the mouth of their pot, and all the rest were little ones."

If you buy berries loose, ask for them to be weighed and packed ½ pound at a time, since this prevents them from being crushed by their own weight on the way home. If you go fruit picking at a farm—every year more of them open their gates to the public—use plenty of small baskets or other containers so that your harvest remains in good condition.

Berries, whether bought or picked, are fragile and perishable, so the sooner you eat them, the better. If they must be stored, spread them out well so that furry casualties do not infect their neighbors. A cool, dark, airy spot other than the refrigerator is in fact the best place to store them because no berries, except perhaps the firmer ones that come in the autumn, will thrive for very long in the refrigerator—it is too humid for them. Also, the more highly scented berries such as strawberries tend to permeate other foods, particularly butter, with their smell. Nevertheless, the refrigerator will be the storage place of necessity for most.

Strawberry

"Doubtless God could have made a better fruit than the strawberry, but doubtless God never did." Best loved among the soft fruits, strawberries conjure up all the well-being of summer. Strawberry shortcake is one of the all-time favorite American desserts. In England, the fruit is built into the summer way of life—garden parties at Buckingham Palace traditionally include what a sixteenth-century writer described as "strawberries swimming in the cream."

The ancestor of the cultivated strawberries we delight in these days was the native wild Virginia berry, introduced to Europe by the early colonists. It was smaller than today's prize specimens, but a positive giant compared with the indigenous European fragrant wood strawberries (fraises des bois) that had long been transplanted into gardens and regarded as a cure for all ills. Alpine strawberries (fraises des Alpes) are slightly larger, and some are white. Both these wild varieties have not changed in their intense fragrance and size, and still remain the best of all strawberries.

The advent of the Virginian strawberry led to unceasing attempts to grow even larger strawberries. Sadly, it was found that what the fruit gained in size it lost in flavor. It was not until a particularly fragrant strawberry arrived from Chile and was crossbred with the Virginian that the balance between size and taste was finally adjusted. This hybrid is the ancestral strawberry of all modern varieties cultivated on both sides of the Atlantic.

Today new varieties of strawberries are regularly introduced and old ones discarded as being too fragile or not sufficiently resistant to disease, or too small: size rather than flavor has been the important factor in marketing, and the big strawberries command the highest prices. They may look luscious, but from the eater's point of view, bigger is not necessarily better; nor do the deep scarlet varieties necessarily taste best.

Do not be put off by the lighter berries or those that have paler tips, but make sure that the strawberries are plump and glossy. They should be bought with their green frills intact, and if washing them, do so immediately before hulling. Hulled strawberries yield their juice when they are sugared. Only in jam making should strawberries be cooked at all. Even when making strawberry sauce to go with ice creams or sorbets, simply pureé the fresh fruit with sugar and perhaps with a little lemon juice.

The way in which strawberries are served is really a matter of personal preference. Some people like their strawberries simply hulled and sugared, or—using a serving method that is especially pretty—hulled and arranged in a pyramid with strawberry leaves tucked in here and there. Others prefer to eat them with a dusting of black pepper or a sprinkling of orange or lemon juice or balsamic vinegar to bring out the flavor. There is also a school of thought that considers a sprinkling or even a dousing of Beaujolais, claret, or Champagne perfection on strawberries.

Raspberry

This beautiful, velvety berry, from which the liqueur crème de framboises is made, is at its best when a deep garnet red. Black raspberries taste much like the red ones, as do the golden ones, which do not often find their way onto the market. Raspberries are always sold hulled, which makes them fragile and particularly vulnerable to crushing. When picking them, gently slide the beaded lantern shape off its conical center, as this will turn brown and mushy, quickly spoiling the flavor of the fruit.

The flavor of raspberries is intense, and their presence will be apparent even if only a handful is mixed with other fruit, or if the juice of a few is mixed with the juice of, say, red currants, for the Scandinavian dessert called rødgrød.

Raspberry juice is much loved in Germany and Scandinavia as a refreshing drink. And in Berlin, when you order a weisse mit Schuss in a beerhall, you will be served a goblet containing a drink made from pale ale, raspberry syrup, and soda. Finally, among the raspberry-flavored liquids is raspberry vinegar, which is

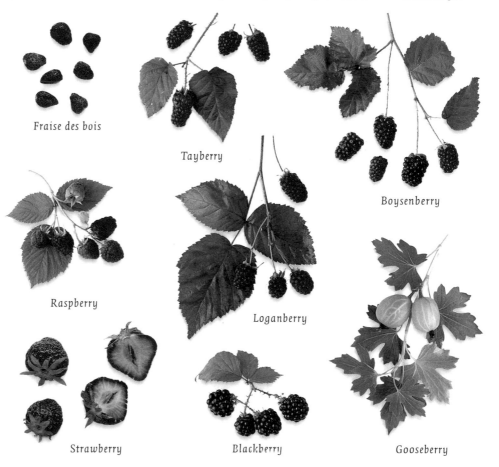

Fraise des bois

Tayberry

Boysenberry

Raspberry

Loganberry

Strawberry

Blackberry

Gooseberry

grouse 82–3
mackerel 15

made by steeping crushed berries in wine vinegar. It is a delicious addition to fruit salads, and when mixed with sugar and water and poured over ice, it makes a cool, thirst-quenching drink.

A few savory dishes are improved by the addition of raspberries—the Scots stuff grouse with the wild raspberries that grow in abundance in the hedges. It is in desserts, however, that raspberries come into their own, either served quite plain with a dollop of whipped cream, or crushed into fresh sorbets, or puréed with a little sugar and served as a sauce.

Blackberry and dewberry

From the shopper's point of view, the distinction between these two berries is purely academic. From the picker's point of view, these relations of the raspberry are distinguished by their growing habits: upright plants are thought of as blackberry bushes, trailing ones as dewberries.

Although blackberries are generally larger than dewberries, and shiny while dewberries are dull, sometimes with a white bloom, their names are used interchangeably in many places. In the United States, the word blackberry is almost always used for any variety. Neither their taste nor their properties differ, and both are exceptionally rich in vitamin C. Both remain sour for a long time after turning black and are only fully ripe when they are soft to the touch.

The plant, which is a bramble, grows freely and can often be found growing along the roadside. In peak season, pickers who know where to look are out in full force, and kitchens are filled with the aroma of the berries, which, besides preserves, are also made into syrup, wine, and any number of desserts. Like raspberries, blackberries can also be eaten with sugar and cream, but this is a success only when the berries are ripe and fresh—once off the brambles, wild blackberries lose their flavor fast.

Cultivated blackberries are more stable and keep their taste longer. They are always sold with their core but without their green stem. They, too, make lovely pies, tarts, crisps, and fools. Blackberries are particularly good cooked with apples, not only because apples give an agreeable texture to the dish, but also because their mellowness accentuates the blackberry's delicious acidic flavor.

Hybrid berries

Whether in an attempt to improve the humble blackberry or to make the raspberry more robust, Messieurs Logan, Young, and Boysen in turn did us a great service in crossbreeding. All three of these hybrid berries can be made into cooked and uncooked desserts and preserves using any recipe in which raspberries are called for.

Loganberry The loganberry is essentially a cross between a blackberry and a raspberry; it is more acidic than the blackberry but less intensely flavored than the raspberry. It is purple with a delicate bloom, is almost conical in shape, and has no seeds. It needs plenty of sugar if eaten uncooked.

Youngberry This is the result of crossing a dewberry with a raspberry. It looks like an elongated blackberry and tastes rather like a loganberry.

Boysenberry This is a cross between a youngberry and a raspberry. Dark red to black and very juicy, it is similar in taste and shape to the raspberry. The size of this fruit causes amazement to those unfamiliar with it, as it is twice or even three times the size of its ancestors.

Marionberry A cross between wild and cultivated blackberries, the marionberry is dark black or scarlet, with a sweet-tart flavor. It is eaten sprinkled with sugar or cooked in pies or preserves.

Tayberry Another blackberry/raspberry cross, the tayberry was bred in Scotland. Large and scarlet-red, it is quite tart.

Cloudberry and mulberry

Cloudberry This is the raspberry's slow-ripening, cold-weather cousin. It has been found as far north as the Arctic Circle, and grows in Siberia, Canada, cold districts of the northern United States, and in Scandinavia, where it forms the basis of many fruit desserts and soups. Fully ripe, it is orange, tinged with red where it catches the sun, and resembles a golden mulberry. Its taste is reminiscent of apples with honey—in Canada it is called the baked-apple berry.

Mulberry Although this berry is not botanically related to the raspberry members of the Rubus tribe, it is used in much the same way. The leaves of the mulberry tree form the silkworm's diet, and many trees of great antiquity are to be found in old gardens, dropping their deep-purple fruit to the ground below.

Mulberries may also be red, and there are even white ones. Ripe and sweet-scented, mulberries are good to eat fresh, although sometimes a little musty and watery. They also make delicious ice creams and sorbets, and a superb jam. They are often used in summer pudding, the traditional English dessert. Take care not to get mulberry juice on your clothes: the stains are hard to remove. One method of removing them, which does work, is to rub the ripe berry juice marks with an unripe mulberry.

Gooseberry

This can be a golden, green, or red globe, translucent or opaque, covered in whiskers or smooth; one variety is also milky-white. The gooseberry is the only berry among the soft fruits that makes the most delicious dishes when it is unripe. No matter what the final color, immature gooseberries are pea-green.

If you find fresh gooseberries, cook them, their spiky stems and tails removed, into a purée with a little water over the lowest heat, adding sugar to taste. They are always sour and require some sweetening even when making the classic sauce for the famous French mackerel dish, to which a little fennel is sometimes added. For pies and crisps or cobblers, gooseberries are also best when they are slightly immature.

When fully ripe, the bigger varieties— full globes of yellow or red— make glorious eating. The common green gooseberries are also good to eat, but are really better for jam making.

Currant

Red currants, white currants, and black currants belong, like gooseberries, to the Rubus tribe, but here the similarity ends. They hang like tiny translucent grapes in little bunches on the bush, and the longer they hang, the sweeter they become. They are, however, never really sweet and even the ripest retain a good percentage of pectin.

Red currant There are those who love eating fresh red currants, raked off their stalks with a fork and covered with sugar and milk. Others prefer them in a berry mixture, or bathed in a real vanilla custard sauce to mitigate their acidity. Red currants are also delicious with melon and are an essential ingredient of summer pudding.

Perhaps best loved of all red-currant preparations, however, is red-currant jelly. Eat this with roast lamb, or with croissants and butter. Add a spoonful when cooking red cabbage or transform it, with the addition of port and orange juice and zest, into a sweet-sharp Cumberland sauce that is ideal for serving with ham and game.

White currant These are less acidic than their red counterparts and can be eaten just as they are, with their thin, almost transparent, silver-gold skins liberally dusted with sugar.

Black currant These, too, make lovely jams and jellies, as well as the liqueur *crème de cassis*, but are rarely eaten fresh, except by those who like sharp-tasting berries.

Black currants are more commonly found in Europe and Central Asia than in America. The Russians, who often add spoonfuls of jam to lemon tea, add black-currant jam to the real brew in cases of colds and coughs. Black currants are rich in vitamin C, and an herbal tea made of their leaves is often taken as a health-giving drink. A few black currant leaves are also sometimes included in a sauce for desserts, and a fragrant spring sorbet can be made with lemons and black currant leaves.

Blueberry

Blueberries, borne by low bushes in Canada and the northern United States and in northern Europe, are one of our oldest berries; they once were an important part of the diet of Native Americans and the Eskimos. The berries have a silvery bloom that intensifies their blueness. They can be small or large, although cultivated blueberries are usually larger than the wild ones.

The bilberry is a European cousin of the blueberry that grows throughout the British Isles. Also called whortleberries, bilberries are usually somewhat tarter and smaller than blueberries.

Wild blueberries were at one time so widespread in both America and northern Europe that there was little to be commercially gained by putting them under cultivation. But their numbers declined as our appetite increased for blueberry pancakes, cheesecake, pie, and cobblers and grunts—those delicious concoctions of cooked fruit and dumplings—and now it is possible to buy cultivated berries that are the size of marbles and twice the size of the wild ones. Flavor has suffered considerably with cultivation, but becomes stronger when the berries are cooked and turn to a deep, teeth-staining purple.

The huckleberry is another wild berry that is sometimes confused with the blueberry. Huckleberries, however, are a darker blue-black, and each berry has ten tiny seeds at its center.

Cranberry

Although their association with Thanksgiving makes cranberries one of the quintessential American berries, they are also plentiful in northern Europe, where they go into a sharp fruit relish that traditionally accompanies venison and roast game birds. Cranberries used to be as popular in Britain as elsewhere, but with the advent of red currants fell out of favor. However, they are still traditional there at Christmas.

A native fruit of North America, cranberries are extensively cultivated in Massachusetts, particularly on Cape Cod, and in Wisconsin and in New Jersey. When buying cranberries, make sure that they are bright, dry, plump, and unshriveled. They will keep, unwashed, in the refrigerator for up to 2 weeks and also freeze well. When preparing them for sauce, chutneys, fritters, jellies, compotes, relishes, or pies, cook them slowly with plenty of sugar and a little water until they pop their skins and turn into a ruby-colored purée.

dried blueberries 184
dried cranberries 184

Blueberry and Corn Muffins 417, 416
Cranberry and Raspberry Mold 361
Cranberry-Orange Sauce 260

Rhubarb

Hothouse rhubarb

Elderberry

White currant

Cranberry

Blueberry

Red currant

Black currant

Rose hip

Elderberry and rose hip

These two berries are not usually found in the market, but each is well worth picking and using for various purposes.

Elderberry Growing black and shiny in flat clusters, elderberries are a good addition to blackberry desserts and ripen at about the same time. On their own they may be a little sour, but a syrup made of the berries can add a delicious flavors to apple pies all winter long.

Sprigs of the cream-colored flowers can be dipped in batter and eaten as fritters; they are surprisingly good, light and delicate.

Rose hip Either the scarlet oval fruits that appear when wild roses have gone to seed, or the flat, squat fruits of the Rugosa roses, these are the essential ingredients of delicate rose-hip jelly. They also make a health-giving syrup, which is full of vitamin C.

Care must always be taken to strain out the sharp, prickly hairs that surround the abundant seeds found in each rose hip, so after steeping the finely chopped hips in boiling water, you must pass the liquid at least twice through a double layer of cheesecloth.

Rhubarb

Odd man out in the world of fruit, rhubarb is used for the same types of dishes that call for apples and plums. It is probably best known stewed and in pies—in fact, it used to be known as the pie plant—and its tart taste combines well with blander, sweeter fruits and particularly with strawberries. When you are buying rhubarb, look out for stalks that are crisp and firm. Use the rhubarb as soon as possible, because the stalks are very perishable; keep them in the refrigerator until you are ready to cook them.

Hothouse rhubarb, with its brilliant pink stalks of a delicate texture, needs only the briefest of cooking, as it softens so quickly. Tougher, greenish field-grown rhubarb takes longer, and both need lots of sugar. If the rhubarb is particularly tart, a teaspoon of red-currant jelly added to the cooking water will often help.

Rhubarb is sometimes sold with its leaves because these prevent it from wilting, but the leaves must be discarded before cooking, as they contain toxic amounts of oxalic acid.

GRAPE

Grapes can be pale, straw-colored or amber, shades of green, rose or scarlet, or deepest blue-black with a rich silvery bloom. They can be tear-shaped, oval or round, large or small, and in tight or straggly bunches. All of today's grapes are descended from the wild grape.

The main role of grapes, of course, is to provide us with "God's choicest gift to man"—wine. The grape contains all that is necessary for making wine: it has yeast in its bloom, natural sugar to feed the yeast, tannin in the skin and seeds, and natural acids to help provide the right environment for the yeast to make alcohol.

But grapes have long been celebrated for more than the wine they yield. Fresh grape juice was much used in medieval kitchens. The acid juice that characterizes grapes when they are unripe and sour was pressed out for verjuice—a piquant green liquid used in place of vinegar for flavoring tart sauces. The sweet juice of mature grapes, when not concentrated by sun-drying, which transforms the grapes into raisins, or currants, was boiled down into a syrup that was used as an alternative to honey.

Grape "cures," too, were once very popular. In the early days of this century, British society, after a season's overeating, would spend a week or so eating nothing but grapes, in an attempt to restore the figure and cleanse the system. These grapes would probably have been huge, perfectly flavored hothouse Muscats—still the most elegant of all the dessert grapes—which became the pride of landowners all over northern Europe as soon as greenhouses appeared in the seventeenth century.

Grapes are to be seen in the market almost all the year round, the hothouse varieties swaddled in tissue paper to protect their yeasty bloom. They may be translucent green with a golden tinge, a deep blue, or anywhere from scarlet to purple. Grapes can be classified by their color—white (or green) and black (or red)—or as table or wine grapes, although some varieties can both be eaten out of hand and made into wine.

Most of the grapes in the United States come from California. All California grapes are of the European type, descended from the *Vinifera* grape. They include the Muscat grapes and others. Muscats in their turn actually encompass a number of different varieties, but all of them are large, with the richly perfumed flesh that makes muscatel wines so distinctive. Muscat grapes are more common on European tables than in America.

Grapes with seeds

White/green grape These grapes include the Italia Muscat, large, golden-amber, and very sweet and flavorful; the Calmeria, long and oval-shaped, with a sweet flavor and few seeds; and the fleshy green Almeria, of Spanish stock. Popular in Europe are the green (or amber when fully ripe (oval-shaped Muscat of Alexandria, with a bloom that rubs off easily unless carefully handled; and the prized Golden Chasselas, green with an amber tinge.

Black and red grapes Among the blue-black grapes are the Ribier, oval-shaped and sweetly perfumed, with a vine-like flavor; and the beautiful Exotic, large black grapes with a milder flavor. Among the best of these grapes in Europe are the delicately flavored Gros Colmar and the large round Royal, with a heavy bloom, and very juicy and sweet.

Red grape These range from the Cardinal, scarlet, crisp, and aromatic; to the Flame Tokay, a deep red; and the Emperor, red or purple, firm, and bland.

Labrusca and Muscadine The *Vitis labrusca*—not to be confused with Lambrusco, the sparkling red wine of Lombardy—is the native American vine that thrives in the colder climate of the eastern United States, where more tender varieties of grape refuse to grow. (Some of these are now grown in the Pacific Northwest as well.) Labruscas, such as the round, blue-black Concord, are rich in pectin and ideal for making grape juice and grape jam. Delaware, small and a pale rose-red, has a juicy, sweet flesh, and Catawba is red-purple and sweet.

Muscadines, such as the large, bronze, sweet-fleshed Scuppernong, are grown mainly in the southern states. They have a rich, spicy flavor.

Seedless grapes

These grapes, which have much less tannin than the varieties with seeds, dominate the market in the United States. Sweet, juicy, and green, with smallish fruit, varieties such as Thompson

Seedless and the smaller Perlette Seedless, both descendents of the European Sultana, are among the most abundant grape varieties in the world. Flame Seedless is a red-skinned variety with sweet flesh. Ruby Seedless have purplish-red skin and are also sweet.

Buying grapes Although some grapes have ceased to be seasonal, and are either issued from greenhouses all the year round, or imported from the Southern Hemisphere, the end of summer is the traditional grape season.

When buying grapes, make sure that the red or black kinds have lost any tinge of green, and that green or white ones have a tone of amber about them. The stems of both kinds should be fresh-looking but show a few brown patches, excepting Emperor grapes, whose stems should be woody-brown all over.

From the trade's point of view, the perfect bunch consists of grapes that are uniform in size, with no lurking tiny ones, and all of them firmly attached to their stems. From the consumer's viewpoint, bunches with a tendency to shedding are often the sweetest, as anyone who has bought local grapes from a huge mound in an open market,

through a haze of wasps, can testify, for these straggly bunches and loose grapes can be delicious and more aromatic than the cosseted sort. But if perfect fruit is desired, it should be plump with no wrinkling and no brown patches at the stems. Avoid bunches with little or no bloom, which shows they have been handled too much, or with any small, shriveled grapes; these will be sour.

Storing grapes Grapes will keep in good condition for about 2 weeks if stored in the refrigerator, wrapped in their perforated plastic bags—a long way from the barrels in which the ancient Romans sealed their oil-dipped grapes, hoping to keep them fresh and luscious. But since part of the pleasure of grapes is their appearance, it seems a pity to banish them from sight. A fine bunch placed in a glass bowl or a basket makes a perfect centerpiece on the dining table for a special meal.

Serving grapes Grapes are usually eaten as a snack or served at the end of a meal, either on their own or with one of the soft French cheeses from Normandy—or perhaps a hard cheese from Switzerland, where grapes are a frequent accompaniment to cheese. In Italy, you may be offered your grapes

in a huge bowl of ice water, with a few floating ice cubes.

In the kitchen, grapes are used to make pies and tarts, jam, jelly, and juice, and sorbets. They can also be frosted with egg white and sugar. In France, grape juice is sometimes boiled down until syrupy, then boiled again with sliced apples, quinces, pears, or lemons until sticky: such fruit is called *raisiné*.

Sole becomes *sole Véronique* when the rolled, poached fillets in a light white wine sauce are garnished with scented Muscat grapes. Richly flavored grapes are good, too, with duck foie gras, and pheasant is sometimes stuffed with peeled, seeded grapes.

If you wish to peel grapes, you will find that some types slip easily from their skins, while others may need to be dipped in scalding water for a minute. Seeding grapes is easy if you halve them first.

If you like salads with fresh fruit, try grapes in a mixture of apples and watercress, dressed with oil and lemon juice. Grapes and cottage cheese also combine well. Make fruit salads prettier with the addition of black grapes, seeded but not peeled, even though the skins of black grapes may be tougher than those of the white varieties.

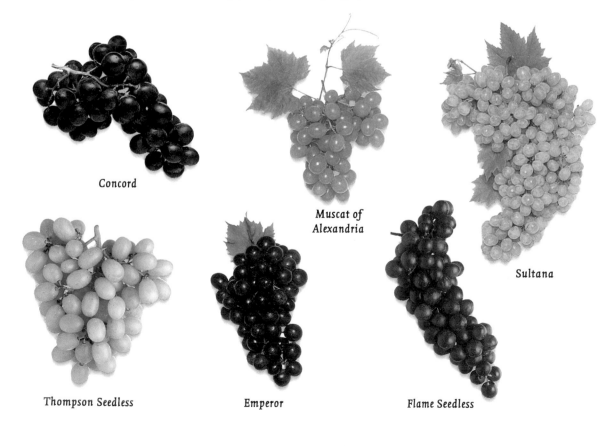

Concord

Muscat of Alexandria

Sultana

Thompson Seedless

Emperor

Flame Seedless

MELON

A melon is a luxurious thing. Beautiful and intricately patterned on the outside, a ripe melon no larger than an orange can entirely fill a good-sized room with its fragrance. Inside, cool and full of juice, it offers to quench your thirst and provide you with a delicate sensation rather like eating snow. "There is," say the Arabs, "a blessing in melons. He who fills his belly with melons fills it with light."

Sweet melons, ribbed and encrusted with lacy patterns, were brought to Spain by the Moors, who had in turn received them from Persia or from the depths of Africa—both the Middle East and Africa claim to be the home of this honey-sweet fruit, described as "the masterpiece of Apollo" and celebrated for being as beneficial as the sun itself.

Melons appeared in France toward the end of the fifteenth century, to extravagant praise, and were eaten in astonishing quantities by the royal court. Served piled in pyramids and mountains, "as if it were necessary to eat to the point of suffocation, and as if everyone in the company ought to eat a dozen," they were washed down with glasses of Muscat wine.

Melons were brought to the New World by Christopher Columbus. At that time, of course, sweet melons were no larger than oranges, but over the centuries, they have been cultivated and expanded in both their size and their variety.

Muskmelon and cantaloupe

It is most likely that the muskmelon, or "nutmeg" melon as it is sometimes known, was the kind eaten by the ancient Romans, who served it with a sprinkling of powdered musk in order to accentuate the delicate flavor.

Muskmelons, which include the cantaloupe, are easily recognized by the distinctive raised netting on their skin, which may be coarse like crochetwork or fine like lace. It is for this reason that cantaloupes are also called "embroidered" melons in France and "netted" melons in North America and Britain. They may be sharply segmented or grooved, with a green or yellow-orange skin, and the flesh ranges from green to salmon-pink.

The cantaloupe is among the most aromatic types of muskmelon. Despite the mounds of netted fruit seen in every produce market, however, the true cantaloupe is not grown commercially in the United States. Named for the Italian town of Cantalupo, it is seen all through Europe. Its rind is ribbed and warty, and the flesh is usually a pale orange, rich and juicy.

The French prefer to grow this type, especially the Charentais, with its deep-orange, faintly scented flesh, although new similar hybrids are always being introduced. The delicate, pale yellow-fleshed Ogen melon from Israel is a small, smooth-skinned cantaloupe hybrid. The Persian melon is another of the netted melons, large with flavorful salmon-colored flesh.

Winter melon

The skin of this melon is either smooth or shallowly ribbed. It is less aromatic than the cantaloupe and other netted melons. Principal varieties are the onion-shaped Casaba, with its thick golden-yellow skin and creamy-white to golden flesh; the Crenshaw, with green-gold skin and aromatic golden-salmon flesh; and the ubiquitous pale green or yellow honeydew melon, which has delicate pale green flesh.

Buying sweet melons Whatever type of melon you buy, there are a few sound rules to follow. Choose firm, plump melons with clean scars at the stem ends (a roughness here indicates they were picked before they were fully ripe). Netted melons should have no bald patches on their skins, as these are a sure indication that the melon has suffered a setback of some kind during its development.

You should reject any fruits that are soft or scarred or that show moist bruises on the skin. It is a bad sign, too, if the stem end has started to rot; however, light cracking at this end is a sign of ripeness. If you press them gently at the blossom end with your fingers, both the cantaloupe and the honeydew melon should feel slightly springy to the touch.

If you are able to shake the melon before buying it and you hear a sloshing sound as you do so, this indicates that the fruit is too ripe and

may have started to deteriorate. All melons should feel heavy for their size and—most importantly—ripe melons should have a pleasant, sweet melon scent about them.

Storing melons A cool, airy place is best for storing all types of melons—although this should be warmer if you suspect that your melon is not quite ripe. When you think that it is ready to eat, and if you do not want it to scent everything in your refrigerator, put your melon to chill in a tightly closed plastic bag before cutting it up, ready for serving.

Serving melons Although the most-scented varieties are nicest when served all on their own for desserts, melon can also be served in salads with leaves of fresh mint and an oil and lemon dressing; with oranges and watercress; or with finely chopped celery, onions, olives, and mayonnaise. This last mixture may sound rather strange, but it rests on an old tradition: a seventeenth-century list of "sallet" herbs includes the melon, and ideas for eating it with salt and pepper.

Sugar or a squeeze of fresh lime juice has today taken the place of pepper—which had ousted powdered musk—as the melon's usual condiment. Even the sweetest melon will be enhanced by a fine dusting of sugar, but to pour port or another type of fortified wine into the cavity of a small scented melon, as some people like to do, is a mistake, since it actually ruins both.

Fragrant melon slices, resting on the rind from which they have been separated with a sharp knife, beside thin, translucent slices of prosciutto, is as delicious a start to a meal as one could hope for.

The French traditionally used to offer melons only as an hors d'oeuvre—these were usually chilled, halved cantaloupes sitting in a bowl of crushed ice, but sometimes, in the case of larger light-fleshed varieties, the melon was served in wedges, the flesh already cut and resting on the rind in an attractive sawtooth arrangement.

These days, melons have rightly taken a place in the dessert course and are to be met in fruit salads, filled with an assortment of fresh fruit, or diced and mixed with grapes or red currants. Or they may appear as melon sorbet or even melon ice cream, made with orange and lemon juices and served, if possible, together with wild strawberries. The best melons, of course, really need no dressing up at all, but a very cool and refreshing sweet melon salad can be made with an assortment of melon balls or cubes—orange, white, green, and scarlet—sugared and chilled: this will provide a feast for the eye as well as an opportunity for the palate to distinguish between all the slightly different flavors of the fruits.

Watermelon

The watermelon—which Mark Twain once memorably described as "the food that angels eat"—is a different proposition altogether. Considerably larger in size than the sweet melons, and either oblong or round in shape, this is an entirely separate species of fruit that originated in tropical Africa and in India.

Small round watermelons, weighing anywhere from 6 to 10 pounds, with sweet red flesh and pitch-black seeds, may have deep green rinds with a bloom, as found on the Sugar Baby, or they may be striped on a light green background, such as on the appropriately named Tiger watermelon.

However, the favorites at family picnics are the large spherical or oblong watermelons, which are often sold in wedges. These usually have a much paler flesh than the smaller varieties because of their higher water content. There are also yellow-fleshed varieties, as well as seedless watermelons—which, in spite of their name, usually do have a few small edible seeds in their flesh.

When you buy a watermelon, there are various things to look out for. The spot where the melon rested on the ground should be amber-colored, not white or green. The fruit should sound hollow when tapped. If you buy your melon by the piece, avoid pieces with visible fibers: the flesh should not have any hard white streaks in it.

Watermelon is often eaten chilled in slices. When cut into smaller pieces, it makes a decorative and delicious addition to a fruit salad.

wild strawberries 171

Sugar Baby watermelon

Cantaloupe

Casaba

Ogen

Charentais

Honeydew

Tiger watermelon

Crenshaw

Watermelon

177

TROPICAL AND EXOTIC FRUIT

Before steamships began to cross the seas regularly in the nineteenth century, trading in perishable tropical fruits such as bananas and pineapples was an impossibility. Now, unfamiliar fruits appear by boat or plane and make strange, exotic-looking piles among the more familiar fruits, appearing, conveniently, just at the time of year when most fresh fruit, apart from apples and oranges, is usually scarce.

Banana and plantain

There are many varieties of this perfectly packaged fruit. One is grown only for making beer, and there are red bananas, purple bananas, and pink bananas, slim bananas, and fat ones like little pigs. Plantains, also called cooking bananas, tend to be starchier and less sweet than the eating variety and are often used before they ripen. Bananas for the table are picked while they are still hard and green, and may not be perfectly ripe when they reach the market. They will, however, ripen quickly at room temperature, turning first yellow, when they are ready for eating, then spotted, when they become softer and more scented, and finally black, when they can still be used to make banana bread. Buy them in the bunch rather than loose, since the skin of loose bananas may well be ripped at the top, thus exposing the flesh.

The first bananas to reach us came from the Caribbean, and many early desserts using bananas have a distinctly Latin flavor: raw brown sugar and rum, coffee flavoring and rice, and coffee ice cream feature widely. Bananas Foster, a more recent invention from Brennan's Restaurant in New Orleans, consists of bananas sautéed in butter with brown sugar, then flambéed with rum and orange juice. Bananas are also eaten baked with slices of lemon, or plain in their skins. Chicken Maryland is often accompanied by fried bananas, and in Central America and the Caribbean plantains are found in many dishes.

Bananas, however, are most enjoyed fresh. Sliced, they form part of many savory dishes, including curries. In fruit mixtures, their slightly scented taste and smooth texture complement juicy or crisp fruits such as oranges and apples. They also make a delicious cream pie.

Pineapple

A whole pineapple on the table is a truly luxurious sight. Fresh pineapples form part of many main courses in their native tropical habitat, and it was there that the idea of serving them hot with poultry, pork chops, and ham originated.

It is when fresh and simply served with sugar and perhaps kirsch that the pineapple is really at its best. However, now that bananas from Hawaii and Central America are shipped in quantity, they are sometimes grilled or broiled, baked in the shell, flambéed with cinnamon and rum, sprinkled with lime juice, or used to make relishes or salsas.

When buying a pineapple, look for one that is fully ripe and fragrant. If the stem end is very soft or discolored, the fruit bruised, or the leaves wilting, the pineapple is not at its best. A pineapple will continue to ripen after it is picked, and one that is almost ripe will ripen completely at home—but an unripe pineapple that has no scent and is not uniformly colored will probably never develop its full flavor. Small pineapples often have a more delicate flavor.

Mango

This beautiful fruit may be as large as a melon or as small as an apple. It may be green, gold, rosy, or a mixture of all three. The vivid pinky-golden, yellow, or orange flesh of the best ripe mangoes is smooth, juicy, and fiberless, with a slightly resinous taste that has been compared to that of peaches, apricots, and pineapples.

When buying mangoes, choose fruits that are just soft, with a good perfume. If they are completely green, they will not ripen properly; those with large soft areas or black spots tend to be overripe.

Mangoes can be scored from top to bottom in several places and peeled, or cut in half by slicing down either side of the large, flat pit, and then eaten with a spoon. A better way is to prepare them "hedgehog" fashion: slice them lengthwise into two pieces, discarding the pit, and then score the flesh diagonally at ½-inch intervals in both directions, cutting almost to the skin but without piercing it. Turn each half inside out, and the little squares of mango will be easy to eat with a spoon.

Chilled mangoes are sometimes served halved in their skin, sprinkled with lemon juice, sugar, rum, or ginger. Peeled and cut up, they are delicious in fruit salads, and they make excellent sorbets.

It was in India that the British found their taste for mango chutney, and Major Grey's mango chutney can be found in almost any American supermarket today.

Papaya

Columbus anticipated Mark Twain—in a different context—by declaring that the papaya, which he called a tree melon, tasted, when ripe, like the "food of the angels." The papaya's skin is green to golden, its flesh orangey, and its seeds black. It is sweet and subtly flavored.

When buying papaya, make sure that it is firm, unblemished except for its speckles, and just turning yellow, then

Passion fruit

Kiwifruit

Pomegranate

Papaya

allow it to ripen at home. Ripe papaya is distinctive in fruit salads, pies, and sorbets, and can also be served simply sprinkled with lemon or lime juice and sugar or ginger.

The unripe papaya is used like a vegetable in Latin America. It tastes like a squash and may be served stuffed or baked with butter, added to salads, or pickled. It is good in hot chile salsas.

South American Indians have traditionally wrapped papaya leaves, freshly plucked, around tough meat to act as a tenderizer—the plant contains a powerful enzyme that breaks down protein. A derivative of the leaves, the enzyme papain, is used in commercial tenderizing powders for meat.

The papaya is sometimes called pawpaw, as is another fruit, the papaw, that is similar to look at but is, in fact, related to the cherimoya. The papaw is a wild North American fruit that can be good to eat or unpleasantly scented and flavored, depending on the type.

Guava

Pink- or pale-yellow-fleshed, strongly aromatic, and sweet, this fruit can be as small as a walnut or as large as an apple. It can be puréed or baked, or eaten fresh with sugar and cream, and it goes well with fruit such as pineapple or banana. Guavas make a delicious jelly, and a sauce made from puréed guavas can be served with meat or duck.

Pomegranate

The lark, which Shakespeare's Juliet insisted was a nightingale, "sang on yon pomegranate tree"—a shrub-like plant introduced to the Western world from Persia via Africa. Its beautifully shaped fruit, scarlet or golden flushed with crimson outside and filled with crimson beads, each with its central seed, is an intricate construction.

To admire its crimson glory at its best, cut the fruit in half or into segments, slicing through the leather-like skin. Although the juicy pulp surrounding each of the seeds is beautifully refreshing and aromatic, it can be rather tiresome to eat. You can take a few grains, suck the flesh off the seeds, discard the seeds—

Fuyu persimmon

Hachiya persimmon

Guava

Banana

Pineapple

Mango

and continue to eat and discard until the shell is empty. A much easier way, however, is to crunch and swallow the seeds, which have a nice texture. Avoid the pale yellow pith, which is bitter.

Persimmon

Looking like a golden-red tomato, the persimmon, when it is completely ripe and plumply soft, is often compared in taste to guavas, apricots, tomatoes, and mangoes; however, when less than perfect, its astringency "draws the mouth awry with much torment." Wrinkled fruit of the common acorn-shaped Hachiya type should therefore never be shunned, since by the time it has reached this stage, the acidity and tannin are sure to have disappeared. There is also a

smaller, rounder variety, called the Fuyu, which is not at all astringent and which remains firm when ripe.

The handsome persimmon stays glossy and plump when plucked early and artificially matured. Provided it is ripe, with cap and stem intact, its tough skin can be slit and peeled back, and the soft flesh eaten as is or sliced. A seedless variety of persimmon, the Sharon fruit, has tender, edible skin and less tannic flavor than the Hachiya.

Kiwifruit

The brown furry skin covering this egg-shaped fruit hides glistening, translucent green flesh with decorative edible black seeds. Once known as the Chinese gooseberry, it is now best known by the

name of New Zealand's national bird, the kiwi. The fruit is used to best effect when it is peeled and thinly sliced, since the pattern of the black seeds in the bland but fresh-tasting green flesh is so pleasing.

One kiwi contains huge quantities of vitamin C—as much as ten lemons. Unripe fruit can be ripened in a plastic bag with a ripe banana, apple, or pear; the ethylene gas given off by the ripe fruit accelerates the ripening process.

Passion fruit

This fruit is so called because the flower of the plant is said to symbolize the Passion of Christ. The fruit of some species of the passion flower is also called granadilla (which has yellow skin) or, in the West Indies, calabesh. The size and shape of

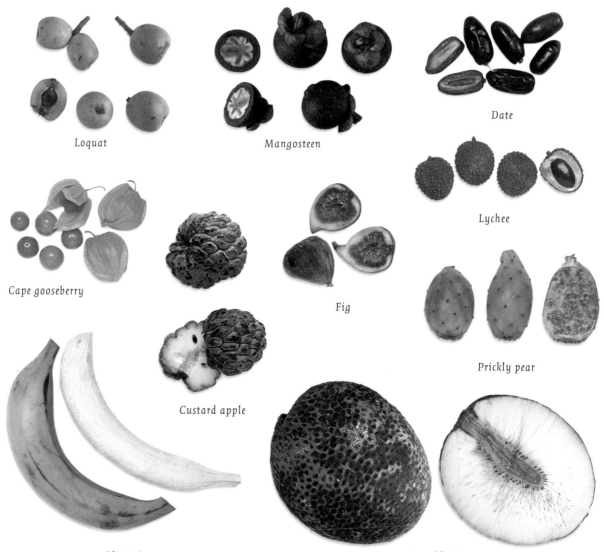

Loquat

Mangosteen

Date

Cape gooseberry

Custard apple

Fig

Lychee

Prickly pear

Plantain

Breadfruit

an egg, the passion fruit normally has a purple-brown, hard skin that becomes crinkly as the fruit gradually ripens.

The richly perfumed, sweet-sour flesh is inseparable from the many small black seeds, which are edible. The fruit is usually halved and perhaps sprinkled with sherry or cream, or the flesh may be scooped out and mixed into fruit salads. It is delicious made into mousses, sorbets or ice cream, or sauces.

Custard apple

This can be any of the fleshy, round or elongated, thick-skinned fruits of the large family of Annona trees in the American tropics. There is the apple-shaped cherimoya, the one most likely to be found in our markets, and the llama, whose taste has been compared

Feijoa

Star fruit

Tamarillo

to that of a banana and pineapple. The soncoya is similar but larger, and the sweetsop, or sugar apple, is green, heart-shaped, and more acidic, with a taste similar to that of a black currant. The atemoya is a cross between a cherimoya and the sweetsop; its delicate flesh tastes of mango and vanilla. All are eaten fresh, the flesh being spooned from the shell. The fruit can also be used for jam and jelly, in milk shakes, and for sorbets.

Loquat

Also known as Japanese medlar, the orangey-yellow loquat is the size of a crabapple but more pear-shaped; it contains a few shiny seeds. Although thirst-quenching, it does not have much flavor when raw and is principally used to make jams, jellies, and sauces. A few of the seeds are usually included, as they add a delicious bitter-almond flavor.

Cape gooseberry

Native to South America, this tart-sweet, pleasant, small fruit of the shrub Physalis peruviana is encased in a papery balloon shaped like a Chinese lantern. In South Africa, the plants are grown on such a large scale that they have come to be known as Cape gooseberries. Golden when ripe, the berries—also called ground cherries—can be eaten out of hand or used decoratively (peel back the papery skin to form "petals" around the golden globe of the fruit), and in Europe they may be coated with fondant and served with *petits fours*, but they are chiefly used to make jellies and jams.

Lychee and rambutan

These fruits, encased in brown, papery shells with a delicate pink lining, both have translucent, colorless flesh enclosing a single brown, glossy seed. Fresh lychees have a delicious perfumed flavor and a refreshing tang that all but disappears when the fruit is canned. In China, the lychee, or *litchi*, has been cultivated for thousands of years. With its sweet-tart flavor, it is used in pork and duck dishes, much as apples and oranges are used in the West.

A rambutan has a hairier shell than a lychee; in Southeast Asia it is peeled and eaten fresh, and is enjoyed for its refreshing, sweet juiciness. Canned rambutans are also available, but these are overly sweet.

Both fruits can be bought in Asian markets in the West—although you are more likely to find lychees—but should be avoided if they look shriveled, since this means their pulp is turning black and their delicate flavor will be lost.

Prickly pear

This is the fruit of a cactus (*Opuntia ficus indica*), and is sometimes known as cactus pear or Indian fig. It is pear-shaped, varies in color from green to rosy, and is covered with small clumps of sharp prickles.

When buying a prickly pear, make sure that it is orange to red and reasonably bright in color, and firm but not too hard. It is mild-flavored and sweet, somewhat pear-like in flavor but more melon-like in texture, and is usually eaten raw. The fruit should be slit lengthwise; the prickly skin will come off easily. The flesh can then be eaten with sugar and cream or sprinkled with lemon juice. Take care when handling prickly pears, as the prickles will irritate the skin. Wear gloves or encase your hand in a paper bag before you pick them up.

Mangosteen

This thick-skinned, glossy, dark-mahogany-colored fruit is very popular in Southeast Asia. The white, soft flesh is segmented like that of an orange; some segments contain a large, inedible seed. The taste of the mangosteen is sweet-sharp, delicate, perfumed, and refreshing.

Fig

This is perhaps the most sensual of all fruits, with its bloomy, bursting skin and luscious flesh. Ancient Greeks thought figs so health-giving that they formed part of the athletes' diet for the original Olympic games, and so delicious that poets and philosophers sang their praises. White, green, brown, or purple, figs are always beautiful. When cut open, they reveal their pulpy flesh, deep purple, red, or pink, embedded with a mass of seeds, which are in fact tiny fruits. Calimyrna, or the Turkish Smyrna, Mission, and Kadota are some of the more familiar varieties.

The entire fruit is edible. In Italy, where the Sicilian figs are most prized, they are served with prosciutto or as a dessert. In France, the purple, white-fleshed Barbillone and many other

dried fig 183
prosciutto 69
tomatillo 152

varieties are also served as a dessert. All are good, especially when eaten fresh and ripe. Being perishable, figs will only keep for up to 3 days in the refrigerator.

Date

In its fresh state, the sumptuous, rich date—called "bread of the desert"—has a glowing brown skin that promises more juice than the flesh actually delivers, and the plumpest date has a warm, fudge-like consistency. When buying fresh dates, pick fat, wrinkly skinned, nonsticky specimens.

Star fruit, carambola

Somewhat cucumber-like in texture, the star fruit, uncut, resembles an elongated yellow Chinese lantern with deep ridges running from top to bottom. When sliced, it reveals that the cross-section is a perfect-star—very beautiful, but when it comes to flavor, it hasn't much to offer. Star fruit can be either sweet or sour and tangy; both are refreshing. They are best sliced and used in a fruit salad, or poached in a sugar syrup.

Tamarillo, tree tomato

Orangey-red, smooth, and glossy, this fruit resembles the small oval eggplant in shape, and, like it, is a member of the family of solanums, together with Cape gooseberries, potatoes and tomatoes. The orange flesh with its black seeds is sweet-tart, but the skin is intensely bitter and should be removed either by plunging the fruit into boiling water for a minute, like a tomato, or, if the fruit is very ripe, by peeling. Eat tamarillos raw with sugar or in fruit salads, or use to make chutney.

Feijoa

A round or oval shiny green fruit related to the guava, the feijoa has a flavor said to resemble pineapple, and it is also known as the pineapple guava. The flesh contains tiny seeds. Eat raw by cutting in half and scooping out the flesh.

Breadfruit

This large and imposing green fruit, covered in short, knobbly spines, can weigh up to 9 pounds. An unripe specimen can be cut up and baked or roasted, while an entirely ripe one may be sliced and eaten raw. Breadfruit is often used in savory dishes.

DRIED AND CANDIED FRUIT

Dried fruit does not so much prolong the taste of summer as provide us with sweetness of a different kind. Drying concentrates the sugar content of the fresh fruit, and although vitamin C is usually lost, vitamin A and the minerals remain. Some dried fruits are completely dried; the larger ones like apricots may need soaking before cooking. Others still contain a percentage of their original moisture. These are succulent and can be eaten as they are or cooked, but tend to be heavy on preservatives.

Dried fruits such as "datyes, figges, and great raysings" have been valued in Europe since they were imported in the thirteenth century from the Levant, to sit in the larder alongside dried domestic "prunellas, apricocks, and pippins [apples]." There were also dried pears (a special delicacy) and the dried cherries and berries that the medieval housewife would prepare in due season. These dried fruits went into a number of what now seem curious dishes. The taste was for the sweet-savory—the sort of dish still found in countries that were once part of the great Ottoman Empire. In Turkey, Iran, Saudi Arabia, Yemen, and North Africa, traditional cookery still allies lamb with prunes, apricots, almonds, honey, and spices. Chicken is simmered with prunes, or with quinces, dates, or raisins.

Medieval Europe ate veal tartlets with prunes and dates, pickled fish was enhanced with raisins and figs, and ducks were smothered with fruit. The "Great Pyes," without which no great dinner was complete, contained a mixture of beef, chicken, bone marrow, eggs, dates, prunes, and raisins, all highly spiced and saffroned before being entombed in the "coffyn," as the crust was called.

The taste for such things lives on. The seventeenth-century recipe for raisin sauce to eat with ham differs very little from that found in modern American cookbooks, or the raisin sauce eaten with boiled tongue in northern Europe. And the eighteenth-century ham stuffed with "apricocks" is not far from Virginia ham with peaches. Indeed, that most British of institutions, the plum pudding, is a descendant of the sweet-savory puddings of the Middle Ages—until the eighteenth century, one of its main ingredients was

a leg or shin of beef. Look farther back and you find that the Christmas pudding is not English at all, but of ancient Greek origin—a less astonishing fact when you think that the very word currant (with which plum pudding is actually made, not plums) is derived from Corinth, its place of origin.

The too-liberal use of sulfur dioxide to keep dried fruit from becoming too dry is a deplorable innovation. The flavor can and occasionally does permeate the fruit and cannot be removed by soaking. So buy unsulfured or organic fruit where possible.

Raisin

The large, sweet raisins made from Spanish Muscat grapes and called muscatels used to be the kings of the tribe. Now, similar giants are produced in other places in the world, especially California. These can be eaten on their own and are also useful in cooking. Sometimes available in specialty markets, Muscat raisins may be sold dried in whole bunches, seedless or complete with seeds. The more familiar smaller dark and golden raisins sold loose and in boxes come from Thompson Seedless grapes; the dark ones are naturally sun-dried, while the golden ones are treated with sulfur dioxide to preserve their color. Raisins are used in cakes, cookies, breads, granola, and mincemeat. They are also good in couscous, and for stuffed vegetables and onions à la grecque. Raisins also come packed together with nuts and other dried fruits, as a snack sometimes called trail mix. Combined with peanuts, hazelnuts, and almonds, they make a mixture known as *Studenten Futter* in Germany, because the sugar content of the raisins and the protein content of the nuts quickly revives the energy of poor scholars while they pore over their books.

Currant and sultana

The dried currant comes from the small, black seedless grape that is a native of the slopes around Corinth in Greece, while sultanas are made from the seedless white grapes once grown only in the neighborhood of biblical Smyrna in Turkey. Although both varieties have long been produced elsewhere, the old names have stuck. In some parts of the world, currants and sultanas are still sun-dried, without the help of chemical treatments. In others, science gives nature a helping hand and the fruit is artificially dried.

Sultanas are rarely seen in U.S. markets; seedless golden raisins can be substituted in any recipe that calls for them. If you mean to use currants or sultanas with yeast for baking, it is a good idea to place them in a strainer over a pot of boiling water for a few minutes. This warms and moistens the fruit just enough to prevent it from retarding fermentation of the temperamental yeast.

Dried fig
The yellow fig of Smyrna was originally the most highly prized, and this is now extensively grown elsewhere, together with many other varieties, including the dark, juicy Mission fig. Calimyrna figs from California are actually Smyrna figs, their name a combination of their place of origin and where they are now grown. Although dried figs pack and travel well, blocks of squashed figs can have

a depressing look; so if you mean to enjoy figs with a dessert wine after a winter dinner, look for those whose plump, cushiony shapes are still discernible. In France, in Provence, a dessert offered at New Year's and known as *les quatres mendiants* (the four mendicants) is a mixture of figs, raisins, hazelnuts, and almonds, their colors recalling the habits worn by the four Roman Catholic mendicant orders.

For compotes or other desserts, dried figs need soaking for a few hours before they are used: try wine instead of water for a good flavor.

Dried banana
Slices of dried banana are eaten as a snack on their own or as part of prepackaged mixes with other dried fruits. Look for banana chips in health food stores and some markets, together with strips of dried banana which can be used in the same way as dried figs.

Date
The date palm has flourished well in favorable places since 5000 BC, and has always been a good and useful friend to mankind. Only the stickiest, juiciest dates—"candy that grows on trees"—are sent into the world from their native Middle East and North Africa. Of them all, the Tunisian date, the Deglet Noor, "date of the light," is considered the finest, although some people prefer Medjool dates, with their wrinkled skins and rich fudge-like texture. Dried dates, black, dark red, or golden yellow, imported from the Middle East, are available year-round, as are those from California; Arizona grows some dates too, but California is the major producer.

Most easily obtained are the shiny or wrinkled dates that have been left on their palm trees to sweeten and mature in the sun, and are then packed in boxes, sometimes with desert scenes on the lid. Most are pitted; dates sold in bulk may

banana 178
fig 181
fresh date 182

Dried cranberry

Dried cherry

Dried blueberry

Sultana

Dried peach

Dried pear

Dried fig

Raisin

Currant

Prune

Dried apricot

Dried apple ring

Dried date

Dried banana

Dried banana chip

sometimes still have their pits. If you plan to stuff dates with nuts or marzipan, making *petits fours* to be offered after dinner, you would, of course, use the handsomest dates you could find. Inexpensive pressed blocks of dates are perfectly adequate to use in breads, cakes, and other desserts.

Prune

Until the nineteenth century, prunes were far more popular than plums. Traditionally eaten with game, goose, and pork, prunes can be cooked with red cabbage. They are also used to make ice creams, soufflés, and delicate whips. Prunes are essential for *tsimmes*, the Jewish-American Passover dish, and they may be used in a stuffing for chicken or turkey. The drying process makes prunes good keepers, and nothing is easier than to reconstitute their plumpness by soaking them overnight. (Better still, keep them in a jar of brandy, ready to eat.)

The finest prunes are from the red and purple plums of Agen and from those of Tours, the orchard of France. It is these varieties that are grown in California and have made the Santa Clara Valley the center of the excellent American prune industry. Some of the French maintain that the flesh of a California plum is less delicate than that of their native produce, but then, in France, plum drying has developed into a fine art. There the Perdrigon plum, for example, is not simply dried. It may be either peeled, pitted, exposed to the sun, and flattened to become a *pistole*, or scalded in its entirety and slowly dried in the shade to become a *brignole* or *pruneau fleuri*. This is plumper and less wrinkled than the humble grocery store prune. It somewhat resembles the Karlsbad plum, a glamorous prune with a blue sheen, tasting strongly of fruit, that is on sale in gourmet shops around Christmastime, packed in handsome wooden boxes. Famous, too, are Elvas plums, semidried and candied greengage plums from Portugal, a very sweet Christmas treat.

Dried peach, pear, and apricot

Dried peaches and pears are most delicious eaten simply as a snack or sweet: their taste is delicate and does not always survive cooking.

On the tart side even when they're ripe, when dried, apricots keep a good deal of their original flavor. Of all the dried fruits, they are the least sickly-sweet. Soaked and cooked, they can be used to make a sharp, fragrant purée, good for desserts, sauces, and jam making. Roughly chopped, they can go into rice pilaf; soaked, they make a good stuffing for poultry and lamb.

Apricots from health food stores are most likely to be sun-dried. Supermarket apricots may have been assisted in drying by sulfur dioxide—the label should reveal the process. If the fruits are sold in bulk, ask if they have been treated. The best dried apricots are tender and chewy, fruit that tastes strongly of itself and doesn't need soaking. Apricot paste, a sweet much appreciated in Arabian countries, where it is called *kem-reddine*, "moon of religion," can be found in the more exotic stores, and apricot leather is available in many markets.

Dried apple

This can be reminiscent of faintly scented rings of soft chamois leather; only by shopping around, particularly at health food stores, can you find dried apples actually tasting of fruit.

Apple rings have only come into fashion during the last century or so. Before that, and before apple drying became a commercial operation, there were several methods for drying apples whole—all of them considerably more trouble than to simply core, peel, and slice apples, soak them for a few minutes in salted water to prevent discoloration (the salt draws out the moisture quickly), and thread them onto string looped around the ceiling, where air can circulate around them until the rings are thoroughly dried.

In whatever way apples have been dried, they have many uses. Chopped and mixed with currants and raisins, they usefully stretch and flavor a cake batter. If you use dried apples for a compote, stew them slowly with cinnamon or cloves and add a dash of lemon juice for tartness. If you make your own granola or mincemeat, you can add chopped dried apple together with the raisins. Indeed, dried apples combined with any other dried fruit and every type of nut, particularly prunes, blanched almonds, and apricots, make nourishing winter fruit salads, steeped either in water or in a syrup.

Dried cherries and berries

Dried cherries can be made from sweet or sour cherries. The sour ones are bright mahogany-red and have a sweet-sour tang and an intense flavor. They can be used in desserts and sweet sauces, and they make a delicious sauce for duck or lamb. Dried sweet cherries are less tangy and lighter in color than the sour ones. Use them in the same way for cooking, or to make a dessert with sugar, lemon juice, and cream. Dried sweet and sour cherries can also be eaten like candy, and are sometimes sold enrobed in chocolate.

Dried blueberries These look like dark raisins and almost lose their blueberry taste in the drying. You may need to soak them for an hour or so before using them, raw or lightly poached and sweetened, in blueberry muffins or with apples in apple and blueberry pies and crisps.

Dried cranberries These dark-rose-colored berries are a great deal sweeter than their fresh counterparts; some have added sugar. They can be eaten raw or soaked and cooked in sauces and stuffings. Or, use them in fruit salads.

Dried mango and papaya

Golden, leathery dried mangoes can be found in health food stores and gourmet shops as small pieces, long strips, or, best of all, whole mango-sized slices. They need to be soaked for several hours before cooking. Like dried apricots, they can eaten in their dried state, making delicious chewy snacks with a full, deep, almost parsnippy mango flavor.

Small cubes of dried papaya, pink and glowing, are usually sugared and eaten like candy. They can also be cut up and used like candied citrus peel in cakes.

Candied citrus peel

The delicate green variety is the candied, aromatic skin of the citron—the large, scented, extremely thick-skinned cousin of the lemon. Orange peel—sometimes sold mixed with citron—and lemon peel may be found in large pieces at gourmet or specialty markets. If you can buy the peel in a large slice, you will find that it has more flavor than the "cut" peel, not only because there has been less chance for its essential oils to evaporate, but also because only the fattest, juiciest peels are sent to market in their entirety. When chopping candied citrus peel, if the pieces are very sticky, separate them with a dusting of flour and then use that much less flour in your recipe. Store candied citrus peel in airtight jars to prevent it from becoming tough and difficult to cut. If it becomes hard, steam it to soften it.

Mixed citrus peel is sold for use in cakes, other desserts, and tea breads, but it is always better to chop your own whenever possible.

Glacé and crystallized fruit

Strictly speaking, crystallized fruit is candied fruit with a coating of granulated sugar, such as that on strips of crystallized orange. *Glacé* refers to the glossy coating of sugar syrup found, for example, on pineapple rings and whole candied fruit such as oranges. The terms, however, have become almost interchangeable.

Cherries for fruitcakes are candied and glazed with a heavy syrup to aid their preservation. This accounts for their extreme stickiness, and makes it advisable to rinse and dry them before adding them to a cake batter; or steam them for 5 to 10 minutes in a strainer placed over a pan of boiling water and then dry them. Without this precaution, they may sink to the bottom of the cake. A dusting of flour helps to keep them suspended in the batter. No need, of course, to wash the cherries you use for decoration—their charm depends on their glistening lusciousness. Candied cherries are often artificially dyed, not just bright red but also yellow or even green; the package label should indicate whether artificial dyes, and other additives best avoided, have been used.

Ginger Made with fiery mature ginger in Asia, and milder, immature ginger in Australia and other parts of the world, crystallized ginger is a delicious alternative to chocolates at Christmas, and far less rich. The Chinese believe that ginger warms and sends energy to the solar plexus, and it certainly cuts the richness after a fatty meal.

Angelica This is an herb related to parsley, and is used primarily for decorating. If you are a gardener, it is quite easy to candy angelica yourself.

Blanch the stalks and peel off the outer skin, then boil the inner stems in a syrup made of ½ cup water and a generous 1 cup sugar. When the stems are soft and translucent, let them cool and then soak in the syrup for two weeks. Finally, dry the sticks in a low oven. The same technique works for all sorts of small fruit, or for chunks or segments of larger fruits.

Crystallized flowers

To crystallize violets or rose petals, or other edible (and nonsprayed) flowers, you will need a light touch.

First prepare a sugar syrup (2¼ cups sugar to each 1 cup water), and boil to just under the hard crack stage (295°F); it will form brittle threads when dropped into cold water. Remove from the heat and dip in the petals or blossoms.

Dry them in a strainer, sprinkling them with a little confectioners' sugar. Shake off the excess sugar and then scatter the flowers over cakes frosted with white buttercream, or use them to decorate chocolate mousse and trifle.

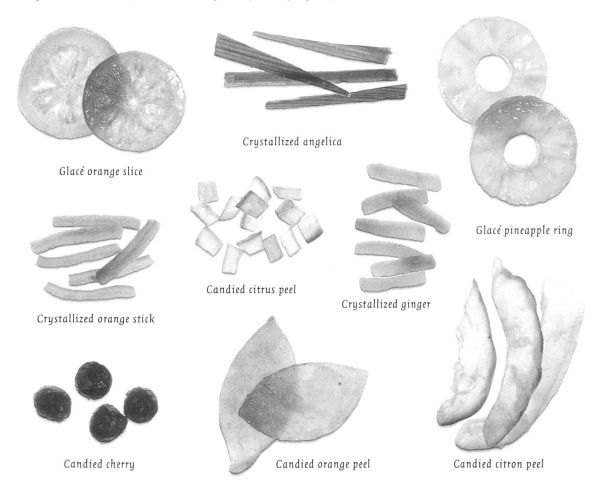

Glacé orange slice

Crystallized angelica

Glacé pineapple ring

Crystallized orange stick

Candied citrus peel

Crystallized ginger

Candied cherry

Candied orange peel

Candied citron peel

Nuts

The sound of cracking nuts has always been a pleasant accompaniment to conversation: "after-dinner talk across the walnuts and the wine" is Tennyson's description of the ritual, while in the Middle East pistachio nuts and cashews are eaten before a meal as part of the varied *mezze*, the morsels that precede a meal, and are "savored accompanied by feelings of peace and serenity."

As well as spreading serenity and tranquil enjoyment, nuts have been used since the earliest times in a huge variety of cooked dishes. Egyptians and Iranians, many of whose favorite recipes have changed very little for almost twelve centuries, may use almonds and pine nuts to thicken their sauces; in stuffings for lamb, chicken and vegetables, and in every kind of pastry and sweet—dates stuffed with walnuts and almonds were one of the earliest sweets invented. In India, pilafs and rich rice dishes are decorated with almonds or cashew nuts, and coconut is a vital ingredient of soups and curries in many areas, particularly in Kerala in the southwest of India. And peanuts are used throughout Africa in all sorts of stews.

Pecan pie is one of the traditional great American dishes, and of course nut-flavored ice creams abound. In Europe, chestnuts are much enjoyed with turkey and with game of all sorts. The French serve wonderful green salads sprinkled with fresh walnuts, while Eastern Europe specializes in rich nut cakes with ground almonds or hazelnuts taking the place of flour.

Since nuts are so rich in protein, vitamins, calcium, iron, and oils (nut cooking oils are used everywhere) and are so extremely versatile, no good cook should be without them. Buy them frequently in small quantities rather than large, preferably in their shells, and store them in a cool environment such as the refrigerator, as their high oil content makes them subject to dire alterations of flavor if they get hot or are kept too long. Make a particular point of enjoying fresh nuts in the autumn and early winter when they are sweet and milky.

Cashew nut (*Anacardium occidentale*) Kidney-shaped cashew nuts come from a tropical tree, which found its way from South America to the rest of the world by way of the early Portuguese explorers. The nuts grow suspended from a large fruit that is liked by monkeys, who ruin the crops in India and Asia. Cashews are widely eaten throughout South America, India, and Asia. They often appear—blanched and plain, roasted, and/or salted—with drinks or as a dessert nut in the colder continents (they are easy to toast and salt yourself at home). Cashews are always sold shelled, as the shells are toxic. In Brazil, they are also used for making wine and producing the famous *anacard*, or cashew nut vinegar. In Chinese cooking, of course, they often appear as an ingredient, especially in chicken dishes. Use raw unsalted cashews for cooking—they are usually sautéed in oil until golden-brown and added to the dish at the last moment.

Pine nut or pignolia (*Pinus pinea*) This nut actually does come from the beautiful glossy cones of pine trees. It is contained inside a hard little torpedo-shaped shell that is covered with a sooty dust. In the southwestern United States, the nuts come from the piñon pine. In the Mediterranean, the shells can be found lying all over the sand or rocks in September, wherever the handsome umbrella-shaped stone pines grow. Chinese and Koreans use the nut of *Pinus kovaiensis* in sweets and desserts.

Pignoli are the classic resinous pine kernels used in Mediterranean cooking. They are delicious in stuffed vegetables—eggplant or zucchini—or wrapped in grape leaves, and are essential for pesto, the smooth green paste of basil that is so irresistible with tagliatelle or linguine. They combine with rice and raisins in a rich stuffing for chicken, duck, or turkey, and are mixed with prunes, dried apricots, pomegranate seeds, and almonds in *khoshaf*—an exotic dried-fruit salad.

Pine nuts can be found in health food stores and other shops. Keep them refrigerated, but don't store them for too long, as their resinous oil spoils easily.

Macadamia nut (*Macadamia ternifolia*) Sweet and buttery, with a waxy texture, this is of the predinner drinks and dessert-nut variety. Native to Australia, where it is sometimes known as the "Queensland" nut, it is also grown extensively in Hawaii and in California and Florida. The hard, shiny shell is cracked open and the kernel roasted in coconut oil before being marketed.

Almond (*Prunus dulcis*) No other nut features as widely in old recipe books as the almond. Milk of almonds—the juice extracted from ground almonds steeped in water—used to take the place of milk on fast days or in hot weather (it is almost as rich in calcium as cow's milk). This technique of dealing with ground almonds is still used in such dishes as almond soup. Slivered almonds, fried golden, were much used for seasoning; they are still sometimes scattered on panfried river fish, particularly trout.

Ground almonds do more than provide their liquor. They can be used in the place of flour for rich, moist cakes and for crisp cookies. Sweet almonds are the chief ingredient of marzipan for coating or decorating cakes, and smooth sugared almonds, ovoids in silver, white, pink, and pale blue, in silver baskets, traditionally grace French wedding feasts (and candy shops). "Burnt almonds," cooked in sugar until caramelized and the color of burnt siena—the classic praline—are superb in ice cream. In India's delicate Mogul dishes, almonds are combined with chicken in a variety of ways, while fresh almonds in their delicate green velvet coats form part of the early autumn fruit baskets in France and Italy—although these must be soaked in cold water before eating.

Almonds can be bought in their shells or out of them, and also come blanched, sliced, slivered, and ground. There are also bitter almonds (*Prunus amara*), which some European recipes for cookies and sweets may specify. The pungent taste of bitter almonds—like that of the crushed peach kernels you would add to jam—is related to the same enzyme reaction by which prussic acid is produced. Although they are inedible raw, bitter almonds, like peach kernels, are quite safe to use in cooking, as the poison is highly volatile and evaporates when heated. However, it is illegal to sell bitter almonds in the United States, although almond extract, made from bitter almonds, is a supermarket staple. Bitter almonds are much used in Italian confectionery and in cookies.

Peanut (*Arachis hypogaea*) Whether one knows them as peanuts, ground nuts, or goobers or goober peas, these are the success story of our age. Dry-roasted, salted, shelled, or unshelled, they come to more cocktail parties than any other nut. In North African countries, you will find whole peanuts scattered over couscous; in Indonesia, ground peanuts go into salads and sauces; and all over the world pressed peanuts give their oil—for use in cooking and as a salad oil.

Raw peanuts have a faint taste of green beans—which is not surprising, as the peanut is a member of the legume family. These are the peanuts that can be so useful in cooking. You can deep-fry, fry, or roast raw peanuts. Try tossing them in a little heated oil and some salt, then toasting them to a light golden color in a moderate oven. To make spiced nuts, first coat them in oil with a little chili powder instead of salt, or season the oil with ground coriander, cumin, and cayenne pepper.

When you buy peanut butter, you may find the highly nutritious oil sitting on top—stir it in before you start spreading. You can make your own peanut butter by grinding shelled whole peanuts, with their skins removed, together with a little peanut oil in a blender. Add a little salt, and do not make too much at a time, because fresh peanut butter is inclined to turn rancid quickly. However, it will soon be used up if you make peanut butter cookies or use it as a foundation for peanut butter fudge, in which to encase chopped blanched nuts.

Pistachio nut (*Pistacia vera*) These exquisite pale-green nuts—marketed with usefully half-open shells and, often, with their papery skins marked by a rosy fingerprint—are the greatest luxury. They are grown in California, Italy, Iran, and Turkey, and are usually roasted and salted, to eat between meals or with drinks. Those from the Middle East are sometimes flavored with rose water or lemon juice. They are also found, blanched and skinned, in mortadella in Italy, and studding the galantines and terrines and even the sausages in provincial French restaurants (you can

use hazelnuts instead in duck pâté). The best halvah, Turkish delight, and nougat contains pistachio nuts. They also make a delicious ice cream.

Betel nut (*Areca catechu*) This is the tough little nut much beloved in India. Chopped and mixed with spices, pink-dyed coconut shreds, other nuts, or tiny candy balls, they are wrapped in betel leaves to make the small triangular packages called *paans* that Indian hostesses (and restaurants) may offer to guests after a meal. Chewing these aromatic little parcels is said to aid the

mortadella 75
peanut oil 112
rose water 195

Lamb with Indian Spices 302, 303

Pine nut

Hazelnut

Fresh hazelnut

Almond

Peanut

Walnut: green, pickled, and mature

Macadamia nut

Chestnut

Cashew nut

Pistachio nut

Betel nut

Pecan nut

Brazil nut and whole husk

Coconut

digestion and sweeten the breath. It can also turn the mouth an alarming red. Betel nuts may be found in some Indian or Asian markets.

Pecan nut (*Carya illinoensis*) Pecans, thin-shelled and richly flavored, are grown mainly in the United States, their natural home. Their very name is Native American, and the nut was widely used in tribal Indian cookery. Heavier in fats than walnuts, which belong to the same family and which pecans somewhat resemble in taste and in the appearance of their kernels, pecans were particularly cherished for their oil. Their flesh, having been ground to a fine meal, was used to thicken soups and stews.

Nowadays, pecans are used to enrich cakes, candies, and ice cream, but their proudest moment comes in pecan pie—that rich, sweet mixture of corn syrup, brown sugar, eggs, vanilla, and nuts in a buttery pastry crust. Pecans can be found in most supermarkets.

Hazelnut, filbert (*Corylus*) In Europe, these are the joy of the autumn countryside, but in the United States, fresh hazelnuts are a rarity. Most of our hazelnuts are imported, from Italy or Turkey, although Oregon does produce a small crop. The best hazelnuts grow on trees, but some are the fruit of a shrub; some varieties are more elongated than the familiar round brown nut.

In America, the terms hazelnut and filbert are used interchangeably. In England, these common nuts are known as hazelnuts or cob nuts, and filbert refers to a larger variety that may be called giant filbert in the United States. Europeans buy the fresh nuts, moist and juicy, in good stores throughout the fall. By Christmas, the pretty leafy husks have shriveled, and the shells hardened and darkened to the familiar hazel color. The nut kernels themselves will be less milky, but, in their own way, still as good to eat as the fresh nuts and to use in cooking.

Hazelnuts are perfect with goat cheese and in green salads, but where they come into their own is in the preparation of candies, tortes, cakes, and other desserts. To make cakes and many other sweets, you need neither fat nor flour: hazelnuts have enough oil, balanced with mealiness, to provide it all. Just combine them, ground, with

eggs and sugar and/or cream, as the case may be, and you have a whole repertoire of rich desserts. In supermarkets, you can buy shelled hazelnuts whole or chopped. In produce markets they'll be sold complete with their shells.

Chestnut (*Castanea sativa*) Edible chestnuts are first cousins to horse chestnuts or buckeyes. They are a prettier shape, but have none of their cousin's flamboyant mahogany sheen. Their pointed shell encloses a truly delicious nut—good to eat with Brussels sprouts, wonderful for stuffings, and warming when roasted over the fire on a winter's day. Unfortunately, most of America's once-common chestnut trees were wiped out by a blight in the early 1900s, and all of the chestnuts in our markets today—or roasted by vendors on the streets of New York—are imported.

Marrons glacés, chestnuts preserved in syrup, are easy to make and are a great treat, although they do not often look as stunning as the French ones bought sitting in individual frilled paper cups. Puréed sweet chestnuts make the basis for the creamy and delicious dessert known as *mont blanc* and for frozen Nesselrode pudding (invented for the nobleman of that name by his gifted cook). In Italy, chestnuts are stewed in wine, and in France, these useful nuts, braised or puréed, provide garnishes for chicken, squab, and turkey.

When shopping for fresh chestnuts, look for smooth, shiny shells and buy nuts that feel heavy for their size. Preserved chestnuts come vacuum-packed, which saves the laborious business of shelling and skinning them—the inner skin is bitter even when cooked, so it must be removed. Less good are chestnuts canned in water. They are also preserved in syrup or, of course, in the form of purée, sweetened or unsweetened. Chestnuts are also sold dried, ready for soaking and making into chestnut purée, a traditional accompaniment for game.

Brazil nut (*Bertholletia excelsa*) This is the seed of a mighty tree that towers above the Brazilian jungle. The trees have never been cultivated: their seeds are gathered and buried by the cotia, the Amazonian hare, and those that the hare forgets to retrieve take root. The fruit that the tree produces is as large as a coconut and

a considerable weight; it falls to the ground when ripe. Inside the hard, woody shell are the twelve to twenty triangular seeds, packed tightly together like segments of an orange. These are the Brazil nuts that we buy, either in their shells (don't buy those that rattle when shaken or that feel light) or shelled, often in containers of mixed nuts.

Rich and creamy-fleshed, Brazil nuts are available all year, but are best in winter. However, they do not keep well—a high oil content gives them a rich flavor but soon turns them rancid.

Walnut (*Juglans regia*) Fresh walnuts have flesh that is pearly-white and soft, easily peeled inner skins, and shells that still have a trace of moisture about them. In Britain and other parts of Europe, these "wet" walnuts are a great delicacy, eaten raw with cheese—particularly goat cheese—and as soon as possible, so that their moisture has had no chance to evaporate. The British like to pickle very young green walnuts, before the shells have hardened, in vinegar, which turns them black.

After the first flush of youth, walnuts become both drier and more oily in consistency. It is in this state that their kernels, halved or chopped, are used raw in salads or in cooking. Walnuts are good in stuffings, pressed into cream cheese, and baked in breads and cakes. They are excellent in a winter fruit compote of prunes, pears, and dried apricots, cooked in spiced red wine. Walnut toffee and walnut fudge are delicious, and so are halved nuts, coated in caramel, to make walnut brittle. In addition, nothing goes better with after-dinner port than a dish of fat walnuts.

The common walnut is also known as the English walnut, although it is a native of the Middle East. The United States is the largest producer of these nuts, grown throughout California. Black walnuts (*Juglans nigra*) and butternuts, or white walnuts (*Juglans cinerea*), are the native North American branch of the family. Black walnut shells are so hard that special nutcrackers are needed. These nuts have a stronger taste than common walnuts, which some find bitter, but are prized in candies, ice creams, and cake. Butternuts are less difficult to crack, and have a rich flavor. Both nuts have a high oil content and turn rancid quickly.

Coconut (*Cocos nucifera*) The coconut is harvested when its outer husk is green, its shell pliable, and its flesh soft and moist. It grows in great clusters on giant palm trees, native to and once found only in Malaysia. It is now cultivated on tropical coasts all over the world. This is because, apart from providing an invaluable source of food, the coconut palm supplies a vast range of products, from coir for rugs and matting to palm wine. And in world kitchens, the coconut proves its worth in any number of ways.

By the time it arrives in our markets, its shell is dark and its flesh thick, and a great deal of the coconut juice—the thin white liquid present in the center of the unripe nut—will have been absorbed. When you buy a fresh coconut, weight is the factor to watch—the heavier the nut, the juicier it will be. When you have opened it and extracted the juice, which makes a sweet, refreshing drink, you only have to peel away the brown skin with a sharp knife and grate your coconut meat to use in pies, cakes, and other desserts, candies, and savory dishes such as curries. You can also mix fresh grated coconut with an equal amount of boiling water and then squeeze the liquid from the shreds to get coconut milk. To make coconut cream, simply use less water—approximately four parts coconut to one part water. Alternatively, buy canned coconut milk, or slabs of creamed coconut. The canned or fresh milk can be used in soups, curries, stews, roasts, drinks, candies, cakes, and other desserts, and even for cooking rice.

Shredded or flaked coconut, usually sweetened, is sold in cans and packages. Unsweetened dried, or desiccated, coconut is also available. It is made from dried coconut meat from which most of the oil has been extracted, and has less flavor than freshly grated flesh, but can be used in desserts and other dishes.

1

2

3

Splitting a coconut

1 Pierce two of the coconut "eyes" with a strong, sharp instrument such as a screwdriver, or, as shown here, an awl.

2 Shake out the juice; bake the empty coconut in a hot oven (400°F) for 15 minutes.

3 Lay the coconut on a board and give the center of the shell a sharp blow with a hammer; it should break cleanly in two.

Blanching almonds

Plunge shelled almonds into boiling water and leave for a few seconds, until the skins expand and loosen. Drain the nuts, and then pinch the almonds out of their skins. (Pistachios are skinned in the same way.)

Skinning hazelnuts

Toast shelled nuts under the broiler or in a moderate oven (350°F) until the skins begin to color and loosen. Put the nuts in a paper bag and then rub them against one another to free most of the skins from the nuts.

Peeling chestnuts

With a sharp pointed knife, score a cross on the flat side of each nut. Blanch the scored chestnuts in boiling water for a few minutes, then drain. While they are still warm, peel away the hard outer shell and the furry inner skin.

Herbs

Each herb used in the kitchen has a special and well-known affinity with certain kinds of food—fresh basil with tomatoes, rosemary with lamb, sage with pork—but there are no rules laid down about these harmonies. One of the great pleasures of cooking is improvising with the fresh green flavors that herbs bring to food, playing around to produce sometimes fierce, sometimes delicate tones. This is especially enjoyable for those who can stroll out into the herb garden for inspiration and cast their eye over the fresh greenery growing there.

The judicious use of dried herbs, too, can lead to some very memorable discoveries, so always keep a wide variety at hand—not simply a jar or two of mixed herbs to fling into everything.

Herbs from the garden can be dried at home, but they must be picked at the right moment, just before they flower, or they will have lost their flavor. Gather them on a dry but gray day, and wash them quickly. Divide the small-leafed herbs such as thyme, tarragon, and summer savory into bunches and tie them loosely with string. Either hang them up in cheesecloth bags or spread them on a cloth or on newspaper laid over a rack, and then leave them to dry in a warm place (this should not be out in the sunshine).

Large-leafed herbs such as bay, sage, and mint can be tied loosely and dried in the same way, or dipped into boiling water for a minute, shaken dry, and dried to a crisp in a very low oven. Parsley is more difficult, as it is a very juicy herb. Dry it on a rack in a hot oven (400°F) for 1 minute, then turn the heat off and leave the parsley in the oven until it is quite crisp.

If you want to crush dried herbs for storage in glass jars, use a rolling pin or whiz them in a little spice grinder, which will turn them a nice green color again. Fill the jars loosely to the top and make sure the tops fit properly, to preserve the herb's aroma.

Most of the more tender herbs—dill, mint, tarragon, parsley, chives, basil, chervil, and so forth—can be frozen. They will darken in color when they are thawed, but the flavor will be well preserved. Since most herbs are very strongly scented, be sure to store them in airtight freezer containers or bags, otherwise they will flavor everything in the freezer.

Bouquet garni Traditionally this is a few sprigs of parsley, some thyme, and a bay leaf. Tied with kitchen twine, it goes into the soup, stew, or whatever dish calls for it and is discarded when the dish is cooked. When used to flavor a stock, the herbs can be tied inside a rib of celery or leek greens. A bouquet garni can also be a mixture of dried herbs tied up in a little square of cheesecloth or muslin. To the basic bouquet can be added a piece of orange peel, a clove of garlic, a few celery leaves, a couple of twigs of fennel, or whatever herbs you choose to go with the particular dish you are making.

Fines herbes This is a delicate mixture of the more tender herbs— parsley, chervil, chives, and sometimes tarragon—all chopped very fine. The alchemy of this mixture has a hundred and one uses, flavoring everything from subtly cooked egg dishes and omelets to poached sole or any delicate fish with a cream and white wine sauce.

Angelica (*Angelica archangelica*) Nobody knows why angelica is associated with angels, although it has been helpful in its time for curing coughs, colds, and colic. It is best known today as a candied stem used for decorating cakes and other desserts. Freshly shredded angelica leaves are a good flavoring for rhubarb, and can also be used in jam making, particularly in rhubarb jam.

Basil (*Ocimum basilicum*) Sweet basil, so necessary to the well-being of anyone who loves the Mediterranean, has large, tender leaves that bruise easily and smell sweetly of cloves. It should be picked young and eaten raw, or almost so, since the aroma and flavor are fleeting. Use it lavishly on tomato salad—it has a great affinity with tomatoes—and with eggplant and zucchini. In the South of France, a few chopped leaves are sometimes thrust into a ratatouille at the last moment. The famous *pesto alla genovese*—basil and pine nut paste—is one of the greatest pasta sauces. And Provençal vegetable soup would be no more than an ordinary vegetable soup were it not for the similar *pommade* made with oil, garlic, and basil pounded together and added to the bowl at the last moment. Fresh basil is also delicious with mozzarella cheese, in a potato salad or a salad of white beans, as well as with steak and chicken.

There are many varieties of basil in addition to common sweet basil. Small-leaved pot basil is particularly sweet, while Thai or Asian basil has a pungent anise aroma, purple stems, and sharply pointed leaves—delicious in salads, stir-fried dishes, and soups. Lemon basil has a citrus fragrance, and purple or opal basil has beautiful dark red-purple leaves with a slightly muted flavor.

To preserve basil, push the leaves into a jar, sprinkling a little salt between the layers, and fill the jar with olive oil. Both leaves (which become black) and oil are good, and impart their flavor to whatever ingredient or dish they are added to. Basil can also be preserved by freezing, after a brief blanching, but the flavor of frozen or dried basil can never compare with that of the freshly picked herb.

Bay (*Laurus nobilis*) Anyone who is familiar with cooking is familiar with the sweet, resinous smell of bay. The leaves or sprigs go into stocks, broths, and marinades, court-bouillons for fish, pickles, stews, and spaghetti sauces— into anything, in fact, that demands a bouquet garni. In the past, fresh bay leaves were used to flavor custards— bay infused in boiled milk adds a very agreeable, subtle flavor.

Fresh bay leaves are not often seen in the United States even in produce markets, but they can sometimes be found at herb growers' stands in farmers' markets. Buy Turkish bay leaves if you can; California bay leaves have a harsher flavor. Avoid buying old bay leaves; if they are more than a year old, they will have lost their flavor as well as their color. In France, bay leaves are called *laurier*, which is sometimes dangerously translated as "laurel leaves" in cookbooks (including Alice B. Toklas's famous cookbook, where there is a laurel soup recipe that would fell a horse), as leaves of laurels other than the sweet bay can be poisonous.

Borage (*Borago officinalis*) A hairy, bristly plant that stings the fingers, borage makes up for the discomfort it inflicts by its flowers, which are a heart-breakingly intense blue. Together with the cucumber-flavored furry leaves, they complete that fruit salad of an English summer drink called Pimms cup. Borage leaves also go into teas and other refreshing summer drinks. The flowers make a pretty garnish for crab salad.

Burnet (*Poterium sanguisorba*) Salad burnet, with its gray-green leaves and cool cucumber flavor, was eaten a great deal by our ancestors. The young leaves of this European plant are very tender and can be sprinkled into the salad bowl with the lettuce. Used a great deal in France and Italy, burnet can also be used, like borage, in cooling drinks, and is an excellent flavoring for vinegar.

Chervil (*Anthriscus cerefolium*) One of the classic fines herbes, chervil has a delicate, anise flavor, so subtle that it needs to be used lavishly. It is good in green salads, with eggs, and in an herb butter for steak or sole. In Korea, it is used as a salad green instead of lettuce, served by itself or with a dish of grilled or curried shrimp. It makes a very good light soup, and chervil and sorrel, both shredded fairly finely, are a traditional garnish for chicken soup. Fresh chervil can be frozen, but it doesn't dry very well.

Chinese chive, garlic chive (*Allium tuberosum*) These garlic-scented and -flavored chives, also known as *ku chai*, have narrow, flat green leaves and edible white flowers. They are much used in Chinese and Indian cooking, and in South Africa they are used for flavoring salads. Usually eaten while still in bud, they can also be picked in full flower and scattered lightly on top of salad greens to add beauty and a delicate garlic flavor. The buds may also be fried.

Chive (*Allium schoenoprasum*) With a flavor faintly redolent of onions but far finer and more delicate, grassy-looking chives are best with eggs, especially in omelets. They are also delicious with potatoes —particularly baked potatoes split open and piled with sour cream mixed with chopped chives—and with raw or cooked tomatoes. As they are such a clean, fresh green, they look pretty snipped and sprinkled over puréed soups—tomato, vichyssoise, avocado, potato, or artichoke—as well as in a mixed green salad and as a garnish for potato salad and glazed carrots. Chives freeze well but lose their flavor if dried.

flavored vinegars 204–5

Cauliflower Vichyssoise 255
Rice Pudding 385
Tomato and Leek Soup 247

Cilantro

Chervil

Tarragon

Curly parsley

Parsley root

Fennel

Flat-leaf parsley

Dill

Bouquet garni

Chinese chive

Cilantro, fresh coriander
(*Coriandrum sativum*) The soft, floppy green leaves of this now well-known herb look like rather lacy, flat parsley. They don't smell particularly strong unless you bruise them, and their taste, on its own, is harsh with a green note (said by some to be reminiscent of soap)—quite unlike the warm flavor of the seeds. But chopped and used in fresh salsas and in many other Mexican and Southwestern dishes, cilantro has a superb flavor. It is also an essential flavor in many types of Indian curry, particularly shrimp, and a very good addition to a Southeast-Asian meat or chicken curry is a paste made from fresh ginger, garlic, hot green chiles, and fresh cilantro, all pounded together. Cilantro can be delicious in meatballs and lamb stews, or with lamb or pork kebabs, and in Mediterranean vegetable dishes. It is widely used in Thai and other Asian cuisines. It does not dry well, but can be frozen or preserved with salt in oil.

The roots of the cilantro plant are also delicious in cooking. In Thailand, the roots are added to dishes that are to be long-simmered, and then the leaves are stirred in at the last moment.

Dill (*Anethum graveolens*) Scandinavians are as fond of dill as they are of summer, the height of which is the first day of the *krefta* season, when thousands of crayfish are cooked with generous amounts of dill and served in their scarlet shells on a bed of the green herb, accompanied by numerous glasses of aquavit interspersed with beer. Dill is the flavor that makes gravlax, the Scandinavian cured salmon, so delicious, and it is also used there with boiled and mashed potatoes. In Greece, it is the herb used to flavor fava beans and artichokes. With white fish, serve dill in melted butter or made into an herb sauce.

To preserve dill, freeze it in plastic bags. (Or use dill seeds when fresh dill is out of season.)

Fennel (*Foeniculum vulgare*) The sweet herb fennel—not to be confused with the bulb vegetable fennel—is used both as an herb and for its seeds. A few of the small twigs are invaluable for bouillabaisse and fish soup and with fresh fish; if you find fresh crayfish and cook them in boiling water with a jungle of fennel, it gives them a most delicate flavor and is a good alternative to the dill the Scandinavians prefer. Burn a few dried twigs when you are grilling fish or lamb outdoors, and put sprigs inside and under a fish when you roast it in the oven. The anise-flavored oils will permeate the food with a wonderful flavor. In Sardinia, wild fennel is often used to flavor a bean and pork stew, and occasionally with lamb.

Horseradish (*Armoracia rusticana*) A fresh, sharp horseradish sauce with roast beef is one of life's pleasures and is very good, too, with hot boiled tongue. In Germany, horseradish is grated and mixed with vinegar as a sauce for fish, and creamed horseradish sauce is particularly good with smoked trout or eel. Bottled horseradish is an adequate substitute for the fresh root but is often quite vinegary; a better substitute, if available, is dried horseradish.

Sage

Sweet woodruff

Sweet cicely

Bay

Thyme

Angelica

Oregano

Rosemary

Basil

Horseradish

Kaffir lime leaf (*Cistus hystrix*) Only the leaves of the Southeast-Asian kaffir lime, or *makrut*, tree and sometimes the peel of its fruit are used in cooking. The glossy, waisted leaves have an aromatic, floral-citrus smell and are used in the same way as bay leaves to flavor Thai and other Southeast-Asian soups and curries. They are usually sold dried in Asian markets, but the fresh leaves are becoming more available. The peel can sometimes be found, dried, and needs soaking before it is used, like the leaves, to flavor soups, marinades, and curries—even marmalade.

Lemon balm, balm (*Melissa officinalis*) Beloved of bees, balm was the vital ingredient of the *elixir vital* created by the Swiss alchemist Paracelsus, which was designed to make man immortal. It now gives its essence to Chartreuse, that green and potent liqueur made by monks, who keep most of the other ingredients a secret. The fresh, lemon-scented leaves and small white flowers of this plant are delicious in a white wine punch, and

a few freshly picked leaves can also go into a green salad, but the taste is rather overpowering and more bitter than you might expect.

Lemon grass (*Ambopogon citratus/ Cymbopogon citratus*) Perfumed, spicy, and balm-like, lemon grass adds a light, rather elusive flavor to many Thai and Indonesian dishes. Tough on the outside, the stalks contain tender inner leaves that are cut into rounds or shredded and used to flavor soups, curries, pork, seafood—particularly crab—and chicken. Lemon grass can be grown in a frost-free place like any other herb. Best fresh, it can also be bought dried: soak for half an hour before use.

Lovage (*Ligusticum officinalis*) This old-fashioned herb looks rather like immensely tall, dark green celery that has gotten out of hand. It has a strange, pleasant but heavy smell (it is called the Maggi plant in Holland because the flavor is reminiscent of the stock cubes, with monosodium glutamate lurking

somewhere in its nuances). It is a strong-flavored herb and should be used sparingly to season stocks or soups when a meaty flavor is wanted; its seeds can be used like celery seed.

Marjoram (*Origanum majorana*) **Sweet, or knotted, marjoram** smells very sweet, both when it is fresh and the bees are enjoying it and when it is cut, just after flowering, and dried in bunches like thyme and sage. Use fresh leaves in a salad, on grilled or roast lamb, or in stuffings for chicken or squab. Dried marjoram can be added to spaghetti and tomato sauces, and to any tomato-based soup or stew.

Pot marjoram (*Origanum onites*) This is less warm-flavored than sweet marjoram, but can be used in all the same ways.

Rigani is the wild marjoram of Greece; the dried herb is sometimes available in specialty markets. Use the dried flowers rather than the leaves to give the authentic Greek flavor to grilled lamb kebabs and to the Greek salad of feta cheese, tomatoes, olives, and onion.

Burnet

Lemon balm

Marjoram

Mint

Borage

Chive

Lovage

Summer savory

Winter savory

Mint (*Mentha*) One of the oldest and most familiar of all the herbs, mint has almost as many varieties as it has uses. Spearmint (*Mentha spicata*), with its pointed leaves and fresh taste, is the most commonly used. Peppermint (*Mentha piperita*) has longer, darker green leaves and a more pungent taste. Pretty apple mint (*Mentha rotundifolia*), which has woolly, rounded leaves, has a superior, fruitier flavor (its woolly texture disappears when it is finely chopped or cooked).

Americans like mint in candies and desserts. For some, an all-too-vividly-green mint jelly is essential with lamb chops or roast lamb. And in Kentucky, mint juleps are always served on Derby Day (and on other days as well). In England, mint is best known in a sauce to accompany roast lamb. A few sprigs of fresh mint are often boiled with new potatoes, when it is delicious, and with garden peas, when it is a mistake. Mint features a good deal in Middle Eastern cookery—for example, finely chopped and stirred into yogurt as a dressing for the cucumber salad called *raita*. In northern India, chopped mint is mixed with hot green chiles and yogurt to make a fresh chutney that is very good with tandoori chicken. In Italy, wild mint is used instead of parsley with grilled or sautéed porcini mushrooms.

Mint is also used with shellfish, particularly grilled shrimp, and in the making of desserts that contain fresh oranges (with which the herb has an affinity). Sprigs of mint go into fruit drinks and iced tea. Sun-brewed mint tea is made by putting mint sprigs and tea bags in a pitcher of cold water and leaving it to brew in the sun—the resulting tea has no hint of bitterness.

Oregano (*Origanum vulgare*) This Mediterranean herb, sometimes known as wild marjoram, has a wonderfully warm, heady scent and flavor. In Italy, it is used for the same dishes as marjoram. The dried leaves give a strong, spicy flavor to an oil and lemon sauce for fish and roast meats, and to pizza and spaghetti sauces, chicken broths, beef stews, and grilled fish, especially the prized red mullet. Oregano is delicious with mozzarella and tomatoes, and is one of the flavors in the best chilis. The oregano of Mexico is stronger than the common Mediterranean variety.

Parsley (*Petroselinum crispum*) The most serviceable of herbs and one that you can always buy fresh, parsley seems to have just as much affinity with garlic and strongly flavor Mediterranean dishes—salty with olives, anchovies, goat cheese, garlic, and capers—as it does with the heartier cooking of cooler northern regions, and many a pallid dish has been saved with a sprinkling of this chopped green. Flat-leaf parsley is tastier and has a better texture than the curled, and parsley root—also called Hamburg parsley—is good for flavoring stews. Use parsley in stock and court-bouillon, soups, and, stews. *Persillade* is the term for garlic and parsley chopped together, and it flavors many dishes; rack of lamb *en persillade*, coated with bread crumbs tossed with this mixture before roasting, is delicious. Parsley can be cooked with cream and served as a vegetable in its own right. Put plenty of coarsely chopped flat-leaf parsley, which is also called Italian parsley, in any green salad.

Rosemary (*Rosmarinus officinalis*) One of the prettiest of shrubs, rosemary loves the baking heat and dryness of the Mediterranean, but will grow to quite a good size in cooler climates if given a warm, dry, sheltered place. It particularly likes the seaside—its name comes from the Latin for "dew of the sea." It has a great affinity with veal, lamb, chicken, and also with rabbit—put a sprig under a rack or leg of veal or lamb before roasting, or into the butter in which you are softening onions for a veal stew, and drop a sprig into the oil in which you are frying potatoes. Rosemary is better fresh than dried, and a fresh rosemary sprig has the added advantage of staying in one piece in the cooking—which is lucky, as it is very disagreeable to get a mouthful of the needle-like leaves. But be miserly, because it is all too easy to overdo the gingery, pungent flavor of this herb.

Sage (*Salvia officinalis*) Sage was once believed to give wisdom and prolong life. It is certainly a powerful herb, musky and fragrant. The leaves go into stuffings for roast pork and turkey, and sage is an important ingredient—usefully cutting the richness of the fat—in pork sausages. Quail and other small game birds are sometimes cooked with sage. In Italy, fresh sage is fried in the oil in which veal or calf's liver is to be cooked, to give it an interesting flavor, and, sprinkled on ravioli, sage leaves fried in butter add a warm, satisfying note.

Savory (*Satureia hortensis*)
Summer savory Aromatic and pleasantly bitter, with a scent a little like thyme, summer savory was used by the Romans to flavor vinegar in much the same way as we use tarragon and other herb vinegars today. In France, where it is called *sarriette*, it is used with thyme to flavor rabbit, and fresh sprigs are cooked with fava beans and peas. It is also good in long-simmered stews and *daubes*. Summer savory dries well, and can be used with other herbs in stuffings for turkey and veal. It is said to be a good antidote to beestings.
Winter savory (*Satureia montana*), with its blue flowers, is a tougher herb than summer savory. Its rough, pointed evergreen leaves cannot be eaten raw, as they tickle the throat. It has a similar, strong earthy flavor, perfect with beef and rabbit stews, and in stuffings.

Sweet woodruff (*Asperula odorata*) A small woodland herb, sweet woodruff is a native European flowering plant that has a ravishing hay-like perfume. In Germany, it is used in May, before it flowers, to flavor the delicate wine punch known as May wine: steep the well-washed plants in a pitcher of white wine overnight in the refrigerator, then add brandy and sugar or Bénèdictine and serve with a garnish of the green leaves.

Tarragon (*Artemisia dracunculus*) Like basil and dill, tarragon has an addictive flavor—that is to say, those who have eaten it fresh can't very well get through the summer without it, since it is so delicious. French tarragon tastes sweetly of vanilla and anise, and harmonizes with all kinds of egg dishes, with cream sauces, and with roast chicken or steak. It is good in green salads and potato salad, and with cold salmon or trout. Tarragon is excellent in homemade mayonnaise for potato salad or chicken, and is essential for béarnaise sauce. Dried tarragon takes on a hay-like flavor, but frozen tarragon is very good.
Russian tarragon (*Artemisia dracunculoides*) Unlike the true French herb, this has a disappointing flavor.

Thyme (*Thymus vulgaris*) Sun-loving, tiny-leafed, but tough, thyme tastes and smells warm, earthy, and flowery. Use it in every kind of long-simmered red-wine dish; with veal and chicken in all their tomatoey incarnations; in a bouquet garni; in marinades; and—instead of rosemary—with lamb. In Marseilles, thyme is sprinkled into everything including vinaigrettes, on fried potatoes, and onto fish to be grilled over a wood fire. It gives pungency to pâtés, terrines, and meatballs and has an affinity with Mediterranean vegetables such as eggplant, zucchini, and sweet peppers.

Lemon thyme (*Thymus citriodorus*) is superb in stuffings for both pork and veal. Home-dried or frozen thyme is incomparably better than commercially dried or ground thyme.

Garden leaves and flowers

Always use only unsprayed (pesticide-free) leaves and flowers.

Geranium (*Pelargonium graveolens*) The curling, slightly furry leaves of the rose-scented geranium add a delicate rose fragrance to a clear amber-pink crabapple jelly or to lemon granita or sorbet. Pick the larger leaves.

Grape (*Vitis*) Every vine that produces edible grapes produces leaves that are edible when young. As rice-filled Greek *dolmades*, and as a wrapping, with bacon, for little birds such as quail, grape leaves impart a delicious, faint lemon flavor. Choose large, tender young leaves; or if they are older, blanch them briefly in boiling salted water to soften them before they are used. Of course, canned grape leaves are also available; rinse them well before using.

Marigold (*Calendula officinalis*) This pretty golden flower was once used a great deal to color and flavor fish soups and meat broths and to decorate salads—especially shrimp, crab, or lobster. Since the petals are surprisingly tough, they are best chopped. Mixed with other chopped petals, such as borage, rose, and hyssop, the effect is colorful and quite charming. Marigolds are still sometimes used as a coloring agent, and can be employed as a substitute for saffron if you don't like the strong flavor of that spice. The petals can be fresh or dried, but don't use the flower centers. The small Signet marigold is one of the nicest.

Nasturtium (*Trapaeolum majus*) Almost every part of this tender plant has a place in the kitchen. The flowers and young leaves can be used in salads—the leaves taste like watercress, but don't use too many, because they are very spicy. The buds and seeds can also be pickled, to make "false capers." Gather the seeds as soon as the blossoms have fallen, before they get hard, rinse them in cold water, and soak overnight in cold salted water. Then drain, cover with cold spiced vinegar, and seal; keep for a year or so before using.

Peach (*Prunus persica*) Fresh peach leaves make a delicate flavoring for custard, more interesting than the usual vanilla and tasting faintly of almonds. Pick five or six fresh leaves and infuse them in the milk for 5 to 10 minutes, then proceed with the custard in the usual way.

Rose (*Rosa*) Although much of life was probably far from rosy in medieval days, it must have been a great pleasure, on a fine day, to gather dark red rose petals to make into rose syrup, rose candy, and rose vinegar. In the Middle East, roses are still definitely the domain of the cook, who will sprinkle rose water into fruit salads made with pomegranates and make clear rose petal jelly with nuts suspended in it, or chewy, scented rose petal jam. In the last century, the American Shakers used their own rose water to flavor apple pie—an unexpectedly exotic touch for such a "plain" people; in England, the Victorians made rose petal sandwiches. Rose petals are also good in cherry pie.

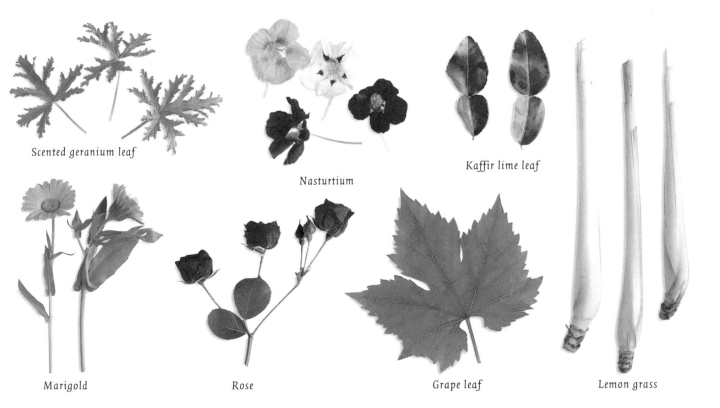

Scented geranium leaf

Nasturtium

Kaffir lime leaf

Marigold

Rose

Grape leaf

Lemon grass

Spices

Although spices have been in wide use since the Middle Ages—and Christopher Columbus would never have landed in America had he not been seeking an easier route to the spices of India—they rather fell into disrepute here as "good plain cooking" took hold. Now the heady, aromatic smells of the spice bazaars are back, with the wave of new ethnic food shops, and with them a revived interest in the cooking of India, the Middle East, and Asia.

Kitchen cupboards are loaded with little pots and jars of cumin, coriander seeds, and cardamom, which are becoming as familiar as the ginger, cloves, and cinnamon many cooks have relied on in the past. Buy in small quantities and use whole spices whenever possible, pounding or grinding them fresh for each dish that calls for ground spice. A small, specially designated coffee grinder can be used for this purpose, as can a spice grinder—but grinding the spices with ingredients such as garlic, fresh cilantro leaves, fresh ginger, and chile pepper in a large mortar and pestle is a pleasure not to be missed.

Mixtures

Five-spice powder This is a Chinese mixture of ground star anise, fennel seeds, cloves, cinnamon, and Sichuan pepper. Its subtle anise flavor is particularly good with roast pork.
Garam masala This Indian mixture of spices is added to a dish toward the end of cooking to enhance the aromas and flavors. It can be bought at Indian markets and well-stocked supermarkets or ground at home from a mixture of whole spices. The powder can be mixed to a paste with water, to be used in curry, stirred into yogurt, or eaten with other foods like a condiment.
Pickling spice Although these mixtures vary according to their manufacturer, most will probably contain a great deal of mustard seed, some small dried chiles, white peppercorns, allspice, cloves, mace, a few coriander seeds, and perhaps some ginger. But it is better to use measured amounts of the individual spices in pickling, because appropriate quantities and ingredients vary from vegetable to vegetable, as well as recipe to recipe.
Quatre épices Although called "four spices" in French, the actual number of spices used in this mixture may vary. The base spices are star anise, cassia or cinnamon, cloves, and fennel seeds; the "extra" spices often added are Sichuan peppercorns, ginger, or cardamom. Quatre épices is used in the making of pâtés, savory pies, and sausages. Buy it from a specialty market or spice purveyor, or make only a small quantity at a time.
Other spice blends commonly available include curry powder and chili powder, and the sweeter mixtures for seasoning pumpkin and apple pies.

Allspice (*Pimenta officinalis*) Allspice, or Jamaica pepper, is a hard brown berry, larger and smoother than a peppercorn. It tastes faintly of cinnamon and strongly of cloves, with a touch of nutmeg, which is why it is sometimes mistakenly thought to be a mixture of spices when it is bought ground. It is called *pimienta* in Jamaica, where it is an essential ingredient in jerk seasoning, the spicy paste rubbed on chicken, pork, and other meats before grilling them. Ground allspice can also go into pâtés and sausages. It is used in gingerbread and spice cake, in marinades, with cured beef, and in chutneys. It seems to impart something of a peppery as well as a spicy flavor.

Anise seeds (*Pimpinella anisum*) Anise seeds, or aniseed, flavor Pernod, ouzo, and other addictive licorice-flavored drinks of the same genre. From a delicate bush of the hemlock family, the seeds give a sweet flavor to fish and particularly to mussels, to some sweets, and, in parts of Europe, to cakes and bread. In the Middle East, anise flavors preserved green figs (it is added to the syrup in which the figs are cooked), and it is a seasoning in some Indian vegetable and fish curries. Buy aniseed in small quantities, as it quickly loses its strength.

Asafoetida (*Ferula asafoetida*) An ingredient in Indian vegetable dishes, curries, and pickles, asafoetida is an evil-smelling resin that is obtained from equally pungent plants of the giant fennel family. It should be used in exceedingly small quantities—or it can be omitted entirely from recipes that call for it.

Anise seeds

Star anise

Dill seeds

Fennel seeds

Juniper berry

Celery seeds

Sesame seeds

Poppy seeds

Indian poppy seeds

Caraway seeds

Caraway seeds (*Carum carvi*) It could be the fact that they aid digestion that makes these an ingredient of so many hearty, delicious rye breads. In Germany, caraway is called *kümmel* and gives the typical flavor to the liquor of the same name—a warm and comforting drink. With anise, star anise, fennel, and coriander, it also flavors aquavit, the superb but lethal white liquor tossed down by the Scandinavians with herring, crayfish, and smoked eel. And there are at least a dozen good cheeses flecked with caraway seeds. Caraway seeds are good in coleslaw, and with cooked cabbage too.

Cardamom (*Elettaria cardamomum*) Genuine cardamom is costly and has a great many inferior relatives, so it pays to look carefully at what you are buying. The best cardamom pods are the size of peas, pale brown or greenish, and the tiny seeds, when you split open a pod, should be dark, shiny, and richly aromatic. The flavor of cardamom is essential in some curries—it has a warm, aromatic, but sharp taste, and an anesthetic effect on the tongue. Sometimes the whole pod is used, but usually the seeds are taken out and ground with other spices. Ready-ground cardamom is sold, but has a much more floury flavor than the freshly ground seeds. In Arab countries, cardamom is put into the sweet coffee, and in Scandinavian countries, it flavors cakes and pastries. White cardamom is dried in the sun—or, more commonly, is bleached with sulfur dioxide—and is the one to use to flavor hot drinks.

Celery seeds (*Apium graveolens*) Although inclined to be bitter, celery seeds give a lift to soups and stews. They can also go into dishes that combine rice with tomatoes, into bread, and into pickling mixtures.

Cinnamon (*Cinnamomum zeylanicum*) Cinnamon sticks are curled, thin pieces of the bark of a tropical evergreen tree. Use them for flavoring the milk for rice pudding and baked custard, or put a few pieces in a rice pilaf. The sticks are also used in hot punches and sweet pickles.

Ground cinnamon is used in baking—in cinnamon rolls and raisin bread, hot-cross buns, apple pie, and cookies, on cinnamon toast, and in sweet and savory spiced dishes all over the Middle East and India. It has a marvelous affinity with chocolate, a combination that is particularly liked in Spain and Mexico. **Cassia** (*Cinnamomum cassia*) is the inner bark of a relative tree. Mainly produced in China and Southeast Asia, it comes in thicker, harder pieces than true cinnamon and is less delicate, more pungent, and less expensive. The cinnamon, ground or in stick form, found on most supermarket shelves is actually cassia. True cinnamon is much more common in Europe and Asia.

Clove (*Eugenia caryophyllus*) Cloves have the scent of the Spice Islands, sweet and warm, with a rather numbing quality that has also made them since the earliest days of medicine an excellent remedy for toothache. They are not, however,

particularly pleasant to bite on, so are usually fixed firmly in an onion—for lamb or oxtail stew, and other long-cooked meat dishes—or used ground. Cloves flavor pumpkin pie, gingerbread, and other baked goods, and they are traditional with cooked apples and pears, in sweet spiced pickles, and in mulled wine. The best cloves are large, dark, and plump, and not easily broken.

Coriander seeds (*Coriandrum sativum*) These round, brittle, easily crushed seeds are the basis of all that is delicious in many curry dishes and in vegetables *à la grecque*, marinated in olive oil and lemon juice. They have a warm, faintly orangey fragrance that is much enhanced if they are toasted by gentle heating in a heavy frying pan just before use. Coriander seeds, together with lemon zest, make a delicate and unusual substitute for vanilla in custards and ice creams, and an excellent flavoring for cooked apples—puréed or in an apple tart or pie. Ground coriander seeds are often used in Scandinavian baked goods.

Cumin (*Cuminum cyminum*) Cumin is an essential spice. Its scent is hard to define: powerful, warm, sweet, and slightly oily, but quite unmistakable—which is fortunate, because it looks rather like caraway and the two are often confused. In Spain, cumin is the traditional seasoning for chickpeas; in Mexico, it is part of the background in chili; and in the Canary Islands, it flavors fish soup. In North Africa and countries

Clove *Ground cinnamon* *Allspice* *Galangal*

Dried ginger *Fresh ginger* *Japanese pickled ginger* *Cinnamon stick*

of the eastern Mediterranean, it is used in couscous, on kebabs, with stewed lamb, and to spice rice and vegetable dishes and yogurt. In India, it is an element of every sort of dish. Toasting the seeds before grinding releases their aroma and makes them easier to grind.

Dill seeds (*Anethum graveolens*) Sprigs of dill complete with half-ripe seeds are a familiar sight in jars of pickles and may be used to make dill vinegar. Dill seeds are also excellent as a flavoring for fish soups and stews and in a court-bouillon. In Scandinavia and other parts of Europe, they are used to flavor cakes and breads.

Fennel seeds (*Foeniculum vulgare*) These have a sweet anise flavor, and a few seeds chewed after meals will help the digestion and sweeten the breath. In Italy, they are used in the manufacture of a marvelous salami called *finocchiona*, and are also found in a kind of nougat called *mandorlotto*. Use them to flavor the liquid in which fish is poached or in fish soups.

Fenugreek seeds (*Trigonella foenum-graecum*) Floury, somewhat bitter, and smelling of maple or fresh hay, the ground seeds of fenugreek are used in many Indian dishes and are a common ingredient of commercial curry powders and garam masala. The seeds need to be lightly toasted before they are ground—don't overdo it, or they become bitter.

Galangal (*Alpinia galanga*) Galangal, popular in European cooking during the Middle Ages and then forgotten, has made a reappearance in Thai and Indonesian markets. An underground rhizome, it takes the place of ginger in Thai cooking. Fresh galangal may occasionally be found in Asian markets, but dried is the more usual form.

Ginger (*Zingiber officinale*) This romantic spice is associated with Asia. The fresh root (actually a rhizome) is used a great deal in Chinese cooking, with pork, beef, chicken, and duck, and with fish, shrimp, and crab. It has a delicious scent and a crisp texture. In India, fresh ginger is a favorite curry ingredient. Ginger has long been used to make ginger beer and ginger ale. Ground ginger—Jamaican is best—goes into ginger snaps, brandy snaps, and gingerbread. It's good in fruit compotes; or mix it with sugar to sprinkle on chilled melon—the pleasant contrast of hot and fiery with icy and juicy being interesting, if slightly detrimental to the flavor of the melon.

Stem ginger preserved in syrup and packed into Chinese jars goes, with its syrup, into many desserts and over—or sometimes into—ice cream. Pickled ginger, called *gari* in Japan, is made from baby ginger, thinly sliced and cured in vinegar, salt, and sugar. It is usually a pale pinky-beige, but it may be dyed red. Serve it with *sushi* or *sashimi*.

Juniper berry (*Juniperus communis*) The flavor of the juniper berry, familiar to gin drinkers and especially to those who drink Dutch gin, is strangely harsh and turpentiney on its own. The hard blue-purple berries, the fruit of a pretty but prickly evergreen bush, take 2 years to ripen, so that green and ripe berries appear together. When combined with game, red cabbage, sautéed pork, chops or tenderloin, or beef stews, they add a delicious, rather somber, spicy background flavor. They are good in pork-based pâtés, in marinades for game, especially venison, and in stuffings for small game birds.

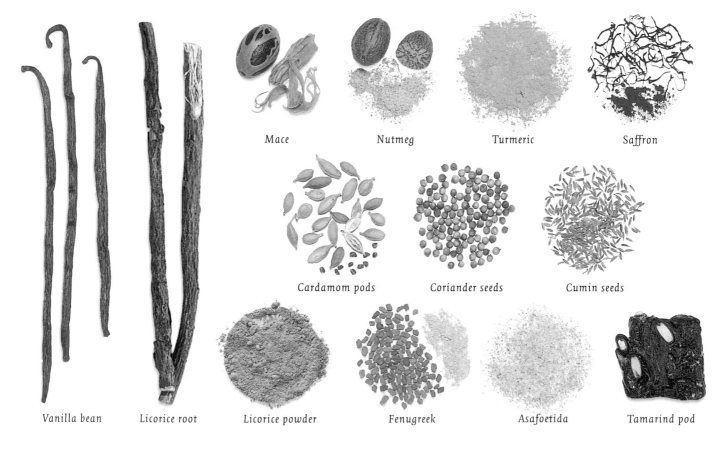

Mace   Nutmeg   Turmeric   Saffron

Cardamom pods   Coriander seeds   Cumin seeds

Vanilla bean   Licorice root   Licorice powder   Fenugreek   Asafoetida   Tamarind pod

Licorice (*Glycrriza glabra*) Licorice root is a natural sweetener and can be made into a strong-flavored herbal tea. Once given to children to chew instead of sweets, it is supposedly an aphrodisiac, especially for women. Licorice extract is used commercially in candies and other sweets, but you may find the dried or ground root in an ethnic market.

Mace (*Myristica fragrans*) This is the frond-like outer coat, or aril, of the nutmeg, dried to an orange-brown. More delicate than nutmeg, it is almost always sold ground. It has an affinity with chicken and shrimp and is invaluable in sausages, pâtés, and terrines, as well as in marinades and chutneys. Its warm, sweet, spicy flavor is delicious in cakes and other desserts, and in Italy it flavors the milk for white and cheese sauces.

Nutmeg (*Myristica fragrans*) Beautifully aromatic, with a warm, slightly bitter flavor, nutmeg is equally at home in sweet and nonsweet dishes. While its pretty outer coating is dried to make mace, the nutmeg or seed is dried and will keep, whole, for months or even years. Buy good-quality, large whole nutmeg rather than ground nutmeg, and grate it as you need it.

Northern Italians use nutmeg in many of their stuffed pastas, and in India it is a frequent ingredient of garam masala. Nutmeg is also essential in eggnog and in mulled wine (an excellent sleeping potion, since nutmeg is mildly narcotic).

Poppy seeds (*Papaver rhoeas*) Although they come from a variety of the opium poppy, there is nothing narcotic about poppy seeds. The blue-gray seeds, scattered over loaves, rolls, and bagels, add a pretty decoration and a warm and dusty flavor. Poppy seed cake or coffee cake is a favorite. The creamy-yellow poppy seeds used in India are ground to make a floury curry spice that adds texture rather than flavor. Because poppy seeds have a high oil content, they turn rancid quickly; they're best stored in a cool spot or in the refrigerator.

Saffron (*Crocus sativus*) Saffron is fabulously expensive—each red-gold shred is a crocus stigma, and each saffron crocus has only three stigmas to be hand-gathered and dried.

It is in Spain that one becomes truly addicted to the flavor of saffron, although it is used a great deal in the South of France for soups, particularly fish soups, and is essential in Milanese risotto. But the Spanish must have it. They like their rice bright yellow, and they have saffron in their fish stews, in vegetable soups, and with mussels and shrimp or prawns. Very little is needed: a pinch soaked in a little warm water or white wine will infuse the liquid with its powerful flavor and characteristic color. Saffron is almost always steeped in the liquid with which the dish is cooked, but sometimes, as in certain types of rice pilaf, it is kept until the end of the cooking and then stirred in for a dish of many shades of yellow and orange.

Saffron powder, also expensive and liable to be adulterated, is a poor substitute for saffron strands. Saffron and turmeric are sometimes substituted for each other, but this is a mistake. Saffron is perfect with garlic, fennel, white wine, mussels, and fish, while turmeric belongs with vegetables and meat; but both can be used to color rice.

Sesame seeds (*Sesamum indicum*) The nutty taste of toasted sesame seeds is probably most familiar topping on bread and crackers, but sesame comes in many guises. Tahini, the oily paste made from the finely ground seeds, is used with chickpeas to make hummus, a delicious smooth, creamy sauce into which pita bread is dipped—an hors d'oeuvre well known to everyone who has eaten a Middle Eastern meal. Halvah, a sweet, compressed, oily bar of crushed sesame seeds, has a delicate scrunch and is good as an unusual dessert. *Gomasio*— a seasoning popular in macrobiotic cooking—is a Japanese mixture of lightly toasted sesame seeds and sea salt. In the American South, sesame seeds are also called benne seeds (*benne* is the African name for these seeds brought over by the slaves), used to make cookies and benne wafers, and in many other recipes.

Star anise (*Illicium verum*) The fruit of a small evergreen tree that belongs to the magnolia family, star anise has the same essential oil that gives aniseed its flavor but is much stronger and more licoricey. It is used in Chinese cooking, particularly with pork and duck.

Tamarind (*Tamarindus indica*) Sharply sour, the sticky, dried pods of the tamarind tree—which are also known as Indian dates—are used instead of limes or lemons to add a sweet-sour tang and a bit of body to many Middle Eastern, Indian, and Southeast-Asian dishes. Tamarind also makes delicious fresh chutneys to eat with curry. The dried pods, shaped into bricks, can be found in ethnic markets; to obtain tamarind juice, steep the pulp in a bowl of hot water until the sour brown juice can easily be squeezed out or strained. Either vinegar or lemon juice makes a reasonable substitute.

Turmeric (*Curcuma longa*) Turmeric, which is a spice much used in Indian cooking, has a harsh taste, somehow reminiscent of freshly scrubbed wood, but its color is indisputably useful. A deep yellow ocher, turmeric is delightful with potatoes and other pale vegetables, such as cauliflower, and in many curries. Use it in moderation, and do not try to use it in place of saffron—the flavor is quite different.

Vanilla (*Vanilla planifolia*) Vanilla is associated with the exotic because of the drowsy, lotus-eating quality of its perfume. In fact, it does have an exotic quality, for it comes from a climbing orchid found in tropical rain forests. It was used to flavor chocolate by the Aztecs, the original chocolate addicts.

The vanilla beans are picked unripe, when they are yellow, and are then allowed to cure to a dark brown. When you buy them, the beans should be somewhat soft, ribbed, and pointed at one end, and they should have a frosting of crystals—the vanillin essence. A favorite way of using vanilla beans is to keep them in a jar of sugar, refilling the jar as you use the sugar in whipped cream, rice pudding, baked custard, and so forth. Another method, useful when making ice cream and crème brûlée, is to infuse the bruised or split bean in the milk or cream. The bean imparts a flowery and spicy aroma, and it can then be gently washed and dried, and stored for another time.

The only vanilla substitute that has genuine flavor is pure vanilla extract; imitation vanilla extract is synthetic and comes nowhere near the real thing.

Salt and Pepper

It has long been considered a measure of a cook's talent as to whether his or her food can be sent perfectly seasoned to the table, and of all the condiments, salt and pepper are the cook's greatest allies. But there are two aspects to the proper seasoning of food. One is what goes into the food in the kitchen, the other is what goes onto it at the table.

SALT

One of the properties of salt—which is an invaluable preservative as well as a seasoning—is to draw the moisture out of foods. This is an advantage with vegetables such as eggplant that may have bitter juices; they can be sliced and salted before cooking so that the bitterness is drawn out. Meat, however, should not be salted before panfrying, grilling, broiling, or roasting, as the moisture raised on its surface will prevent it from searing and browning; salt it only halfway through cooking, after the surface is seared.

Salt also toughens food, which can be helpful, for example, when pickling with vinegar—food salted before being pickled will not turn soggy in the jar. But this is a disadvantage when braising or stewing meat, and with legumes such as dried beans—start these in unsalted water or other cooking liquid and do not add salt until at least 15 minutes after they have reached a simmer.

Sea salt This is the best of all salts for both kitchen and table. It is made by evaporating sea water, either naturally by sun and wind or by artificial heat. The result is large crystals of pure salt that retain their natural iodine and have no bitter aftertaste. They can be sprinkled directly onto foods such as salmon and tuna before cooking, or ground in a salt mill or wooden mortar. This is also the salt to sprinkle over certain breads, rolls, and pretzels before they go into the oven—the crystals dissolve so slowly that they will still be a sparkling presence after baking. Fine sea salt is in most cases the best to use in cooking. Most of our sea salt comes from France, but Britain's Maldon sea salt is considered one of the finest of all.

Sel gris is a coarse, grayish, unrefined French sea salt that contains traces of other minerals. Preferred by some discerning cooks, it is for kitchen use rather than at table.

Kosher salt is widely used in the United States by cooks who prefer its flavor (it is half as salty per volume as table salt) and its coarse-grained, flaky texture; and it contains no additives.

Table salt Ordinary table salt is made by dissolving the salt found in underground deposits and then drying it in a vacuum. It is refined and coated with magnesium carbonate or some other additive to prevent it from absorbing moisture from the air and to keep it free-flowing. Table salt has a decidedly bitter aftertaste, but it is better than any other salt for baking.

Iodized salt is table salt to which iodine has been added. It is useful in areas where the water and soils are lacking in this essential trace element.

Rock salt More widely available in Europe than in the United States (in France it is known as *sel-gemme*), this is a hard, coarse, crystalline salt that needs a salt mill or mortar to make it manageable. At its best, it can be the finest of all the salts. Don't confuse it with the nonedible rock salt, used when making homemade ice cream in an old-fashioned ice cream freezer.

Pickling salt is pure, refined rock salt. It is good for all cooking and is the salt to use for pickling, because it has no additives that might spoil the clarity of the pickling liquid. Other names for it are block salt, cut lump salt, and dairy salt.

Seasoned salts Salts such as garlic salt and celery salt contain extracts of the vegetable—or, in the case of celery salt, the seeds—that give the salt its name, but they add an instantly recognizable "packaged" flavor so often found in convenience foods. Many seasoned salts contain monosodium glutamate plus flavoring agents.

Saltpeter Saltpeter is potassium nitrate, a preservative that has been used in the making of brines and dry salt curing mixtures for hundreds of years. It has the culinary quality of turning meat a beautiful pink—in France, many restaurateurs put a pinch of saltpeter in their pâté to keep it a wholesome rosy color. But saltpeter has been found to be harmful when eaten in large quantities, and, in fact, the U.S. Department of Agriculture no longer recommends it as a curing agent.

PEPPER

The vine that gives us peppercorns and the pepper, or capsicum, plants that give us chili powders, cayenne, and paprika are not related, although all these seasonings add a pungent heat to food.

Preground pepper soon tastes dull and dusty, so buy whole peppercorns—they should be evenly colored, aromatic, free from dust, and too hard to be crushed between the fingers. Nothing could be easier than keeping a peppermill in the kitchen and on the table, and the aroma and flavor of freshly ground pepper, black or white, is quite different from the dry smell and taste of the preground product.

Coarse sea salt

Fine sea salt

Sel gris

Table salt

Rock salt

Kosher salt

Different peppers vary in pungency and size of the peppercorn. Usually they are called after their place of origin—Malabar black, for instance, is one of the best of the black peppercorns; Tellicherry and Lampung are also excellent.

Black peppercorns are the dried, shriveled berries of the pepper vine, *Piper nigrum*. They are picked before they are quite ripe and dried in the sun, where they blacken within a day or two. Coarse "butcher-grind," coarse-ground black pepper, and cracked black pepper are all available in larger supermarkets. These can be used in pâtés to give an aromatic flavor without bringing tears to the eyes, as happens when peppercorns are thrown in whole, and they can also be used for steak au poivre, although freshly crushed whole peppercorns are preferable.

White peppercorns are the ripened berries, soaked, rubbed to remove their husks, and then dried. White pepper is slightly less warm and spicy than black pepper, and has a drier smell. It is useful in pale soups or sauces when black specks would spoil the appearance.

Green peppercorns are unripe pepper berries, milder than the dried black peppercorns and with a crisp texture. Picked when green, they turn black in a day or two and so are rarely seen fresh, but freeze-dried or canned green peppercorns, preserved in brine, are quite good. Use them in a sauce for lamb, steak, or duck, in pâtés and fish terrines, and with shellfish.

Pink peppercorns (*Schinus terepinthifolius*) Not true pepper but the berries of another tree, these are more subtle than green peppercorns and with little of the hotness associated with pepper. They are much used in the South of France in fish dishes. Preserved in vinegar or water and sold in jars, or freeze-dried, they are quite soft.

Sichuan or Szechwan pepper (*Xanthoxylum piperitum*) The dried red berries of a small shrub, this spice comes from the Sichuan region in China. It has a peculiar delayed reaction: nothing happens when you first bite it, but then it floods your mouth with a hot flavor.

Chili or chile powders and chile (red pepper) flakes are dried and ground or crushed chiles. They are usually red but also black, and vary enormously. The powders can be pungent, mild, tasty, or absolutely

red-hot, and only by experience can you know what you are getting. Use chili powder in curry and of course in chili con carne, with beans and chickpeas, and in couscous (although authentically for couscous you should use harissa, a hot Tunisian mixture of crushed dried chiles, ground cumin, and salt). The chili powders that contain spices such as cumin and oregano are made specifically for chili con carne, but pure ground chile pepper is usually preferable. Chile flakes, commonly called crushed red pepper or red pepper flakes, can be used to heat tomato sauces, and will give a lift to many stir-fried and sautéed dishes. They are excellent combined with garlic and anchovies and used to sauce pasta; quickly sautéed slices of pork tenderloin are also splendid with this mixture.

Cayenne pepper is made from ground dried chiles (both pods and seeds), and came originally from Cayenne in French Guiana. The red-orange powder is very hot and rather delicious. Cayenne pepper, or red pepper, is often used in

Cajun cooking. It is also used in dishes with "deviled" in their name, such as deviled chicken, in spiced almonds, and in the gravy served with roasted game birds, particularly duck. Cayenne also makes a pretty finish for deviled eggs.

Paprika Although it may be either sweet or hot, paprika by nature has a sweet flavor and is made from sweet red peppers. In Spain and Portugal, it is used in fish stews and potato and vegetable soups and with salt cod, as well as in most of the chorizos and *salsichas* (sausages). But it is in Hungary that paprika really comes into its own, so the best to buy is the original mild Hungarian paprika, described as "noble and sweet," or, for some dishes, the hot version. The combination of sweet paprika and sour cream has the most appetizing delicacy to it, and, although chicken paprikash and goulash may be somewhat overworked dishes, both are wonderful food. Hungarians sometimes use paprika and cayenne in the same dish—in cabbage soup, for example.

White peppercorns

Black peppercorns

Pink peppercorns

Green peppercorns

Sichuan pepper

Chili powder

Chile flakes

Cayenne pepper

Paprika

Mustard

Mustard has been adding its hot spiciness to food for thousands of years—the ancient Egyptians, and the Greeks and Romans used to crunch the seeds between their teeth during meals, and the Romans used mustard to preserve vegetables—their pickled turnips in mustard were the forerunners of our highly seasoned piccalilli.

In the course of time, it was discovered that mustard helps the digestion, and it came to be eaten particularly with pork dishes and with cheese, which was thought to "sit heavy on the stomach." It had a place in home medicine too: hot mustard poultices were frequently applied to relieve aching joints, and sportsmen, when they came home cold and wet from the hunt, used to thrust their feet into a comforting mustard bath to ward off chills.

Mustard as we know it is basically a paste made from the ground seeds of black (*Brassica nigra*), or brown (*B. juncea*), and white mustard (*B. alba*), which is also called yellow mustard. *Nigra* is hot; *alba* is cooler. It is *alba* that, when young, gives us the tender mustard greens to be added to salads, and when mature, yields the seeds that are used whole in pickling.

B. juncea, the brown variety, is less pungent than *nigra*. It is the seed that is usually called for in Indian recipes. And although black mustard seeds were traditionally used in European mustards, they have mostly been replaced today by the brown seeds.

French mustards

The most famous French mustards are those of Dijon, Bordeaux, and Meaux.

In Dijon, mustard center of the world, the mustard is blended with salt, spices, and white wine or verjuice—an acidic juice made from unripe green grapes. Some Dijon mustards rival powerful English mustard in strength, but are a creamy grayish-lemon color rather than yellow and have a more subtle flavor. Other Dijon mustards are milky-pale and delicate rather than sharp. The famous house of Poupon—one of the sights of Dijon—sells dozens of different blends and exports them all over the world.

Most good cooks use Dijon mustard in preference to any other: for vinaigrettes, for mayonnaise (which mustard helps to emulsify), and for the more delicate creamy sauces to go with egg dishes and chicken or fish. Generally, when mustard is called for in a recipe it is safe to use a strong Dijon, such as Grey Poupon.

Blended with unfermented red wine, Bordeaux mustard is strong, dark brown, and both more acid and more aromatic than that of Dijon. It is unsurpassed for eating with steak, complementing rather than overpowering the flavor of the meat.

Moutarde de Meaux is an interesting mixture of ground and half-ground seeds, with a grainy texture and an attractive musty taste. It is pleasantly hot, and was once described by Brillat-Savarin—the eighteenth-century French gastronome—as "the gourmet's mustard." It comes in widemouthed stoneware jars, their corks secured by

sealing wax. It is made to a formula that has been a closely guarded secret since 1760, when it was handed by the abbots of Meaux to the Pommery family, of Champagne fame. The most superior of the coarse-grained mustards, with a taste all its own, it is best appreciated when eaten with humble food—bacon, sausages, and cold meats.

There are, of course, a thousand other French mustards: sometimes tarragon is added, or a mixture of fresh herbs (which produce a pleasant-tasting but rather alarming-looking result). There is a mustard containing tomato purée, making a red-brown mustard that is designed to go with hamburgers; and a mustard that is basically mild, but with the bite of crushed green peppercorns, called *moutarde au poivre vert*.

American mustards

Owing to the wide range of national tastes, every kind of mustard, plain and spiced, can be found in American supermarkets. What is thought of as the true American mustard, however, is yellow (it's colored with turmeric), mild, and sweet, and has a consistency rather more like a thick sauce than a French mustard. It is made from yellow mustard seeds and is flavored with sugar, vinegar, or white wine—which accounts for its cool character and for the fact that it can be applied in such quantities to hot dogs and be lavished on that other all-American specialty, the hamburger. (It's sometimes referred to as "ballpark mustard.")

This mustard can be used when making homemade mayonnaise, not only to speed up the emulsion of the egg yolks and the oil but also to give the mayonnaise a sweetish mustard flavor. Such mayonnaises are good in egg, potato, and tunafish salads.

A German-style mustard, which is brown, sweet-sour, and spicy, is also very popular, particularly on ham sandwiches. Among the many other flavored mustards on the grocery store shelves are hot, spicy Creole mustard, and sweet, mild honey mustard.

English mustard

This dry mustard is a hot yellow in color and its taste is biting and hot; it is good with plain home-cooked food. For its texture, we owe a debt to an eighteenth-century housewife from Durham, who

Mustard seeds:
Brassica alba

Mustard seeds:
Brassica nigra

Dijon mustard

Dijon mustard
with tarragon

Moutarde de Meaux

Bordeaux mustard

French mustard
with tomato

German mustard
with herbs

decided to grind and sift her mustard seeds rather than pound them. She took her new "mustard flour" to London, where it was championed by King George I, and commercial production followed. Mr. Colman began milling his mustard powder in 1814.

Today you can buy Colman's mustard, the best-known powdered mustard, in its powdered form or—more convenient but perhaps not as good—prepared. A straightforward blend of ground and sifted seeds, wheat flour, and spices, it contains no wine or vinegar to lessen the natural impact of the seeds.

To mix "common" hot English mustard, simply add cold water to the powder, in equal quantities—the water must never be hot, or it will release bitter oils that spoil the taste. To be at its best, the mustard should be freshly prepared in a small quantity. Allow it to stand, well covered, for half an hour before use, to develop its full flavor and heat. For milder mustard, mix 1 teaspoon each of milk and cream and a pinch of sugar, with 2 teaspoons of mustard powder and water. To make a thick mustard, with a more delicate flavor and a biting aftertaste, moisten the powder with wine vinegar, grape or apple juice, or ale or claret.

Common English mustard is perfect with roast beef, its classic partner, as well as with other plain roast meats, ham, English pork pie, and beef or pork sausages. It goes well with Cheddar cheese (especially in Welsh rarebit), and it is the best mustard to use when making strong mustard sauce to go with richly flavored oily fish such as herring or mackerel. But simmered for any length of time in dishes that call for mustard, even English mustard loses some of its taste and piquancy, and in fact mustard sauces of all types benefit from being given a boost of a little more mustard shortly before the end of cooking.

German mustards

Made from a blend of strong mustard flour and vinegar, German mustard— *senf*—generally combines pungency with aroma, and comes halfway between the earthy, aromatic flavor of Bordeaux mustard and that of hot, sharp English mustard. Stronger palates go for mustard that is *scharf* or *extra scharf*— hot or extra-hot

A lot of mustard is consumed in Germany: it is specifically designed to be eaten with the profusion of sausages of the frankfurter type—knackwurst, bockwurst, and of course with frankfurters themselves. So it is not surprising that the Bavarians and other southern Germans, whose pale local sausage is made of veal and called weisswurst, have a mild, pale mustard to go with it: coarse-grained and sweet, it is just right for this bland sausage, which is eaten fried to a golden color. The Rhineland favors a herb mustard, thought to be excellent with lamb.

Mustard preserves

Mostarda di frutta, mostarda di cremona

This is an Italian confection of fruits— figs and cherries, and chunks of pears, lemons, and peaches—candied in a syrup containing mustard oil. Enjoyed from about the sixteenth century on, it is still eaten, like jam, by the spoonful on bread. Its delicate, strange, sweet-sharp flavor makes it an interesting relish for cold meats, particularly ham, boiled beef, and zampone (stuffed pig's foot that is a New Year's Eve specialty). Look for *mostarda di frutta* in gourmet shops and Italian markets. *Bollito misto*—mixed boiled chicken, ham, sausage, and beef—can be served with *mostarda* on the side.

Mostarda di Voghera Even more special is a *mostarda* of whole, translucent pale pears, complete with their stems, in a jar that looks as if it might float off the table; the taste is ethereal too. Eat them with game, particularly roasted venison,

and with the same meats as *mostarda di frutta*. This also comes as a yellow-brown mush—a less extravagant version. It may sometimes be found in gourmet shops.
Piccalilli is a strong, mustardy pickled relish with a crunch to it. It contains cauliflower among other things, including onions, chiles, ginger, and plenty of turmeric to color it a gorgeous bright yellow. Eaten with ham and cold meats, it is very refreshing, cutting the fattiness of the meat.

Making your own mustard

Experimenting with your own blends can produce interesting results. To grind the seeds, use a small coffee grinder (clean it very well after use) or a spice grinder—or, for a coarser mixture, simply pound the seeds in a mortar.

The first time you make your own mustard, use equal amounts of black and yellow seeds and, if necessary, gradually alter the balance according to taste. (Black mustard seeds are available in Indian and Asian markets; if you can't find them, substitute the brown seeds, available in specialty markets.) Moisten the ground mustard with water until just saturated, then add white wine vinegar, salt, and the flavorings of your choice—tarragon, green peppercorns, horseradish, honey, etc.—and leave to ferment for several days. A little olive oil takes the edge off a hot mixture. Store in a tightly sealed jar, in the refrigerator.

To enjoy all mustards at their best, store them in the refrigerator, and keep them for no longer than 6 months.

Hot German mustard   Bavarian mustard   American mild mustard   American spicy brown mustard

Green peppercorn mustard   Mostarda di frutta   Prepared English mustard   English mustard powder

Vinegar

Vinaigre, the French word for vinegar, means sour wine, and this is what wine vinegar is, being produced by an acid fermentation of fresh wine. By the same process, cider vinegar is made from cider, malt vinegar from malted barley, and Chinese and Japanese vinegars from fermented rice.

"The grateful acid," as vinegar was called in the seventeenth century, has had its abuses. In England, in Elizabethan days, salads were served dressed in malt vinegar—a condiment much loved by the British—without benefit of either salt or oil. And in America, until quite recently, the only vinegar found in the kitchen might well have been harsh distilled white vinegar. But things have improved. Although vinegary pickles and relishes still go well with rich foods such as cold roast pork, the biting character of vinegar has been tempered—by the increased use of wine vinegar, which is an altogether milder, subtler, and more flavorful affair than distilled vinegar, by reducing the quantity of vinegar classically used in such things as salad dressings and increasing the proportion of oil, and sometimes—which is rather a pity—by the increased use of sugar in these recipes.

Apart from its role in salad dressings, vinegar can be used instead of lemon juice in mayonnaise, hollandaise, and béarnaise, and is essential in horseradish and fresh mint sauces. It is used in countless marinades for meat, poultry, and game, and a little vinegar can improve the flavor of stews and other dishes—a dash of vinegar sometimes works wonders with a dull sauce or gravy. A little vinegar in the water when steaming food stops the pan from discoloring—but vinegar is corrosive, so when cooking food that includes vinegar, use pans of stainless steel, glass, or earthenware, or enameled ones.

Good vinegars are always worth their price. Cheap vinegars are usually inferior and frequently synthetic.

Wine vinegar The best wine vinegar is produced by a slow, gentle process that allows it to mature naturally. The French wine vinegars from Orléans are expensive but still probably the best and the purest. It is encouraging that a few specialized producers in the United States are making vinegar using the Orléans method (also called the slow method). Wine vinegar can be red or white and is sometimes very powerful, but it has a delicious flavor.

If you are offered a "vinegar mother," accept it with alacrity. It is a fungus that lives in wine and will turn your leftover wine into excellent vinegar. Keep this "mother" in a warm place in an earthenware jar with a loose-fitting lid, so that air can get in, and add wine as often as you have it to spare. If it is not very active, feed it a large dose of cheap wine (avoid the cheapest jug wines) and a pinch of sugar.

When the wine vinegar smells sharp and strongly acetic, decant it carefully into a bottle and let it stand for a month to mature and mellow before using it. Red wine seems to produce the best-flavored vinegar, but white is more useful in mayonnaise.

Cider vinegar Apple cider vinegar has been touted as a cure for all ills, from indigestion to hair loss. As a seasoning, it has a strong, distinctive taste of cider and in sharpness is midway between wine vinegar and malt vinegar. Use it

White wine vinegar

Red wine vinegar

Balsamic vinegar

Sherry vinegar

Raspberry vinegar

when making pickles and fruit chutneys, especially those with apples in them, and for a refreshing vinaigrette to use with fresh tomatoes.

Malt vinegar Brewed from malted barley, malt vinegar is colored with caramel to varying shades of brown. The color is no longer an indication of the strength of the vinegar—although originally a deeper color probably did mean a well-matured vinegar, since it was kept in oak barrels that colored the clear vinegar as it aged.

The best malt vinegar, with an acetic acid content of at least 5 percent, is excellent for pickling, which needs a strong vinegar. This is also the vinegar always served with fish and chips.

Distilled vinegar Being colorless, this is often simply labeled white vinegar. It is the vinegar to use for pickling onions and for any pickling when color is important.

Sherry vinegar A delicious vinegar made from sweet sherry, this varies in strength of flavor—a good-quality one is worth its place in the kitchen and can be used instead of balsamic vinegar for a slightly drier result. Sherry vinegar used with an equal amount of lemon juice in

a vinaigrette gives it a very nutty taste, almost like walnut oil. French chefs sometimes use sherry vinegar in the classic chicken dish *poulet au vinaigre*. The best sherry vinegars come from Spain.

Balsamic vinegar—*aceto balsamico*—is a traditional farm-made vinegar from the Modena region of Italy. It is made from white wine must (the unfermented juice from pressed grapes), which is boiled until it is thick and then matured in barrels. Each year for 5 years, as it reduces in volume by evaporation, it is moved to a smaller barrel made from a different wood: oak, chestnut, mulberry, ash, and cherry are favorites. Then it may be left to age for a further 5 years, or for as many as 50 years. Sweet, dark brown, highly concentrated, and mellow, it was traditionally used sparingly, and often for medicinal purposes. It is exquisite on cold vegetables, both cooked and raw, on fish and shellfish, and on raw steak *carpaccio*. Look out for *Aceto Balsamico di Modena Tradizionale*, as there are many imitations.

Rice vinegar features in Japanese and Southeast-Asian cooking, where its sweet, delicate flavor is used in *sushi* rice. In China, rice vinegar may be "black,"

with a rich, smoky, complex flavor; clear pale red, when it is slightly tart; or white and mild—the vinegar for sweet-and-sour dishes. Black vinegar may also be made from grains, such as wheat, millet, or sorghum. There is also a sweet rice vinegar that is dark, thick, and aromatic.

Flavored vinegars Wine vinegar can be flavored by putting fresh herbs—tarragon, basil, mint, or thyme, for example—into a jar, filling it with vinegar, and then keeping it in a fairly warm place for a week, giving the jar an occasional shake. Then decant the vinegar, keeping a token sprig of herb to show what's what. Three herb sprigs to a scant quart of wine vinegar will be ample. Fruits such as raspberries can be used to flavor vinegar in the same way.

To make garlic vinegar, crush the garlic and then leave it in the vinegar for 24 hours. For a really good chile vinegar, steep the dried chiles for 10 days, and give the jar a daily shake.

Tarragon vinegar is excellent for hollandaise. Use chile vinegar with shellfish, and garlic vinegar for salad dressings when sharp flavors such as anchovies and capers are used.

Tarragon vinegar *Rice vinegar* *Cider vinegar* *Distilled vinegar* *Malt vinegar*

Sauces, Flavorings, and Colorings

There is no dispute that sauces, relishes, and other condiments are best made at home, although in a busy world it is often not possible to brew great batches of ketchup, to crack the secret formula of Worcestershire sauce, or to find the time to make a zesty tomatillo salsa.

Sauces, ketchups, and pastes

Some store-bought sauces have been able to withstand the test of time and changing tastes, and are to be found in almost every kitchen.

Tomato ketchup must head the list. Properly made, it is thick and almost chunky in appearance. It should be bright red and contain no artificial coloring. Homemade ketchup is delicious, but only viable if you grow your own tomatoes. We tend to think of ketchup as solely a tomato condiment, but walnut and mushroom ketchups were once very popular. Even fruits such as peaches can be made into ketchup.

Salsa A wide range of bottled salsas can be found in any grocery store. Larger supermarkets often carry fresh salsas as well, and specialty shops may offer a mind-boggling array of salsas.

Tomato paste is used in cooking rather than at the table and is highly concentrated—a tablespoonful will improve the taste and texture of Mediterranean casseroles and provide melting juices for Greek braised lamb.

Worcestershire sauce There is only one true variety, which is of Indian origin, although there are many similar concoctions, including bottled steak sauces. The real thing is hot, spicy, and vinegary and contains tamarind, molasses, sugar, anchovies, garlic, salt, and other natural flavors. This sauce, besides adding its own ineffable taste, heightens the flavor of whatever is being cooked. It is essential for Bloody Mary.

Chile or chili sauce is thick and bright red and can vary considerably in hotness. This Asian condiment also goes under the names Sichuan chile sauce and, in Malaysia, sambal oelek. Use it sparingly in stews and discreetly as a dip for Chinese and Southeast-Asian food or spareribs.

Chile or chili paste is used in Chinese cooking. Most of these red pastes are quite hot; some include soybeans or black beans.

Tabasco sauce is an exceedingly hot, peppery liquid made from vinegar, red chiles, and salt. The label suggests a multitude of uses: soup, gravy, breakfast eggs, even milk, and insists "no seafood to be eaten without it." It also adds its heat to Creole and Cajun cookery. There is also now a jalapeño Tabasco sauce, but the original is still the favorite. There are dozens of other hot sauces on the market—some good, some less so.

Hoisin sauce This anise-flavored sweet and spicy red-brown sauce is, like soy sauce, soybean-based. The texture varies from a thick, creamy sludge to a sauce that can be poured, and the flavor is inclined to be overpowering, containing as it does garlic, chiles, and several spices. However, it is served to advantage, mixed with sugar and sesame oil, with Peking duck, when it is spread over the pancakes before the cucumber, scallions, and shredded duck are placed on top.

Plum sauce Thick and sweet-tart, this is made from plums preserved with chiles, ginger, vinegar, sugar, and spices. Also called duck sauce, it is a popular ingredient in Chinese cookery.

Fish sauce This is made by fermenting barrels of small fish (often anchovies) in brine for several months under the tropical sun. The end result is a strange-smelling, salty brown liquid, highly nutritious, which is a major element of the cooking of Southeast Asia. It is called *nam pla* in Thailand and *nuoc nam* or *nuoc cham* in Vietnam and Laos. Fish sauce is mixed with garlic, lime juice, sugar, and chile oil to make a wonderful dipping sauce for fried foods or dumplings. It can be added to chopped tomatoes together with red onion, vinegar, and plenty of fresh cilantro, to make a salsa to serve with braised chicken and pork.

Anchovy paste comes in tubes and is good in a green herb sauce for fish. It is also nice in canapés or on buttered toast.

Shrimp paste (*terasi, kapee,* or *blachan*) is a common general flavoring in Asian cookery. It is pungent and salty, so use it sparingly. Chinese shrimp paste is the consistency of a thick sauce; the Southeast-Asian version comes either fresh, in jars and bottles, or dried in cakes. Before using the dried paste, bake it, wrapped in foil, then crumble it. Shrimp paste keeps well, but store it well wrapped because of its pungent odor.

Oyster sauce is a flavoring used a great deal by the Chinese. It is a thick brown sauce made with oysters cooked in soy sauce and brine.

Tahini This is a Middle Eastern, Turkish, and Greek staple. A thick, oily beige paste made from ground toasted sesame seeds, tahini resembles peanut butter in texture, being rich and dense. It forms the basis of several delicious *mezze*, such as hummus, a mixture of cooked chickpeas, tahini, lemon juice, and olive oil, puréed and eaten with pita bread.

Wasabi or Japanese horseradish Unrelated to our horseradish, despite its popular name, wasabi root, grated or powdered, makes the eye-watering accompaniment that gives *sushi* and *sashimi* such a fresh lift. Wasabi powder, available in Japanese and specialty markets, is mixed with water to make the familiar stiff paste. Wasabi paste is also sold, in tubes, but the fresh root is only found in Japan.

Tomato paste Tomato ketchup Chile sauce Anchovy paste

Shrimp paste Fish sauce Hoisin sauce Tahini

Soy sauce

True soy sauce is a thin liquid distilled from a naturally fermented mixture of soybeans, wheat or barley flour, and water. Most commercially prepared brands are chemically fermented from defatted soybean pulp. When selecting soy sauce, shake the bottle vigorously until bubbles form at the top. Naturally fermented soy will form a thick, foamy head that takes quite a while to disperse.

Good soy sauce has a rich aroma and a flavor both salty and pungent. It heightens the flavor of whatever is being eaten with it. In China and Japan, it is a staple condiment, used extensively in cooking and at the table in place of salt. In Western cooking, it has become a common ingredient in marinades and barbecue sauces.

Tamari is pure, naturally fermented soy sauce complete with nutritious oils and free from coloring and flavorings.
Light soy sauce is sometimes labeled "superior soy," and is salty, while **dark soy sauce** is thick and sweet. Use light soy for cooking, and dark for dipping.
Miso is a thickened paste made from soybeans, and tastes much like soy sauce. It is used in Asian cooking to make soups and to enrich sauces.
Teriyaki marinade or sauce can be bought prepared in bottles, and is a mix of soy sauce, sugar, ginger, and spices.

Angostura bitters

Originally created as a remedy for fever, as they contain quinine, Angostura bitters are clove-scented, spiced, and pink in color. Found more often at the bar than in the kitchen, this bitter liquid can do a great deal more than flavor Champagne cocktails. In cooking, it makes a good contribution to several sauces, particularly mustard sauce and tarragon sauce.

Capers

These little green flower buds, tasting of goats and the sea, are both a seasoning and a condiment. They are an essential part of Italian and Provençal cooking. Use capers in any sharp sauce to be eaten with fish, such as the Italian herb sauce, or with "black" butter and lemon juice in the classic sauce for skate. Steak tartare would be unthinkable without its caper seasoning. The buds imported from Spain are usually called caperberries.

Chutneys, pickles, and relishes

Chutneys (the Indian word *chatni* means literally "to lick something in small amounts") form an important part of every meal in India and accompany most basic curries. We are used to seeing them in jars, but they are often freshly made, from a wide range of ingredients. One of the most popular is mango chutney, which comes in several different guises, some hot, some sweet, but all made from green, unripe mangoes. A chutney that takes just 10 minutes to make consists of green mangoes, onion, hot green chiles, fresh cilantro, and salt, all blended together with a little water to make a smooth paste.

Pickles are made from vegetables and fruits—just one kind or a mixture—preserved in a seasoned and often highly spiced vinegar. Like chutneys, they are mainly eaten as a condiment. Vegetables commonly pickled include cucumbers, peppers, beets, onions, and red cabbage. Other foods that are pickled are ginger and radishes (both popular in Japan), walnuts (in Britain), and herring (especially in Scandinavia and the United States); watermelon rind is a popular pickle in the American South.
Relish is the term often used for pickles made from chopped vegetables and/or fruit. Because of their texture, relishes are ideal in sandwiches.

Flavoring extracts

These volatile substances are the essential oils extracted from flowers, nuts, fruits, and herbs, mixed with alcohol—vanilla, orange extract, almond extract, peppermint extract, and so on. There are, of course, endless artificial flavorings that are cheaper than the true extracts, but these imitation extracts have little of the flavor of the real thing and are best avoided. Even more intense are citrus and herb oils, such as lemon oil and oil of peppermint, which can be used in candy making and some baking; these are usually available only at specialty shops or through mail-order sources.

Colorings

In countries where the sun shines at its brightest—in Sicily, for example, and southern Italy, India, and also South America—food tends to be extravagantly brightly colored.

Shocking pink and silver, bright orange and magenta, and glaring yellow and green make the dinner table look like a carnival and the food rather exotic to most of us. Ideally these hues are achieved with vegetable colorings, but even in these locales food may be artificially colored with chemicals that are potentially harmful.

Cooks at home can avoid artificial colorings: forget about the garish chemical food colorings and gravy brownings and use the gentler natural colorings. Use saffron or annatto for a beautiful golden yellow and turmeric for a brighter, harsher yellow; onion skins for golden broths; spinach juice or chopped herbs for green sauces and mayonnaise; beet juice for a ruby-colored soup; and tomato paste for healthy reddish-brown stews or delicately pink sauces for shellfish.

Capers   Fruit relish   Mango chutney

Pickled walnuts   Pickled radish   Wasabi powder

Cooking with Wine and Spirits

In a good restaurant kitchen there will be, within easy reach of the bubbling and simmering pots and pans, a lineup of interesting bottles of wines, fortified wines, and *eaux-de-vie*. This alcohol supply is not for fortifying the cooks but to be used judiciously as an ingredient in cooking—an ingredient as vital as butter, flour, salt, pepper, or eggs.

There is no reason why the home cook should not emulate the professional here. Use leftover wine for cooking, and raid the liquor cabinet or buy small bottles of sherry, port, rum, vermouth, brandy, and the more exotic spirits. Do not make false economies—"cooking" sherry, cheap brandy, and wine-flavored extracts will defeat the purpose, which is not to swamp food in alcohol (which evaporates in cooking anyway) but to add flavor. If a wine or spirit is too awful to drink, then it is too awful to cook with. **Wine** is an important ingredient in marinades. It impregnates food with its flavor, and it will soften the fibers of meat and draw out the juices from fruit. Wines for cooking should, in general, be young and dry. It is easy enough to find a reasonably priced red, but cheap white wines do tend to sourness—a light French vermouth such as Noilly Prat is an excellent substitute. Cooking with Champagne may seem extravagant, but

often a glass or two is all that is required to make a superlative sauce for sole or scallops, or an unforgettable sorbet. **Liqueurs and *eaux-de-vie*** (clear fruit brandies or spirits) will turn a simple dish of fruit into a deliciously alcoholic dessert worthy of any occasion. Apart from the fact that it is fun, flaming or *flambéing* crêpes Suzette or an elegant dessert can add to the dish. The purpose of pouring spirits over food and igniting it is, of course, to flavor the food—but also to lose the raw taste of the straight alcohol.

Liqueurs and *eaux-de-vie* distilled from fruit or flavored with it have an obvious affinity with the fruit from which they were made—hence oranges in Grand Marnier—and they share with the parent fruit affinities with certain foods—hence pork cooked with Calvados, the dry French apple brandy. The same logic applies to liqueurs flavored with herbs and essences.

Rice wines are enjoyed in Japan and China. Crystal-clear colorless sake is used in Japanese cooking to remove strong flavors and enhance delicate ones. The Japanese like the lightness of vegetables that are cooked with sake, and also use it in marinades for chicken and other meats. In one recipe, the chicken is pricked all over and marinated in sake, soy sauce, and salt for 20 minutes before being steamed with ginger and scallions. (Although sake

is thought of as a wine, this is not really accurate, because the rice is boiled and yeast is then added, in a method more akin to brewing than wine making.)

Mirin, a sweet, lustrous, amber-colored Japanese rice wine, contains 10 percent alcohol and a huge 40 percent sugar. It is used as a seasoning for *sushi* and, together with dark soy sauce, as an ingredient in marinades and for basting grilled foods such as *teriyaki*, when it forms a sticky golden glaze.

Shaoxing, a very clear yellow wine, is more like a sherry in color and flavor than sake. This Chinese wine has been made for thousands of years and is always aged before drinking. It is traditional to buy it when a daughter is born, and to keep it to celebrate her coming-of-age at 15 and her wedding. It is used in stir-fried dishes to moisten the ingredients and in the marinades for cuttlefish and for *char-siu* pork. When drunk, it is served warm, as sake often is.

Beers and ales have their place in the kitchen too. The dry taste of beer makes an interesting addition to a soup or a stew, fruity hard cider complements pork and rabbit, and bittersweet English stout is a good addition to beef stews.

These charts are not intended to be exhaustive lists—merely a guide to inspire you to tip the right bottle into the dish that will benefit from the added flavor.

Liqueurs/*Eaux-de-vie*	Made from	Uses
Advocaat	Eggs and brandy	Whip into cream for trifles and rich custards
Apricot brandy	Apricots	Flame over roast chicken; use to soak dried apricots
Cointreau, Curaçao, Grand Marnier	The rind of bitter oranges, oranges	Chicken, duck; lemon soufflé, chocolate mousse, sweet omelets, crêpes, fruit salads; apples, pears, figs, strawberries, oranges
Crème de cassis	Black currants	Pour over ice cream; use in sorbets
Amaretto, crème d'amandes	Almonds and apricot kernels	Cookies, icings, cakes, tiramisù
Crème de cacao	Chocolate flavored with vanilla	Ice cream, mousses, cakes
Calvados	Apples	Pheasant and other game birds; pork and veal dishes; cooked apple desserts
Maraschino (sweet), Kirsch (dry)	Cherries	Black Forest cake, fruit compotes, clafoutis; cheese fondue; fruit salad; strawberries, pineapple, cherries, figs, peaches, apples
Izarra	Herbs and mimosa honey	Sweet fruity desserts
Kahlúa; Tía Maria; Bailey's	Coffee; coffee and cream	Cakes, ice creams, other desserts
Kümmel	Caraway, cumin, and fennel	Cabbage, sauerkraut
Crème de menthe	Peppermint	Pour over chocolate ice cream; use in chocolate milk shakes and puddings
Pernod, Anis, Pastis	Anise	Trout, sea bass, striped mullet; fennel; pork
Mirabelle, Slivovitz, plum brandy	Yellow plums, plums	Plum desserts, compotes
Southern Comfort	Bourbon flavored with peaches	Peach desserts
Poire Williams', *eau-de-vie de poire*	Pears	Pear desserts
Eau-de-vie de fraise, de framboise, de pêche	Strawberries, raspberries, peaches	Strawberries, raspberries, melon; sorbets

THE PURCHASE AND PREPARATION OF FOOD

Wines and Spirits	Soup	Fish and shellfish	Poultry	Game	Meat	Vegetables	Sauces	Fruit and desserts	Cheese and eggs
Red wine	Cherry	Salmon, mackerel, sole	Chicken, duck, goose, squab	Duck, pheasant, squab, venison; marinades for all game	Beef stews, steaks and braises; lamb, liver, oxtail, pork, veal; marinades for all cuts of beef	Broccoli, leeks, red cabbage	Gravy (meat); anything à la bordelaise (in red wine sauce), such as steak, etc.	Cherries, peaches, pears, prunes, raspberries, strawberries	Poached eggs
White wine (or substitute dry vermouth or hard cider)	Crab and lobster bisque, strawberry	Haddock, salmon, sole, trout, turbot, herring, mackerel; Clams, lobster, mussels, scallops, shrimp	Pâtés; chicken, duck, squab	Pâtés; duck, squab, rabbit	Pâtés; beef stews; ham, lamb, liver, pork, veal, sweetbreads, sausages	Artichoke bottoms, carrots, cauliflower, green beans, leeks, sauerkraut	Court-bouillon; sauces for fish, poultry, vegetables	Peaches, raspberries; sorbet	Fondue, sabayon
Rosé wine	Shrimp	Salmon	Chicken						
Champagne		Salmon, sole, turbot; Oysters	Chicken		Ham, sweetbreads		Sauces for fish, poultry, oysters	Peaches, raspberries, strawberries; sorbet	
Sherry	Asparagus, tomato, chicken consommé, game consommé	Salmon, any firm-fleshed white fish; lobster	Pâtés; chicken, chicken livers, duck, turkey; foie gras	Pâtés; pheasant	Pâtés; beef, veal	Stir-fried vegetables; avocado	Applesauce; gravy (meat), sauce for poultry, seafood sauces	Apricots, oranges, fruitcake, trifle	Cheese spread, Welsh rarebit; sabayon, zabaglione
Port	Duck	Scallops	Duck	Duck, rabbit		Mushrooms	Applesauce	Cherries, melon, peaches, plums, prunes, strawberries	
Madeira	Consommé	Crab, lobster	Pâtés; chicken, duck	Pâtés; quail	Pâtés; veal		Sauce for veal	Cakes, tea breads	
Marsala (dry)			Chicken livers		Veal scallops		Sauce for sweetbreads	Pears	Zabaglione
Vermouth (dry)		Sole			Pork		Sauce for fish		
Brandy	All bisques	Sole; all shellfish, especially lobster	Pâtés; chicken, chicken livers, duck, squab	Pâtés; quail, rabbit, venison, partridge	Pâtés; beef stews and steaks, lamb	Mushrooms	Brandy butter, brandy cream, lobster sauce	Apricots, cherries, oranges, peaches; fruitcake, mince pies	Custard
Rum		Oysters					Rum butter	Apple desserts, baked apples, baked bananas, fruit compotes, ice cream, mixed berries, babas au rhum, anything flambéed; oranges	Omelets, soufflés
Whisky (scotch) and whiskey (bourbon, rye)		Lobster					Sauce for lobster	Mincemeat pie, trifle, bourbon balls	
Gin				Quail	Venison, pork				

Honey, Syrups, Sugars, and Chocolate

Man was probably born with a sweet tooth. Wild fruits and honey taken from wild bees provided the first sweet foods, and since then the craving for sweet things has continued unabated.

Obviously, any sensible household is now aware that it is unwise to eat too many sweet things, but sweeteners do have an important part to play in the kitchen. As seasonings and preservatives, they have always been as important as salt to the cook. There are many foods too bitter, like cocoa; too sour, like lemons and sour cherries; too acid, like some plums and rhubarb; or too bland, like applesauce, to be enjoyable without added sweeteners.

Without sugar it would not be possible to preserve strawberries and raspberries as jam, and there would be no breakfast marmalade. By using honey, syrups, and sugars in their original roles, and cutting down on highly sweetened convenience and other manufactured foods and drinks, it is possible to enjoy sweet things without undue concern.

HONEY

Like all natural things, honey can vary enormously. It can be runny, or gritty, or so stiff that you can hardly dig it out of the jar. It can vary in color from darkest amber to almost white. Connoisseurs look out for a honey with a clean flavor, with no undertones of bitterness.

For a single pot of honey, bees have to visit myriad flowers, and the honey's taste, color, and runniness depend on the sort of flowers they choose. Normally, the bees' main diet will be written on the label—clover, lavender, heather, and so on.

Generally, the paler honeys, gathered from meadow flowers such as clover, have a mild, clean, delicate flavor. Orange blossom honey from California has its own distinctive flavor, and heather honey is light golden with an aromatic tang to it. Other honeys, such as lavender from Provence or the dark Greek Hymettus honeys, have heavily scented flavors. Although not the finest, blended honeys are reliable.

Clover honey is best for all-round cooking and eating. If you bake yeast breads or rolls sweetened with honey, note that the presence of honey will slightly lengthens the rising time. If you substitute honey for sugar in any recipe, remember that honey is much sweeter than sugar, so you need less of it. Frozen yogurt and ice creams that are made with honey will usually have a softer consistency than those sweetened with sugar, because the freezing point of honey is lower.

Honeycombs, or comb honey, give us the honey sealed in the cells with a capping of wax (scoop horizontally, so that the honey does not run out); chunk-style honey includes pieces of the comb bottled in liquid honey. Clear, runny honeys have usually been heat-treated to prevent them from crystallizing—which most honeys will do naturally within a few weeks of being taken out of the comb. If your honey does begin to crystallize, loosen or remove the top and set the jar in hot water (no hotter than 160°F) until it reliquifies. Creamed or whipped honeys should be smooth and fine-grained, with no coarse crystals.

SYRUPS

Some syrups are made by God, others are made by man.

Maple syrup is among the former, and is the best known and most delicious: the grades generally considered to be among the best are light in color and crystal-clear and come from the maples of Vermont. The clear, thin sap tapped from the trunks of the maple trees is boiled for hours to reduce it to the syrup that goes onto hot buttered waffles and pancakes, and over ice cream. There are also various maple-flavored syrups on the market, less pure, less fragrant, and less expensive. Maple sugar is produced by boiling the syrup until most of the liquid has evaporated. Much sweeter than ordinary granulated sugar, it is used to make the candies sold all over New England.

Palm syrup Another natural syrup, this is the sap of date palms (which also gives us the sugar known as jaggery). Very dark and extremely sticky, it can be bought in Asian grocery stores, and often features in Indian recipes.

Corn syrup is produced from corn. It can be light or dark (the dark syrup tastes stronger), and is used in baking and candy making.

Golden syrup is a byproduct of sugar refining that has been through its own refining process. It can be used in cakes and other desserts, and as a substitute for corn syrup in most recipes. It is less sweet than sugar, so when it is used in baking, sugar is usually added. It can be useful when making such things as brandy snaps, since it is not as granular as sugar when heated.

Sorghum syrup, molasses This comes from the sorghum plant, which grows throughout the American South. Sweet and thick, it is used like molasses and as a pancake syrup. A rich source of vitamins and minerals, it can be found in health food stores.

Honeycomb

Clear clover honey

Creamed clover honey

Orange blossom honey

Hymettus honey

Scottish heather honey

Molasses This dark, heavy syrup is a good friend to the cook. Far less sweet than honey, it goes into gingerbreads and hefty fruitcakes and into such traditional dishes as Boston baked beans and Indian pudding. A byproduct of sugar refining, molasses comes light and dark—the darker the molasses, the less sugar it contains. Molasses can be sulfured or unsulfured; unsulfured has a somewhat richer flavor and a lighter color.

Being slightly bitter, molasses should be used in smallish amounts for the best flavor. It is much more nutritious than sugar. Britain's black treacle is a molasses-like syrup, but it contains more sugar and is sweeter than molasses.

SUGAR

Sugar first started to replace honey as a sweetener in European kitchens in medieval times, although it was being used in China and India over two thousand years ago. It was introduced into the Americas by Columbus, and it was the first sugar plantations that formed the basis for the slave trade.

While the natural brown sugars still bring us some of the flavor and goodness of the sugarcane from which they come, the white sugars contain no proteins, no minerals, and no vitamins—simply instant energy. For the cook, sugar, used discriminatingly, is an indispensable ally.

Brown sugar

The natural brown sugars come from raw sugarcane, and if you like the warm taste of molasses that still clings to them, you can use them all the time. Any "raw" brown sugar sold in the United States has been purified and cleaned, a process that also removes some of the flavor and nutrients. Being moist, brown sugar has a tendency to harden in the bag or box, but if covered with a damp cloth for a few hours, it softens up again.

Light and dark brown sugar The ordinary brown sugars used so much in baking are simply fully refined white sugar combined with molasses. Dark brown sugar, which has a greater proportion of molasses added, has a somewhat deeper flavor than the light.

Muscovado sugar is sometimes also called Barbados sugar. It is soft, fine-grained, and very moist. It is good in dark, rich fruitcakes and in desserts made with dried fruit, gingerbread,

and homemade toffee. Molasses sugar, popular in Britain, is similar to dark muscovado and can be used in the same ways. Pale muscovado sugar is excellent for making crunchy toppings, and in pickles and chutneys.

Demerara is gritty, with golden crystals; it is crystallized from partly refined sugar syrup and contains 2 percent molasses. It can be used in the same ways as pale muscovado sugar. Although, like honey, demerara slightly retards the action of yeast in the early stages of rising, it is particularly useful in spiced breads and other yeasted baked goods, giving them a creamy color and a nice flavor.

Turbinado is refined one stage beyond demerara and lighter in color. It can be used in recipes that call for demerara.

White sugar

All white sugars are equally sweet, but the finer the sugar, the faster it dissolves and the sweeter it seems. There is one thing that white sugars have in common: they taste sweeter when hot than when cool. This is why ice cream mixtures, before freezing, need to taste almost too sweet, and why recipes for warm desserts specify, as a rule, less sugar than for cold ones.

Granulated or white sugar is a highly refined white crystal sugar, primarily made from sugarcane but sometimes from sugar beets (both are pure sucrose). If there is such a thing as an all-purpose

sugar, this is it, used in all sorts of desserts and candies, cooking, and in coffee and tea. Use it, too, to make your own vanilla sugar by sticking a vanilla bean or two into a large jar of sugar and leaving it for at least two weeks. Make cinnamon-scented sugar—good on pancakes, French toast, and even creamy fresh dessert cheese—in the same way, substituting two cinnamon sticks for the vanilla beans. Or try rosemary sugar: clean and dry sprigs of rosemary, put them in the sugar, and shake well; after 24 hours, shake again, and then leave for a week. This unusual sugar is good in puddings and other creamy desserts.

Lump sugar Once hacked from cones of sugar, this is now granulated sugar pressed into cubes to use in coffee or tea.

Superfine sugar is a smaller-grained crystal. It is very fine and dissolves easily: use it when cooking soft fruit and in meringues, in custards or mousses, and, in fact, whenever it is desirable for the sugar to dissolve before the mixture starts cooking. Because it dissolves so quickly, it is often used to sweeten iced tea and other cold drinks, and it is the best sugar to use in sorbets made with uncooked fruit purées.

Confectioners' or powdered sugar tastes the sweetest of all and dissolves the fastest. It is known as icing sugar in Britain, and, of course, there are countless icings made with confectioners' sugar.

Light corn syrup

Dark corn syrup

Golden syrup

Maple syrup

Molasses

In the new wave of restaurant cooking, it is sifted over many desserts—especially those made with dark red berries and pastry—and over the edges of dessert plates as decoration.

Decorating, coarse, or pearl sugar has large, round granules. Because it dissolves less quickly than granulated, it is often sprinkled on cookies before baking and on other baked goods. It's found in gourmet markets and cake-decorating supply stores.

Preserving sugar is a coarse sugar used for jam making: the large crystals retain enough air between them to prevent the sugar from sinking in a solid mass to the bottom of the pan, so they dissolve evenly and quickly without burning or forming too much scum. Jams, jellies, and marmalades will then need less skimming, and will be crystal clear. Unfortunately, preserving sugar has become difficult to find in the United States, although some ethnic or specialty shops may have it.

Jaggery

In India and Southeast Asia, sugar is regarded as quite good for you, and many of the little sweet snacks eaten during the day, rather than at meals, are intensely sweet. The dark, coarse unrefined sugar used is called jaggery, and it may be processed from the sap of palm trees or from sugarcane.

COCOA, CHOCOLATE, AND CAROB

A century before coffee arrived in the West, the Spanish conquistadores had brought chocolate home with them from the New World. They had seen the Aztecs whisk up a hot, frothy drink called *cacahuatl* ("bitter water,") and at the court of Montezuma, the Mexican emperor, they had savored a richer brew that the Mexicans called *chocolatl*.

Cocoa beans, each the size of an almond, grow thirty or forty at a time in large pods. Their characteristics vary widely depending on the region in which they are grown, and a closely guarded secret of the chocolate industry is the formula for handling and blending different varieties.

When cocoa beans are fermented, roasted, hulled, and ground, a rich reddish-brown liquid, the chocolate liquor, is extracted, which contains a fat called cocoa butter. It is at this stage that cocoa and chocolate undergo their separate processes.

Cocoa

To make cocoa, a proportion of the cocoa butter—it varies from one maker to the next—is removed from the chocolate liquor. The remaining liquid sets hard and is then pulverized. The result, pure, naturally acid cocoa, needs sweetening before it becomes palatable. Dutch, or

alkalized, cocoa undergoes a further process known as Dutching to neutralize the acids, making it mellower and darker.

Cocoa powder contains starch, so when it is being made into a hot drink it should, like flour, be mixed to a paste with a little milk or water before being added to the heated milk, or it will turn lumpy. Instant cocoa, or cocoa mix, is precooked cocoa to which sugar and flavorings have been added. When buying cocoa powder, avoid any that is labeled "chocolate-flavored."

Hot cocoa is very popular in Europe, as well as in America, particularly during the long winters. In the United States, steaming cups of cocoa are traditionally topped with whipped cream, or have a melting marshmallow floating on the top. In France, cream is often added, and in Spain, they make a rich chocolate drink thick enough to eat with a spoon. In Russia and Brazil, coffee is added (when coffee is added to cocoa or chocolate, the flavor is called mocha).

Cocoa powder can also be used as a flavoring for cookies, cakes, and other desserts. When unsweetened baking chocolate is called for in a recipe, you can substitute 3 tablespoons cocoa plus 1 tablespoon vegetable shortening or unsalted butter for each 1 ounce chocolate. If bittersweet or semisweet chocolate is required, do the same, but add an extra 3 tablespoons sugar.

Light brown sugar

Dark muscovado sugar

Dark brown sugar

Demerara sugar

Molasses sugar

Granulated sugar

Lump sugar

Superfine sugar

Confectioners' sugar

Preserving sugar

Chocolate

The quality of chocolate is a subject of great interest to chocolate lovers and serious connoisseurs alike. Whole books have been written about chocolate, discussing the merits and drawbacks of the many types and the individual characteristics of the beans from which chocolate is made. This should not be surprising, though, considering that good chocolate makers use a blend of as many as twelve different varieties of beans to achieve just the right balance of richness, aroma, and depth of flavor.

Unlike cocoa, chocolate may retain all the natural cocoa butter found in the liquor extracted from the beans. However, the proportion of cocoa butter varies considerably; in some instances extra cocoa butter is added to the liquor to make the chocolate even richer. The higher the cocoa butter content, the more delectable the chocolate—and also the more expensive. Sugar may be added too, and the sweetness or otherwise is another quality to consider. Connoisseurs like bittersweet chocolate, but more popular by far is chocolate with lots of added sugar and, often, milk solids. Chocolate to which sugar and extra cocoa butter have been added ranges from the darkest bitter chocolate to mild milk chocolate.

When cooking with chocolate, it is generally best to use the least-sweet variety that you can find (the less sugar that is added to chocolate, the stronger and more chocolaty will be the flavor—you can always add more sugar). To ensure the best flavor, unsweetened or bittersweet chocolate with at least 50 percent cocoa butter content is ideal, though 60 to 70 percent is even better, whether it is for cooking or eating. However, although a few imported European chocolates may include these percentages on their labels, most brands of chocolate do not. Experiment to find the ones you like best; higher price often indicates better quality and fuller flavor, but this is not always the case. For icings and frostings, semisweet chocolate is better: it has a higher fat content than unsweetened or bittersweet chocolate so is easier to melt, and the sugar in it produces a good sheen when dry. Beware of cheap baking chocolates, which have often been blended from rather inferior beans, or may not even be real chocolate: as with cocoa mixes, products that are labeled "chocolate-flavored" or "artificial chocolate" are to be avoided. Liquid chocolate, although it may seem convenient for baking, is made with vegetable oil rather than cocoa butter.

Great care is needed when melting any sort of chocolate: it should be done in a bowl set over a pan of boiling water or a double boiler—if it is overheated, it scorches. It is also important to prevent any steam or the smallest drop of water from coming into contact with the melting chocolate, as this will cause it to "seize," or become a thick, lumpy mass.

Chocolate is, of course, essential to the making of some of the world's most delicious cakes and tortes, truffles, pastries, and other desserts and candies. It has a special affinity with rum and brandy, particularly in mousses and ice creams. To make a particularly rich and glorious-tasting drink, melt grated chocolate slowly with sugar and then whisk in hot milk.

Unsweetened chocolate is also used as a flavoring in extraordinary dishes, such as the Mexican holiday dish, *mole poblano de guajolote* (turkey in Pueblan sauce); while in Spain, two casseroles, one of veal tongue *a la aragonesa* and one of braised pigeon, *pichones estofados*, are served in sauces containing chocolate. It can be used very sparingly to improve the color and texture of other sauces—with rabbit and other game, for example.

White chocolate is made with cocoa butter, milk solids, and sugar, and contains no chocolate liquor. Some types, in fact, do not even contain cocoa butter; these, however, cannot be labeled white chocolate. It is not suitable for much in cooking except decoration, and is more cloying than real chocolate.

Carob

Naturally sweet and nutritious, carob provides a satisfying alternative to chocolate. In their natural state, carob beans are the long, elegant pods of a Mediterranean tree belonging to the legume family (it is the carob, or locust bean, on which St. John reputedly lived in the wilderness—hence another of its names, St. John's bread).

Carob contains fewer calories than chocolate and none of the substance theobromine, found in chocolate, that can be a cause of migraine. Carob powder is ground from the whole pod, which is also very palatable in its natural state. As a powder, carob can be used in the same way as cocoa in cakes, cookies, and homemade candies, but carob is sweeter than cocoa, so use less sugar or other sweetener with it. Its mild, milk-chocolate taste is good in cake icings, ice creams, and some baked goods, but it is not recommended for use in recipes that require a really strong chocolate flavor, such as mousses and rich chocolate cakes.

White chocolate

Milk chocolate

Bittersweet chocolate

Cocoa powder

Carob powder

Carob pod

Coffee, Tea, and Herbal Tea

COFFEE

In the Arab world, where coffee is drunk throughout the day in countless ceremonial cups, the old rule for a good brew is that it should be "as black as hell and as sweet as sin."

Good coffee, to suit the Western palate, is made from freshly roasted beans of the particular kind you like best, preferably ground just before brewing. Freshness is vital: coffee rapidly loses quality if exposed to air. There must be a generous amount of beans to the cup, the grind must be suitable for your method of making coffee, and the water sparkling fresh. Our breakfast coffee loses nothing by the addition of milk, however, or our after-dinner coffee by a layer of cream.

Sadly, however, the promise in the delicious smell of real coffee is not always fulfilled. This is one of the reasons why coffee making has become surrounded by mystique—quite unnecessarily, for it is really only a matter of knowing a little bit about the properties of coffee, the way it has been roasted, the grind, and the method of infusion. But the beginning of a good cup of coffee lies in the beans.

The beans

These are, in fact, not beans at all but the twin seeds of the cherry-red fruit produced by the tropical coffee plant. The seeds lie, flat sides facing, in a parchment-like covering. If, as occasionally happens, only one seed develops, it is called a peaberry, because of its rounded shape. (This is noted for its even roasting qualities and so is especially good for home-roasting.)

Once picked and with some of its pulp removed, the fruit is usually fermented in water for varying periods. The seeds are then extracted from their natural wrapping, dried, washed, dried again, and graded according to size.

Before roasting, coffee beans are quite pale. The type called Mochas are yellowish, small, uneven beans; the Bourbon Santos are the same color but oblong and a little larger; and the Martiniques are greenish, rounder, and larger still.

The true Mocha that comes from the Yemen is now a rarity. There had been hardly enough to go around when only the Arab and Levantine world drank what was described by an astonished British traveler as "that black liquid called *kahveh.*" But when Europe took to coffee in the seventeenth century, enterprising colonists were quick to spread the tree now known as *Coffea arabica* to new parts of the world. The Dutch were soon providing coffee from plantations in their East Indian possessions, while in France the ever-growing demand for coffee led to its cultivation in Martinique. France was also to grow coffee on its Indian Ocean island of Bourbon (now called Réunion); it was from here that the Brazilians imported the seed for the famous Bourbon Santos coffee.

These *arabica* coffees all do best at high altitudes; they are often labeled "mountain grown" and are a good deal more temperamental than the group of coffees called *robusta.* The *robustas* can be grown in lower regions and are, as the name implies, hardier, easier to grow, and therefore cheaper. Mostly grown in Africa, the *robustas* are less delicately flavored, but are steadily improving.

However, the *arabicas,* which the trade now also divides into the Brazilians and the Milds, make up most of the coffees you are likely to find at a specialty store. If you buy preground, vacuum-packed coffee, always look for "100 percent arabica" or "Pure arabica" on the package.

Brazil is the world's largest coffee grower, and produces all grades from exquisite to indifferent. Santos is the word to look out for: the Brazilian Santos, especially Bourbon Santos, give a good, full-bodied cup of coffee. "Prime Brazilian" on a coffee label is actually meaningless as far as flavor goes.

Colombia Second only to Brazil as a coffee exporter, Colombia produces some excellent coffees that brew so well that you need fewer beans than of other coffee to the amount of water. Among the best Colombians are Medellin, mildly acid, which means that it has a much-valued sharpness, just short of being sour; Manizales, a little sharper; and Excelsio, which is slightly bitter.

Jamaica If you find Jamaican Blue Ridge Mountain coffee, which is all too rarely available, you can be sure that it will be mellow and "sweet"—it is rich in natural sugars, which caramelize in the roasting. It is hailed by many as the best coffee in the world. The Jamaican High Mountain Supremes are less full-bodied.

Venezuela Coffee from Venezuela, if it has grown in the mountain districts, can be rich, winy, and light in body.

Guatemala Mountain-grown coffees from Guatemala are noted for their acidity and fullness. Antiquas and Cobans are the best varieties.

Costa Rica Coffee grown in the high areas of Costa Rica is renowned for its acidity—it has the reputation of being able to curdle milk in the cup—but other Costa Rican *arabicas* are famed for their fragrance, mild flavor, and full body.

Mexico Coffee grown in Mexico is light, mellow, and on the bitter side.

Hawaii This is where Kona coffee comes from. It is rich, mellow, full-bodied, and full of flavor.

Sumatra and Java Sumatra *arabica* coffee is wonderful: sweet, mellow, and full-bodied. It is Sumatra coffee that is still most sought after by the Dutch, who take great pride in perfect coffee making. However, both Sumatra and Java now also grow *robustas,* so ask specifically for a Sumatran *arabica.* Take the same precaution when you buy Java coffee. Old Java ("old" means that it has been stored in tropical conditions for a decade or so) is always of the *arabica* variety; *robustas* are not worth storing for so long and would not in a hundred years develop the fine flavor associated with Old Java.

Mysore This Indian coffee is velvety, acidy, and aromatic. It is delicious, especially when blended with Mocha.

Malabar Monsooned Malabar, from India, is coffee grown throughout the monsoon period, which is supposed to give a very aromatic and mellow flavor. It is indeed wonderful coffee.

Ethiopia This coffee is acid and has a slightly spicy aroma. A type known as Longberry Harrar is now replacing the traditional descendants of Yemen Mocha, and in this there is a poetic justice: the Yemen's first coffee came from Ethiopia, after a legendary Abyssinian goatherd observed his goats skipping and dancing after feeding off the hitherto-ignored coffee plant growing in the wild.

Kenya The *arabicas* of Kenya are among the best-quality coffees: one, the Kenya Peaberry, a variant producing a single round bean, is much admired for its flavor and is one of the coffees always drunk straight, unmixed with any other.

Although there are these, and many more, distinctive varieties of coffee beans, most coffees are blended, producing a pleasant balance of body, flavor, sweetness, and acidity. This is where the skill and knowledge of a discerning coffee merchant, or of a knowledgeable department manager in a large gourmet market, is an invaluable help. The names of house blends—Connoisseur and such like—signify nothing, so it will pay to cultivate a discerning coffee merchant who can be relied upon to offer freshly roasted beans and will explain which combinations of beans constitute his particular blends.

The roast

Roasting brings out the flavor of the bean and determines the mellowness, richness, nuttiness, smoothness, or otherwise of the final brew. The roast does not determine the strength of the coffee—this depends on the ratio of coffee to water when brewing.

Light roast is also called light city roast. It results in a cinnamon-colored bean and a brew called delicate by those who like it and thin by those who don't.

Medium or American roast, regular roast, or city roast will give beans a stronger character and flavor, but the flavor is still on the acid side.

French roast produces shiny beans, burnt umber in color, for coffee that is still smooth, but only just.

Heavy roast or continental roast produces dark brown beans and a flavor that is deeper still.

High roast, dark continental roast, or dark French roast burns the beans almost black, for after-dinner coffee with a strong kick. Dark continental roast is a favorite of gourmets.

Viennese roast is two thirds regular-roasted beans and one third heavy roast.

European roast is stronger, with the proportions reversed: two thirds heavy-roasted beans and one third regular roast.

Espresso or Italian roast is dark to the point of carbonization, but can be mellow in flavor.

The higher the roast, the lower the acidity of the bean and the less varied the aroma, so the most precious beans are not used for very high roasts. However, the high-roasted coffees are preferred by many coffee connoisseurs who dislike the acid flavors of lightly roasted beans.

Only countries that take their coffee drinking very seriously go in for large-scale home-roasting, with appropriate machinery. If you want to try roasting your own "green" beans (which you can buy from specialty coffee merchants and which will keep, before roasting, for long periods) but lack an electric roaster, use a frying pan, shaking it continuously over the heat until the beans are the right color all over. However, for the very best coffee, it is easier to buy your beans freshly roasted and in small quantities. Store them in an airtight container to preserve their aroma. In this state they will keep in good condition for up to 3 weeks. You can also freeze them.

If you buy your coffee preground in vacuum packs, you may not be told on the package the exact types of beans used to make the blend, but you should be informed of the degree of roast and the grind. Many of these coffees are excellent, and blended for consistency

of flavor, although coffees, like wines, do vary according to conditions during the growing season. Once the package has been opened, store the ground coffee in an airtight container and use it up within a week if possible, or freeze it.

The grind

Choosing the right grind is essential. The finer the grind, the greater the surface area of coffee that is exposed to the water, and the longer the water takes to run through it as it is brewed. A coarser grind has less surface area and the water passes through more rapidly. The various machines for making coffee are designed so that with the right grind the coffee is exposed to the water for just the right length of time. If the grind is not right, it will result in underextraction, which is wasteful and gives a weak-bodied brew, or overextraction, which makes coffee bitter and can leave a lot of sediment in the cup. If you don't grind your coffee yourself, tell the store where you buy the beans by what method you make your coffee and have it ground accordingly.

Turkish grind Powder-fine, this is the grind that is used to make intensely strong, sweet Greek and Turkish coffee.

Very fine grind (sometimes referred to as Melitta grind) is the grind to use for the paper-filter method. It is too fine to use in an infusion—the fine grounds would turn into an unstrainable mud.

Fine or drip grind is the coffee to use in an espresso machine and in the Italian-style drip pot, or Neapolitan. Brillat-Savarin, the French gastronome,

Unroasted peaberry

Light roast

Medium roast

Turkish grind

Very fine grind

Heavy roast

High roast

Espresso roast

Fine grind

Regular grind

writing on coffee in the early eighteenth century, preferred this type to others; it is what the French still call for when they order *un filtre*.

Medium-fine grind This is the grind for the cafetière method, using the glass pots that have a pump filter. The coffee comes up through the mesh filter and the grounds stay at the bottom.

Regular grind is the one to use in an electric coffee maker or percolator, since it requires an extraction time of 6 to 8 minutes.

The brew

When making coffee, it is important to use coffee and water in the right proportions. Nineteenth-century visitors to England—notorious for its awful coffee—once were urged by experienced travelers to specify the precise number of beans to the cup, or they would be served with a prodigious quantity of pale brown liquid. "Waiter, is this tea? Bring me a cup of coffee. Or is this coffee? In that case bring me a cup of tea"—ran a famous joke in *Punch*. Sixty-five beans to the cup was Brillat-Savarin's recipe, but he and his peers liked their coffee extra-strong. ("I know it is a poison," said Voltaire, whose clarity of thought Brillat-Savarin ascribed to copious coffee consumption, "but it is a slow one." He was over eighty at the time.) Today, the recommended amount of ground coffee is 2 tablespoons per regular coffee cup, or per each cup of water used.

There is much controversy among experts over which proportions produce the best brew. Internationally recognized styles of serving coffee include:

Café au lait or café con leche, the breakfast drink served in France and in Spain, is made with equal amounts of strong dark-roasted coffee and hot milk.

Demitasse, an after-dinner coffee that is a regular medium-roasted coffee served double-strength.

Espresso, the Italian favorite. The small, strong, foaming cup is the product of a machine that forces steam and boiling water through finely ground Italian-roast coffee. Use a high-roast coffee at double strength to make espresso, if you haven't bought espresso roast. It should be drunk immediately.

Cappuccino, espresso served with steaming, frothy milk from the espresso machine. It can be dusted with cocoa powder or cinnamon. In France, *café crème* is espresso with milk but without the froth, while in Italy, *caffè latte* is espresso combined with a much larger quantity of steamed milk.

Viennese coffee, made with dark-roasted beans and topped with sweetened, whipped cream, often spiced with cinnamon and nutmeg.

Turkish or Greek coffee, usually drunk very sweet and after dinner. It is traditionally made in an *ibrik*, a long-handled copper pot. The powdered coffee beans, sugar—plenty of it—and water are slowly brought to a boil and simmered to a froth, then left to stand for a few seconds to allow the grounds to settle. This rich, thick coffee is served in a tiny cup and should not be drunk until the grounds have settled at the bottom.

By long tradition, the enjoyment of really good coffee is something of an event. There are still individual flourishes to be seen in Africa and the Middle East. The Moroccans, for instance, add whole peppercorns to the brew for extra kick. The Ethiopians take it with a pinch of salt, and in some Arab countries pounded saffron or cardamom pods are added to a foam called the "face of the coffee." Most evocative of all, perhaps, when the Turks gather around the polished *ibrik*, is the practice of taking coffee with extra sugar for happy occasions such as a wedding, but with no sugar at all at somber gatherings such as funerals.

Additives and extractions

Unless you are positively fond of the taste, avoid coffees that are "stretched" with additives, or coffee substitutes. The reason for using them is, of course, economy, but chicory "coffee" and other mixtures that appear in abundance whenever the Brazilian crops are decimated by frost are, even so, quite popular in their own right. In New Orleans, a chicory-coffee blend that is sometimes called Creole coffee is often served. In various parts of the world, such things as dandelion roots, toasted and ground, sometimes feature in mass-produced coffee; so do toasted figs and barley, which make what is called malt coffee. If you buy packaged coffee, the label will tell you what it contains.

Decaffeinated coffee is pure coffee from which the stimulating properties have been extracted. With them, alas, goes a proportion of the aromatics, too: using the traditional extraction method, to produce a product that is 97 percent caffeine-free, the beans have to swirl in a solvent and then be dried off twenty-four times. Some coffee is decaffeinated using the Swiss water method. With this process, rather than using a solvent the beans are steamed and then their outer layers, where the caffeine is concentrated, are removed. Decaffeinated coffee beans need a higher, darker roast than the unprocessed ones to develop their flavor.

"Gourmet" coffee If tea can be flavored with anything God can create in the way of fruits, flowers, and spices, it seems to follow that coffee can be too. So we now have designer coffees, with flavors such as vanilla nut crème, Irish crème, chocolate hazelnut, and so on. Many coffee lovers don't seem interested, but if you like the idea, the time to serve these coffees is after dinner. Look for those without artifical flavorings.

Instant coffee

Purists may despise them, but these are nevertheless pure coffee, if not of the most delicately flavored sort; few (but discriminating) are the people who insist on making the real thing for every cup they drink. Instant coffee is also an asset in the kitchen when you want just a coffee flavor, not a pot of liquid.

What is true is that instant coffees vary. Their taste is affected not only by the blends of coffee going into their making (they are made entirely from *robustas*) but also by the way they are produced. The freeze-dried varieties are most like the real thing. For these, brewed coffee is frozen and the resulting ice is ground and vacuum-dried. The strongest and most flavorful of all are the individual sachets of Italian espresso coffee, recently introduced in the United States. Other, cheaper varieties are spray-dried at high temperatures, a process that drives away the aromatics. These are sometimes reintroduced by means of a spray of coffee oil, which evaporates as soon as the jar is opened—the result is a poor apology for the real thing. Some instant coffees are composed of partly freeze-dried and partly heat-dried types.

Of course, with instant coffee one gains in convenience but loses in flavor and the delicious aroma that heralds a pot of fresh coffee in the making.

TEA AND HERBAL TEA

When, in the early seventeenth century, the Dutch first brought tea to the West— it had been cultivated in China for centuries—it was the rich who savored its various aromas, not the poor. For another century or more, ordinary people continued drinking their habitual cheap ale and wine, while the gentry sipped the costly new brew from the East.

It was not until the middle of the eighteenth century that tea became a popular drink as a result of the British East India Company cutting prices and opening up the trade. Today, still single-minded about their tea, the British lead the field in consumption, drinking three times as much as the Japanese (to whom tea is as much a ceremony as a refreshment) and ten times as much as the Americans, who much prefer coffee. In Russia, tea is served very strong, sometimes with lemon but never with milk, while Moroccans like their milkless tea very sweet, adding great quantities of sugar and honey and, frequently, mint leaves. Indian masala tea is brewed with spices—cinnamon, cardamom, and so on—and, usually, made with milk and plenty of sugar. It is deliciously reviving for the traveler.

What is a curious anomaly, now that tea is such a universal beverage, is that the terminology under which it is graded and sold remains utterly cryptic to the bulk of the tea-buying public. True, most people readily distinguish black tea, the kind most commonly drunk in the West, from green, which is the favorite in the East. But other terms are for the most part incomprehensible outside the trade. The term Orange Pekoe, for example, on the label of many black teas, simply indicates the size of the leaf and has nothing to do with the taste of the tea.

Although all tea comes from variants of the same evergreen plant, *Camellia sinensis*, it varies noticeably according to the region in which it is grown and after which it tends to be named. The factors mainly associated with superior teas are good soil and water conditions, high elevation, attentive picking, or plucking, and a favorable harvest season.

Generally, the finest flavors are to be found among what are known as high-grown teas—varieties cultivated on terraced hillsides at high altitude. Scarcer and more difficult to harvest, these hill varieties invariably cost more than the lowland teas.

Following the harvest, what happens to the leaf during its processing has a considerable bearing on the quality of tea in the cup. Tea processing not only changes the leaf to bring out its inherent qualities, but also ensures that the finished leaf will not spoil. In addition, it confirms it in one of the three classifications into which all teas are grouped: black tea, fermented and with the highest concentration of essential oil; green tea, which is unfermented and retains the closest resemblance to the natural leaf; and oolong, semi-fermented tea.

Black tea

Rich, aromatic, and full flavored, black teas make up by far the largest proportion of international tea sales. The oxidization that takes place during fermentation largely accounts for their flavor, strength, body, and color—all characteristics that hinge on chemical changes in the tea tannin and the development of the essential oil. The longer the tannin ferments, the more color it has and the less pungent it is to the taste, so that a very black tea might, in fact, have little pungency—in tea terms, astringency without bitterness.

Black teas are graded by the size of the leaf into leaf teas—those with large leaves, which develop flavor and color more slowly to make a lighter, more fragrant brew—and broken-leaf teas, covering the smaller, broken leaves, which yield a stronger, darker, quicker brew.

Among the leaf teas, the term Orange Pekoe means that the leaves are long and well defined, perhaps with a few yellow tips or mixed with a few leaf buds. (1000 years ago, the term pekoe—"white haired"— was applied by the Chinese to teas that showed a touch of white on the leaves and to which they sometimes added orange blossoms for extra fragrance, but the name no longer denotes this agreeable custom.) Pekoe, with smaller and more tightly rolled leaves, produces a brew that is darker in color but not necessarily stronger in taste than Orange Pekoe. Souchong, the largest, coarsest leaf picked, makes a tea that is pale and quite pungent.

Crystal-Clear Iced Tea 268

Black: Darjeeling

Black: Ceylon spiced with lemon

Black: Keemun

Black: Ceylon

Black: Assam

Japanese Three-year tea

Green: Taiwan Special Chun Mee

Green: China Young Hyson

Green: Japanese Sencha (pan-fired)

Green: China Gunpowder

bergamot 165

Of the broken-leaf teas, Broken Orange Pekoe, which yields good strength and color in the cup, is the one most often used as the mainstay of a blend. Fannings, much smaller, make a strong, quick brew, as does Dust, the smallest grade produced.

Outstanding among the black teas are Keemun, a full-bodied, aromatic tea from North China, and the rich, tarry-flavored, smoke-cured Lapsang Souchong from South China and Taiwan, which is best without milk. With its penetrating bouquet, Keemun makes a good alternative to after-dinner coffee.

The classic Indian teas include high-grown Darjeeling, the Champagne of teas and one of the world's most prized, with a rich, pale liquor and exquisite, penetrating aroma; and the full, strong, malty-tasting Assam. Ceylon teas (from what is now known as Sri Lanka) are generally softer in character than other blacks, and the high-grown varieties are known for their strength, delicacy of flavor, and scented aroma. Dimbula, a rich, mellow Ceylon, makes a good bedtime drink. Indonesian black teas are favored mainly by Dutch blenders and packers.

Green tea

Primarily from China, Japan, and Taiwan, green tea is cool, clean, and refreshing. Said to aid digestion, it is often served with highly flavored or fried foods. It has a mellow, subtle flavor and brews to a pale golden-green. But where green tea is concerned, pallor does not signify lack of strength: the lighter the liquor, the younger the leaf and the better the brew.

Green tea is steamed and heat-dried but not fermented. It is graded by the age as well as by the size of the leaf. The top grades are Gunpowder (young leaves rolled into tiny balls), and Young Hyson (long, thinly rolled leaves). Other grades are Imperial (loosely balled leaves), and Hyson, which is a mixture of Young Hyson and Imperial.

Among the Chinese green teas, look for the type known as Moyunes, celebrated for its richness and clarity, and Dragon Well, a variety that takes its name from a spring outside Hanzhou and is considered the best in China.

Japan, which meets a good deal of the U.S. demand for green tea, grows its finest varieties in the district of Yamashiro, near Kyoto. Sadly, the most prized, Gyokuro or "Pearl Dew," is not normally exported, nor is the leaf from which Mattcha, the ceremonial tea of Japan, is made. Most of Japan's tea is Sencha, or "ordinary" tea, which finds its way abroad as pan-fired teas—delicate, light-colored, and similar to the Young Hyson of China—and the long-leafed, basket-fired teas, which have been cured to a dark olive-green.

The green teas of Taiwan are graded as Special Chun Mee, Chun Mee, Sow Mee, and Gunpowder.

Oolong tea

Named after the Chinese words *wu* (black) and *lung* (dragon), the oolongs combine the characteristics of black and green teas. Best known—and the best of all teas, some experts believe—are those from Taiwan, known as Formosa oolongs, with their deep amber color and magnificent fruity taste. Also very distinctive is Pouchong—oolong mixed with highly scented flowers such as jasmine and gardenia.

Much better than other countries (China included) at cultivating oolongs, Taiwan is the one exception to the high-altitude rule: here on this subtropical island, the best teas are grown on the yellow clay soils of the *teela*, or broken lands, many of which are at sea level. It is the summer pluckings that yield the highest-grade, rich golden oolongs.

Blended teas

Perhaps not surprisingly, the hub of the tea trade is London. Here firms base their bidding on the verdicts of tea tasters, who are much preoccupied with appearance, aroma, and taste. For although there are only three basic types of tea, there are something like three thousand commercial blends.

Given the fluctuations in price and availability from year to year, the major tea packers mostly market products that are blends using perhaps fifteen or twenty varieties. The most distinguished of these tea blends include English Breakfast, traditionally a straight Keemun but now more likely to be a strong blend of India and Ceylon teas; Irish Breakfast, high-grown Ceylon with hearty Assam; Russian Style (also known as Russian Caravan or Russian Blossom), a blend of Keemun, Assam, and China green well suited to the samovar; and Uva, a blended Ceylon, golden when brewed and with a distinctive flowery bouquet.

Another well-known blend is Earl Grey—so called because its secret was said to have been passed by a Chinese mandarin in 1830 to the Earl Grey, who had it made up for himself by a London tea merchant. Earl Grey is made from Indian and Chinese teas, and is scented with oil of bergamot. Ideal for afternoon tea, it yields a pale, clear liquor with a slight citrus flavor—a reminder of how well a hint of citrus combines with tea.

Spiced blends on the market, such as the orange-flavored teas particularly popular in the United States, usually feature a smooth-drinking Ceylon tea

Oolong: Formosa Blend: Earl Grey Blend: Uva

Oolong: Pouchong with jasmine Blend: English Breakfast Blend: Irish Breakfast with added cloves, dried orange peel, or lemon. Various teas can also be deliciously spiced with cinnamon, anise, or cardamom.

Japanese three-year tea, also known as twig tea or *kukicha*, is a natural tea with no caffeine, made from the roasted 3-year-old twigs and leaves of the tea bush. It is best sipped slowly after meals.

Herbal teas

Long eclipsed by ordinary tea, herbal teas, also known as tisanes, are making a comeback as more and more people realize that, as well as being refreshing in summer and a fragrant reminder in winter of sunny gardens, herbal teas can be soothing and beneficial. And, of course, they are caffeine-free.

Modern-day herbal teas and blends are sold either in packages, complete with instructions, in the ubiquitous tea bag, or loose, by retailers who should be able to advise on their use. The ingredients can also be gathered from the garden, as long as one keeps to the absolutely safe, well-known plants (be sure that they have not been sprayed with pesticides). The flowers, leaves, seeds, and/or roots can then be used fresh or dried gently, out of the sun, to use later.

Most of the teas made from dried herbs, flowers, and leaves are infused—made like regular tea—in a stainless steel or ceramic container (never aluminum). Measure about 1 teaspoonful of the dried herb or 2 teaspoonfuls of the fresh (or a few sprigs) per cup of water, add boiling water as if making ordinary tea, cover,

and allow to stand for no more than 5 minutes—long enough to bring out the fragrance, but not too long, or the tea will become bitter. Strain and, if you like, flavor with lemon or honey. Teas made from seeds, roots, or bark are prepared by boiling them to extract the flavors: allow 2 tablespoons of seeds, or a small handful of roots or bark, per 2 cups water. Bring to a boil, cover, and allow to simmer gently for about 15 minutes. Strain into a teapot, cover, and leave the tea to steep for a few minutes.

Ginseng (*Panax quinquefolium*) An ancient Chinese cure-all and aphrodisiac, said to be good for the mind, ginseng makes a tea with a licorice-like taste. Ginseng root, with fifteen other herbs, features in the powerful, spicy Japanese mu tea.

Linden (*Tilia americana, T. vulgaris*) Beautifully scented flowers from the linden tree, which may be called lime flowers in Europe, are dried to yield relaxing linden-blossom tea, which can be drunk hot or cold (disconcertingly, some recent studies say that frequent consumption of linden tea may affect the heart). A pale amber liquid, this is sometimes known as basswood tea.

Bergamot (*Monarda didyma, M. citriodora, M. fistulosa*) Tea made from the leaves and flowers has a slightly bitter taste.

Mint (*Mentha*) A great Arabian beverage, mint tea, which contains both mint and tea leaves, is served hot and heavily sweetened, in glasses, with sprigs of fresh mint. This refreshing tea is stimulating to drink and is also a good aid to digestion. The many mint teas

include peppermint, with menthol coolness, giving a pungent tea, and sharp, aromatic spearmint.

Chamomile (*Anthemis nobilis*) The dried flowers of chamomile make a rather bitter but soothing tea, excellent for settling the stomach and supposed to induce tranquil sleep. (It should be drunk in moderation.)

Maté (*Ilex paraguensis*) This stimulating tea, made from the dried leaves of a small tropical tree, is a favorite South American drink. Also known as yerba maté, it can be drunk hot or cold.

Lemon verbena (*Lippia citriodora*) The lemon-scented leaves make a delicious tea, strongly reminiscent of lemon and excellent for the digestion.

Marigold (*Calendula officinalis*) The warm orange flowers of pot marigold make a very pretty but somewhat bitter tea, supposed to be healing and to have antiseptic properties. Make it weak and sweeten it, or mix a few marigold flowers with lemon verbena tea.

Raspberry, black currant The leaves from both bushes make lightly flavored teas faintly evocative of the fruits.

Rose hip (*Rosa*) Wild rose hips yield a sweet, astringent tea popular for its high vitamin C content.

Fruit teas Refreshing and astringent, these are often spiced with cinnamon or cloves. Some common ones include a fragrant apple-based tea, a refreshing orange-based tea, a spicy ginger and red fruit blend, and lemon and ginger, a good morning tea. To sweeten a fruit tea, use honey rather than sugar.

Mint Bergamot Rose hip Ginseng Japanese mu

Maté Linden Raspberry leaf Chamomile Lemon verbena

Equipment:
How to choose it
and use it

Equipment

KNIVES

A good sharp knife that is comfortable to hold is the most essential tool to have in the kitchen—and one that makes the preparation of food a pleasure rather than a troublesome chore.

Quality and materials

Before selecting the right knife for the particular task you have in mind, it is important to know what qualities raise a kitchen knife into the top-quality class.
Balance It is critical that the weight of a knife be evenly distributed along the blade and handle, as an unbalanced knife is tiring to use. Knives are balanced by a tang (the metal that extends from the base of the blade through the handle), and in the case of heavy-bladed knives, the tang should run the full length of the handle. A full tang will also lend extra strength to a knife designed for tough tasks. Whether the knife is light- or heavy-bladed, the tang should be securely fixed inside the handle, preferably with rivets.
Machine-ground edge Grinding gives a blade both sharpness and strength. The best knives are taper-ground, with grinding marks at right angles to the cutting edge.
Hollow-ground blades are recognizable by their profile—a thick blade abruptly punched in at the cutting edge. The blade is machined so it cannot be sharpened, and it does not make a good edge for a chopping knife, but hollow grinding does make the hardest, most durable serrated edge.
Handles on the best-quality kitchen knives will be either of close-grained hardwood, which will not split or warp—and the slight texture of which gives a secure grip—or of plastic, or plastic-impregnated wood, which combines extreme toughness with the natural properties of wood. High-quality plastic handles are practical.
Stainless steel is a rust-resisting alloy of iron and chromium. Many people are disparaging of stainless steel, claiming that it is impossible to give it a really sharp edge. This is certainly true of inferior-quality knives stamped out of a flat piece of metal, but those forged from tempered stainless steel with a high carbon content (sometimes described as carbon stainless) are among the best knives you can buy, and they hold a very fine edge indeed.

Carbon steel has the advantage of being cheaper to buy than stainless steel, and it will sharpen to a razor-sharp edge. The disadvantage is that it is particularly susceptible to corrosion and staining, especially when used for foods with a high acid content, such as lemons and tomatoes, so it needs careful looking after and cleaning.

Shape and size

There are dozens of knives available today, designed for all the specialized tasks a professional chef may have to perform, but a carefully chosen collection of six or seven will equip most kitchens admirably.
Chopping To finely chop vegetables, herbs, garlic, nuts, and so on, you will need a tough, well-balanced, general-purpose cook's, or chef's, knife with a deep, smoothly curved blade that tapers toward a pointed tip. The handle should be shaped to the grip, with a downturned curve at the end to prevent the hand from slipping backward. It should have a full tang in order to balance the weight of the blade and to absorb the chopping vibrations as the knife is used.

The bolster (the thicker back end of the blade, also called the shoulder or guard) must be thick and deep to shield the hand and to allow the full length of the cutting edge to be used without hitting the knuckles on the chopping surface. The correct way to use this type of knife for fine chopping is to rest one hand lightly on the back of the blade at the tip to keep the blade in contact with the cutting board, while the other hand simply rocks the handle up and down, gradually moving the knife across the food. For coarser chopping, raise and lower the whole blade.

For tough chopping jobs, a cleaver should be used. This tool relies for its strength on a wide, really hefty, full-tanged blade, and it is one of the few instances where an imbalance between handle and blade is desirable. Butchers may be seen wielding this implement with considerable force and accuracy, but ferocious hacking can chip and blunt the cutting edge very quickly. To chop through bones, rest the cleaver in the proper position and hit the back of the blade with a mallet.

Cleavers are traditionally used for all the chopping and shredding that goes

into the preparation of Asian dishes. Chinese and Japanese chefs are able to cut a thin scallop of meat or fish by placing the ingredient under one palm and passing the cleaver through the meat or fish, their palm acting as a sort of radar device. This skill takes years of practice, however, and nonprofessionals should always treat cleavers with respect—and a fair amount of caution.
Slicing The type of knife you use will depend entirely on what you are slicing.
Bread A long serrated edge is good for cleanly penetrating the rough outer crust. Choose a straight, firm knife with hollow-ground serrations.
Cold meats The compact, tender fibers of cooked cold meats offer little resistance to a sharp knife and thus can be sliced very thin. Choose a knife with a long, narrow blade, which should be flexible and strong. Special ham slicers have a rounded tip to prevent accidental slashes to the meat and a fluted edge that gives a little purchase to the first stroke and reduces friction. Fluted or scalloped smoked salmon knives are also available; they make light work of slicing smoked salmon wafer-thin, and are also useful for cutting raw meat and fish for carpaccio.
Fruit and vegetables A small serrated stainless steel blade is wonderfully efficient for slicing lemons, tomatoes, cucumbers, peppers, and all those other fruits and vegetables with tough or slippery outer skins. The serration pierces the skin so easily that the flesh beneath is not bruised or squashed, and each slice keeps all its juice.
Paring, peeling, and scraping Everyone has a favorite little knife that tucks under the index finger and can be used almost as an extension of the hand. As the hand should be in close contact with the food, choose a light knife with a comfortable, well-shaped handle. The blade should be short and made of good-quality stainless steel capable of holding a really sharp edge.
Boning This operation is carried out in a series of small cutting movements, using the tip of the knife to follow the contours of the bone, so good control of the blade is important. For lightweight cuts of meat or poultry, a short, rigid knife is best, with a slim, pointed blade and a broad handle. The larger the piece of meat to be boned, the larger and more rigid the blade should be.

Filleting Choose a pointed straight-edged knife with a flexible blade that will feel its way around soft cartilaginous fish bones—this is a task requiring precision and dexterity. The blade should be protected by a bolster and the knife should have a full-tanged handle. This kind of knife is useful for almost every sort of cutting, slicing, carving, etc., except chopping.

Mincing The Italians have a very practical instrument called a *mezzaluna* ("half-moon"). It is a double-handled knife with a crescent-shaped single or double blade that is rocked over herbs, peppers, strips of meat, garlic, and already sliced vegetables, mincing them to fine bits. Small *mezzalunas* are sometimes sold together with a wooden herb-chopping bowl.

Carving Happily the days are past when carving was a competitive performance, but a good sharp knife is still a reassuring ally on these occasions. So too is a strong carving fork, traditionally used to hold the roast steady while slicing. A chicken can be carved with a small, handy knife, while a bulky hot roast with a bone requires a straight, sharply pointed knife. It helps when carving meat around a bone if the blade curves slightly upward toward the tip. The handle should be shaped to the hand, preferably with a full tang and a bolster to prevent the hand from slipping onto the blade. A slim blade that is slightly flexible will enable the carver to slice the meat quite thin.

Care and cleaning

Dishwashers can be very unkind to knives. The high temperature and harsh detergents loosen, warp, and split the handles, so it is better to wash them by hand unless they are guaranteed dishwasherproof. Wash them in hot, soapy water and dry immediately. Knives made of carbon steel are inclined to become rusty very quickly, so they must be cleaned and dried immediately after use. If the blades do become stained, polish them with a cork sprinkled with an abrasive cleaning powder, or scrub with a plastic scouring pad and a scouring cream or powder.

If by any chance a knife gets put in the dishwasher, you may find that its handle turns out of alignment with the blade. This will be because the tang is fixed to the handle not with rivets, but with resin

that softens with heat. To realign the knife, put the handle in boiling water for a few minutes, then twist it straight.

Sharpening Knives should always be kept in razor-sharp condition. A blunt knife is frustrating and dangerous to use—it performs badly, needing a great deal of force, and it can all too easily slip out of control. To help preserve their cutting edges, always chop on a wooden or polyethylene or acrylic board.

The best way to keep a sharp edge on a knife is to use a hand-held steel: draw the blade lightly down the steel at a shallow angle. Repeat, drawing the knife first down one side of the steel, then the other. To resharpen a dull blade you will have to resort to a whetstone—a block made of very hard Carborundum or very hard stone. There are many other devices for sharpening knives, but these usually grind down blades quickly and are not recommended.

Storage Kitchen knives should not be stored in drawers where the blades will clash together, bending the tips and dulling the fine edges. Each knife should be separated from its neighbors and clearly visible to the cook, who can then easily select the right knife for the job.

The best solution is to slot the knives into a wooden knife block or into a wall-fixed rack within easy reach of the work surface (but inaccessible to children.) Magnetic racks are good, but they may not be strong enough to hold very heavy knives or cleavers.

OTHER CUTTING UTENSILS

There are some cutting tasks that are really quite difficult to carry out with a straight-bladed knife, however sharp it may be. Fortunately, over the centuries a wide variety of special tools has been invented to do these jobs more quickly, safely, and efficiently. Some tools, like scissors, are strokes of genius, invaluable in the kitchen and elsewhere. Other tools are so specialized that it is advisable to examine your needs quite dispassionately before you go ahead and acquire them, as they might well spend more time collecting dust than attracting compliments for your prowess.

The following tools, used in conjunction with a basic collection of knives, should equip the cook to deal with most cutting tasks in the kitchen.

Graters

Choose a sturdy stainless steel box (or octagonal) grater that will sit firmly in a bowl or on a work surface without slipping or sliding. Each face should offer a different grating surface, and the grater should be large enough for the food to collect neatly inside without being squashed.

The face with fine holes is useful for Parmesan and other hard cheeses, while the abrading face consists of a series of jagged puncture holes for rasping tough or brittle foods, such as lemon zest and nutmeg. (Some graters have two abrading faces, one with large puncture holes, the other with small ones, rather than a side with fine slightly oval holes.) The smoother directional face cuts smooth slices or slivers from softer cheeses and vegetables.

A small flat or conical abrading grater is useful for holding over dishes to add a dash of nutmeg or lemon zest at a stroke.

Hand-operated rotary graters are speedy and pleasant to use, keeping the fingers at a safe handle's length from the grating surface. A curved plate holds the food tightly against the grating drum, which is turned by hand. Choose a model with a selection of drums of fine and coarse gauges.

Small nutmeg graters are nice to have, but are not essential.

Peelers and corers

Potato peeler It is perfectly possible to peel a potato quickly and easily with a small sharp knife, but the chances are that the discarded peel will contain more nourishment and flavor than the potato on the table. The *raison d'être* of a good potato peeler is to shave off the skin so finely that nothing of value is lost.

Fixed-blade peelers are used in the same way as knives, but left-handed people should make sure they buy a left-handed version. The slotted blade of the swivel-action peeler adapts to the shape of the fruit or vegetable as it is moved quickly over it; the sharp steel blade will cut equally well in either direction, meaning it is adaptable to either right-handed or left-handed use.

Citrus zester and canelle knife There are several types of peeler available that will remove only the zest, the thin colored top layer of citrus peel. A zester has a row of small holes that remove the zest in tiny strips, while a canelle knife, also called a citrus stripper, has a V-shaped tooth that removes the zest in ribbons or fatter strips—it's especially good for making martini-sized twists. The object of these specialized peelers is to leave behind the bitter pith, which is harder to do when using a knife.

Apple corer The end of this tool should be placed over the target area and pushed firmly through the apple; when it is withdrawn, the core will be retained in the center of the corer. It is a most useful gadget for preparing baked apples, the only drawback being that not every apple has an obligingly straight core of a standard size. Choose a corer with a sharp bottom edge.

Olive or cherry pitter This little gadget ejects pits from cherries and olives, and a sturdy stainless steel pitter will do the job very efficiently—a boon if you make a great deal of cherry pies or want pitted olives for cooking.

Slicers

Mandoline This instrument is used for high-speed slicing of firm, crisp foods—such as potatoes, onions, zucchini, carrots, cucumbers, or celeriac. While the cutting disks of a food processor can be used for slicing and shredding, they are never as fine and precise as the blades of a mandoline. Professional mandolines made of stainless steel have several blades and attachments for a variety of thicknesses and shapes; wooden mandolines usually have just two adjustable blades (preferably of high-carbon stainless steel), for slicing thick or thin. Plastic mandolines may have several interchangeable blades. In any case, the mandoline is held firmly in place with one hand while the other hand moves the food over the chosen blade with a regular strumming movement.

Cheese plane, cheese slicer These slicers are intended for semi-hard cheeses, such as Edam, that are traditionally cut very thin, and they are extremely good once you are accustomed to using them.

Cheese wire This is only useful if you buy cheese in large pieces. However hard or crumbly the cheese, a stainless steel cutting wire, when drawn taut, will melt through it and leave a clean, straight cut.

Egg slicer Wire slicers are a very good way of cutting hard-boiled eggs without displacing or crumbling the yolk. Some kinds cut wedges, some slices. Make sure that the wires are of stainless steel.

French fry cutter If you make a lot of french fries, then this gadget is quite useful. The whole peeled potato is placed under it, the stainless steel cutter pushed down, and within a few minutes you have a bowl of neatly cut potatoes ready for frying. Instruments for cutting raw potatoes must be sturdy, so be prepared to pay for a heavy-duty steel model. A flimsy cutter is worse than useless.

Scissors and shears

Kitchen scissors should be very sharp, strong, and chrome-plated or made of stainless steel with plastic handles because they must be impervious to rust. For tough jobs, their power will be strengthened if the lower handle is large enough to take the first three fingers of the cutting hand, and a serrated edge is sometimes useful for giving an extra bite to the first cut.

The blades should cut evenly right down to their tips—in fact, especially at the tips, because snipping is an important function of this tool. Scissors should be professionally sharpened when they become blunt.

Poultry shears Like garden clippers, this tool gains its strength from the tension in the coiled spring just below the pivot point of the blades. Usually one blade is serrated to give a firm grip when tackling tough assignments such as small bones, and the pointed tips enable the shears to reach and operate effectively in small awkward places.

Some versions are quite attractive, and as well as being invaluable in the kitchen, they can be used at the table for dividing a roast duck (or a small game bird) into neat and manageable portions. This is an especially good way to serve duck, as its bony carcass makes carving awkward.

Cutters

Graded sets Tin-plated steel plain- and crinkly-edged cutters are basic equipment for small pastries and can be used for cookies; the top edge should be rolled for strength, the cutting edge sharp. For convenient storage, buy graded sets that fit inside each other in their own tin.

Fancy cutters These are usually tin-plated steel, although occasionally stainless steel or plastic, in every imaginable shape and for every possible occasion. In addition to making cookies, these are fun to use for pastries, cakes, icings, marzipan, canapés, etc.

Pastry wheel This can cut straight or crimped lines through pastry or through sheets of pasta for pappardelle and ravioli with professional panache, dividing dough with a smooth, even pressure.

Ravioli cutter This is a fluted-edged metal cutter with a wooden handle, for stamping out individual rounds of ravioli. Different sizes are available. Ravioli trays are used for sheets of pasta—a rolling pin is rolled over the stuffed sheets and up to forty small squares of ravioli are cut at one time.

Pizza cutter This is a wheel with a sharp cutting edge to cut through cooked pizza dough and its toppings to make neat portions.

Specialty knives

Oyster and clam knives These tough knives are designed to open the shells of oysters and clams while they are raw and still alive. The blades of oyster knives and some supposedly dual-purpose knives have cutting edges on both sides to pry open the shells, and there is usually a guard to protect your hands. Clam knives usually have just one sharp side. Shucking raw shellfish is a tricky task. For safety's sake, choose one of the short, stubby knives, and hold the shellfish in a cloth—this will improve your grip and also protect your hand.

Grapefruit knife This double-edged, serrated knife is curved to fit the shape of a grapefruit half. It's easier than using a straight-edged knife for separating and removing individual grapefruit segments from tough membranes.

Sandwich spatula, sandwich spreader This is similar to a metal icing spatula, but has a shorter, broader, and more flexible blade. It is useful for spreading butter and sandwich fillings, whipped cream, icings, and frostings.

Cleaning

It is an unpleasant fact that behind every meal there looms the inevitable pile of dirty dishes. Even if there is a dishwasher in the kitchen, there will still be a hard core of gadgets, knives, and pots that has to be hand-washed. Some of the items listed in this section come into this rather unfortunate category.

Mandolines should be cleaned with a brush, rinsed, and dried quickly to preserve the cutting edge of their blades; wooden ones should never be left to soak, or they will warp. Brushing is also the best way to clean graters, although the larger box-shaped ones usually come clean perfectly well in the dishwasher.

Storage

Most of these implements have sharp cutting edges, so do not jumble them all into a drawer. This will ruin the blades and you will most probably cut your fingers as you root about searching for the appropriate gadget. Some can be hung from a rack or a rail on hooks, while larger items can be kept on a shelf. In all cases, the cook must be able to see and reach them easily.

GRINDERS, MASHERS, AND SIEVES

When you look at a collection of modern kitchen tools—efficient, easy to use, light, and simple to clean—it is easy to believe that they are all twentieth-century inventions. But most of them have a long and interesting lineage, and this is certainly true of the diverse group of tools in this section, designed to refine or change the texture of food.

Even before the advent of bread, our ancestors had realized that seeds and grains could be made more digestible or aromatic by pounding and grinding; pieces of cloth filled with berries and then wrung tightly were the first juice extractors. And loosely woven cloths suspended on wooden frames were the predecessors of modern sieves and strainers.

Grinders

Mortar and pestle This elegant descendant of the primitive pounding pole is still the most effective tool for pulverizing nuts, garlic, berries, grains, seeds, herbs, and spices.

The mortar should have a smooth, regularly curved bowl and a compatibly shaped pestle. The grinding surfaces should be slightly rough to provide the necessary friction and prevent the food sliding away from the pestle.

Mortars and pestles are available in wood, glass, tough unglazed porcelain, stone, metal, and marble. The small wooden ones are excellent for crushing most things, but because they are fairly lightweight, they require a fair amount of force to crush seeds, grains, and spices. The off-white vitrified porcelain versions are probably the most handsome and best all-round performers at a reasonable price.

Peppermill Peppercorns should be ground when and where they are needed so that their fugitive pungency can be enjoyed before it fades. The mealtime musings of many designers have resulted in an enormous variety of pepper mills to choose from, but perhaps the favorite is still the classic wooden mill with a removable top for easy filling and a highly efficient steel grinding mechanism.

Salt mill Where the pepper goes, salt goes too, so many manufacturers make a salt mill to match their peppermill. They will reduce coarse sea salt to usable size.

Coffee grinder Freshness is the essence of good coffee, and one way to ensure it is to grind your own. Hand-operated mills are preferred to electric grinders by some purists, as the beans are truly ground rather than cut, and the grind is cooler.

Grinder, meat grinder A hand-operated grinder should be very strong and have clamps or suction cups for fixing it rigidly to the work surface. The handle turns a small Archimedean screw, which inexorably pushes the food from the hopper onto the rotating stainless steel grinding plates, or disks, which will process almost anything except bones. Make sure that the machine has been designed to come apart completely so that every part can be easily cleaned.

Pounders and tenderizers

Meat pounder, meat mallet Thin slices of raw meat, such as veal scallops that are to be cooked quickly, should be flattened to half their original thickness. This is best done by gently pounding the meat, using a stroking motion, with a smooth, heavy meat pounder. Doing this homogenizes the texture of the flesh and breaks down the fibers, which will otherwise contract when the meat is cooked, causing shrinkage and toughness.

Meat tenderizer A mallet with a flat grid-shaped face is less brutal than the type with steel protuberances—which cut through fibrous tissues. Use a tenderizer only on very thick, tough cuts of meat.

Mashers

Potato masher Choose a strong masher that deals severely with the food and will not collapse under pressure. Traditional-style mashers are extremely efficient at mashing and puréeing cooked potatoes and other root vegetables, and can be used in the pan in which the vegetables were cooked. Stylish, modern mashers, which are made of zigzagging stainless steel are quite efficient, but they do seem to require more hard work than the traditional kind.

Ricer Chrome-plated steel ricers are excellent for making ultrasmooth mashed potatoes and other vegetable and fruit purées. The food is put into a mesh basket or hopper, then pressed through by means of a metal pusher attached to a handle. The end result is light, dry, and fluffy. Buy a ricer of a decent size, and preferably one that is dishwasherproof, as the basket can be a bore to clean by hand.

Garlic press For all those who are wary about impregnating a wooden cutting board or a mortar and pestle with the all-pervading odor and flavor of garlic, the garlic press is the answer. Select a sturdy cast aluminum or stainless steel press with a fairly coarse mesh—then there is no need to peel the clove of garlic before you squeeze. (Beware—crushed garlic is more overpowering than chopped.)

Sieves and strainers

There are sieves for sifting, sieves for straining, and sieves for puréeing: versatility breeds variation, and the sieve family is no exception.

Round stainless steel sieves are suitable for all sifting and puréeing tasks. They are preferable to the wire- or nylon-mesh type because they do not stain or corrode in contact with acid, and they do not wear out as quickly or come apart with constant pushing. To help with puréeing, you can use a wooden mushroom-shaped pestle called a *champignon* (French for mushroom) or the back of a spoon.

Sieves should not be filled too full for sifting—simply knock the side of the frame gently against the palm of the free hand to help the contents pass through.

Sieves can be very difficult to clean, and for this reason the wood-framed drum sieves, or tamis, are best avoided for puréeing—metal-framed drum sieves are better, as they are stronger and can be immersed in really hot, soapy water, or, better still, left for the dishwasher.

Conical strainer For fine puréeing jobs, a stainless steel *chinois*, or cone-shaped strainer, is preferable. Look for one with the frame and perforations formed from one piece of metal, with no seams or welds. The food is forced through the perforations by a pumping action using a small ladle or a wooden spoon, or by a long narrow pestle that fits right into the tip. A conical strainer is also excellent for straining, the tapering point channeling the liquid neatly down in a trickle into a deep bowl or saucepan.

Food mill This rotary sieve produces a range of purées, from the most delicate tomato sauces to a robust vegetable soup. A food processor, of course, would do the same, but a hand-cranked food mill often gives better results as it does not rob the food entirely of its intrinsic texture—it takes out, rather than chops up, lumps, fibers, or fine bones. Most food mills have a set of interchangeable plates or disks for a coarse, medium, or fine finish, and are easily dismantled for cleaning. The best food mills have bodies of stainless steel.

Juicers

A citrus fruit juicer must be able to extract the maximum amount of juice free of seeds, pith, and other solids. There are good models available with the reamer and strainer molded in one piece, which fits onto a container with a lip for pouring. Stainless steel versions are the most stylish, although plastic ones do the job just as well.

More traditional but not so efficient is the familiar glass version. It has teeth, which only halfheartedly trap the seeds and pieces, and a moat that barely holds the juice of one lemon.

For extracting just a few drops of juice without sacrificing a whole lemon or lime, there is a very clever little gadget called a citrus spigot. When plugged into the fruit, it will produce the required number of drops.

Ultramodern citrus presses are made of stainless steel. They look beautiful on the kitchen countertop, and most do the job exceedingly well. The most efficient types have a geared mechanism with sufficient power to squeeze every last drop of juice out of the fruit. Electric juicers are also widely available.

ESSENTIAL KITCHEN TOOLS

Some tools are never far from the cook's hand—usually tucked into a jar by the stove ready in an instant to tend those dishes that need stirring, whisking, or skimming while they cook.

Cutting boards

Wooden cutting boards are tough, but they are porous and so not only stain easily but also take on the flavors of foods that are chopped on them. If you choose wooden boards, you need to have several, each one for a specific task—chopping onions and garlic, rolling out pastry, slicing bread, etc. When you clean wooden boards, they should never be saturated or left to soak in water, as this will warp and crack the wood, and they should be kept away from heat. Polyethylene or acrylic boards are easier to keep clean than wood, but wooden boards are often preferred for their natural look and feel.

Whisks and beaters

Substances are whisked to lighten their texture by the introduction of air, to emulsify and blend ingredients, or to thicken those substances that contain fat. Egg whites, for example, have an almost infinite capacity for trapping air as they are whipped—when gently folded into sponge cakes, soufflés, or meringues, the air bubbles expand on heating to give the food a texture of honeycombed lightness.

A brisk whisking will rescue a lumpy sauce, and transform egg yolks and oil into a pale-golden mayonnaise.

There are many varieties of whisks. These are the most effective types:

Balloon whisk Made of several loops of stainless steel or tin-plated steel wire bound together around a central handle, these are simple and very effective instruments with no moving parts to break. However, they do need a strong arm to keep up the whisking motion for some minutes without tiring. Sizes range from large heavy-duty models for egg whites to small, dainty ones for light sauces and delicate dressings.

Rotary beater This can be heaven or hell depending on the quality. A cheap version is really a waste of money; unless the gear mechanism is carefully made of high-quality materials, the beater will not operate smoothly at high speed. The best types work very well indeed and are

less tiring to use than balloon whisks, but they do not achieve the same volume, particularly in the case of egg whites. They also require both hands, which is sometimes a disadvantage.

Flat coiled whisk, whip This is a neat spoon-shaped tool that can get right into the corners of a pan, or control one or two egg whites so well that they can be whisked on a plate. It is most effective at beating lumps out of sauces.

Spoons

Wooden spoons The wooden spoon is regarded by most people with affection, not only because it is associated with childhood treats like scraping the mixing bowl, but also because it is one of the most useful tools in the kitchen. A wooden spoon is invaluable for beating, mixing, and stirring; it will never burn your hand, because wood is a very bad conductor of heat; it will not scratch saucepans; and it is quiet and strong in use.

Choose a spoon of a close-grained wood that is not likely to split. The bowl of the spoon should have a fairly thin edge that can get right into the bottom corner of deep saucepans—some spoons are specially shaped to help you do this.

Metal spoons Although wooden and metal spoons share the same shape, their functions do not often overlap. While wooden spoons are good for stirring and beating, metal ones excel at transferring food quickly from pan to dish, and at gently folding together delicate mixtures. A metal spoon should always be used for last-minute taste checks on soups and sauces, as wood can hold a tiny bit of the flavor from its last use.

Perforated and slotted metal spoons are excellent for removing and serving pieces of food that have been cooked in liquid; the excess liquid drains through the holes or slots, keeping the food whole and fairly dry.

Ladle The familiar shape of the ladle has remained unchanged since very ancient times. Like most classics, ladles are satisfying to use because of their geometric balance, and they are also pleasing to the eye. Soups and stews can be dexterously served without fear of spilling a drop; just the right quantity of batter can be poured into a crêpe pan for feather-light crêpes; and lipped ladles will transfer punches from serving bowl to glasses with ease.

Essential kitchen tools

1 colander
2 wooden cutting board
3 wooden spoons
4 polyethylene cutting board
5 wooden spatula
6 can opener
7 angled spatula
8 tongs
9 large metal spoon
10 bottle opener
11 slotted turner
12 fish lifter
13 ladle
14 metal icing spatula
15 flat coiled whisk
16 balloon whisk
17 plastic spatula
18 corkscrew

Skimmers

Wire mesh skimmer Sometimes called a spider, a mesh skimmer is a shallow lightweight wire basket on a long handle that will scour bubbling oil, soup, or stock, gathering up impurities or removing food as it cooks. It is also good for scooping up fritters from hot oil at just the right moment to be rolled crisp and hot in sugar.

Solid perforated disk skimmer This can both skim liquids and remove pieces of food from their cooking liquid. They are not as good as mesh skimmers for deep-frying, because their bulk lowers the oil temperature and the perforations are not large enough to allow the oil to drain freely from the food.

Turners, spatulas, and tongs

Metal turner The flexibility of a good turner must be finely judged: slim and flexible enough to slide under the food without causing damage, but broad and firm enough to support it as it is turned or lifted from the pan. Perforations in the blade will allow excess fat or oil to escape, and a sturdy handle will help insulate the hand from the transferred heat of the pan. A fish lifter is a specialized metal turner

designed for removing a nicely cooked whole fish from its poaching liquid. (Turners are sometimes called spatulas, although this is incorrect.)

Wooden spatula It is strange that this archaic tool should be the perfect companion to the nonstick pan—that culinary spin-off from our space-age technology—and although as a turner it is somewhat lacking in flexibility, nothing harsher than wood should be used on this vulnerable finish.

Wooden spatulas are available in rounded spoon shapes, or with a flat blade and a slanted straight end, which fits snugly against the sides of pans and bowls, and gathers up everything in its path. Pierced or slotted wooden spatulas are useful for lifting and draining off fried food.

Rubber or plastic spatula These tools are the delight of a frugal cook's heart. Nothing else can scrape a bowl or jar as clean. Their rubber or plastic heads have a rounded side and an angular edge so they will fit a wide variety of pots, pans, and surfaces. Unless it's of the more expensive heat-resistant type, never put a rubber spatula into the dishwasher or very hot liquid—it will perish.

Metal spatula The long, thin, flexible blade of a metal icing spatula, also called a palette knife, is ideally suited to large-scale spreading jobs—like professionally smoothing a layer of buttercream on a cake or deftly distributing its filling. It is also a handy tool for lifting and turning pancakes or crêpes.

Angled or offset spatula This is useful for removing slices of tart or pie from rimmed pans without breaking them, and for lifting very delicate items like meringues.

Tongs These reach like heatproof fingers into sizzling pots and pans to grip small or awkwardly shaped items. They are invaluable for removing individual strands or pieces of pasta from the water to test for doneness, or for serving pasta.

Forks

Metal fork The long two-pronged kitchen forks, which are also known as pot forks or cook's forks, are mostly for various tasks such as removing a whole chicken from a deep pot or turning a roast. Smaller three-tined forks are called granny forks.

A strong fork with two long tines is necessary for holding meat firmly while it is carved. The best forks have a full tang riveted to a wooden or plastic handle. A carving fork may have a guard to protect the hand.

Wooden fork This friendly giant is ideal for gently swirling spaghetti while it cooks in the pot. Some cooks also find its light touch useful when adding liquid to pastry or dough mixtures.

Colander For the speedy separation of food from liquid, a round, double-handled metal bowl standing on a firm base and laced with a pattern of perforations is the most effective instrument to use. Choose the most roomy colander you can find so that when you are washing fruit, vegetables, or greens, there is plenty of space to swish them around.

Corkscrew There are so many different corkscrews that it's difficult to decide which is best for you. Corkscrews are very personal things—some people swear by one type of mechanism, others by another. The coil (or worm) should be a very sharp, thin spiral, preferably of a triangular section so that it really cuts into the cork. It should have a solid, comfortable handle, and should be long enough so that it can penetrate the whole cork.

The corkscrew that is known as the Screwpull is very simple and effective because it involves no pulling, and the screw itself is wider than most, making it extremely effective at holding the cork firmly. As you turn the handle, the screw goes into the cork and lifts it out in one action. Some models incorporate a blade for cutting the foil.

The winged or double-lever corkscrew is also easy to use. No pulling is required: the coil is screwed in and the two arms slowly depressed to raise the cork.

The simple waiter's corkscrew needs only a little strength to use and is quite efficient and reliable, if it is inserted and pulled out straight—otherwise, it breaks the cork. The classic corkscrew with a simple wooden crossbar can require a lot of effort, especially if the cork is stubborn.

Bottle opener Choose the simplest and sturdiest bottle opener you can find. Wooden handles have a nice feel to them. Make sure that the shape fits your hand comfortably.

Can opener Easy to use is the type that clamps onto the rim of the can and then cuts through the metal by means of two gear-driven cutting wheels, which are turned by means of a butterfly handle. It grips the can very firmly and leaves a very clean cut edge. Dishwasherproof, this type of can opener is a sophisticated and much improved version of the original all-metal butterfly-action opener.

A wall-mounted opener is also very convenient to use, in that the can is slotted into the jaws and held there by a lever as the lid is removed.

The old-fashioned scythe-cutting-action manual can opener has no moving parts to wear out, but it requires a firm pushing action to cut through the lid, and makes a rather messy job of it.

OTHER USEFUL ITEMS
Depending on the kind of cooking you do, you may consider some, or all, of the following to be essential.

Pasta machine This operates in a similar way to an old-fashioned clothes mangle with adjustable rollers. It has attachments to produce different shapes and sizes of pasta. The best machines are made of chrome-plated steel with stainless steel rollers.

Salad basket and spinner A salad basket, that airy balloon of wire, will contain a leafy salad with the minimum of restriction while it is whirled around out in the garden by energetic arms to extract the water by centrifugal force. If you don't have revolving arm sockets, try instead one of the ingenious plastic salad spinners operated by a handle.

Bulb baster A useful tool, this looks rather like a large syringe and acts on the same principle. Inserting the plastic tube of the baster into a liquid and squeezing the rubber bulb at the top draws the liquid up into the tube. It can then be squirted back out again, for basting meat during roasting. The added advantage of a bulb baster is that it can also be used as a fat separator—any fat in the liquid settles at the top of the tube, and can be left behind. Some basters come with a needle that can be screwed onto the tip and used to inject the basting liquid into the meat, or under the skin of a roasting chicken or turkey.

Gravy separator As a fat separator, this is an alternative to the bulb baster. The original version of the gravy separator, which was invented by the French, is an ingenious gravy boat with two spouts, one at either side. One spout has a deep funnel that pours the nonfatty gravy (*maigre*) from the bottom of the pitcher, while the other is shallow and pours the fat (*gras*) on the surface; its French name is *maigre et gras*, or *gras-maigre*. The newer plastic types have just one spout for pouring out the nonfatty gravy or pan juices.

Funnel This can be made of stainless steel, aluminum, or plastic, and is an invaluable tool for decanting liquids into bottles or other narrow-necked containers.

Lobster crackers These look like nutcrackers in the shape of lobster claws. They are hinged, with ridges inside near the hinge, and are indispensable for cracking open the very hard shells of both lobster and crab claws.

Lobster pick These are for extracting every last bit of meat from the awkward parts of lobsters and crabs. The most efficient picks have a two-pronged fork at the end, which helps pull the meat from hidden crevices.

Lobster pincer This is a two-in-one tool that in essence combines both lobster crackers and pick.

Nutcrackers Heavy chrome- or silver-plated crackers with a squeezing action are probably the most popular shape, but people with weak wrists may find them difficult; a wooden version of the screw-type nutcracker is a good alternative.

Cake tester Resembling a long needle with a handle, a cake tester is inserted into a cake to check for doneness. A toothpick will often do this job, but cake testers are especially useful for tall cakes baked in deep Bundt or other such pans.

Wire cake rack Raised wire racks are essential for cooling just-baked pastries, cookies, and cakes. If the steamy moisture is not allowed to escape after baking, it will condense inside the dough, making it leaden. Choose large racks made of strong stainless steel.

Useful utensils, bowls, and measuring equipment

1 gravy separator
2 meat thermometer
3 deep-fry/candy thermometer
4 bulb baster
5 glass mixing bowls
6 English pudding basins
7 ceramic mixing bowl
8 wooden salad bowl with salad servers
9 salad spinner
10 stainless steel bowls
11 blowtorch
12 pasta machine
13 lobster cracker
14 nutcracker
15 lobster pick
16 cake tester
17 wire cooling rack
18 dry measuring cups
19 glass measuring cups
20 funnel
21 electronic scale
22 ice cream scoop
23 measuring spoons

Blowtorch This is used by chefs to rapidly caramelize the sugared tops of desserts such as crème brûlée. Buy a small blowtorch for your kitchen from a hardware store—it will be invaluable for that professional touch with desserts that would otherwise melt or overcook if caramelized using the conventional broiler method.

Ice cream scoop There are two main types. One has a blade that sweeps between the bowl of the scoop and the ice cream, shaping the ice cream into a perfect ball as if by magic. This is the traditional kind used in ice cream parlors; it is easy to use, but needs to be dunked in water in between each scooping or the ice cream will stick. It is also useful for serving mashed potatoes and other vegetable purées, and for making cookies (especially the smaller sizes).

A second, rather more sophisticated type of ice cream scoop has no blade mechanism, but inside the handle there is a type of (nontoxic) antifreeze fluid. This enables you to scoop out very hard ice cream, sorbets, and granitas (be sure not to put this type of scoop in the dishwasher, or the antifreeze fluid will solidify). A similar version is made without the antifreeze.

Trussing equipment For the simple trussing of whole birds, especially small ones, kitchen string is usually sufficient. Short metal skewers or poultry lacers are useful for larger birds and those that are stuffed. Trussing with a needle and butcher's twine keeps a large stuffed bird in good shape. Trussing needles have very sharp points and eyes that are large enough for threading the quite thick twine. The length of a trussing needle is important—it should be at least 10 inches long so that it can be used to pierce a bird from one side to the other, through wings or legs and the body in between. The butcher's twine or kitchen string should be strong, undyed, and not waxed.

Larding needle This is the type of needle used for larding roasts of meat with bacon or other fat. It is long and hollow, and often has one pointed end and a clasp at the other end to hold the fat.

BOWLS

Bowls are used for food preparation, cooking, storing, and serving. They are available in a huge variety of materials and sizes, each having qualities suited more to one purpose than another. Bowls must be suited to the job in hand—too large, and the ingredients spread themselves in a thin film around the sides; too small, and the contents will overflow.

Every serious kitchen needs at least one huge bowl, suitable for soaking dried beans, or perhaps a country ham, and for mixing layer cake batters and bread doughs. It will also be useful for salads.

Glass bowls Tempered glass bowls are good for all mixing tasks, and the sets of different sizes that fit neatly inside one another are most convenient for easy storage. All are heatproof, and some are also ovenproof. Many of us grew up mixing cookie dough in—or licking icing from—the nested set of colored Pyrex bowls, and Pyrex bowls are still the cornerstone of many a cook's collection.

Ceramic bowls The classic yellow mixing bowl with a white interior, made of stoneware, is a favorite of many cooks, especially those who bake their own bread, as it is the ideal bowl for dough making. At the bottom of one side, there is a small flat area that acts as a base for holding the bowl steady when tilting the bowl for beating or creaming.

China pudding basins These useful bowls are a standard of the English kitchen. The sides of a pudding basin are steeper and more tapered than those of a regular mixing bowl because this shape gives support to the center of the cooked dessert or pudding, and prevents it from collapsing when turned out. The tough glazed finish will withstand even the high temperatures of a pressure cooker when steaming a pudding, and its raised rim holds a cover and string in place.

Plastic bowls Good-quality plastic bowls are quiet, nonporous, virtually unbreakable, and good insulators, but they have to be treated carefully, as they are vulnerable to scratching and to distortion through heat. And of course they cannot be used in the oven. A rubber-ringed base will keep the bowl anchored safely in place. Melamine is one of the toughest plastics used to manufacture mixing bowls, and it can be put in the dishwasher.

Stainless steel bowls It is not surprising that most restaurant kitchens choose to use stainless steel bowls almost to the exclusion of all others. The conductivity of metal makes these bowls ideal for ingredients that need to be cooled or heated over water; stainless steel is also an excellent alternative to the once-popular copper for beating egg whites.

Wooden bowls A handsome wooden bowl is the perfect setting for fresh green lettuce leaves. It should be wide and deep enough to contain an exuberant curly salad while it is being tossed.

Wooden bowls need to be washed briefly soon after they have been used, as they absorb the flavor of food. When washing, use the minimum amount of detergent, and never soak these bowls, or dry them next to direct heat.

Other bowls There are all sorts of small porcelain, earthenware, terracotta, and stoneware bowls of ancient and modern design that are endlessly useful. Handmade bowls with slightly rough interiors are good for making mayonnaise and vinaigrette—the surface helps the mixture to emulsify.

MEASURING EQUIPMENT

It is obvious from just a cursory glance at any cookbook that artistry needs to be underpinned by a solid foundation of knowledge. Ingredients must often be measured in exact amounts, assembled and prepared in an ordered sequence, and then cooked at precise temperatures for a predetermined length of time. Measuring equipment is therefore an important component of the *batterie de cuisine*, enabling recipes to be perfectly balanced every time.

In these days of international recipe exchanges, measuring is complicated by the different systems used in America and Europe. Americans mete out their ingredients, liquid and dry, in cups (which sounds like a vague term for what is in fact a precise volume), and only rarely weigh ingredients in ounces and pounds, whereas Europeans measure their dry ingredients by metric weights. (To further complicate the issue, the American pints, quarts, and gallons are quite different from English imperial measures, their counterparts that share the same names.) So it makes sense, whenever possible, to buy measuring devices that are marked with metric calibrations, as well as with our regular American measures.

Scales

Balancing quantities of goods against weights of constant or standard size is a very ancient practice that began in the marketplace as a fair method of trading. In these days of high technology, scales are more important than ever, not least in the kitchen, where serious cooks know they are one of the keys to successful baking and useful for some other recipes as well.

Balance scale A strong balance scale will last a lifetime because it operates on a simple seesaw principle and there is no complicated mechanism to wear out. The weight is not indicated on a register, but when the weights on the two sides exactly match, a pointer lines up with a central marker on the fulcrum. These scales are usually so sensitive that two or three crumbs added to either side are enough to tip the balance.

American or metric weights may be used according to the manufacturer,

and these are available in brass or, less expensively, in cast iron, especially for the heavier weights. The pan for containing the food should ideally be a pear-shaped brass, stainless steel, or enamel bowl that, when tipped, will funnel its contents neatly into a mixing bowl or saucepan.

Electronic battery-operated scales have a digital display that shows either just American weights or both American and metric weights. Many models incorporate an ingenious device by which the display can be returned to zero when weighing more than one ingredient in the bowl at the same time. The disadvantage of these scales is that they are not very accurate with small amounts (under 1 ounce).

Spring-balance scale In this type of scale, the weights have been replaced by a metal coil or spring. The ingredients are balanced against the tension stored in the spring and the weight is registered on a calibrated scale, usually marked with both American and metric measures. The capacity is limited by the power of the spring, so check before purchase that the

scale is not just suited to light loads—the best balance scales will weigh up to 26 pounds. There is a tendency for spring balance scales to wander out of true, so choose one where accuracy can be restored by means of an adjustment screw when the scale is at rest.

Measuring cups

For cooking purposes, ingredients are usually measured in cups, or fractions thereof (and smaller amounts in teaspoons and tablespoons). Many cooks who do a lot of baking, especially bread making, however, prefer to weigh dry ingredients such as flour and sugar for more accurate measurement.

For liquids, a measuring cup made of tempered glass is the most useful; the glass, which can withstand the impact of boiling liquids, enables the cook to see exactly how much is in the cup, and, because glass is such a poor conductor of heat, the handle always remains cool.

Clear plastic measuring cups are cheaper than glass, but they must be treated more carefully; heat can craze or distort the plastic, and if the shape of the

cup changes, it may no longer provide an accurate measure. Liquid measuring cups come in 1-cup, 2-cup, 1-quart, and even larger sizes. Most also have metric markings.

The best dry measuring cups are sturdy metal ones; cheaper plastic ones are often inaccurate. Dry measuring cups come in sets that nest neatly inside each other. Most sets include ¼-cup, ⅓-cup, ½-cup, and 1-cup measures; some have an ⅛-cup measure too, and 2-cup dry measuring cups are also available. Dry ingredients should be spooned or scooped into the cup, without packing (except for brown sugar, which is measured by the packed cup), and the top leveled off with a knife or other straight edge.

Measuring spoons

Smaller amounts of ingredients, both liquid and dry, are measured using measuring spoons. The best are metal, but plastic ones are also common; avoid cheaper sets, which are likely to be inaccurate. Measuring spoons always come in sets, which usually include ⅛-teaspoon, ¼-teaspoon, ½-teaspoon, and 1-tablespoon measures; some also have a handy ½-tablespoon measure (which is, of course, the same as 1½ teaspoons). The ingredients in the spoon should be leveled off with a knife unless the recipe specifies a heaped measure.

Thermometers

A well-equipped kitchen will ideally have a variety of thermometers to cope with the whole gamut of culinary needs, from monitoring the coldest depths of the freezer to recognizing the different stages of cooking sugar. Precise temperature control is also essential for the safety and the success of many dishes and methods, such as making custard or yogurt, yeast baking, deep-fat frying, and jam making.

Freezer thermometer There are two enemies to be faced when preserving food by freezing: first, the bacteria that cause the food to decay, and second, the enzymes that break down its structure and impair the flavor. Food frozen to 0°F will be safe from bacteriological activity. You should check that this temperature is constantly maintained, as the enzymes will begin to function at 14°F.

Deep-fry and sugar/candy thermometers These register the highest temperatures that are encountered in cooking. The secret of successful deep-frying lies in preheating the oil until it registers about 375°F on a deep-fry thermometer before adding the food. At this temperature, the oil will sear the food instantly, preventing the escape of any juices or flavor; conversely, the food will not absorb the oil.

When sugar is heated, it passes through various stages of crystallization at certain critical temperatures, until at 356°F it becomes dark caramel. A candy thermometer is required to catch the sugar at just the right moment before it passes to the next stage. Combination deep-fry/candy thermometers are also widely available. Some of these high-temperature thermometers are made of glass, so warm them in hot water before use to avoid any danger of cracking.

Oven thermometer In a perfect world this would be superfluous, but ovens are notorious for their idiosyncrasies and their temperature variations between the top and bottom racks and the front and back. You can establish the temperature pattern inside your oven by standing or hanging a mercury-filled or spring-type thermometer in various positions and noting the differences.

Meat thermometer This will take all the guesswork out of roasting meat by enabling you to gauge the exact degree of doneness. A meat thermometer is also vital for checking the internal temperature of whole roast chickens and turkeys—this should be at least 180° to 185°F to kill any dangerous bacteria such as salmonella. "Instant-read" meat thermometers are used for spot checks, but the more common type is inserted into the meat or poultry before cooking begins and left until the hand points to the appropriate place on the dial.

Timers

Automatic timer Very often it is the sense of smell that alerts a busy or forgetful person that something is not only cooked but overcooked. An automatic timer preset to ring at a certain time will help avoid disaster.

Sand timer Egg timers and hourglasses have now been largely superseded by automatic timers, but they are quiet and accurate, and cost a fraction of the price.

STOVETOP POTS AND PANS

Before purchasing, take care to find out what the qualities of good saucepans are and the various properties of the metals they are made from. Equipped with this information, it is possible to make a selection that will suit all needs and give a lifetime's reliable service.

The materials

Stainless steel The most durable metal found in the kitchen, stainless steel will retain a polished finish throughout its long life and is completely impervious to acid or alkaline ingredients. Alas, this promising metal is not the best conductor of heat—which is of course an enormous drawback in a pan—but thankfully, modern technology has found a solution. Good-quality stainless steel pans now have heavy-gauge bases made of a "sandwich" of stainless steel with a metal filling that is a good conductor of heat. This may be copper, copper and silver alloy, or aluminum or aluminum alloy. These types of pans are expensive, but they should last a lifetime. *Care* Soak pans to loosen food deposits, then clean with a brush and hot soapy water. Scouring pads and powders can be used without risk of damage.

Iron and steel In spite of its propensity to rust, cast iron is popular for some pans, such as stovetop griddles, frying pans, paella pans, blini pans, and Belgian waffle pans, when cooking the food evenly at high temperatures is important.

Untreated black steel pans are very susceptible to corrosion and distortion by heat, and although a well-seasoned heavy steel frying pan, crêpe pan, or omelet pan is a very satisfying thing to use, saucepans made of steel are always covered with a layer of vitrified enamel. *Care* Maintenance is a continuous battle against rust. Pans should be thoroughly dried before being stored, and if they are not used very often, coated with a light layer of vegetable oil before being put away. New cast-iron and black steel pans should be prepared for use by seasoning them: first heat the pan slightly and then wash thoroughly in hot soapy water to remove any protective coating. Dry the pan and heat again, with some vegetable oil in the pan, over fairly high heat until it smokes. Keep the pan at this high temperature for several minutes, tilting the pan so that the oil runs over the

Stovetop pots and pans, ovenware, and bakeware

1 pasta pot
2 enameled cast-iron casseroles
3 baking and gratin dishes
4 ramekins
5 soufflé dish
6 glass custard cups
7 stainless steel roasting pan with rack
8 nonstick frying pan
9 baking sheet
10 cast-iron griddle
11 long chopsticks
12 wooden spatula
13 wok
14 ridged cast-iron grill pan
15 cast-iron frying pan
16 stainless steel saucepans

bottom and up the sides until the whole surface of the pan has been covered. Cool, then vigorously rub and wipe out excess oil using a pad of paper towels and some coarse salt. Cast-iron pans may also be seasoned in the oven: brush with oil and add about ¼ inch oil to the pan. Heat in a 300°F oven for 1 hour, then cool and wipe out the excess oil.

Enameled cast iron and steel Enameled cast iron is a good, even conductor of heat, and it does not rust. It makes very strong, sturdy vessels, which are excellent for both stovetop and oven cooking—ideal for casseroles and stews or braises that are started off on top of the stove and then left to simmer slowly in the oven. Allow time for the metal to heat up at the start of cooking, and remember that it will retain the heat exceptionally well, so it is rare that a very high heat need be used.

Care Wash these types of pans in hot soapy water, scrubbing off any food that has adhered during cooking with a brush. Soaking helps loosen stubborn food stuck on the inside of pans. Plastic scouring pads can be used, and if all else fails, diluted bleach.

Enameled steel pans need to be treated with care—don't allow empty pans to sit over the heat, or they will distort and shed their protective enamel coating, and never clean them with an abrasive substance, or you will eventually expose the metal. Harsh scouring powders or pads will destroy the glassy surface and eventually wear through the enamel; any stains can be easily removed by soaking the pan in a solution of diluted bleach. Be careful not to bang or knock these pans, particularly when they are hot, as the enamel may chip. They scorch easily, are not very flat, and are not good conductors of heat, so are only really appropriate when cooking with gas, not on an electric stove.

Copper The great advantage of copper is that it is an excellent conductor of heat, and its rich golden-red color adds a warm glow to the kitchen. But it is expensive and, regrettably, readily combines chemically with food, liquids, and the air to form a poisonous layer of green verdigris. For this reason, copper cooking vessels must always be lined. Tin or silver were the traditional lining materials, but nowadays the more durable stainless steel is preferred.

Care Copper needs constant polishing to keep it bright, and for some this is just one chore too many. Salt and lemon halves will keep copper pans shining— commercial cleaners give the copper a light finish that is difficult to maintain. Avoid using harsh scouring pads, cream, or powder when cleaning the copper outside of the pans.

Nonstick Nonstick surfaces are a gift from modern technology and daily appear in more durable and long-lived forms. They are particularly useful for lining frying pans, where, for example, eggs and fillets of fish will cook happily with little or no fat and be released completely intact at the end, leaving scarcely a trace in the pan.

Care Clean with a plastic scouring pad or cloth in hot soapy water, rinse, and dry. Avoid using metal spoons: these will scratch, exposing the metal beneath.

The perfect metal Unfortunately, no one particular metal is capable of providing the perfect pan, but until a single hybrid alloy can be produced combining the beauty and conductivity of copper and the stability of stainless steel, the next best thing is to laminate the various metals in such a way as to combine all their best qualities and minimize their negative points. Combinations that give excellent results are: aluminum sandwiched between an outer layer of copper and an inner lining of stainless steel; copper lined with stainless steel; aluminum lined with a nonstick finish; cast iron coated with enamel; and stainless steel with a thick copper or aluminum base.

Choosing pans

Once you have decided on the best metal or combination of metals, you should consider the design and quality of the pan. Look for the following points:

- Thick, heavy-gauge metal, particularly at the bottom, which will not distort or dent and will spread the heat evenly from the source to all parts of the pan.
- Sides that curve gently into the base so that no part of the pan will be inaccessible to the spoon. This is a good feature to look for in a frying pan—curved sides enable delicate omelets, for example, to be rolled gently onto a plate without damage.
- Handles should be strong, securely riveted to the pan, and preferably

insulated so they always remain cool enough to hold. They should have well-rounded contours—thin angular shapes cut into the hand when you are pouring or lifting heavy pans. Plastic or wooden handles are the best insulators, but may loosen and split if cleaned in a dishwasher, and of course they can't go in the oven. A sturdy ring or a hole at the end of the handle is useful for hanging the pan on a rack.

- Lids must give a tight seal and be shaped so that condensed water vapor is returned to the pan and does not escape in trickles down the outside of it. Lid knobs, like handles, should remain cool enough to touch—again, plastic or wood is best.

Storage

If possible, pans should be kept at eye level, or at least above the waist, either hanging from a rack or lined up on a shelf. Crowded, low cupboards infuriate the busy cook, while pans piled together indiscriminately are very likely to become scratched, or will be pushed to inaccessible corners.

Useful pots and pans

The following pans will make a good "starter pack" if you are equipping a kitchen from scratch. There are many more pans you can have, but most are suited to specific tasks, so it is best to buy them only if and when you need them. Good-quality pans are expensive, but they will last a very long time.

Set of stainless steel pans A stacking set of three or four saucepans is adequate for most tasks. Sizes vary enormously, so choose the ones that suit your needs and size of household. A large pot with two handles is an essential purchase even if you normally cook small quantities—you can use it for cooking pasta and making stocks and soups, and it can also double as a casserole to be used in the oven.

Frying pan Cast-iron frying pans are traditional, especially for sautéing and making pancakes. They improve with age and can last a lifetime. However, they are heavy and not always easy to clean, so a couple of good-quality nonstick frying pans will also come in handy. These will not last as long as cast iron, so expect to replace them from time to time.

OVENWARE AND BAKEWARE

From everyday roasting pans and baking sheets to "country kitchen" casseroles, porcelain ramekins, and fancifully shaped metal molds, this section covers items that you will use time and again, and more specialized equipment that may be used only once a year.

The materials

Stainless steel This conducts heat slowly, so its use in the oven is generally limited to roasting pans, although some other baking equipment is made in stainless.

Enamel High-quality enamel on steel or cast iron is a most durable, hard-wearing combination—the glassy finish will not be affected by even the most corrosive ingredients. Its weakness lies in the different expansion rates of the enamel and base metal, so it is particularly vulnerable to chipping when it is heated or cooled.

Glass Ovenproof glass behaves in the same way as dark metal surfaces when it is heated, and oven temperatures should be reduced slightly (by about 25°F) when using glass baking dishes. The brittleness, however, and sensitivity of glass to temperature changes means that

careful handling is essential. It is not as good a conductor of heat as metal, so if used for pies and other pastry-based dishes, the pastry bottom will never achieve such a crisp result.

Porcelain This is especially suitable for dishes such as soufflés that must be served straight from the oven. Although porcelain is prone to chipping, the highly vitrified surface is very tough.

Stoneware is another tough ceramic, with a homey quality and the ability to withstand high temperatures in the oven.

Glazed earthenware is not as highly fired as stoneware, so will chip more easily.

Unglazed terracotta pots for cooking meats or vegetables without fat will be essential for the diet-conscious, or for those who enjoy the flavor of meat and vegetables stewed in their own juices.

The equipment

Casserole Casseroles require slow, lengthy cooking, so conservation of moisture is of paramount importance. Whatever the material the dish is made from, it should be heavy so that it absorbs heat slowly and then retains heat and moisture for the longest possible time. The lid must fit very tightly to prevent the

Sauté pan Deeper than ordinary frying pans, sauté pans have straight or slightly rounded sides. A good sauté pan is very versatile; it can be used both as a regular frying pan and for risottos, sautés, stir-fries, sauces, etc., and for poaching.

Pasta pot This is stainless steel, with a perforated inner basket. It is expensive, but ideal for cooking pasta in a large quantity of water, and the basket makes for easy draining. Some pasta pots also come with a second insert for steaming.

Steamer set The best is stainless steel, with one or two stackable steamer compartments. The bottom pot can also serve as a stovetop pot. The Chinese bamboo steamer that fits in a wok is cheaper, but its use is more limited.

Wok and accessories An inexpensive carbon-steel wok is more than adequate, but the more expensive preseasoned carbon steel woks are easier to keep clean. Carbon steel is the best metal because it is such an excellent conductor of heat. The most useful accessories are wooden spatulas and long chopsticks, plus a long-handled spatula or scoop.

Clean your wok with hot soapy water, and dry it well. To prevent rusting, wipe it with vegetable oil before putting away.

Cake and pastry making equipment

1 loaf pan
2 rolling pin
3 tube pan
4 flour sifter
5 Bundt pan
6 deep pie dish
7 ceramic tart pan
8 dough scraper
9 jellyroll pan
10 pastry brush
11 marble slab
12 pastry blender
13 madeleine pan
14 muffin pan
15 round cake pan
16 brioche mold
17 springform pan
18 ring mold
19 removable-bottomed tart pan
20 pastry bag with tips

escape of steam, and the seal must be designed so that condensed water vapor is channeled back into the dish. Handles should be easy to grip, yet small enough for the dish to fit easily into the oven.

Casseroles made of enameled cast iron, or other suitable heavy-gauge metals, can be used on top of the stove, for searing the meat over high heat (if required) and for lengthy simmering. Earthenware or heat-resistant glass dishes should only be used in the oven.

It is useful to have casseroles of various sizes because the contents should fill the pots in the correct proportion—a small stew in a large casserole, for instance, will dry out long before it is cooked.

Baking dish and gratin dish It is impossible to have too many of these, in different shapes and sizes, full-size and individual. They are used for lasagne and other baked pastas, moussaka, chicken pot pie, vegetable gratins and roasts—in fact any dish with a topping that needs to be crisped and browned at a high temperature. Baking dishes may be rectangular or oval and made of porcelain, enameled cast iron or steel, glass, or earthenware or stoneware. French gratin dishes were traditionally made of copper, but nowadays enameled cast iron, porcelain, and stoneware are more common. They can be put safely under the broiler or into a very hot oven and yet still look presentable enough for the table.

Roasting pan Roasting pans in one or two sizes are useful, in stainless steel or anodized aluminum, which are both easy to clean—an important consideration with a roasting pan. Buy them with racks that fit inside for keeping meat and poultry above the fat as it runs out during roasting. Racks are especially good for fatty birds like duck and geese, and long-cooking poultry such as turkey.

Ovenproof skillet A useful pan for dishes that need to start off on top of the stove, finish cooking in the oven, and then be turned out for serving. French tarte tatin and potato galette are such dishes, as are some Italian frittatas. Most frying pans do not have ovenproof handles, so would not be suitable, whereas cast iron is.

Soufflé dish These are traditionally straight-sided so the soufflé mixture can rise unimpeded above the edge. Made of porcelain, glass, or stoneware, they can be taken straight from oven to table. Available in different sizes and as individal ramekins, they are also useful for general baking, and for such things as baked custard and gelatin-based cold mousses and soufflés.

Terrine Deep enameled cast-iron or earthenware terrines are traditional for baking pâtés and terrines. They are often long and narrow, which makes for elegant presentation.

Baking sheet Heavy-duty steel sheets are best. Flat and rigid, they are good conductors of heat, and will not buckle or warp in the hottest of ovens. Baking sheets usually have four slightly flared upturned edges. Cookie sheets have only one, or sometimes two, rims; the flat sheet allows hot air to circulate around the cookies for more even baking.

CAKE AND PASTRY MAKING EQUIPMENT

When food is placed in the dry, hot atmosphere of the oven, it is cooked equally from all directions, and the containers do not have to withstand and conduct heat from a single intense source as saucepans do. The function of a baking pan is to mold and contain, and to respond as quickly as possible to the ambient heat of the oven.

The materials

Some baking pans have bright shining surfaces, which deflect the heat away from the contents so that they will not scorch. Others have dark finishes, which absorb and hold the heat and need an oven temperature reduction of 25°F to achieve the same results.

Tinned steel, black steel This is the most widely used material for baking containers. It is really worth spending money on good-quality baking pans that have the minimum number of seams, as nooks and crannies are difficult to clean and dry. Corrosion is the chief enemy of tinned steel, for underneath the shining exterior lurks a metal that is addicted to oxidation through even the smallest pinhole in the tin coating. Never use steel wool or other abrasive cleaning materials; wash and dry baking pans as soon as possible after use. A good-quality, well-treated tinned steel baking pan will last a lifetime.

Some baking equipment, such as tart pans and loaf pans, is made of plain black or blue steel. Black steel conducts heat well and evenly, but it rusts easily and so must be well dried after washing.

Aluminum Impervious to atmospheric oxidation, aluminum is a metal that is often used for cake pans, but it is thinner and lighter than tinned steel, making it unsuitable for dense rich fruit mixtures or other cakes that need a long baking time. They are likely to dry out and even burn if baked in aluminum pans. In any case, choose heavier-weight aluminum pans.

Stainless steel Stainless steel baking pans are sturdy, nonreactive, and easy to clean. However, stainless steel does not conduct heat well, and can be expensive.

Nonstick silicone surfaces These can be applied to tinned steel or aluminum, but the surface will not last if metal utensils are used to cut or scoop out the contents of the pan. To clean nonstick surfaces, soak for a few minutes, then wipe with a soapy cloth and rinse.

Aluminum foil If you are baking for the freezer, it is a nuisance to lose the use of baking containers for weeks on end. Aluminum foil dishes can be used in the oven, then put in the freezer once cool.

Cake pans

Even if you are not a prolific baker or cake maker, a few basic pans are very versatile and well worth buying.

Round cake pan The standard size of these is 8 or 9 inches in diameter and about 1 inch deep; some, which are usually of better quality, are 2 inches deep. Shiny metal pans are best for these because they deflect the heat and the cake cooks quickly and evenly. Loose-bottomed pans facilitate unmolding.

Square cake pan Used for brownies and gingerbread as well as for cakes, the standard sizes are 8 and 9 inches square. Square cake pans are available in the same materials as round cake pans, and also in glass.

Springform pan This is one of the most useful pans in that it can be used for most cake batters. It can also be used for cheesecakes and for layered mousse cakes. The combination of the spring-clip mechanism and loose bottom makes it an excellent pan for easy unmolding of delicate or crumbly textures.

Jelly-roll pan Indispensable for making jelly rolls and other rolled cakes, this pan is also useful as a baking sheet.

Loaf pan These are sold in different sizes, but 5 by 9 inches and 4½ by 8½ inches are the most common. Also called bread pans, these are useful for pound cakes and tea breads as well as the daily loaves, and are the standard pan for meat loaf. Nonstick pans are useful for both bread and cakes.

Muffin pan Muffin pans have 6 or 12 cups and come in three sizes, for regular, miniature, and giant muffins. Related pans, with cups of varying sizes, include those for making mini Bundt cakes, miniature tea cake pans, and fancy bun or muffin pans. These latter, often in cast iron, have decorative cups. Nonstick pans make for easy unmolding.

Specialty cake pans and molds

Some traditional and classic cakes require specially shaped pans; among these is the tube pan used for angel food cake. Pans with loose bottoms are best. Some have three little feet along the top edge for raising the cake up during its upside-down cooling. Bundt pans, used for dense cakes like pound cakes, are fluted tube pans that come in various sizes; a 10-inch pan with a 12-cup capacity is the most useful. The Austrian *kugelhopf* pan is a fluted tube pan used for the enriched sweet bread of the same name.

Other special pans include those for savarins, brioches, and charlottes, all of which can double as molds for mousses and other gelatin-based desserts, so are worth buying to add interest to your culinary repertoire. Pans or molds with depressions for individual madeleines, éclairs, and petits fours are more specialized and therefore less generally useful. Molds for cannoli and cream horns, *coeurs à la crème*, and darioles, etc., also fall into this latter category.

Decorating equipment

Desserts, pastries, and cakes are often decorated using a pastry bag for piping, whether it is writing messages on frosting or making a ring of whipped cream rosettes. Pastry bags are also used for shaping meringues and choux pastry.

Pastry bag These cone-shaped bags are usually made of flexible nylon fabric or plastic-lined cotton that can be easily washed and dried after use. A decorating tube or tip is fitted into the opening in the tip of the bag and the contents are forced through by twisting the top of the bag and then applying gentle hand pressure.

Pastry tube or tip A good set of these will contain large, plain round tips for shaping meringues, cream puffs, or

éclairs, large star tips for piping whipped cream, and a galaxy of smaller tips for delicate and intricate cake icing.

Revolving turntable When decorating a cake, you must have the part you are working on facing you; turntables can be rotated with just a flick of a finger.

Pastry making

Anyone who makes pastry needs good tools because pastry is not improved by handling, and because pastry making turns from a chore to a pleasure if your equipment is well designed and efficient.

Rolling pin Some cooks are perfectly happy to be up to their elbows in flour; those who have this tactile approach to baking will probably opt for a rolling pin made from a single length of wood, which keeps the palms near the dough.

The handled pin is more likely to suit people who prefer to keep food at a distance. The two handles, which are set on an axle and remain stationary in the hands, guide the pin.

The best rolling pins of either type are heavy and of a good size, made of hard, close-grained wood smoothed to a fine, silky finish. Ceramic and marble rolling pins are available, but these break easily and do not roll as well—the smooth surface will not hold a dusting of flour.

Boards and slabs Pastry can be rolled perfectly well on smooth kitchen countertops. A large wooden board can also be used, but to preserve its smooth surface, it should only be used for pastry and not as a bread or cutting board. Polyethylene or acrylic boards are very good for pastry because they are smooth, stay cool, and are easy to clean after use.

Marble slabs These are satin-smooth, impervious to flavors, and keep the pastry cold while it is being worked.

Pie and tart pans

Pie pan Aluminum or black or tinned steel are best. The bottom crust of a pie really needs metal beneath it to crisp—glass and ceramic do not conduct heat well enough and so result in a soggy crust under the filling. This is especially true with wet or juicy fruit fillings.

Deep-dish pie pan For deep-dish pies, choose from earthenware, tempered glass, or porcelain. Pans for deep-dish apple pie and the like are ½ to 1 inch deeper than regular pie pans; there is also a deeper oval pie dish, used for fruit pies and, traditionally, for British savory pies.

Tart pan These are for open-faced tarts, quiches, and flans. Usually fluted for attractive presentation, they come in different shapes and sizes, and may be made of metal or porcelain (when they are sometimes called quiche pans). Removable-bottomed pans are especially good for sweet, rich pastries that are likely to break. To unmold, the bottom is pushed up from the side of the pan so that the tart comes out in one piece. For serving, the tart can be slid off the bottom or left on.

Flan ring and frame An alternative to removable-bottomed tart pans, these come in many more shapes and sizes. Some rings are also called cake or tart rings. All of these are used on a baking sheet and lift off so that the quiche, tart, or other pastry can be easily transferred to a plate or dish.

Other useful equipment

Flour sifter This both aerates flour and blends it with other dry ingredients as called for in a recipe. Sifters come in various sizes and in stainless steel, tinned steel, or plastic. Some have a triple screen rather than just a single one, for finer sifting.

Pastry blender This ingenious tool is most adept at cutting fat into flour and aerating it at the same time. It is made of a series of stainless steel wires curved into a half-oval shape and attached to a handle. The best have deep wires to cope with a large volume of ingredients.

Dough scraper This piece of flexible plastic is used by bakers for scraping up rich pastry doughs from marble slabs and other work surfaces, and for marking and dividing dough into portions. Some dough scrapers are rigid and have handles; these are also called bench scrapers, and look more like tools for smoothing plaster.

Pastry brush Soft natural or nylon bristles will spread egg washes, glazes, jam, or melted butter without damaging the surface of delicate or uncooked pastry. They are also useful for buttering or oiling the awkward grooves and ridges in patterned baking pans and molds.

Sugar and flour dredgers are useful items, usually made of aluminum or stainless steel. They can be used for sprinkling cakes and other desserts with confectioners' sugar or cocoa, and for dusting a work surface with flour.

Electrical appliances

1 toaster
2 coffee grinder
3 combination espresso/ cappuccino and drip coffee machine
4 blender
5 immersion blender
6 ice cream machine
7 heavy-duty stand mixer
8 juice extractor
9 hand-held mixer
10 food processor
11 waffle iron

ELECTRICAL APPLIANCES

There is an ever-increasing choice of electrical appliances for the kitchen. Think hard before you purchase, and don't clutter up valuable counter and cupboard space with bulky machines you hardly ever use.

Blender For blending soups and making vegetable purées, pâtés, and baby food, a blender gives excellent results. Many blenders claim to be able to pulverize nuts, chop vegetables, and grate cheese, but few have the power and the capacity to do so, and it is often just as quick to use a sharp knife. Some blenders offer over a dozen speeds, but these are really unnecessary; in fact, the machines called professional or bar blenders have only two speeds, but they are powerful and efficient.

Choose the largest blender you can, because they rarely work well when the container is more than half-full, and it is time-consuming trying to purée a huge pan of soup in a blender that takes a cup or two at a time. The container should be clear, tempered glass or heavyweight plastic to enable you to see how things are going on; avoid lightweight plastic, which may chip or crack. A small "trap door" in the lid allows you to dribble in your oil for mayonnaise without spattering the kitchen.

Hand-held immersion blender This is excellent for puréeing soup in the pan, thus saving on dish washing. It is also very good for whipping cream, making mayonnaise, and blending small quantities of ingredients.

Food processor The ultimate in kitchen machines, this chops, slices, shreds, pulverizes, and grinds, makes pastry and bread dough, and purées soups and pâté mixtures. Some models go even further and, with attachments and different blades, squeeze citrus fruit,

grind coffee beans, and peel potatoes. They will not beat egg whites effectively, however, so a separate mixer or a rotary beater, or whisk, is still essential.

The more compact the design, the better for countertop storage, but you will still have to find room for the extra blades, disks, and attachments.

Choose a model that has a heavy-duty motor and a large bowl, as, like blenders, they work better if they are no more than half-full. Rubber foot pads will make the machine stay put during any operation.

Hand-held mixer The main advantage of a hand-held electric mixer is that it is faster than a whisk or old-fashioned rotary beater. It also frees one hand to hold the bowl or add ingredients as you beat, and you can move the mixer to beat in every part of the bowl. Choose a mixer with three speeds (high, medium, low) and a switch that is easy to change using your thumb. The beaters should be easy to remove for cleaning. Unless you want a stand mixer, buy a hand mixer with a heavy-duty motor and beaters for tough jobs such as mixing dough.

Stand mixer A heavy-duty stand mixer is useful for many jobs besides cake making. Most have a dough hook attachment and some a separate blender and/or coffee grinder, which can be used with the same motor and base. When a mixer also has such varied attachments as a food grinder, a juice extractor, a pasta maker, a potato peeler, and a shredder and slicer, it has really moved into the next function and price bracket of the all-in-one food processor. Before buying a multifunction apparatus, check that the motor can cope with heavy-duty jobs and is not just a glorified blender/mixer.

The mixer bowl may be made of plastic, stainless steel, or tempered glass; stainless steel or tempered glass is best for durability. In some mixers, the beaters are simply inserted into the motor housing and rotate only in one spot; these often leave a ring of unbeaten ingredients around the bowl. The best machines are those with beaters that travel in a circle as they rotate and thus beat every part of the mixture efficiently. Make sure, too, if you can, that the beaters can handle a small quantity, such as one egg. Mixers with light plastic bases and bowls may be lighter to move around, but a solid base with a rubber pad or feet will prevent the machine from "creeping" during prolonged activity.

Toaster Toasters are very simple electrical gadgets and the vast majority of them do their job efficiently. Some take four slices—a must for the large family—but standard models take two. Some have adjustable slots that are wide enough to take items like thick slices of bread, English muffins, bagels, and croissants without burning; others have one wider and one narrower slot. When selecting a toaster, look for a removable crumb tray—and a long guarantee.

Waffle iron Most waffle iron griddles have the traditional honeycombed surface, but others are embossed with figures or decorative scenes. A nonstick surface prevents waffles from sticking, and thermostat controls ensure the ideal crisp finish.

Juice extractor This offers effortless juice extraction from all kinds of fresh fruits and vegetables. A juice extractor is a worthwhile purchase if you drink a lot of fresh juice, as it will be less expensive than store-bought juices in the long run. Models range from simple and small citrus juicers to large machines with two juicing functions—one for extracting juice from vegetables and fruits such as apples and peaches, the other for juicing citrus fruits. Some models have filters and strainer baskets to separate the juice from the seeds, pulp, and pith.

Deep-fryer A thermostatically controlled, electric deep-fryer with a lid not only takes the guesswork and odor out of deep-frying, it is also the safest way to deep-fry at home. It brings the fat up to the chosen temperature and holds it there; the best models have a light that indicates the desired temperature is reached. Deep-fryers come in various capacities and designs, some with nonstick linings that are easy to keep clean. A good design feature in some models is a basket with handles that clip on the pan so that the fat from the fried food can drain before serving.

Ice cream machine Old methods of ice cream making involved a great deal of cranking and stirring over buckets of crushed ice and rock salt. The latest state-of-the-art ice cream machines have their own compressors and freezers so they sit on the countertop to make ice cream. This kind works very fast and doesn't take up freezer space—it also makes the most velvety smooth ice creams and sorbets. Professional-style models make a large quantity in a very short time. Less expensive electric ice cream machines with rotation motors are not quite as convenient, because they must be put into the freezer, but they also achieve very good results in a very short time. Choose a compact shape, and check that it makes a generous quantity.

Pasta machine A machine that makes the dough from start to finish, cutting out all the hard work of kneading and rolling by hand. The dough can be extruded in a variety of shapes according to the cutting disk used—from long and thin spaghetti and tagliatelle to ridged ziti, flat sheets of lasagne, and noodles.

Bread machine This popular machine mixes all the ingredients, then kneads the dough and bakes it. Most machines are quite compact and sit neatly on the countertop. A programmer allows you to set the time the machine operates, so you can wake up to freshly baked bread in the morning. The machine itself bakes different types of dough in a set loaf shape, but if you want rolls, different-shaped loaves, pizza, or pita bread, etc., you can use the machine just to ready the dough for shaping by hand and then bake it conventionally.

Coffee grinder The advantage of electric coffee grinders over the manual type is that they are quicker, but they are often noisy. The ideal grinder is quiet, efficient, and neat. It is also useful if you can preselect the grind required, from powder to coarse ground. The safest electric coffee grinders are those that will not work unless the lid is on.

Drip coffee machine The electric drip or filter coffee machine is an elaborate version of the drip coffeepot. It heats the water to the right temperature and pulses it through the ground coffee into the pot below; a hotplate under the pot keeps the coffee warm. As long as you put the correct type and amount of coffee in the filter, it's a foolproof way to make decent coffee. You should avoid leaving the pot on the hotplate for too long, however, or the coffee will taste stewed.

Combination coffee machine The most versatile coffee machine is the type that makes filter coffee in a pot on one side and espresso or cappuccino on the other, thus eliminating the need for two separate machines. Before you buy, check that the instructions are easy to follow, and ask for a demonstration if possible. Some espresso and cappuccino machines may look very glamorous and stylish, but they can be fiendishly difficult to use. Other considerations are whether the pump mechanism for frothing the milk for cappuccino is fast and efficient, and whether the water reservoir can be refilled during brewing for uninterrupted use. Pump espresso machines make the best coffee; also available are steam-type machines, which are less expensive but often produce disappointing results.

GRILLING

Cooking outdoors is one of the greatest pleasures of summertime and, to many, grilling is one of the easiest and the most enjoyable ways of preparing food.

Devotees of grilling will not need to be convinced of its benefits, but those who have not tried it should not be put off by the apparently vast selection of tools and equipment available: the rule is, the simpler the better. Food that has been cooked on a piece of chicken wire over a driftwood fire on a beach tastes just as good as—if not better than—food prepared on a elaborate gas-fired grill with a motorized spit.

Types of grills

For those with large backyards, a built-in brick barbecue is worth considering; it allows you to design extra warming racks, cupboards, and preparation surfaces. Sturdy grills made of heavy-gauge metals may be more expensive, but cheaper, flimsier ones are best avoided. Heavy metal and cast-iron grates—also called grids and, of course, just grills—are less likely to bend or become misshapen with repeated use than lightweight nickel-plated and chrome-plated grates, which do have the advantage of being rustproof. The grill wires should be positioned fairly close together for grilling chicken wings, sausages, and the like.

Most people find it is convenient to cook at table height and this is certainly safer for the usual grilling conditions of outdoor light and uneven ground; if you buy a small portable grill or hibachi, you will need to set it on a table or on a board on two stools. Some portable braziers have very short legs—check that they are high enough to cook on in comfort.

Kettle grill As the name suggests, kettle grills are totally enclosed by means of a hinged lid. This may be left open during grilling—it also provides a windbreak—but often the food is cooked with the lid down, which reflects the heat like an oven so that even whole chickens and roasts can be grilled. Made from cast-aluminum or vitreous-enameled steel, kettle grills are popular and versatile—they can also be used for smoke-cooking food.

Wagon-type grill Probably the most elaborate of grills, these carts are usually on wheels and sometimes covered. The

Grilling equipment

1 large grill basket
2 portable grill
3 bamboo and metal skewers
4 fish grill basket
5 sardine grill basket
6 long matches
7 long-handled tongs
8 kettle grill

larger kinds are gas-fired and have all manner of modern cooking aids, such as warming racks, electric rotisseries, thermometers, cutting surfaces, equipment racks, and even gas side burners for stovetop-style cooking. They are bulky and need storage room in winter, but they come into their own if you are cooking for a lot of people.

Hibachi These are small Japanese-style black cast-iron troughs, rectangular or round, with strong wooden-handled grids. The height of the grids is adjustable. Especially useful for taking on picnics and other outings, hibachis come with single, double, or even triple grids, which can be raised to different heights, but they are not adaptable for spit-roasting.

Brazier Often made in unsuitably lightweight materials, braziers are basically round or square trays on legs, and sometimes on wheels. Some have hoods, and spits can be fitted, but the main drawback of braziers is that they are often too low to cook on comfortably. Some models have legs that screw in or fold up, making them as portable as picnic grills.

Portable or picnic grill This is a term that may be applied to the small compact types of brazier that can be easily packed for travel. They may be rectangular or round in shape and are usually made of lightweight metal.

The accessories

There is no real need to assemble a battery of gadgets for grilling, but some specialized items will aid the cook considerably and some are essential for safety reasons.

Heatproof gloves and apron
Protective gloves and an apron are a must when cooking over an open fire to save you from grease splashes and prevent burns from unexpectedly hot grill rack handles. Choose really thick gloves and heavy aprons—and avoid plastic aprons.

Long-handled fork
Useful for lifting and turning food over the heat; those with wooden handles are best.

Tongs
Long-handled tongs are useful, both for moving glowing coals and for lifting and turning pieces of food without piercing them. Wooden handles are best.

Basting brush and bulb baster
Succulent grilled food needs frequent basting. For steaks and chops, a long-handled basting brush is easiest to use, but for large roasts cooked on a rotisserie, a bulb baster allows you to baste over the heat without burning your arms. (Alternatively, use a bunch of rosemary twigs or bay leaves dipped in the marinade or juices as a brush.)

Stiff wire brush
This is ideal for removing burned-on fragments of food from the grill.

Skewers
Long ones are preferable because they enable you to leave the handles outside the fire. Stainless steel skewers will not rust, and those with wooden handles will be easier to use.

Grill baskets and hamburger grill
For tender fish and crumbly hamburgers, you need a wire grill basket to cradle them gently while cooking and to keep them in one piece. Usually made of stainless steel or chrome- or tin-plated steel, grill baskets consist of two sides made of close-set wires hinged together, with two long, flat wire handles. Steaks and hamburgers are cooked in a flat round, square, or rectangular grill; if heated before use, it sears the food with a lovely pattern. Fish grills are curved so that the delicate flesh is not crushed. They are usually shaped in the form of a single large fish, and some have legs on each side to allow them to stand in the coals. Sardine grills are round, with twelve small fish shapes nose-to-nose. All wire baskets and grills need to be greased with oil or butter and heated before use, or the food will stick to them.

Rotisserie
The simplest rotisserie has a long stainless steel spit with a plastic or wooden handle, and two or four sharp angled tines that can be adjusted to hold the bird or roast in place. This sort of rotisserie is usually made to slot into the hood of a barbecue grill. A motor-driven spit with either battery or electrical power is essential for roasting evenly.

Make sure the spit is strong enough to take the heaviest roast without bending, and when loading, always test it for balance before cooking, or you will wear out the motor and the meat will cook most on the heaviest side.

SMOKING

Home smoking—to cook food or to cure it—offers great scope to the adventurous cook. Simply adding aromatic herbs, to enhance the fragrant wood smoke, will produce wonderful flavors.

Hot smoking
Hot smoking is a refinement of grilling: the food is cooked and smoked at the same time. Those people who plan to do a great deal of hot smoking will want to purchase a smoker, but food can also be smoked using an ordinary covered barbecue grill. Sawdust or wood chips are added to the fire to cause a fragrant smoke to flavor and preserve the food. Resinous woods such as pine must never be used, because they will make the food taste more like disinfectant. Favorite woods are apple, hickory, and oak, but any hardwood will do.

The temperature in the smoker depends on the food you are smoking and how strong a smoke flavor you want. Fish and shellfish take well to smoking; most is hot-smoked at temperatures ranging from 120 to 200°F.

Many hot smokers are available, all of which come with full instructions—some use sawdust, or smoke dust, and others use wood chips. No matter what type you have, these are always used outdoors, because there will be a fair amount of smoke and fumes escaping.

Electric smoker
This type of smoker is expensive but convenient. With the combination of a heating element and lava rocks, it keeps an even, constant heat and can be used for fish, meat, and poultry. Wood chips are an optional extra, if you like the additional flavor.

Small stovetop hot smoker
This type of smoker is convenient for smoking small quantities of food indoors. A stovetop smoker looks like a large covered rectangular baking pan; it is fitted with a wire rack and a drip tray. Sawdust is used for the smoke, most of which is contained by the sliding cover (look for a sturdy smoker with a tight-fitting lid), but good ventilation is still important.

Cold smoking
Hot smoking is essentially a method of cooking, but cold smoking, with which it is often confused, is a long process that does not cook the food—with the exception of very small fish—but instead cures it. Before being cold-smoked, all foods must be brined and air-dried.

You can make your own cold smoker from a barrel, or you can convert a hot smoker to a cold smoker. Cold smoking must always be done outdoors.

3

Recipes

Stocks

Making homemade stock is not a costly proposition—inexpensive meat bones, fish frames, chicken giblets, or even a leftover roast chicken carcass can all be made into stock with very little effort. Add whatever vegetables you have to the stock pot, or do without. Or, if you only have vegetables, you can make a good meatless stock. Homemade stock is always the first choice when preparing a recipe, although you could use canned broth (the low-sodium variety has the best flavor) or the good but pricey fresh or frozen stocks now carried by many specialty butchers. But it is well worth trying to get in the habit of making your own stock when convenient, and freezing it for future use in a range of recipes.

Most stocks consist of a straightforward broth of bones and vegetables, and they may be either **white** (a pale stock, made from unbrowned bones, that won't add significant color to the dish in which it is used) or **brown** (a dark stock, achieved with deeply browned bones, that gives a rich color to the end result). There are also two variations to these basic types. **Jellied stock** is a chicken or meat stock that sets lightly when chilled; this is due to the inclusion of a high proportion of gelatinous veal bones or calf's or pig's feet. This stock gives an especially velvety texture to sauces, gravies, and soups, and is an essential component of some cold dishes. If you reduce jellied stock to about one fourth of its original quantity, you will have **meat glaze**, a syrupy jelly used to enrich many classic sauces. Meat glaze is an important ingredient in French restaurant cooking, where it is called *glace de viande*.

Do not salt long-simmered stocks until the very end of the cooking time (or don't salt at all, as you will be salting the dish the stock is used in), because as the stock reduces during simmering, the saltiness will increase. With long-simmered stocks, add the seasoning vegetables after the bones have already simmered for a couple of hours. If the vegetables are cooked from the beginning, together with the bones, they will certainly be overcooked at the end, and can then give a bitter flavor to the stock.

ROAST CHICKEN STOCK

Don't ever throw away the leftover carcass from a roast chicken dinner—it is the beginning of an excellent light-colored, but full-flavored chicken stock that is perfect for soups, stews, and braising. For a jellied stock, add some veal bones—even if you don't need to have the stock jell, the gelatin extracted from the bones will add body to the stock. Be flexible in your choice of seasoning vegetables; leeks and celery are especially good. Cruciferous vegetables such as cabbage or broccoli should be avoided because they are just too strong in flavor, and too many carrots will give an oversweet note. To give a golden tint to the stock, chop the onions with their skins and add the skins to the pot, too.

MAKES ABOUT 1½ QUARTS

1 roast chicken carcass, the larger the better, plus the giblets (no liver) if you have them
1 pound veal bones, sawed into 1-inch-thick pieces by the butcher, or 1 calf's or pig's foot, halved lengthwise (optional)
½ cup dry white wine (optional)
2 medium onions, coarsely chopped
2 medium carrots, coarsely chopped
2 medium leeks, white part only, coarsely chopped
2 medium celery ribs, coarsely chopped
1 bouquet garni of 1 sprig fresh thyme, 1 sprig fresh parsley, and 1 bay leaf
6 whole black peppercorns
Salt, to taste

Break up the chicken carcass and place in a large soup pot with the optional giblets and veal bones. Add enough cold water to cover by 2 inches. Slowly bring to a simmer over medium heat, skimming off any foam that rises to the surface. Add the wine, if using, along with the onions, carrots, leeks, celery, bouquet garni, and peppercorns. Reduce the heat to low. Simmer until the flavor is well concentrated, at least 2 and up to 3 hours. Do not allow the stock to boil, or it will become cloudy. Season with salt.

Strain the stock into a large bowl, pressing lightly on the vegetables to extract all the flavor. (If you want a clear stock, do not press the vegetables.) Let the stock cool to room temperature, then cover and refrigerate until chilled. Scrape off the solidified fat on the surface (save it, if desired, to use in other recipes as an excellent cooking fat). The stock can be kept in the refrigerator for up to 3 days, or frozen for up to 3 months.

Roast Duck Stock: Substitute a roast duck carcass for the chicken carcass.

WHITE VEAL STOCK

Veal stock is very versatile, and can be used for veal, beef, or even chicken dishes, especially stews and roasts. Although marrow bones give lots of flavor to the stock, always include some additional meat, or choose meaty bones like shanks. Not only does the meat enrich the stock, it also helps to keep it relatively clear. Long, slow cooking is very important to draw out the gelatin, salts, and flavor deep in the bones.

MAKES ABOUT 2 QUARTS

- 3 pounds veal bones, sawed into 1-inch pieces by the butcher
- 12 ounces boneless veal shoulder, cut into 1-inch pieces
- ½ cup dry white wine (optional)
- 2 medium onions, coarsely chopped
- 2 medium carrots, coarsely chopped
- 3 small leeks, white part only, coarsely chopped
- 2 medium celery ribs, coarsely chopped
- 1 bouquet garni of 1 sprig fresh thyme, 1 sprig fresh parsley, and 1 bay leaf
- 6 whole black peppercorns
- Salt, to taste

Place the veal bones and shoulder in a large soup pot, and add enough cold water to cover by 2 inches. Slowly bring to a simmer over medium heat, skimming off any foam that rises to the surface. Reduce the heat to low. Simmer for 2 hours. Add the wine, if using, along with the onions, carrots, leeks, celery, bouquet garni, and peppercorns. Continue simmering until the flavor is well concentrated, 2 to 3 more hours. Do not allow the stock to boil at any time. Season with salt.

Strain the stock into a large bowl. Let cool to room temperature, then cover and refrigerate until chilled. Scrape off the solidified fat on the surface. The stock can be kept in the refrigerator for up to 3 days, or frozen for up to 3 months.

White Beef Stock: Use 3 pounds beef bones and 1 pound veal bones, sawed into 1-inch pieces by the butcher, instead of the 3 pounds veal bones. Substitute beef chuck for the veal shoulder.

White Chicken Stock: Substitute 3 pounds chopped chicken bones (such as backs, necks, or wings) and giblets (no liver) for the veal bones and veal shoulder.

BROWN BEEF STOCK

When a hearty, meaty flavor is required in robust soups, stews, and sauces, use this stock. The bones from a roast prime rib of beef would be an excellent addition to the stock pot. Veal stock can be made using veal bones and veal shoulder, and lamb stock using meaty lamb neck bones.

MAKES ABOUT 2 QUARTS, OR ABOUT 3 QUARTS IF USING PRIME RIB BONES

- 4 tablespoons lard or vegetable oil
- 3 pounds beef bones, sawed into 1-inch pieces by the butcher
- 12 ounces boneless beef chuck, cut into 1-inch pieces
- Leftover roast prime rib bones (optional)
- 2 medium onions, unpeeled, coarsely chopped
- 2 medium leeks, coarsely chopped
- 2 medium carrots, coarsely chopped
- 2 medium celery ribs, coarsely chopped
- ½ cup hearty red wine (optional)
- 2 medium tomatoes, seeded and coarsely chopped
- 2 whole cloves
- 4 sprigs fresh parsley
- 3 sprigs fresh thyme
- 1 bay leaf
- ¼ teaspoon whole black peppercorns
- Salt, to taste

In a large stock pot, heat 2 tablespoons of the lard over medium-high heat. In batches, and without crowding, brown the bones and beef chuck on all sides, about 8 minutes. Transfer to a plate. Pour off the fat from the pot. (Alternatively, the bones and chuck can be roasted in a preheated 425°F oven. Put them in a roasting pan, without the fat, and roast, turning occasionally, until well browned, about 45 minutes; remove the bones and set aside. Deglaze the browned bits in the pan on top of the stove with 2 cups water; add this liquid to the stock pot.)

Return the bones and beef chuck to the stock pot, along with the optional roast prime rib bones. Add enough water to cover by 2 inches. Slowly bring to a simmer over medium heat, skimming off any foam that rises to the surface. Simmer for 2 to 3 hours, skimming occasionally.

In a saucepan, heat the remaining 2 tablespoons lard over medium heat. Add the onions, leeks, carrots, and celery and then cook the vegetables, stirring occasionally, until browned, 10 to 15 minutes. Drain off the fat, then add the vegetables to the stock, along with the optional wine, the tomatoes, cloves, parsley, thyme, bay leaf, and peppercorns. Continue simmering until the stock is well flavored, about 2 more hours. Season with salt.

Strain the stock into a large bowl. Let cool to room temperature, then cover and refrigerate the stock until chilled. Scrape off the solidified fat on the surface. The stock can be kept in the refrigerator for up to 3 days, or frozen for up to 3 months.

Meat Glaze: In a large pot, bring the degreased and unsalted stock to a boil over high heat. Reduce the heat to medium and cook at a steady simmer until the stock has reduced to about 1½ quarts, about 1 hour. Transfer to a medium saucepan and continue simmering until reduced to a thick, dark syrup, about 30 minutes. The yield will be about 3 cups. Transfer to small containers (meat glaze is usually used in small quantities). The glaze can be kept in the refrigerator for up to 2 weeks, or frozen for up to 6 months.

Brown Chicken Stock: Substitute 3 pounds chopped chicken bones (such as backs, necks, or wings) and giblets (no liver) for the beef bones and chuck. Roast the chicken bones in a roasting pan in a preheated 400°F oven until browned, about 45 minutes. Discard any fat in the roasting pan, and deglaze the browned bits in the bottom of the pan with 2 cups water. Continue as for Brown Beef Stock above, using white wine instead of red.

Brown Duck Stock: Substitute the chopped carcass, wing tips, neck, giblets (no liver), and excess skin of a 5-pound duck (or 3 pounds chopped duck wings and giblets, available at many Asian butchers) for the beef bones and chuck. Roast the duck bones, following the instructions above for Brown Chicken Stock. Continue as for Brown Beef Stock above.

COURT-BOUILLON

Court-bouillon is used as a poaching medium for fish, and also forms the basis for many fish soups. Before adding fish to court-bouillon for poaching, cool the liquid to room temperature.

MAKES ABOUT 1½ QUARTS

2½ cups dry white wine or 1¼ cups white wine vinegar
1 medium onion, sliced
3 medium carrots, sliced
1 tablespoon unsalted butter
6 sprigs fresh parsley
2 slices of lemon
6 whole black peppercorns
2 bay leaves
Salt, to taste

Combine all of the ingredients in a pot. Season well with salt if using as a poaching liquid for fish; do not salt if using in a soup. Add 5 cups cold water. Bring to a simmer over medium heat. Cook for 20 minutes. If using in a soup, strain the court-bouillon. The court-bouillon can be prepared up to 3 days ahead and kept in the refrigerator.

FISH STOCK

Fish stock is an important ingredient in seafood soups and stews, and, when reduced, is excellent in sauces for fish. Use the bones of white-fleshed fish, such as flounder or cod, and avoid oily, strong-flavored varieties, such as salmon, mackerel, and bluefish. Fish stock is simmered just long enough to release the flavors and gelatin from the bones—long cooking will make the stock bitter. If desired, substitute 1 to 1½ cups dry white wine for some of the water.

MAKES ABOUT 1½ QUARTS

2 pounds fish bones and heads without gills, well rinsed in cold water
3 medium celery ribs, sliced
2 medium onions, sliced
1 medium carrot, sliced
1 bay leaf
Salt, to taste

Place all the ingredients in a large pot (do not add salt if you intend to use the reduced stock in a sauce). Add 10 cups cold water. Bring to a boil over medium heat. Reduce the heat to low and simmer, occasionally skimming off the foam that rises to the surface, until the stock is well flavored, 30 to 45 minutes. Strain into a bowl. The stock can be kept in the refrigerator for up to 3 days, or frozen for up to 3 months.

VEGETABLE STOCK

This vegetable stock may appear to include some unusual ingredients, but these have in fact been carefully chosen to give a very satisfying, savory flavor. You can use this vegetable stock in recipes as a substitute for chicken stock, or in any recipe that is based on legumes, onions, root vegetables, or mushrooms (it is especially good when used as a base for yellow pea, onion, beet, or mushroom soups).

MAKES ABOUT 1½ QUARTS

¾ cup dry white wine
2 tablespoons light soy sauce
2 medium leeks, chopped
1 medium red onion, chopped
4 large mushrooms, sliced
½ cup yellow split peas
½ cup pearl barley
1 teaspoon brown mustard seeds
½ teaspoon fenugreek seeds
Sprigs of fresh parsley
1 bay leaf
A pinch of sugar
Salt and freshly ground pepper, to taste

Place all of the ingredients in a large pot and then add 10 cups water. Bring to a boil over high heat, skimming off all the foam that rises to the surface. Reduce the heat to low and simmer for 1 hour. Strain into a bowl, discarding the last bit of stock, which will be dark and cloudy with sediment. Taste the stock to check the seasoning and adjust if necessary. The stock can be kept in the refrigerator for up to 3 days, or frozen for up to 1 month.

Soups

DELICATE CARROT SOUP

Carrots and potatoes, simmered until tender, are blended to make a light-bodied, pale orange soup.

MAKES 6 SERVINGS

6 medium carrots, coarsely grated
2 medium boiling potatoes, coarsely grated
2 medium onions, coarsely grated
2 tablespoons unsalted butter
3¾ cups chicken stock
3 tablespoons heavy cream
Salt and freshly ground pepper, to taste
2 teaspoons chopped fresh chervil or parsley

In a large, heavy-bottomed saucepan, combine the carrots, potatoes, onions, and butter. Stir over medium heat until the butter melts, then cover the pan and reduce the heat to low. Cook, stirring occasionally, until the vegetables are softened, about 10 minutes. Stir in the stock and bring to a simmer. Cook, uncovered, until the vegetables are very tender, about 20 minutes.

In batches, purée the soup in a blender. Stir in the cream, and season with salt and pepper. At the last minute, stir in the chervil. Serve hot.

CREAMY WILD MUSHROOM SOUP

Mushrooms of all sizes and shapes now fill the produce shelves—make this soup with your favorite, or use a combination. For a richer soup, you can thicken with an egg yolk and cream mixture (called a *liaison* in classic French cooking) rather than flour: in a small bowl, lightly whisk the cream with 3 egg yolks, add a few ladles of the soup, and stir this mixture into the rest of the soup in the pan, along with the parsley and seasoning. Cook over very low heat, stirring, until the soup thickens; do not let it boil or it will curdle.

MAKES 6 SERVINGS

4 tablespoons unsalted butter
½ cup minced shallots
1 garlic clove, minced
8 ounces cultivated wild mushrooms (such as oyster or cremini mushrooms), finely chopped
2 tablespoons all-purpose flour
3 tablespoons dry vermouth
5 cups chicken or vegetable stock
1 cup heavy cream
2 teaspoons chopped fresh parsley
Salt and freshly ground pepper, to taste

In a large saucepan, melt the butter over medium heat. Add the shallots and garlic and cook until softened,

about 3 minutes. Add the mushrooms and stir to mix with the shallots and garlic. Sprinkle with the flour and cook, stirring often, for 2 minutes. Stir in the vermouth. Add the stock and bring to a simmer. Cook over medium-low heat until the mushrooms are very tender, about 15 minutes. Reduce the heat to low. Stir in the heavy cream and parsley, and season with salt and pepper. Heat thoroughly, stirring all the time. Serve hot.

TOMATO AND LEEK SOUP

This is a simple, yet sophisticated, soup, without any need for herbs or spices—as long as you use ripe tomatoes that are full of flavor.

MAKES 6 SERVINGS

1 pound ripe plum tomatoes, cut into quarters
2 medium leeks, white part only, chopped
2 small boiling potatoes, peeled and cut into ½-inch cubes
5 cups chicken stock
Salt and freshly ground white pepper, to taste
3 to 4 tablespoons crème fraîche or sour cream

Place the tomatoes, leeks, and potatoes in a large saucepan. Cover with the stock and bring to a boil over medium heat. Simmer over low heat just until the vegetables are tender, 25 to 30 minutes. In batches, purée the soup in a blender, then strain through a sieve to remove the tomato seeds and skin. Season to taste, and stir in half the crème fraîche. Serve in soup bowls, topping each serving with a swirl of the remaining crème fraîche.

SPRING GREENS SOUP

Sorrel gives this soup a beautiful velvety consistency and a refreshing, slightly acidic edge that will lift jaded appetites. If desired, top with freshly made small croutons.

MAKES 4 TO 6 SERVINGS

3 tablespoons unsalted butter
1 medium onion, chopped
12 ounces fresh sorrel, tough stems discarded and leaves chopped
1 small head Boston lettuce, cored and coarsely chopped
1 tablespoon chopped fresh chervil or parsley
3¾ cups chicken stock, heated to boiling
3 large egg yolks
Salt and freshly ground pepper, to taste
4 to 6 tablespoons heavy cream, for garnish

RUSSIAN BORSCHT

In a large saucepan, melt the butter over medium-low heat. Add the chopped onion and cook until soft and translucent, about 5 minutes. Add the sorrel, lettuce, and chervil. Continue cooking until the greens have all wilted, about 5 minutes, turning them over occasionally. Add the boiling stock. Simmer over low heat until the greens are very tender, 10 to 15 minutes.

In batches, purée in a blender. Strain the soup through a fine wire sieve to remove the sorrel fibers. Return the soup to the saucepan and heat to just below a simmer. Reduce the heat to low. In a small bowl, whisk the egg yolks. Gradually whisk in about 3 to 4 tablespoons of the hot soup. Stir this mixture into the remaining soup in the saucepan and continue stirring just until the soup is slightly thickened. Do not boil, or the soup will curdle. Season with salt and pepper. Serve the soup in individual bowls, adding a tablespoon of cream to each serving.

Cream of Spinach Soup: Substitute 1 pound fresh spinach leaves, tough stems discarded and leaves coarsely chopped, for the sorrel and lettuce.

PUMPKIN SOUP

Cheese or sugar pumpkins make better soup than the jack o'lantern variety. Rather than using a whole pumpkin, you can also use a wedge of pumpkin or another large winter squash such as calabasa or hubbard. For a dramatic presentation, hollow out a pumpkin and use it as a soup tureen (double the quantities for a large pumpkin).

MAKES 8 OR MORE SERVINGS
  1 small (1-pound) pumpkin or 1-pound winter squash
  2 large leeks
  5 cups chicken stock
  2 cups milk
  2 sprigs fresh basil, leaves chopped, or ½ teaspoon
    dried basil

A pinch of grated nutmeg
Salt and freshly ground pepper, to taste
2 tablespoons unsalted butter
3 tablespoons heavy cream

Cut the pumpkin into 1-inch cubes, discarding the seeds and fibers, and pare away the skin. Thinly slice the white part of the leeks into rounds. Thinly slice enough of the tender pale green part of the leeks to make ½ cup; set aside. Place the pumpkin cubes and white leek rounds in a medium saucepan. Add ⅓ cup water. Cover and cook over medium-low heat, stirring often to be sure the vegetables aren't sticking to the pan, until they are very soft and can be mashed, about 20 minutes. Transfer to a blender in batches and purée.

Return the purée to the cleaned saucepan and stir in the stock, milk, basil, and nutmeg. Season with salt and pepper. Let cook over low heat, stirring often, until heated through. Meanwhile, in a medium saucepan, melt the butter over medium-low heat. Add the pale green leek rounds and cook just until tender, about 5 minutes. Stir the green leek rounds and cream into the soup and heat through. Serve immediately.

RUSSIAN BORSCHT

Borscht can be made with either beef stock, which gives it more depth of flavor, or vegetable stock, which lightens its character considerably.

MAKES 8 OR MORE SERVINGS

2 tablespoons unsalted butter
2 medium beets, peeled and finely chopped
½ small head white cabbage, cored and finely chopped
2 medium onions, finely chopped
2 medium leeks, white part only, finely chopped
2 medium celery ribs, finely chopped
2½ quarts beef stock, well skimmed of fat, or vegetable stock
1 teaspoon caraway seeds
1 bouquet garni of 1 sprig fresh thyme, 1 sprig fresh parsley, and 1 bay leaf
A pinch of grated nutmeg
Salt and freshly ground pepper, to taste
½ cup hearty red wine
2 tablespoons red wine vinegar
2 teaspoons granulated sugar
1 large cooked beet, grated or cut into thin strips
⅔ cup sour cream, for garnish

In a large soup pot, melt the butter over medium-low heat. Add the beets, cabbage, onions, leeks, and celery, and cook until the vegetables are softened, about 5 minutes. Add the stock, caraway seeds,

bouquet garni, and nutmeg, and season lightly with salt and pepper. Bring to a simmer over medium heat, then reduce the heat to low. Simmer for 1 hour. Add the wine, vinegar, and sugar, and simmer until the vegetables are very tender, about 20 minutes longer. Add the grated cooked beet and heat through. Remove the bouquet garni and taste the soup to check the seasoning. Serve in soup bowls, garnishing each serving with a dollop of sour cream.

CLASSIC FRENCH ONION SOUP

In France, this famous and filling soup is often enjoyed in trencherman proportions as a late-night meal in itself, but here it is usually presented in more manageable servings as a first course. While a French cook would traditionally use beef stock, vegetable stock makes this an excellent meatless soup. One important note of authenticity is the spoonful of caramelized sugar; this is added to give a mellow brown color to the soup.

MAKES 6 SERVINGS

4 tablespoons unsalted butter
2 to 3 Spanish onions (1 pound), thinly sliced
5 cups beef stock, heated to boiling
2 sprigs fresh fennel leaves or ¼ teaspoon fennel seeds
1 whole clove
Salt and freshly ground pepper, to taste
1 teaspoon granulated sugar
12 (½-inch-thick) slices crusty French bread, cut on the diagonal
1 tablespoon brandy
1½ cups shredded Gruyère or other Swiss cheese

In a large saucepan, melt the butter over medium-low heat. Add the onions and cook, stirring occasionally, until they are very soft, translucent, and golden, about 10 minutes. Add the boiling stock, fennel, and clove, and season with salt and pepper.

Place the granulated sugar in a long-handled, large metal spoon. Hold it under a broiler or, alternatively, over a gas flame and heat until the sugar melts and caramelizes to a deep brown color. Stir this into the soup. Bring the soup to a boil, then simmer over low heat for 30 minutes.

Preheat the broiler. Toast the slices of bread under the broiler, turning once, until golden-brown on both sides. Discard the fennel sprigs from the soup, and stir in the brandy. Ladle the soup into heatproof bowls. Thickly cover each piece of toast with shredded Gruyère. Float 2 pieces of toast on top of each serving. Broil until the cheese is melted and bubbling, 1 to 2 minutes. Serve immediately.

OLD-FASHIONED CHICKEN SOUP

The best chicken soup has a golden broth so delicious you can enjoy it all by itself—the extras, like rice and noodles, are really superfluous. Chicken soup is best understood by the Italians, who use it in delicate ways such as *stracciatella* (with just a couple of eggs stirred into it to form tender flakes). Start with a good chicken, preferably free-range. If you can find one, a stewing hen will give superior flavor. For a really terrific, doubly delicious soup, simmer the chicken in previously made chicken stock.

MAKES 6 TO 8 SERVINGS

    1 (4-pound) roasting chicken or 1 (5-pound) stewing
       hen, with the giblets (no liver), rinsed and patted dry
    2 medium onions, unpeeled, coarsely chopped
    1 medium leek, coarsely chopped
    1 medium carrot, coarsely chopped
    1 medium celery rib, coarsely chopped
    2 medium shallots, coarsely chopped
    ½ cup dry white wine
    6 whole black peppercorns
    8 sprigs fresh parsley
    2½ quarts chicken stock or water
    Salt, to taste

Place the chicken, breastside down, in a large pot. Add the remaining ingredients. Bring to a simmer over medium heat, skimming off any foam that rises to the surface. Reduce the heat to medium-low and simmer, skimming occasionally, until the chicken is tender, about 1 hour for the roasting chicken and 2 to 2½ hours for the stewing hen.

   Remove the chicken from the broth. Strain the broth, but do not press on the vegetables. Let the broth stand for about 5 minutes, then skim off the clear yellow fat from the surface. Season with salt. Serve the soup in bowls, with the carved chicken served as a separate main course. Or, discard the chicken bones and skin, cut the meat into bite-sized pieces, and stir into the soup. If desired, save any leftover soup for use as a chicken stock.

Stracciatella: In a large saucepan, bring the strained broth to a boil over medium heat. In a small bowl, lightly beat 2 large eggs with an optional 2 tablespoons freshly grated Parmesan cheese and a seasoning of salt and pepper. Whisking constantly, pour the eggs into the boiling broth, and continue whisking until the eggs form tiny flakes, about 2 minutes.

Chicken and Rice Soup: In a large saucepan, bring the strained broth to a boil over medium heat. Add ½ cup long-grain rice and cook until the rice is tender, about 15 minutes.

Chicken and Noodle Soup: In a large saucepan, bring the strained broth to a boil over medium heat. Add 6 ounces dried egg noodles and cook until the noodles are tender, about 15 minutes.

RIBOLLITA

This hearty Tuscan soup is called *ribollita* (reboiled) because it was originally made with leftover vegetables, cooked with the addition of beans and their liquid. The version here reheats very well. It is traditional to douse chunks of day-old country bread in the soup. Try using rosemary bread for a particularly delicious winter lunch.

MAKES AT LEAST 8 SERVINGS

    4 tablespoons olive oil, plus extra for serving
    1 medium red onion, chopped
    2 garlic cloves, chopped
    ½ cup chopped fresh parsley
    1 small head green cabbage, preferably Savoy,
       coarsely chopped
    8 ounces Swiss chard, including stems,
       coarsely chopped
    4 large ripe tomatoes, peeled, seeded, and chopped
    3 medium boiling potatoes, peeled and cut into
       ½-inch cubes
    2 quarts chicken or vegetable stock
    2 medium yellow squash or zucchini, cut into
       ½-inch pieces
    1 cup dried white beans, cooked and drained
    Salt and freshly ground pepper, to taste
    Chunks of day-old country-style bread
    Freshly grated Parmesan cheese, for serving.

In a large soup pot, heat the oil over medium heat. Add the onion, garlic, and parsley and cook until the onion is softened, about 5 minutes. Add half of the cabbage (with the thick ribs) and the chard stems, reserving the more tender leaves. Stir in the tomatoes and potatoes. Cook, stirring all the time, for about 2 minutes. Add the stock and bring to a boil over high heat. Reduce the heat to low and simmer for 1 hour. Add the squash or zucchini and cooked white beans and simmer about 20 minutes longer. Season with salt and pepper.

   In another large pot, plunge the reserved cabbage and chard leaves into lightly salted boiling water and cook until just tender, about 2 minutes. Drain well and add to the soup. Bring it back to a boil.

   Put chunks of bread into warmed soup bowls and ladle the hot soup over the top. Pass a bowl of Parmesan cheese and a cruet of olive oil on the side, so each guest can add them to taste.

VARIATION: After adding the cabbage and chard to the soup, put it into a casserole. Cover the surface of the soup with slices of toasted Italian bread and sprinkle with freshly grated Parmesan cheese. Bake in a preheated 350°F oven for 30 minutes.

NEW MEXICAN CHICKEN POZOLE

Pozole (which is also the Mexican word for hominy) is usually made with pork. This is a lighter, but equally satisfying, version. Each guest can sprinkle their serving with an assortment of garnishes to taste.

MAKES 6 TO 8 SERVINGS

2 tablespoons olive oil
6 chicken thighs
1 large zucchini, cut into ½-inch-thick rounds
1 medium onion, chopped
1 medium bell pepper, seeded and chopped
1 fresh hot green chile pepper (such as jalapeño), seeded and minced
2 garlic cloves, minced
4 cups chicken stock
1 teaspoon dried oregano
1 bay leaf
2 cups canned hominy, drained and rinsed
Salt and freshly ground pepper, to taste
Grated radishes, cubed avocado, shredded Monterey Jack cheese, lime wedges, and chopped black olives, for garnish

In a soup pot, heat the oil over medium heat. Add the chicken thighs and brown on both sides, about 8 minutes. Transfer to a plate and set aside. Add the zucchini, onion, bell pepper, chile pepper, and garlic to the pot. Cover and cook, stirring occasionally, until the vegetables are softened, about 10 minutes. Return the chicken to the pot. Stir in the chicken stock, oregano, and bay leaf. Bring to a simmer, then reduce the heat to low and simmer until the chicken is tender, about 40 minutes. Remove the chicken, discard the skin and bones, and chop the meat into bite-sized pieces. Stir the chicken back into the soup, along with the hominy, and season with salt and pepper. Cook until the hominy is heated through, about 5 minutes. Serve the soup in deep soup bowls, accompanied by small bowls of the garnishes.

SAUSAGE AND BEER GUMBO

Gumbo is a spicy, rib-sticking meal-in-a-pot that has dozens of variations. The name probably comes from the Bantu word for okra, the vegetable whose juices act as a natural thickening.

MAKES 8 SERVINGS

2 tablespoons vegetable oil
1 pound Cajun andouille or kielbasa sausage, cut into ½-inch-thick rounds
1 large onion, chopped
1 medium green bell pepper, seeded and chopped
2 medium celery ribs with leaves, chopped
2 garlic cloves, minced
¼ cup all-purpose flour
1 teaspoon sweet or hot Hungarian paprika
1 teaspoon dried basil
1 teaspoon dried thyme
½ teaspoon freshly ground pepper
¼ teaspoon cayenne pepper
4 cups chicken stock
1½ pounds ripe plum tomatoes, peeled, seeded, and chopped; or use drained canned tomatoes
1 (12-ounce) bottle or can lager beer
10 ounces fresh or frozen okra, cut into ¼-inch-thick rounds
Salt, to taste
Hot cooked rice, for serving

In a large soup pot, heat the oil over medium heat. Add the sausage and cook, turning once, until browned on both sides, about 5 minutes. Transfer to paper towels to drain, leaving the oil in the pot. Add the onion, bell pepper, and celery to the pot. Cover and cook, stirring often, until the vegetables are well softened, about 10 minutes. Add the garlic and cook for 1 minute. Stir in the flour and cook, stirring almost constantly, until well browned but not scorched, about 4 minutes. Stir in the paprika, basil, thyme, pepper, and cayenne and stir for 1 minute. Add the chicken stock, tomatoes, and beer and bring to a boil. Reduce the heat to low and simmer for 30 minutes. Stir in the okra and the reserved sausage, and cook until the okra is tender, about 10 minutes. Season with salt. To serve, spoon rice into individual soup bowls, and ladle in the gumbo.

BOUILLABAISSE

It is often argued that bouillabaisse is very much a fish stew of its birthplace, and cannot be made authentically outside of Provence. Authenticity is hardly to the point when something is as delicious as this, made with the best local fish at hand. If possible, buy fish with bones and have it filleted, so that you will have the bones to make the stock. Bouillabaisse is traditionally served in two courses, with the broth served first, then the fish presented as the entrée, both accompanied by the spicy garlic mayonnaise, rouille. Here, bouillabaisse is served as a hearty main course soup.

MAKES 6 TO 8 SERVINGS

3 pounds assorted boneless fresh fish (fillets or steaks),
   such as monkfish, cod, haddock, snapper, and bass

3 large ripe tomatoes, peeled, seeded, and chopped

2 medium onions, chopped

3 garlic cloves, minced

½ cup olive oil

1 bouquet garni of 4 sprigs fresh fennel or ½ teaspoon
   fennel seeds, 3 sprigs fresh thyme, a 3-inch strip of
   orange zest, and 1 bay leaf

A large pinch of saffron threads, soaked in ½ cup
   white wine

Salt and freshly ground pepper, to taste

6 cups fish stock

6 slices crusty French bread, dried in the oven or toasted

Rouille, for serving

1 cup shredded Gruyère or Swiss cheese

2 tablespoons chopped fresh parsley

Cut all the fish into thick slices or chunks. Cover and
refrigerate until ready to add to the soup.

   In a large saucepan, combine the tomatoes,
onions, garlic, olive oil, bouquet garni, and saffron
and wine mixture. Season with salt and pepper. Bring
to a boil over medium-high heat and boil rapidly,
stirring often, until the onion is softened, about
5 minutes. Add the fish stock. Return to a rapid boil
and boil furiously for 10 minutes. (It is important that
the broth is boiled, to amalgamate the oil and stock.)
Reduce the heat to low and add the fish. Cook at a
gentle simmer until the fish is just firm and opaque,
4 to 5 minutes.

   Remove the bouquet garni. Ladle the soup into
individual bowls. Spread each slice of bread with rouille
and sprinkle with a little Gruyère cheese. Float a slice
on each serving and sprinkle with chopped parsley.
Serve immediately.

PROVENÇAL VEGETABLE SOUP WITH BASIL

Another vegetable and bean soup from the
Mediterranean canon, this one is made especially
aromatic with the addition of *pistou*, a basil purée that
is very closely related to Italian pesto. The soup can
be made ahead and reheated, but don't add the *pistou*
until just before serving, as the heat will eventually
darken the basil.

MAKES 6 SERVINGS

3 tablespoons olive oil

1 large onion, finely chopped

1 pound ripe plum tomatoes, peeled, seeded, and
   chopped, or use canned

Salt and freshly ground pepper, to taste

8 ounces green beans, cut into ½-inch lengths

1 large zucchini, cut into ½-inch cubes

2 medium boiling potatoes, peeled and cut into
   ½-inch cubes

¾ cup dried white beans, cooked (reserve the cooking
   water), or 1 (16-ounce) can cannellini beans, drained

¼ cup broken (½-inch pieces) thin pasta, such
   as vermicelli

1 cup coarsely shredded Emmentaler or Swiss cheese

Pistou

   1 cup packed fresh basil leaves

   3 garlic cloves, chopped

   3 tablespoons olive oil

   Salt and freshly ground pepper, to taste

In a large soup pot, heat the oil over medium heat.
Add the onion and cook, stirring often, until soft and
translucent, about 5 minutes. Add the tomatoes and
cook, stirring often, until they form a sauce, 10 to
15 minutes. Add 6 cups water, and season with salt
and pepper. Increase the heat to medium-high and
bring to a boil. Add the green beans, zucchini, and
potatoes, and simmer for 10 minutes. Add the cooked
white beans, along with their cooking water (if using
canned beans, add them with 2 cups water). Add the
vermicelli. Cook until all the vegetables and the pasta
are tender, about 5 minutes longer.

   Meanwhile, to make the *pistou*, place the basil and
garlic in a blender or a food processor fitted with the
metal blade and blend to a coarse paste. With the
machine running, add the oil to make a thick, green
paste. Season with salt and pepper.

   Stir the *pistou* into the soup. Serve the soup in
individual bowls, passing a bowl of Emmentaler
cheese so each guest can add it to taste.

SALMON CIOPPINO

From Monterey to Seattle, Italian and Portuguese
fishermen argue about whose cuisine introduced the fish
soup, cioppino, into West Coast cookery. It can be made
with just about any Pacific fish, but its sturdy tomato,
wine, and herb basis is especially good with salmon.

MAKES 6 SERVINGS

3 tablespoons olive oil

1 medium onion, chopped

2 medium celery ribs, chopped

½ cup chopped fennel bulb, or 1 additional celery rib

2 garlic cloves, minced

1 cup hearty red wine

2 pounds ripe plum tomatoes, peeled, seeded, and
   chopped; or use drained canned tomatoes

PROVENÇAL VEGETABLE SOUP WITH BASIL

¼ cup chopped fresh parsley
1 teaspoon dried basil
1 teaspoon dried oregano
1 bay leaf
¼ teaspoon chile flakes
3 cups fish stock
1½ pounds skinless salmon fillets, cut into 1-inch cubes
Salt and freshly ground pepper, to taste

In a very large soup pot, heat the oil over medium heat. Add the onion, celery, fennel, and garlic. Cover and cook until the vegetables are softened, about 10 minutes. Add the wine and cook, uncovered, until reduced by half, about 5 minutes. Add the tomatoes, parsley, basil, oregano, bay leaf, and chile flakes and cook for 5 minutes. Stir in the fish stock and bring to a boil. Reduce the heat to low and simmer, with the pot partially covered, for 30 minutes. Add the cubes of salmon and cook, covered, until the fish is firm, about 5 minutes. Season with salt and pepper to taste, and serve hot.

NEW ENGLAND FISH CHOWDER

This ivory-colored stew, slightly thickened with potatoes and cream, is appetizing in both appearance and taste.

MAKES 6 TO 8 SERVINGS
  1½ pounds cod or haddock steaks
  4 ounces salt pork or slab bacon, rind removed, cut into small dice
  1 large onion, thinly sliced
  3 large boiling potatoes, peeled and sliced into rounds
  Salt and freshly ground pepper, to taste
  2 cups milk
  ⅔ cup heavy cream, heated
  2 to 4 tablespoons unsalted butter

Remove the skin and bones from the fish and place in a medium saucepan. Cut the fish into 1-inch pieces and set aside. Add 2 cups water to the skin and bones in the saucepan and bring to a boil. Reduce the heat to low and simmer for 15 minutes. Strain the fish stock into a bowl and set aside.

In a medium saucepan, cook the salt pork over medium-low heat until the fat begins to render, about 5 minutes. Stir in the onion, cover the pan, and cook until the onion is translucent and very soft, about 10 minutes. Set aside.

In a large saucepan, combine the potatoes, 2 cups water, and a pinch of salt. Bring to a boil over medium heat, then reduce the heat to low. Cover and simmer for 15 minutes. Add the reserved fish stock, the milk, and the onion and salt pork mixture. Bring to a simmer. Add the pieces of fish and cook, uncovered, until firm and opaque, about 10 minutes. Add the hot cream and butter, and heat through without boiling. Season with pepper and serve hot.

Clam Chowder: Omit the cod or haddock steaks. Place 2 dozen littleneck clams, well scrubbed, in a large pot with ½ cup water. Cover tightly and cook over high heat, shaking the pot often, until the clams are opened, about 5 minutes. Discard any unopened clams. Remove the meat from the shells and reserve. Strain the clam broth through cheesecloth; if necessary add enough water to make 2 cups. Use the clam broth instead of the fish stock. After adding the broth (with the milk and onion/salt pork mixture) simmer for about 10 minutes. Stir in the reserved clams with the cream and butter.

Oyster Chowder: Omit the cod or haddock. Shuck 16 oysters, reserving and straining the oyster liquor. Set the oyster meat aside. Add enough fish stock or water to the oyster liquor to make 2 cups and use instead of the fish stock. Stir in the oysters with the cream and butter.

SHRIMP AND CORN CHOWDER

A fine representative of New American cooking that blends regional specialties to make a delicious hybrid.

MAKES 6 TO 8 SERVINGS
    1 pound medium shrimp, peeled (shells reserved) and deveined
    3 cups fish or chicken stock
    4 strips bacon
    2 medium celery ribs, chopped
    1 medium red bell pepper, seeded and chopped
    2 cups fresh or defrosted corn kernels
    4 scallions, white and green parts, chopped
    2 cups half-and-half
    Salt and Tabasco sauce, to taste
    Chopped fresh parsley, for garnish

In a small pot, simmer the shrimp shells with the stock over medium-low heat for 10 minutes. Strain the broth and reserve. In a large soup pot, cook the bacon over medium heat until crisp, about 5 minutes. Transfer to paper towels to drain, leaving the bacon fat in the pot. Add the celery, red bell pepper, and corn to the pot. Cook until the peppers are softened, about 5 minutes. Add the scallions and cook until wilted, about 3 minutes. Stir in the reserved broth and the half-and-half. Bring to a simmer and then cook for 5 minutes over low heat. Stir in the shrimp and cook just until firm and pink, about 5 minutes. Season with salt and Tabasco sauce. Serve hot, sprinkled with the parsley and crumbled bacon.

Crab and Corn Chowder: Use fish stock and do not simmer the shrimp shells. Substitute ½ pound crabmeat, picked over for cartilage, for the shrimp.

SHRIMP AND FENNEL BISQUE

Bisques, the richest and creamiest of soups, are usually made from shellfish. This version is enhanced with the licorice-like taste of fennel. If you like, set aside some of the fennel greens to sprinkle on the soup as a garnish.

MAKES 6 SERVINGS
    1 pound medium shrimp, peeled (shells reserved), deveined, and coarsely chopped
    5 cups fish stock
    ⅔ cup dry white wine
    1 small head fennel, white bulb sliced and leafy green tops reserved
    2 medium onions, thinly sliced
    1 sprig fresh parsley
    2 bay leaves
    4 tablespoons unsalted butter
    1 sprig fresh thyme
    4 tablespoons all-purpose flour
    1¼ cups milk
    ¼ cup heavy cream
    1 tablespoon brandy
    Salt and freshly ground white pepper, to taste

Combine the shrimp shells, fish stock, wine, fennel greens, 1 sliced onion, parsley, and 1 bay leaf in a medium saucepan. Bring to a boil over high heat. Reduce the heat to low and simmer for 25 minutes. Strain the stock and set aside.

In a large saucepan, heat 3 tablespoons of the butter over medium heat. Add the remaining sliced onion and bay leaf with the thyme. Cook, stirring often, until the onion has softened, about 5 minutes. Add the shrimp and cook for 2 minutes. Sprinkle with the flour and stir well. Gradually add the reserved stock, stirring. Bring to a simmer, then cook over medium-low heat for 20 minutes. Discard the bay leaf and thyme sprig. In batches, purée the soup in a blender, and return to the saucepan. Add the milk and set aside.

In a saucepan, heat the remaining 1 tablespoon butter over medium-low heat. Add the sliced fennel bulb. Cover and cook until tender, 15 to 20 minutes. Stir the fennel into the soup, with the cream and brandy, and heat gently. Season and serve hot.

HOT-AND-SOUR SHELLFISH SOUP

This soup is loosely based on a Thai soup, with a bit of hot-and-sour Chinese influence thrown in. You can use any kind of shellfish, but mussels will contribute a good amount of juices to the broth.

MAKES 4 SERVINGS
2 tablespoons vegetable oil
2 medium onions, finely chopped
4 garlic cloves, sliced
2 pounds mussels, scrubbed and debearded, if necessary
2½ cups chicken stock
2 stems lemon grass, tender inner leaves only, chopped
1 (2-inch) piece fresh ginger, sliced
6 kaffir lime leaves, or grated zest of 1 lime
12 fresh cilantro sprigs with stems and leaves chopped separately
3 tablespoons rice vinegar
1 teaspoon granulated sugar
¼ cup fish sauce
2 tablespoons lime juice
1 pound medium shrimp, cooked, peeled, and deveined
1 teaspoon arrowroot or cornstarch, mixed with 1 tablespoon water
3 hot fresh chile peppers (such as bird or serrano), seeded and finely chopped

In a large saucepan, heat the oil over medium heat. Add the onions and garlic and cook until lightly browned, about 8 minutes. Add the mussels. Cover the pan and cook until the mussels have opened, about 5 minutes. Using a slotted spoon, lift out the mussels and set aside on a plate. When cool enough to handle, shell the mussels and reserve the meat.

Add the chicken stock to the mussel juices in the saucepan, along with the lemon grass, ginger, lime leaves, and cilantro stems. Bring to a boil. Reduce the heat, and simmer for 30 minutes. Add the vinegar and sugar and simmer for 3 or 4 minutes. Strain the broth.

Return the broth to the pan, add the fish sauce and lime juice, and bring to a simmer. Add the shrimp and mussels. Stir in the arrowroot mixture and cook until

the broth is slightly thickened, 1 minute. Stir in the chiles and cilantro leaves. Remove from the heat, cover, and leave to stand for 5 minutes before serving.

COLD CUCUMBER AND MINT SOUP

This refreshing soup is for occasions calling for an elegant first course that can be prepared quickly.

MAKES 4 TO 6 SERVINGS
1½ large English cucumbers, coarsely chopped
1¼ cups sour cream
1¼ cups plain low-fat yogurt
2 cups cold chicken stock, well skimmed of fat
¼ cup chopped fresh mint leaves
Salt, to taste
½ cup heavy cream, chilled
Sweet Hungarian paprika, for garnish

In batches, purée the cucumbers, sour cream, and yogurt in a blender. Transfer to a bowl and stir in the stock and mint. Cover and chill, about 2 hours. Season with salt. Whip the cream. Serve topped with a dollop of cream and a sprinkling of paprika.

CAULIFLOWER VICHYSSOISE

A particularly fresh and delicate version of the classic summertime soup. Serve with croutons.

MAKES 8 SERVINGS
4 tablespoons unsalted butter
1 (1-pound) head cauliflower, trimmed and cut into small florets
2 small boiling potatoes (8 ounces), peeled and cut into ½-inch cubes
2 shallots or 1 small onion, chopped
2 cups chicken stock, well skimmed of fat
⅔ cup dry white wine
A pinch of grated nutmeg
Salt and freshly ground white pepper, to taste
4 cups milk
⅔ cup heavy cream

In a heavy-bottomed saucepan, melt the butter. Add the cauliflower, potatoes, and shallots and cook, stirring, until softened but not browned, 5 minutes. Add the stock and wine and bring to a boil. Add the nutmeg, and season. Simmer over medium-low heat until the vegetables are very tender, about 25 minutes.

In batches, purée the soup in a blender. Transfer to a large bowl and stir in the milk. Cover and refrigerate until well chilled, at least 2 hours. Check the seasoning and serve, drizzling each serving with heavy cream.

Sauces and Marinades

WHITE SAUCE

White sauce is one of the most versatile of all sauces. To name just three variations, it can be turned into a classic *sauce béchamel*, or flavored with cheese, or made with stock to achieve a totally different result. To make a thin white sauce, suitable for serving as an accompaniment to poached fish or chicken, use 1 tablespoon each butter and flour. The secret of a fine white sauce is to let the roux bubble gently at the beginning without browning.

MAKES ABOUT 2 CUPS
- 3 tablespoons unsalted butter
- 2 tablespoons all-purpose flour
- 2 cups milk
- Salt and freshly ground white pepper, to taste

In a medium saucepan, heat 2 tablespoons of the butter over medium-low heat. Stir in the flour. Let cook and bubble gently without browning for 1 to 2 minutes. Gradually stir in the milk, using a wooden spoon. Season with salt and pepper. Cover the pan and simmer the sauce over very low heat, stirring occasionally, for about 15 minutes. Off the heat, whisk in the remaining 1 tablespoon butter in small pieces to give the sauce a velvety texture.

Béchamel Sauce: Pour the milk into a medium saucepan and add 1 sliced onion, 1 bay leaf, and 4 or 5 whole cloves. Scald the milk over medium heat, then remove from the heat, cover the pan, and let infuse for 10 minutes. Strain the flavored milk. Make the roux as for White Sauce, then let it cool a little before stirring in the hot milk. Continue making the sauce as above.
Cheese Sauce (*Sauce Mornay*): Remove the White Sauce or Béchamel Sauce from the heat, and stir in ¼ cup freshly grated Parmesan cheese and ¼ cup shredded Emmentaler cheese. Do not season the sauce until after the cheese has been added, as the cheese is salty. Add a little cayenne pepper and a pinch of grated nutmeg, too.
Velvety White Sauce (*Sauce Velouté*): Substitute 3 cups white chicken stock (or 2¾ cups stock and ¼ cup dry white wine) for the milk. Season with salt, pepper, and a pinch of grated nutmeg. If desired, add a bouquet garni. Cover and cook for about 25 minutes. Remove the bouquet garni before serving.

BROWN SAUCE

Brown sauce is an important component of classic French cooking, used as an ingredient and to create other sauces. Originally thickened with a flour and butter roux, most contemporary chefs prefer the lighter (and quicker) results achieved with arrowroot or potato starch. The sauce is only as good as the stock it is made with, so always use homemade.

MAKES ABOUT 2 CUPS
- 2 cups brown beef or veal stock
- 4 teaspoons arrowroot, potato starch, or cornstarch
- 2 tablespoons Madeira or dry sherry

In a medium saucepan, bring the stock to a simmer over medium heat. Mix the arrowroot with the Madeira, and whisk into the stock. Simmer, whisking constantly, just until the sauce is thickened. The sauce can be kept, covered, in the refrigerator for up to 3 days; reheat gently for serving.

Red Wine Sauce (*Sauce Bordelaise*): This is a classic sauce for grilled beef steaks. In a medium saucepan, melt 1 tablespoon butter over medium heat. Add 2 tablespoons minced shallot and cook until softened, about 3 minutes. Add 1 cup red wine. Bring to a boil and boil until reduced to 2 tablespoons. Stir in the Brown Sauce and bring just to a simmer.

HOLLANDAISE SAUCE

Serve warm with poached fish (especially salmon) or shellfish, and with asparagus or broccoli.

MAKES ABOUT 1 CUP
- 2 extra large egg yolks
- 1 tablespoon white wine vinegar or lemon juice
- 10 tablespoons (1¼ sticks) unsalted butter, at room temperature
- Salt and freshly ground white pepper, to taste

Whisk the egg yolks and vinegar in a double boiler insert. Place the insert over a saucepan of hot, not simmering, water, over low heat (do not let the base of the insert touch the water). Stirring constantly with a wooden spoon, add the butter, 1 tablespoon at a time. Stir until each addition of butter is thoroughly incorporated before adding the next. Occasionally scrape down any sauce that splashes onto the side of the insert. If the sauce seems to be thickening too fast, immediately remove the insert to a bowl of cold water and stir the sauce to cool it quickly. If the sauce isn't thickening at all, increase the heat slightly. The finished sauce should be smooth and creamy. If desired, thin the sauce slightly with a small amount of cold water or milk. Season with salt and pepper.

Hollandaise can be prepared up to 1 hour ahead, and kept warm over hot water, off the heat; cover with plastic wrap pressed directly onto the surface of the sauce.

BÉARNAISE SAUCE

A tarragon-scented derivative of hollandaise, this is one of the best sauces for lamb or beef.

MAKES ABOUT 1 CUP

⅓ cup minced shallots
3 tablespoons white wine vinegar
12 whole black peppercorns, coarsely crushed
3 sprigs fresh tarragon
3 large egg yolks
10 tablespoons (1¼ sticks) unsalted butter, at room temperature
Salt, to taste

Place the shallots, vinegar, peppercorns, and tarragon in a small saucepan and bring to a boil over medium-high heat. Cook until the liquid is reduced to about 1 tablespoon. Let cool and then strain into a double boiler insert. Beat the egg yolks into the strained liquid. Place the insert over a saucepan of hot, not simmering, water, over low heat (do not let the base of the insert touch the water). Whisk until the egg mixture is slightly thickened and creamy. Still whisking constantly, add the butter, 1 tablespoon at a time. Whisk until each addition of butter is thoroughly incorporated before adding the next. Occasionally scrape down any sauce that splashes onto the side of the insert. If the sauce seems to be thickening too fast, immediately remove the insert to a bowl of cold water and stir the sauce to cool it quickly. If the sauce isn't thickening at all, increase the heat slightly. When all the butter has been added, season with salt.

Béarnaise can be prepared up to 1 hour ahead, and kept warm over hot water, off the heat; cover with plastic wrap pressed onto the sauce. If it is too thick, add a few drops of cold water just before serving.

BEURRE BLANC

Beurre blanc, a smooth sauce perfect for grilled fish, depends on the gentle melting and emulsion of butter to create a creamy consistency. It can be seasoned with your choice of fresh herbs—tarragon or dill are very good.

MAKES ABOUT ¾ CUP

3 shallots, finely chopped
3 tablespoons white wine vinegar
3 tablespoons dry white wine
8 tablespoons (1 stick) unsalted butter, chilled
A few drops of lemon juice
Salt and freshly ground white pepper, to taste

Place the shallots, vinegar, and wine in a small saucepan and bring to a boil over medium-high heat.

Boil until reduced to about 2 tablespoons. Remove from the heat and let cool slightly. Whisking constantly, add the butter, 1 tablespoon at a time. Whisk until each addition of butter is thoroughly incorporated before adding the next. After 2 or 3 tablespoons have been added, return the saucepan to very low heat. Continue gradually whisking in the butter. When it has all been incorporated, season the sauce with lemon juice, salt, and pepper. If desired, strain the sauce before serving.

DELICATE TOMATO SAUCE

Not all tomato sauces need to be long-simmered with olive oil and garlic. This one is best served right after preparation, and is excellent with pasta or gnocchi, and with grilled meat or fish.

MAKES ABOUT 2½ CUPS

4 tablespoons unsalted butter
2 pounds ripe plum tomatoes, peeled, seeded, and coarsely chopped
2 teaspoons chopped fresh basil or 1 teaspoon dried basil
1 teaspoon chopped fresh tarragon or ½ teaspoon dried tarragon
Salt, to taste

In a medium saucepan, melt the butter over low heat. Add the tomatoes and cook gently for about 10 minutes. Purée in a blender or food processor fitted with the metal blade. Stir in the basil and tarragon, and season with salt. Let stand for at least 10 minutes to allow the flavors to blend. If necessary, reheat the sauce before serving.

ROASTED TOMATO SAUCE

Roasting is an easy way to add flavor to less-than-perfect tomatoes. When made with the best summer tomatoes, the results are spectacular.

MAKES ABOUT 2 CUPS

2 pounds ripe plum tomatoes
4 tablespoons unsalted butter
2 teaspoons chopped fresh parsley
Salt and freshly ground pepper, to taste

Preheat the oven to 400°F. Place the whole tomatoes on a baking sheet. Roast until the skins are split and blackening, about 30 minutes. Let stand until cool enough to handle, then remove the peels and gently squeeze out the seeds. Purée the tomato flesh in a blender or a food processor fitted with the metal blade.

In a medium saucepan, heat the puréed tomatoes with the butter over medium heat, stirring all the time until the butter melts. Stir in the chopped parsley, and season with salt and freshly ground pepper. The sauce can be prepared up to 2 hours ahead, and reheated gently for serving.

HERB BUTTER

Place a small spoonful of this butter (called *beurre maître d'hôtel* in classic French cuisine) on top of piping hot grilled fish, steaks, or chops. You can form the butter into a log and keep it in the freezer to slice and use as needed.

MAKES ABOUT ½ CUP
  8 tablespoons (1 stick) unsalted butter, at room temperature
  2 tablespoons finely chopped fresh parsley
  1 tablespoon lemon juice

In a small bowl, combine all of the ingredients and work them together with a fork until well mixed. Cover and refrigerate until slightly firmed. The butter can be kept in the refrigerator for up to 2 days, or frozen for up to 3 months.

Garlic and Herb Butter: Add 1 shallot and 2 garlic cloves, both finely minced. Substitute 1 tablespoon finely chopped fresh tarragon for the parsley, if desired. **Horseradish Butter:** Add 2 tablespoons grated fresh horseradish, 1 teaspoon Dijon mustard, and 1 teaspoon red wine vinegar (or more of any of these ingredients according to taste). If you are unable to find fresh horseradish, use drained, prepared horseradish and omit the vinegar.

ASIAN PEANUT SAUCE

Use this sauce to dress Sichuan Chicken Salad, or serve as an accompaniment to crab cakes or grilled chicken or pork. If you are unable to find stem ginger preserved in syrup, you can substitute 2 tablespoons minced fresh ginger plus 2 tablespoons honey.

MAKES ABOUT 2½ CUPS
  1½ cups smooth peanut butter
  7 tablespoons soy sauce
  ⅓ cup lemon juice
  ⅓ cup Asian dark sesame oil
  3 pieces candied stem ginger in syrup plus 3 tablespoons syrup from the jar
  1 teaspoon chile flakes
  2 garlic cloves, minced

Place all the ingredients in a blender with a scant ½ cup water, and purée until smooth. Strain through a fine sieve, pressing hard on the solids. The sauce should be thick and creamy, but if it is too thick, thin with a little water. The sauce can be kept, covered, in the refrigerator for up to 1 week.

MEXICAN SALSA CRUDA

Salsa has many uses beyond being a dip for tortilla chips. Serve it as a condiment for broiled meat, fish, or chicken, or with steamed vegetables.

MAKES ABOUT 2½ CUPS
  3 large ripe tomatoes, peeled, seeded, and chopped
  3 hot fresh chile peppers (such as serrano or jalapeño), seeded and minced, or less to taste
  ½ small red onion, finely chopped
  2 tablespoons chopped fresh cilantro
  2 garlic cloves, minced
  Salt, to taste
  A splash of red wine vinegar (optional)

Combine all the ingredients in a bowl and stir to mix. Season with salt. If you feel the salsa needs a bit of acidity, add the vinegar. Cover and chill, about 1 hour. The salsa can be made up to 1 day ahead and kept, covered, in the refrigerator, but the fresher, the better.

CIDER BBQ SAUCE

Apple juice gives a fruity edge to this thin grilling sauce. It works best brushed onto meats and chicken during the last 10 or 15 minutes of grilling, because the sugars in the tomatoes and cider will scorch if it is applied sooner.

MAKES ABOUT 1½ CUPS
  1¼ cups dry apple cider, or 1 cup apple juice and ¼ cup dry white wine
  ½ cup tomato paste
  2 tablespoons cider vinegar
  2 tablespoons packed light brown sugar
  1 teaspoon soy sauce
  1 garlic clove, crushed
  ¾ teaspoon salt
  3 good dashes Tabasco sauce

Combine all the ingredients in a medium, heavy-bottomed saucepan. Bring to a simmer over medium heat. Reduce the heat to low and then simmer, stirring occasionally, until slightly thickened, about 20 minutes. Let cool completely. The sauce can be kept, covered, in the refrigerator for up to 3 days.

SOUTHERN-STYLE BBQ SAUCE

Once you've made BBQ sauce at home, you may never buy another bottle.

MAKES ABOUT 2 CUPS
- 2 tablespoons unsalted butter
- 1 medium onion, chopped
- 2 garlic cloves, minced
- 1 cup tomato ketchup
- 1 cup prepared American-style chile sauce
- 1/3 cup lemon juice
- 1/3 cup honey
- 2 tablespoons spicy brown mustard
- 2 tablespoons Worcestershire sauce
- 1/4 teaspoon cayenne pepper (optional)

In a medium, heavy-bottomed saucepan, melt the butter over medium heat. Add the onion and garlic. Cover and cook until the onion is golden-brown, about 8 minutes. Stir in the remaining ingredients and bring to a simmer. Reduce the heat to low. Simmer, uncovered, stirring often, until the sauce has thickened, about 30 minutes. The sauce can be kept, covered, in the refrigerator for up to 1 month.

HORSERADISH SAUCE

One of the most popular sauces for hot or cold roast beef, this is also excellent with smoked trout. For a milder sauce (or if using prepared horseradish instead of fresh), omit the vinegar.

MAKES ABOUT 3/4 CUP
- 2/3 cup heavy cream
- 3 tablespoons grated fresh horseradish, or use drained prepared horseradish
- 1 tablespoon white wine vinegar
- 1 teaspoon Dijon mustard
- A pinch of granulated sugar

In a small bowl, whisk together all of the ingredients until smooth. Taste the sauce and add more vinegar or sugar, if desired. Serve immediately.

MAYONNAISE

Homemade mayonnaise is a real treat. Remember to have all of the ingredients at room temperature. If you use extra virgin olive oil, mix it with another oil, in equal parts, because mayonnaise made with all extra virgin oil tends to "break" after a day or two in the refrigerator. If you prefer to avoid raw egg yolks, use 1/4 cup liquid egg substitute; this is pasteurized and makes a surprisingly good mayonnaise.

MAKES ABOUT 1 1/4 CUPS
- 2 large egg yolks, at room temperature
- 1 teaspoon Dijon mustard
- Salt and freshly ground white pepper, to taste
- 1 1/4 cups olive oil, or sunflower oil, peanut oil, or a mixture of olive and peanut oils
- 2 tablespoons lemon juice or white wine vinegar

In a medium bowl, combine the egg yolks, mustard, and salt. Beat together with a wire whisk or wooden spoon. Gradually add the oil, 1/2 teaspoon or so at a time, thoroughly mixing in each addition of oil before adding the next. As the mixture thickens, you can increase the flow of oil, to about 2 teaspoons at a time. After about half of the oil has been added and the mayonnaise is thick, beat in the lemon juice. By this stage it is almost impossible to curdle the mayonnaise, so you can whisk in the rest of the oil quite fast. Taste the mayonnaise, and add more salt and lemon juice if desired. Serve immediately. Or, cover and refrigerate until ready to serve (the mayonnaise can be prepared up to 1 day ahead); before serving, whisk the mayonnaise briefly.

Tartar Sauce: Stir 2 chopped hard-boiled eggs, 1/3 cup finely chopped fresh parsley, 2 tablespoons finely chopped sweet dill pickle, 2 tablespoons capers, chopped, and 2 tablespoons minced shallot into the mayonnaise.
Remoulade Sauce: Stir 1/2 cup finely chopped scallions, 2 tablespoons chopped fresh parsley, 1 tablespoon Creole or spicy brown mustard, 1 tablespoon prepared horseradish, and 1 teaspoon Worcestershire sauce into the mayonnaise.
Garlic Mayonnaise (Aïoli): Add 3 garlic cloves, crushed, to the egg yolks before adding the oil. Use a mixture of half peanut oil and half olive oil.

ROUILLE

Rouille is the traditional Provençal accompaniment to fish soups, in particular Bouillabaisse. It looks like mayonnaise with a warm red tint, but its gentle color belies its heat.

MAKES ABOUT 1 CUP
- 1 small red bell pepper
- 1 fresh hot red chile pepper (such as serrano), or 1/2 teaspoon chile flakes
- 1 slice white bread, crusts removed
- 3 garlic cloves, chopped
- 1 large egg yolk, at room temperature
- Salt, to taste
- 2/3 cup olive oil

Roast, peel, and seed the red bell pepper and fresh chile pepper, then chop them. Moisten the bread with a little water to soften it, then squeeze out the excess water. In a blender or food processor, combine the bread, bell pepper, chile pepper or chile flakes, garlic, egg yolk, and salt. Blend to a paste. With the machine running, gradually drizzle in oil. The finished rouille should have a thick, smooth, mayonnaise-like texture. Rouille can be kept, covered, in the refrigerator for up to 1 day.

ITALIAN HERB SAUCE

This emerald-green sauce, called *salsa verde* in Italy, is extremely good with poached chicken and fish.

MAKES ABOUT 1½ CUPS
  4 scallions, finely chopped
  3 tablespoons finely chopped mixed fresh herbs
    (flat-leaf parsley and chives)
  2 tablespoons capers, finely chopped
  8 anchovy fillets in oil, drained and finely chopped
  1 hard-boiled egg, chopped
  Grated zest of 1 lemon
  1 garlic clove, minced
  ½ tablespoon wine vinegar or 1 tablespoon lemon juice
  6 tablespoons olive oil
  Salt, to taste

In a medium bowl, combine the scallions, herbs, capers, anchovies, egg, lemon zest, and garlic. Add the vinegar, then gradually whisk in the oil. Season with salt. Cover and let stand for 1 hour to blend the flavors. Serve at room temperature. The sauce can be kept, covered, in the refrigerator for up to 1 day.

CRANBERRY-ORANGE SAUCE

Cranberry sauce's affinity with turkey is well known, but try this with pork and venison as well.

MAKES ABOUT 3 CUPS
  2 large oranges
  2 cups cranberries (12 ounces)
  1½ cups granulated sugar
  2 tablespoons orange-flavored liqueur (optional)

Grate 2 teaspoons of zest from the oranges and set aside. Cut off and discard the thick white pith, then carefully cut between the membranes to release the orange sections.

  In a medium, heavy-bottomed saucepan, combine the cranberries, sugar, 1 cup water, the oranges, and zest. Bring to a boil over medium heat, stirring often to help dissolve the sugar. Reduce the heat to low and

simmer until the sauce is thick and the cranberries have burst, 10 to 15 minutes. Stir in the liqueur, if using. Let cool completely before serving.

MANGO COULIS

A coulis is nothing more than the French culinary term for a simply prepared sauce made from puréed fruit or vegetables. This vibrant gold mango coulis is excellent in a tropical fruit salad, spooned over exotic-flavored ice creams and sorbets, or stirred into plain yogurt.

MAKES ABOUT 1½ CUPS
  2 large ripe mangoes
  ¼ cup lime juice
  ¼ cup granulated sugar

The mango pit lies lengthwise in the center of the fruit. Lay one mango on your work surface, plump side down. Holding the mango firmly, use a sharp, thin-bladed knife to slice off the top third of the fruit, cutting around the pit. Turn the mango over and slice off the other side. Repeat with the other mango. Using a large spoon, scoop the flesh from each piece.

  In a blender, purée the mango flesh with the lime juice and sugar. Taste, and add more lime juice or sugar to get the proper balance of acid and sweetness. The coulis can be kept, covered with plastic wrap pressed directly onto the surface, in the refrigerator for up to 4 hours.

WARM CHOCOLATE SAUCE

Poured over ice cream, this sauce will harden slightly and be deliciously chewy. Or, serve it as a sauce with pastries such as cream puffs.

MAKES ABOUT ⅔ CUP
  6 tablespoons unsalted butter
  ⅓ cup heavy cream
  8 ounces bittersweet or semisweet chocolate,
    finely chopped
  2 tablespoons honey
  2 tablespoons dark rum or additional heavy cream

In a saucepan, bring the butter and heavy cream to a simmer over medium heat. Remove from the heat and add the chocolate. Let stand for 3 minutes, then whisk until the chocolate has melted and the mixture is smooth. (If necessary, return to very low heat, stirring constantly, until the chocolate has melted.) Stir in the honey and rum. Serve warm. The sauce can be kept, covered, in the refrigerator for up to 5 days; reheat in a double boiler insert over simmering water.

ORANGE CARAMEL SAUCE

The rich flavor of caramelized sugar adds another dimension to many desserts. For a simple dessert, pour this sauce over ripe fresh peach slices garnished with a few raspberries. There are a couple of tips for making this sauce. First, be sure the cream is hot before adding it to the caramel—if cold, it will stiffen the sauce. Also, be careful when adding the liquids, because they will boil up dramatically.

MAKES 1¼ CUPS
1 cup granulated sugar
¼ cup heavy cream, heated until very hot
½ cup orange juice, at room temperature

Put ¼ cup water in a deep, medium saucepan. Add the sugar. Bring to a boil over high heat, stirring to help dissolve the sugar. Then let boil, without stirring, but occasionally swirling the syrup around in the pan, until the syrup is a medium amber color, 3 to 5 minutes. Remove from the heat. Gradually stir in the hot cream, being careful of the sauce bubbling up, then stir in the orange juice. Cool slightly before serving; the sauce will thicken upon cooling. The sauce can be kept, covered, in the refrigerator for up to 3 days; reheat in a double boiler insert over simmering water before serving, adding additional heavy cream or orange juice as needed to thin the sauce to the desired consistency.

PROVENÇAL LEMON MARINADE

Grilling marinades should include enough oil to keep the food from sticking to the grill, but don't use too much oil, or it will drip onto the coals and cause flareups. This marinade uses full-flavored extra virgin olive oil, which adds its own character to the fragrant blend of herbs and garlic.

MAKES ABOUT 1¼ CUPS, ENOUGH FOR 3 POUNDS MEAT, POULTRY, OR FISH
½ cup extra virgin olive oil
½ cup lemon juice
2 garlic cloves, crushed
1 tablespoon chopped fresh rosemary or 1½ teaspoons dried rosemary
1 tablespoon chopped fresh thyme or 1½ teaspoons dried thyme
1 tablespoon chopped fresh oregano or 1½ teaspoons dried oregano
1 teaspoon fennel seed, crushed
Grated zest of 1 orange
¼ teaspoon chile flakes
Salt, to taste

In a medium bowl, combine all of the ingredients. Use the mixture to marinate meat and poultry for up to 8 hours, covered, in the refrigerator. Marinate fish and shellfish for no longer than 2 hours, covered, in the refrigerator.

ITALIAN RED WINE MARINADE

Choose a robust dry red wine, such as Chianti or Zinfandel, to make this Tuscan-inspired marinade. It makes an especially delicious marinade for either lamb or beef.

MAKES ABOUT 1¼ CUPS, ENOUGH FOR 3 POUNDS MEAT, POULTRY, OR VEGETABLES
1 cup hearty red wine
⅓ cup extra virgin olive oil
2 garlic cloves, minced
1 tablespoon chopped fresh rosemary or 1½ teaspoons dried rosemary
1 tablespoon chopped fresh thyme or 1½ teaspoons dried thyme
¼ teaspoon freshly ground pepper
Salt, to taste

In a medium bowl, combine all of the ingredients. Use the mixture to marinate meat and poultry for up to 8 hours, covered, in the refrigerator. Marinate vegetables for no longer than 2 hours, covered, in the refrigerator.

CAJUN DRY RUB

Blackened fish took America by storm, and along with it the concept of rubbing foods with spicy seasoning blends before cooking them became very popular. This Cajun dry rub is a particularly good mixture. New Orleans cooks almost always include both onion and garlic powders, as used in this recipe, in their dry rubs.

MAKES ABOUT ¼ CUP, ENOUGH FOR ABOUT 3 POUNDS MEAT, POULTRY, OR FISH
1 tablespoon sweet Hungarian paprika
1 teaspoon dried oregano
1 teaspoon dried thyme
½ teaspoon garlic powder
½ teaspoon onion powder
½ teaspoon freshly ground pepper
¼ teaspoon cayenne pepper

In a small bowl, combine all of the ingredients. The dry rub, stored in a covered container, will keep indefinitely in a cool, dry spot.

Appetizers, Snacks, and Beverages

CRUDITÉS WITH GARLIC MAYONNAISE

The more vegetables you have on a crudité platter, the better, as you want to create a colorful, eye-catching combination. Other possibilities to use include boiled small new potatoes, slices of fresh fennel bulb, steamed baby beets, sticks of celeriac, and tiny globe artichokes the size of a walnut.

MAKES 6 TO 8 SERVINGS

1 English cucumber
8 ounces small zucchini
8 ounces green beans
1 large red bell pepper, seeded and cut into 2- by 1/4-inch sticks
3 medium carrots, cut into 2- by 1/4-inch sticks
2 celery ribs, cut into 2- by 1/4-inch sticks
4 ripe plum tomatoes, cut into 1/4-inch-thick rounds
1 bunch radishes
2 heads Belgian endive, separated into leaves
1 1/2 cups Garlic Mayonnaise
3/4 cup black Mediterranean olives

Peel the cucumber, cut crosswise into 2-inch pieces, and cut these into 1/4-inch-thick sticks, removing the seeds. Bring a small saucepan of lightly salted water to a boil over high heat. Add the zucchini and cook until they are crisp-tender, about 3 minutes. Remove them with a slotted spoon and let cool. Bring the water back to a boil. Add the green beans and cook until crisp-tender, 1 to 2 minutes. Drain, refresh, and dry on paper towels. When the zucchini are cool, cut them across in half and then into 1/4-inch-thick sticks.

Bring another small saucepan of lightly salted water to a boil over high heat. Add the red pepper strips and cook just to soften slightly, about 1 minute. Drain, refresh, and pat dry with paper towels.

Arrange all the vegetables on a large platter, cover with plastic wrap, and chill, about 1 hour. Place the garlic mayonnaise and olives in bowls. Serve the vegetables and olives with the mayonnaise as a dip.

FARMHOUSE CHEESE SPREAD WITH PITA CRISPS

Yogurt, when drained of its whey, has a cheese-like consistency that makes it an admirable low-fat ingredient. Mixed with vegetables, it becomes a versatile spread that can be served with pita crisps or crackers, or even used as a sandwich filling.

MAKES ABOUT 3 CUPS

2 medium kirby cucumbers or 1 large cucumber
1/4 teaspoon salt
1 quart plain low-fat yogurt, drained
1 cup shredded radishes (about 6 medium radishes)
2 scallions, finely chopped
2 tablespoons chopped fresh dill
Freshly ground pepper, to taste
6 pita breads
Olive oil, for brushing

Scrub the cucumbers well and cut them in half lengthwise. (Leave kirby cucumbers unpeeled, but peel regular cucumber, if using.) With the tip of a spoon, scoop out and discard the seeds. Chop the cucumbers into 1/4-inch dice and place in a small bowl. Toss with the salt, and let stand until they release their juices, about 30 minutes. Rinse well, drain, and squeeze out the excess moisture. Transfer to a medium bowl.

Stir in the drained yogurt, radishes, scallions, and dill. Season with salt and pepper. Cover and refrigerate for at least 2 hours. The spread can be prepared up to 1 day ahead and kept, covered, in the refrigerator.

To make the pita crisps: Preheat the oven to 350°F. Pull apart the two layers of the pita breads. Cut into wedges and arrange in single layers on baking sheets. Lightly brush with olive oil. Bake until crisp and golden-brown, about 10 minutes.

GUACAMOLE

This mixes hot and cool sensations, which stimulates the appetite—no wonder it's so hard to stop eating it.

MAKES 6 TO 8 SERVINGS

3 ripe Hass avocados
2 tablespoons lime juice
1 scallion, chopped
2 small hot chile peppers (such as jalapeño), seeded and chopped, or to taste
1 garlic clove, minced
1 large ripe tomato, peeled, seeded, and chopped
Salt and freshly ground pepper, to taste
2 tablespoons chopped fresh cilantro (optional)

Cut the avocados in half and scoop out the flesh. In a medium bowl, use a fork to mash the avocado flesh with the lime juice. Using a mortar and pestle, or a mini food processor, work the scallion, chiles, and garlic to a paste. Add to the avocado mixture. Fold in the chopped tomato. Season with salt and pepper. Garnish with the cilantro, if using. Press plastic wrap

FARMHOUSE CHEESE SPREAD WITH PITA CRISPS

directly onto the surface of the guacamole, and then refrigerate until well chilled, at least 1 hour. The guacamole can be prepared up to 8 hours ahead; keep it covered with plastic wrap to prevent discoloration.

OLIVADA

Olivada, and its French twin, tapenade, are olive pastes that have many uses in the Mediterranean kitchen. Spread onto toasted baguette slices, they make an admirable antipasto, but they can also be incorporated into recipes as a seasoning.

MAKES ABOUT 1 CUP
    2 cups black Mediterranean olives, pitted
    3 tablespoons extra virgin olive oil
    2 tablespoons coarsely chopped capers
    1 tablespoon Dijon mustard
    1 tablespoon brandy
    2 teaspoons anchovy paste
    1 teaspoon chopped fresh rosemary or ½ teaspoon
        dried rosemary
    2 teaspoons chopped fresh thyme or 1 teaspoon
        dried thyme
    ¼ teaspoon chile flakes

In a food processor fitted with the metal blade, process all the ingredients together just long enough so that they form a coarse purée. Transfer the paste to a suitable container, cover tightly, and keep refrigerated until you are ready to use it. The olivada can be kept, covered, in the refrigerator for up to 1 week.

Sun-Dried Tomato Olivada: Substitute ½ cup coarsely chopped sun-dried tomatoes packed in oil, well-drained, for 1 cup of the black olives.

BLACK BEAN AND BACON DIP

This is a zesty Southwestern-style bean dip.

MAKES ABOUT 2½ CUPS
    4 strips bacon
    1 medium onion, chopped
    1 hot fresh chile pepper (such as jalapeño), seeded
        and minced
    2 garlic cloves, minced
    3 ripe plum tomatoes, seeded and chopped
    1 teaspoon dried oregano
    ½ teaspoon ground cumin
    3 cups cooked black beans
    ¾ cup beef stock, approximately
    Tortilla chips, for dipping

In a large frying pan, cook the bacon over medium heat until crisp, about 5 minutes. Transfer to paper towels to drain, leaving the fat in the frying pan. Add the onion, chile pepper, and garlic to the pan and cook, stirring often, until the onion is softened but not browned, about 5 minutes. Stir in the tomatoes, oregano, and cumin, and cook for 5 minutes. Add the cooked black beans. Continue cooking over low heat, mashing the beans with a large spoon and gradually adding the stock, to make a chunky, but soupy, purée. Remove from the heat and stir in the crumbled bacon. Let the dip cool completely—it will thicken as it cools.

The dip can be kept, covered, in the refrigerator for up to 3 days. Before serving, thin down the dip, if necessary, with additional beef stock. Serve with tortilla chips for dipping.

CHICKPEA HUMMUS

Hummus is most delicious when made with freshly cooked chickpeas, but it can also be made with high-quality canned chickpeas—the ones sold at health food stores are the best.

MAKES 4 TO 6 SERVINGS
    1 cup dried chickpeas, cooked and drained,
        or 2½ cups drained canned chickpeas
    2 garlic cloves, crushed
    ⅓ cup tahini
    ¼ cup lemon juice
    2 teaspoons ground cumin
    2 teaspoons chili powder
    Salt, to taste
    2 tablespoons olive oil
    Cayenne pepper, for garnish
    1 tablespoon chopped fresh parsley
    Pita bread, for serving

In a food processor fitted with the metal blade, process the chickpeas until they are smooth. If desired, press the purée through a sieve to remove any bits of skin. Add the garlic, tahini, and lemon juice. Beat in just enough cold water to make a smooth paste with the consistency of mayonnaise, about 5 tablespoons. Add the cumin and chili powder, and season with salt.

Pour the hummus into a serving bowl and smooth over the surface with the back of a spoon or a spatula. Pour the olive oil on top, and sprinkle generously with cayenne pepper in the center and parsley all over the surface. The hummus can be kept, covered, in the refrigerator for up to 3 days; garnish with oil, cayenne, and parsley just before serving. Serve the hummus as a dip, with pita bread.

EGGPLANT CAVIAR

Sometimes called "poor man's caviar," this has an intriguing smoky flavor. Serve it as a delicious snack accompanied by warm pita bread and olives, or as part of a combination of salads, perhaps with hummus and tomatoes.

MAKES 4 TO 6 SERVINGS
    2 medium eggplants
    1 teaspoon cumin seeds
    2 ripe plum tomatoes, peeled, seeded, and
        finely chopped
    2 scallions, finely chopped (optional)
    2 garlic cloves, minced
    6 tablespoons olive oil
    1 teaspoon lemon juice, or more to taste
    Salt and freshly ground pepper, to taste

Preheat the broiler. Broil the eggplants until the skins have blackened and the eggplants are becoming soft, about 20 minutes. Turn the eggplants and continue broiling until completely soft, about 15 minutes longer. Cool until easy to handle, then split the eggplants open and remove the flesh from the skin with a large spoon. Coarsely chop the flesh and transfer to a medium bowl.

In a small frying pan, toast the cumin seeds over medium heat, stirring often, until fragrant, about 2 minutes. Transfer to a mortar and pestle, and crush. (Or, place the seeds on a work surface and crush under a heavy pot.) Add to the eggplant, along with the tomatoes, optional scallions, and most of the garlic. Stirring constantly, gradually add the oil. Add the lemon juice, and season with salt and pepper. Taste the caviar and add more lemon juice, garlic, and/or seasoning if desired. Serve at cool room temperature. The eggplant caviar can kept, covered, in the refrigerator for up to 2 days.

CRAB CHILE CON QUESO

Hot dips are always a hit at parties, especially when made with sweet crabmeat. This one can be prepared well ahead of serving.

MAKES 12 APPETIZER SERVINGS
    1 pound, 3 ounces cream cheese, at room temperature
    1 cup Mexican Salsa Cruda, finely chopped, or use
        bottled salsa, drained slightly to remove excess liquid
    ⅔ cup mayonnaise
    1 teaspoon chili powder
    ½ teaspoon Worcestershire sauce
    1 pound fresh lump crabmeat, picked over to remove
        any cartilage

    Tabasco sauce, to taste
    ½ cup finely crushed unsalted tortilla chips
    Assorted raw vegetables, tortilla chips, or crackers,
        for serving

Preheat the oven to 350°F. In a medium bowl, mix together the cream cheese, salsa, mayonnaise, chili powder, and Worcestershire sauce. Fold in the crab, and season with Tabasco sauce. Transfer to a shallow 1-quart baking dish. (The dip can be kept, covered, in the refrigerator for up to 8 hours before baking.)

Sprinkle the top with the crushed tortilla chips. Bake until bubbling, about 30 minutes. Serve warm with vegetables or chips, for dipping.

SQUASH FRITTERS WITH GARLICKY YOGURT DIP

Serve these crispy fritters as a snack with drinks, or as a Mediterranean-style first course.

MAKES 4 TO 6 SERVINGS
    1 cup all-purpose flour
    2 tablespoons vegetable oil
    3 small pattypan squash (1 pound)
    Vegetable oil, for deep-frying
    1 large egg white
    Salt, to taste
Garlicky Yogurt Dip
    4 ounces cream cheese, at room temperature
    ½ cup thick, drained plain yogurt
    2 garlic cloves, chopped and mashed to a paste with
        a sprinkle of salt

Put the flour in a medium bowl. Make a well in the center, and pour in the oil and ¾ cup water. Stir just until smooth. Let the batter stand for at least 30 minutes and up to 1 hour.

Meanwhile, for the dip, mash all the ingredients until smooth. Let stand so the flavors can blend.

Slice the pattypan squash vertically into ¼-inch-thick slices. (If there are seeds in the squash, remove them, and peel the squash rounds.) Pour enough oil into a deep saucepan to come 2 inches up the sides of the pan. Heat to 360°F. Preheat the oven to 200°F. In a small bowl, beat the egg white until it forms stiff peaks, then fold into the batter. Working in small batches, dip the squash slices one at a time in the batter, shake off the excess, and place in the hot oil. Fry until pale golden on both sides, 2 to 3 minutes. Using a slotted spoon, transfer to paper towels to drain, and keep warm in the oven while making the rest of the fritters. Sprinkle the fritters with salt, and serve hot with the dip.

the bottom of the pan. In a medium saucepan of lightly salted water, cook the carrots until very tender, about 20 minutes. Drain well. In a medium frying pan, heat the butter over medium heat. Add the shallots and cook until softened, about 3 minutes. In a small bowl, soak the bread crumbs in the cream until soft.

In a food processor fitted with the metal blade, purée the carrots with the shallots and crumb mixture. Add the beans, eggs, egg yolk, and lemon juice, and purée until smooth. Transfer to a bowl and stir in 1 tablespoon each of the dill and parsley, along with all the tarragon. Season well with salt and pepper. Spoon into the prepared pan and spread evenly. Top with a buttered piece of waxed paper, buttered side down. Put the loaf pan in a larger roasting pan and place in the oven. Pour enough water into the roasting pan to come ½ inch up the sides. Bake until the center of the pâté is firm and an instant-read thermometer inserted in the center reads 160°F, about 1¼ hours.

Remove the loaf pan from the bain marie. Remove the top piece of waxed paper, and cool the pâté in the pan on a wire cake rack. Then run a knife around the edges of the pâté, unmold onto a serving platter, and remove the waxed paper. Cover with plastic wrap and refrigerate until chilled, at least 4 hours or overnight (the pâté can be kept, covered, in the refrigerator for up to 3 days). Before serving, sprinkle the pâté with the remaining dill and parsley. Serve with slices of French bread.

PAN CATALAN

The simplest of ingredients—-toasted bread, fine olive oil, robust garlic, and ripe tomatoes—combine in a form of alchemy to make the perfect appetizer. Similar to its better-known Italian cousin, bruschetta, this Spanish specialty has a charm all of its own. You could also toast the bread under the broiler or on a ridged cast-iron grill pan.

MAKES 4 SERVINGS
4 large, thick slices country-style bread
2 or 3 garlic cloves, peeled
1 or 2 large ripe tomatoes, cut in half horizontally
Extra virgin olive oil, for drizzling
Salt, to taste
4 large basil leaves, cut into thin strips (optional)

Light a charcoal (or wood) fire in an outdoor grill and let burn until the coals are covered with ashes. Grill the bread on both sides until toasted and very lightly charred. Fiercely rub one side of each toast with a garlic clove, using as much garlic as you like. (The rough surface of the toast will grate the garlic and the

toast will absorb all the garlic juices.) Now rub the same surfaces with the cut side of the tomato halves. Drizzle oil over the tomato-soaked toasts and sprinkle with salt, both to taste. Serve at once, topped with the basil leaves, if desired.

CRYSTAL-CLEAR ICED TEA

The best iced tea takes time—if tea brewed from hot water is chilled, it will become cloudy.

MAKES 5 CUPS, ABOUT 5 SERVINGS
4 tea bags of your favorite tea
Sprigs of fresh mint or lemon slices, or both
Sugar, to taste

Place the tea bags in a large pitcher. Add 5 cups of cold water. Cover and refrigerate until the tea is brewed, at least 4 hours or overnight. Serve over ice cubes, garnishing each serving with mint or lemon, or both. Let each guest sweeten with sugar to taste.

PINK RASPBERRY LEMONADE

Lemonade is the ultimate summer thirst-quencher. It only takes a second to muddle some berries in the bottom of a glass before pouring in the lemonade, producing a lovely pink-colored drink.

MAKES 3 QUARTS, ABOUT 12 SERVINGS
2 cups fresh lemon juice
1½ cups granulated sugar
1 pint fresh raspberries

In a blender, process 1 cup of the lemon juice with the sugar until the sugar dissolves. Pour into a pitcher and stir in the remaining juice and 2 quarts of ice-cold water. Chill until ready to serve.

Just before serving, place a few raspberries in the bottom of each serving glass. Then, using a long spoon, crush the raspberries to release their juices. Pour the lemonade over the top. Add ice cubes, if desired, and serve.

GLÖGG

Mulled wine can be tame, but when it is made the Scandinavian way, it becomes a delicious, heady drink. Glögg is traditionally presented spectacularly flaming.

MAKES ABOUT 8 SERVINGS
5 cups hearty red wine
2½ cups Muscat wine
⅔ cup raisins

SANGRÍA

⅔ cup packed light brown sugar
3 (3-inch) strips orange zest
5 whole cloves, lightly crushed
5 whole cardamom pods, lightly crushed
1 cinnamon stick, lightly crushed
⅔ cup aquavit
¼ cup slivered blanched almonds

Combine the red wine, Muscat wine, raisins, light brown sugar, strips of orange zest, cloves, cardamom pods, and cinnamon in a large nonreactive bowl. Let the mixture stand at room temperature overnight to infuse the flavors.

The next day, pour the mixture into a large nonreactive pot and bring just to a boil over medium heat. Pour 1 tablespoon of the aquavit into a small saucepan and set aside. Stir the remaining aquavit and the almonds into the pot. Heat the aquavit in the saucepan just until warm. Pour it over the top of the

glögg, and, averting your face, set it alight with a match. Serve immediately in tumblers with teaspoons, so the guests can eat the raisins and almonds.

SANGRÍA

Rioja is the best wine to use to give sangría an authentic Spanish flavor.

MAKES ABOUT 8 SERVINGS
1 medium orange, cut into ¼-inch-thick rounds
1 medium lemon, cut into ¼-inch-thick rounds
1 (750-ml) bottle red wine, preferably Rioja
¼ cup brandy, preferably Spanish
⅔ cup sparkling mineral water
Superfine sugar, to taste
Sprigs of fresh mint

Half-fill a pitcher with ice cubes. Add the orange and lemon slices. Stir in the wine and brandy, then pour in the sparkling water. If needed, sweeten with sugar. Serve immediately, garnishing each glass with mint.

Preserves

MAKING PRESERVES AND PICKLES

Making good jams, jellies, preserves, and pickles does not necessarily mean an afternoon's devotion to the kitchen. Preparing small quantities is perfectly practical and doesn't take long. Many recipes don't even need to be processed in a water bath—just be sure to store them in the refrigerator instead of on the pantry shelf. Before you start, here are a few guides to success.

Pectin This substance is naturally present in many fruits, and when combined with sugar and the fruit's acids, ensures that your jam or jelly will set properly. Slightly underripe fruit contains more pectin than ripe. Tart fruits, such as apples, quinces, currants, oranges, and lemons, are particularly rich in pectin. When making preserves low in pectin, the setting is helped by the addition of some lemon juice. Some recipes (not in this book) call for liquid pectin, extracted from apple pulp, which is available at supermarkets during canning season.

Preparation Check jars to be sure they are free of nicks and cracks, and only use brand-new rings and lids. Do not use leftover jars from, say, mayonnaise, as they are not made to withstand the high heat of water-processing. Jars should be washed with soap, and rinsed thoroughly with very hot water. Both jars and rings must be sterilized in boiling water for 10 minutes before using. Have everything else ready and scrupulously clean. If you wish, warm the sugar in a 200°F oven while preparing the fruit—warm sugar will dissolve more quickly.

Setting Point After the jam, jelly, or preserve has boiled for 10 minutes, test it by dropping a spoonful onto a cold plate, and cooling until it looks set (you can speed the cooling in the refrigerator). Nudge with your finger; if the jam, jelly, or preserve wrinkles and clings to where it was dropped, it is ready. Skim the batch at this point to remove any scum or froth on the surface.

Packing into Jars Always pack your preserves in hot jars. After sterilizing, leave the jars standing in the hot water until ready to use, then remove with long tongs. Dry them with a very clean kitchen towel. The lids only need to be placed in a bowl of hot water to soften the rubber seal slightly; drain the lids right before using. To fill the jars most easily, use a widemouthed funnel. Don't fill the jars completely: leave about ½ inch of headspace. Use a clean towel to wipe the rims clean of any drips. Screw on the lids and rings.

Processing in a Water Bath Have a large pot of boiling water ready, filled with enough water to cover the jars by 1 inch. A processing pot with a removable basket works best, but any large pot with a rack on the bottom is fine. Submerge the jars in the water and process for the time indicated in the recipe. Lift the jars out of the hot water with tongs and place on a folded kitchen towel (this helps insulate the bottom of the jars to prevent them from cracking.) Let cool at room temperature.

Checking the Seal The jars must be checked for a proper seal. Unscrew the band and pick up the jar, holding by the seal. If the seal holds, all is well. If it is loose, return the screw band, and use the preserve promptly (or refrigerate and plan to use within the average refrigerated life of the food). If a stored jar shows an unsightly bulge on top, throw the preserve away—do not taste it to see if it is edible.

Storage Store preserves in a cool, dark, dry place.

STRAWBERRY JAM

There is no use making strawberry jam with inspid berries—wait until they are at their peak.

MAKES ABOUT 8 CUPS

4 pounds fresh strawberries, hulled
¼ cup lemon juice
4 pounds granulated sugar, warmed

Put the strawberries and lemon juice in a large, heavy-bottomed pot. Cook over very low heat, stirring from time to time, until the strawberries have softened and released their juices, 20 to 30 minutes.

Gently stir in the warmed sugar until it dissolves. Increase the heat to high and bring to a rapid boil, stirring frequently. Boil until the jam reaches the setting point (the syrup will look thick and the fruit will mound slightly in a metal spoon). Remove the pot from the heat. Draw the scum to the sides and carefully skim it off. Let the jam cool slightly, then ladle into hot, sterilized jars and seal.

PEACH PRESERVES

When peaches are in season and plentiful, but maybe just a little too ripe for eating out of hand, make peach preserves so that you can continue to enjoy the fruit's sweetness until next year's crop comes around.

MAKES ABOUT 5 CUPS

3 pounds ripe peaches, peeled, halved, and pitted
2¼ cups granulated sugar
2 tablespoons lemon juice
⅓ cup brandy

Place the peaches in a pan with 1 tablespoon water. Simmer gently until very soft, about 45 minutes.

STRAWBERRY JAM

Measure the cooked peaches; you should have about 4 cups. Return to the saucepan. Stir in the sugar and lemon juice. Stir over low heat until the sugar dissolves. Increase the heat to medium-high and boil for 6 minutes. Remove from the heat, cover, and let stand in a cool place overnight.

The next day, return the saucepan to medium-high heat and bring to a boil. Remove from the heat and stir in the brandy. Ladle into hot, sterilized jars and seal.

LEMON CURD

Lemon curd is not only an admirable tart filling, but is excellent spread onto English muffins or toast.

MAKES 2 CUPS

8 tablespoons (1 stick) unsalted butter

1 cup granulated sugar

½ cup fresh lemon juice, strained

Zest of 2 lemons, removed with a vegetable peeler

3 large eggs, at room temperature

In a double boiler insert set over a saucepan of hot, not simmering, water, combine the butter, sugar, lemon juice, and zest. When the mixture is smooth, stir in the eggs. Cook, stirring occasionally with a wooden spoon, until the curd is thick enough to coat the spoon (an instant-read thermometer will read about 185°F), about 6 minutes. Strain into a medium bowl. If using within 24 hours, press a sheet of plastic wrap directly onto the surface of the curd, and pierce with a few holes to allow the steam to escape. Let cool to room temperature, then transfer to a covered container and refrigerate for up to 1 week. Otherwise, ladle into hot, sterilized jars and seal, and store, refrigerated, for up to 3 months.

SWEET PEPPER CHUTNEY

This excellent chutney is a good accompaniment to all cold meats and game, and could even replace the cranberry sauce at the Thanksgiving meal.

MAKES ABOUT 2 PINTS

¼ cup olive oil

3 medium onions, chopped

2 medium red bell peppers, seeded and cut into 1-inch pieces

2 medium green bell peppers, seeded and cut into 1-inch pieces

1 garlic clove, minced

12 allspice berries, coarsely crushed

¾ teaspoon ground cinnamon

½ teaspoon ground ginger

⅛ teaspoon ground cloves

Salt, to taste

1 pound ripe plum tomatoes, peeled, seeded, and chopped

⅔ cup raisins

¾ cup granulated sugar

⅔ cup white wine vinegar

In a heavy-bottomed saucepan, heat the oil. Add the onions and cook until soft, about 5 minutes. Add the peppers, garlic, allspice, cinnamon, ginger, cloves, and a seasoning of salt. Reduce the heat and cook for 10 minutes. Stir in the tomatoes and raisins, and cook for another 10 minutes. Add the sugar and vinegar. Increase the heat to medium and, stirring, bring to a simmer. Return the heat to medium-low and simmer until the chutney is thick and a beautiful bronze color, about 2 hours. Ladle into hot, sterilized jars and seal. Let stand in a cool, dark place for at least 2 weeks.

PICKLED BABY CARROTS

This blue-ribbon recipe turns a bag of peeled baby carrots into crisp and crunchy pickles. For crisp-tender pickles, cook the carrots in boiling lightly salted water for 2 minutes and drain before placing in the jar.

MAKES 1 QUART

1 pound peeled baby carrots

2 large sprigs fresh dill

1 garlic clove, cut in half

1½ cups distilled white vinegar

1¼ teaspoons pickling salt

1¼ teaspoons granulated sugar

1½ teaspoons dill seeds

¼ teaspoon whole black peppercorns

In a hot, sterilized quart jar, arrange the carrots (quite a few will stand upright; lay the others across the top). Add the dill sprigs and garlic. In a saucepan, combine the vinegar, ½ cup water, the salt, sugar, dill seeds, and peppercorns. Bring to a boil. Pour the liquid into the jar, adding boiling water, if needed, to bring the liquid up to ½ inch from the top. Screw on the lid and ring, and let stand at room temperature overnight. Store in the refrigerator for 3 days before eating. The pickles will keep in the refrigerator for 1 month.

To store longer, or at room temperature, you must process the pickles in a water bath: Submerge the sealed jar in a saucepan of boiling water and boil for 5 minutes. Remove and let cool to room temperature.

New-Fashioned Dill Pickles: Substitute 6 medium kirby cucumbers for the carrots.

SPICY BREAD AND BUTTER PICKLES

The taste of homemade pickles is incomparable, and this recipe lets you enjoy it.

MAKES 1 QUART

    4 medium kirby cucumbers, unpeeled, cut into
       ¼ inch-thick rounds (about 3 cups)
    1 large onion, cut into ¼-inch-thick half-moons
    1 medium red bell pepper, seeded and cut into
       ¼-inch-thick strips
    2 tablespoons pickling salt
    1 cup cider vinegar
    1 cup granulated sugar
    ¼ teaspoon yellow mustard seeds
    ¼ teaspoon celery seed
    ¼ teaspoon coriander seeds
    ¼ teaspoon whole cloves
    ¼ teaspoon ground turmeric
    ¼ teaspoon chile flakes

In a large bowl, toss the cucumbers, onion, and red pepper with the salt. Add enough cold water barely to

SWEET PEPPER CHUTNEY

cover the vegetables, then stir in 2 trays of ice cubes. Let stand for 3 hours. Drain the vegetables, and rinse well under cold water. In a medium pot, combine the vinegar, sugar, and spices, and bring to a boil over high heat. Reduce the heat to low and simmer for 5 minutes. Add the drained vegetables and return just to boiling point. Spoon the hot vegetables into a hot, sterilized quart jar. Pour enough of the syrup into the jar to come up to ¼ inch from the top. Wipe the rim of the jar clean with a dish towel, and then close it with the lid and ring. Let stand at room temperature overnight, then refrigerate for at least 3 days before eating. The pickles can be kept in the refrigerator for up to 1 month.

For longer storage, the pickles must be processed in a water bath: Submerge the sealed jar in a deep saucepan of boiling water and boil for 5 minutes (counting from when the jar is put in the pot). Remove from the water, and let cool to room temperature.

Fish

Where most meat is cooked to make it tender, fish is naturally tender, so heat is only applied to develop the fish's flavor. Cooking fish beyond the moment when the flesh has turned from translucent to opaque will make it tough and dry. Fish is done if the fleshiest part flakes when it is prodded with the tip of a knife. You should start this testing about halfway through the recommended cooking time, in order to ensure succulent results.

There are a number of different ways to cook fish:
Poaching When cooking fish in a court-bouillon or other liquid, take care that the liquid never passes a bare simmer. Boiling extracts flavor from fish, which is fine for soups and stews, but disastrous when you want to serve simply prepared fish fillets or steaks. The poaching liquid should be well salted.
Steaming As the fish will not be cooked in a medium that lends much flavor, the fish itself must be impeccably fresh. Season the fish well with herbs, salt, and pepper, or it could end up as bland as hospital food. Place the fish on a buttered or oiled plate, and steam on a rack in a large covered pan of simmering water until just done.
Baking There is only one firm rule about baking fish—don't let it dry out. Be sure the oven is preheated well. The fish is often protected with a foil or paper wrapping, or insulated with a sauce or stuffing. If you are baking a whole fish, try to leave the head and tail on, as it will then retain more moisture.
Frying Fish should be fried as quickly as possible to seal the exterior and hold in the juices. Clarified butter is a good fat for sautéing, but only use enough to stop the fish from sticking to the pan. When deep-frying fish, preheat the oil to 375°F. Large pieces of fish should be sealed in a batter or with egg and crumbs; small fish, like whitebait, only need a quick dip in milk and seasoned flour.
Broiling The broiler should be preheated so the fish can start to cook immediately, to seal in the juices. If you are cooking a whole fish, leave the head and tail on, and make two diagonal slashes in the thickest parts of the body to help the heat to penetrate. Brush fish steaks or fillets with oil or clarified butter to add moisture. Fish fillets do not need turning over halfway during broiling, but do turn whole fish and steaks.
Grilling Brush the grill well with oil so the fish won't stick. Let the coals burn down for a few minutes after they are covered with white ash—they should be medium-hot, not blazing. For whole fish, use a fish-shaped grilling basket, which makes turning the fish very easy.
Marinating For dishes such as *seviche*, very fresh fish is "cooked" in an acidic marinade (the acids turn the fish opaque, which makes it look as if it has been cooked by heat, when it is actually raw). Fish to be cooked by heat is often marinated in a well-seasoned liquid, to add flavor and, sometimes, moisture (it is important not to marinate fish for longer than 2 hours or the acids will do their "cooking" trick and make the cooked flesh mushy). Always marinate fish in a glass or ceramic dish, as the acids will react with metal and give the marinade a metallic taste.

FILLET OF SOLE MEUNIÈRE
This is a delicious, useful recipe for a quick supper. For the best results, use Dover sole fillets, or another firm fish fillet like snapper, since sole's ubiquitous cousin, flounder, has a tendency to fall apart when panfried. Be sure the butter is good and hot before adding the fish in order to create a nice crust.

MAKES 4 SERVINGS
4 (7-ounce) sole fillets
Salt and freshly ground pepper, to taste
½ cup all-purpose flour
7 tablespoons unsalted butter
3 tablespoons lemon juice
2 tablespoons finely chopped fresh parsley

Season the fillets with salt and pepper, then coat lightly with flour, shaking off the excess flour. In a large frying pan, heat 2 tablespoons of the butter over medium-high heat until very hot and starting to brown. Add the fillets and cook, turning once, until golden-brown on both sides, about 4 minutes. Transfer the fish to warm dinner plates. Wipe out the pan and then return it to medium-high heat. Add the lemon juice and parsley to the pan, then the remaining 5 tablespoons butter. Swirl the butter in the pan until melted, then pour equal portions of the lemon butter over each fillet. Serve immediately.

Trout Meunière: Substitute 4 whole trout (about 12 ounces each) for the sole. Cook until golden-brown on both sides, turning once, about 8 minutes. If necessary, cook the fish in batches and keep warm.

BAKED HALIBUT STEAKS WITH MUSHROOMS
A delicate dish for a special meal. Serve with boiled new potatoes and brightly colored vegetables such as baby carrots or young peas.

MAKES 4 SERVINGS
4 tablespoons unsalted butter
1 cup sliced button mushrooms
4 shallots, sliced

4 (6- to 8-ounce) halibut steaks
¾ cup dry white wine
Salt and freshly ground pepper, to taste
2 tablespoons heavy cream

Preheat the oven to 350°F. In a flameproof baking dish or an ovenproof frying pan, heat 2 tablespoons of the butter over medium heat. Add one fourth of the mushroom and shallot slices and cook until they absorb the butter, about 1 minute. Place the halibut steaks on top and pour the wine over the fish. Lay the remaining mushrooms and shallots on the fish. Season with salt and pepper, and dot with small pieces of the remaining 2 tablespoons butter. Cover with foil and bake until the fish is barely opaque when flaked with the tip of a sharp knife, 10 to 15 minutes.

Using a perforated metal turner, transfer the halibut steaks, mushrooms, and shallots to a warm platter, and cover with foil to keep warm. Strain the cooking liquid into a small saucepan. Add the cream, bring to a boil over high heat, and cook until slightly thickened, about 3 minutes. Season the sauce with salt and pepper. Transfer the halibut steaks and mushrooms to four warm dinner plates, and spoon the sauce over each serving.

STEAMED COD WITH GINGER AND SCALLIONS

Cantonese restaurants all over the world serve steamed seafood—just about anything that swims, from sea bass or sole to lobster or crab. However, cod is especially good prepared like this. Chinese woks often come with a large steaming rack that will fit a standard dinner plate. Lacking a wok, use a large covered roasting pan with a rack, and place the fish on an oval platter that will fit the pan.

MAKES 4 SERVINGS
    4 (6-ounce) cod fillets, with skin
    2 tablespoons vegetable oil
    2 tablespoons light soy sauce
    1½ teaspoons dry sherry
    2 teaspoons rice vinegar
    1 teaspoon Asian dark sesame oil
    1 (2-inch) piece fresh ginger, peeled and cut into
        matchstick-sized strips
    6 scallions, thinly sliced on the bias
    4 sprigs fresh cilantro

Place the fish on a plate or platter that will fit your steaming utensil. Pour the vegetable oil over the fish. Pour enough water into the steamer to come about 1 inch up the sides. Place the plate of fish in the steamer, cover, and then bring the water to a full boil over high heat.

While the water is coming to a boil, in a small saucepan, combine the soy sauce, sherry, rice vinegar, sesame oil, and ginger. Bring to a simmer over medium heat and cook for 2 minutes. Pour the soy sauce mixture over the fish. Cover again and steam until the fish is barely opaque when flaked in the thickest part with the tip of a knife, 6 to 8 minutes. Sprinkle with the scallions and steam for 2 more minutes.

Using a perforated metal turner, transfer the fish to individual plates. Spoon over the cooking juices, and garnish with the cilantro. Serve immediately.

WHOLE BAKED SEA BASS WITH TOMATOES

A whole baked fish always makes an impressive main dish. This method of preparation is appropriate for any large fish, such as snapper, sea trout, or grouper. To estimate baking times for whole fish, measure the height of the fish in its thickest part, and allow 15 minutes for each inch. For example, a 2-inch-thick fish will take about 30 minutes.

MAKES 4 SERVINGS
    1 (3- to 4-pound) whole sea bass, cleaned and scaled
    3 garlic cloves, halved lengthwise
    2 lemon slices, halved
    Salt and freshly ground pepper, to taste
    A few sprigs fresh fennel leaves, or ½ teaspoon
        fennel seed
    3 large ripe tomatoes, peeled, seeded, and quartered
    2 small onions, sliced
    ¼ cup olive oil

Preheat the oven to 375°F. Butter a large baking dish or roasting pan. Rinse the fish and pat dry with paper towels. Make two deep diagonal slashes in the thickest part on both sides of the fish. In each slash, place a piece of garlic and a half lemon slice, peel side outward. Place a piece of garlic in the head. Put the remaining garlic in the body, and season with salt and pepper. If using fennel seed, sprinkle it inside the fish. Put the fish in the prepared dish and surround with the tomatoes and onions. Pour the olive oil over all, and season with salt and pepper.

Bake in the bottom third of the oven until the fish is opaque in the thickest part when flaked with the tip of a knife, about 35 minutes. If using fennel sprigs, scatter them over the fish 15 minutes before the end of cooking. Lift the fish off the bone, in serving-sized pieces, and serve hot with the vegetables. The fish can also be served cold, with a garlicky tomato sauce.

FISH FILLETS IN BASQUE PEPPER SAUCE

Pipérade, a zesty vegetable mixture featuring different-colored bell peppers, tomatoes, and onions, can be found in various dishes throughout the Pyrenees mountains. Here it acts as a flavorful sauce for baked fish fillets, where the colors of the ingredients add to the appeal of the finished dish.

MAKES 4 SERVINGS

4 tablespoons olive oil

2 medium onions, sliced

2 medium red or yellow bell peppers, seeded and cut into ¼-inch-wide strips

2 garlic cloves, minced

3 large ripe tomatoes, peeled, seeded, and coarsely chopped

Salt and freshly ground pepper, to taste

4 (6-ounce) skinless fish fillets, such as porgy, sea bass, or snapper

12 black Mediterranean olives, pitted

In a large frying pan, heat 2 tablespoons of the olive oil over medium heat. Add the onions and cook until they are soft and translucent, about 5 minutes. Add the peppers and garlic, and cook until the peppers have softened, about 10 minutes. Stir in the tomatoes and cook until the mixture forms a thick sauce, about 15 minutes. Season with salt and pepper. Transfer to a bowl and set aside.

Preheat the oven to 350°F. Lightly oil a shallow baking dish. Season the fish with salt and pepper. Heat 1 tablespoon of the remaining oil in the cleaned frying pan over medium-high heat until very hot but not smoking. Add the fish and cook, turning once, until lightly browned on both sides, about 2 minutes. Place in the baking dish and cover with the tomato-pepper sauce. Bake until the fish is cooked through, about 15 minutes. About 3 minutes before the fish is done, scatter the olives on top and drizzle with the remaining 1 tablespoon oil. Serve hot.

BAKED BLUEFISH WITH SWEET MUSTARD GLAZE

East Coast bluefish has a rich, oily flesh that needs a sharp accent to bring out its flavor. This mustard glaze does the job perfectly.

MAKES 4 SERVINGS

4 (8-ounce) bluefish fillets
⅓ cup Dijon mustard
1 tablespoon packed light brown sugar
2 teaspoons chopped fresh tarragon or 1 teaspoon dried tarragon
1 teaspoon soy sauce

Preheat the oven to 375°F. Place the bluefish, skin side down, in a lightly oiled baking dish. In a small bowl, mix together the Dijon mustard, light brown sugar, fresh or dried tarragon, and soy sauce. Spread evenly over the bluefish. Bake until the fish appears opaque when flaked in the center with the tip of a knife, 15 to 20 minutes. Serve hot.

FRIED SARDINES WITH LEMON

Whenever you see plump fresh sardines in the fish market, think about preparing them this way—simply sautéed in olive oil and served with a good squeeze of lemon juice to offset their oily flesh. This quick preparation is also applicable to other small fresh fish, such as anchovies.

MAKES 4 SERVINGS AS A FIRST COURSE, OR 2 SERVINGS AS A MAIN COURSE

1½ pounds fresh sardines
2 lemons
Salt, to taste
4 tablespoons olive oil

Rinse the sardines well under cold running water, rubbing them to remove their tiny scales. To clean the fish, pinch off their heads and gills, and pull out the innards at the same time. Otherwise, run your finger down the belly to open, and remove the innards. Rinse again and pat dry with paper towels. Place the sardines in a glass baking dish. Squeeze the juice of 1 lemon over the fish and let stand for 30 minutes. Season with salt.

In a large frying pan, heat the oil over medium-high heat until very hot but not smoking. Carefully add the sardines to the pan, standing well back to avoid any spitting fat. Cook, turning once, until golden-brown, about 5 minutes. Transfer to paper towels to drain. Serve hot, with the second lemon cut into wedges.

MEDITERRANEAN SWORDFISH IN TOMATO-ONION SAUCE

The meaty quality of swordfish makes it a good candidate for baking. For an interesting variation of this sauce, substitute ½ teaspoon fennel seed for the oregano, and add ¼ teaspoon crushed saffron threads.

MAKES 4 SERVINGS

½ cup olive oil
1 tablespoon dry white wine
3 sprigs fresh thyme
4 (6-ounce) swordfish steaks
3 medium onions, sliced
2 garlic cloves, minced
1 pound ripe plum tomatoes, peeled, seeded, and coarsely chopped
1 teaspoon finely chopped fresh oregano or ½ teaspoon dried oregano
Salt and freshly ground pepper, to taste
4 slices white bread, cut into triangles

Mix 2 tablespoons of the oil, the wine, and the thyme in a shallow glass baking dish. Add the swordfish. Cover and let marinate in the refrigerator, turning the fish occasionally, for 1 to 2 hours, no longer.

Preheat the oven to 375°F. In a large frying pan, heat 2 tablespoons of the oil over medium heat. Add the onions and garlic and cook, stirring occasionally, until softened, about 5 minutes. Stir in the tomatoes and oregano, and season with the salt and pepper. Pour the tomato-onion sauce over the swordfish steaks and stir to mix with the marinade. Bake until the swordfish is medium-rare (pink) when pierced in the center with a sharp knife, about 20 minutes.

Meanwhile, in a frying pan, heat the remaining oil over medium-high heat. Fry the triangles of bread until golden-brown on both sides, 3 to 4 minutes. Drain on paper towels. Arrange the bread triangles around the fish and serve immediately.

SICILIAN BROILED TUNA

Tuna plays a large part in Sicilian cuisine, and is often cooked in large portions like a meat roast.

MAKES 4 SERVINGS

1 (2-pound) tuna steak, in one piece, skin removed
4 anchovy fillets, cut in half
6 tablespoons lemon juice
6 tablespoons olive oil
1 teaspoon chopped fresh marjoram or oregano, or ½ teaspoon dried oregano
Salt and freshly ground pepper, to taste
Delicate Tomato Sauce, for serving

Using the tip of a sharp knife, make eight incisions all over the tuna, and stuff the incisions with the anchovies. In a medium bowl, whisk the lemon juice with the oil. Add the tuna and cover. Let marinate in the refrigerator, turning often, for at least 1 and up to 2 hours.

Preheat the broiler, and line the broiler pan with aluminum foil. Remove the tuna from the bowl and shake off excess marinade. Place the tuna on the foil-lined pan. Season the tuna with the marjoram, salt, and pepper. Broil, turning once, and occasionally basting with the marinade, until the fish looks medium-rare in the center when flaked with the tip of a knife, 15 to 20 minutes. Serve immediately, with the tomato sauce passed on the side.

BAKED STUFFED POMPANO

A tarragon and chive stuffing adds flavor and keeps the fish succulent during baking. Removing the backbone and ribs makes for easy serving.

MAKES 4 SERVINGS
    1 (2½-pound) whole pompano, cleaned and scaled
    1 cup fresh bread crumbs
    ¼ cup milk
    6 tablespoons butter, at room temperature
    2 large egg yolks
    1½ teaspoons finely chopped fresh tarragon
    1½ teaspoons finely chopped fresh chives
    Salt and freshly ground pepper, to taste
    ⅔ cup dry white wine
    3 tablespoons heavy cream
    2 teaspoons finely chopped fresh parsley

Preheat the oven to 325°F. Lightly oil a baking dish large enough to hold the fish. Using a long, flexible, sharp knife, make a long slit down the back of the fish. Running the knife along the rib bones, cut out and remove the backbone and ribs.

In a medium bowl, moisten the bread crumbs with the milk, and then squeeze out the excess milk. Add 4 tablespoons of the butter, the egg yolks, tarragon, chives, and some salt and pepper. Mix well. Stuff the fish with the herb mixture, and use kitchen string to sew up the back and belly incisions.

Place the fish in the prepared baking dish. Pour the wine over the fish, season with salt and pepper, and dot with the remaining butter. Bake until the thickest part of the fish feels tender when pressed with a fingertip, about 30 minutes. Using a fish lifter, carefully transfer the fish to a warmed serving platter. Cover with foil to keep warm.

Pour the cooking juices into a medium saucepan. Bring to a boil and cook until reduced by half, about

5 minutes. Add the cream and parsley and continue cooking until the sauce has thickened slightly, about 3 more minutes. Season with salt. Pour the sauce around the fish and serve immediately.

TUNA WITH HOT RED CHILE SAUCE

Adapted from a North African recipe, this is an aromatic, boldly colored dish. Serve it with fried potatoes or couscous.

MAKES 4 SERVINGS
    4 (6-ounce) tuna or swordfish steaks
    4 garlic cloves: 2 crushed to a paste with ½ teaspoon salt, and 2 minced
    1 teaspoon ground cumin
    3 medium red bell peppers, roasted, peeled, and seeded
    3 medium yellow or orange bell peppers, roasted, peeled, and seeded
    ¼ cup olive oil, plus more as needed
    1¼ pounds ripe plum tomatoes, peeled, seeded, and quartered, or use canned
    2 hot fresh green chile peppers, seeded and chopped
    Salt and freshly ground pepper, to taste
    Shredded fresh mint and lemon wedges, for garnish

Rub the tuna steaks with the garlic paste and ground cumin. Cover and refrigerate while making the sauce.

Cut the roasted peppers into thin strips. Set aside about ½ cup of the pepper strips to use as a garnish. Stack the remaining strips and cut them crosswise into ¼-inch pieces. In a large frying pan, heat the oil over medium-high heat. Add the tomatoes, chiles, and minced garlic. Cook rapidly, stirring often, until the tomato juices have evaporated and the mixture is caramelizing and beginning to stick to the pan, about 10 minutes. Add a little more oil, if needed. Remove from the heat. Crush the tomatoes with a large spoon, then stir in the chopped peppers. Season this sauce with salt and pepper.

Preheat the oven to 400°F. In the center of four 12-inch squares of aluminum foil, place a heaping tablespoon of the sauce. Top with a tuna steak and cover with the remaining sauce, dividing it equally. Bring up the edges of the foil squares over the fish and tightly crimp together to seal closed. Place the foil packets on a baking sheet. Bake for about 15 minutes.

Open the packets and turn the tuna and sauce onto four dinner plates. Sprinkle each serving with mint, and serve with lemon wedges.

TUNA WITH HOT RED CHILE SAUCE

SKATE WITH BROWN BUTTER SAUCE

Skate, with its deliciously sweet flesh, is finally finding the recognition in America that it has long enjoyed in Europe. This is a classic preparation.

MAKES 4 SERVINGS

1 quart Court-Bouillon
2 (1- to 2-pound) skate wings, skin removed
4 tablespoons unsalted butter
1 teaspoon red wine vinegar
2 teaspoons drained capers (optional)
Salt and freshly ground pepper, to taste
1 teaspoon finely chopped fresh parsley

In a large frying pan, bring the court-bouillon to a simmer over medium heat. Add the skate wings and return to the simmer. Cover and remove from the heat. Let the retained heat cook the fish until it looks opaque when flaked in the center with the tip of a sharp knife, about 15 minutes. Using a perforated metal turner, transfer the skate to a platter and cover to keep warm.

In a small frying pan, heat the butter over medium heat until it is hazelnut brown in color, 1 to 2 minutes. Off the heat, swirl in the red wine vinegar and the optional capers. Season with salt and pepper, and stir in the chopped parsley. To serve, lift off the top fillets from the skate wings and place on dinner plates. Remove the cartilage, and serve the bottom fillets. Pour the sauce over the skate and serve.

NORMANDY FISH STEW

The French province of Normandy is famous for an abundance of apples from its orchards and fish from its coast. Monkfish is used in this rich fish stew, called *matelote normande* in France, but sea bass or snapper is also very good, and if you like eel, this recipe is a traditional way to serve it. Hard, alcoholic apple cider, which is quite dry, almost like a fruity white wine, acts as the cooking liquid. A few American companies are beginning to make hard cider, but if you can't find it and you want to keep an apple flavor in the stew, use a combination of ¾ cup dry white wine and ½ cup regular apple cider.

MAKES 4 SERVINGS

2 pounds mussels, scrubbed and debearded if necessary
6 tablespoons unsalted butter
2 medium onions, finely chopped
1¼ cups dry hard cider or dry white wine

NORMANDY FISH STEW

2 pounds monkfish, boned and cut into 2-inch pieces
3 tablespoons all-purpose flour
8 medium shrimp, cooked, peeled, and deveined
2 tablespoons chopped fresh parsley
Salt and freshly ground pepper, to taste
Juice of ½ lemon (optional)

Place the prepared mussels and 3 tablespoons cold water in a large saucepan. Cover and bring to a boil over high heat. Cook, shaking the saucepan often, until all the mussels have opened, about 5 minutes. Remove the mussels to a platter and leave them to cool. Strain the cooking liquid. When the mussels are cool enough to handle, shell them, discarding the shells, and set them aside.

In a large saucepan, heat 2 tablespoons of the butter over medium heat. Add the onions and cook until they are soft and translucent, about 5 minutes. Add the strained mussel liquid and the cider. Bring to a simmer. Add the monkfish. The liquid should just cover the fish, so add hot water, if necessary. Simmer gently over medium-low heat until the fish is almost cooked through, about 5 minutes.

In a small bowl, work the remaining 4 tablespoons butter and the flour together to make a paste. Add this to the simmering liquid in small pieces, stirring constantly. Continue to simmer until the sauce is lightly thickened and the fish is opaque when pierced in the center with the tip of a knife, 3 to 5 minutes longer. Add the reserved mussels, the shrimp, and the chopped parsley. Season with salt and pepper, and add the optional lemon juice. Cook just until the mussels and shrimp are heated through, about 1 minute. Transfer to a warm soup tureen and serve immediately, accompanied by plenty of fresh, crusty French bread.

OVEN-FRIED CATFISH WITH REMOULADE SAUCE

Crispy catfish fillets in a cornmeal crust, served with a spoonful of spicy remoulade sauce alongside, are a specialty of Southern cuisine. These fillets are oven-fried—a quick and healthy way to prepare this old-fashioned dish.

MAKES 4 SERVINGS

¾ cup buttermilk
1 tablespoon Cajun Dry Rub
1 cup yellow cornmeal, preferably stoneground
Salt, to taste
4 (7-ounce) catfish fillets
3 tablespoons vegetable oil
½ cup Remoulade Sauce

Preheat the oven to 400°F. Lightly oil a large baking sheet and then place this in the oven to heat up for about 3 minutes.

In a shallow dish, mix together the buttermilk and the Cajun dry rub. Place the cornmeal in another shallow dish and season with a little salt. Dip each catfish fillet first in the buttermilk and Cajun dry rub mixture, shaking off the excess, and then coat with the cornmeal.

Place the prepared catfish fillets on the hot baking sheet, and drizzle them with the vegetable oil. Bake until the coating is a lovely golden-brown color, about 20 minutes. Serve hot, accompanied by the remoulade sauce.

SALMON WITH HERBED YOGURT SAUCE

This fish dish is based on an Indian recipe, and is very easy to make. Boiled new potatoes would go well with the salmon.

MAKES 4 SERVINGS
4 (5- to 6-ounce) skinless salmon fillets
2 tablespoons lemon juice
Salt, to taste
½ cup packed fresh cilantro leaves
½ cup packed fresh flat-leaf parsley leaves
¼ cup coarsely chopped fresh chives
3 hot fresh green chile peppers (such as serrano),
    seeded and chopped
3 garlic cloves, peeled
1 cup plain yogurt, drained
½ cup vegetable oil

Place the salmon fillets in a shallow glass baking dish and sprinkle them with lemon juice and salt. Cover the dish and leave the salmon to marinate in the refrigerator, turning the fillets from time to time, for 1 to 2 hours, no longer.

In a food processor fitted with the metal blade, purée the cilantro, parsley, chives, chiles, and garlic to a mush, adding a little water if needed to help smooth out the mixture. Pour the processed herb mixture into a shallow dish, and put the thick drained yogurt in another shallow dish.

Heat the vegetable oil in a large frying pan over medium-high heat. Dip each salmon fillet in the yogurt to coat well, and then dip into the herb mixture. Quickly place the fillets in the frying pan, being careful of hot spitting oil. Cook, turning the fish over once, until it looks barely opaque when pierced in the thickest part with the tip of a sharp knife, 6 to 8 minutes. Transfer the fish to paper towels to drain. Serve immediately.

SOY-MARINATED SALMON BROCHETTES

Salmon's inherent oiliness makes it a perfect fish for grilling. Charcoal grilling really brings out the fish's flavor, but these brochettes can also be broiled indoors or cooked on a ridged cast-iron grill pan. Serve the brochettes on a bed of Sesame Spinach.

MAKES 4 SERVINGS
1½ pounds skinless salmon fillet, cut into 1-inch pieces
Chopped garlic chives or scallions, and lime wedges,
    for garnish
Marinade
¼ cup light soy sauce
¼ cup rice wine or dry sherry
1 (2-inch) piece fresh ginger, unpeeled, thinly sliced
Thinly pared zest and juice of 1 lime
2 teaspoons Chinese chile oil
1 tablespoon syrup from a jar of candied stem ginger,
    or 1 tablespoon honey
½ teaspoon five-spice powder
½ teaspoon chile flakes

To make the marinade, mix all of the ingredients in a medium nonreactive bowl. Add the salmon. Cover and let marinate in the refrigerator, stirring occasionally, for 1 to 2 hours, no longer.

Build a hot charcoal fire in an outdoor grill. Lightly oil the grill. Drain the salmon, reserving the marinade, and thread onto metal skewers. (If using bamboo skewers, soak them for 30 minutes, then drain.) Grill for 5 minutes, then turn the brochettes over and grill until the salmon is just cooked, about 3 more minutes. The outside should be lightly charred and blistered.

Place the brochettes on dinner plates. If desired, gently heat the marinade in a small saucepan and brush it onto the brochettes to give a glossy finish. Sprinkle with garlic chives or scallions and serve with lime wedges.

GRILLED SALMON WITH COOL AND HOT CUCUMBERS

This combination of hot grilled salmon with cool, spiced cucumber is very pleasing, particularly eaten outdoors on a hot summer day.

MAKES 4 SERVINGS
4 (9-ounce) salmon steaks
1 tablespoon vegetable oil
Salt and freshly ground pepper, to taste
Cucumber Salad
1 large cucumber, peeled, halved lengthwise, seeded,
    and sliced into ⅛-inch-thick half-moons
½ teaspoon salt

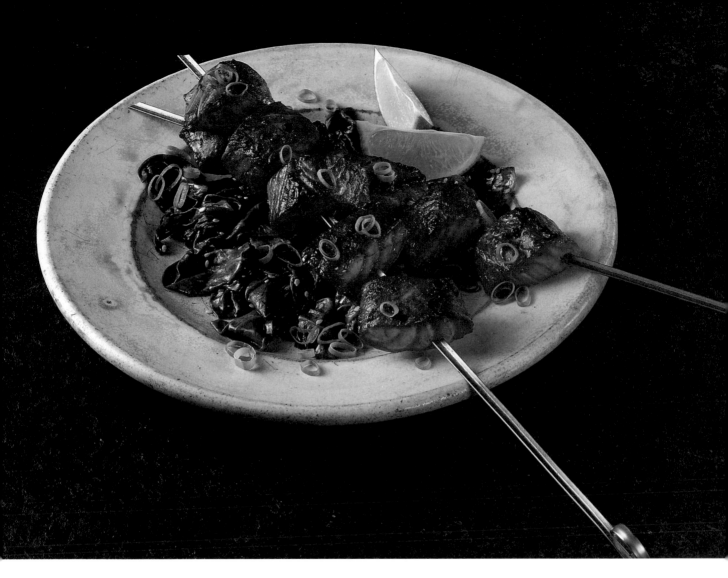

2 tablespoons plain yogurt

2 tablespoons chopped fresh cilantro

1 tablespoon chopped fresh mint

1 or 2 hot fresh chile peppers (such as jalapeño or
serrano), seeded and minced

1 garlic clove, minced

2 teaspoons lime juice

1 teaspoon granulated sugar

½ teaspoon ground cumin

Cayenne pepper, to taste

To make the cucumber salad, toss the cucumbers with the salt and then refrigerate for 1 hour to draw out some of the cucumber juices. Drain, rinse under cold water, drain again, and pat dry with paper towels. Add the remaining salad ingredients and toss to combine. Cover and refrigerate until ready to serve. (The salad can be prepared up to 8 hours ahead.)

Build a hot charcoal fire in an outdoor grill. Lightly oil the grill. Brush the salmon on both sides with oil, and season with salt and pepper. Grill, turning once, until the fish looks barely opaque when pierced in the thickest part, 8 to 10 minutes. Serve the salmon steaks with the cucumber salad.

SOY-MARINATED SALMON BROCHETTES
WITH SESAME SPINACH

BAKED WHOLE SALMON FILLET WITH LEMON AND HERBS

A lovely main course for a spring buffet, this recipe proves that some of the simplest foods are the best.

MAKES 8 TO 12 SERVINGS

1 (3-pound) salmon fillet, fine bones removed
with tweezers

Salt and freshly ground pepper, to taste

¼ cup chopped mixed fresh herbs, such as tarragon,
dill, and parsley

2 tablespoons minced shallots

2 lemons, very thinly sliced and seeds removed

Italian Herb Sauce or Remoulade Sauce, for serving

Preheat the oven to 375°F. Lightly oil a large piece of heavy-duty aluminum foil. Place the fillet on the foil, skin side down. Season with salt and pepper, sprinkle with the herbs and shallots, and top with the lemon slices. Wrap well in the foil. Place on a baking sheet.

Fish/Shellfish

Bake until the salmon looks barely opaque when pierced in the thickest part (unwrap the salmon to check this), 35 to 40 minutes. Open the foil and cool the salmon to room temperature, then rewrap it and refrigerate until chilled. To serve, transfer the salmon onto an oval serving platter. Cut the fish into individual servings, and serve with a bowl of the sauce on the side.

TROUT WITH MUSHROOMS EN PAPILLOTE

Other small fish under 1 pound can also be prepared in this manner, baked in an envelope of parchment paper or foil with a finely chopped mushroom mixture, called a *duxelles* in French.

MAKES 4 SERVINGS
2 cups finely chopped button mushrooms
1 tablespoon lemon juice
2 tablespoons unsalted butter, plus softened butter for the parchment paper or foil
1/4 cup chopped shallots
1 tablespoon chopped fresh parsley
Salt and freshly ground pepper, to taste
4 (12-ounce) whole trout, cleaned and scaled
Velvety White Sauce, made with fish stock, for serving

Toss the mushrooms with the lemon juice, which will help keep the mushrooms white. In a large frying pan, melt the butter over medium heat. Add the mushrooms and shallots, and cook, stirring often, until the mushrooms give off their liquid. Continue cooking until the liquid has evaporated and the mixture is quite dry, 4 to 5 minutes. Stir in the parsley, and season with salt and pepper.

Preheat the oven to 400°F. Cut four 12-inch rounds of parchment paper or foil. Butter one side of each round, leaving the borders unbuttered. Using a sharp knife, cut two deep slashes on both sides of each trout, in the thickest part. Season the fish, inside and out, with salt and pepper.

Reserve about 1/3 cup of the mushrooms for the sauce. Place a spoonful of the remaining mushrooms on one half of each paper round, buttered side up. Top with a trout, and spoon the remaining mushrooms over the fish. Fold over the paper round to enclose the fish, and pleat the edges together twice to seal them. Place the packets on a baking sheet and bake for 15 minutes. Meanwhile, if necessary, reheat the white sauce; stir in the reserved 1/3 cup mushrooms, and keep warm. Serve the fish in their paper packets, letting each guest open his or her own, and passing the sauce on the side.

VERMOUTH-MARINATED TROUT PIEDMONTESE

Italians love cold marinated fish, served either as a piquant first course or as a cool entrée. This recipe, from the Val d'Aosta, should be made at least a day ahead.

MAKES 6 SERVINGS
6 (12-ounce) trout, cleaned and scaled
1/2 cup all-purpose flour
1/4 cup vegetable oil
Marinade
6 tablespoons vegetable oil
2 tablespoons olive oil
2 medium onions, sliced
2 garlic cloves, sliced
6 tablespoons dry vermouth
3 tablespoons white wine vinegar
4 strips lemon zest
4 fresh sage leaves
1 sprig fresh rosemary
1 teaspoon whole black peppercorns, coarsely crushed
Salt, to taste

Coat the fish lightly with the flour, shaking off excess flour. Heat the oil in a frying pan over medium heat. Add the fish and cook, turning once, until golden on the outside and opaque when flaked in the thickest part, about 12 minutes. Drain on paper towels. Place the fish, side by side, in an earthenware or glass dish.

To make the marinade, heat both oils in a medium saucepan over medium heat. Add the onions and garlic and cook until softened, about 5 minutes. Add the remaining marinade ingredients and bring to a boil. Pour the hot marinade over the trout. Let cool to room temperature, then cover. Let marinate in the refrigerator, turning the fish occasionally, for at least 1 and up to 3 days. Serve lightly chilled.

VARIATION: Substitute orange zest for the lemon zest, and add 2 tablespoons dark raisins to the marinade.

BACALAO WITH POTATOES

Salt cod is a beloved ingredient of Hispanic cooks, and this way of preparing it with potatoes in a garlicky tomato sauce is known from Spain to Puerto Rico. Salt cod needs at least 24 hours' soaking, to desalt it.

MAKES 4 SERVINGS
1 pound salt cod fillet
3 tablespoons olive oil
1/2 cup all-purpose flour
2 pounds boiling potatoes, peeled and cut into 1/4-inch-thick rounds

3 medium onions, thinly sliced
4 large ripe tomatoes, peeled, seeded,
  and sliced
1 garlic clove, chopped
1 tablespoon chopped fresh parsley
⅛ teaspoon crushed saffron threads
Salt and freshly ground white pepper, to taste

Place the salt cod in a bowl. Add enough cold water to cover the fish by at least 2 inches. Refrigerate for 24 hours, changing the water twice. Drain.

Place the cod in a large frying pan and add enough cold water to cover. Bring to a boil over medium-low heat. Remove from the heat and let the cod cool in the liquid. Drain, and cut into 1-inch squares.

Heat the oil in a large frying pan over medium-high heat until hot but not smoking. Coat the squares of cod in the flour, shaking off the excess flour. Cook until golden-brown on all sides, about 4 minutes. Using a perforated metal turner, transfer the cod to paper towels to drain, leaving the oil in the pan.

Reduce the heat to medium-low. Add the potatoes, onions, tomatoes, and garlic to the pan and cook, stirring occasionally, for about 2 minutes. Add the parsley and enough boiling water to cover the vegetables. Cover and simmer until the potatoes are almost tender, about 15 minutes.

Stir in the saffron, and return the cod to the pan. Season with pepper; taste and add a little salt, if desired. Cover and continue cooking until the cod is heated through and the potatoes are tender, about 10 more minutes. Serve hot from the pan.

———————— • ————————

CRAB CAKES WITH ROASTED TOMATO SAUCE

These crab cakes are quick and easy to make, and the roasted tomato sauce provides a tasty alternative to tartar sauce.

MAKES 4 SERVINGS
1 pound crabmeat, preferably lump
¾ cup fresh bread crumbs
4 tablespoons unsalted butter
1 medium onion, grated
2 garlic cloves, minced
¼ teaspoon dried thyme
⅛ teaspoon hot Hungarian paprika, or a large pinch
  of cayenne pepper
1 tablespoon chopped fresh parsley
Salt and freshly ground pepper, to taste
Lemon wedges, for serving
Roasted Tomato Sauce, for serving

Pick over the crab and discard any cartilage. In a medium bowl, toss the bread crumbs together with 2 to 3 tablespoons water, just to moisten. Add the crabmeat and set aside. In a medium frying pan, melt 2 tablespoons butter over medium heat. Add the onion, garlic, thyme, and paprika. Cook until the onions soften, about 5 minutes. Add to the crab mixture, along with the parsley. Season with salt and pepper. Using floured hands, form into eight cakes. In a large frying pan, heat the remaining butter over medium heat. Add the crab cakes and cook, turning once, until browned on both sides, about 5 minutes. Serve with lemon wedges and the warm tomato sauce.

SOFT SHELL CRABS WITH MACADAMIA-LIME BUTTER

Soft shell crabs are a summertime delicacy on the Atlantic seaboard. Here they are served perfectly crisp, topped with sizzling macadamia nuts. Cook soft shell crabs with caution, as they tend to sputter and spit hot oil when you least expect it.

MAKES 4 SERVINGS
8 large soft shell crabs, cleaned
2 cups all-purpose flour
Salt and freshly ground pepper, to taste
1 cup milk
2 large eggs
Vegetable oil, for frying
4 tablespoons unsalted butter
1 cup coarsely chopped unsalted macadamia nuts
2 tablespoons lime juice

Pat the crabs dry with paper towels. In a shallow dish, combine the flour with a seasoning of salt and pepper. In another dish, beat the milk and eggs together. Dip each crab in the flour to coat lightly, then into the milk mixture, and finally back into the flour again, shaking off excess flour. Place the crabs on a wire cooling rack and refrigerate for 30 minutes to set the coating.

Preheat the oven to 200°F. Pour oil into a frying pan to come ¼ inch up the sides. Heat over medium-high heat until very hot, but not smoking. Carefully add four crabs to the pan. Cook, turning once with kitchen tongs, until golden-brown, 3 to 4 minutes. Transfer to a paper-towel-lined baking sheet, and keep warm in the oven while you cook the remaining crabs.

Discard the oil from the frying pan. Put the butter in the pan and melt over medium heat. Add the macadamia nuts and cook just until lightly browned, about 2 minutes. Remove from the heat and stir in the lime juice. Serve the crabs on dinner plates, spooning the macadamia-lime mixture over the top.

GRILLED LOBSTER

Lobster cooked in this way has a wonderful flavor, and has to be one of summer's greatest pleasures. If you want to broil the lobsters indoors, be sure you can fit the amount of lobsters you want to serve in your broiler at the same time—it may only be large enough to hold two or three.

MAKES 4 SERVINGS

4 (1½-pound) lobsters, freshly killed

¼ cup olive oil

Salt and cayenne pepper, to taste

8 tablespoons (1 stick) unsalted butter, melted

Build a hot charcoal fire in an outdoor grill and let the coals burn down until they are just medium-hot, rather than blazing. Lightly oil the grill. Using a heavy, sharp knife, carefully cut each of the lobsters in half lengthwise, and remove the sacs found in both sides of the head. Using the back of the knife, crack the claw shells, but do not remove them. Brush the lobsters all over with the olive oil and season with salt and cayenne pepper.

Grill the lobsters, shell sides up and covered with the grill lid, for 5 minutes. Turn the lobsters and spoon some of the melted butter over the top. Grill until the flesh is just firm when pressed with a finger, 5 to 7 more minutes. Place the cooked lobsters, with their cut sides up, on four dinner plates. Pour the remaining melted butter over the lobsters and then serve immediately.

GRILLED BUTTERFLIED SHRIMP WITH LEMON

This is an easy and extremely tasty way to serve large shrimp. They will be eaten with your fingers, so serve them at a casual dinner with good friends. If desired, you can thread the shrimp onto skewers, piercing them crosswise to keep them open and butterflied, before grilling them.

MAKES 4 SERVINGS

2 pounds jumbo or extra-large shrimp, unpeeled

2 tablespoons lemon juice

Salt and freshly ground pepper, to taste

¼ cup extra virgin olive oil

Devein and butterfly the shrimp, then flatten them lightly. In a large bowl, whisk together the lemon juice and a seasoning of salt and pepper. Gradually whisk in the olive oil. Add the shrimp and toss to coat them all thoroughly with the marinade. Leave to stand for about 30 minutes.

Build a hot charcoal fire in an outdoor grill, and lightly oil the grill. Put the shrimp on the grill cut sides down, and grill for 2 minutes. Turn them over, baste well with the marinade, and grill until they are pink in color and firm in texture, about 2 more minutes. Serve immediately.

SHRIMP BROCHETTES WITH MINT BUTTER

Mint may seem to be an unusual seasoning for shrimp, but it is both delicious and refreshing. Use a large-leafed variety, such as spearmint.

MAKES 4 SERVINGS

1 large bunch fresh mint

1½ pounds medium or large shrimp, peeled and deveined

8 tablespoons (1 stick) unsalted butter

2 tablespoons lemon juice

Salt and cayenne pepper, to taste

Soak four or eight bamboo skewers in a bowl of cold water for about 30 minutes.

Discard the mint stems, and reserve about 40 of the largest leaves; chop enough of the remaining mint leaves to measure 1 tablespoon and set aside. Thread the shrimp, alternating with the whole mint leaves, onto the skewers (if you use two parallel skewers for each brochette, instead of one skewer, the brochettes will be easier to turn, and this will also prevent the shrimp from twirling around on the skewer). When threading the shrimp onto the skewers, pierce each shrimp through the top and bottom, and keep the natural curve of the shrimp.

Preheat the broiler. In a small saucepan, melt the butter with the lemon juice and a seasoning of salt and cayenne pepper. Baste the brochettes well with the lemon butter.

Broil the brochettes, basting them occasionally and turning once, until the shrimp are firm and pink, 3 to 4 minutes. Stir the chopped mint into the remaining melted butter. Serve the shrimp brochettes immediately, with a little of the mint butter poured over each serving.

GRILLED THAI-MARINATED SHRIMP

During grilling, the shells of the shrimp scorch and blacken, leaving the flesh inside deliciously moist and juicy. A simple salad of thinly sliced English cucumber, seasoned with salt and sugar and moistened with a little white wine vinegar, would be an ideal accompaniment to this dish.

SHRIMP BROCHETTES WITH MINT BUTTER

MAKES 4 SERVINGS

2 pounds large shrimp, unpeeled

Marinade

3 tablespoons vegetable oil

2 tablespoons syrup from a jar of candied stem ginger, or 2 tablespoons honey

¼ cup fish sauce

¼ cup lime juice

4 kaffir lime leaves, torn into pieces, or grated zest of 1 lime

½ cup coarsely chopped cilantro stems

3 tablespoons chopped shallot

1 (2-inch) piece fresh ginger, unpeeled, thinly sliced

4 small hot green chile peppers (such as Thai or serrano), seeded and chopped, or to taste

2 garlic cloves, sliced

Dipping Sauce

½ cup chopped fresh cilantro leaves

6 tablespoons lime juice

¼ cup chopped fresh mint leaves

3 small hot chile peppers (such as Thai or serrano), seeded and chopped, or to taste

5 tablespoons fish sauce

2 teaspoons granulated sugar

2 garlic cloves, chopped

To make the marinade, mix all of the ingredients together in a large bowl. Add the shrimp and turn to coat them thoroughly. Cover and let marinate in the refrigerator, occasionally tossing the shrimp, for at least 6 hours or overnight.

To make the dipping sauce, combine all of the ingredients in a blender or food processor fitted with the metal blade. Add 5 tablespoons water, and blend until well mixed but not completely smooth. Pour into four small serving dishes.

Build a hot charcoal fire in an outdoor grill (or you can use a ridged cast-iron grill pan or the oven broiler if you prefer). Lightly oil the grill. Remove the shrimp from the marinade and heap them onto the grill. Cook, turning once, until the shrimp are pink and firm to the touch, 4 to 5 minutes. Serve together with the dipping sauce.

SHRIMP AND CUCUMBER CURRY

Cucumber is an unusual addition to this curry, but their mild taste and slight crunch are the perfect foil to the spicy sauce. If you wish, you can substitute 2 medium zucchini.

MAKES 4 SERVINGS

1½ pounds medium shrimp, peeled and deveined (shells reserved)

3 or 4 scallions, coarsely chopped

5 garlic cloves, 2 whole and 3 minced

1 large English cucumber, quartered lengthwise and cut into 2-inch pieces

5 tablespoons unsalted butter

1 large onion, thinly sliced

2 tablespoons finely chopped fresh ginger

2 teaspoons garam masala

1 teaspoon turmeric

½ teaspoon ground cinnamon

½ teaspoon ground cloves

1 teaspoon granulated sugar

½ teaspoon salt

1 tablespoon all-purpose flour

1¼ cups thick coconut milk

3 small hot fresh green chile peppers (such as serrano), seeded and cut into thin strips

1 tablespoon lemon juice

Hot cooked rice, preferably basmati rice

Combine the shrimp shells, scallions, whole garlic cloves, and 3 cups water in a large saucepan. Bring to a simmer over medium heat, then cook for 20 to 30 minutes. Strain the broth and reserve 1¼ cups. Cut each shrimp in half lengthwise.

Bring a medium saucepan of lightly salted water to a boil over high heat. Add the cucumber and 1 tablespoon of the butter. Simmer until the cucumber is barely crisp-tender, 4 to 5 minutes. Drain and set aside.

In a saucepan, heat the remaining 4 tablespoons butter over medium heat. Add the onion, ginger, and minced garlic and cook, stirring often, until softened but not browned, about 5 minutes. Sprinkle in the garam masala, turmeric, cinnamon, cloves, sugar, and salt and stir well. Cook for 2 minutes, stirring constantly. Add the flour and stir for 1 minute. Gradually stir in half of the reserved shrimp-shell broth and half of the coconut milk. Bring to a simmer and cook until lightly thickened, about 10 minutes. Remove from the heat, and stir in the shrimp, cucumber, and chiles. Let stand for 30 minutes.

Stir in the remaining broth and coconut milk, along with the lemon juice. Return to a simmer and cook over medium-low heat until heated through, about 2 minutes. Serve hot, with rice.

JAMBALAYA CLASSIQUE

Jambalaya, one of the masterpieces of Louisiana cookery, is a deliciously spicy meal-in-a-pot. It can be prepared in various ways according to the cook's whim on different occasions——for instance, you could try adding spicy smoked sausage (such as Cajun andouille) instead of the ham, or substituting shucked oysters for the shrimp.

MAKES 4 TO 6 SERVINGS

4 tablespoons vegetable oil

1 pound medium shrimp, peeled and deveined

6 ounces smoked ham, coarsely chopped

1 medium onion, chopped

1 medium green bell pepper, seeded and chopped

2 medium celery ribs with leaves, chopped

1 garlic clove, minced

½ teaspoon sweet Hungarian paprika

½ teaspoon dried basil

½ teaspoon dried thyme

½ teaspoon salt

½ teaspoon cayenne pepper

1 (28-ounce) can peeled plum tomatoes, drained (juices reserved) and chopped

1½ cups long-grain rice

1½ cups chicken stock

Chopped scallions, for garnish (optional)

In a large Dutch oven, heat 2 tablespoons vegetable oil over medium heat. Add the shrimp and smoked ham and cook until the shrimp is firm to the touch and pink in color, about 3 minutes. Transfer to a plate and set aside.

Heat the remaining 2 tablespoons vegetable oil in the Dutch oven. Add the onion, bell pepper, celery, and garlic. Cover and cook until the vegetables soften, about 10 minutes. Uncover the pan. Add the paprika, basil, thyme, salt, and cayenne pepper and stir for 1 minute. Add the tomatoes with their juices and bring to a simmer. Cook, uncovered, over medium heat, stirring often, until a thick sauce is formed, 15 to 20 minutes.

Meanwhile, combine the rice, chicken stock, and 1½ cups cold water in a medium saucepan. Bring to a boil over high heat, then cover and reduce the heat to low. Simmer gently until the rice is tender, about 15 minutes, then remove from the heat and leave to stand for 5 minutes.

Stir the shrimp and ham into the sauce and heat through gently, about 2 minutes. Remove from the heat and then stir in the rice until thoroughly mixed. Serve hot, sprinkling each serving with chopped scallions, if desired.

STUFFED SQUID

Baked, stuffed squid is a wonderful way to make a sumptuous main course from a range of inexpensive ingredients.

MAKES 4 SERVINGS

12 squid, cleaned

Stuffing

1 cup fresh bread crumbs

½ cup milk

2 tablespoons olive oil

1 large onion, finely chopped

5 ripe plum tomatoes, peeled, seeded, and chopped

2 garlic cloves, minced

1 tablespoon chopped fresh parsley

2 large egg yolks

Salt and freshly ground pepper, to taste

Sauce

3 tablespoons olive oil

1 medium onion, chopped

1 garlic clove, crushed

1 bay leaf

2 teaspoons all-purpose flour

¾ cup dry white wine

Salt and freshly ground pepper, to taste

Preheat the oven to 350°F. Lightly oil a shallow baking dish. Cut the tentacles from the squid, leaving the body sacs intact, and coarsely chop the tentacles. Set aside.

To make the stuffing, soak the bread crumbs in the milk in a small bowl for 5 minutes. Squeeze out excess milk and set the softened crumbs aside. Heat the oil in a large frying pan over medium heat. Add the onion and cook until translucent, about 5 minutes. Add the chopped squid tentacles, tomatoes, and garlic and mix until well combined. Add the bread crumbs and chopped parsley. Remove from the heat, and stir in the egg yolks to make a thick stuffing. Season with salt and pepper. Spoon into the squid (the stuffing will expand during cooking, so don't pack it in tightly) and close the ends with wooden toothpicks. Place in the prepared dish.

To make the sauce, in a medium saucepan, heat the olive oil over medium heat. Add the onion, garlic, and bay leaf and cook until the onion is softened and translucent, about 4 minutes. Add the flour and stir for 1 minute. Gradually stir in the wine and ¾ cup hot water, and season well with salt and pepper. Bring to a simmer and cook over low heat until lightly thickened, about 15 minutes. Pour the sauce over the stuffed squid.

Bake, basting occasionally, until the squid is very tender, about 1 hour. Serve hot.

FRIED SQUID WITH AÏOLI

Golden, tender morsels of fried squid can be problem-free if you observe a simple rule: be sure your oil is hot enough, and allow it to return to the proper temperature before frying each batch. Don't fry the squid until deep golden-brown, or it will be overcooked. The garlic mayonnaise called *aïoli* is a perfect accompaniment.

MAKES 4 SERVINGS

Vegetable oil, for deep-frying

½ cup all-purpose flour

Salt and cayenne pepper, to taste

1 pound squid, cleaned, sacs cut crosswise into ⅓-inch-thick rings, and tentacles intact

Garlic Mayonnaise (Aïoli), for serving

Preheat the oven to 200°F. Pour enough oil into a large, heavy saucepan to come to a depth of about 2 to 3 inches. Heat the oil to 350°F. In a shallow dish, combine the flour and a seasoning of salt and cayenne pepper. Working in batches, toss the squid in the flour, shaking off excess flour, and fry until golden-brown, 1 to 2 minutes. Drain on a paper-towel-lined baking sheet, and keep warm while preparing the remaining squid. Serve hot, with garlic mayonnaise.

FRIED SCALLOPS WITH LEMON AND GARLIC

Scallops should be sautéed in small amounts—if they are crowded into a pan they will steam and not brown. Do not overcook them, so they remain tender.

MAKES 2 TO 3 SERVINGS

4 tablespoons unsalted butter

1 pound sea or bay scallops

3 tablespoons all-purpose flour

2 garlic cloves, chopped

1 tablespoon chopped fresh parsley

2 tablespoons lemon juice

Salt and freshly ground pepper, to taste

Preheat the oven to 200°F. In a large frying pan, heat 2 tablespoons of the butter over medium-high heat until lightly browned. Toss half of the scallops with about 1½ tablespoons of the flour to coat them lightly, then add to the pan with half of the garlic and parsley. Cook briskly, turning occasionally, until the scallops are golden-brown in color and barely cooked through, 2 to 3 minutes. Transfer to a baking sheet, and keep warm while sautéing the remaining scallops, lightly floured, with the rest of the butter, garlic, and parsley. Add the lemon juice to the pan, swirl it around, and pour over the scallops. Season, and serve immediately.

SCALLOPS WITH TOMATO, BASIL, AND SAFFRON VINAIGRETTE

Serve this on its own as a first course, or add some tender mixed greens to present it as an entrée salad. Use the very best extra virgin olive oil and red wine vinegar available for the vinaigrette.

MAKES 4 SERVINGS

3 tablespoons olive oil (not extra virgin)
12 large sea scallops
Salt and freshly ground pepper, to taste

Vinaigrette

2 tablespoons red wine vinegar
½ garlic clove, minced and crushed to a paste with a sprinkle of salt
Freshly ground pepper, to taste
6 tablespoons extra virgin olive oil
1 teaspoon saffron threads, infused in 2 tablespoons hot water for 2 minutes
2 large ripe tomatoes, peeled, seeded, and chopped into ¼-inch dice
2 tablespoons coarsely chopped fresh basil

To make the vinaigrette, whisk together the vinegar, garlic, and pepper in a medium bowl. Gradually whisk in the oil until emulsified. Stir in the saffron (do not whisk it, as the saffron will become entangled in the whisk). Stir in the tomatoes and basil.

Divide the oil between two large, heavy frying pans and heat over medium-high heat. Add the scallops and cook, turning once, until browned on both sides, 2 to 3 minutes. Do not overcook the scallops.

Place 3 scallops in the center of each warmed plate. Spoon the vinaigrette over, and serve immediately.

MOULES À LA MARINIÈRE

Probably the most classic way to prepare mussels, this is the method preferred by French fishing communities.

MAKES 5 SERVINGS

⅔ cup dry white wine
1 medium onion, chopped
½ cup chopped shallots
4 pounds mussels, scrubbed and debearded if necessary
Salt and freshly ground pepper, to taste
2 tablespoons chopped fresh parsley

Place the wine, onion, and shallots in a large pot and add ⅔ cup water. Bring to a boil over medium-high heat. Cook briskly until reduced by about half, 6 to

MUSSELS WITH COCONUT MILK AND CHILES

8 minutes. Add the mussels. Cover and cook, shaking the pan occasionally, until the mussels open, 4 to 5 minutes. Spoon the mussels into individual bowls. (Leave any unopened mussels in the pot and cook for another couple of minutes. If they remain firmly shut, discard them.) Season the cooking liquid, then strain it through a fine sieve (or a regular sieve lined with moistened paper towels). Divide among the bowls of mussels, sprinkle with parsley, and serve immediately.

Moules à la Crème: Add ⅔ cup heavy cream to the strained cooking liquid and heat through before spooning over the mussels.

MUSSELS WITH COCONUT MILK AND CHILES

The wonderfully aromatic Thai flavorings used here— coconut milk, fish sauce, lemon grass, and kaffir lime leaves—enhance the delicate flavor of mussels.

MAKES 4 SERVINGS

5 pounds mussels, scrubbed and debearded, if necessary
1¾ cups coconut milk
6 scallions, chopped
⅓ cup chopped fresh cilantro stems
4 hot fresh green chiles (such as jalapeño), seeded and chopped
2 stalks lemon grass, tender inner leaves only, chopped
1 (2-inch) piece galangal or fresh ginger, peeled and thinly sliced
¼ cup lime juice
6 kaffir lime leaves or grated zest of 1 lime
1 garlic clove, crushed
⅔ cup heavy cream
3 tablespoons fish sauce
¾ cup chopped fresh cilantro leaves

Place the mussels in a pot with 1¼ cups water. Bring to a boil over high heat. Cover and cook, shaking the pan occasionally, until the mussels open, 3 to 5 minutes. Drain in a colander over a clean saucepan, and reserve the broth. Let the mussels cool, then remove the empty shell halves. Set the mussels aside.

Add the coconut milk, scallions, cilantro stems, chiles, lemon grass, galangal, lime juice, lime leaves, and garlic to the broth. Bring to a simmer and cook over low heat until well flavored, about 30 minutes. Strain into the pot in which you cooked the mussels.

Add the heavy cream, fish sauce, and cilantro leaves and stir well. Return to a simmer. Add the reserved mussels. Cook gently until the mussels are reheated, about 3 minutes. Serve immediately in shallow soup bowls.

Meat

FILETS MIGNONS WITH SHALLOT SAUCE

Filets mignons are a good size for sautéing, making this a quick bistro-style meal. They should be served in the classic way, with french-fried potatoes.

MAKES 4 SERVINGS

    8 tablespoons (1 stick) unsalted butter
    2 tablespoons olive oil
    1 cup chopped shallots
    ⅔ cup dry white wine
    Salt and freshly ground pepper
    4 (6-ounce) filet mignon steaks, each about 1 inch thick
    1 tablespoon chopped parsley

In a medium saucepan, heat 2 tablespoons of the butter and 1 tablespoon of the oil over medium-low heat. Add the shallots and cook gently until softened, about 3 minutes. Add the wine and increase the heat to high. Boil rapidly until the liquid is syrupy and reduced to about 2 tablespoons, 5 to 10 minutes. Season with salt and pepper. Remove from the heat and keep warm.

In a large frying pan, heat 2 tablespoons butter and the remaining 1 tablespoon oil over medium-high heat until very hot. Add the steaks and cook, turning them once, until well browned, about 6 minutes for medium-rare meat. Season. Transfer the steaks to four warmed dinner plates. Pour off any fat from the pan, leaving the browned bits. Return the pan to low heat. Add the shallot mixture and stir with a wooden spoon to mix in the browned bits on the bottom of the pan. Stir in the remaining 4 tablespoons butter and the parsley, and season. Spoon equal amounts of the shallot sauce over each steak. Serve hot.

STEAK AU POIVRE

Pick a frying pan that is large enough to hold all of the steaks at once, or choose smaller steaks, like filets mignons or rib eye steaks. Another alternative is to cook the steaks in two pans. However, do not, under any circumstances, crowd the steaks, or they will not get a nicely browned exterior. Use freshly crushed peppercorns for the best flavor.

MAKES 4 SERVINGS

    4 (6- to 8-ounce) beef steaks (such as club, rib eye, or filet mignon)
    1 teaspoon olive oil
    2 teaspoons black peppercorns, coarsely crushed
    2 tablespoons unsalted butter
    Salt, to taste
    ¾ cup chicken stock
    1 tablespoon dry sherry
    2 teaspoons Cognac

Rub the steaks lightly with the oil, and press the peppercorns into them on both sides. In a large frying pan, heat 1 tablespoon of the butter over medium-high heat until very hot. Add the steaks and cook, turning once, until browned on both sides, about 6 minutes for medium-rare meat. Season the steaks with salt. Transfer the steaks to four warmed plates and tent with aluminum foil to keep warm.

Add the remaining 1 tablespoon butter to the pan and melt. Add the stock and bring to a boil over high heat, scraping up the browned bits in the pan with a wooden spoon. Add the sherry and boil rapidly until reduced by half. Add the Cognac and cook for another 30 seconds. Season with salt and pepper, and drizzle the sauce evenly over the steaks.

RIB EYE STEAKS WITH CHIMICHURRI SAUCE

In Argentina, countless restaurants specialize in grilled beef, and this is the sauce found on every table.

MAKES 4 SERVINGS

    4 (10-ounce) rib eye steaks
    Salt and freshly ground pepper, to taste
Chimichurri Sauce
    ⅓ cup chopped fresh parsley
    ¼ cup minced onion
    ¼ cup red wine vinegar
    4 garlic cloves, minced
    1 teaspoon dried oregano
    ½ teaspoon salt
    ½ teaspoon freshly ground pepper
    ½ cup olive oil

To make the sauce, whisk together all of the ingredients, except the oil, in a medium bowl. Gradually whisk in the oil. Cover and refrigerate for at least 1 hour before serving. (The sauce can be prepared up to 1 day ahead.)

Build a charcoal fire in an outdoor grill or preheat a broiler. Lightly oil the grill. Grill or broil the steaks, turning once, for 8 to 10 minutes for medium-rare meat (or cook longer, if desired). Season the steaks with salt and pepper. Serve the steaks with a bowl of the sauce passed on the side.

ROAST BEEF TENDERLOIN

Roast beef tenderloin is a perfect party entrée. It is quick to prepare, has very little waste, and is equally good served hot or cold. The interior temperature of the meat will continue to rise by about 5 degrees as it rests before serving, so be careful not to overcook.

MAKES 8 TO 12 SERVINGS
1 (4-pound) trimmed whole beef tenderloin, all fat and
    silver membrane removed
Asian Marinade or Italian Red Wine Marinade
2 tablespoons vegetable oil
Freshly ground pepper, to taste

Fold the thin ends of the tenderloin underneath so the
tenderloin is the same thickness throughout its length,
and tie with kitchen string. Immerse the tenderloin
in the marinade. Cover and leave to marinate in the
refrigerator for at least 8 hours and up to 24 hours.

Drain the tenderloin and let stand at room
temperature for 1 hour before roasting.

Preheat the oven to 450°F. Pat the tenderloin dry
with paper towels. Rub it all over with the oil, and
season with pepper. Place on a rack in a large roasting
pan. Roast until a meat thermometer inserted in the
center of the roast reads 130°F for medium-rare meat,
about 45 minutes. Let the tenderloin stand for 10
minutes before carving.

T-BONE STEAKS WITH SMOTHERED VIDALIA ONIONS

Here is another good way to add interest to familiar
grilled steak. This sweet-and-sour condiment is an
opportunity to use sweet Vidalia, Maui, or Walla Walla
onions, but if these are not available, regular Spanish
onions will work, too.

MAKES 4 SERVINGS
4 (12-ounce) shell (sirloin) steaks
Smothered Vidalia Onions
2 tablespoons unsalted butter
2 pounds sweet onions (such as Vidalia), cut into
    ¼-inch half-moons
⅓ cup balsamic vinegar
2 tablespoons light brown sugar
2 teaspoons chopped fresh thyme or 1 teaspoon
    dried thyme
Salt and freshly ground pepper, to taste

To make the smothered onions, heat the butter in
a large saucepan over medium heat. Add the onions.
Cover and cook, stirring often, until the onions
are softened, about 8 minutes. Stir in the balsamic
vinegar, light brown sugar, and fresh or dried thyme,
then reduce the heat to medium-low. Cover the pan
once again and continue to cook until the onions
are very tender, about 30 minutes. Uncover the pan
and cook over medium-high heat until the liquid
has reduced to a glaze, about 3 minutes. Season with
salt and pepper. Set aside.

Build a charcoal fire in an outdoor grill or preheat
the broiler. Lightly oil the grill. Grill or broil the
steaks, turning once, for 8 to 10 minutes for medium-
rare meat. Top each steak with a mound of onions.

SHORT RIBS BERBERE

There's more to African cuisine than couscous, as
these short ribs in a well-spiced sauce will prove.
It is based on the Ethiopian spice paste, *berbere*,
which oddly resembles the moist red curry pastes
of Southeast Asia, thousands of miles away.

MAKES 4 TO 6 SERVINGS
6 (1-pound) meaty beef short ribs
4 tablespoons vegetable oil
2 medium onions, cut into ½-inch-thick half-moons
6 garlic cloves, minced
½ teaspoon fenugreek seeds
½ teaspoon coriander seeds
½ teaspoon whole black peppercorns
2 tablespoons sweet Hungarian paprika
1 teaspoon chile flakes
½ teaspoon ground ginger
¼ teaspoon ground cardamom
¼ teaspoon grated nutmeg
¼ teaspoon ground cinnamon
Salt, to taste
1 cup hearty red wine
2 tablespoons tomato paste

Preheat the oven to 325°F. In a large Dutch oven or
flameproof casserole, heat 2 tablespoons oil over
medium-high heat. In batches, add the ribs and brown
on all sides, about 10 minutes. Transfer to a plate.
Heat the remaining oil in the Dutch oven, and add
the onions and garlic. Cook, stirring, until the onions
are translucent, about 5 minutes.

Meanwhile, heat a dry medium frying pan over
medium heat. Add the fenugreek seeds, coriander seeds,
and peppercorns. Cook, stirring often, until very fragrant
and lightly toasted, about 1 minute. Transfer to a spice
grinder. Let cool completely, then grind to a powder.
Add the paprika, chile flakes, ginger, cardamom,
nutmeg, and cinnamon, and pulse to combine. Season
the browned short ribs with the salt and spice mixture.

Pour the wine and tomato paste into the Dutch
oven and bring to a boil, stirring to dissolve the paste.
Return the short ribs to the Dutch oven and cover.
Transfer to the oven and bake until the meat is fork
tender, about 1½ hours. Transfer the short ribs to a
deep serving platter and tent with foil to keep hot.
Skim off the fat from the cooking liquid, and boil to
reduce by half. Pour the sauce over the ribs and serve.

FRENCH BEEF DAUBE WITH OLIVES

A rich *boeuf en daube*, with its aromas of red wine, orange zest, herbs, and garlic, is the pride of many a Provençale cook. If at all possible, let the stew stand for a few hours (preferably overnight), to allow the flavors to mellow, then reheat for serving.

MAKES 6 SERVINGS

3 tablespoons olive oil, approximately
4 ounces thick-sliced pancetta or slab bacon
    rind removed, diced
1 large onion, chopped
4 garlic cloves, minced
2½ pounds beef chuck or round, cut into
    1½-inch pieces
⅓ cup dry vermouth
1 cup hearty red wine, heated to boiling
⅔ cup beef stock, heated to boiling
1 tablespoon tomato paste
1 bouquet garni of 3 sprigs fresh thyme, 1 bay leaf,
    and 1 (3-inch) strip orange zest
Salt and freshly ground pepper, to taste
5 ounces black Mediterranean olives, pitted

Preheat the oven to 300°F. In a large Dutch oven or flameproof casserole, heat 1 tablespoon of the oil over medium heat. Add the pancetta and cook until browned, about 5 minutes. Using a slotted spoon, transfer to paper towels to drain, leaving the fat in the Dutch oven. Add the onion and garlic and cook until the onion is golden-brown, 8 to 10 minutes. Transfer to a plate. Add the remaining 2 tablespoons oil to the Dutch oven and heat over medium-high heat. In batches, without crowding, add the beef and brown on all sides, about 8 minutes; add more oil as needed. As the batches of beef are browned, transfer to a plate.

Return all the beef and its juices, the pancetta, onions, and garlic to the Dutch oven. Pour in the vermouth, boiling wine, and stock. Stir in the tomato paste, then add the bouquet garni. Season with pepper. Cover and transfer to the oven. Cook until the beef is almost tender, about 1½ hours. Add the olives and continue cooking until the beef is very tender, about 30 more minutes. Season with salt. Skim off any fat from the surface of the sauce, and remove the bouquet garni. Serve hot.

BELGIAN BEEF AND BEER STEW

Lots of onions add a delicious touch of sweetness to this stew, which is known as *carbonnade de boeuf* in its country of origin, Belgium. Use a mellow lager beer for this dish, not anything too dark or strong like ale or stout.

MAKES 6 TO 8 SERVINGS

3 tablespoons vegetable oil, approximately
4 ounces slab bacon, rind removed, cut into
    ½-inch-wide sticks
3 pounds beef chuck or round, cut into 1-inch pieces
3 large onions, sliced
2 tablespoons all-purpose flour
2½ cups lager beer
1 tablespoon red wine vinegar
1 teaspoon granulated sugar
2 garlic cloves, minced
2 bay leaves
Salt and freshly ground pepper, to taste

Preheat the oven to 300°F. In a large Dutch oven or flameproof casserole, heat 1 tablespoon of the oil over medium heat. Add the bacon and cook until browned, about 5 minutes. Using a slotted spoon, transfer to paper towels to drain, leaving the fat in the Dutch oven. Increase the heat to medium-high.

In batches, without crowding, add the beef and brown on all sides, about 8 minutes; add more oil as needed. As the beef is browned, transfer to a plate, then set aside. Add the remaining 2 tablespoons oil to the Dutch oven and heat. Add the onions and cook, stirring often, until golden brown, about 10 minutes. Sprinkle the vegetables with the flour and cook, stirring, for 2 minutes. Gradually stir in the beer, then add the vinegar, sugar, garlic, and bay leaves. Season with salt and pepper. Return the beef and its juices to the Dutch oven, along with the bacon. Bring the liquid to a simmer, then cover the pot and transfer to the oven. Cook until the meat is very tender, about 2 hours. Skim off any fat from the surface of the stew. Serve hot.

TRATTORIA BEEF STEW WITH POLENTA DUMPLINGS

When the weather is cool, practically every Italian trattoria serves its own version of a hearty, aromatic beef stew. Topped with plump polenta dumplings, this will become a favorite at home, too.

MAKES 6 TO 8 SERVINGS

1 cup dried porcini (1 ounce)
4 tablespoons olive oil, approximately
3½ pounds beef chuck, cut into 1½-inch pieces
2 medium red onions, chopped
4 medium celery ribs with leaves, cut into 1-inch
    lengths and leaves chopped
6 garlic cloves, minced
1 cup hearty red wine
2 cups ripe plum tomatoes, peeled, seeded, and
    chopped; or use canned

1 cup beef stock

2 teaspoons chopped fresh rosemary, or 1 teaspoon
   dried rosemary

1 bay leaf

Salt and freshly ground pepper, to taste

Beurre Manié made with 2 tablespoons each unsalted
   butter and all-purpose flour

Polenta Dumplings

½ teaspoon salt

1 cup polenta (not quick-cooking) or yellow cornmeal

In a small bowl, soak the porcini in 1 cup boiling water until softened, 20 to 30 minutes. Lift from the water and chop coarsely. Strain the liquid through a paper-towel-lined sieve over a bowl. Set aside.

In a large Dutch oven or flameproof casserole, heat 2 tablespoons oil over medium-high heat. In batches, without crowding, add the beef and brown on all sides, about 8 minutes; add more oil as needed. As the beef is browned, transfer to a plate, then set aside. Heat the remaining 2 tablespoons oil in the Dutch oven, and add the onions, celery, and garlic. Cover and cook over medium heat until the onions are very soft and translucent, about 10 minutes. Add the wine and strained mushroom liquid. Bring to a boil, scraping up the browned bits on the bottom of the pot. Cook, uncovered, until the liquid has reduced by half, about 8 minutes. Add the tomatoes, beef stock, rosemary, and bay leaf. Return the beef to the Dutch oven, along with the soaked mushrooms, and season. Bring to a boil, then reduce the heat to low. Simmer, covered, until the meat is tender, about 2 hours.

Skim the fat off the top of the cooking liquid. Whisk about 1 cup of the cooking liquid into the beurre manié in a small bowl until smooth. Stir the mixture into the stew, and let simmer over medium-low heat while you make the polenta mixture.

In a saucepan, bring 2 cups water to a boil. Add the salt, then gradually whisk in the polenta. Whisk over medium-low heat until very thick, about 2 minutes. Drop the polenta in six large spoonfuls onto the surface of the stew. Cover the pot and cook until the dumplings are set, 10 to 15 minutes. Serve hot.

BEEF POT ROAST WITH ROOT VEGETABLES

Tender, juicy pot roast is even more delectable when paired with naturally sweet root vegetables.

MAKES 4 TO 6 SERVINGS

2 tablespoons vegetable oil

1 (3½-pound) beef bottom round roast

1 large onion, chopped

3 medium carrots, cut into 1-inch lengths

3 medium parsnips, cut into 1-inch lengths

6 small turnips, scrubbed and quartered

3 medium boiling potatoes, scrubbed and quartered

1 teaspoon dried thyme

Salt and freshly ground pepper, to taste

½ cup beef stock

Preheat the oven to 325°F. Heat the oil in a large Dutch oven or flameproof casserole over medium-high heat. Add the roast and brown on all sides, about 10 minutes. Transfer to a plate and set aside. Add the onion, carrots, parsnips, turnips, potatoes, and thyme to the pot. Cover and cook over medium heat until the onions are soft and golden, about 10 minutes. Season with salt and pepper. Return the roast to the Dutch oven and add the beef stock. Bring to a boil. Cover and transfer to the oven. Cook until the roast is fork-tender, 2½ to 3 hours. To serve, slice the roast across the grain, and serve with the vegetables and juices.

CHINESE BEEF BRISKET

A blend of Chinese spices makes an interesting brew for simmering beef brisket. Serve with plain boiled potatoes—unexpected but very good.

MAKES 4 TO 6 SERVINGS

1 (3-pound) beef brisket, well trimmed

½ cup soy sauce

½ cup sake or dry sherry

2 tablespoons sherry vinegar

1 teaspoon granulated sugar

⅓ cup sliced peeled fresh ginger

10 garlic cloves, peeled

3 whole star anise

4 (3-inch) strips orange zest

2 small dried hot red chile peppers

½ cinnamon stick

12 large Pacific oysters (optional)

Sliced scallions, ¼ teaspoon chile flakes (optional),
   and cilantro sprigs, for garnish

Preheat the oven to 275°F. Place the brisket in a large flameproof casserole that is just large enough to hold it. Add enough cold water to cover the brisket, and bring to a boil over medium heat. Cook for 2 minutes, then drain. Rinse the beef, drain again, and pat dry with paper towels.

Return the brisket to the casserole and add all of the remaining ingredients, except the oysters (if using) and those for the garnish. Stir well to mix the liquid and flavorings. Bring to a simmer over medium-low heat, and then cook for 5 minutes. Cover the casserole and transfer to the oven. Cook until the brisket is very tender, about 3 hours. Check occasionally to be sure that the braising liquid isn't boiling away; if necessary, add a little more water to the casserole.

Shuck the oysters, if using, and reserve them along with their juice.

Transfer the brisket to a warmed serving platter and cover it loosely with a sheet of foil to keep warm. Strain the braising liquid into a saucepan, and carefully skim off any fat that rises to the surface. Bring the liquid to a boil and cook until it is rich and syrupy, 1 to 2 minutes. Add the oysters with their juices and warm through until they are just firm to the touch. Slice the meat, and pour the sauce over. Sprinkle with the scallions and optional chile flakes, and garnish with cilantro sprigs. Serve immediately.

GRILLED FAJITAS WITH CHILE-LIME MARINADE

For first-class fajitas, you need a zesty marinade to flavor and tenderize the meat. This one is so good, you may want to try it on chicken breasts, too.

MAKES 4 TO 6 SERVINGS
  1½ pounds flank steak
  2 tablespoons olive oil
  1 large onion, cut into half-moons
  1 large red bell pepper, seeded and cut into strips
  1 teaspoon dried oregano
  12 (6-inch) flour tortillas, warmed
  Mexican Salsa Cruda, for serving
  Guacamole, for serving
Marinade
  ¼ cup lime juice
  ¼ cup olive oil
  1 tablespoon Worcestershire sauce
  2 scallions, trimmed
  1 hot fresh chile pepper (such as jalapeño), seeded
    and chopped
  2 garlic cloves, chopped
  ⅛ teaspoon cayenne pepper
  Salt, to taste

In a blender, blend all the marinade ingredients until smooth. Pour into a glass baking dish. Add the steak. Cover and let marinate in the refrigerator for at least 4 and up to 8 hours, turning the steak occasionally. Remove from the refrigerator 1 hour before cooking.

In a large frying pan, heat the oil over medium heat. Add the onion, bell pepper, and oregano. Cook, stirring often, until the onions are soft and golden, about 10 minutes. Remove from the heat, cover, and keep warm.

Build a charcoal fire in an outdoor grill and let burn until the coals are covered with white ash. Lightly oil

the grill. Remove the steak from the marinade. Grill, turning once, for 6 to 8 minutes for medium-rare meat. Leave to stand for about 5 minutes, then cut the meat across the grain into thin slices. Serve the sliced steak accompanied by the warm tortillas and bowls of the vegetables, salsa, and guacamole. Let each guest roll up the steak in a tortilla, adding the condiments to taste.

VEAL SCALLOPINE MARSALA

Veal scallopine make a quick, elegant, and delicious meal. Be sure to use only dry Marsala in the sauce for this dish—sweet Marsala should always be reserved for desserts.

MAKES 4 SERVINGS
  2 tablespoons olive oil
  4 tablespoons unsalted butter
  4 veal scallops (1 pound), pounded until less than
    ⅛ inch thick
  ⅓ cup all-purpose flour
  Salt and freshly ground pepper, to taste
  ⅔ cup dry Marsala

In a large frying pan, heat the olive oil together with 2 tablespoons of the butter over medium-high heat until very hot, but not smoking. Dip each piece of veal in the flour to coat, shaking off any excess flour. Working in batches, if necessary, place the veal in the pan and cook, turning once, until browned on both sides, about 2 minutes. Season with salt and pepper. Transfer to a large heated platter and tent with a sheet of foil to keep warm.

Pour the Marsala into the pan. Bring to a boil over a medium heat and cook until the liquid is slightly reduced, about 1 minute. Add the remaining butter and let it melt, swirling it into the Marsala. Return the veal to the pan, along with any juices from the platter, and turn to coat the veal all over with the sauce. Serve immediately.

VEAL STUFFED WITH PROSCIUTTO AND MOZZARELLA

These stuffed veal rolls are excellent dinner party fare, as they can be prepared well ahead of time, and then only need a brief browning and baking to serve. A simple fresh green salad is the only accompaniment that you will need.

GRILLED FAJITAS WITH CHILE-
LIME MARINADE

MAKES 4 SERVINGS

1 pound veal scallops, pounded until less than ⅛ inch thick and cut into 8 pieces

Salt and freshly ground pepper, to taste

4 ounces thinly sliced prosciutto, cut into 8 pieces to fit veal

6 ounces mozzarella cheese, thinly sliced and trimmed to fit veal

8 fresh sage leaves or 1 teaspoon crumbled dried sage

½ cup all-purpose flour

4 tablespoons clarified or unsalted butter

⅓ cup freshly grated Parmesan cheese

Preheat the oven to 375°F. Place a piece of veal on a work surface, and season. Cover with a slice of prosciutto, a couple of slices of mozzarella, and a sage leaf. Roll up into a cylinder and secure with a wooden toothpick. Repeat with the remaining veal, prosciutto, mozzarella, and sage. Coat the veal rolls with the flour, shaking off the excess flour.

In a large flameproof casserole or ovenproof skillet, heat the butter over medium-high heat until very hot. Add the veal and cook, turning occasionally, until browned on all sides. Remove the casserole from the heat and sprinkle the veal with Parmesan cheese. Baste with the melted butter from the casserole, and bake until the cheese melts, about 10 minutes. Remove the toothpicks and serve hot.

OSSO BUCCO

Osso bucco, the Italian way of preparing veal shank, has an especially luscious sauce due to the gelatinous quality of the meat. The sauce is accented by *gremolata*, a zesty lemon, parsley, garlic, and anchovy garnish.

MAKES 4 SERVINGS

½ teaspoon saffron threads

⅔ cup dry white wine

6 tablespoons unsalted butter, approximately

3 pounds veal shank, cut in 1½-inch-thick pieces

¼ cup all-purpose flour

1 medium onion, finely chopped

1 medium carrot, finely chopped

1 medium celery rib, finely chopped

1 pound ripe plum tomatoes, peeled, seeded, and chopped; or use drained canned tomatoes

1 tablespoon tomato paste

Zest of 1 small lemon, removed in strips with a vegetable peeler

2 teaspoons minced fresh parsley

OSSO BUCCO

1 large garlic clove, minced

2 anchovy fillets packed in oil, drained and minced (optional)

Salt and freshly ground pepper, to taste

Combine the saffron and wine in a small bowl. Let infuse while you prepare the veal.

In a large Dutch oven, heat 2 tablespoons of the butter over medium-high heat. Dust the veal lightly with the flour. In batches, without crowding, add the veal to the pot and cook, turning occasionally, until browned on all sides, about 8 minutes; add more butter as needed. As the veal is browned, transfer to a plate, then set aside.

Melt 2 tablespoons of the remaining butter in the Dutch oven over medium heat. Add the onion, carrot, and celery and cook until the onion is softened, about 5 minutes. Return the veal to the pot. Add the wine and saffron mixture and cook until the wine has almost completely evaporated, about 3 minutes. Stir in the tomatoes, tomato paste, and 2 strips of lemon zest. Bring to a simmer. Cover and cook until the veal is very tender, 1½ to 2 hours; check occasionally to be sure the liquid isn't evaporating too quickly, and add a little water if needed.

Meanwhile, finely chop the remaining lemon zest and place in a small bowl. Add the parsley, garlic, and optional anchovies. Set this *gremolata* aside. When the veal is tender, sprinkle with half of the *gremolata*, turn the veal over, and cook for about 2 more minutes.

Transfer the veal to a heated serving platter. Swirl the remaining 2 tablespoons butter into the sauce. Season with salt and pepper. Spoon the sauce over the veal, sprinkle with the remaining *gremolata*, and serve immediately.

VEAL POT ROAST WITH MUSHROOMS AND ONIONS

Veal shoulder, which can be dry, benefits from being cooked slowly in this way. If you wish, the sauce can be thickened with a teaspoon or so of beurre manié.

MAKES 6 SERVINGS

1 (3-pound) boneless veal shoulder roast, tied

½ teaspoon fresh thyme leaves or ¼ teaspoon dried thyme

Salt and freshly ground pepper, to taste

4 tablespoons unsalted butter

3 ounces slab bacon, rind removed, cut into ¼-inch-thick sticks

12 ounces small button mushrooms

20 small white boiling onions, peeled

3 tablespoons white veal stock, white wine, or water

Preheat the oven to 325°F. Rub the veal with the thyme and some pepper. In a large Dutch oven just big enough to hold the veal comfortably, heat 2 tablespoons of the butter over medium-high heat. Add the bacon and cook until browned, about 5 minutes. Remove the bacon with a slotted spoon and set aside. Add the veal to the Dutch oven and cook, turning occasionally, until browned on all sides, about 10 minutes. (Reduce the heat as needed so the butter doesn't get too brown.) Pour out the excess fat, and return the bacon to the pot. Cover and transfer to the oven. Cook for 1½ hours, turning the veal over occasionally.

Meanwhile, in a large frying pan, heat the remaining 2 tablespoons butter over medium heat. Add the button mushrooms and cook, stirring occasionally, until lightly browned, about 10 minutes. Set the mushrooms aside. Bring a medium saucepan of lightly salted water to a boil over high heat. Add the onions and blanch for 5 minutes. Drain well. After the veal has cooked for 1½ hours, add the onions to the pot. Continue cooking until the veal is tender, 30 more minutes. Add the mushrooms to the pot for the last 15 minutes of cooking.

Transfer the veal to a warmed serving platter, and use a slotted spoon to place the mushrooms, onions, and bacon around the veal. Skim off the fat from the cooking liquid. Add the stock and bring to a boil over high heat. Cook until slightly reduced, 1 to 2 minutes. Pour into a sauceboat. Slice the veal and serve.

BREADED VEAL CHOPS MILANESE

At the end of cooking the butter will be very dark, but don't worry about it because the chops will be golden and crusty outside, juicy and tender within.

MAKES 4 SERVINGS

    4 veal loin chops, cut about ½ inch thick
    Salt and freshly ground pepper, to taste
    2 large eggs
    1 cup fine fresh bread crumbs
    4 tablespoons unsalted butter
    Lemon wedges, for serving

One at a time, place the chops between two sheets of moistened waxed paper, and pound out the meat, still attached to the bone, until it is about ¼ inch thick. Season with salt and pepper. In a shallow dish, beat the eggs lightly to mix. In another shallow dish, spread out the bread crumbs. Dip each chop in beaten egg and shake off the excess, then coat on both sides with the crumbs, patting them on gently. Let the chops stand on a wire rack for about 15 minute to set the coating.

In a very large frying pan (or use two pans, if necessary), heat the butter over medium-high heat until it is very hot and starting to brown. Add the veal loin chops and cook for 1 minute on each side to brown the crumb coating. Reduce the heat to medium-low and continue cooking, turning once, until the chops are thoroughly cooked, 15 to 20 minutes. Transfer to paper towels to drain. Serve immediately, with lemon wedges.

BREAST OF VEAL WITH RICOTTA AND SPINACH STUFFING

This recipe uses boneless breast of veal, which can be rolled around a stuffing and sliced into neater servings; the bones add richness to the simple sauce.

MAKES 6 TO 8 SERVINGS

    1 (7- to 8-pound) whole veal breast, bones removed
        and reserved, well-trimmed of excess fat (about
        3 pounds after boning)
    4 tablespoons vegetable oil
    1 medium onion, chopped
    1 medium carrot, chopped
    1 medium celery rib, chopped
    1 cup dry white wine
    Salt and freshly ground pepper, to taste
Stuffing
    2 tablespoons unsalted butter
    1 medium onion, chopped
    2 garlic cloves, minced
    1 pound fresh spinach, stems removed, coarsely
        chopped
    ½ cup dry bread crumbs
    ½ cup freshly grated Parmesan cheese
    ½ cup ricotta cheese
    2 tablespoons finely chopped fresh basil
    2 tablespoons finely chopped fresh parsley
    1 large egg
    A pinch of grated nutmeg
    Salt and freshly ground pepper, to taste

To make the stuffing, heat the butter in a large frying pan over medium heat. Add the onion and garlic and cook, stirring often, until the onion is translucent, about 5 minutes. Add the spinach. Cover and cook until the spinach is wilted and tender, about 8 minutes. Transfer to a sieve and drain. Let cool until easy to handle, then squeeze out the excess liquid from the spinach by handfuls, and place the spinach in a medium bowl. Add the remaining stuffing ingredients and mix well, seasoning with salt and pepper.

Place the veal flat, smooth side down, on a work surface. Spread with the cheese mixture, leaving a

1-inch border around all sides. Starting at a long side, roll up the veal into a cylinder. Tucking in the ends of the veal cylinder to enclose the filling, tie up the veal horizontally and vertically using kitchen string.

Preheat the oven to 300°F. In a heavy roasting pan, heat 2 tablespoons of the oil over medium-high heat. Add the veal and cook, turning often, until browned on all sides, about 10 minutes. Transfer to a platter and set aside.

Add the remaining 2 tablespoons oil to the pan and heat. Add the veal bones and cook, turning occasionally, until browned, about 10 minutes. Add the onion, carrot, and celery and cook for 1 minute. Pour in the wine and bring to a simmer. Place the veal breast on top of the bones and vegetables. Cover the pan and transfer to the oven. Cook until the veal is tender and a meat thermometer inserted in the center reads 160°F, about 1½ hours. Transfer the veal to a platter, tent with foil, and let stand for 10 minutes before slicing.

Strain the cooking liquid, and skim off the fat that rises to the surface. Return the liquid to the roasting pan and cook over high heat until reduced and slightly thickened. Season with salt and pepper. Remove the strings from the veal, then cut crosswise into thick slices. Serve with the sauce.

POMEGRANATE-MARINATED LEG OF LAMB

That harbinger of autumn, the pomegranate, has a vibrant red juice that can be the beginnings of a sensational marinade for lamb. Pomegranates are only available for a short time, so you may want to freeze some juice for making this dish throughout the year.

MAKES 8 TO 10 SERVINGS
  1 (4-pound) leg of lamb
  1 cup brown beef or lamb stock
  Salt and freshly ground pepper, to taste
Marinade
  3 medium pomegranates
  2 tablespoons balsamic vinegar
  1 small onion, thinly sliced
  1 teaspoon ground cumin
  1 teaspoon dried oregano
  2 garlic cloves, minced
  ¼ teaspoon salt
  ¼ teaspoon freshly ground pepper
  ⅓ cup extra virgin olive oil

To make the marinade, remove the seeds from the pomegranates. Place the seeds in a strainer set over a medium bowl. Using a large spoon, crush the seeds to

extract the juice. You should have 2 cups pomegranate juice. In the bowl, combine the juice with the balsamic vinegar, onion, cumin, oregano, garlic, salt, and pepper. Whisk in the oil. Pour into a large nonreactive baking dish and add the lamb. Cover and let marinate in the refrigerator, turning the lamb often, for at least 8 and up to 24 hours. Remove from the refrigerator 1 hour before cooking.

Preheat the oven to 450°F. Remove the lamb from the marinade, reserving the marinade, and pat the lamb dry with paper towels. Place the lamb on a roasting rack set in a large roasting pan. Roast for 10 minutes. Reduce the heat to 350°F. Continue roasting, basting often with the marinade, until a meat thermometer inserted in the thickest part of the lamb reads 130°F for medium-rare lamb, about 50 minutes. Transfer the lamb to a serving platter. Let the lamb stand for 10 minutes before carving.

Meanwhile, skim off any fat from the roasting juices in the pan. Place the pan over two stove burners on medium heat. Add the stock and bring to a boil, scraping up the browned bits in the pan with a wooden spoon. Boil until slightly reduced, about 2 minutes. Season with salt and pepper. Carve the lamb and serve with the sauce.

ROAST LEG OF LAMB WITH WHITE BEANS

Roasting a boned leg of lamb makes slicing much easier. While white beans are delicious in the tomato-wine sauce, other legumes work well too. Try tiny dried green flageolets, reducing the cooking time.

MAKES 6 TO 8 SERVINGS
  6 tablespoons unsalted butter
  ¼ cup chopped fresh parsley
  3 garlic cloves, minced
  1 (4-pound) boneless leg of lamb
  Salt and freshly ground pepper, to taste
White Beans
  1 pound dried white beans, soaked overnight
    and drained
  1 (1-pound) smoked ham hock, sawed in half
  1 tablespoon olive oil
  1 large onion, finely chopped
  2 tablespoons tomato paste
  1 cup dry white wine
  Salt and freshly ground pepper, to taste

To prepare the beans, place them in a large saucepan with the ham hock and add enough cold water to cover. Bring to a boil over high heat. Reduce the heat to low and simmer until the beans are tender, 1 to

1½ hours. Remove and reserve 1 cup of the liquid. Drain the beans, discard the ham hock, and set aside.

Preheat the oven to 425°F. In a small frying pan, heat 4 tablespoons of the butter over medium-low heat. Add the parsley and garlic and cook, stirring often, until the garlic is softened, but not browned, 1 to 2 minutes. Let cool, then push into the cavity left by the bones in the leg of lamb. Season with salt and pepper. Roll up the lamb and tie crosswise in places with kitchen string. Spread the remaining butter over the lamb. Place on a roasting rack set in a roasting pan. Roast for 30 minutes, basting occasionally with the fat in the pan. Reduce the heat to 350°F, and continue roasting until a meat thermometer inserted in the center of the roast reads 130°F (medium-rare), about 40 minutes. Transfer the lamb to a platter and let stand for 10 minutes before carving.

While the lamb is roasting, finish the beans. In a medium saucepan, heat the oil over medium heat. Add the onion and cook until soft and translucent, about 5 minutes. Stir in the tomato paste and bubble for 1 to 2 minutes. Add the wine and the reserved bean cooking liquid. Bring to a simmer, stirring, and simmer for 1 to 2 minutes. Add the beans and let simmer over low heat until the lamb is cooked.

Skim off any fat from the roasting juices in the pan, and stir the juices into the beans. Season. Transfer the beans to a large platter. Slice the lamb crosswise, and overlap the slices on the beans. Serve hot.

LAMB WITH INDIAN SPICES

This is a fine dish for a dinner party, and looks as beautiful as it tastes. Plan ahead, as it should marinate overnight in the refrigerator. Serve with spiced rice—steamed with 4 cardamom pods and 2 cinnamon sticks—to complement the rich cooking juices.

MAKES 6 SERVINGS
  1½ cups plain yogurt
  3 tablespoons lemon juice
  1 medium onion, minced
  2 garlic cloves, minced and mashed to a paste
    with a sprinkle of salt
  1 teaspoon ground ginger
  1 tablespoon chili powder
  Salt, to taste
  1 (3-pound) boneless leg of lamb or lamb shoulder,
    well trimmed
  ¾ cup raisins
  ½ cup chopped blanched almonds
  ¼ cup chopped pistachio nuts
  4 tablespoons unsalted butter
  1 tablespoon honey

Reserve 2 tablespoons of the yogurt. In a medium bowl, mix together the remaining yogurt, the lemon juice, onion, garlic, ginger, chili powder, and salt. Prick the lamb all over with a metal skewer, and place in a shallow nonreactive dish. Spread on both sides with the yogurt mixture. Cover and let marinate in the refrigerator overnight.

Preheat the oven to 325°F. Remove the lamb from the dish, reserving the marinade, and place on the work surface. In a medium bowl, combine the raisins, almonds, pistachios, and reserved 2 tablespoons yogurt. If using a leg of lamb, push the nut mixture into the cavity left by the bones; if using a shoulder of lamb, place it boned side up and spread the nut mixture over the surface. Roll up the lamb and tie it crosswise in several places with kitchen string.

Place the lamb in a deep medium casserole, and add the reserved yogurt marinade and the butter. Cover and cook in the oven for 1 hour. Turn the lamb over and drizzle with the honey. Cook, covered, for another 1 hour, basting about every 30 minutes with the juices in the casserole. Uncover and continue cooking until a meat thermometer inserted in the center of the roast reads 140°F (medium), about 30 more minutes.

Transfer the lamb to a large heated platter and let stand for 5 minutes before removing the string and carving crosswise into fairly thick slices. Skim off the fat from the surface of the cooking liquid, and serve the liquid with the lamb.

FRENCH LAMB RAGOUT WITH PEAS AND POTATOES

The French would call this lamb stew a *navarin*. The best ones are made in the spring with baby new potatoes and fresh peas.

MAKES 6 TO 8 SERVINGS
  3 tablespoons vegetable oil
  4 pounds boneless lamb shoulder, well trimmed and
    cut into 1-inch chunks
  1 large onion, chopped
  3 garlic cloves, crushed
  2 tablespoons all-purpose flour
  2 tablespoons tomato paste
  2 cups chicken stock
  2 cups dry white wine
  1 bouquet garni of 2 sprigs fresh thyme, 2 sprigs
    fresh parsley, and 1 bay leaf
  Salt and freshly ground pepper, to taste
  1½ pounds boiling potatoes, cut into
    ¼-inch-thick rounds
  1 cup shelled fresh peas (from 1 pound unshelled),
    or use frozen

Preheat the oven to 325°F. In a large Dutch oven, heat 2 tablespoons of the oil over medium heat. In batches, without crowding, add the lamb and brown on all sides, about 8 minutes. As the lamb is browned, transfer to a plate.

Add the remaining 1 tablespoon oil to the Dutch oven. Add the onion and garlic, and cook until the onion is golden-brown, about 8 minutes. Sprinkle with the flour and stir for 1 minute. Stir in the tomato paste. Pour in the stock and the wine, and stir to mix. Return the lamb to the pot, and add the bouquet garni. Season with salt and pepper. Bring to a boil, then cover and transfer to the oven. Cook for 1 hour.

Skim off any fat on the surface of the cooking liquid. Layer the potatoes over the lamb, seasoning the slices with salt and pepper as they are layered and pushing them down into the cooking liquid to moisten them. Cover again and cook for 30 minutes. Increase the heat to 375°F. Uncover the pot, and cook until the potatoes are browned and tender, about 30 more minutes.

Meanwhile, in a medium saucepan of lightly salted boiling water, cook the peas over medium heat until barely tender, about 4 minutes. Drain well and keep warm. Scatter the peas over the surface of the stew just before serving.

LAMB WITH INDIAN SPICES

GARLIC-BRAISED LAMB SHANKS WITH SWEET PEPPERS

Cooking lamb shanks on the bone gives a wonderful sauce that is made more delicious by the addition of sweet peppers. Yellow peppers add a pleasing color, but red peppers, or even a combination of red and yellow, could also be used.

MAKES 6 SERVINGS

6 tablespoons olive oil, or more as needed

6 (1-pound) lamb shanks

2 medium red onions, cut into ¼-inch-thick half-moons

20 garlic cloves, peeled

1 teaspoon dried oregano

12 ounces ripe plum tomatoes, peeled, seeded, chopped, and well drained, or use drained canned tomatoes

6 tablespoons hearty red wine

Salt and freshly ground pepper, to taste

4 medium yellow bell peppers, seeded and cut into 1½-inch pieces

Preheat the oven to 325°F. In a large Dutch oven, heat 3 tablespoons of the oil over medium-high heat. In batches, without crowding, add the lamb shanks and brown on all sides, about 8 minutes. As the shanks are browned, transfer to a plate. Add more oil to the Dutch oven if needed, then add the onions, garlic, and oregano. Cook until the onions are lightly browned, about 8 minutes. Stir in the tomatoes and cook for 3 minutes. Pour in the wine and bring to a simmer. Return the lamb shanks to the pot, and season with salt and pepper. Cover and transfer to the oven. Cook, turning the lamb occasionally, for 1 hour.

Meanwhile, in a large frying pan, heat the remaining 3 tablespoons oil over medium heat. Add the peppers and cook, turning often, until lightly browned, about 5 minutes. When the lamb has cooked for 1 hour, add the peppers to the Dutch oven. Continue cooking, covered, until the lamb is tender, 30 to 45 more minutes, depending on the size of the shanks.

Transfer the shanks to a serving dish. Skim off any fat that has risen to the surface of the sauce. If the sauce is too thin, bring to a boil and reduce until thickened and velvety. Pour the sauce over the shanks and serve hot.

LAMB, ZUCCHINI, AND RED PEPPER KEBABS

You can create a new kebab recipe simply by using a different marinade. Provençal Lemon Marinade is just one alternative to the one suggested here.

MAKES 4 SERVINGS
2½ pounds boneless leg of lamb, cut into 1½ inch cubes
Italian Red Wine Marinade
1 medium zucchini, cut into 8 rounds
1 small red bell pepper, seeded and cut into 8 pieces
Salt and freshly ground pepper, to taste

In a medium bowl, combine the lamb with half of the marinade. Cover and leave to marinate in the refrigerator for at least 4 and up to 12 hours. In another bowl, combine the rounds of zucchini and the pieces of bell pepper with the remaining marinade, and let stand at room temperature for at least 1 and up to 2 hours.

Build a hot charcoal fire in an outdoor grill or preheat the broiler. Lightly oil the grill. Drain the lamb and vegetables, patting the lamb dry with paper towels. Thread the lamb cubes onto metal skewers, alternating them with the pieces of zucchini and red pepper. Grill or broil the kebabs, turning occasionally, until the lamb is browned on all sides and medium-rare, about 10 minutes. Season with salt and pepper.

LAMB RIB CHOPS WITH ROASTED GARLIC BUTTER

This recipe calls for tender rib chops, but of course you could use less expensive lamb shoulder chops instead. The flavor of roasted garlic with a hint of thyme goes perfectly with grilled lamb.

MAKES 6 SERVINGS
8 lamb rib chops, cut about ¾ inch thick
Roasted Garlic Butter
1 large head garlic, with firm, plump cloves
1 tablespoon extra virgin olive oil
6 tablespoons unsalted butter, at room temperature
1 teaspoon chopped fresh thyme or ½ teaspoon dried thyme
Salt and freshly ground pepper, to taste

Preheat the oven to 350°F. To make the butter, cut the head of garlic in half horizontally, then put the two halves back together to form the original shape. Place on a piece of aluminum foil, drizzle with the oil, and wrap tightly. Bake until the garlic feels tender when squeezed, 20 to 30 minutes. Unwrap and let cool. Squeeze the tender garlic pulp out of the hulls into a small bowl. Add the butter and thyme, and mash. Season. Scrape out onto a square of waxed paper. Use the waxed paper to form the butter into a 4-inch-long log. Refrigerate until the butter is firm, at least 2 hours. (The butter can be kept, wrapped in foil, in the freezer for up to 2 months.)

Build a hot charcoal fire in an outdoor grill or preheat the broiler. Lightly oil the grill. Grill or broil the chops, turning once, until medium-rare, 8 to 10 minutes. Cut the butter into eight rounds. Serve the chops hot, topping each with a butter round.

GRILLED BUTTERFLIED LEG OF LAMB WITH DIJON AND HERBS

Here the lamb is grilled by the indirect cooking method (covered, and not directly over the coals), so it cooks through without scorching the outside.

MAKES 4 TO 6 SERVINGS
½ cup Dijon mustard
2 scallions, minced
2 garlic cloves, minced
1 tablespoon chopped fresh rosemary or 1½ teaspoons dried rosemary
1 tablespoon chopped fresh mint or 1½ teaspoons dried mint
Salt and freshly ground pepper, to taste
1 (4-pound) butt portion leg of lamb, boned and butterflied (about 2½ pounds after boning)

In a small bowl, combine the mustard, scallions, garlic, rosemary, and mint with a seasoning of salt and pepper. Place the lamb in a glass baking dish and slather the mustard mixture on both sides. Cover and let marinate in the refrigerator for at least 2 and up to 8 hours. Remove from the refrigerator 1 hour before grilling.

Build a hot charcoal fire in an outdoor grill, banking the coals to one side and leaving the other side empty. Lightly oil the grill. Grill the lamb over the coals, turning once, until seared on both sides, about 5 minutes. Place the lamb over the empty side of the grill and cover. Grill, basting occasionally with the remaining marinade, until a meat thermometer inserted in the thickest part of the lamb reads 130°F, about 20 minutes for medium-rare lamb. (To use a gas grill, heat one side of the grill on High, leaving the other side off. Sear the lamb on the hot side for 5 minutes. Move to the unheated side of the grill and close the lid. Continue cooking as directed.) Transfer to a carving board and leave to stand for about 10 minutes before carving.

ROAST LOIN OF PORK

A fine pork roast needs little attention to make it into a delicious meal. Applesauce and roast potatoes are ideal accompaniments.

MAKES 6 SERVINGS

    1 (3½-pound) pork loin roast with bone, chine bone
        cracked by butcher
    2 sprigs fresh rosemary
    2 garlic cloves, unpeeled
    2 tablespoons lemon juice
    ⅔ cup dry white wine or hard cider
    1 cup chicken stock
    2 teaspoons all-purpose flour
    Salt and freshly ground pepper, to taste

Preheat the oven to 350°F. Place the pork roast in a roasting pan, bones down (the bones will act as a natural rack). Tuck the rosemary under the pork, and push the garlic cloves into the roast next to the bones. Rub the meat with the lemon juice. Roast, basting occasionally, until a meat thermometer inserted in the center of the roast reads 155°F, about 2 hours. Transfer the pork to a platter and let stand for at least 10 minutes before carving.

Meanwhile, make the gravy. Spoon off the fat from the roasting pan, and discard the rosemary. Squeeze the garlic cloves from their skins into the pan. Place the roasting pan over medium heat. Add the wine and bring to a boil, mixing in the garlic and scraping up all the browned bits and pieces in the pan with a wooden spoon. Cook until the wine is reduced to

about 2 tablespoons. In a small bowl, gradually whisk the broth into the flour until completely dissolved. Pour into the roasting pan and bring to a simmer, stirring. Reduce the heat to low and simmer until the gravy has thickened, with no trace of raw flour taste, about 5 minutes. Season with salt and pepper. Strain, if desired. Pour into a warmed sauceboat. Carve the roast and serve with the gravy.

PORK TENDERLOIN WITH CHERRY AND PORT SAUCE

Pork tenderloin is an excellent choice for a special but speedy entrée. Here a dry rub adds extra flavor to the mild meat, and the sauce is an intriguing, sweet-and-sour blend of dried cherries, port, and chile pepper.

MAKES 4 TO 6 SERVINGS

    2 (12-ounce) pork tenderloins
    1 teaspoon granulated sugar
    1 teaspoon dried marjoram
    ½ teaspoon salt
    ¼ teaspoon freshly ground pepper
Cherry and Port Sauce
    1½ cups dried cherries or cranberries (6 ounces)
    ¾ cup ruby or tawny port
    3 tablespoons unsalted butter
    ¼ cup minced shallots or scallions (white part only)
    1 small hot fresh chile pepper (such as jalapeño),
        seeded and minced
    1 cup chicken stock
    Salt, to taste

Rinse the pork and pat dry with paper towels. Mix together the sugar, marjoram, salt, and pepper, and rub all over the pork. Place in a plastic bag and refrigerate for at least 4 hours or up to 24 hours. When ready to cook, drain the pork of its released juices, and gently pat dry with paper towels. Fold the thin, elongated end of each tenderloin underneath and tie with kitchen string so each tenderloin is the same thickness along its length, thus ensuring that it will cook evenly.

To start the sauce, soak the cherries in the port in a small bowl until plumped, about 30 minutes.

Build a hot charcoal fire in an outdoor grill or preheat the broiler. Lightly oil the grill. Grill or broil the pork, turning occasionally, until browned on all sides and a meat thermometer inserted in the thickest part reads 155°F, about 20 minutes.

Meanwhile, finish the sauce. In a small saucepan, melt 1 tablespoon butter over medium-low heat. Add the shallots and chile pepper and cook, stirring often, until the shallots are lightly browned, about 3 minutes. Add the cherries and their soaking liquid, along with the chicken stock, and bring to a simmer. Reduce the heat to low and cook until the liquid is reduced by half, about 10 minutes. Remove from the heat, and swirl in the remaining 2 tablespoons butter. Season with salt, and keep warm.

Let the grilled pork stand for 5 minutes before slicing crosswise, and serve with the warm sauce.

NEW MEXICAN PORK AND VEGETABLE CHILI

In the Southwest, whole dried chile peppers are turned into a brick-red cooking sauce that is preferred to one seasoned with chili powder.

MAKES 4 TO 6 SERVINGS

10 mild whole dried chile peppers (preferably New Mexico)
1½ cups beef stock
2 garlic cloves, minced
4 tablespoons olive oil
3 pounds boneless pork shoulder, cut into 1½ inch cubes
1 tablespoon ground cumin
1 tablespoon dried oregano
Salt and freshly ground pepper, to taste
¼ cup yellow cornmeal
3 medium zucchini, cut into ½-inch cubes
1½ cups corn kernels, fresh or defrosted frozen
Chopped fresh cilantro, for garnish

Discard the stems and seeds from the peppers, and tear into pieces. Place in a bowl and add boiling water to cover. Let stand until soft, about 30 minutes. Drain the peppers and place in a blender. Add the beef stock and garlic, and purée. Set the sauce aside.

In a large Dutch oven or flameproof casserole, heat 2 tablespoons oil over medium-high heat. In batches, without crowding, add the pork and brown on all sides, about 8 minutes. Return all the pork to the Dutch oven, and stir in the pepper sauce, the cumin, and oregano. Season with salt and pepper. Bring to a simmer, then reduce the heat to low. Cover and simmer until the pork is tender, about 1½ hours. Carefully skim off any fat that has risen to the surface of the cooking liquid, and then stir in the cornmeal and simmer until it has thickened, about 5 minutes.

Meanwhile, in a large frying pan, heat the remaining 2 tablespoons oil over medium heat. Add the zucchini and cook until lightly browned, about 5 minutes. Stir in the corn and cook until heated through, about 5 minutes. Stir the zucchini and corn into the stew. Serve hot, sprinkling each serving with cilantro.

DOUBLE-COOKED PORK CHOPS

The trouble with panfried pork chops is that by the time they have cooked through, they are very likely to have dried out. But by browning the chops in a frying pan first, and then stacking them in a warm oven where they continue to cook gently, they will turn out perfectly tender and juicy.

MAKES 4 SERVINGS

4 (7-ounce) center-cut loin pork chops
2 tablespoons vegetable oil
1 teaspoon chopped fresh thyme or ½ teaspoon dried thyme
2 garlic cloves, minced
Salt and freshly ground pepper, to taste

Preheat the oven to 350°F. Rub the pork chops with 1 tablespoon of the oil and then the thyme, garlic, and pepper (do not add salt yet). In a large frying pan, heat the remaining 1 tablespoon oil over medium-high heat until very hot, but not smoking. Add the chops and cook, turning once, until seared on both sides, about 2 minutes. Reduce the heat to medium and cook, turning occasionally, until both sides are browned and the meat feels a little resistant when pressed in the center, about 8 minutes. Transfer the pork chops to a baking dish, stacking them on top of each other into a tower. Cover lightly with foil. Place in the oven, and leave the oven door slightly ajar. Cook for about 10 minutes. Season with salt and serve hot.

SHERRY-GLAZED HAM

Here's a nice way to dress up ham.

MAKES 8 TO 12 SERVINGS

1 (4- to 5- pound) boneless smoked ham
¾ cup packed light brown sugar
3 tablespoons sherry vinegar
1 tablespoon dry sherry
1 teaspoon dry mustard
¼ teaspoon ground cloves

Place the ham in a large pot or deep roasting pan and add enough cold water to cover as much as possible. Bring to a simmer over high heat. Reduce the heat to low and simmer for 45 minutes, turning the ham occasionally in the water. Drain and let cool slightly.

Preheat the oven to 325°F. Cut off the rind from the ham, leaving a thin layer of fat. Using the tip of a sharp knife, score the fat in a diamond pattern. Place the ham on a roasting rack set in a foil-lined roasting pan. Mix together all of the remaining ingredients in a medium bowl and set aside.

Bake the ham until a meat thermometer inserted in the thickest part reads 160°F, about 2 hours. During the last 30 minutes of baking, spread the ham with the glaze, and baste occasionally with the melted glaze in the pan.

Increase the oven temperature to 450°F, and continue baking until the glaze is tinged with brown spots, about 10 minutes. Transfer to a platter and let stand for at least 15 minutes before carving, or let cool completely and serve cold.

OVEN-BARBECUED SPARERIBS

Spareribs are almost as delicious when cooked indoors as out.

MAKES 6 SERVINGS

6 pounds spareribs, cut between the ribs into
   2-rib pieces
¼ cup Cajun Dry Rub
Salt, to taste
2 cups Southern-Style BBQ Sauce

Preheat the oven to 350°F. Season the spareribs with the Cajun dry rub and salt. Place in a large roasting pan and cover with aluminum foil. Bake for 1 hour. Pour off the fat from the pan, and increase the heat to 400°F.

SHERRY-GLAZED HAM

Bake until the ribs are beginning to brown and are almost tender, about 20 minutes. Baste with some of the sauce, and continue baking, turning and basting often, until the ribs are tender, about 15 more minutes. Serve immediately, with any remaining sauce passed on the side.

Outdoor BBQ Spareribs: Leave the ribs in 6- to 8-rib slabs, and season with the Cajun dry rub and salt. Wrap each slab in a piece of heavy-duty aluminum foil. Build a hot charcoal fire in an outdoor grill. Place the ribs on the grill and cover with the grill lid. Cook, turning occasionally, until the ribs are almost tender, about 1 hour. Unwrap the ribs, and discard any fat and juices remaining in the foil.

Add more coals to the grill and allow them to continue burning until they are covered with white ash. Lightly oil the grill grate. Grill the parcooked ribs (this time without the aluminum-foil covering), turning them occasionally and basting with the sauce, until they are tender and well glazed, 10 to 15 minutes.

If you are using a gas grill, cook the foil-wrapped ribs at low heat, and then glaze them, turning and basting with the sauce, over medium heat.

Game

GRILLED VENISON WITH RED WINE AND ROSEMARY

Smoldering fresh rosemary branches add a distinctive smokiness to these grilled venison filets mignons. Try serving them with Sweet Pepper Chutney.

MAKES 6 SERVINGS

1 cup hearty red wine
¼ cup olive oil
1 teaspoon chopped fresh rosemary
6 (6- to 8-ounce) boneless venison tenderloin steaks
20 to 40 (5-inch) sprigs fresh rosemary
Salt and freshly ground pepper, to taste

In a shallow glass dish, whisk together the wine, oil, and chopped rosemary. Add the venison steaks. Cover and let marinate in the refrigerator until ready to grill, at least 2 and up to 8 hours.

Build a hot charcoal fire in an outdoor grill. Lightly oil the grill. Remove the venison from the marinade and pat the steaks dry with paper towels. Toss the rosemary sprigs on the coals, and cover to build up a good head of smoke. Place the venison on the grill and cover again. Grill until seared, about 3 minutes. Turn and continue grilling until the steak is medium-rare, about 3 more minutes. Season and serve.

SPICED VENISON AND BEER RAGOUT

A heady blend of aromatic spices sets this ragout apart. Suitable accompaniments are new potatoes, creamed celeriac, and red-currant jelly.

MAKES 6 TO 8 SERVINGS

2 tablespoons unsalted butter
1 tablespoon olive oil, approximately
3 pounds venison stew meat, such as shoulder, cut into 1½-inch cubes
2 medium onions, chopped
Salt, to taste
1 teaspoon whole black peppercorns, coarsely crushed
1¼ cups stout (such as Guinness)
⅔ cup beef or chicken stock
3 tablespoons malt or cider vinegar
1 teaspoon brown sugar or 1 tablespoon red-currant jelly
8 whole allspice berries
4 whole cloves
3 bay leaves
2 tablespoons heavy cream
About 2 tablespoons Beurre Manié (optional)

In a large Dutch oven, heat the butter and oil over medium-high heat. In batches, without crowding, add the venison and cook until browned on all sides, about 8 minutes. As the venison is browned, transfer to a plate. Add more oil to the Dutch oven, if needed, then add the onions and cook until golden-brown, about 6 minutes. Return the venison to the Dutch oven, and season with salt. Add the peppercorns.

Add the stout, stock, vinegar, sugar, allspice, cloves, and bay leaves. Bring to a simmer, then reduce the heat to low and simmer, partially covered, until the meat is tender, about 1½ hours. Discard the bay leaves. Stir in the cream and heat through. The sauce should be nicely thickened. If not, remove the venison to a heated serving tureen using a slotted spoon, and cover to keep warm. Boil the sauce over high heat until reduced to the consistency of heavy cream. Or, bring the sauce to a boil, whisk in enough beurre manié to thicken the sauce, and simmer over medium heat for 5 minutes.

BRAISED RABBIT WITH PRUNES

At one time, vinegar was used in recipes like this to help mellow the flesh of wild game. Even today's farmed game benefits from a spell in a vinegar- and wine-based marinade.

MAKES 4 SERVINGS

1 (2½- to 3-pound) rabbit, cut into serving pieces
4 tablespoons unsalted butter
2 tablespoons all-purpose flour
1 medium onion, chopped
Salt and freshly ground pepper, to taste
1 cup hearty red wine
½ cup chicken stock
1½ cups packed dried pitted prunes
Marinade
2 cups hearty red wine
½ cup wine vinegar
2 garlic cloves, crushed
1 sprig fresh thyme or ¼ teaspoon dried thyme
3 to 4 sprigs fresh fennel or ¼ teaspoon fennel seed
1 bay leaf
Salt, to taste
6 whole black peppercorns, crushed

Combine all of the marinade ingredients in a large nonreactive bowl. Add the rabbit and cover with plastic wrap. Let marinate in the refrigerator, turning the rabbit pieces occasionally, for at least 4 hours but not longer than 12 hours. Remove the rabbit from the marinade and pat dry with paper towels. Discard the marinade.

In a large Dutch oven, heat 2 tablespoons of the butter over medium-high heat. Dust the rabbit pieces

BRAISED RABBIT WITH PRUNES

lightly with the flour. In batches, without crowding, add the rabbit to the Dutch oven and cook, turning occasionally, until browned on all sides, about 8 minutes. As the pieces are browned, transfer to a plate.

Add the remaining 2 tablespoons butter to the Dutch oven and reduce the heat to medium. Add the onion and cook until soft and translucent, about 5 minutes. Return the rabbit to the Dutch oven, and season with salt and pepper. Add the wine, stock, and prunes and bring to a simmer. Reduce the heat to low, cover, and simmer, turning the rabbit occasionally, for 30 minutes. Uncover and continue simmering until the rabbit is tender, about 15 more minutes. Serve hot.

RABBIT WITH MUSTARD AND THYME
Smothered with a zesty mustard sauce, this rabbit would go well with steamed new potatoes.

MAKES 4 SERVINGS
½ cup all-purpose flour
Salt and freshly ground pepper, to taste
2 tablespoons unsalted butter
1 tablespoon olive oil, approximately
1 (2½- to 3-pound) rabbit, cut into serving pieces
1 medium onion, thinly sliced
1 cup dry white wine
½ cup chicken stock
3 teaspoons Dijon mustard
3 teaspoons prepared "common" English mustard
3 sprigs fresh thyme or ½ teaspoon dried thyme
3 tablespoons heavy cream

Put the flour and a seasoning of salt and pepper in a shallow dish. In a large Dutch oven, heat the butter and olive oil together over medium-high heat. Coat the rabbit pieces in the flour, shaking off the excess, then in batches, without crowding, add to the Dutch oven. Cook, turning occasionally, until browned on all sides, about 8 minutes. As the pieces are browned, transfer them to a plate.

Add more oil to the Dutch oven, if needed, and reduce the heat to medium. Add the onion and cook until lightly browned, about 8 minutes. Return the rabbit to the Dutch oven, and pour in the wine and stock. Stir in 1 teaspoon each of the Dijon mustard and English mustard, along with the thyme. Bring to a simmer, then cover and reduce the heat to low. Simmer, turning the rabbit occasionally, for 20 minutes. Stir in the remaining 2 teaspoons of Dijon mustard, and continue simmering until the rabbit is tender, about 25 more minutes. Stir in the heavy cream and the remaining 2 teaspoons of English mustard. Serve hot.

MARINATED ROAST QUAIL
The marinade gives a delicious glossy finish to the birds. Eat them with your fingers so you can really savor every morsel.

MAKES 4 SERVINGS
8 quail
Sprigs of fresh cilantro, for garnish
Lime wedges, for serving
Marinade
⅔ cup rice wine or dry sherry
½ cup light soy sauce
⅓ cup fresh orange juice
¼ cup hoisin sauce
2 tablespoons honey
1 (2-inch) piece fresh ginger, unpeeled, thinly sliced
1 tablespoon Asian dark sesame oil
1 teaspoon five-spice powder
1 teaspoon chile flakes
1 teaspoon freshly ground white pepper
Zest of 1 orange, removed in strips with a vegetable peeler
1 garlic clove, crushed

To make the marinade, combine all of the ingredients in a food processor fitted with the metal blade, and process for 30 seconds. Pour the marinade into a large nonreactive bowl. Add the quail. Cover and let marinate in the refrigerator, turning the quail occasionally, at least overnight or preferably for 24 hours.

Preheat the oven to 425°F. Remove the quail from the marinade, shaking off any clinging marinade solids. Place the birds, well apart, on a rack in a heavy roasting pan. Pour about 1¼ cups water into the pan (to prevent the drippings from burning).

Strain the marinade into a medium saucepan. Bring to a boil over high heat and boil until reduced to a syrup, about 10 minutes. Spoon a little of the reduced marinade over each bird, reserving the remaining marinade. Roast the quail for 5 minutes. Remove from the oven, and spoon a bit more of the marinade over. Roast for 10 more minutes, then spoon all the remaining marinade over the birds. Continue roasting until the quail are tender and a rich, glossy golden-brown, 5 to 10 minutes. There may be a few scorched patches, which will add to the flavor.

Transfer the quail to a serving platter and place in the turned-off oven to keep warm. Strain the roasting liquid into a medium saucepan and bring to a boil over high heat. Boil until syrupy, about 5 minutes; taste the liquid occasionally and stop boiling if it is becoming very salty. Garnish the quail with the cilantro and lime wedges, spoon the sauce over the birds, and serve.

MARINATED ROAST QUAIL

PHEASANT WITH CHESTNUTS

Pheasant braised in red wine and stock, with fresh chestnuts, is a succulent dish for a winter's night.

MAKES 2 OR 3 SERVINGS

6 ounces slab bacon, rind removed, cut into
   ¼- by 1-inch strips
1 (2- to 3-pound) pheasant
2 tablespoons all-purpose flour
2 tablespoons unsalted butter
4 medium carrots, thinly sliced
2 medium onions, thinly sliced
2 shallots, thinly sliced
½ cup hearty red wine
1 bouquet garni of 1 sprig fresh thyme, 1 sprig fresh
   parsley, and 1 bay leaf
Salt and freshly ground pepper, to taste
8 ounces fresh chestnuts, cooked and peeled
   (about 1½ cups)
1 teaspoon cornstarch, mixed with 2 teaspoons water

Stock

2 teaspoons vegetable oil
Neck, heart, and gizzard from the pheasant
1 small onion, chopped
1 small carrot, chopped
1 bay leaf

To make the stock, in a medium saucepan, heat the oil over medium-high heat. Add the pheasant neck, heart, and gizzard and cook until browned, about 5 minutes. Add the onion and carrot, and cook until softened, about 5 minutes. Pour in 3 cups cold water and bring to a simmer. Skim off any foam that rises to the surface. Add the bay leaf. Reduce the heat to low, and simmer until well flavored, 2 to 3 hours. Strain the stock. If necessary, return to the saucepan and boil over high heat until reduced to 1½ cups. Set aside.

   Preheat the oven to 325°F. In a medium Dutch oven or flameproof casserole, just large enough to hold the pheasant, cook the bacon over medium-high heat until crisp and brown, about 5 minutes. Using a slotted spoon, transfer the bacon to paper towels to drain, leaving the fat in the Dutch oven. Dust the pheasant with the flour, shaking off any excess flour. Place in the Dutch oven and cook, turning often, until browned on all sides, about 10 minutes. Set aside on a plate. Pour excess fat from the Dutch oven, then add the butter and heat it. Add the carrots, onions, and shallots to the pot, and reduce the heat to medium.

Game/Poultry

Cook until softened, but not browned, about 5 minutes. Add the red wine, bring to a simmer, and cook for 3 minutes. Return the bacon to the Dutch oven, then the pheasant, placed on one side. Add the stock and bouquet garni, and season with salt and pepper. Cover and cook in the oven for 20 minutes.

Add the chestnuts to the Dutch oven, and turn the pheasant onto its other side. Cover again and continue cooking until the legs of the pheasant show the barest hint of pink when pierced at the bone with the tip of a sharp knife, 20 to 30 more minutes. Transfer the pheasant, chestnuts, and vegetables to a deep serving platter, and cover with aluminum foil to keep warm.

Skim the fat from the sauce. Bring it to a simmer, stir in the cornstarch, and simmer for 2 minutes to thicken. Carve the pheasant and serve with the vegetables and chestnuts, with the sauce on the side.

BRAISED SQUAB WITH CABBAGE

Squabs, those little farm-raised pigeons, turn out beautifully tender after being braised on a bed of cabbage and bacon cooked in white wine.

MAKES 4 SERVINGS

- 4 (12-ounce to 1-pound) squabs
- 2 tablespoons all-purpose flour
- Salt and freshly ground pepper, to taste
- 3 tablespoons unsalted butter
- 1 tablespoon vegetable oil
- 2 medium onions, thinly sliced
- 1 (1-pound) head green cabbage, cored and finely sliced
- 3 ounces thick-sliced bacon, coarsely chopped
- ⅔ cup chicken stock
- ¼ cup dry white wine
- 2 tablespoons cider vinegar
- 2 teaspoons granulated sugar
- 6 juniper berries, crushed
- 4 allspice berries
- 1 bay leaf

Preheat the oven to 325°F. Dust the squabs with the flour, shaking off the excess, and season inside and out with salt and pepper. In a large Dutch oven, heat 2 tablespoons of the butter and the oil over medium-high heat. In batches, so they aren't crowded while browning, add the squabs to the Dutch oven and cook, turning occasionally, until browned on all sides, about 8 minutes. Transfer to a plate.

Pour excess fat from the Dutch oven, then add the remaining butter to the pot and heat. Add the onions

and cook, stirring occasionally, until they are lightly browned, about 8 minutes. Add the cabbage and bacon. Cover and cook until the cabbage is softened, about 5 minutes. Add the stock, wine, vinegar, sugar, juniper berries, allspice, and bay leaf. Season with salt and pepper. Bring to a simmer, then reduce the heat to low. Cook, covered, until the cabbage is tender, about 30 minutes.

Return the squabs to the pot, placing them on the bed of cabbage. Cover and place in the oven. Cook until the squabs are tender and the juices run a pale pink when pierced at the bone, 20 to 30 minutes; if you prefer well-done squab, cook for longer. Serve them on a bed of the braised cabbage.

———————— • ————————

ROAST CHICKEN WITH MARJORAM BREAD STUFFING

Everyone loves a simply roasted chicken with an herby bread stuffing. Marjoram is a great flavoring for poultry, but if not available you can substitute fresh parsley or thyme.

MAKES 4 SERVINGS

- 1 (3½-pound) chicken, rinsed and patted dry
- Salt and freshly ground pepper, to taste
- 5 tablespoons unsalted butter, at room temperature
- 1 small onion, finely chopped
- 1 cup fresh bread crumbs
- 1 tablespoon chopped fresh marjoram or 1½ teaspoons dried marjoram

Preheat the oven to 375°F. Season the chicken inside and out with salt and pepper. In a small frying pan, heat 1 tablespoon of the butter over medium heat. Add the onion and cooked until soft and translucent, about 5 minutes. Transfer to a bowl. Add the bread crumbs, marjoram, and 2 tablespoons of the butter to the bowl. Season with salt and pepper, and mix well. Use to stuff the body cavity, then truss the bird.

Place the chicken on a rack in a roasting pan, and rub the bird with the remaining 2 tablespoons butter. Roast, basting occasionally with the juices in the pan, until golden-brown and the juices show no sign of pink when the chicken's thigh is pierced, about 1 hour.

CHICKEN ON A BED OF GARLIC

Once a regional Provençal favorite, this dish's popularity has traveled far from its place of origin. The quantity of garlic may seem too much, but baking makes the cloves soft and mellow in flavor. Serve this with mashed potatoes to sop up the delicious butter.

BRAISED SQUAB WITH CABBAGE

MAKES 4 SERVINGS

1 (3½-pound) chicken, rinsed and patted dry
2 heads garlic (about 30 cloves), each clove peeled
5 tablespoons unsalted butter
Salt and freshly ground pepper, to taste

Preheat the oven to 375°F. Place 2 garlic cloves and 1 tablespoon butter in the chicken cavity. Season the bird inside and out with salt and pepper. Place the chicken on a rack in a roasting pan. Rub the bird with 2 tablespoons of butter, and put the remaining 2 tablespoons butter into the roasting pan. Roast for 30 minutes.

Add the remaining garlic cloves to the roasting pan. Continue roasting, basting often with the garlic-flavored butter in the pan, until the chicken is golden-brown and the juices show no sign of pink when the thigh is pierced, about 30 more minutes. (If the garlic is tender before the chicken is done, transfer the cloves to a bowl with a slotted spoon and keep warm.) Transfer the chicken to a platter and let stand for 5 minutes before carving. Serve the chicken, spooning a portion of the garlic and butter over each serving.

GRILLED CHICKEN DRUMSTICKS WITH DEVILED SAUCE

Deviled dishes always contain hot and/or spicy seasonings—here mustard, cayenne pepper, and Worcestershire sauce are used. Serve the drumsticks with rice and a green salad for a simple meal.

MAKES 4 SERVINGS

¼ cup dry sherry
1 tablespoon tarragon vinegar, or 1 tablespoon white wine vinegar with ½ teaspoon dried tarragon
2 teaspoons Worcestershire sauce
2 teaspoons Dijon mustard or prepared English mustard
A pinch of cayenne pepper
¼ teaspoon freshly ground black pepper
Salt, to taste
8 chicken drumsticks
3 tablespoons olive oil

In a shallow glass baking dish, mix the sherry, vinegar, Worcestershire sauce, mustard, cayenne, black pepper, and a seasoning of salt. Cut deep slashes in the thickest parts of the drumsticks, parallel to the bone. Place in the marinade, and rub it over the drumsticks and into the slashes. Cover and marinate at room temperature for 1 hour, or in the refrigerator for up to 8 hours.

Build a hot charcoal fire in an outdoor grill. Lightly oil the grill. Remove the drumsticks from the marinade, reserving the marinade. Brush the drumsticks with half of the oil. Grill the drumsticks directly over the coals, turning occasionally, until seared on all sides, about 8 minutes. Move the chicken to the cooler outside edges of the grill. Cover with the grill lid and continue cooking, basting alternately with the marinade and the remaining oil, until the meat of the drumsticks shows no sign of pink at the bone, about 30 minutes. Serve hot.

CHICKEN POT PIE

This is one of the best examples of delicious farmhouse cooking. If you don't have the time to make your own crust, you could use store-bought puff pastry.

MAKES 4 TO 6 SERVINGS

6 chicken thighs
4 small boiling potatoes, cut into cubes
8 small white boiling onions, peeled and an "X" cut into each end
3 medium carrots, cut into ½-inch lengths
3 medium celery ribs, cut into ½-inch lengths
2 tablespoons chopped fresh parsley
¼ teaspoon dried thyme
Salt and freshly ground pepper, to taste
3 tablespoons unsalted butter
3 tablespoons all-purpose flour
½ cup heavy cream
Basic Pie Dough
1 egg yolk, beaten with 1 tablespoon milk

Place the chicken in a large saucepan with the potatoes, onions, carrots, and celery. Add enough cold water to cover by 2 inches. Bring to a simmer over high heat, skimming off the foam that rises to the surface. Add the parsley and thyme, and season with salt and pepper. Reduce the heat to low and simmer until the chicken meat shows no sign of pink near the bone, about 25 minutes. Drain the chicken and vegetables, reserving the cooking liquid. Discard the skin and bones from the chicken, and cut into bite-sized pieces. Set the chicken and vegetables aside. Strain the chicken broth, skim off any fat from the surface, and reserve 2 cups of the broth.

In a medium saucepan, melt the butter over medium-low heat. Whisk in the flour and let bubble without browning for 2 minutes. Gradually whisk in the reserved broth. Bring to a simmer, and simmer for 5 minutes. Stir in the cream and simmer for 5 more minutes. Season. Add the chicken and vegetables to the sauce and stir to mix. Let cool completely.

Meanwhile, on a lightly floured work surface, roll out the pastry dough into a ⅛-inch-thick circle. Trim into a circle about 2 inches larger than the top diameter of a 2½-quart round casserole. Place the circle of dough on a large baking sheet, cover with plastic wrap, and refrigerate for 20 minutes.

Preheat the oven to 375°F. Transfer the cooled chicken mixture to the casserole. Place the circle of dough over the top of the casserole, and press the dough to the sides. Brush the crust lightly with some of the egg mixture, and cut an "X" in the center. Place the casserole on a baking sheet, and bake until the crust is golden-brown, 35 to 45 minutes.

CHICKEN WITH RICE, ALMONDS, AND RAISINS

Dried fruits and nuts are often combined with meat or poultry in Middle Eastern cooking. If you like, make the chicken stock from the chicken giblets, simmering them with a small chopped onion and a few parsley sprigs in 4 cups water and ½ cup dry vermouth or white wine for about 45 minutes.

MAKES 4 SERVINGS

1 (3½-pound) chicken, rinsed and patted dry
3 tablespoons unsalted butter
2 tablespoons lemon juice
Salt and freshly ground pepper, to taste
⅛ teaspoon saffron threads
½ cup dry vermouth or white wine
¾ cup blanched almonds, each separated in half
½ cup raisins
1 cinnamon stick
2 to 3 whole cloves
3 tablespoons olive oil
½ cup chopped shallots
2 cups long-grain rice
3½ cups light chicken stock
2 tablespoons chopped fresh parsley

Preheat the oven to 375°F. Place 1 tablespoon of the butter inside the chicken's body cavity. Rub the outside of the chicken with the lemon juice, then rub with the remaining 2 tablespoons butter. Season inside and out with salt and pepper. Place the bird on a rack in a roasting pan. Roast, basting occasionally with the juices in the pan, until the chicken is golden-brown and the juices show no sign of pink when the thigh is pierced, about 1 hour.

Meanwhile, put the saffron and vermouth in a small bowl and set aside to soak. In a dry medium frying pan, cook the halved almonds and the raisins with the cinnamon and cloves over medium heat, stirring often, until the almonds are lightly toasted, about 3 minutes. Transfer to a plate. In the same frying pan, heat the oil over medium heat. Add the shallots and cook until softened, about 3 minutes. Add the rice and cook, stirring often, until opaque, about 3 minutes. Add the stock, saffron mixture, and reserved spiced almonds and raisins, and season with salt and pepper. Bring to a simmer, then reduce the heat to low. Cover and simmer, without stirring, until the rice has absorbed the liquid and is tender, about 20 minutes.

Pour out all of the juices in the chicken cavity into the roasting pan, and transfer the roasted chicken to a warmed platter. Stir the contents of the roasting pan into the rice, along with the parsley. Carve the chicken and serve with the rice.

CHICKEN WITH POTATOES AND MUSHROOMS

The potatoes and mushrooms play important roles in this dish, so try to get the best ones available at your farmers' market.

MAKES 4 SERVINGS

4 tablespoons unsalted butter
2 tablespoons vegetable oil
1 (3½-pound) chicken, rinsed, patted dry, and cut into 6 pieces
18 small new or fingerling potatoes (preferably no bigger than walnuts), scrubbed, or 1 pound red-skinned potatoes, scrubbed and cut into 1-inch pieces
4 ounces fresh wild mushrooms such as chanterelles, or cultivated mushrooms such as cremini or oyster, sliced
Salt and freshly ground pepper, to taste
1 tablespoon chopped fresh parsley
2 garlic cloves, minced
⅔ cup light chicken stock

In a large frying pan, heat 2 tablespoons of the butter and 1 tablespoon of the oil over medium heat. Add the chicken and cook, turning the pieces occasionally, until golden-brown all over, about 10 minutes.

Meanwhile, in another frying pan, heat the remaining butter and oil over medium heat. Add the potatoes and cook until lightly browned, about 7 minutes. Add the sliced mushrooms, stir to mix with the potatoes, and cook for 2 minutes. Add the potatoes and mushrooms, along with their butter, to the chicken. Season with salt and pepper. Cover and reduce the heat to low. Cook gently until the potatoes are tender and the chicken meat shows no sign of pink at the bone, about 30 minutes. Stir the parsley and garlic into the chicken and vegetables. Cook, uncovered, until the garlic is softened, 3 to 4 minutes.

Transfer the chicken, potatoes, and mushrooms to a serving platter and keep warm. Skim off the fat from the cooking juices in the pan. Add the stock to the pan and bring to a boil, scraping up the browned bits with a wooden spoon. Boil until the liquid has reduced by half, 2 to 3 minutes. Pour over the chicken and serve immediately.

COQ AU VIN

Chicken simmered in red wine is one of the best dishes to make for an autumn supper. All it needs is plain boiled potatoes or turnips, and a green salad.

MAKES 4 SERVINGS

4 tablespoons unsalted butter, at room temperature

1 tablespoon vegetable oil

4 ounces slab bacon, rind removed, cut into
    ¼- by 1½-inch sticks

1 (3½-pound) chicken, rinsed, patted dry, and cut into
    8 pieces

½ cup all-purpose flour

2 garlic cloves, crushed

2 cups hearty red wine

1 bouquet garni of 2 sprigs fresh thyme and 2 sprigs
    fresh parsley

Salt and freshly ground pepper, to taste

12 white boiling onions, peeled

12 button mushrooms

Beurre Manié, made with ½ tablespoon each unsalted
    butter and all-purpose flour (optional)

Preheat the oven to 350°F. In a large flameproof casserole, heat 2 tablespoons of the butter and the oil over medium heat. Add the bacon strips and cook until lightly browned, about 4 minutes. Using a slotted spoon, transfer the bacon to paper towels to drain, leaving the fat in the casserole. Dip the chicken pieces in the flour, and shake off the excess. In batches if necessary, add the chicken pieces to the casserole and cook, turning once, until nicely browned on all sides, about 10 minutes. Return the bacon to the casserole, and add the garlic. Cook until the garlic is fragrant, about 1 minute. Add the wine and bouquet garni, and season with salt and pepper. Bring to a simmer, then cover and transfer to the oven. Cook until the chicken is tender and the meat shows no sign of pink near the bone, about 1 hour.

Meanwhile, bring a medium saucepan of lightly salted water to a boil over high heat. Add the boiling onions and cook until barely tender, about 10 minutes. Drain and pat dry. Heat the remaining 2 tablespoons of butter in a medium frying pan over medium heat. Add the onions and cook, turning occasionally, until lightly browned, about 5 minutes. Remove with a slotted spoon, and set aside on a plate. Add the mushrooms to the pan, with a little more butter, if needed, and cook until lightly browned, about 8 minutes. Add to the onions.

When the chicken is tender, add the onions and mushrooms to the casserole. Cook, covered, for 5 more minutes, just to heat the vegetables through. Using a slotted spoon, transfer the chicken, bacon, and vegetables to a deep serving bowl. Cover with foil to keep warm. Skim the fat from the surface of the cooking liquid. Bring to a simmer over medium heat, and cook until reduced, 5 to 10 minutes. Taste to check the seasoning, and discard the bouquet garni. If you prefer a thicker sauce, reduce the heat to low, whisk in the beurre manié, and simmer until no trace of raw flour flavor remains, about 5 minutes. Pour the sauce over the chicken and serve immediately.

CHICKEN PAPRIKA

This recipe represents simple home cooking at its best—just a few ingredients cleverly combined to make a satisfying meal. Serve with hot buttered noodles, perhaps sprinkled with poppy seeds.

MAKES 4 SERVINGS

2 tablespoons unsalted butter

1 tablespoon vegetable oil

1 (3½-pound) chicken, rinsed, patted dry, and cut into
    6 pieces

2 large onions, chopped

2 tablespoons sweet Hungarian paprika

Salt, to taste

⅔ cup canned tomato purée

⅔ cup sour cream

Preheat the oven to 300°F. In a flameproof casserole, heat the butter and vegetable oil together over medium-high heat. In batches, if necessary, add the chicken pieces and cook, turning once, until nicely browned all over, about 8 minutes. Transfer to a plate, leaving the fat in the casserole.

Add the onions to the casserole and reduce the heat to medium. Cook, stirring often, until golden-brown, about 8 minutes. Stir in the paprika and cook for 1 minute. Return the chicken to the pot, and season with salt. Cover the casserole with foil, then with the lid to make a tight seal. Transfer to the oven and cook until the chicken shows no sign of pink at the bone, about 1 hour. Stir in the tomato purée. Continue cooking until the purée is heated through, about 5 minutes. Serve on warmed dinner plates, topping each serving with a dollop of sour cream.

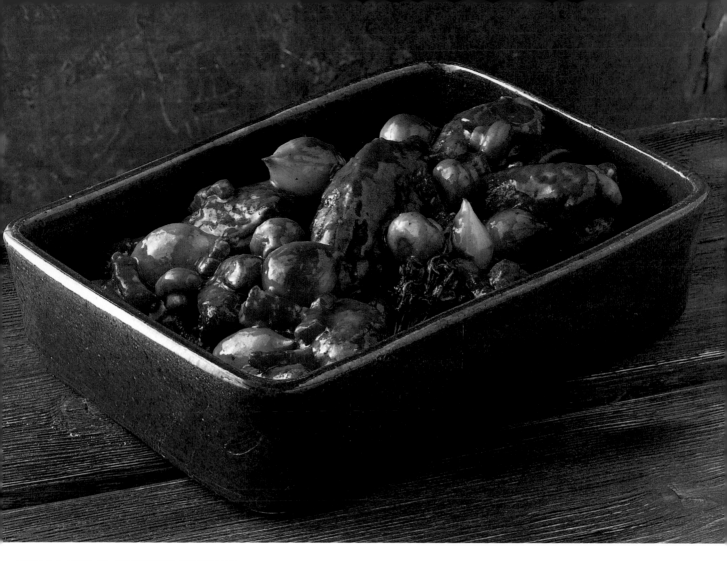

TEXAS FRIED CHICKEN BREAST WITH SALSA

This buttermilk-dipped version of popular fried chicken gives a crisp crust with a juicy interior.

MAKES 4 SERVINGS
  1 cup buttermilk
  1 teaspoon Tabasco sauce
  4 (7-ounce) boneless, skinless chicken breast halves,
     lightly pounded to an even thickness
  1 cup all-purpose flour
  Salt and freshly ground pepper, to taste
  Vegetable oil, for frying
  Mexican Salsa Cruda, for serving

In a shallow dish, mix together the buttermilk and Tabasco sauce. Add the chicken breasts and turn to coat. Cover and refrigerate for at least 1 and up to 8 hours.

   In another shallow bowl, mix the flour with a seasoning of salt and pepper. Wipe off the excess buttermilk from the breasts. Dip each chicken breast in the flour, then back into the buttermilk, and then into the flour again. Shake off the excess flour. Place the coated breasts on a wire cake rack and refrigerate for 1 hour to set the coating.

Coq au Vin

   Pour enough oil into a large frying pan to come approximately ¼ inch up the sides. Heat the oil over medium heat until it is very hot, but not smoking. Add the chicken breasts and cook them, turning once, until they are golden-brown on both sides, 12 to 15 minutes. (The oil should be bubbling steadily, but not furiously. Adjust the heat as necessary.) Drain the chicken breasts thoroughly on paper towels, and serve with the salsa.

BAKED CHICKEN WITH LEMON AND OLIVES

Mediterranean olives are the key to the success of this dish. Use either brine-cured black olives, such as Kalamata or Gaeta, or cracked Sicilian green olives. The best way to pit the olives is to smash them underneath a large frying pan, one at a time, and then to discard the pits (it doesn't matter that the olives themselves are slightly crushed). Serve the tangy roasting juices from the chicken and the olives over hot cooked rice.

ROAST CHICKEN BREASTS WITH
ASIAN MARINADE

MAKES 4 SERVINGS

1 (4-pound) chicken, rinsed, patted dry, and cut into
   8 pieces

2 large lemons

2 tablespoons extra virgin olive oil

8 garlic cloves, unpeeled

1 tablespoon chopped fresh rosemary or 1½ teaspoons
   dried rosemary

1½ teaspoons dried oregano

Salt, to taste

½ teaspoon chile flakes

1 cup pitted black or green Mediterranean olives

Place the chicken, skin side up, in a large baking dish.
Squeeze the juice of 1 lemon over the chicken. Add the
oil, garlic, rosemary, oregano, salt, and chile flakes,
and toss well. Cover and let marinate for 30 minutes
at room temperature, or put in the refrigerator and let
marinate for up to 4 hours.

Preheat the oven to 400°F. Slice the other lemon
into thin rounds and place over the chicken. Bake,
basting occasionally, for 35 minutes. Scatter the olives
around the chicken, and continue baking until the
chicken meat shows no sign of pink at the bone,
about 10 more minutes. With a large spoon, crush the
garlic cloves in the pan and discard the skins. Serve
the chicken hot, with the roasting juices and olives.

QUICK-FRIED CHICKEN WITH GARLIC AND CHILE PEPPERS

Cooked like this, chicken legs are very succulent. Ask
your butcher to chop the thighs and drumsticks.

MAKES 4 SERVINGS

6 tablespoons soy sauce

3 tablespoons dry sherry

1 tablespoon honey

½ teaspoon freshly ground white pepper

4 chicken thighs, chopped into 3 pieces

4 chicken drumsticks, chopped in half

¾ cup cornstarch

Peanut or vegetable oil, for frying
10 garlic cloves, sliced
5 hot red chile peppers, seeded and sliced
Salt, to taste
Crisp lettuce leaves, for serving

In a shallow dish, combine the soy sauce, sherry, honey, and white pepper. Add the chicken thighs and drumsticks and toss to combine. Cover and let marinate in the refrigerator, turning the chicken pieces occasionally, for about 2 hours. Drain the chicken and pat dry with paper towels.

Preheat the oven to 200°F. Toss the chicken in the cornstarch, shaking off the excess. Pour enough oil into a large frying pan to come about ¼ inch up the sides. Heat the oil over medium-high heat until very hot and almost smoking. In batches, and without crowding, add the chicken pieces to the pan and cook, turning once, until the chicken is crusty and deep golden-brown all over, 8 to 10 minutes. Transfer to a plate and keep warm in the oven while cooking the rest of the chicken.

Pour off all but 2 tablespoons of the oil from the pan. Add the garlic and chile peppers and cook until crisp and slightly browned, about 2 minutes. Return the chicken to the pan, and mix with the garlic and chiles. Using a slotted spoon, transfer to a warmed serving platter. Season with salt and serve immediately, with a bowl of lettuce leaves passed on the side.

ROAST CHICKEN BREASTS WITH ASIAN MARINADE

Boneless chicken breasts are quick to prepare. You will get more succulent results if you cook them with the skin and bones still attached.

MAKES 6 SERVINGS
  6 chicken breast halves
  3 tablespoons vegetable oil
  Roasted Tomato Sauce, made without butter
Asian Marinade
  ¼ cup light soy sauce
  ¼ cup dark soy sauce, or 3 tablespoons light soy sauce and 1 tablespoon molasses
  2 tablespoons light brown sugar
  1 tablespoon rice vinegar or sherry vinegar
  2 teaspoons Asian dark sesame oil
  1 (2-inch) piece fresh ginger, thinly sliced
  3 garlic cloves, sliced

To make the marinade, mix all the ingredients together in a medium bowl. Place the chicken breasts side by side in a shallow earthenware or glass baking dish. Pour the marinade over the breasts, and cover. Let marinate in the refrigerator, turning the chicken occasionally, for at least 2 and up to 8 hours.

Preheat the oven to 350°F. Drain the chicken breasts, reserving the marinade. In a large frying pan, heat the oil over medium heat. Add the chicken breasts and cook, turning once, until a golden mahogany color on both sides, about 6 minutes.

Transfer the chicken breasts to a large roasting pan. Roast, basting often with the reserved marinade, just until the juices run clear yellow when the breasts are pierced with a knife, about 20 minutes. Remove from the oven, place on a heated serving platter, and cover with foil. Return to the turned-off oven to keep warm while making the sauce.

Tilt the pan and skim off any fat on the surface of the cooking juices. (If there are burned bits on the bottom of the roasting pan, pour the juices into a saucepan.) Add the tomato sauce to the juices. Place the pan over medium heat and bring to a boil, scraping up any browned bits on the bottom of the roasting pan with a wooden spoon. Bubble the sauce for a minute or two, stirring. Serve the chicken with the sauce.

Grilled Chicken Breasts: Build a charcoal fire in an outdoor grill, and let the coals burn until they are covered with white ash. Grill the marinated, drained breasts, basting often with the reserved marinade, until the juices run clear when a breast is pierced with a knife, 20 to 25 minutes. If the coals flare up, move the chicken to the outside edges of the grill, not over the coals. Cover the grill with the lid, leaving all the vents open, and continue grilling. Serve with Asian Peanut Sauce, instead of the roasted tomato sauce.

CHICKEN BREAST WITH SUN-DRIED TOMATOES AND BASIL

Here's a low-fat recipe that is easy to make after a day's work, yet elegant enough for a dinner party.

MAKES 4 SERVINGS
  1 tablespoon extra virgin olive oil
  4 (6-ounce) boneless, skinless chicken breast halves, lightly pounded to an even thickness
  Salt and freshly ground pepper, to taste
  ⅔ cup dry vermouth
  ⅓ cup chopped sun-dried tomatoes (packed without oil), soaked in water until plumped and drained
  1 garlic clove, minced and mashed to a paste with a sprinkle of salt
  2 tablespoons chopped fresh basil
  2 tablespoons unsalted butter (optional)
  2 tablespoons fresh basil, cut into thin strips

Heat the oil in a large nonstick frying pan over medium heat. Add the chicken breasts and cook, turning once, until browned on both sides and cooked through, about 8 minutes. Season with salt and pepper. Transfer to a plate, and cover to keep warm. Add the vermouth, tomatoes, and garlic to the pan and bring to a boil, scraping up any browned bits from the bottom with a wooden spoon. Cook until reduced by half, about 2 minutes. Stir in the chopped basil. Off the heat, swirl in the optional butter. Place the chicken breasts on dinner plates, spoon the sauce over the breasts, and garnish with the strips of basil.

INDIAN CHICKEN KEBABS

This exotic marinade is a great way to add excitement to chicken, which sometimes can seem just a little too familiar.

MAKES 4 SERVINGS

8 boneless, skinless chicken thighs, cut into 1-inch pieces

1/3 cup lime juice

1/2 teaspoon salt

2/3 cup plain yogurt

1 small onion, coarsely chopped

1 (2-inch) piece fresh ginger, coarsely chopped

3 garlic cloves, halved

2 teaspoons ground cumin

1 teaspoon turmeric

1 teaspoon ground coriander

1 teaspoon paprika

1 teaspoon garam masala

1/2 teaspoon freshly ground black pepper

1/4 teaspoon ground cloves

1/8 teaspoon cayenne pepper

8 sprigs fresh cilantro, for garnish

1 lime, quartered, for garnish

In a shallow glass dish, combine the chicken thighs, lime juice, and salt. Cover and let stand at room temperature for 30 minutes.

In a food processor fitted with the metal blade or a blender, process all of the remaining ingredients, except the cilantro and lime wedges, to make a smooth paste. (If the mixture seems too thick to process smoothly, add a little water.) Rub the paste through a sieve. Add to the chicken and mix well with your fingers. Cover and let marinate in the refrigerator for at least 3 and up to 8 hours.

Build a charcoal fire in an outdoor grill and let burn until the coals are covered with white ash. Lightly oil the grill. Thread the chicken onto eight small skewers. (If you will be using wooden skewers, soak them in water for at least 30 minutes, then drain.) Grill the chicken kebabs until a crust forms on the side nearest the coals, about 5 minutes. Turn the kebabs and continue grilling until they are cooked through, about 5 more minutes. Serve the kebabs garnished with cilantro and lime wedges.

GLAZED CORNISH GAME HENS WITH RICE AND PINE NUT STUFFING

Cornish game hens always add a festive touch, whether they are simply for a family meal or for a company dinner party. These have an Asian accent, with a delicious gingered rice stuffing and glazing of plum sauce. Serve accompanied by a colorful stir-fry of vegetables.

MAKES 4 SERVINGS

4 (1½-pound) Cornish game hens, rinsed and patted dry

½ cup plum sauce

Rice Stuffing

½ cup long-grain rice

¼ cup pine nuts

2 teaspoons vegetable oil

2 scallions, chopped

2 teaspoons minced fresh ginger

1 garlic clove, minced

1 tablespoon dry sherry

Salt and freshly ground pepper, to taste

To make the rice stuffing, bring a medium saucepan of lightly salted water to a boil over high heat. Add the long-grain rice and boil, uncovered, until tender, about 15 minutes. Drain and rinse under cold water, then transfer to a bowl.

In a dry medium frying pan placed over medium heat, cook the pine nuts, stirring often, until they are lightly toasted, about 2 minutes. Add these to the rice. In the same pan, heat the vegetable oil. Add the scallions, ginger, and garlic and cook until fragrant, about 30 seconds. Stir in the sherry and cook until evaporated, about 30 more seconds. Stir into the rice. Season with salt and pepper.

Preheat the oven to 450°F. Fill the hens with the stuffing, and close with toothpicks. Place the hens on a rack in a large roasting pan. Roast for 15 minutes. Reduce the oven to 350°F. Roast for 45 minutes longer. Brush the hens lightly with the plum sauce. Continue roasting, brushing occasionally with the remaining plum sauce, until the hens are well glazed and a meat thermometer inserted in the thickest part of the thigh, not touching a bone, reads 180°F, 20 to 30 minutes. (The total baking time for this dish is about 1½ hours.)

ROAST DUCK WITH BACON AND LIVER STUFFING

The stuffing in this duck is quite rich: just a spoonful each will suffice. As to how many people a duck will serve, consider your side dishes—with several, you could serve a quarter of a duck per person.

MAKES 2 TO 4 SERVINGS

1 (5-pound) duck, neck and giblets reserved
1 small onion, chopped
1 medium carrot, chopped
1 medium orange, halved
1 small bunch fresh thyme, or 1 teaspoon dried thyme
⅓ cup chopped shallots
2 strips bacon, chopped
Salt and freshly ground pepper, to taste
1 tablespoon olive oil
½ cup dry white wine, heated
2 teaspoons all-purpose flour

Rinse the duck and pat dry. Pull out the fat from both sides at the end of body cavity. Cut off the excess neck skin and coarsely chop. Chop the neck into 1-inch pieces. Return the duck and its liver to the refrigerator.

In a medium saucepan over medium heat, cook the chopped neck skin until it begins to render its fat, about 5 minutes. Add the chopped neck and giblets and cook, turning occasionally, until browned, about 10 minutes. Add the onion and carrots, and cook until softened, about 5 minutes. Add 5 cups water, half of the orange, and the thyme. Bring to a simmer over medium heat, and skim off the foam that rises to the surface. Reduce the heat to low and simmer for at least 2 and up to 4 hours. Strain the stock and skim off any fat that rises to the surface. Measure out 2 cups of stock, saving the remainder for another use.

Preheat the oven to 425°F. Using a pot fork, prick the duck skin all over, being sure not to pierce the duck meat. Chop the duck liver into ¼-inch pieces. In a small bowl, combine the liver, shallots, and bacon, and season with salt and pepper. Spoon the liver mixture into the duck body cavity. Squeeze the juice from the remaining orange half all over the duck. Score the skin of the orange half with the tines of a fork, and rub all over with salt. Place the orange half inside the duck with the stuffing. Place the duck on a rack in a roasting pan, and drizzle with the oil.

Roast for 15 minutes, then reduce the oven to 350°F. Continue roasting, basting alternately with hot wine and the pan drippings, until the juices are mostly yellow with a hint of pink when the duck is pierced in the thigh, about 1¼ hours. Transfer to a serving dish.

Spoon off all but 1 tablespoon of the fat from the roasting pan. Place the pan over medium-low heat.

Whisk in the flour and cook until lightly browned, 1 to 2 minutes. Whisk in the reserved stock, scraping up the browned bits in the bottom of the pan, and bring to a simmer. Simmer until the sauce has thickened, about 5 minutes. Season, and pour into a warmed sauceboat. Carve the duck, discarding the orange half, and serve with the sauce.

BALLOTINE OF DUCK WITH PRUNE AND MADEIRA STUFFING

A boned roast duck, filled with a luxurious stuffing of veal, pork, and wine-soaked prunes, is a spectacular centerpiece for a special meal. Reserve the bones and giblets for making the stock, which will become a sauce for the sliced duck. Wild rice, baby carrots, and tiny green beans are perfect accompaniments.

MAKES 6 TO 8 SERVINGS

1 (5-pound) duck, boned
Salt and freshly ground pepper, to taste
6 cups brown duck or chicken stock
2 teaspoons cornstarch mixed with 1 tablespoon Madeira

Stuffing

⅓ cup coarsely chopped prunes
⅓ cup Madeira or tawny port
1 tablespoon unsalted butter
⅓ cup chopped shallots
½ cup fresh bread crumbs
1 large egg
2 tablespoons coarsely chopped pistachios
1 tablespoon chopped fresh parsley
1¼ teaspoons salt
¼ teaspoon freshly ground pepper
12 ounces ground pork
12 ounces ground veal or turkey

To make the stuffing, put the prunes and Madeira in a small bowl and let soak for at least 15 minutes or up to 1 hour. In a medium frying pan, heat the butter over medium heat. Add the shallots and cook until they are lightly browned, about 4 minutes. Transfer to a bowl and let cool completely. Add the prunes and the Madeira to the shallots, along with the bread crumbs, egg, pistachios, parsley, salt, and pepper. Mix together, then add the ground pork and veal, and mix well.

Place the duck, skin side down, on the work surface. Spread the stuffing inside the duck. Use a sturdy needle and kitchen string to sew it up, pressing the stuffing inside the duck to help form it back into its original shape. Season the duck, and prick the skin all over with a skewer (do not pierce into the meat). (The duck can be prepared up to 2 hours ahead of cooking and kept, covered, in the refrigerator.)

Preheat the oven to 400°F. Place the duck on a rack in a roasting pan. Slowly pour 1 cup boiling water over the duck. Roast, basting occasionally with the pan juices, until a meat thermometer inserted in the center of the duck reads 165°F, about 1½ hours. Transfer to a serving platter and let stand for 10 minutes.

While the duck is roasting, bring the duck stock to a boil in a large saucepan, and boil until reduced to 2 cups, 30 to 40 minutes. Stir in the cornstarch mixture, and cook until slightly thickened. Set the sauce aside; reheat when ready to serve.

Remove the kitchen twine from the duck. Using a sharp, thin knife, slice the duck into ½-inch-thick slices. Serve the duck, spooning a little of the sauce over each portion.

SAUTÉED DUCK BREASTS WITH GINGERED PEARS

In this recipe the duck breasts are sautéed until medium-rare, then ripe pears are tossed in the pan to make a quick side dish that complements the rich duck meat beautifully. In season, you can substitute peaches or nectarines for the pears.

MAKES 4 SERVINGS

4 (10-ounce) boneless duck breasts (magrets)

½ teaspoon ground allspice

Salt and freshly ground pepper, to taste

2 tablespoons minced shallots

1 tablespoon minced fresh ginger

2 large ripe pears (such as Bartletts), cored and cut into ¼-inch-thick wedges

1 teaspoon granulated sugar

1 tablespoon lemon juice

1 teaspoon chopped fresh mint or cilantro

Season the duck breasts with the allspice, salt, and pepper. Place skin side down in a large cold frying pan, preferably nonstick. Cook over medium heat until the skin is deep golden-brown, about 10 minutes, pouring off the fat as it accumulates. Turn the breasts over and continue cooking until they are medium-rare, about 2 more minutes. Transfer to a plate and cover loosely with foil to keep warm.

Pour out all but 1 tablespoon of the fat from the pan. Return the pan to medium heat. Add the shallots and ginger and cook until softened, about 2 minutes. Add the pears, and sprinkle with the sugar. Cook until the pears are lightly browned, about 2 minutes. Gently stir in the lemon juice and mint. Season with salt and pepper. Slice the duck breasts on the bias into thick slices. Place a duck breast on each dinner plate, fanning out the slices, and serve with the gingered pears.

ROAST GOOSE WITH APPLE STUFFING

Geese are not very meaty, but the meat is rich. Good side dishes are sweet and sour cabbage, braised celery, and potato dumplings. A lot of fat will run out of the bird during cooking—you could skim it off the top of the liquid in the roasting pan and save it in a jar in the refrigerator. It makes excellent fried potatoes.

MAKES 6 TO 8 SERVINGS

1 (10- to 12-pound) goose, including the neck and giblets

3 cups chicken stock

Salt and freshly ground pepper

4 or 5 medium Golden Delicious apples, unpeeled, cored and left whole

½ cup semi-dry white wine, such as Riesling

1 medium onion, thinly sliced

1 tablespoon chopped fresh sage or 1½ teaspoons dried crumbled sage

1½ tablespoons all-purpose flour mixed with 3 tablespoons water

Use a cleaver or heavy knife to chop the neck into 2-inch pieces. Place the neck, giblets, and stock in a medium saucepan. Bring to a simmer over medium heat, and simmer for 30 minutes. Strain the stock.

Preheat the oven to 425°F. Place the goose in the sink and slowly pour about 1 quart boiling water all over the top of the bird. (This helps to release the fat.) Season the inside of the bird with salt and pepper. Stuff the goose with the apples. Using wooden skewers or a sturdy needle and kitchen string, close the body cavity and secure the neck skin to the back.

Pour the goose stock and wine into a roasting pan, and add the onion and sage. Place the goose, breast side down, on a rack in the pan. Roast for 1 hour, occasionally basting with the liquid in the pan and pricking the skin all over with a meat fork to help the fat run out (do not pierce the meat). Turn the goose breast side up, and reduce the oven to 350°F. Continue roasting, occasionally basting and pricking with the fork, until a meat thermometer inserted in the thickest part of the thigh reads 180°F, about 1½ hours longer (allow about 15 minutes per pound total roasting time). Transfer to a warmed platter, and keep warm by tenting with foil or returning to the turned-off oven.

Strain all the liquid in the pan into a glass bowl or measuring cup. Let stand for 5 minutes, then skim off all the clear fat. Return the degreased liquid to the pan, and bring to a simmer on the stove over medium heat. Whisk in the flour mixture, and simmer until thickened and no taste of raw flour remains. Season, and pour into a sauceboat. Carve the goose and serve with the sauce and the apples from inside the bird, which will have softened into a delicious stuffing.

ROAST TURKEY WITH HERB AND APPLE BREAD STUFFING

A gorgeous roast turkey is an icon of the holiday table, but a turkey's size alone (what other food does one cook that averages 20 pounds?) can make this a tricky proposition. Here are some basic tips for roasting a perfect bird:

Always choose a fresh bird over one that has been frozen or that has been injected with flavorings and fats. If you must use a frozen bird, defrost it in the refrigerator according to the instructions on the package.

Estimate at least 1 pound turkey for each guest, more if you want plenty of leftovers. Large tom turkeys have a higher proportion of meat to bone than smaller hens.

Roast the turkey in a preheated 325°F oven. This temperature promotes even browning and discourages shrinkage. For large tom turkeys (16 pounds and above), estimate 15 minutes per pound. For smaller hen turkeys (below 16 pounds), estimate 20 minutes per pound. If the birds are not stuffed, decrease the estimated cooking times by 2 minutes per pound.

Turkey roasting times are always an estimate, as there are many variables (from exact oven temperature to the density of the stuffing) that affect the final timing, so always test with a meat thermometer or an instant-read thermometer.

Covering the breast with foil will help keep the breast meat (which is much leaner than dark meat) from drying out. Remove the foil for the last hour of roasting so that the breast will be as browned as the rest of the bird.

Baste every 30 minutes to promote a brown skin.

Let the turkey stand for at least 20 minutes and up to 1 hour before carving. (It will stay perfectly warm—it takes quite a long time for a large bird to get cold.) Not only will this allow the juices to settle in the turkey meat and make for easier carving, but it also gives the cook extra time to gather all of the side dishes and finish the gravy.

MAKES 12 TO 16 SERVINGS

1 (18-pound) fresh turkey, neck and giblets (not liver) reserved, rinsed, patted dry, and excess fat removed
A double recipe of Herbed Bread Stuffing with Onions and Apples
4 tablespoons unsalted butter, softened
Salt and freshly ground pepper, to taste
1 medium onion, chopped
1 medium carrot, chopped
1 medium celery rib, chopped
4 cups chicken stock
2 sprigs parsley
6 tablespoons all-purpose flour

Preheat the oven to 325°F. Fill the neck and body cavities loosely with the stuffing. (Place the excess stuffing in a buttered baking dish, cover, and refrigerate to bake later: put in the oven just before the turkey has finished cooking and bake for 30 to 40 minutes.) Truss the turkey. Rub the bird with 3 tablespoons butter, and season with salt and pepper. Cover the breast tightly with a piece of aluminum foil.

Place on a roasting rack in a large, shallow roasting pan. Pour 1 cup of water into the pan. Roast, basting every 30 minutes with the pan drippings, for 3¼ hours. Remove the foil and continue roasting until a meat thermometer inserted in the thickest part of the thigh reads 180°F, about 1 more hour. If the drippings start to burn during roasting, add additional water to the pan. Transfer the turkey to a serving platter and let stand for at least 20 minutes before carving.

While the turkey is roasting, prepare a turkey stock. In a large saucepan, heat the remaining 1 tablespoon butter over medium heat. Chop the turkey neck into 2-inch pieces. Add the turkey neck and giblets to the pot and brown them all over, about 10 minutes. Add the onion, carrot, and celery. Cover and cook until the vegetables are soft, about 10 minutes. Add the chicken stock and 2 cups water and bring to a simmer, skimming off any foam. Add the parsley. Reduce the heat to low and simmer, uncovered, for 3 hours. Strain. (If desired, chop the giblets and boned turkey neck meat, and reserve to stir into the gravy.) Skim off any fat that rises to the surface of the turkey stock.

To make the gravy, pour off all the drippings from the roasting pan into a glass bowl and let stand for 5 minutes. Skim off and reserve any clear yellow fat that rises to the surface. Measure out 6 tablespoons fat, and discard the remainder. Add enough of the turkey stock to the degreased pan drippings to measure 4 cups. Place the roasting pan over two stove burners at medium-low heat. Pour the reserved fat into the pan, then whisk in the flour. Let cook until lightly browned, 1 to 2 minutes. Whisk in the turkey stock/cooking liquid and bring to a simmer. Cook until thickened and no taste of raw flour remains, about 5 minutes. Season with salt and pepper.

Pour the gravy into a warmed sauceboat and serve with the carved turkey.

VARIATIONS: Use Herbed Bread Stuffing with Sausage; Cornbread Stuffing with Ham and Pecans; or Oyster, Ham, and Cornbread Stuffing instead of the stuffing suggested above.

OVERLEAF: ROAST TURKEY WITH HERB AND APPLE BREAD STUFFING

Eggs and Cheese

Eggs are not always as wholesome as they should be, so care must be taken to be sure they are very fresh, clean, and uncracked. Unfortunately, some raw eggs have been found to be contaminated by the bacteria salmonella. While cooks are warned against serving undercooked eggs, this bacteria will be killed at temperatures about 170°F—a temperature that is easily reached with a hard-boiled egg, for example, but is impossible to achieve for a soft-boiled one. If you want to serve soft-boiled, poached, or sunnyside-up eggs, which will not reach the safe temperature of 170°F, realize that there is a small amount of risk involved. People with impaired immune systems, and the elderly or very young, may want to avoid undercooked eggs completely. The key is not to be alarmed, just sensible.

Soft-Boiled Eggs The old remark about not even being able to boil an egg is no joke. Often, the egg cracks from being bounced around in the boiling water, and the white pours out, and other times the egg yolk gets too hard. The term "boiled" is a misnomer—the eggs should be gently simmered. To cook soft-boiled eggs, bring a medium saucepan of unsalted water to a boil over medium heat (salt toughens the whites). Reduce the heat to low so the water is simmering. Gently lower the eggs into the water, and simmer for 3 to 5 minutes, depending on how soft you like your eggs.

Coddled Eggs These are a foolproof variation of soft-boiled eggs. Place the eggs in a saucepan and add enough unsalted cold water to cover. Bring the water to a boil over high heat. Immediately remove from the heat, cover, and let stand for 5 minutes.

Hard-Boiled Eggs The timing for hard-boiled eggs is crucial—don't overcook them, or the sulfur compounds in the white will be transformed into ferrous sulfide and create a dark gray ring around the yolk. Simmer the eggs in unsalted water for 10 to 12 minutes. Immediately drain the water out of the saucepan, and fill the pan with cold water to stop the eggs from cooking further. Run a gentle stream of cold water into the pan for a couple of minutes until the eggs are cool enough to handle. Shell the eggs as needed. Store hard-boiled eggs in the refrigerator.

Poached Eggs Use the freshest eggs available. Pour enough cold water into a large frying pan to come about halfway up the sides. Add 1 tablespoon vinegar (any type) to help set the whites, but no salt. Bring to a boil over high heat, then reduce the heat so the water is boiling steadily, but not rapidly. One at a time, holding the eggs just over the surface of the water, break them into the pan. For a nice, oval poached egg, use a large spoon to coax the white into shape, spooning the spreading white back over the egg. If the yolks aren't covered by the simmering water, spoon the water over them to help cook the tops. Simmer the eggs just until the whites are set and are no longer translucent. Use a slotted spoon to transfer them to a bowl of very hot water. They can now wait for a few minutes. If desired, trim off any untidy edges from the whites.

Scrambled Eggs These should be rich and creamy, not tough and overcooked. To make them, you need patience and a nonstick pan. Crack the eggs into a medium nonstick frying pan, and season with salt and pepper. Add about 2 tablespoons unsalted butter for every 3 eggs. Now place the pan over low heat. (If you don't have a nonstick frying pan, beat the eggs in a bowl with salt and pepper, and then melt the butter in the pan before adding the eggs.) Using a wooden spoon, constantly stir the eggs with intelligence— that is, moving all of the eggs around, not just stirring them clockwise in the center of the pan. Gradually, the eggs will begin to thicken. When they start to hold shape, but are still runny, remove the pan from the heat, and continue to stir until they become a soft, creamy mass.

Serve the scrambled eggs immediately, preferably with hot buttered toast. If you like, add any of the following to the eggs before they are scrambled: chopped fresh parsley or chives, chopped ham or prosciutto, or shredded fresh truffle. Scrambled eggs are also delicious topped with smoked salmon.

OLIVADA-STUFFED EGGS

These are extraordinary stuffed eggs, a far cry from the usual picnic fare.

MAKES 2 DOZEN
  1 dozen large eggs, hard-boiled
  3 tablespoons Olivada
  3 tablespoons mayonnaise
  Salt and freshly ground pepper, to taste
  Chopped fresh parsley, for garnish

Cut the eggs in half lengthwise; place the yolks in a medium bowl, and reserve the whites. Add the olivada and mayonnaise to the yolks, and mash with a fork until smooth. Season with salt and pepper. Put the mixture in a pastry bag fitted with a large open star pastry tube (Number 5). Pipe the olivada filling into the whites, and sprinkle with the parsley. The eggs can be kept, covered, in the refrigerator for up to 8 hours.

TUNISIAN EGGS IN VEGETABLE SAUCE

This dish originated in Tunisia, where it is called *chakchouka*, but is now enjoyed throughout the Middle East. Here, the eggs are poached directly in a sweet pepper and tomato sauce, rather than in water.

MAKES 4 SERVINGS

- 2 tablespoons olive oil
- 1 garlic clove, crushed under a knife and peeled
- 2 red or green bell peppers, seeded and cut into
½-inch-wide strips
- 1½ cups peeled, seeded, and chopped ripe plum
tomatoes, or use drained canned tomatoes
- Salt and freshly ground pepper, to taste
- 4 large eggs

In a medium frying pan, heat the oil over medium heat. Add the garlic and cook until golden-brown, about 2 minutes. Remove and discard the garlic clove. Add the peppers to the pan and reduce the heat to medium-low. Gently cook the peppers until soft, about 15 minutes. Stir in the tomatoes, and season with salt and pepper. Bring to a simmer, then partially cover the pan and cook until the sauce has thickened, about 15 minutes. Taste to check the seasoning, and adjust if necessary.

One at a time, carefully break the eggs onto the vegetable sauce. Cover and cook just until the eggs are set, about 5 minutes. Serve immediately, directly from the pan.

SCRAMBLED EGGS WITH PEPPERS

Here's the Basque way to cook eggs with peppers and tomatoes, in a dish called *pipérade*. It's traditionally eaten with Bayonne ham.

MAKES 4 SERVINGS

- 2 tablespoons olive oil
- 2 medium onions, thinly sliced
- 2 bell peppers, 1 red and 1 green, seeded and cut into
½-inch-wide strips
- 2 garlic cloves, crushed and minced to a paste with a
sprinkle of salt
- 1½ cups peeled, seeded, and coarsely chopped ripe
plum tomatoes, or use drained canned tomatoes
- Salt and freshly ground pepper, to taste
- 4 large eggs

In a large frying pan, heat the oil over medium heat. Add the onions and cook until soft and translucent, about 5 minutes. Add the peppers and garlic and cook until the peppers are softened, about 5 minutes. Stir in the tomatoes, and season with salt and pepper. Bring to a simmer, then reduce the heat to medium-low. Cook until the sauce has thickened, about 15 minutes.

In a medium bowl, beat the eggs. Stir them into the pepper stew. Cook, stirring, until the eggs are just beginning to set, 1 to 2 minutes. Serve immediately, directly from the pan.

OMELETS

For a quick meal, an omelet is hard to beat, and the possibilities for flavorings and fillings are practically endless. For each omelet, break 2 or 3 large eggs into a bowl, and season with salt and pepper to taste. Beat just enough to break the eggs down, but not so much that they get foamy and filled with air. Heat 1 tablespoon unsalted butter in a medium nonstick frying pan until it is very hot and the butter foam subsides. Pour in the egg mixture. Using a rubber spatula, lift up the cooked, set edges of the omelet, and tilt the pan to let the uncooked portion run underneath. When the top of the omelet is barely set, but still shiny, use the spatula to fold one third of the omelet toward the center. Then roll the omelet onto a heated plate so that it is folded in three. It should look like a plump golden cushion. Eat at once: speed is essential when serving an omelet, too.

Omelet with Herbs: Add 1 teaspoon each finely chopped fresh tarragon, chives, and parsley and 1½ teaspoons freshly grated Parmesan cheese to the beaten eggs. If you have it, add 1 teaspoon chopped fresh chervil, too.

Cheese Omelet: Just before folding the omelet, sprinkle with ⅓ cup shredded Emmentaler or Gruyère cheese. Or, use half Emmentaler or Gruyère with half freshly grated Parmesan cheese.

Mushroom Omelet: In a medium frying pan, heat 1 tablespoon unsalted butter over medium heat. Add ½ cup sliced mushrooms, 1 tablespoon chopped fresh parsley, and ½ clove garlic, minced. Cook until the mushrooms have given off their liquid and are lightly browned, about 8 minutes. Season with salt and pepper. Scatter the mushrooms over the omelet before folding.

Shrimp Omelet: In a medium frying pan, combine 6 medium shrimp, peeled and deveined, and ⅓ cup heavy cream. Bring to a simmer over medium heat, and cook until the shrimp are firm and pink and the cream has thickened, about 3 minutes. Stir in 2 teaspoons chopped fresh chives, and season with salt and pepper. Spoon over the omelet before folding.

Spinach and Cheese Omelet: In a medium frying pan, heat 1 tablespoon unsalted butter over medium heat. Add 2 cups shredded fresh spinach leaves, and cook until the spinach is wilted and tender, about 5 minutes. Place the spinach in a colander and press to remove any excess moisture. Let cool completely. Add to the beaten eggs, along with 2 tablespoons freshly grated Parmesan cheese.

Ham Omelet: In a frying pan, heat 1 tablespoon unsalted butter over medium heat. Add ¼ cup finely chopped smoked ham and cook until heated through, about 5 minutes. Let cool completely. Add to the beaten eggs (season with less salt than usual, as the ham may be salty).

OMELET WITH ARTICHOKES AND PARSLEY

If you have a 12-inch nonstick frying pan, you can make a single large omelet: in this case, beat all the eggs together, and then use just 2 tablespoons butter for cooking the omelet.

MAKES 4 SERVINGS

Juice of 1 lemon
8 large artichokes
8 tablespoons (1 stick) unsalted butter
1 garlic clove, crushed under a knife and peeled
Salt and freshly ground pepper, to taste
1 tablespoon chopped fresh parsley
8 large eggs

Stir the lemon juice into a large bowl of cold water. Working with 1 artichoke at a time, trim off all the leaves and remove the hairy choke, leaving just the artichoke bottom. Cut the bottom into ¼-inch-thick slices, and drop into the bowl of water.

Drain the artichoke slices thoroughly and then pat them dry with paper towels. In a large frying pan, heat 4 tablespoons of the butter over medium-low heat. Add the artichokes and the crushed garlic, and season with salt and pepper. Cover and cook until the artichokes are beginning to soften, about 10 minutes. Uncover and cook until golden-brown and tender, about 10 more minutes. Stir in the chopped parsley. Transfer to a large plate and cover with aluminum foil to keep warm.

In a bowl, lightly beat 2 of the eggs with a seasoning of salt and pepper. Heat 1 tablespoon of butter in a 7-inch nonstick frying pan over medium-high heat. Pour in the beaten eggs. Using a rubber spatula, lift up the cooked, set edges of the omelet, and tilt the pan to let the uncooked portion run underneath. Cook until the top of the omelet is barely set, but still shiny, about 2 minutes. Spoon about one fourth of the artichokes into the center of the omelet, arranged neatly in a vertical strip. Use the spatula to fold one third of the omelet toward the center, and then roll the omelet onto a heated platter so that it is folded in thirds. Serve the omelet immediately, or keep it warm in a 200°F oven while making the remaining three omelets in the same way.

Artichoke Frittata: Prepare the omelet in a 9-inch nonstick frying pan. When the eggs are barely set, spread the artichokes evenly over the surface of the omelet. Place in a preheated broiler and cook until the eggs are set and the artichokes are golden-brown in color, 1 to 2 minutes. Do not fold the omelet. Instead, cut it into wedges for serving.

FRITTATAS AND TORTILLAS

A frittata is a thick, flat, fairly solid omelet made with eggs and lightly cooked vegetables. It is cut into wedges like a cake, and served hot, warm, or at cool room temperature—the Italians prefer the latter.

A tortilla is the Spanish version of the frittata (not to be confused with the Mexican corn or flour flatbread, also called tortilla). Fried potatoes and onions are the usual ingredients, although spicy chorizo sausage, sweet peppers, and garlic may also be added. Wedges of cold tortilla are an essential part of the appetizers called *tapas*, available at almost every Spanish bar. Frittatas and tortillas are perfect picnic fare.

SPINACH FRITTATA

Serve this frittata accompanied by a bowl of juicy black olives.

MAKES 4 SERVINGS

2 tablespoons olive oil
2 garlic cloves, crushed
8 ounces spinach leaves, tough stems discarded
Salt and freshly ground pepper, to taste
6 large eggs
A pinch of grated nutmeg
¾ cup shredded Gruyère cheese
2 tablespoons heavy cream

In a medium frying pan, heat 1 tablespoon of the oil over medium heat. Add the garlic and crush it into the oil with a large spoon to release the flavor. Cook until the garlic is lightly browned, about 1 minute. Add the spinach, and season with salt. Stir until the spinach has wilted, about 1 minute. Then continue cooking until the most of the liquid has evaporated, about 10 minutes. Let cool completely. Transfer to a sieve and press the spinach to release any excess moisture. Chop coarsely and set aside.

Preheat the oven to 350°F. In a large bowl, lightly beat the eggs with the nutmeg and a seasoning of salt and pepper. Stir in the spinach, cheese, and cream. In a 10-inch flameproof round earthenware dish, or a metal cake pan, heat the remaining 1 tablespoon oil over medium heat. Pour in the egg mixture. Place in the oven and bake until firm and set, 20 to 25 minutes. Cut into wedges and serve hot, directly from the dish, or allow to cool to room temperature.

POTATO AND ONION TORTILLA

If you wish, add ½ cup chopped Serrano ham or prosciutto to the potatoes about 5 minutes before they have finished cooking.

MAKES 6 SERVINGS

5 tablespoons olive oil

3 medium boiling potatoes, peeled, quartered, and thinly sliced

2 medium onions, thinly sliced parallel to the layers

Salt and freshly ground pepper, to taste

8 large eggs

In a large nonstick frying pan, heat 3 tablespoons of the oil over medium heat. Add the potatoes and onions, and season with salt and pepper. Cover and cook, stirring occasionally, until the potatoes are tender, about 20 minutes.

In a large bowl, lightly beat the eggs with a little salt and pepper. Pour the eggs into the frying pan. Cook uncovered, lifting up the set edges of the tortilla and tilting the pan to let the uncooked portion run underneath, until the eggs are set but the top is still shiny, 4 to 5 minutes. Place a plate on top of the tortilla, and invert the pan and plate together so the tortilla falls out onto the plate. Return the pan to the heat and add the remaining 2 tablespoons oil. When the oil is hot, slide the tortilla, cooked side up, off the plate back into the pan. Continue cooking until the underside is golden-brown, 2 to 3 minutes. Serve hot, warm, or at room temperature.

ZUCCHINI AND GOAT CHEESE FILO TART

A flaky, golden-brown crust of filo pastry encloses a rich zucchini, cheese, and nut filling. Serve the tart cut into wedges with a crisp green salad dressed with a simple vinaigrette.

MAKES 8 SERVINGS

1 pound zucchini (about 3 medium), shredded

Salt and freshly ground pepper, to taste

5 ounces soft goat cheese

3/4 cup ricotta cheese

1 large egg

1 teaspoon lemon juice

2 tablespoons olive oil

1 medium onion, chopped

1 garlic clove, sliced

1 cup chopped pecans or walnuts

1 tablespoon chopped fresh basil or 1 teaspoon dried basil

1 teaspoon chopped fresh thyme or 1/4 teaspoon dried thyme

5 (12- by 17-inch) sheets filo pastry, thawed if frozen

4 tablespoons butter, melted

Toss the shredded zucchini with 1/2 teaspoon salt in a medium bowl. Let stand for 20 minutes. Meanwhile,

in a large bowl, mash together the goat cheese, ricotta, egg, and lemon juice with a fork until combined. Set aside. In a medium frying pan, heat the oil over medium heat. Add the onion and garlic, and cook until the onion softens, about 5 minutes. Add to the cheese mixture. In the same pan, cook the pecans over medium heat, stirring often, until they are toasted and fragrant, about 3 minutes. Stir half of the pecans into the cheese mixture, setting the remainder aside. A handful at a time, squeeze the zucchini to remove excess juice, and add the zucchini to the bowl. Add the basil and thyme, and season with salt and pepper. Mix well.

Preheat the oven to 325°F. Lightly butter a 10-inch pie pan. Place the filo sheets on the work surface and cover with a damp towel. Lay one filo sheet on the work surface (keep the remaining filo sheets covered to prevent them from drying out), and brush lightly but completely with melted butter. Center the sheet in the pie pan, letting the corners hang over the sides. Repeat with a second filo sheet, placing the corners at different points of the compass from the first. Sprinkle with some of the reserved pecans. Continue with 3 more filo sheets, placing the corners of the progressive sheets at different points and sprinkling with the remaining pecans. Fill the tart with the cheese mixture. Loosely bring up the overhanging filo to enclose the filling completely and form a crown. Brush the top of the tart with the remaining butter. Place on a baking sheet and bake until crisp and golden, 35 to 45 minutes. Remove from the oven, cover with a damp cloth, and let cool for 10 minutes. Remove the cloth and cool until warm on a wire cake rack. To serve, slice into wedges with a serrated knife.

QUICHE

Quiche went through a raging fad in the 1960s, but then fell out of fashion. However, it makes such a pleasant brunch, lunch, or supper entrée, and can so easily be varied, that it is well worth keeping in the cook's repertoire. Like frittatas and tortillas, quiches are excellent served at just about any temperature, from piping hot to tepid.

The basic custard for a 9-inch quiche is 3 large eggs, 1 cup milk, and 1/3 cup heavy cream, seasoned with salt and pepper. Solid ingredients, such as cheese or cooked vegetables, are placed in a partially baked pastry shell, then the custard is poured into the shell. (To avoid spills, it is a good idea to set the quiche pan, filled with the solid ingredients only, on a baking sheet and place it in the oven before pouring in the custard.) You may need slightly more or less custard, depending on the quantity of solid ingredients. If you need more, whisk together 1 large egg, 1/3 cup milk,

BACON AND PARMESAN QUICHE

and 1½ tablespoons heavy cream with a pinch each of salt and pepper. To bake the quiche, follow the recipe for Bacon and Parmesan Quiche below.

Red and Yellow Pepper Quiche: Roast and peel 1 red and 1 yellow bell pepper, then seed and cut into thin strips. Sprinkle ½ cup freshly grated Parmesan cheese over the bottom of the warm, partially baked pastry shell, then arrange the strips of pepper on top and sprinkle with 2 tablespoons chopped fresh basil. Pour in the custard and bake.

Provençal Quiche: Heat ¼ cup olive oil in a large frying pan over medium heat. Add 2 cups diced (¼-inch) eggplant and cook until the eggplant is lightly browned, about 5 minutes. Add 2 peeled, seeded, and coarsely chopped ripe plum tomatoes, and cook until the tomatoes are softened, about 3 more minutes. Season with salt and pepper. Let cool completely. Sprinkle ½ cup shredded Gruyère cheese over the bottom of the warm, partially baked pastry shell. Add the eggplant mixture and sprinkle with 1 teaspoon chopped fresh thyme. Pour in the custard and then bake.

Leek Quiche: In a medium frying pan, heat 2 tablespoons unsalted butter over medium heat. Add 3 medium leeks, white part only, cut into thin rounds. Cook, stirring often, until the leeks are golden, about 8 minutes. Add ⅛ teaspoon crumbled saffron threads. Let cool completely. Sprinkle ½ cup shredded Gruyère cheese over the bottom of the warm, partially baked pastry shell. Add the leek mixture and sprinkle with 1 tablespoon chopped fresh parsley. Pour in the custard and bake.

BACON AND PARMESAN QUICHE

This version of the classic quiche Lorraine uses Parmesan instead of Gruyère cheese.

MAKES 4 TO 6 SERVINGS
  Basic Pie Dough
  4 slices thick-cut bacon, cut into ½-inch-wide strips
  3 large eggs
  1 cup milk
  ⅓ cup heavy cream
  ½ cup freshly grated Parmesan cheese
  Salt and freshly ground pepper, to taste
  A pinch of grated nutmeg

Preheat the oven to 400°F. On a lightly floured work surface, roll out the pastry dough to a ⅛-inch-thick circle. Use to line a 9-inch round tart pan with a removable bottom. Line the pastry shell with foil and fill with dried beans or rice. Bake until the pastry is set (peek under the foil), about 10 minutes. Remove from the oven, keeping the oven on. Lift out the foil with the beans.

In a medium frying pan, cook the bacon over medium heat until crisp, about 5 minutes. Drain on paper towels; reserve 1 tablespoon fat in the pan.

In a medium bowl, whisk the eggs with the milk and cream. Stir in the Parmesan cheese, and season with salt (very lightly as the bacon and cheese may be salty), pepper, and nutmeg. Place the tart pan on a baking sheet. Sprinkle the bacon into the pastry shell, then drizzle with the bacon fat. Pour in the egg mixture. Bake for 10 minutes. Reduce the heat to 375°F, and continue baking until the filling is puffed and browned, and a knife inserted near the center comes out clean, 30 to 40 minutes. Serve hot, warm, or at room temperature.

Spinach and Chèvre Quiche: In a medium frying pan, heat 1 tablespoon unsalted butter over medium heat. Add 2 cups shredded fresh spinach leaves and cook until the spinach is wilted and tender, about 5 minutes. Place the spinach in a colander and press to remove any excess moisture. Let cool completely. Add to the filling, along with ½ cup crumbled soft goat cheese and ⅓ cup chopped scallions.

SOUFFLÉS

The classic French soufflé has an unfair reputation for being difficult. In fact, it is quite simple, and lends itself to advance preparation. The trick is to make the base (actually a thick sauce) a couple of hours ahead. Use a fairly large saucepan, and cover the sauce with plastic wrap pressed onto the surface so a crust won't form. When ready to bake, reheat the sauce until just warm, beat the egg whites, and fold them in.

ASPARAGUS SOUFFLÉ

A delicious way to celebrate spring.

MAKES 4 SERVINGS
8 ounces fresh asparagus, woody ends trimmed
4 large eggs, separated
4 tablespoons unsalted butter
¼ cup all-purpose flour
1¼ cups milk, heated
6 tablespoons freshly grated Parmesan cheese
Salt and freshly ground pepper, to taste

Preheat the oven to 400°F. Lightly butter a 1½-quart soufflé dish and set aside.

In an asparagus cooker or a wide pan of lightly salted water, cook the asparagus until tender, about 8 minutes. Drain and rinse well under cold running water. Cut off the top 2 inches or so from each asparagus spear and set aside. Place the asparagus stalks in a blender with the egg yolks and process into a purée. Set the purée aside.

In a large saucepan, melt the butter over medium heat. Stir in the flour and reduce the heat to low. Let bubble without browning for 1 to 2 minutes. Gradually stir in the milk to make a thick, smooth sauce. Bring to a simmer and cook, stirring frequently to prevent sticking, for 5 minutes. Remove from the heat, and stir in the Parmesan cheese. Let cool slightly, then stir in the asparagus purée. Season with salt and pepper.

In a large, greasefree bowl, beat the egg whites until soft peaks form. Stir about one fourth into the asparagus mixture to lighten it, then fold in the remaining whites. Pour half of the soufflé mixture into the prepared dish, then sprinkle with the asparagus tips, and pour in the remaining mixture. Bake until the soufflé is puffed and golden-brown, about 20 minutes. Serve immediately.

APPLE, CHEDDAR, AND PECAN QUESADILLAS

The concept of the quesadilla, that Tex-Mex favorite, is applied here to the Yankee grilled cheese sandwich. It makes a terrific quick lunch or snack, or can be served as an appetizer.

MAKES 4 SERVINGS
8 (6-inch) flour tortillas
2 cups shredded sharp Cheddar cheese
1 tart green apple, such as Granny Smith, quartered, cored, and cut into very thin wedges
4 tablespoons finely chopped pecans

Preheat the oven to 200°F. For each quesadilla, sprinkle one tortilla with about ¼ cup of the cheese. Arrange one fourth of the apple slices in a spoke pattern on the cheese, then sprinkle with 1 tablespoon pecans and another ¼ cup of the cheese. Top with a second tortilla. Heat an empty large frying pan over medium heat. One at a time, cook the quesadillas in the pan, turning them once, until both sides are lightly browned and the cheese has melted, about 3 minutes. Keep the quesadillas warm in the oven until they are all prepared. Cut them into wedges and serve hot.

MOZZARELLA IN CARROZZA

Mozzarella in carrozza, or "in a carriage," consists of cheese sandwiches dipped in egg and fried to an appetizing golden-brown.

MAKES 4 SERVINGS

6 ounces mozzarella cheese, cut into 4 thick slices
8 slices firm white sandwich bread, crusts removed
8 anchovy fillets (optional)
3 large eggs
Salt, to taste
Olive oil, for frying

Make four sandwiches out of the cheese and bread, including the anchovies, if desired. Cut each sandwich in half. In a small bowl, beat the eggs with a pinch of salt.

Put enough oil in a large frying pan to come ½ inch up the sides. Heat over medium heat until very hot but not smoking. Dip each sandwich into the beaten egg to coat both sides, shaking off the excess egg, and place in the oil. Fry the sandwiches, turning once, until golden, about 3 minutes. Drain briefly on paper towels. Sprinkle lightly with salt and serve hot.

HAM AND MUSHROOM BREAKFAST CASSEROLE

This must be refrigerated overnight before serving, so it is perfect for holiday brunches. It is actually a savory bread pudding with sautéed mushrooms and ham.

MAKES 8 SERVINGS

2 tablespoons unsalted butter
1 pound button mushrooms, thinly sliced
12 ounces smoked ham, cut into ¼-inch cubes
6 scallions, chopped
20 (¼-inch-thick) slices French or Italian bread, approximately
2 cups shredded Cheddar cheese
4 cups milk
6 large eggs
2 tablespoons Dijon mustard
2 tablespoons chopped parsley
1 teaspoon dried thyme
½ teaspoon salt
¼ teaspoon freshly ground pepper

In a large frying pan, heat the butter over medium heat. Add the mushrooms and cook, stirring often, until lightly browned, about 10 minutes. Stir in the ham and scallions, and cook until the scallions are softened, about 2 minutes. Set aside.

Lightly butter a 9- by 13-inch baking dish. Arrange enough bread slices, slightly overlapping or trimmed to fit, in the dish to cover the bottom. Spread the mushroom-ham mixture over the bread, then sprinkle with the cheese. Top with another layer of bread. In a large bowl, whisk together the milk, eggs, mustard, parsley, thyme, salt, and pepper. Slowly pour all over the bread. Cover and refrigerate overnight.

Preheat the oven to 325°F. Set the dish in a larger roasting pan, and place in the oven. Add hot water to the pan to come ½ inch up the sides. Bake until a knife inserted in the center of the casserole comes out clean, about 1½ hours. Remove from the water bath and let stand for 10 minutes before serving.

SWISS FONDUE

Like the quiche, fondue went through a period of decline. But as busy cooks realized that this fun way to enjoy supper with friends was also easy, it returned to the culinary scene. If you don't have a fondue set, improvise with a plate warmer and a saucepan.

MAKES 6 SERVINGS

2 garlic cloves, peeled
1 cup dry white wine
1¼ pounds shredded Emmentaler cheese (about 5 cups), or a mixture of Emmentaler and Gruyère
1 teaspoon potato flour or cornstarch
2 tablespoons kirsch
A drop of corn or vegetable oil
A pinch of grated nutmeg
Freshly ground pepper, to taste
Crusty French or Italian bread, cut into 1-inch cubes

Rub a cheese-fondue pot, a medium earthenware dish, or a medium saucepan with 1 crushed garlic clove; discard the garlic. Add the wine and the remaining whole clove of garlic. Bring to a simmer over medium-low heat on top of the stove. Toss the cheese with the potato flour. Gradually add the cheese to the pot, stirring constantly, until it has melted into a thick sauce. If the fondue seems too thick, add a little more wine. Stir in the kirsch mixed with the corn oil, and season with the nutmeg and freshly ground pepper.

Transfer the fondue in the cooking utensil to the fondue burner and place over a medium flame. Allow each guest to serve themselves, piercing a bread cube onto a fork and dipping into the cheese sauce. Maintain the heat so the fondue is very hot and gently bubbling. A delicious crust will form on the bottom of the pot; this can be scraped up and eaten.

MOZZARELLA IN CARROZZA

Pasta

FRESH PASTA DOUGH

Whether you make this dough by hand or in a food processor, the results will be equally fine. You will have to be flexible with the amount of flour and liquid, as the flour will absorb differently according to the humidity of the day and exact size of the eggs.

MAKES ABOUT 1 POUND

2 cups unbleached all-purpose flour
3 large eggs

To make the dough by hand, place the flour in a large bowl and make a well in the center. Put the eggs in the well. Using the fingers of one hand like a fork, break up the eggs. Then, stirring the eggs in a circle, gradually draw the flour into the eggs to make a moist, pliable ball of dough. If the dough is too dry, sprinkle with 1 tablespoon water. If the dough seems too sticky, sprinkle with a tablespoon of flour. Turn the dough onto a lightly floured work surface and knead until the dough is supple, about 5 minutes. If the dough feels at all sticky while you are kneading, sprinkle it with a little flour.

To make the dough in a food processor, fit the bowl with the metal blade and put in the flour. With the food processor running, gradually pour in the beaten eggs through the feed tube. Process until the dough forms a ball that rides on top of the blade. Feel the dough to test its consistency. If it is too dry, sprinkle with 1 tablespoon water. If it is too sticky, sprinkle with 1 tablespoon flour. Process for about 30 seconds and check again. To knead the dough, process for 1 more minute.

Wrap the dough in plastic wrap and allow to relax at room temperature for 30 minutes before rolling out.

Tuscan Pasta Dough: Substitute 1 tablespoon each olive oil and milk for 1 of the eggs.

Rolling Pasta Dough in a Machine

Be sure the pasta machine is very clean and dry. Attach the machine to your work surface. Set the rollers at the widest setting. Cut the dough into thirds. Work with one piece at a time, keeping the remaining dough covered with plastic wrap. Dust the piece of dough lightly with flour and press it into an oblong shape. Cranking the handle of the machine, feed the dough through the rollers. Fold the dough into thirds, dust with flour, and feed it through the rollers again. Do this several times to smooth out and finish kneading the dough.

Now set the rollers one notch closer together. Fold the dough, dust with flour, and feed through the rollers again. Move the machine up another notch, and repeat the procedure, without folding the dough into three. The dough will now be getting fairly long, and you will have to hold it up over the machine. Set the rollers to the next setting, dust the dough with flour, and feed through the machine. Set the rollers to the next-to-last setting, and pass the dough through a final time. (The finest setting is reserved for very thinly rolled pasta, like ravioli, where the edges of each raviolo will have a double thickness.)

Spread out the dough strip on a lightly floured work surface. Repeat the procedure with the remaining dough. If you will be cutting the dough into noodles or other shapes, let the dough strips dry, uncovered, for 15 to 30 minutes (depending on the weather and humidity), turning them over once so that they dry evenly. The dough should be supple and leathery, but not so dry that it will crack when cut. For stuffed pasta, do not let the dough dry at all, and keep the strips covered with a slightly damp dish towel.

Making Pasta Shapes

Tagliatelle (sometimes called fettuccine) are narrow ribbons of pasta. They are eaten with all sorts of sauces—cream, tomato, or meat. To make tagliatelle by hand, roll up each strip of pasta like a jelly roll, and slice across at ¼-inch intervals all the way along the roll. Unroll each spiral of dough. If you wish, hang the tagliatelle on a cloth placed over the back of a chair to dry, but the pasta can be cooked immediately. You can also cut tagliatelle by running the strip of dough through the wide cutters on the pasta machine.

Linguine are ⅛-inch-wide ribbons of pasta. They are normally cut by hand, as most pasta machines do not have cutters of the required width.

Tagliarini are very narrow strands of pasta, about 1/16 inch wide. They can be cut by hand like tagliatelle, but it is easier to run the strips of dough through the thinnest cutters on the pasta machine.

Pappardelle are ¾-inch-wide ribbons of pasta that are about 12 inches long. Use a fluted pastry wheel, or even a plain pizza cutter, to cut the flat strips of dough into pappardelle.

Farfalle are eaten with the same sauces as tagliatelle. To make them, use a fluted pastry wheel to cut the dough into 2-inch squares. With the forefinger and thumb of one hand, pinch each square across the middle to make an even fold, thus creating a butterfly or bow-tie effect.

Lasagne are large strips of pasta that are cooked and then layered with meat or vegetable sauces, cheese, and, sometimes, béchamel sauce. The assembled lasagne is then baked until it is bubbling and browned. To fit a typical 9- by 13-inch lasagne pan,

1

2

Making pasta dough

1 Put the flour in a bowl and make a well in the center. Add the eggs to the well.

2 Using your fingertips, break up the eggs to mix them. Gradually mix the flour into the eggs to make a moist, pliable dough. The dough can now be kneaded and rolled by hand, or using a pasta machine.

flour dredger
237
pasta machine
229, 239

**Fresh Pasta
Dough** 334
**Tuscan Pasta
Dough** 334

3

3 If using a pasta machine, turn the dough out onto a lightly floured work surface. Cut the dough into three portions (or into as many pieces as there are eggs in the dough). Work with one piece at a time and keep the others covered to prevent them from drying out.

Rolling and cutting pasta dough

1 To knead the dough, set the rollers on the pasta machine to the widest setting. Flatten the piece of dough and feed it through the rollers, then fold the dough into thirds.

2 Feed the dough through the rollers again. Repeat several times, folding it into thirds each time.

3 To roll out the dough, set the rollers one notch closer together. Feed the dough through again, but do not fold it into thirds. Continue moving the rollers closer together, one notch at a time, and feeding the dough through, rolling it gradually into a long, thin strip. Repeat with the remaining dough.

4 To cut noodles, let the dough strips dry until they look leathery. Then fit the appropriate cutting rollers onto the machine. Feed through the strips, and catch the emerging nooodles on your hand.

1

2

3

4

Cutting tagliatelle by hand (*right*)
Roll up the sheet of pasta loosely, like a jelly roll. Using a small, sharp knife, cut across the roll at ¼-inch intervals and then unroll the little spirals of dough.

Making farfalle (*far right*)
With a fluted pastry wheel, cut the sheet of dough into strips 2 inches wide, then cut across the strips to make 2-inch squares. Pinch the middle of each square between your thumb and forefinger, to make a butterfly shape.

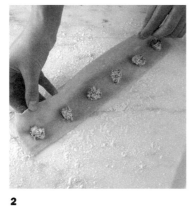

Making ravioli

1 Roll the pasta dough as thinly as possible. With a fluted pastry wheel, cut the pasta sheet into strips about 3 inches wide.

1

2

3

2 Put heaped teaspoonfuls of the filling down each strip, spacing the mounds of filling about 1½ inches apart and about ¾ inch from one long edge. Lightly moisten the dough around the mounds of filling, then fold the dough over the filling.

3 Press the edges of the dough together, and press all around the mounds of filling to seal the dough.

4

4 With the pastry wheel, carefully cut between the mounds of filling to form the ravioli.

cut the dough with a fluted pastry wheel into 3 ½- by 13-inch strips (this allows a little extra so the strips can overlap slightly in the pan).

Cooking and Serving Pasta

Pasta in Italy is most often served as a first course, but in other parts of the world it is also served as an entrée. If you are serving pasta as an appetizer, 1 pound of pasta will feed six to eight people; as a main course, each pound of pasta will give four to six servings (according to the sauce used to dress the pasta, and individual appetites).

Bring a large pot of water—this should be at least 4 quarts—to a boil over high heat. Salt the water, allowing 2 tablespoons salt for every 4 quarts of water. When cooking fresh pasta, add it to the boiling water all at once and then stir gently for 1 minute to be sure the strands or shapes don't stick together. Continue to cook until the pasta is just tender but still a little resilient (al dente): test a strand or piece by biting into it. This will take between 2 and 4 minutes, depending on how dry the pasta is.

To cook dried pasta, add it to the water all at once (spaghetti should be gradually pushed down into the pot as it softens), then stir well for 1 to 2 minutes to be sure the strands or shapes don't stick together. Boil until al dente, 10 to 12 minutes or according to the package instructions; test often to be sure the pasta is not overcooked.

Drain spaghetti and other noodles and pasta shapes in a colander, shaking it around gently. Leave a tiny bit of water on the pasta—if it is too well drained it will stick together. Transfer the pasta to a warmed bowl or return it to the empty pot. Add the sauce and toss briefly. Serve immediately, into warmed bowls or onto warmed plates, and provide a bowl of freshly grated Parmesan cheese so each diner can add this to taste (unless you have dressed the pasta with a fish sauce, which in Italy is never accompanied by Parmesan).

To drain lasagne properly, lift the strips out of the water using either a perforated metal turner or a fish lifter. Dip each strip briefly into a bowl of cold water, and then spread it flat on a clean damp cloth to drain and dry completely.

SPAGHETTI WITH TOMATO AND VEGETABLE SAUCE

Tomato sauce is the everyday sauce of northern Italy, where everyday means at least once or even twice a day. Italians make a batch large enough to last a week, and may eat it with pasta, semolina gnocchi, and polenta, with plenty of Parmesan cheese.

MAKES 4 TO 6 SERVINGS
1 pound spaghetti
Freshly grated Parmesan cheese, for serving
Tomato and Vegetable Sauce
¼ cup olive oil
2 medium onions, finely chopped
2 small carrots, finely chopped
2 small celery ribs, finely chopped
3 garlic cloves, minced
1½ pounds ripe plum tomatoes, peeled, seeded, and chopped, or 2 cups canned tomato purée
¾ cup chicken stock or water
Salt and freshly ground pepper, to taste
3 tablespoons unsalted butter

In a large saucepan, heat the oil over medium heat. Add the onions, carrots, celery, and garlic. Cook, stirring often, until softened and starting to brown, about 8 minutes. Add the tomatoes and stock and bring to a simmer. Season with salt and pepper. Reduce the heat to low and simmer until the sauce has thickened, about 1 hour. If desired, purée the sauce in a food processor fitted with the metal blade or in a blender. Stir in the butter, and taste the sauce to check the seasoning. Keep the sauce warm. (The sauce can be cooled and then kept, covered, in the refrigerator for up to 2 days; reheat before serving.)

In a large pot of boiling salted water, cook the spaghetti until *al dente*, about 10 minutes. Drain the pasta and add to the sauce. Cook, stirring to mix the pasta with the sauce, for 1 to 2 minutes. Transfer to a heated bowl and serve, with the cheese on the side.

SPAGHETTI ALLA CARBONARA

This rich and creamy sauce, whose name means "in the charcoal-burner's style," is justifiably popular. The trick is to work very quickly once the pasta has been drained so everything is served piping hot.

MAKES 4 TO 6 SERVINGS
2 tablespoons unsalted butter
5 ounces thick-sliced pancetta or slab bacon, rind removed, cut into ¼-inch-wide sticks
3 large eggs
4 large egg yolks
⅔ cup heavy cream
Freshly ground pepper, to taste
1 pound spaghetti
⅔ cup freshly grated Parmesan cheese

In a frying pan, heat the butter over medium heat. Add the pancetta and cook until lightly browned, about 5 minutes. Remove from the heat and keep warm.

In a medium bowl, whisk together the eggs and yolks, then whisk in the cream. Season with plenty of pepper, and set aside.

In a large pot of boiling salted water over high heat, cook the pasta until *al dente*, about 10 minutes. Drain and return to the empty pot in which the pasta was cooked. Stir in the pancetta and its cooking fat, then add the egg mixture and Parmesan cheese. Toss well, transfer to a warmed bowl, and serve immediately.

SPAGHETTI WITH QUICK TOMATO AND BALSAMIC VINEGAR SAUCE

Make this when tomatoes and basil are at their best. A splash of balsamic vinegar works magic with this simple sauce.

MAKES 4 TO 6 SERVINGS

   1 pound spaghetti
   ¼ cup olive oil
   2 garlic cloves, minced
   2½ pounds ripe plum tomatoes, seeded and
      coarsely chopped
   3 tablespoons chopped fresh basil
   2 tablespoons balsamic vinegar
   Salt and freshly ground pepper, to taste
   Freshly grated Parmesan cheese, for serving

In a large pot of boiling salted water over high heat, cook the spaghetti until *al dente*, about 10 minutes.

Meanwhile, heat the oil in a large nonreactive frying pan over medium heat. Add the garlic and cook until softened, about 1 minute. Add the tomatoes and cook, stirring often, until just heated through, about 3 minutes. Stir in the basil and balsamic vinegar, and season with salt and pepper.

Drain the pasta and transfer to a warmed serving bowl. Add the sauce and toss well. Serve, with a bowl of Parmesan cheese on the side for sprinkling.

PAPPARDELLE WITH RAGÙ BOLOGNESE

Here is the classic meat sauce of northern Italy. Wide strips of pappardelle match the heartiness of the sauce, but tagliatelle is a good choice, too, either fresh or dry.

MAKES 4 TO 6 SERVINGS

   1 pound fresh pappardelle
Ragù
   3 tablespoons olive oil, or 1½ tablespoons each olive
      oil and unsalted butter
   1 medium onion, finely chopped
   1 large carrot, finely chopped
   1 large celery rib with leaves, finely chopped
   2 garlic cloves, minced
   8 ounces ground veal or beef
   8 ounces ground pork
   3 large ripe tomatoes, peeled, seeded, and chopped,
      or 1 cup drained, chopped canned tomatoes
   3 chicken livers, cut into ¼-inch dice
   ½ teaspoon chopped fresh thyme or ¼ teaspoon
      dried thyme
   Salt and freshly ground pepper, to taste
   ⅔ cup chicken stock
   ⅔ cup hearty red wine
   2 tablespoons heavy cream

To make the *ragù*, heat the oil in a large saucepan over medium heat. Add the onion, carrot, celery, and garlic. Cook until the vegetables are softened, about 5 minutes. Add the ground veal and ground pork and increase the heat to medium-high. Cook, uncovered, breaking up the meat with a spoon, until the meat is browned, about 10 minutes. Stir in the tomatoes, chicken livers, and thyme, and season with salt and pepper. Bring to a simmer, and cook until most of the liquid from the tomatoes has evaporated. Add half of the stock and red wine. Reduce the heat to medium-low, and simmer for 30 minutes. Add the rest of the stock and red wine, and simmer until the sauce is thick, about 1 more hour. Remove from the heat and stir in the cream. Taste the sauce to check the seasoning. (The sauce can be prepared, without the cream, then cooled and kept, covered, in the refrigerator for 1 day; reheat, then remove from the heat and add the cream. The cream may curdle if allowed to boil.)

In a large pot of boiling salted water over high heat, cook the pasta until *al dente*, 3 to 5 minutes. Drain and transfer to a warmed serving bowl. Add the hot sauce and toss. Serve immediately.

TAGLIATELLE WITH PESTO SAUCE

This is a memorable dish, especially when prepared with homemade pasta. The pesto is delicious—an aromatic partner for many kinds of pasta.

MAKES 4 TO 6 SERVINGS

   1 pound fresh tagliatelle or fettuccine
Pesto Sauce
   3 tablespoons pine nuts
   2 cups packed fresh basil leaves
   2 large garlic cloves, coarsely chopped
   2 tablespoons freshly grated Parmesan cheese, plus
      more for serving
   6 tablespoons olive oil
   Salt, to taste

In a small dry frying pan over medium heat, cook the pine nuts, stirring often, until lightly toasted. Transfer to a plate to cool.

In a food processor fitted with the metal blade or a blender, process the basil leaves and garlic until finely chopped. Add the pine nuts and pulse briefly. Add the cheese and pulse again. With the machine running, gradually add the oil to make a smooth, thick sauce. Season with salt. (The pesto can be kept, in a covered container, with a film of olive oil poured over the top of the sauce, for up to 3 days.)

In a large pot of boiling salted water over high heat, cook the pasta until *al dente*, 3 to 5 minutes. Drain well, but reserve ½ cup of the pasta cooking liquid. Transfer the pasta to a heated serving bowl. Add the pesto and toss, adding enough of the reserved pasta liquid to make a smooth sauce. Serve the pasta immediately, with additional grated Parmesan cheese passed on the side.

TAGLIARINI WITH FRESH ARTICHOKES AND GREMOLATA

This is a very light and refreshing pasta dish that is also easy to make.

MAKES 4 TO 6 SERVINGS

1 large lemon
2 tablespoons chopped fresh parsley
4 garlic cloves, thinly sliced
½ cup extra virgin olive oil
8 large artichoke bottoms, cut into ⅛-inch-wide slices
Salt and freshly ground pepper, to taste
1 pound fresh tagliarini or linguine
Freshly grated Parmesan cheese, for serving

Grate the zest from the lemon and put it into a small bowl. Mix in the parsley and garlic, and set this *gremolata* aside. Squeeze the juice from the lemon and set aside.

In a large frying pan, heat ¼ cup of the oil over medium heat. Add the artichoke slices, and season with salt and pepper. Cook until the artichokes are golden-brown and tender, 10 to 15 minutes. Stir in the lemon juice. Remove the frying pan from the heat and keep warm.

In a large pot of boiling salted water over high heat, cook the pasta until *al dente*, 3 to 5 minutes. Drain, and return to the empty pot. Add the remaining ¼ cup of oil, season generously with pepper, and toss well. Divide among warmed pasta bowls. Top with the artichokes, and sprinkle with the *gremolata*. Serve immediately, with the Parmesan cheese passed on the side.

TAGLIATELLE WITH TUSCAN MEAT SAUCE

This exquisite meat sauce, fundamental to the Tuscan kitchen, is a delicious change from its more familiar Bolognese cousin. While beef or veal are excellent in the sauce, a Tuscan cook would use whatever meat were handy or abundant—rabbit, chicken, or squab.

MAKES 4 TO 6 SERVINGS

1 pound fresh tagliatelle
Sauce
10 ounces boneless beef round or veal shoulder, cut into 2-inch pieces
2 chicken livers, coarsely chopped
1 medium onion, chopped
2 medium carrots, chopped
1 medium celery rib, chopped
6 large fresh basil leaves, chopped
¼ cup olive oil
Salt and freshly ground pepper, to taste
1 cup hearty red wine
1¼ cups chicken stock
½ cup dried porcini mushrooms (½ ounce)
¾ cup peeled, seeded, and chopped plum tomatoes, or use drained canned tomatoes

In a large saucepan, combine the beef, chicken livers, onion, carrots, celery, and basil. Drizzle with the oil and stir to coat the ingredients. Season with salt and pepper. Place over medium-high heat and then cook, stirring often with a wooden spoon, until the ingredients are well browned, 10 to 15 minutes. Don't worry if the vegetables stick to the bottom of the pan, but take care not to let them burn. Add the red wine. Scrape up the browned bits and pieces on the bottom of the pan, and blend them with the wine. Bring to a boil over medium heat and then cook until the wine has reduced to ¼ cup, about 10 minutes. Add the stock and bring to a simmer. Reduce the heat to low, cover, and simmer until the beef is tender, about 1½ hours.

Meanwhile, in a small bowl, soak the porcini in 1 cup hot water until softened, about 30 minutes. Lift the mushrooms out of the liquid and chop coarsely. Strain the soaking liquid through a sieve lined with a wet paper towel, and reserve the liquid.

Remove the beef and chop coarsely. Return the beef to the sauce, along with the mushrooms and their liquid and the tomatoes. Cook over medium heat, stirring often, until the sauce is thick, about 15 minutes. If the sauce seems too dry, add a little stock or water. (The sauce can be cooled and kept, covered, in the refrigerator for 1 day; reheat before serving.)

In a large pot of boiling salted water over high heat, cook the pasta until *al dente*, 3 to 5 minutes. Drain and put in a warmed bowl. Add the sauce, toss, and serve.

Tuscan Game Sauce: Substitute 2 (1½-pound) squabs, including their giblets, chopped through the bones into 2-inch pieces, for the beef. When the sauce has simmered for 1½ hours, remove the squab pieces and giblets. Discard the skin and bones, and chop coarsely. Return the chopped squab and giblets to the sauce and continue cooking.

RIGATONI WITH SPICY TOMATO AND PANCETTA SAUCE

This dish, known in Italy as *rigatoni all' amatriciana*, should be good and spicy. If you can't find pancetta, just use rindless slab bacon. As pancettá is unsmoked, you may want to remove some of the bacon's smokiness by simmering it in water for 3 minutes, then draining and patting dry before browning it.

MAKES 4 TO 6 SERVINGS

1½ tablespoons olive oil
4 ounces thick-sliced pancetta, cut into ¼-inch dice
1 small onion, chopped
¼ teaspoon chile flakes, or to taste
2 cups peeled, seeded, and chopped ripe plum tomatoes; or use drained canned tomatoes
Salt, to taste
1 pound rigatoni or ziti
½ cup freshly grated Parmesan cheese, plus more for serving

In a medium saucepan, heat the oil over medium heat. Add the pancetta and cook until lightly browned, about 5 minutes. Using a slotted spoon, remove the pancetta to a plate.

Add the onion and chile flakes to the fat in the pan and cook until the onion is softened, about 5 minutes. Add the plum tomatoes and bring the mixture to a simmer. Cook, stirring often, until the sauce is thick, about 10 minutes. Return the pancetta to the sauce, and season with salt.

In a large pot of boiling salted water over high heat, cook the pasta until *al dente*, about 10 minutes. Drain and place in a warmed serving bowl. Add the sauce and toss well to combine, then add the cheese and toss again. Serve immediately, with more cheese passed on the side.

SEA SHELLS WITH SHRIMP, FETA, AND OLIVES

The flavors in this dish are as lively as a busy Greek taverna. The sauce is made with uncooked tomatoes, so they must be very flavorful. Make it when they are at their summertime peak.

MAKES 4 TO 6 SERVINGS

3 large ripe tomatoes, chopped
1 cup Mediterranean black olives, pitted and coarsely chopped
4 tablespoons extra virgin olive oil
2 tablespoons minced fresh dill or oregano
1 garlic clove, minced
Salt and freshly ground pepper, to taste
1 pound medium shrimp, peeled and deveined
1 pound conchiglie (sea shells)
6 ounces feta cheese, crumbled

In a large bowl, combine the tomatoes, olives, 2 tablespoons oil, the dill, garlic, and a seasoning of salt and pepper. Let stand for 1 hour.

Heat the remaining 2 tablespoons oil in a large frying pan over medium-high heat. Add the shrimp and cook, stirring occasionally, until firm and pink, about 3 minutes. Remove from the heat, and cover the pan to keep the shrimp warm.

In a large pot of boiling salted water over high heat, cook the pasta until *al dente*, 10 to 12 minutes. Drain well. Return the pasta to the empty pot, and add the tomato mixture, shrimp, and feta. Toss until the feta begins to melt, then season with salt and pepper, and serve.

BUCATINI WITH TOMATOES, VEGETABLES, AND HAM

If you were to order pasta with tomato sauce in the Marches, in the central part of Italy, this is what you would be given. The cooking of this region features pork, so try to cook the sauce with lard to create an authentic flavor. Bucatini is a long, hollow macaroni, but if you prefer you can use other hollow pasta such as penne.

MAKES 4 TO 6 SERVINGS

2 tablespoons lard or olive oil
1 medium onion, finely chopped
1 medium carrot, finely chopped
1 medium celery rib, finely chopped
4 ounces (¼-inch-thick) sliced boiled ham, cut into ¼-inch-wide strips
½ cup hearty red wine
3 cups peeled, seeded, and chopped ripe plum tomatoes, or use drained canned tomatoes
2 tablespoons tomato paste
A pinch of dried marjoram
A pinch of dried thyme
Salt and freshly ground pepper, to taste
1 pound bucatini
1 cup freshly grated Parmesan cheese

In a medium saucepan, heat the lard over medium heat. Add the onion, carrot, and celery. Cook, stirring often, until lightly browned, about 10 minutes. Add the ham and stir for 2 minutes. Add the wine, increase the heat to high, and bring to a boil. Boil until the wine has almost all evaporated, about 5 minutes. Stir in the tomatoes, tomato paste, marjoram, and thyme. Season with salt and pepper. Bring to a simmer, then reduce the heat to low and let simmer until rich and thick, about 30 minutes.

In a large pot of boiling salted water, cook the pasta until *al dente*, about 10 minutes. Drain and place in a heated bowl. Mix in half of the sauce and a few heaping tablespoons of cheese. Serve immediately, with the remaining sauce and cheese on the side.

PASTA WITH GRILLED VEGETABLES AND MOZZARELLA

Grilled vegetables add a smoky dimension to this pasta sauce that works in harmony with the mozzarella's creaminess. It is easiest to grill the onion rounds on a perforated vegetable grilling grid,

SEA SHELLS WITH SHRIMP, FETA, AND OLIVES

available at kitchenware stores, so they don't fall onto the coals. An alternative is to chop the onion and sauté in a little olive oil.

MAKES 4 TO 6 SERVINGS
- ¼ cup extra virgin olive oil
- 2 garlic cloves, coarsely chopped
- 8 ripe plum tomatoes, cut in half lengthwise
- 1 medium eggplant, cut into ½-inch-thick rounds
- 2 medium zucchini, cut in half lengthwise
- 1 medium red onion, cut into ½-inch-thick rounds
- 1 large red bell pepper, seeded and cut in half lengthwise
- 3 tablespoons chopped fresh basil
- Salt and freshly ground pepper, to taste
- 1 pound penne or ziti
- 2 cups shredded mozzarella

In a small saucepan, heat the olive oil with the garlic over medium heat until the garlic is golden, about

3 minutes. Discard the garlic, and then set the garlic-flavored oil aside.

Build a hot charcoal fire in an outdoor grill or preheat a gas grill. Lightly oil the grill. Brush the vegetables lightly with the garlic-flavored oil. Grill the vegetables, turning and basting with the oil occasionally. Cook the tomatoes until tender but still holding their shape, about 8 minutes. Cook the eggplant and zucchini until browned on both sides, about 10 minutes. Cook the onion until crisp-tender and the edges are charred, 10 to 12 minutes. Cook the red pepper until the skin is charred, about 12 minutes. As the vegetables cook, transfer them to a large bowl and cover with a sheet of foil to keep warm. When the pepper is cool enough to handle, remove and discard the charred skin.

Transfer the vegetables to a food processor fitted with a metal blade and coarsely chop. (The sauce can be prepared up to 1 hour ahead, and kept at room temperature; reheat until hot in a medium saucepan over medium heat.) Stir in the basil, and season with salt and pepper. Keep warm.

LASAGNE WITH PORTOBELLO MUSHROOMS, ARTICHOKES, AND PANCETTA

In a large pot of boiling salted water, cook the pasta until *al dente*, about 10 minutes. Drain well, but reserve ½ cup of the pasta cooking water. Place the hot pasta in a warmed serving bowl. Add the sauce and mozzarella and toss thoroughly to combine, adding enough of the reserved water to make a creamy sauce. Serve immediately.

PENNE WITH EGGPLANT AND RICOTTA

A satisfying vegetarian pasta dish, this is both easy and quick to make.

MAKES 4 TO 6 SERVINGS

4 tablespoons olive oil
1 medium onion, chopped
1 medium red bell pepper, seeded and chopped
1 medium eggplant, unpeeled, cut into ½-inch cubes

2 garlic cloves, minced
1 teaspoon dried oregano
¼ teaspoon chile flakes
2 cups peeled, seeded, and chopped ripe plum
   tomatoes, or use canned tomatoes
Salt, to taste
1 pound penne or ziti
1 cup ricotta cheese
⅓ cup grated pecorino romano cheese, plus more
   for serving
2 tablespoons chopped fresh basil (optional)

In a large frying pan, heat 2 tablespoons oil over medium heat. Add the onion and bell pepper and cook until the onion is golden, about 8 minutes. Add the remaining 2 tablespoons oil, then the eggplant, garlic, oregano, and chile flakes. Cover and cook until the eggplant softens, about 5 minutes. Add the tomatoes and bring to a boil. Reduce the heat to low and simmer, uncovered, until the eggplant is tender and the sauce is thick, about 20 minutes.

In a large pot of boiling salted water over high heat, cook the penne until *al dente*, about 10 minutes. Drain well and return to the empty pot. Add the sauce, ricotta and romano cheeses, and the optional basil, and toss well. Season with salt. Serve immediately, with a bowl of romano cheese passed on the side.

LASAGNE WITH PORTOBELLO MUSHROOMS, ARTICHOKES, AND PANCETTA

Made without the pancetta, this is an excellent vegetarian main course.

MAKES 6 SERVINGS
   Béchamel Sauce, made with 2½ cups milk flavored
      with onion, bay leaf, and cloves, 4 tablespoons
      unsalted butter, and ⅓ cup all-purpose flour
⅔ cup half-and-half
A pinch of grated nutmeg
Salt and freshly ground pepper, to taste
1 pound large portobello mushrooms
3 tablespoons olive oil
2 tablespoons lemon juice
2 garlic cloves, sliced
6 ounces thick-sliced pancetta or thinly
   sliced bacon
6 large artichoke bottoms
12 dried lasagne strips (9 ounces)
1 tablespoon chopped fresh oregano
3 tablespoons freshly grated Parmesan cheese
6 tablespoons unsalted butter
12 large fresh sage leaves

Preheat the oven to 400°F.
   Add the half-and-half to the béchamel sauce, and simmer until it returns to its original thickness, about 5 minutes. Season with the nutmeg, salt, and pepper. Remove from the heat. Press a piece of buttered waxed paper directly onto the surface of the sauce, and set aside.
   Cut off the stems from the mushrooms. Put the mushroom caps and stems in a baking dish just large enough to hold them. Drizzle with the oil and lemon juice. Tuck the garlic slices under the mushrooms, and season. Bake until the mushrooms are tender, 30 to 40 minutes. Let cool. Discard the garlic. Cut the mushroom caps into ¼-inch-thick slices, and the stems into ¼-inch-thick rounds. Set aside.
   Cook the pancetta in a preheated broiler until crisp and golden-brown. Set aside.
   In a large pot of lightly salted water over high heat, cook the artichoke bottoms until tender, about 20 minutes. Drain and rinse under cold running water to cool. Cut into ¼-inch-thick slices. Set aside.
   In a large pot of boiling salted water over high heat, cook the lasagne until it is barely tender, about 10 minutes. Do not overcook. Drain.
   Oil a 9- by 13-inch baking dish well. Spread with a thin layer of the béchamel sauce. Place an overlapping layer of four lasagne strips in the dish (three placed horizontally, and one vertically). Spread with another thin layer of béchamel, then sprinkle with half of the oregano. Arrange half of the mushrooms on top. Spread with another thin layer of béchamel, then add half of the pancetta and half of the artichokes. Top with another layer of four lasagne strips. Repeat the layering process, using thin layers of béchamel and the remaining oregano, mushrooms, pancetta, and artichokes. Finish with the final four lasagne strips and a thick coating of béchamel. Cover with plastic wrap and then refrigerate until firm, at least 6 hours or overnight.
   Preheat the oven to 400°F. Lightly oil two baking sheets. Using a sharp knife, cut the lasagne into six portions. Carefully lift out each of the portions with a metal spatula, and place on the baking sheets, being sure to space the portions well apart. Sprinkle each portion with some grated Parmesan cheese. Bake until the tops are bubbling and golden-brown in color, about 30 minutes.
   Just before serving, heat the butter in a medium frying pan over medium heat. Add the sage leaves and cook until they are crisp, 1 to 2 minutes. Season the leaves with salt.
   Transfer each lasagne portion to a warmed dinner plate. Spoon equal amounts of the sage leaves and butter over each, and serve immediately.

LASAGNE WITH TWO SAUCES

Authentic *lasagne alla bolognese* is prepared with two sauces—a rich, meaty tomato sauce and a creamy béchamel (or, as the Italian would say, *besciamella*).

MAKES 8 SERVINGS

6 (3½- by 13-inch) strips fresh lasagne

Béchamel Sauce, made with 4 cups milk flavored with onion, bay leaf, and cloves, 6 tablespoons unsalted butter, and ½ cup all-purpose flour

1 pound mozzarella cheese, shredded

¾ cup freshly grated Parmesan cheese

Meaty Tomato Sauce

¼ cup olive oil

2 medium onions, chopped

1 pound ground round

8 ounces ground pork

1½ cups peeled, seeded, and chopped ripe plum tomatoes; or use drained canned tomatoes

¾ cup chicken or beef stock

1 heaping teaspoon dried oregano

1 heaping teaspoon dried basil

3 garlic cloves, minced

Salt and freshly ground pepper, to taste

To make the meaty tomato sauce, heat the oil in a large saucepan over medium heat. Add the onions and cook until soft and translucent, about 5 minutes. Add the ground round and pork, and cook, stirring with a spoon to break up the meat, until browned, about 10 minutes. Add the tomatoes, stock, oregano, basil, and garlic, and season with salt and pepper. Bring to a simmer, then reduce the heat to low. Let simmer, adding more stock if the sauce seems too dry, until thickened, about 1 hour. Set aside.

In a large pot of boiling salted water over high heat, cook the lasagne until barely tender, 3 to 4 minutes. Do not overcook. Drain.

Preheat the oven to 350°F. Lightly butter a 9- by 13-inch baking dish. Spread one third of the meat sauce in the bottom of the dish, then spoon on one third of the béchamel. Top with half of the mozzarella and Parmesan cheeses, then add a neat layer of half of the lasagne. Repeat the layers of meat and béchamel sauces and pasta, then top with the remaining meat and béchamel sauces. Sprinkle with the remaining mozzarella, then with the rest of the Parmesan cheese. Bake until the cheese topping is golden-brown, about 45 minutes.

BAKED RIGATONI WITH CREAMY PROSCIUTTO SAUCE

This is incredibly rich and satisfying. Don't overcook the pasta, as it will be baked with the sauce.

MAKES 4 SERVINGS

2½ cups heavy cream, or 1½ cups heavy cream and 1 cup half-and-half

A pinch of grated nutmeg

Salt and freshly ground pepper, to taste

5 ounces (⅛-inch-thick) sliced prosciutto or boiled ham, cut into thin strips

1 pound rigatoni or ziti

1 cup freshly grated Parmesan cheese

5 tablespoons unsalted butter, cut into small pieces

Preheat the oven to 400°F. In a medium saucepan, bring the cream to a simmer. Season with the nutmeg, salt, and pepper. Stir in the prosciutto and set aside.

In a large pot of boiling salted water over high heat, cook the pasta until barely tender, about 9 minutes. Do not overcook. Drain and return to the empty pot. Add the cream mixture and ½ cup of the Parmesan cheese and toss well.

Transfer to a well-buttered 9- by 13-inch baking dish. Sprinkle with the remaining ½ cup of Parmesan cheese and dot with the butter. Bake until the top is golden-brown and the sauce is bubbling nicely, about 15 to 20 minutes.

MACARONI AND THREE CHEESES

In this delicious trio of cheeses, each adds its own characteristics to create a special version of this well-loved dish.

MAKES 4 TO 6 SERVINGS

1 pound elbow macaroni

8 ounces cream cheese, at room temperature

2 cups shredded sharp Cheddar cheese

1 cup heavy cream or milk

½ cup fresh bread crumbs

½ cup freshly grated Parmesan cheese

⅛ teaspoon cayenne pepper

1 tablespoon unsalted butter, cut into bits

Preheat the oven to 350°F. Lightly butter a 2½-quart round baking dish. In a large pot of boiling salted water over high heat, cook the macaroni until just tender, about 8 minutes. Do not overcook, as it will cook further in the sauce. Drain and return to the empty pot. Add the cream cheese and stir until it melts. Stir in the Cheddar cheese and cream. Transfer to the prepared baking dish.

In a small bowl, combine the bread crumbs, Parmesan cheese, and cayenne pepper. Sprinkle this mixture over the macaroni, and dot with the butter. Bake until the top is golden-brown and the macaroni is bubbling, about 35 minutes.

SPINACH AND RICOTTA RAVIOLI

Homemade ravioli are a real treat. They require a bit of effort, however, so are not everyday fare. Save them for very special holiday meals, which is exactly what the Italians would do.

MAKES 4 SERVINGS

1 pound Fresh Pasta Dough
⅔ cup light cream
2 tablespoons unsalted butter
Freshly grated Parmesan cheese, for serving
Filling
1 pound fresh spinach, tough stems
   discarded
⅔ cup ricotta cheese
¼ cup freshly grated Parmesan cheese
3 tablespoons chopped fresh basil leaves
¼ teaspoon freshly grated nutmeg
Salt and freshly ground pepper, to taste

To make the filling for the ravioli, place the spinach (with the rinsing water still clinging to its leaves) in a large saucepan. Cover and cook over medium-low heat until wilted and just tender, 4 to 5 minutes. Drain thoroughly and let cool. Chop finely and place in a medium bowl. Add the remaining filling ingredients and mix well.

Roll out the pasta dough to the thinnest setting on the pasta machine. It is important for the pasta to be very thin, as each raviolo will have a double thickness around the edges. Using a fluted pastry wheel, cut the pasta into strips about 3 inches wide (they can be as long as you like). Place heaped teaspoons of the filling about 1½ inches apart along the length of one strip, about ¾ inch from one long edge. Dampen the pasta dough around the filling. Fold the dough over so the long edges meet. Press all around the mounds of filling, sealing carefully. Using the fluted pastry wheel, cut between the mounds of filling to form ravioli. Place the ravioli on baking sheets lined with flour-dusted dish towels. Repeat with the remaining filling and dough. Cover with plastic wrap and refrigerate until ready to cook.

Preheat the oven to 350°F. Bring a large pot of salted water to a boil over high heat. In a small saucepan, heat the cream and butter together gently over low heat, stirring. Season with salt and pepper, and keep warm.

In batches, without crowding, cook the ravioli in the boiling water until al dente, 3 to 4 minutes. Using a slotted spoon or a skimmer, remove the ravioli from the water and transfer to a warmed heatproof serving dish. Sprinkle each layer of ravioli with a little of the cream sauce. When all the ravioli are in the dish, bake until heated through, 5 to 10 minutes. Sprinkle with grated Parmesan cheese and serve immediately, with more Parmesan passed on the side so that guests can help themselves.

SEMOLINA GNOCCHI

Semolina flour is a golden and gritty-textured flour that is ground from durum wheat. It is used to make very light Italian dumplings, which are known as *gnocchi alla romana*. If you would like to serve the gnocchi with a sauce, Delicate Tomato Sauce would be a very good choice.

MAKES 4 TO 6 SERVINGS

2½ cups milk
1 small onion, thickly sliced
1 bay leaf
1 mace blade or a pinch of grated nutmeg
¾ cup semolina flour
1 large egg yolk
4 tablespoons unsalted butter
½ cup freshly grated Parmesan cheese
Salt and freshly ground pepper, to taste

In a large saucepan, heat the milk with the thickly sliced onion, the bay leaf, and mace over low heat until bubbles start forming around the edge of the milk. Spoon the onion, bay leaf, and mace out of the milk and discard them. Stirring constantly, gradually add the semolina, and continue stirring until the mixture is very thick, 2 to 3 minutes. Cover the pan, reduce the heat to very low, and cook very gently, stirring often, for 15 minutes. Remove from the heat. Stirring briskly, add the egg yolk, 2 tablespoons of the butter, and ¼ cup of the Parmesan. Season with salt and pepper. Wet a baking sheet with water. Pour the semolina onto the baking sheet and, using the palm of your hand, spread into a ½-inch-thick slab. Leave to cool until firm.

Preheat the oven to 325°F. Lightly butter a 9- by 13-inch baking dish. Using a 1½-inch round biscuit cutter (or, alternatively, the top of a wine glass if you do not have a biscuit cutter), cut out rounds from the semolina. Or, if you prefer, use a sharp knife to cut it into squares or triangles. When you have cut out as many shapes as you can, press the leftover scraps together until smooth, and cut out more rounds until the semolina is all used.

Arrange the semolina rounds in rows, slightly overlapping, in the dish. Sprinkle with the remaining Parmesan cheese and dot all over with the remaining 2 tablespoons butter. Bake until nicely browned, about 30 minutes.

SPINACH GNOCCHI WITH BUTTER AND SAGE

These gnocchi are actually quite easy to make, and have a sublime texture. To guarantee success with this recipe, be sure not to overhandle the gnocchi when you are shaping them.

MAKES 4 SERVINGS

 1½ pounds fresh spinach leaves, thick
   stems discarded
 1 cup freshly grated Parmesan cheese
 ½ cup ricotta cheese
 3 large egg yolks
 ¼ teaspoon freshly grated nutmeg
 Salt and freshly ground pepper, to taste
 All-purpose flour, for coating
 8 tablespoons (1 stick) unsalted butter
 16 large fresh sage leaves
 1 lemon, cut into quarters

In a large pot of boiling salted water, cook the spinach until wilted and tender, about 3 minutes. Drain and refresh the spinach in cold water, then squeeze by handfuls in a clean dish towel to remove all the excess moisture.

In a food processor fitted with the metal blade, process the spinach with ¾ cup Parmesan cheese, the ricotta, egg yolks, nutmeg, and a seasoning of salt and pepper until the spinach is evenly chopped and the mixture is well combined. Spread in a shallow baking dish, cover with plastic wrap, and refrigerate until firm, at least 2 hours.

Using a pair of tablespoons, form the spinach mixture into small egg shapes, and roll each one in flour. As they are shaped, place the gnocchi on a lightly floured baking sheet.

Preheat the oven to 200°F. In a large saucepan, bring 2 quarts salted water to a boil over high heat, then reduce the heat so that the water remains just at a steady simmer. In batches, and taking care not to crowd them, cook the gnocchi until they are swollen and floating buoyantly on the surface, about 5 minutes. Remove the gnocchi from the water with a slotted spoon or skimmer and transfer them to a heatproof serving bowl. Cover loosely with aluminum foil and keep warm in the oven while cooking the remaining gnocchi.

In a medium frying pan, melt the butter over medium heat and continue to cook until it is a nut-brown color. Add the sage leaves and cook until slightly crisp, about 1 minute. Pour the sage and butter over the gnocchi, sprinkle with the remaining grated Parmesan cheese, and serve immediately, with lemon wedges.

CHINESE EGG NOODLES WITH BROWNED GARLIC, CHILES, AND CILANTRO

Garlic fans will love this easy lunch or supper dish. Whenever you find them, purchase fresh Chinese egg noodles—they freeze very well. You can make this dish with fresh or dried tagliatelle or linguine, too.

MAKES 4 SERVINGS

 1 pound fresh Chinese egg noodles
 6 tablespoons peanut oil
 2 tablespoons Asian dark sesame oil
 8 garlic cloves, thinly sliced
 2 hot green chile peppers (such as jalapeño), seeded
   and thinly sliced
 ⅓ cup chopped fresh cilantro leaves

In a pot of boiling salted water, cook the egg noodles until just tender, about 3 minutes. Drain well.

Meanwhile, in a wok or large nonstick frying pan, heat the peanut and sesame oils over medium heat until hot. Add the garlic and stir-fry until golden-brown, about 1 minute. Ad the chiles and stir briefly. Add the drained noodles and toss to coat with the flavored oil. Stir in the cilantro, and serve.

VEGETABLE STIR-FRY ON A NOODLE PILLOW

You'll need a 12-inch nonstick frying pan to prepare this colorful dish. The vegetables can be stir-fried in a wok, or a frying pan works just as well.

MAKES 6 SERVINGS

 2 cups broccoli florets
 2 tablespoons vegetable oil
 2 scallions, chopped
 2 tablespoons minced fresh ginger
 2 garlic cloves, minced
 3 medium celery ribs, thinly sliced on the diagonal
 2 medium carrots, thinly sliced on the diagonal
 1 medium red bell pepper, seeded and cut into
   ½-inch-wide strips
 2 medium zucchini (or 1 zucchini and 1 yellow
   squash), cut in half lengthwise and then into
   ¼-inch-thick slices
 1 (10-ounce) can baby corn, drained and rinsed
 1 cup bean sprouts
Noodle Pillow
 1 pound fresh Chinese noodles or linguine
 3 tablespoons vegetable oil
Stir-Fry Sauce
 ¾ cup chicken stock
 ¼ cup soy sauce

1 tablespoon rice vinegar

1 tablespoon dry sherry

1 tablespoon light brown sugar

½ teaspoon chile sauce with garlic, or ¼ teaspoon
chile flakes

4 teaspoons cornstarch

Preheat the oven to 200°F.

To make the noodle pillow, cook the noodles in
a large pot of boiling salted water until just tender,
about 3 minutes. Drain, rinse well under cold water,
and drain again. Toss with 1 tablespoon of the oil.
Heat the remaining 2 tablespoons oil in a 12-inch
nonstick frying pan over medium heat. Add the
noodles and spread into a thick cake. Cook until the
underside is golden-brown, about 5 minutes. Slide the
noodle cake out of the pan onto a large rimless baking
sheet. Return to the pan, crisp-side up, and cook until
the other side is golden, about 4 minutes. Transfer
the noodle cake to a paper-towel-lined baking sheet,
and keep it warm in the oven while you are stir-frying
the vegetables.

VEGETABLE STIR-FRY ON A NOODLE PILLOW

To make the stir-fry sauce, mix together all of the
ingredients except the cornstarch in a medium bowl.
Add the cornstarch and whisk to mix thoroughly, then
set the bowl aside.

In a medium saucepan of boiling salted water,
cook the broccoli until crisp-tender, about 2 minutes.
Drain, refresh, and set aside.

Heat the oil in the frying pan over high heat. Add
the scallions, ginger, and garlic and stir until very
fragrant, about 30 seconds. Add the celery, carrots,
and red pepper and stir-fry for 1 minute. Add the
zucchini and stir-fry for 1 more minute. Add the
broccoli florets and corn, and stir-fry until all the
vegetables are heated through, about 1 minute longer.
Add the bean sprouts and the sauce mixture and cook,
stirring, until the sauce thickens, about 1 minute.
Place the noodle pillow on a large serving platter,
and pour the vegetables on top. Serve immediately.

Rice, Grains, and Legumes

PLAIN STEAMED RICE

This method works well with any kind of long-grain rice, from basmati and jasmine to supermarket extra-fancy. There is no need to rinse domestic rice. If you are feeling lazy, and don't want to measure the rice, it can be cooked in boiling water, just like pasta.

MAKES 4 SERVINGS

    ½ teaspoon salt

    1½ cups long-grain rice

In a medium saucepan, bring 3 cups water and the salt to a boil over high heat. Add the rice and return to the boil. Reduce the heat to low, cover, and simmer until the rice is tender, about 15 minutes. Remove from the heat and let stand, covered, for 5 minutes before serving.

BROWN RICE PILAF

Brown rice is much denser than white rice, and takes longer to cook. When plainly steamed, it can be a bit stodgy, but cooking it in a flavorful stock makes it much more interesting.

MAKES 4 SERVINGS

    4 tablespoons unsalted butter

    2 tablespoons olive oil

    1 medium onion, chopped

    1 cup brown rice

    3½ cups chicken stock

    ¼ teaspoon salt

In a medium saucepan, heat the butter and oil over medium heat. Add the onion and cook until softened, about 5 minutes. Add the rice and stir until completely coated with butter and oil, about 1 minute. Add the stock and salt, and bring to a boil. Reduce the heat to low, cover, and simmer until all of the liquid has been absorbed and the rice is tender, about 1 hour.

RISOTTO MILANESE

Risotto must be made with Italian rice, such as Arborio or Carnaroli, as only they have the proper amount of starch to give a creamy quality to the sauce. The stock is added gradually so the rice swells and cooks slowly. Serve this as a first course, or as the classic accompaniment to osso bucco.

MAKES 4 SERVINGS

    5 cups chicken or beef stock

    ¼ teaspoon crushed saffron threads

    4 tablespoons unsalted butter

    2 tablespoons olive oil

    1 small onion, finely chopped

    1⅓ cups Italian rice for risotto

    ½ cup freshly grated Parmesan cheese

    Salt and freshly ground pepper, to taste

In a medium saucepan, heat the stock with the saffron until simmering. Reduce the heat to very low, and keep the stock at the barest simmer while making the risotto.

In a large, heavy-bottomed frying pan or sauté pan, heat 2 tablespoons of the butter and the oil over medium heat. Add the onion and cook until softened, about 5 minutes. Add the rice and cook, stirring often, until it becomes a little translucent, about 2 minutes. Reduce the heat to medium-low. Add about ½ cup of the simmering stock: it will hiss and bubble violently, but will then subside to a fairly quiet simmer. Stir constantly until the rice absorbs almost all the stock, then add another ½ cup of the stock, and stir until this has been absorbed. Continue adding stock and stirring until the rice is barely tender (*al dente*, like pasta, with a slightly resistant bite), about 25 minutes. The finished risotto should have a creamy, but not soupy, consistency. If you run out of stock, you can use hot water. (Conversely, you may not use all of the stock.) Stir in the Parmesan cheese and the remaining butter, and season with salt and pepper. Serve hot.

Chicken Liver Risotto: Omit the saffron, and add 6 large sage leaves to the stock. Cook 3 chopped chicken livers with the onion. Before adding the stock to the rice, stir in ½ cup dry Marsala or vermouth.

ASPARAGUS RISOTTO

If you use vegetable stock, this can be a vegetarian main course.

MAKES 4 SERVINGS

    1 pound asparagus spears, woody stems discarded

    5 cups chicken stock

    ½ cup dry white wine

    4 tablespoons unsalted butter

    1 medium onion, finely chopped

    1⅓ cups Italian rice for risotto

    1 heaped tablespoon chopped fresh mint or tarragon

    3 tablespoons freshly grated Parmesan cheese

    Salt and freshly ground pepper, to taste

Cut off the top 3 or 4 inches from each asparagus spear; cut each asparagus tip into 3 pieces, and set aside. Coarsely chop the asparagus stalks. In a medium saucepan, bring the stock and wine to a boil over high heat. Add the chopped asparagus stalks and reduce the heat to low. Cover and simmer until the stock is flavored with asparagus, about 20 minutes. Strain the stock and discard the stalks. Return the strained stock to the saucepan and bring back to a boil. Add the reserved asparagus tips and cook until just tender, about 3 minutes. Remove the tips with a slotted spoon and set aside. Keep the stock at a bare simmer while making the risotto.

In a large, heavy-bottomed frying pan or sauté pan, heat the butter over medium heat. Add the onion and cook until softened, about 5 minutes. Add the rice and stir until slightly translucent and coated with butter, about 2 minutes. Reduce the heat to medium-low. Add about ½ cup of the simmering stock; it will hiss and bubble violently, but will then subside to a fairly quiet simmer. Stir constantly until the rice absorbs almost all the stock, then add another ⅓ cup of the stock, and stir until this has been absorbed.

Continue adding stock and stirring until the rice is barely tender (al dente, like pasta, with a slightly resistant bite), about 25 minutes. The finished risotto should have a creamy, but not soupy, consistency. If you run out of stock, you can use hot water instead. (Conversely, you may not use all of the stock.) When the rice is almost tender, add the reserved asparagus tips and mint. Just before serving, stir in the Parmesan cheese, and season with salt and pepper. Serve immediately in warmed soup bowls.

WILD RICE PILAF WITH WILD MUSHROOMS

An interesting mix of European and American ingredients makes an enticing side dish for poultry, game, or pork. When cleaning the fresh mushrooms, wipe them with a damp cloth, and only rinse them quickly under cold water if absolutely necessary.

MAKES 6 SERVINGS
1 cup dried wild mushrooms, such as porcini (1 ounce)
1½ cups wild rice, soaked in water overnight and drained well
2 cups chicken stock
6 tablespoons olive oil
1 pound assorted fresh mushrooms, preferably a mixture of cremini, oyster mushrooms, and stemmed shiitakes, trimmed and sliced
1 medium red onion, chopped
2 garlic cloves, minced
1 tablespoon chopped parsley
2 tablespoons unsalted butter
3 tablespoons freshly grated Parmesan cheese, plus more for serving

In a small bowl, soak the dried mushrooms in 1 cup warm water until they are softened, about 30 minutes. Lift the mushrooms out of the liquid and squeeze them dry over the bowl of soaking liquid. Drain the liquid through a cheesecloth- or paper-towel-lined sieve to remove the grit. Set the mushrooms and liquid to one side.

In a medium saucepan, combine the drained wild rice and chicken stock, and bring to a simmer. Cover and cook over medium-low heat until the rice is just tender, about 30 minutes.

Meanwhile, in a frying pan, heat 4 tablespoons of the oil over medium heat. Add the fresh mushrooms and cook, stirring often, until golden-brown, about 10 minutes. Transfer to a bowl and set aside. In the same pan, heat the remaining 2 tablespoons oil and cook the onion and garlic until softened, about 5 minutes. Add the soaked mushrooms and parsley, and cook for 2 more minutes. Stir into the wild rice, along with the strained soaking liquid. Cook, uncovered, over low heat, stirring often, until rice absorbs almost all of the liquid, about 10 minutes. Stir in the cooked mushrooms and continue cooking until the liquid is totally absorbed, about 5 minutes. Add the butter and cheese, and stir until melted.

Serve immediately, passing a bowl of Parmesan cheese on the side.

SPICED BASMATI RICE

Spiced rice makes a wonderful accompaniment to curries as well as roast chicken. However, you should warn your guests in advance to look out for the spice pieces!

MAKES 4 SERVINGS
1 (2-inch) cinnamon stick
8 cardamom pods
4 whole cloves
4 tablespoons clarified butter
1 large onion, cut into very thin rings
2 bay leaves
1⅓ cups basmati rice
⅓ cup raisins
¼ cup blanched slivered almonds
¼ teaspoon salt

Coarsely crush the cinnamon, cardamom, and cloves with a rolling pin or under a heavy pan. In a medium frying pan, heat 1 tablespoon of the butter over medium heat. Add the onions and cook, stirring occasionally, until the onions are a deep cinnamon-brown, about 12 minutes or so. Transfer them to a plate and then set aside.

In the same pan, melt the remaining 3 tablespoons of butter over low heat. Stir in the crushed spices and bay leaves. Add the rice and cook, stirring often, until translucent, about 7 minutes. Add 2⅔ cups water, and stir in the raisins, almonds, and salt. Bring to a boil, then cover and reduce the heat to low. Simmer until the rice is tender and has absorbed the liquid, about 15 minutes. Remove from the heat and let stand, covered, for 5 minutes. Scatter the onion rings over the rice and serve.

PAELLA

What a great dish for a party! It can be prepared with clams instead of mussels if you prefer, or with 6 ounces chopped smoked chorizo sausage, sautéed with the onions. Use Italian rice for risotto, as this most closely resembles the Spanish rice that gives the dish its character.

MAKES 4 TO 6 SERVINGS

1 (2½-pound) chicken, rinsed, patted dry, and cut into 4 pieces; or 2 pounds chicken thighs
¼ teaspoon crumbled saffron threads
5 cups chicken stock
1 pound mussels, scrubbed and debearded if necessary
4 tablespoons olive oil
1 medium onion, finely chopped
1 medium red bell pepper, peeled, seeded, and finely chopped
2 garlic cloves, minced
1½ cups drained and chopped canned plum tomatoes
1 bay leaf
2 cups Italian rice for risotto
8 ounces squid, cleaned, bodies cut into ¼-inch rings, and tentacles coarsely chopped
Salt and freshly ground pepper, to taste
¾ cup shelled fresh or frozen peas
12 medium shrimp, unpeeled
½ cup black Mediterranean olives
1 lemon, thinly sliced into rounds

Chop the chicken pieces, except the drumsticks, through the bone into 1½-inch pieces; leave the drumsticks whole. Add the saffron to the stock and let soak. In a large saucepan, combine the mussels and ½ cup water, and bring to a boil over high heat. Cover and cook until all the mussels have opened, 4 to 5 minutes. Remove the mussels and set aside. Strain the mussel liquid through a sieve lined with a damp paper towel, and reserve the liquid.

PAELLA

In a very large, heavy-bottomed paella pan or frying pan, heat the oil over medium-high heat. Add the pieces of chicken and cook until browned on all sides, about 8 minutes. Add the onion, red pepper, and garlic and cook, stirring often, until the vegetables soften, about 5 minutes. Add the chicken stock mixture, tomatoes, and bay leaf and bring to a simmer. Stir in the rice and squid, and season with salt and pepper. Spread out the ingredients in the pan.

Reduce the heat to low, put a heat diffuser under the pan, cover, and simmer gently until the rice is almost tender, about 20 minutes. Stir in the peas, and arrange the shrimp and mussels over the rice. Place the olives around the edge. Add the reserved mussel liquid, then cover and continue cooking until the rice has absorbed all of the liquid and is tender, about 5 more minutes.

Serve from the frying pan, garnishing each serving with a slice of lemon.

CURRIED FRIED RICE WITH SHRIMP AND ASPARAGUS

There is a trick to cooking good fried rice—the rice must be well chilled, or it will clump up in the pan. This version uses basmati rice and curry to make fragrant fried rice, Indian style.

MAKES 4 SERVINGS

2 tablespoons vegetable oil
8 ounces medium shrimp, peeled and deveined
1 medium onion, chopped
1 medium red bell pepper, seeded and chopped
1 tablespoon minced fresh ginger
2 garlic cloves, minced
1 tablespoon Madras-style curry powder
3 cups cold cooked basmati rice
3 tablespoons chicken stock
1 tablespoon soy sauce
Chopped scallions, for garnish

In a large wok or frying pan, heat 1 tablespoon of the oil over medium heat. Add the shrimp and cook until firm and pink, about 3 minutes. Transfer the shrimp to a plate and set aside.

In the same pan, heat the remaining 1 tablespoon oil over medium heat. Add the onion, red pepper, ginger, and garlic, and cook until the onion is translucent, about 5 minutes. Add the curry powder and stir for 30 seconds. Add the rice, chicken stock, and soy sauce and stir-fry until the rice is heated through, about 3 minutes, returning the shrimp to the pan during the last minute. Serve, garnishing each serving with chopped scallions.

BULGUR PILAF

Bulgur pilaf is a wonderful alternative to rice as a side dish, but can also serve as a light entrée.

MAKES 4 SERVINGS

2 tablespoons olive oil
1 small onion, chopped
2 garlic cloves, minced
1⅓ cups medium or coarse bulgur
3 cups chicken stock
Salt, to taste
A pinch of cayenne pepper
¼ cup chopped fresh parsley
3 tablespoons lemon juice
⅔ cup plain yogurt, for serving

In a large frying pan, heat the oil over medium heat. Add the onion and cook, stirring occasionally, until golden-brown, 6 to 8 minutes. Add the garlic and cook for 1 more minute. Add the bulgur and stir until well coated with the oil. Add 1½ cups of the stock, and season with salt and cayenne. Bring just to a boil, then reduce the heat to low. Cover and cook gently for 10 minutes. Add the remaining 1½ cups of the stock, cover again, and continue cooking for 10 minutes.

Remove from the heat. Stir the bulgur, then cover the pan with a dish towel and the lid. Let steam until the grains are light and separate, about 10 minutes. Stir in the parsley and lemon juice, and taste to check the seasoning. Serve hot or cold, with the yogurt on the side.

TABBOULEH

Tabbouleh is the perfect hot weather salad, since it doesn't need to be cooked. The bulgur is merely soaked until it is nice and tender, and then mixed with lots of good things.

MAKES 4 SERVINGS

1 cup fine bulgur
1 cup chopped scallions
2 large tomatoes, peeled, seeded, and chopped
¼ cup chopped fresh parsley
¼ cup chopped fresh mint
¼ cup lemon juice, or more as needed
3 tablespoons olive oil, or more as needed
Salt and freshly ground pepper, to taste
Crisp romaine lettuce leaves, for garnish

In a bowl, combine the bulgur with enough cold water to cover by 2 inches. Let soak for 15 minutes. Drain in a fine sieve. By handfuls, squeeze the excess water from the bulgur, then place in a large bowl.

Add the scallions, tomatoes, parsley, and mint. Mix in the lemon juice and oil. Taste and balance the flavors with more lemon juice and oil, if needed, and season with salt and pepper. Place the tabbouleh on a deep platter, and surround with lettuce leaves. To eat, scoop up the tabbouleh in a lettuce leaf.

SOFT POLENTA VENETO-STYLE

There are two ways to enjoy polenta, soft and firm. Cooked soft, as in this method, the polenta can be served as an accompaniment to stews, or even served as a main course, topped with a spoonful of *ragù*. To vary, you could stir in chopped ham or minced fresh herbs, instead of or in addition to the Parmesan.

MAKES 6 TO 8 SERVINGS

1½ teaspoons salt
4 cups polenta (not quick-cooking) or stoneground yellow cornmeal
½ cup freshly grated Parmesan cheese
4 to 6 tablespoons unsalted butter, cut into pieces

Bring 2 quarts water to a boil in a large, heavy-bottomed saucepan over high heat. Add the salt. Reduce the heat to low so the water is simmering steadily. Gradually whisk in the polenta. Whisk the polenta vigorously to dissolve any lumps. Reduce the heat to very low and cook, whisking often (if you have a heavy-bottomed pan, you don't have to whisk constantly as old recipes state), until the polenta is tender and pulls away from the sides, about 20 minutes. Remove from the heat, and whisk in the Parmesan and butter. Serve immediately.

Grilled Polenta: Pour the hot polenta mixture into an oiled straight-sided rectangular pan, to make a layer ¾ inch thick. Cover with plastic wrap and let cool until firm. Then cut into squares. Heat a ridged cast-iron grill pan over medium heat. Brush the polenta squares with olive oil, then cook until crisp and lightly charred on both sides, 4 to 5 minutes. Serve hot.

POLENTA FRITTI

Firm, golden, fried polenta is perfect with lightly sauced meat and poultry. It can also be a luscious first course, topped with crumbled Gorgonzola cheese.

MAKES 4 TO 6 SERVINGS

1 cup milk
¼ teaspoon salt
1 cup yellow cornmeal, preferably stoneground
½ cup freshly grated Parmesan cheese
Olive oil, for frying

Lightly oil a 6- by 11-inch baking dish. In a heavy-bottomed saucepan, bring the milk, 1 cup water, and salt to a boil. Gradually whisk in the cornmeal. Reduce the heat to low and cook until very thick, about 2 minutes. Remove from the heat, and whisk in the cheese. Immediately pour into the pan and spread evenly. Let cool until firm, about 1 hour.

Cut the polenta into eight rectangles. Lightly oil a griddle or a large frying pan and heat over medium heat. Cook the polenta squares, turning once, until golden-brown on both sides, about 4 minutes. Serve hot.

TAMALE SPOONBREAD

This cornmeal-based side dish is almost a cornbread, but its spoonable quality resembles a zesty polenta. It has a firm topping and a creamy layer underneath.

MAKES 6 SERVINGS
1 cup yellow cornmeal, preferably stoneground
½ cup all-purpose flour
2 teaspoons chili powder
1 teaspoon baking soda
1 teaspoon salt
1 cup buttermilk
2 large eggs, beaten
1½ cups milk
1 cup shredded sharp Cheddar cheese
1 hot fresh green chile pepper (such as jalapeño), seeded and minced
1 cup fresh or defrosted frozen corn kernels
2 tablespoons unsalted butter, cut into pieces

Preheat the oven to 400°F. Whisk the cornmeal, flour, chili powder, baking soda, and salt. Stir in the buttermilk and eggs. Add 1 cup of the milk, the cheese, chile pepper, and corn, and mix just until they are all combined.

Put the butter in a 10-inch round cake pan and heat in the oven until the butter has melted. Pour in the cornmeal mixture, and top with the remaining ½ cup milk. Bake until a toothpick inserted 2 inches from the center comes out clean and the center is barely set, about 25 minutes. Let stand for 5 minutes, then serve.

KASHA WITH APPLES

Kasha has an elusive nutty flavor that blends well with apples. Serve this with roast pork, duck, or chicken.

MAKES 4 SERVINGS
2 tablespoons unsalted butter
1 tart green apple (such as Granny Smith), peeled, cored, and cut into ¼-inch pieces
1 large egg
1 cup kasha
2 cups chicken stock
Salt and freshly ground pepper, to taste

In a medium nonstick frying pan, heat 1 tablespoon butter over medium heat. Add the apple and cook until tender and lightly browned, about 4 minutes. Transfer the apple to a plate and set aside.

Add the remaining 1 tablespoon butter to the pan and heat over medium-low heat. In a medium bowl, beat the egg. Add the kasha and mix well to coat with egg. Pour into the pan and cook, stirring often, until the egg is set, about 3 minutes. Add the chicken stock, and season with salt and pepper. Bring to a simmer. Cover tightly and cook until the kasha is tender and the liquid is absorbed, about 15 minutes. Stir in the apple and cook for 1 more minute. Transfer to a warmed serving bowl and serve.

INDIAN MILLET

Here, cauliflower and zucchini add their color to a simple pot of spiced millet, to make a delicious lunch, supper, or side dish.

MAKES 6 SERVINGS
4 tablespoons unsalted butter
2 medium onions, 1 thinly sliced and 1 chopped
½ small head cauliflower, cut into small florets (about 3 cups)
2 medium zucchini, cut into ¼-inch dice
1 cup millet
2 garlic cloves, minced
1 teaspoon cumin seeds
4 whole cardamom pods
4 whole cloves
Salt and freshly ground pepper, to taste

In a medium frying pan, heat 2 tablespoons of the butter over medium heat. Add the sliced onion and cook, stirring occasionally, until a deep cinnamon-brown, about 12 minutes. Transfer to a plate, and cover to keep warm.

In the same pan, heat the remaining 2 tablespoons of butter over medium heat. Add the chopped onion, cauliflower, and zucchini, and cook, stirring often, until lightly browned, about 6 minutes. Add the millet, garlic, cumin, cardamom, and cloves, and cook, stirring often, until well combined and the spices are fragrant, about 4 minutes. Pour in enough water just to cover the millet. Season. Bring to a boil, then reduce the heat to low. Cover and cook, fluffing the millet occasionally with a fork, until just tender,

20 to 25 minutes. Remove from the heat. Cover the pan with a dish towel and then the lid, and let steam for 5 minutes. Fluff the millet a final time with a fork. Scatter the onions on top, then serve hot.

BOSTON BAKED BEANS

Long, slow cooking and a good heavy cooking utensil (preferably an old-fashioned earthenware bean pot) are the keys to this traditional dish's success.

MAKES 4 TO 6 SERVINGS
1 pound dried Great Northern or navy beans, soaked overnight and drained
2 tablespoons unsalted butter
¼ pound rindless salt pork or bacon, thickly sliced
1 medium onion, peeled
2 tablespoons unsulfured molasses
2 tablespoons tomato paste
1 tablespoon spicy brown mustard
1 teaspoon cider vinegar
1 teaspoon salt

Place the drained beans in a large pot and add enough cold water to cover by 2 inches. Bring to a boil over high heat. Reduce the heat to medium-low and simmer until the beans are tender, about 1 hour, depending on their dryness. Drain, reserving the cooking liquid. Place the beans in a 4- to 5-quart bean pot or Dutch oven.

Preheat the oven to 300°F. In a medium frying pan, heat the butter over medium heat. Add the salt pork and cook until browned on both sides, about 5 minutes. Bury the salt pork and onion in the beans, and stir in the fat from the frying pan. Stir the molasses, tomato paste, mustard, vinegar, and salt into the reserved cooking liquid, and pour over the beans. Cover tightly and bake for 2 hours. Remove the lid and continue baking until the liquid has thickened, about 30 minutes. Let stand for 10 minutes; serve hot.

WHITE BEAN, VEGETABLE, AND ROSEMARY STEW

This makes a large batch of hearty vegetarian stew, and it reheats well. You can substitute 6 cups canned cannellini beans, well rinsed, for the freshly cooked beans.

MAKES 8 TO 12 SERVINGS
¼ cup olive oil
1 large onion, chopped
1 large red bell pepper, seeded and chopped
2 medium zucchini, cut into ½-inch pieces
2 medium carrots, cut into ½-inch pieces
2 medium celery ribs, chopped
2 garlic cloves, chopped
1 cup hearty red wine
1 pound dried white beans, cooked and drained
1½ cups peeled, seeded, and chopped ripe plum tomatoes; or use drained canned tomatoes
1¼ tablespoons chopped fresh rosemary or 2 teaspoons dried rosemary
1 bay leaf
½ teaspoon chile flakes
Extra virgin olive oil, for serving
Freshly grated Parmesan cheese, for serving

In a large Dutch oven or flameproof casserole, heat the oil over medium heat. Add the onion, bell pepper, zucchini, carrots, celery, and garlic. Cover and cook, stirring often, until the onion is soft and golden, about 10 minutes. Add the red wine and bring to a boil over high heat. Stir in the cooked white beans, tomatoes, rosemary, bay leaf, and chile flakes, and bring to a simmer. Reduce the heat to low and simmer, uncovered, until the vegetables are tender, about 30 minutes. Serve hot, drizzling each serving with extra virgin olive oil, and passing a bowl of Parmesan cheese on the side.

CUBAN BLACK BEANS AND RICE

Bean and rice dishes are daily fare in many Central and South American countries. This Cuban recipe is one of the most tasty examples.

MAKES 6 SERVINGS
1 cup dried black beans, soaked overnight and drained
2 tablespoons olive oil
1 large onion, chopped
1 small green bell pepper, seeded and chopped
1 hot fresh green chile pepper (such as jalapeño), seeded and minced
1 garlic clove, minced
½ cup coarsely chopped smoked or boiled ham (optional)
⅔ cup long-grain rice
2 ripe plum tomatoes, peeled, seeded, and chopped
Salt, to taste

Put the beans in a medium saucepan, and add enough cold water to cover by 1 inch. Bring to a boil over medium heat. Reduce the heat to medium-low and simmer until just tender, about 1 hour.

Meanwhile, in a medium frying pan, heat the oil over medium heat. Add the onion and cook until soft and lightly browned, about 7 minutes. Stir in the green pepper, chile pepper, and garlic, along with the ham, if using. Continue cooking for about 5 minutes. Add the rice and stir until well coated with the oil, about 2 minutes. Stir in the tomatoes.

Add the rice mixture to the pot of beans and stir to mix. Pour in enough cold water so that all the ingredients are covered by liquid. Bring to a boil over high heat, then return the heat to medium-low. Season with salt to taste. Simmer until the rice is tender, about 20 minutes. If necessary, add a little more water during cooking: the beans and rice should be bathed in a light sauce.

LENTILS AND RICE WITH FRIED ONIONS

This dish from Baghdad, called *magedra*, is known as "the food of the poor." Serve it with a spoonful of plain yogurt or chopped tomatoes and scallions.

MAKES 4 SERVINGS
⅔ cup brown lentils
3 tablespoons olive oil
2 large onions, thinly sliced

CUBAN BLACK BEANS AND RICE

1⅓ cups long-grain rice
Salt, to taste

Put the lentils in a saucepan with 5 cups cold water. Bring to a boil, then simmer until tender, about 30 minutes. In a frying pan, heat 1½ tablespoons of oil. Add the onions and cook, stirring occasionally, until cinnamon-brown, about 12 minutes. Transfer to a plate, and cover to keep warm.

Drain the lentils, reserving the liquid. Return this to the saucepan and bring to a boil. Add the remaining 1½ tablespoons oil, then the rice and salt. Reduce the heat to medium-low. Partially cover the pan and cook until the rice has absorbed most of the liquid and is tender, about 15 minutes. Let stand, uncovered, until all of the liquid has been absorbed, about 5 minutes. Stir in the lentils and cook over low heat, stirring constantly, just until heated through, 1 or 2 minutes. Transfer to a dish and scatter with onions. Serve hot.

Salads

ARUGULA AND BACON SALAD

The slightly bitter edge of arugula is tempered by the crisp saltiness of bacon in this great salad. Another time, substitute dandelion or curly endive for the arugula, or use tender young spinach leaves plus a diced avocado.

MAKES 4 TO 6 SERVINGS

1 tablespoon white wine vinegar or sherry vinegar
A pinch of granulated sugar
Salt and freshly ground pepper, to taste
2 tablespoons olive oil
6 strips thick-sliced bacon, cut into ¼-inch-wide pieces
1 pound arugula (about 2 large bunches), tough stems discarded

In a small bowl, whisk the vinegar with the sugar and a seasoning of salt and pepper. Gradually whisk in the oil, and set the dressing aside.

Just before you are ready to serve, cook the bacon in a medium frying pan over medium heat until crisp, about 5 minutes.

Toss the arugula with the dressing. Pour the bacon with its fat over the arugula and toss again. Taste a leaf and balance the flavor of the dressing with more vinegar or oil if needed. Serve immediately.

SPINACH AND WALNUT SALAD

This simple but delicious salad can easily be varied, for example by sprinkling over about 2 ounces crumbled Gorgonzola cheese or 1 or 2 chopped hard-boiled eggs.

MAKES 4 SERVINGS

12 ounces fresh young spinach leaves, tough stems removed
1 cup walnut halves or pieces, preferably freshly shelled
Dressing
½ tablespoon white wine vinegar
½ tablespoon white wine
¾ teaspoon Dijon mustard
1 garlic clove, minced with a sprinkle of salt
Salt and freshly ground pepper, to taste
¼ cup walnut oil
1 tablespoon extra-virgin olive oil

To make the dressing, whisk together the white wine vinegar, wine, Dijon mustard, minced garlic, and a seasoning of salt and pepper. Gradually whisk in the walnut and olive oils.

Put the spinach in a large salad bowl, and sprinkle with the walnut halves or pieces. Add the dressing, toss, and serve immediately.

ROMAINE SALAD WITH BALSAMIC CAESAR DRESSING

The original Caesar salad used a coddled egg in the dressing, but this updated version leaves it out as a concession to modern tastes.

MAKES 4 SERVINGS

1 large head romaine lettuce, torn into bite-sized pieces
1 cup croutons, fried or baked
½ cup freshly grated Parmesan cheese
Dressing
2 tablespoons balsamic vinegar
1 teaspoon anchovy paste
1 garlic clove, crushed through a press
½ cup olive oil
Salt and freshly ground pepper, to taste

To make the dressing, in a bowl, whisk together the vinegar, anchovy paste, and garlic. Gradually whisk in the oil. Season with salt and pepper.

In a large bowl, toss the lettuce thoroughly with the dressing until well combined. Add the fried or baked croutons and the Parmesan cheese, and toss again. Serve immediately.

Romaine Salad with Balsamic Herb Vinaigrette: In a medium bowl, whisk together 2 teaspoons each balsamic vinegar and lemon juice with a seasoning of salt and pepper. Gradually whisk in ¼ cup each olive oil and vegetable oil, then add 2 shallots, finely chopped, and 2 teaspoons each chopped fresh tarragon, chopped fresh chives or scallions, and chopped fresh parsley or chervil. Toss the lettuce thoroughly with the dressing and serve immediately.

BIBB LETTUCE WITH LEMON-POPPY SEED DRESSING

A sweet-and-sour dressing with roots in Pennsylvania Dutch cooking, this is excellent on Bibb lettuce.

MAKES 4 SERVINGS

2 large heads Bibb lettuce, torn into bite-sized pieces
1 medium cucumber, peeled and thinly sliced
Dressing
3 tablespoons lemon juice
Grated zest of 1 lemon
1 tablespoon red wine vinegar
1 tablespoon brown sugar
1 tablespoon Dijon mustard
2 tablespoons poppy seeds
¾ cup vegetable oil
Salt and freshly ground pepper, to taste

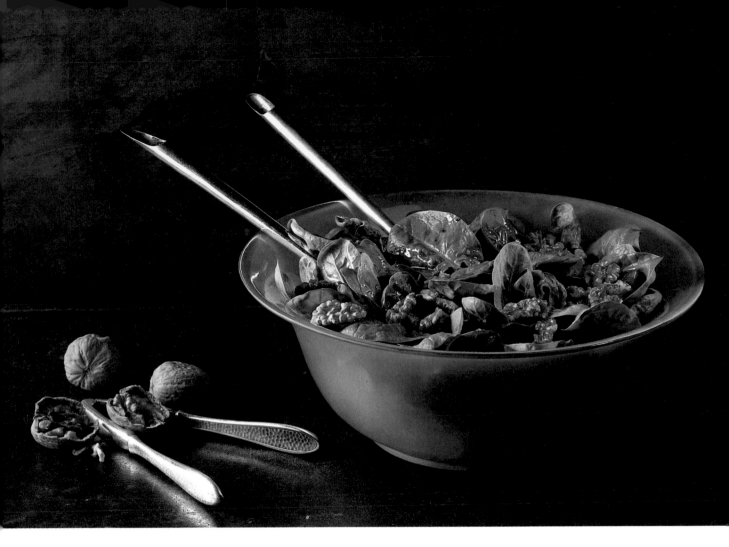

To make the dressing, combine all of the ingredients except the vegetable oil in a blender. With the machine running, gradually pour in the oil until the dressing is thick and smooth. Season with salt and pepper. (The dressing can be kept, covered, in the refrigerator for up to 3 days.)

Place the lettuce and cucumber in a large bowl and add the dressing. Toss well, and serve immediately.

CELERY AND PARMESAN SALAD

Serve this simple salad as an unusual first course, or as a separate salad course after roast veal or pork. Use a piece of fresh Parmesan that is young and moist, not aged and dry.

MAKES 6 SERVINGS

1 (2-ounce) piece Parmesan cheese
8 medium celery ribs, thinly sliced
¼ cup olive oil
1 tablespoon lemon juice (optional)
Salt and freshly ground pepper, to taste

Using a Parmesan knife or a small, sharp knife, cut the Parmesan into the thinnest possible flakes. (This can also be done by using a swivel-bladed vegetable

SPINACH AND WALNUT SALAD

peeler, shaving off the cheese in curls.) Place the flakes of Parmesan in a medium bowl and add the sliced celery ribs. Sprinkle with the olive oil and optional lemon juice, and season to taste with salt and pepper. Toss the salad gently to mix, and then serve it immediately.

CELERIAC REMOULADE

Celeriac, also called celery root, is a very popular vegetable in France, but it really deserves to be better known with American cooks. The brief blanching will keep the celeriac white, although many people prefer it raw and crunchy.

MAKES 4 SERVINGS

2 tablespoons lemon juice
1 pound celeriac (2 medium heads)
1 large egg yolk, at room temperature
1½ teaspoons Dijon mustard, or more as needed
2/3 cup peanut or vegetable oil
3 tablespoons light cream or half-and-half
Salt and freshly ground pepper, to taste

Fill a medium bowl with cold water and add the lemon juice. Using a sharp paring knife, remove the thick brown skin from the celeriac. Cut the celeriac into quarters and remove any soft core. Using a mandoline, cut the celeriac into thin shreds. (The celeriac can also be shredded on a box grater or with a food processor fitted with the shredding blade.) Drop the celeriac immediately into the acidulated water to prevent discoloration.

Bring a large saucepan of salted water to a boil over high heat. Add the celeriac and stir briefly, then immediately drain. Rinse the celeriac under cold water until cooled. Drain thoroughly and pat dry with paper towels. Cover and refrigerate until well chilled, at least 2 hours.

Whisk the egg yolk and mustard. Gradually whisk in the oil as if making mayonnaise, then add the cream. Season. Taste and add more mustard if the dressing is too bland. Add the celeriac and toss with the dressing. Serve within 8 hours.

TOMATO AND CHÈVRE SALAD WITH PESTO VINAIGRETTE

This is a twist on the classic tomato and basil salad. Make it with the best summer tomatoes you can find for the tastiest results.

MAKES 6 TO 8 SERVINGS
  ¾ pound arugula, tough stems removed
  6 large ripe tomatoes, sliced into ½-inch-thick rounds
  3 ounces chèvre (goat cheese) or feta, crumbled
  ½ cup black Mediterranean olives, pitted
Pesto Vinaigrette
  ⅓ cup packed chopped fresh basil leaves
  2 tablespoons red wine vinegar
  1 garlic clove, crushed
  Salt and freshly ground pepper, to taste
  ⅔ cup extra virgin olive oil

To make the dressing, combine the basil, vinegar, garlic, and a seasoning of salt and pepper in a blender. With the machine running, gradually pour in the olive oil.

Arrange the arugula on a round platter. Top with the tomatoes, overlapping the slices in a circle. Sprinkle with cheese and olives. Serve immediately, with the pesto vinaigrette on the side.

ROASTED SWEET PEPPER SALAD

This is frequently served as part of an antipasto plate, along with fresh cheese, olives, and bread. The salad can also accompany main courses, from grilled chicken to roast beef tenderloin.

MAKES 4 SERVINGS
  2 medium red bell peppers, roasted, peeled, seeded, and cut into 1-inch-wide strips
  2 medium yellow bell peppers, roasted, peeled, seeded, and cut into 1-inch-wide strips
  1 tablespoon lemon juice
  ¼ cup olive oil
  1 garlic clove, minced
  Salt, to taste
  A handful of small basil leaves

On a serving platter, arrange the peppers, alternating the two colors. Sprinkle with the lemon juice, olive oil, and garlic, and season with the salt. Turn the pepper strips over in this dressing to coat both sides. (The peppers can be prepared up to 4 hours ahead of serving, and kept at room temperature.) Just before serving, scatter the basil leaves over the top.

APPLE AND CABBAGE SLAW

This is a delicious year-round salad.

MAKES 6 SERVINGS
  12 ounces green cabbage (about ½ medium head), cored and shredded
  1 medium carrot, shredded
  1 medium celery rib, cut into ⅛- by 1½-inch strips
  1 tart green apple (such as Granny Smith), peeled, cored, and cut into ⅛- by 1½-inch strips
  ⅓ cup chopped walnuts
  1 tablespoon red wine vinegar
  1 teaspoon Dijon mustard
  1¼ cups mayonnaise
  3 tablespoons light cream or half-and-half
  Salt and freshly ground pepper, to taste

In a bowl, combine the cabbage, carrot, celery, apple, and walnuts, and toss. In a small bowl, mix the vinegar with the mustard. Add the mayonnaise and cream, and blend. Season. Add to the vegetables and toss to coat.

GREEN BEAN SALAD WITH ANCHOVY-CREAM DRESSING

In Italy, green-vegetable salads with a creamy anchovy dressing are often enjoyed during the summer. If you don't want to use all the dressing for the beans, keep the remains in a covered jar in the refrigerator.

MAKES 4 SERVINGS
  1 pound haricots verts or thin green beans
  2 tablespoons minced shallot
  Lemon wedges, for garnish

Dressing
- 1 tablespoon red wine vinegar
- 1 tablespoon Dijon mustard
- 1 small garlic clove, chopped
- ⅔ cup peanut or vegetable oil
- ⅔ cup extra virgin olive oil
- 1 (2-ounce) can anchovy fillets packed in oil, undrained
- Freshly ground pepper, to taste

To make the dressing, place the vinegar, mustard, garlic, and ¼ cup water in a blender. Blend until smooth. With the machine running, gradually add the peanut and olive oils to make a thick dressing. Add the anchovies and their oil, and blend until smooth. Season with pepper. Taste the dressing, and add salt and more vinegar if needed.

Bring a large saucepan of lightly salted water to a boil over high heat. Add the haricots verts and cook until crisp-tender, 2 to 4 minutes. Drain and refresh, then pat dry with paper towels.

Arrange the haricots verts in bundles on four chilled salad plates. Spoon the dressing over the green beans. Sprinkle with the shallots. Serve with the lemon wedges for squeezing over the salad.

MEXICALI BEAN SALAD

Great as an extra for a picnic or barbecue, this salad is also filling enough to make a good lunch on its own.

MAKES 6 SERVINGS
- ¼ cup red wine vinegar
- 1 tablespoon chili powder
- 1 hot fresh chile pepper (such as jalapeño), seeded and minced
- 2 garlic cloves, minced
- ¾ cup olive oil
- 3 cups cooked pinto beans
- 3 cups cooked black beans
- 2 medium celery ribs, finely chopped
- 1 medium red onion, finely chopped
- 1 medium red bell pepper, seeded and chopped
- 1 pint cherry tomatoes, cut in half horizontally
- 2 tablespoons chopped fresh cilantro
- Salt and freshly ground pepper, to taste
- 1 cup shredded sharp Cheddar cheese

In a medium bowl, whisk together the vinegar, chili powder, chile pepper, and garlic. Gradually whisk in the oil. Set the dressing aside.

In a large bowl, combine the pinto and black beans, celery, red onion, red pepper, cherry tomatoes, and cilantro. Add the dressing, season with salt and pepper, and toss well. Cover and refrigerate until chilled, about 1 hour. (The salad can be prepared up to 2 days ahead and kept, covered, in the refrigerator.) Just before serving, sprinkle with the cheese.

RICE SALAD WITH ORANGES AND OLIVES

Rice hardens when chilled, so serve this Moroccan-inspired salad at room temperature.

MAKES 6 TO 8 SERVINGS
- 1½ cups long-grain rice
- Salt and freshly ground pepper
- 3 tablespoons balsamic vinegar
- Grated zest of 1 orange
- ⅔ cup olive oil
- 2 oranges, peeled and sectioned
- 1 cup black Mediterranean olives, pitted and chopped
- 4 scallions, chopped

Bring 4 cups of water to a boil over high heat. Add the rice and ½ teaspoon salt. Reduce the heat to low, cover, and simmer until the rice is tender, about 15 minutes. If necessary, drain the cooked rice of excess water. Transfer to a large bowl and let cool to lukewarm.

In a medium bowl, whisk together the balsamic vinegar and orange zest with a seasoning of salt and pepper. Gradually whisk in the oil. Pour half of the dressing over the rice, and reserve the remainder. Toss the rice with the orange sections, olives, and scallions. Cover and let stand at room temperature for 1 hour to blend the flavors. (The salad can be kept, covered, in the refrigerator for up to 1 day, but bring to room temperature before serving.) Just before serving, toss with the remaining dressing, and taste to check the seasoning.

CREAMY SCANDINAVIAN POTATO SALAD WITH DILL

Everyone loves potato salad. Here's an unusual version with dill and capers.

MAKES 6 TO 8 SERVINGS
- 3 pounds boiling potatoes, scrubbed
- 2 tablespoons white wine vinegar or cider vinegar
- ¾ cup mayonnaise
- ½ cup sour cream
- 4 hard-boiled eggs, chopped
- 3 scallions, chopped
- 3 tablespoons chopped fresh dill
- 3 tablespoons capers, rinsed
- Salt and freshly ground pepper, to taste

ITALIAN SEAFOOD SALAD

Bring a large pot of lightly salted water to a boil over high heat. Add the potatoes and cook until they are just tender, about 20 minutes. Drain well and leave until cool enough to handle. Peel the potatoes, if desired (this is not essential), and use a sharp knife to cut them into thick rounds.

Put the potatoes in a large bowl and sprinkle them with the vinegar, tossing the potatoes around in the bowl so that they are all moistened. Add the mayonnaise, sour cream, hard-boiled eggs, chopped scallions, dill, and capers, and season with salt and pepper. Fold all the ingredients together gently but thoroughly. Cover the bowl and put in the refrigerator to chill for at least 2 hours.

Just before you wish to serve the salad, taste the potatoes to check the seasoning, and adjust if necessary. The salad can be kept, covered, in the refrigerator for up to 1 day.

INDIAN POTATO SALAD WITH YOGURT AND SCALLION DRESSING

This is just the dressing to complement a potato salad, with its smooth, creamy texture; it is also good over greens.

MAKES 6 SERVINGS
  2 pounds new potatoes, unpeeled
Dressing
  6 scallions, cut into thin rounds
  Salt, to taste
  ⅔ cup plain yogurt, preferably goat-milk yogurt
  4 ounces cream cheese, at room temperature
  1 teaspoon chopped fresh dill

In a small bowl, sprinkle the scallion rounds lightly with salt. Let stand until limp, 20 to 30 minutes. Drain, rinse, and pat dry with paper towels. In a bowl, mash the yogurt with the cream cheese until well blended and smooth. Stir in the scallions and dill, and season with salt.

Bring a large pot of lightly salted water to a boil. Add the potatoes and cook until they are just tender, about 20 minutes. Drain the potatoes thoroughly and leave on one side to cool. Peel the potatoes, if desired, and then cut them into thick rounds. Add to the dressing and toss well to combine. Cover the potatoes and then place in the refrigerator to chill until you are ready to serve them.

CRANBERRY AND RASPBERRY MOLD

For many families, the American Thanksgiving menu would be incomplete without a deliciously chilled gelatin fruit-salad mold. The version that is given here eschews artificially-flavored gelatin in favour of a combination of cranberries and raspberries that is truly mouthwatering. If fresh raspberries are not available, frozen ones, thawed before use, will be just as good.

MAKES 12 SERVINGS

2 envelopes unflavored gelatin
4 cups apple juice
1 (12-ounce) bag fresh cranberries
2 cups sugar
1 cup heavy cream
2 cups fresh or defrosted
    frozen raspberries

In a medium bowl, sprinkle the gelatin over ½ cup of the apple juice. Let stand while preparing the cranberry mixture.

In a medium saucepan over medium-high heat, bring the cranberries, sugar, and remaining 3½ cups apple juice to a boil, stirring to dissolve the sugar. Cook until all of the cranberries have burst, about 3 minutes. Reduce the heat to very low. Add the softened gelatin mixture and stir until the gelatin has completely dissolved, about 2 minutes. Transfer to a large bowl set in a larger bowl of ice water. Let stand, stirring occasionally, until cool, but not set, about 20 minutes.

In a chilled medium bowl, whip the cream until it forms stiff peaks, and then fold it into the cooled gelatin mixture. Fold in the raspberries. Spoon the mixture into a lightly oiled 12-cup fluted mold. Cover the mold and refrigerate until it is set, at least 4 hours or overnight.

When you are ready to serve the mold, dip the outside of the mold into a large bowl filled with hot water and let stand in the water for about 10 seconds or so. Wipe the outside of the mold dry with a dish towel, then invert the mold onto a chilled serving platter. Serve cold.

ITALIAN SEAFOOD SALAD

This makes a perfect luncheon salad, or a special first course. If you prefer, use 8 ounces of thinly sliced white mushrooms instead of the squid (there is no need to cook the mushrooms), and let the salad marinate for an hour or two before serving so that the flavors can mingle together.

MAKES 6 SERVINGS

20 mussels, scrubbed well and debearded,
    if necessary
12 littleneck clams
8 small squid, cleaned, bodies cut into ¼-inch-thick
    rings and tentacles left whole
12 ounces medium shrimp
24 Dublin Bay prawns or jumbo shrimp
1 tablespoon lemon juice
6 tablespoons olive oil
⅛ teaspoon chile flakes
2 tablespoons chopped fresh parsley, oregano,
    or dill (optional)
Salt and freshly ground pepper, to taste

In a large saucepan, combine the mussels, clams, and 1¼ cups water. Bring to a boil over high heat, then cover and cook, shaking the pan often, until all the shells have opened, about 5 minutes. Using a slotted spoon, transfer the mussels and clams to a bowl and set to one side.

Return the cooking liquid to a simmer over medium-low heat. Add the prepared squid and cook, uncovered, until barely tender, 1 to 2 minutes. Do not overcook. Using a slotted spoon, quickly transfer the squid to another bowl. Add the shrimp and Dublin Bay prawns to the saucepan, cover, and cook until they turn pink and firm, about 3 minutes. Drain the shrimp and prawns. When the seafood is cool enough to handle, discard the mussel shells, and peel and devein the shrimp and prawns.

Add the mussels, shrimp, and prawns to the squid, along with the clams still in their shell (or shelled if you prefer). Toss the seafood, adding the lemon juice, then the oil, chile flakes, and optional herbs. Season with salt and pepper. Refrigerate the seafood salad until ready to serve, up to 2 hours.

SALADE NIÇOISE

While salade niçoise conjures up an image of a glorified tuna salad to many cooks, it can be simply a wonderful combination of colorful vegetables dressed with vinaigrette. If you wish, add canned tuna, preferably an excellent imported brand packed in olive oil, to the center of the platter.

MAKES 4 TO 6 SERVINGS

4 small boiling potatoes, unpeeled

8 ounces haricots verts or thin green beans

1 small head romaine lettuce, separated into
individual leaves

1 small head curly-leaved red lettuce, separated
into individual leaves

3 large ripe tomatoes, sliced

2 medium red bell peppers (or 1 red and 1 yellow),
peeled, seeded, and cut into thin strips

3 hard-boiled eggs, cut in half lengthwise

12 anchovy fillets packed in oil, drained

¼ cup drained capers, rinsed

½ cup black Mediterranean olives

Balsamic Herb Vinaigrette, made with 1 garlic clove,
crushed through a press

1 small red onion, thinly sliced

A handful of small fresh basil leaves

In a medium saucepan of boiling salted water,
cook the potatoes until they are just tender, 15 to
20 minutes. Drain the potatoes and rinse under cold
running water until cool enough to handle, then slice
into thick rounds. In another medium saucepan of
boiling salted water, cook the haricots verts until they
are crisp-tender, about 2 minutes (if using green
beans, cook for 4 minutes). Drain and refresh, then
pat dry with paper towels.

Arrange the lettuce leaves around the edge of
a large serving platter. Place the sliced tomatoes and
potatoes in rings in the center. Arrange the pepper
strips, radiating outward, on top of the lettuce leaves.
Add small bundles of haricots verts here and there,
and place the egg halves on the peppers. Lay 1 anchovy
over each yolk. Add little mounds of capers, and place
the olives on the tomato slices. Drizzle ½ cup of the
dressing over the salad, and pour the remainder into
a sauceboat. Scatter the red onion and basil leaves
over all. Serve immediately, with the remaining
dressing passed on the side.

GRILLED SHRIMP LOUIS

This classic seafood salad (named after its forgotten
originator) gets an update with grilled shrimp.

MAKES 4 SERVINGS

2 tablespoons olive oil

2 tablespoons lemon juice

16 jumbo shrimp, peeled, with last tail section left
attached, deveined, and butterflied

Salt and freshly ground pepper, to taste

6 cups *mesclun* salad leaves

1 cup halved cherry tomatoes

1 medium cucumber, peeled, seeded, and cut into
thin half-moons

2 hard-boiled eggs, chopped

Dressing

⅓ cup finely chopped sun-dried tomatoes packed in
oil, well drained

1 cup mayonnaise

2 tablespoons lemon juice

2 tablespoons chopped capers, rinsed

1 scallion, finely chopped

1 teaspoon chili powder

2 tablespoons lemon juice

Salt and freshly ground pepper, to taste

2 tablespoons milk, approximately

To make the dressing, mix all of the ingredients in
a small bowl, thinning with milk as needed. Cover
and refrigerate for 1 hour to blend the flavors.

In a medium bowl, whisk together the olive oil and
lemon juice. Add the shrimp, and season with salt and
pepper. Cover and let marinate in the refrigerator for
1 to 2 hours, no longer.

Build a hot charcoal fire in an outdoor grill. Lightly
oil the grill. Place the shrimp on the grill, opened up,
cut side down. Grill, turning once, until firm, about
3 minutes. Set aside.

Divide the *mesclun*, cherry tomatoes, and cucumber
among four large plates. Top each with four grilled
shrimp, and sprinkle with the hard-boiled egg. Serve
immediately, with the dressing passed on the side.

CHICKEN, FENNEL, AND PEAR SALAD

The crisp texture and herbaceous flavor of fennel
make it a fine addition to this luncheon salad.

MAKES 4 TO 6 SERVINGS

4 (10-ounce) chicken breast halves

2 cups chicken stock

2 cups chopped fennel bulb

2 ripe medium pears (such as Bartlett), peeled, cored,
and chopped

1 cup mayonnaise

2 scallions, chopped

1 tablespoon chopped leafy fennel tops or herb fennel

1 cup chopped pecans

Salt and freshly ground pepper, to taste

3 cups watercress leaves, tough stems removed

Fresh fennel or tarragon sprigs, for garnish

Place the chicken breasts and stock in a large frying
pan, and add enough cold water so that the breasts are
just covered with liquid. Bring to a simmer over high
heat, then reduce the heat to low. Cover and simmer

for 20 minutes. Remove from the heat and let stand, covered, until cool and the chicken meat shows no sign of pinkness at the bone, about 1 hour. Discard the skin and bones, and use a sharp knife to cut the chicken into bite-sized pieces. (You can save the broth for another use.)

In a large bowl, combine the chicken with the fennel, pears, mayonnaise, scallions, and fennel leaves. Stir in the pecans, and season with salt and pepper. Cover and refrigerate until chilled, about 1 hour. (The salad can be prepared up to 8 hours ahead.)

Place the watercress leaves on large plates, and top each with a large spoonful of the chicken salad. Garnish with fennel sprigs and serve immediately.

SICHUAN CHICKEN SALAD

In Chinese restaurants, this tasty chicken salad often goes by the name bang-bang chicken. It's a good way of using up leftover roast chicken—substitute 3 cups shredded cooked chicken for the chicken thighs.

MAKES 4 SERVINGS

    4 (6-ounce) chicken thighs
    2 teaspoons sesame seeds

Sichuan Chicken Salad

    1 large English cucumber, cut into
        1/8- by 3-inch strips
    1 large carrot, cut into 1/8- by 3-inch
        strips
    8 scallions, shredded lengthwise
    2 tablespoons lime juice
    1/2 teaspoon granulated sugar
    Salt, to taste
    1 cup Asian Peanut Sauce
    1/2 teaspoon chile flakes
    2 teaspoons Asian dark sesame oil
    Sprigs of fresh cilantro, for garnish
Poaching Liquid
    3 tablespoons soy sauce
    2 tablespoons rice vinegar
    2 teaspoons Asian dark sesame oil
    4 scallions, sliced
    2 garlic cloves, crushed
    4 slices fresh ginger, unpeeled
    2 small hot fresh chile peppers (such as serrano),
        thinly sliced
    2 star anise

**Asian dark
sesame oil** 112
**English
cucumber** 155
chile pepper 153
ginger 198
rice vinegar 205
scallion 143
sesame seeds
199
star anise 199

**Asian Peanut
Sauce** 258

Put the chicken thighs in a saucepan just big enough to hold them snugly. Add all the ingredients for the poaching liquid, and pour in enough cold water to cover the chicken. Shake the pan to mix everything together. Bring to a simmer, then cover and simmer gently for 30 minutes. Remove from the heat and let stand, still covered, until cool, about 1 hour. Remove the chicken from the poaching liquid. Discard the skin and bones, and shred the meat. Cover and refrigerate the chicken until chilled, about 2 hours. (You can strain the poaching liquid and keep it in the freezer for the next time you want to make this salad.)

In a small dry frying pan over medium heat, cook the sesame seeds until nicely toasted. Tip them onto a plate to cool.

Toss the cucumber, carrot, and scallions with the lime juice, sugar, and salt. Place on a serving platter. Top with the shredded chicken, and spoon the peanut sauce over the chicken. Sprinkle with the toasted sesame seeds, chile flakes, and sesame oil, and garnish with cilantro.

Six Vegetable Couscous Salad

LIDO PASTA SALAD

Summer is the time to make this simple, delicious salad. Salted capers, available at many Italian grocers, are the best, although you could use bottled ones.

MAKES 6 TO 8 SERVINGS

3 tablespoons salted capers

5 ounces black olives (preferably herb-marinated Kalamata olives), pitted

1 large red onion or 6 scallions, chopped

20 anchovy fillets packed in oil, drained and chopped (optional)

5 garlic cloves, minced

2 tablespoons lemon juice

½ cup olive oil

1 pound penne, ziti, or rigatoni

1 pound cherry tomatoes, halved crosswise

3 tablespoons chopped fresh basil

Salads/Vegetables

3 tablespoons chopped fresh parsley
2 tablespoons chopped fresh mint
Salt and freshly ground pepper, to taste

Soak the capers in cold water for 5 minutes, then drain and pat dry with paper towels. In a large bowl, combine the capers, olives, onion, optional anchovies, and garlic. Mix in the lemon juice, then the oil.

In a large pot of boiling salted water over high heat, cook the pasta until *al dente*, 10 to 12 minutes. Drain thoroughly, and add to the bowl. Toss well with the olive mixture. Reserve about one fourth of the tomatoes and herbs, and mix the remainder into the salad. Check the seasoning. Scatter the reserved tomatoes and herbs on top, and serve warm.

SIX VEGETABLE COUSCOUS SALAD

The combination of vegetables here is typically Moroccan, but other mixes are possible, according to the cook's inspiration. Serve with a green salad.

MAKES 6 TO 8 SERVINGS
  1 (1-pound) acorn squash, halved crosswise and
    seeds discarded
  8 ounces green beans, cut in half crosswise
  3 medium zucchini, sliced into ½-inch-thick
    rounds
  3 tablespoons butter
  Salt and freshly ground black pepper
  1¾ cups instant couscous
  2 tablespoons vegetable oil
  ½ cup dark raisins
  1 teaspoon cumin seeds
  ½ teaspoon chile flakes
  2 medium red bell peppers, peeled, seeded,
    and chopped
  1½ cups cooked chickpeas, either fresh
    or canned
  10 scallions, thinly sliced
  1 tablespoon chopped fresh cilantro
  1 tablespoon chopped fresh parsley
Harissa Dressing
  2 tablespoons lemon juice
  2 teaspoons harissa
  6 tablespoons vegetable oil
  2 tablespoons olive oil

Preheat the oven to 350°F. Place the acorn squash, cut side down, on a lightly oiled baking sheet. Bake until tender, 30 to 40 minutes. Let cool, then peel and cut into 1-inch chunks. In a medium saucepan of boiling salted water, cook the green beans until crisp-tender, 3 to 5 minutes. Drain and refresh, then pat dry with paper towels. In another medium saucepan, steam the zucchini, covered, over simmering water until crisp-tender, about 4 minutes. Drain well and pat dry with paper towels. Set the acorn squash, green beans, and zucchini aside.

In a medium saucepan, combine 1¾ cups water, the butter, and 1 teaspoon salt. Bring to a boil over high heat. Stir in the couscous, then immediately remove from the heat. Cover tightly and let stand until the couscous absorbs the water, about 5 minutes. Uncover, and stir over low heat to separate the couscous grains and evaporate any excess moisture, 1 to 2 minutes. Transfer to a large bowl.

In a medium frying pan, heat the oil over medium heat. Add the raisins, cumin seeds, and chile flakes, and stir until the cumin seeds are lightly toasted, about 1 minute. Stir into the couscous, and season with salt and pepper.

To make the dressing, whisk the ingredients in a small bowl. Stir about one third of the dressing into the couscous. In another bowl, combine the green beans, zucchini, acorn squash, red peppers, chickpeas, and scallions. Add the remaining dressing to the bowl, and season with salt and pepper. Toss gently to mix, then arrange the vegetables on top of the couscous.

The salad can be made up to 4 hours ahead, and kept in a cool place. Just before serving, sprinkle with the cilantro and parsley.

———————— • ————————

ORANGE-GLAZED ACORN SQUASH

Here baked acorn squashes are finished with a simple marmalade and butter glaze. These go well with grilled pork chops.

MAKES 6 SERVINGS
  2 (1-pound) acorn squashes, halved horizontally and
    ends trimmed
  ¼ cup orange marmalade, preferably bitter orange
  2 tablespoons unsalted butter
  ¼ teaspoon ground cinnamon

Preheat the oven to 350°F. Line a baking sheet with foil, then butter it lightly. Place the squash halves, cut side down, on the baking sheet. Bake until the squash is tender when pierced with the tip of a sharp knife, 30 to 40 minutes.

Meanwhile, in a small saucepan over low heat, heat the marmalade, butter, and cinnamon until melted; set aside. Preheat the broiler. Turn the squash cut sides up, and brush with the marmalade mixture. Broil until glazed, about 2 minutes.

STIR-FRIED ASPARAGUS WITH GINGER

Asparagus lends itself beautifully to stir-frying.

MAKES 4 SERVINGS

   1½ pounds asparagus

   2 tablespoons vegetable oil

   1 tablespoon shredded fresh ginger

   1 garlic clove, minced

   ¼ cup chicken stock or water

   Salt and freshly ground pepper, to taste

Snap off and discard the woody ends from the asparagus. Cut the spears into 1-inch lengths. In a large wok or frying pan, heat the oil over medium-high heat until very hot. Add the asparagus and stir-fry for 2 minutes. Add the ginger and garlic and stir until fragrant, about 30 seconds. Add the stock, then cover tightly and reduce the heat to medium-low. Cook until the asparagus is crisp-tender, 2 to 3 minutes. Season with salt and pepper, and serve hot.

GREEN BEANS WITH PORTOBELLO MUSHROOMS AND PROSCIUTTO

This is a super blend of flavors that could well become a favorite, especially at holiday meals.

MAKES 6 SERVINGS

   ½ cup dried porcini (½ ounce)

   2 tablespoons unsalted butter

   2 large portobello mushrooms, stems discarded, caps cut into ½- by 3-inch strips

   4 ounces prosciutto, chopped into ¼-inch pieces

   12 ounces green beans

   Salt and freshly ground pepper, to taste

In a small bowl, soak the porcini in 1 cup boiling water until softened, about 20 to 30 minutes. Lift the mushrooms out of the water and coarsely chop. Strain the soaking liquid through a paper-towel-lined sieve set over a bowl. Set aside.

   In a large frying pan, heat the butter over medium heat. Add the portobello strips and cook, stirring occasionally, until the mushrooms give off their liquid, about 5 minutes. Add the chopped porcini and their soaking liquid, and cook until the mushrooms are tender and the liquid has reduced to about 2 tablespoons, about 5 more minutes. Add the prosciutto and stir for 1 minute.

   Meanwhile, in a large saucepan of lightly salted boiling water, cook the green beans over high heat until crisp-tender, about 4 minutes. Drain and refresh. (The mushrooms and beans can be prepared up to 2 hours ahead, and kept at room temperature.)

Stir the green beans into the mushroom mixture, and cook over medium heat, stirring often, until heated through, 3 to 5 minutes. Season with salt and pepper, and serve hot.

GREEN BEANS ATHENA

The Greeks appreciate long-cooked vegetables where the flavors have time to mingle. Here, green beans and tomatoes are combined.

MAKES 6 SERVINGS

   2 tablespoons olive oil

   1 large onion, cut into thin half-moons

   2 garlic cloves, minced

   1 pound green beans

   6 ripe plum tomatoes, peeled, seeded, and chopped

   Salt and freshly ground pepper, to taste

   2 ounces feta cheese, crumbled

In a large frying pan, heat the oil over medium heat. Add the onion and garlic and cook, stirring often, until the onion is soft and translucent, about 5 minutes. Add the green beans, tomatoes, and 2 tablespoons water, and season with salt and pepper. Cover and cook over medium-low heat until the green beans are very tender and the tomatoes have softened into a sauce, about 40 minutes. Sprinkle with the cheese, and serve hot or warm.

ROASTED BEETS WITH GREENS

Roasting beets emphasizes their natural sugars, and helps them keep their vibrant color. Try to purchase beets with the tops attached. Not only are the greens a good sign of freshness, they are also delicious. Balsamic vinegar, with its sweet note, is a perfect condiment.

MAKES 4 TO 6 SERVINGS

   6 medium beets, with green tops attached

   3 tablespoons balsamic vinegar

   Grated zest of 1 orange

   3 tablespoons extra virgin olive oil

   Salt and freshly ground pepper, to taste

Preheat the oven to 350°F. Cut off the beet greens about 1 inch from the top of the beets, and set the greens aside. Wrap each beet in aluminum foil. Bake until tender, about 1 hour, depending on the size of the beet. Unwrap the beets and let cool until easy to handle. Slip off the skins and slice into rounds.

Stir-Fried Asparagus with Ginger

While the beets are cooling, rinse the beet greens well. Coarsely chop the tough stems. Bring a medium saucepan of lightly salted water to a boil over high heat. Add the stems and cook for 5 minutes. Add the beet greens and continue cooking until the greens and stems are tender, about 10 minutes. Drain well.

Place the beet greens and stems on a platter and top with the sliced beets. In a bowl, whisk together the balsamic vinegar, orange zest, and olive oil, and season with salt and pepper. Pour over the beets and greens, and serve warm or at room temperature. (If the latter, add the dressing just before serving.)

CREAMED BELGIAN ENDIVE

Belgian endive is usually thought of as a salad vegetable. Here it is eaten hot, cloaked in a suave cream sauce.

MAKES 4 SERVINGS

- 4 plump heads Belgian endive, tough cores removed
- 1 cup chicken stock
- 2 tablespoons unsalted butter
- 1 tablespoon lemon juice
- 6 tablespoons heavy cream
- Salt, to taste

Cut the endive lengthwise into ½-inch-wide strips. Cut the strips crosswise into pieces about 2 inches long. Place in a medium frying pan with the stock, butter, and lemon juice. Bring to a simmer over medium heat. Cook, stirring occasionally, until the stock has reduced to 2 tablespoons, about 8 minutes.

Add the cream and cook until the liquid has reduced by half and the endive is coated with a light sauce. Season with salt. Serve hot. (The endive can be prepared up to 2 hours ahead; reheat gently to serve.)

IRISH CABBAGE AND POTATOES

Called colcannon in Ireland, this hearty side dish is just the thing for a St. Patrick's Day dinner. Leftovers can be shaped into patties and fried in butter until crisp.

MAKES 4 TO 6 SERVINGS

- 1 (1½-pound) head green cabbage (about 1 medium head), quartered and cored
- 1 pound boiling potatoes, peeled and cut into 2-inch chunks
- 2 small leeks, chopped
- 1 cup half-and-half
- A pinch of ground mace or nutmeg
- Salt and freshly ground pepper, to taste
- 4 tablespoons unsalted butter, melted

Bring a large pot of salted water to a boil over high heat. Add the cabbage and cook until just tender, about 15 minutes. Drain and rinse under cold running water until cool enough to handle. Cut the cabbage into shreds.

In a medium saucepan of boiling salted water, cook the potatoes until tender, about 15 minutes. Meanwhile, in a small saucepan, bring the leeks and half-and-half to a simmer over medium-low heat. Cook until the leeks are tender, about 10 minutes. Drain the potatoes well and return to the pan. Mash the potatoes, then add the leeks and cream. Beat in the shredded cabbage. Cook over low heat, beating continuously, until hot and fluffy, 2 to 3 minutes. Season with the mace, salt, and pepper.

Transfer to a heated serving dish. Make a little hollow in the potato mixture and fill with the melted butter. Serve hot.

BRAISED RED CABBAGE

Is there anything that goes better with roast pork or game than tangy red cabbage?

MAKES 4 SERVINGS

- 1 tablespoon unsalted butter
- 1 medium onion, finely chopped
- 1 (1-pound) head red cabbage, halved lengthwise, cored, and cut into ¼-inch-thick slices
- 2 tart green apples (such as Granny Smith), peeled, quartered, and cored
- ⅔ cup red wine
- ⅓ cup red wine vinegar, or more to taste
- 3 tablespoons light brown sugar, or more to taste
- 1 (3-inch) strip orange zest
- 3 juniper berries, crushed (optional)
- 2 bay leaves
- Salt and freshly ground pepper, to taste

Preheat the oven to 325°F. In a Dutch oven or flameproof casserole, heat the butter over medium heat. Add the onion and cook until softened, about 5 minutes. Add the cabbage and stir until well coated with butter. Stir in the remaining ingredients, and season with salt and pepper. Bring to a simmer.

Cover with aluminum foil and then a lid. Transfer to the oven and cook, stirring occasionally, until the cabbage is very tender, about 1¼ hours. If the casserole is well sealed, there will be enough liquid; however, if the cabbage seems to be getting too dry, add a little more red wine or water. During the last 30 minutes of cooking, taste the cabbage and add more vinegar or sugar, if needed—some cabbages are full-flavored, but others are bland and need the extra seasoning. Serve hot.

GLAZED BABY CARROTS

Peeled baby carrots make a lovely side dish for many different entrées, especially roasts.

MAKES 4 SERVINGS

1 pound peeled baby carrots
2 teaspoons granulated sugar
4 tablespoons unsalted butter
2 teaspoons chopped fresh chives or parsley

Bring a pan of lightly salted water to a boil. Add the carrots and cook until barely tender, 6 to 8 minutes. Drain off all but 2 tablespoons of the cooking water. Reduce the heat to medium-low. Add the sugar and let it dissolve in the cooking water. Add the butter and melt. Increase the heat to medium-high and cook until the liquid reduces to a thick, golden-brown syrup, rolling the carrots in this to glaze, about 5 minutes. Sprinkle with the herbs, and serve hot.

CAULIFLOWER AU GRATIN

This is an excellent way to prepare broccoli, too.

MAKES 4 TO 6 SERVINGS

4 tablespoons unsalted butter
3 tablespoons all-purpose flour
2 cups milk
1 large head cauliflower, broken into florets
½ cup light cream or half-and-half
¾ cup shredded Emmentaler or Gruyère cheese,
    or freshly grated Parmesan cheese
Salt and freshly ground pepper, to taste
1 cup fresh bread crumbs

In a saucepan, melt 2 tablespoons of the butter over medium-low heat. Stir in the flour and let bubble gently without browning for 1 to 2 minutes. Gradually stir in the milk, then bring to a simmer. Cover and simmer over low heat, stirring occasionally, for about 15 minutes.

Meanwhile, bring a large saucepan of lightly salted water to a boil. Add the cauliflower and cook until just tender, about 8 minutes. Drain and keep warm.

Preheat the broiler. Stir the cream into the sauce, then remove from the heat. (The sauce should be thin but creamy.) Reserve 3 tablespoons of the cheese for the topping, then stir the remaining cheese into the sauce. Season with salt and pepper. Keep warm.

In a medium frying pan, heat the remaining 2 tablespoons of butter over medium-high heat. Add the bread crumbs and cook, stirring often, until golden-brown, about 3 minutes. Add the cauliflower, and stir and mix until each floret is coated with bread crumbs. Transfer to a buttered baking dish. Pour the sauce around the cauliflower, and sprinkle the reserved cheese over the top. Broil until the top is lightly browned, 1 to 2 minutes. Serve hot.

CAJUN SMOTHERED CORN

Cajun cooks know how to season humble ingredients and get delicious results. If desired, substitute ¼ cup olive oil for the bacon and its rendered fat.

MAKES 6 TO 8 SERVINGS

6 strips thick-sliced bacon
1 medium onion, chopped
1 medium red bell pepper, seeded and chopped
2 medium celery ribs, chopped
4 cups fresh or defrosted frozen corn kernels
2 garlic cloves, minced
½ teaspoon Hungarian paprika
½ teaspoon dried thyme
½ teaspoon dried basil
¼ teaspoon freshly ground pepper
2 large ripe tomatoes, seeded and chopped
Salt, to taste

In a large frying pan over medium heat, cook the bacon until crisp, about 5 minutes. Transfer to paper towels to drain. Pour out all but 2 tablespoons of the bacon fat from the pan. Add the onion, bell pepper, and celery to the pan, and cook until the onion is golden-brown, about 10 minutes. Add the corn, garlic, paprika, thyme, basil, and pepper, and cook, stirring frequently, until the corn is beginning to brown around the edges, about 5 minutes. Stir in the tomatoes and cook until they are heated through, about 5 minutes. Crumble the bacon, stir it in, and season with salt. Serve hot.

STIR-FRIED EGGPLANT WITH CHILES AND CILANTRO

This vegetable dish is just as good hot or warm as it is cool. If you can find them, use Asian eggplants.

MAKES 4 SERVINGS

¼ cup vegetable oil
1 pound eggplant, cut into 1-inch cubes
¼ cup balsamic vinegar
2 tablespoons soy sauce
2 tablespoons finely sliced scallions
1 tablespoon shredded fresh ginger
½ teaspoon chile flakes, or more to taste
Salt and freshly ground pepper, to taste
Fresh cilantro sprigs, for garnish

In a wok or large nonstick frying pan, heat the oil over medium-high heat until very hot. Add the eggplant and cook, turning often, until browned on all sides, about 3 minutes. Transfer to paper towels to drain.

Add the vinegar and soy sauce to the pan and heat to boiling. Return the eggplant to the pan. Reduce the heat to medium-low and simmer for 5 minutes. Stir in the scallions, ginger, and chile flakes, and season with salt and pepper. Cook until the liquid is reduced and the eggplant is very tender, about 2 more minutes. Transfer to a serving dish and garnish with cilantro sprigs. Serve hot, warm, or at room temperature.

BAKED EGGPLANT PARMESAN

Melanzane alla parmigiana, a dish that is found on menus in Italian restaurants all around the world, is a good example of how peasant food has been popularized, if not glamorized, in recent years. Until recently, only the wealthiest Italian families could afford meat, and recipes like this were served in its stead, so deliciously that one wonders how much the meat was missed.

MAKES 6 SERVINGS

2 (1-pound) eggplants, cut lengthwise into
    ¼-inch-thick slices
Salt and freshly ground pepper, to taste
¾ cup vegetable oil, plus more as needed
All-purpose flour, for dusting the eggplant
⅓ cup olive oil
1 medium onion, chopped
2 garlic cloves, minced
2 pounds ripe plum tomatoes, peeled, seeded, and
    chopped, or use drained canned tomatoes
3 tablespoons chopped fresh basil
2 tablespoons chopped fresh parsley
12 ounces mozzarella cheese, cut into cubes
1 teaspoon dried oregano
¼ cup freshly grated Parmesan cheese

Sprinkle the eggplant slices lightly with salt. Let stand for 30 minutes to draw out the juices. Pat dry with paper towels.

In a large frying pan over medium-high heat, heat the vegetable oil until very hot, but not smoking. In batches, dust the eggplant slices with flour and add to the oil. Cook, turning once, until golden-brown on both sides, about 5 minutes. Add more oil to the pan, if needed. As the eggplant is browned, place on paper towels to drain.

In a medium saucepan, heat the olive oil over medium heat. Add the onions and garlic and cook, stirring often, until softened and translucent, about 5 minutes. Stir in the tomatoes and 1 tablespoon each of the basil and parsley. Season with salt and pepper. Bring to a simmer, then reduce the heat to low and simmer until the tomatoes have formed a thick sauce, about 30 minutes.

Preheat the oven to 350°F. Lightly oil a 9- by 13-inch baking dish. Layer half of the eggplant slices in the dish, then spread with half of the tomato sauce and half of the mozzarella cheese. Sprinkle with half of the remaining basil and parsley, and half of the oregano. Top with the remaining eggplant, tomato sauce, and mozzarella. Sprinkle with the Parmesan and the remaining herbs. Bake until the cheese has melted and the juices are bubbling, about 30 minutes. Let stand for 5 minutes before serving hot.

FENNEL PARMIGIANO

This superior side dish makes an excellent accompaniment for grilled pork chops or roast pork tenderloin.

MAKES 6 SERVINGS

3 heads fennel
Salt and freshly ground pepper, to taste
¾ cup freshly grated Parmesan cheese
5 tablespoons unsalted butter, cut into small pieces

Preheat the oven to 375°F. Cut the fennel bulbs crosswise into ⅓-inch-thick slices, or cut them lengthwise into quarters. Bring a large pot of lightly salted water to a boil over high heat. Add the fennel and cook until barely tender, about 5 minutes for slices and 8 minutes for quarters. Drain thoroughly and pat dry with paper towels.

Lightly butter a medium-sized baking dish. If you have cut the fennel into slices, layer them in the dish, seasoning each layer lightly with salt and pepper, sprinkling with cheese, and dotting with butter; finish with a layer of cheese dotted with butter. If you have cut the fennel into quarters, arrange them in the dish and sprinkle with seasoning and cheese, then dot with butter. Bake until the top is golden, 20 to 25 minutes. Serve hot.

GLOBE ARTICHOKES ROMAN-STYLE

Romans treat their artichokes with loving care. Instead of simply serving them boiled, they braise them in a fragrant broth of olive oil, mint, and garlic. Serve with plenty of bread for mopping up the cooking juices.

MAKES 4 APPETIZER SERVINGS

2 tablespoons lemon juice

8 or 12 small artichokes (preferably less than 2 inches across)

⅔ cup extra virgin olive oil

3 tablespoons chopped fresh mint

4 garlic cloves, chopped

Salt and freshly ground pepper, to taste

Fill a large bowl with cold water and add the lemon juice. If using very small artichokes, peel the stems and lower parts, cutting away the outer layer of leaves. If using larger artichokes (but still no more than 3 inches across), you will need to remove the hairy choke in the center. As each artichoke is prepared, place it in the bowl of acidulated water.

In a medium frying pan, heat 1 tablespoon of the oil over medium-low heat. Add the mint and garlic and cook gently until the garlic is fragrant, about 2 minutes. Drain the artichokes and shake each one upside-down to remove excess water. Divide the mint mixture evenly among the artichokes, randomly stuffing teaspoonfuls of it between the leaves (and in the center if you have removed the chokes).

Pack the artichokes in a saucepan just large enough to hold them snugly. Pour in 1¼ cups water and the remaining olive oil. Season lightly with salt and pepper. Bring to a boil over high heat, then cover and reduce the heat to low. Simmer until the artichokes are tender, 30 to 45 minutes. Uncover, increase the heat to high, and cook until the liquid has reduced by about half, 10 to 15 minutes. Transfer the artichokes to a platter and spoon the cooking juices over them. Serve hot, warm, or at room temperature.

STEWED ARTICHOKE BOTTOMS WITH SPINACH

You can also make this springtime dish with sorrel instead of spinach. Serve with plainly grilled or broiled meat or fish.

MAKES 4 SERVINGS

2 tablespoons unsalted butter, cut into small pieces

1 pound fresh spinach leaves, tough stems discarded

10 fresh artichoke bottoms, or 1 (10-ounce) package frozen artichoke hearts, defrosted, cut into quarters

2 tablespoons olive oil

1 garlic clove, peeled

A pinch of granulated sugar

Salt and freshly ground pepper, to taste

Scatter the butter on the bottom of a large, heavy-bottomed saucepan. Add one fourth of the spinach (still wet from its rinsing), then one fourth of the artichoke pieces. Repeat the layers until all the spinach and artichokes are in the pan. Drizzle with the oil, add the garlic clove and sugar, and season with salt and pepper. Cover the pan tightly. Cook over very low heat for 1 hour, checking occasionally to be sure the bottom layer of spinach isn't sticking and burning, and adding a few tablespoons of water, if needed. (If using frozen artichokes, cook for about 30 minutes.) If too much liquid remains, remove the lid for the last few minutes of cooking so the excess moisture can evaporate. Serve hot.

MUSHROOMS WITH SWEET PEPPERS

Serve this as an unusual first course for a summer lunch.

MAKES 4 APPETIZER SERVINGS

3 tablespoons olive oil

2 medium red or yellow bell peppers, seeded and cut into ¼-inch-wide strips

8 ounces button mushrooms, thinly sliced

3 tablespoons hearty red wine

1 tablespoon lemon juice

2 tablespoons chopped fresh parsley

½ tablespoon chopped fresh thyme or 1 teaspoon dried thyme

12 coriander seeds, crushed, or ⅓ cup chopped fresh cilantro

1 garlic clove, thinly sliced

Salt and freshly ground pepper, to taste

In a medium frying pan, heat the oil over medium heat. Add the peppers and cook until softened, about 5 minutes. Add the mushrooms, 3 tablespoons water, the wine, lemon juice, parsley, thyme, coriander, and garlic. Season. Simmer, uncovered, stirring occasionally, until the mushrooms are tender, about 15 minutes. Cool to room temperature before serving.

GRATINÉED ONIONS IN GORGONZOLA SAUCE

Creamed onions are given a very sophisticated finish in this recipe.

MAKES 8 SERVINGS

2 pounds small white boiling onions

5 tablespoons unsalted butter

3 tablespoons all-purpose flour

1½ cups milk

3 ounces Gorgonzola cheese, crumbled

Salt and freshly ground pepper, to taste

½ cup fresh bread crumbs

In a large saucepan of boiling water, blanch the onions for 1 minute. Drain well and refresh under cold running water. Using a small sharp knife, peel and trim the onions. Cut a small "X" in the end of each onion. In a large saucepan of lightly salted boiling water, cook the onions over medium heat until they are just tender, 10 to 15 minutes, then drain well.

Preheat the oven to 350°F. Lightly butter a 2-quart round baking dish. Transfer the cooked onions to the dish. In a medium, heavy-bottomed saucepan, heat 4 tablespoons of the butter over medium-low heat until melted. Stir in the flour and let bubble gently without browning for 2 minutes. Gradually stir in the milk and bring the sauce to a simmer. Reduce the heat to low and simmer for 2 minutes. Remove from the heat, and stir in the Gorgonzola cheese until melted. Season with salt and pepper.

Pour the sauce over the onions. Sprinkle with the crumbs and dot with the remaining 1 tablespoon butter. Bake until bubbling and the top is golden-brown, about 30 minutes.

GLAZED PEARL ONIONS

Pearl onions are now available in many supermarkets in a variety of colors—yellow and red, as well as white. If you can, use an assortment. To peel the onions, drop them in a large saucepan of boiling water and boil for 1 minute, then drain and rinse under cold water—this blanching loosens the skins and makes them easier to peel.

MAKES 4 TO 6 SERVINGS

1½ pounds pearl or small white boiling onions, peeled
⅔ cup chicken or beef stock
2 teaspoons granulated sugar
Salt, to taste

Choose a frying pan just large enough to hold the onions snugly in one layer. Half fill the pan with salted water and bring to a boil over high heat. Add the onions and cook for 5 minutes, then pour off all but 3 tablespoons of the water. Add the stock, sugar, and just a pinch of salt (the saltiness will intensify as the liquid cooks and reduces).

Bring to a simmer, then reduce the heat to low. Cook gently until the onions are very tender and the liquid has reduced to a glaze, 15 to 20 minutes. Shake the pan occasionally during cooking to turn the onions, so they become evenly coated with the glaze. The onions can be prepared up to 30 minutes before serving, and kept covered; reheat gently before serving, if necessary.

FRESH PEAS WITH LETTUCE FRANÇAISE

The French like to cook fresh peas with lettuce hearts—both are sweet vegetables and complement each other very well.

MAKES 4 SERVINGS

4 sprigs fresh savory or thyme, or ¼ teaspoon dried savory or thyme
2 heads Bibb lettuce, outer leaves removed (reserve for another use)
2½ cups shelled fresh peas (about 2 pounds unshelled)
4 tablespoons unsalted butter
A pinch of granulated sugar
Salt, to taste

Tuck the herb sprigs into the lettuce hearts and then place them in a medium saucepan. Add the peas, butter, and sugar, and season with salt. Pour in ½ cup water. Bring to a simmer over medium heat, then cover and reduce the heat to low. Simmer gently until the peas are tender, 10 to 15 minutes (this will depend on the age of the peas; older ones will take slightly longer). Drain well. Serve hot.

PEAS IN THE INDIAN FASHION

Here fresh peas are cooked together with Indian seasonings. This method can also be adapted to add interest to frozen peas—just adjust the cooking time accordingly.

MAKES 4 SERVINGS

3 tablespoons clarified butter, or 2 tablespoons vegetable oil and 1 tablespoon unsalted butter
1 large onion, finely chopped
½ teaspoon ground cumin
2½ cups shelled fresh peas (about 2 pounds unshelled)
1 small hot fresh chile pepper (such as serrano), seeded and minced
3 tablespoons chopped fresh cilantro
Salt, to taste

In a medium frying pan, heat the clarified butter over medium heat. Add the onion and ground cumin and cook until the onion is soft and golden, but not browned, about 6 minutes. Add the peas, minced chile pepper, and chopped cilantro, and stir for 1 to 2 minutes. Add ¼ cup water and season with salt. Cover and cook over medium-low heat until the peas are tender, 10 to 15 minutes, depending on the age of the peas.

Serve the peas hot, with the fragrant cooking juices poured over them.

STUFFED RED PEPPERS WITH TOMATOES AND ANCHOVIES

Elizabeth David included this simple recipe in her book *Italian Food*, published in the 1950s.

MAKES 4 SERVINGS

4 medium red bell peppers, halved lengthwise
  and seeded
4 garlic cloves, sliced
Salt and freshly ground pepper, to taste
4 large ripe tomatoes, peeled and halved crosswise
½ cup olive oil
16 anchovy fillets packed in oil, drained

Preheat the oven to 375°F. Lightly oil a baking dish. Arrange the pepper halves, cut side up, in the dish, and distribute the garlic evenly in the cavities. Season with salt and pepper. Push a halved tomato, cut side down, into each pepper half. Season lightly with pepper, then drizzle with the oil.

Bake until the peppers are very tender, with scorched edges, about 1 hour. Remove from the oven, and criss-cross 2 anchovy fillets over each stuffed pepper. Let cool to room temperature before serving.

ROASTED POTATOES

If you are cooking a roast, you can add the potatoes to the roasting pan, using the meat drippings in the pan instead of the butter and oil.

MAKES 8 SERVINGS

4 large russet potatoes, peeled and halved
6 tablespoons unsalted butter, or goose or duck fat
¼ cup vegetable oil
Salt and freshly ground pepper, to taste

Preheat the oven to 400°F. Place the potatoes in a large saucepan of lightly salted water and bring to a boil over high heat. Cover and cook for 5 minutes. Drain. Return the potatoes to the pan and cook uncovered over low heat, shaking the pan occasionally, to dry out them out and give them a rough surface, 1 to 2 minutes.

Put the butter and oil in a roasting pan, and heat in the oven. Arrange the potatoes in the pan and baste with the hot fat. Roast, turning occasionally, until golden-brown and tender, about 1 hour. Using a slotted spoon, transfer to a warmed serving bowl. Season with salt and pepper, and serve hot.

POTATO AND GRUYÈRE TIMBALE

This satisfying potato dish can be prepared with whatever favorite cheese you have in the house.

MAKES 6 SERVINGS

6 tablespoons unsalted butter, at room
  temperature
2 tablespoons dry bread crumbs
2 pounds boiling potatoes, peeled and quartered
½ cup milk
2 large eggs, beaten
1½ cups shredded Gruyère cheese
Salt and freshly ground pepper, to taste

Preheat the oven to 350°F. Grease a 9-inch round cake pan with 1 tablespoon of the unsalted butter, and then coat it with about 1 tablespoon of the dry bread crumbs.

In a large pot of lightly salted boiling water, cook the potatoes until tender, about 20 minutes. Drain well. Return to the pot and cook over low heat, stirring constantly, to evaporate any excess moisture, about 3 minutes. Using a potato masher or a hand-held electric mixer on low speed, mash the potatoes with the milk. Stir in the eggs and cheese. Season with salt and pepper.

Spread the potatoes in the prepared pan. Sprinkle the top with the remaining 1 tablespoon bread crumbs, and dot with the remaining 1 tablespoon butter. Bake until the top is golden-brown, 30 to 35 minutes. Let stand for 5 minutes, then invert and unmold onto a serving plate. Serve hot.

BAKED STUFFED POTATOES

Serve these with grilled steak or a vegetable stew.

MAKES 8 SIDE DISH SERVINGS

4 large russet potatoes, unpeeled, pricked all over
  with a skewer
⅔ cup half-and-half or milk, heated
1½ cups shredded sharp Cheddar cheese
4 tablespoons unsalted butter
1 large egg, beaten
Salt and cayenne pepper, to taste

Preheat the oven to 400°F. Place the potatoes directly on the oven rack and bake until tender, about 1 hour. Let cool until easy to handle. Cut each potato in half lengthwise, then use a fork to scrape out the flesh into a bowl, leaving a ¼-inch-thick layer of flesh in the skins to form shells. Set the skins aside.

Add the half-and-half to the potato flesh, mashing with a fork until smooth. Add the cheese, butter, and egg, and mix well. Season with salt and cayenne pepper. Heap into the potato skins and place on a lightly greased baking sheet. Bake until the tops are golden-brown, about 15 minutes. Serve hot.

PARSLEY MASHED POTATOES

Plain mashed potatoes are just fine, but they can also be embellished with herbs and other flavorings. This version is one of the most versatile.

MAKES 4 SERVINGS

2 pounds boiling potatoes, peeled
½ cup packed fresh flat-leaf parsley leaves
1¼ cups heavy cream
8 tablespoons (1 stick) unsalted butter, cut up
Salt and freshly ground pepper, to taste

Bring a large saucepan of lightly salted water to a boil over high heat. Add the potatoes and cook until tender, about 20 minutes, depending on the size of the potatoes.

Meanwhile, bring a small saucepan of water to a boil over high heat. Add the parsley and blanch for 1 minute. Drain and refresh. Squeeze dry in a dish towel. Place the blanched parsley in a blender. In another small saucepan, bring the cream and butter to a simmer over low heat, stirring to melt the butter. Pour into the blender and process until smooth. Season with salt and pepper.

Drain the potatoes and return to the warm saucepan. Mash the potatoes, adding the parsley cream. Taste to check the seasoning. Serve hot.

Pesto Mashed Potatoes: Subsitute ½ cup packed fresh basil leaves for the parsley. Stir ½ cup freshly grated Parmesan cheese into the mashed potatoes.

PAN-ROASTED NEW POTATOES

Sometimes you want roasted potatoes, but the oven is packed with other foods. This method gives delicious results on top of the stove. If you can find very small new potatoes about the size of a large walnut, leave them whole.

MAKES 4 SERVINGS

6 tablespoons unsalted butter
1½ pounds small new potatoes, unpeeled, cut into 1-inch pieces
Salt and freshly ground pepper, to taste

In a large frying pan that will hold the potatoes in a single layer, heat the butter over medium heat. Add the potatoes and cook, turning occasionally, until browned on all sides, 8 to 10 minutes. Season with salt and pepper. Cover and reduce the heat to medium-low. Cook until the potatoes are tender when pierced with the tip of a sharp knife, about 30 minutes. Remove the lid, increase the heat to medium-high, and cook, shaking the pan often, until the potatoes become a bit crispier, 2 to 3 minutes. Using a slotted spoon, transfer to a warmed serving bowl and serve hot.

FRIED NEW POTATOES WITH MINTED YOGURT DRESSING

Many Indian vegetable dishes include potatoes, which are an ideal bland background for the aromatic blends of onions, garlic, chiles, and spices.

MAKES 4 SERVINGS

8 medium boiling potatoes (2 pounds), peeled and cut into 1½-inch pieces
½ cup clarified butter or vegetable oil
1 large onion, thinly sliced
4 garlic cloves, thinly sliced
1 tablespoon shredded fresh ginger
2 teaspoons ground coriander
1 teaspoon ground cumin
2 small hot fresh chile peppers (such as serrano), seeded and chopped
Salt and freshly ground pepper, to taste
2 tablespoons chopped fresh cilantro
1 tablespoon lime juice
Dressing
⅔ cup plain yogurt
2 tablespoons chopped fresh mint
¼ teaspoon cayenne pepper, or more to taste
Salt, to taste

To make the dressing, combine all of the ingredients in a small bowl. Let stand at room temperature while preparing the potatoes.

Bring a large pot of lightly salted water to a boil over high heat. Add the potatoes and cook until half done, about 10 minutes. Drain well.

In a large frying pan, heat the clarified butter over medium heat. Add the onion and garlic and cook until the onion is golden-brown, about 7 minutes. Add the ginger, coriander, and cumin, and reduce the heat to very low. Cook, stirring often, until very fragrant, 3 to 5 minutes. Stir in the chiles, and season with salt and pepper. Add the potatoes and mix well to coat with the spices. Add ½ cup water, and increase the heat to medium-low. Simmer the potatoes until they are tender and the water has almost completely evaporated, about 15 minutes. Sprinkle with the cilantro and lime juice. Increase the heat to high and continue cooking, stirring often, until the potatoes are crisped, about 3 more minutes. If desired, drain the potatoes to remove excess fat. Allow to cool to warm, then spoon the dressing over the potatoes and serve.

BAKED NEW POTATOES WITH SAFFRON, CREAM, AND GARLIC

Prepared this way, the potatoes become wonderfully soft and creamy in texture, and the saffron adds a new flavor dimension.

MAKES 8 SERVINGS

8 medium boiling potatoes (2 pounds), peeled and cut into 1½-inch pieces
⅔ cup heavy cream
⅔ cup milk
2 garlic cloves, minced
½ to 1 teaspoon crushed saffron threads
Salt and freshly ground pepper, to taste
Chopped fresh chives, for garnish

Preheat the oven to 350°F. Lightly butter a baking dish large enough to hold the potatoes in a single layer. Bring a large saucepan of lightly salted water to a boil over high heat. Add the potatoes and cook until half done, about 10 minutes. Drain and refresh. Place in the prepared baking dish.

In a medium saucepan, combine the heavy cream, milk, garlic, and saffron, and season with salt. Bring to a simmer over medium heat. Remove from the heat and let stand for 5 minutes or so. Pour evenly over the potatoes. Bake until the potatoes are tender when pierced with the tip of a sharp knife and the cream has thickened, about 30 minutes. Sprinkle generously with pepper and with chives, and serve hot.

CARAMELIZED SWEET POTATOES

These are perfect with baked ham, roast pork, and, of course, the holiday turkey.

MAKES 6 SERVINGS

4 medium sweet potatoes (about 2 pounds), unpeeled
3 tablespoons sugar
4 tablespoons butter, cut into pieces

In a saucepan of boiling salted water, cook the sweet potatoes until barely tender when pierced with a knife, 20 to 25 minutes. Cool until easy to handle, then peel. Cut into 1½-inch rounds, and cover to keep warm.

In a large frying pan, heat the sugar over medium heat, shaking the pan often, until the sugar melts and caramelizes to a golden amber color. Add the butter, and swirl the pan to incorporate the butter into the caramel. Quickly rinse the sweet potatoes under cold running water, shake off excess water, and carefully place the sweet potatoes in the pan. Turn them in the caramel until well coated, then heat through for about 2 minutes. Serve hot.

BAKED SWEET POTATOES WITH PINEAPPLE

Use either yellow-fleshed sweet potatoes or orange-fleshed sweet potatoes (often called yams) for this holiday specialty.

MAKES 8 TO 12 SERVINGS

1 small ripe pineapple
3 pounds sweet potatoes, peeled and cut into ¼-inch-thick slices
8 tablespoons (1 stick) unsalted butter
1½ cups unsweetened pineapple juice, fresh or canned
¾ cup packed light brown sugar
3 tablespoons dark rum, bourbon, or additional pineapple juice
1 tablespoon minced fresh ginger
2 tablespoons cornstarch mixed with 2 tablespoons water

Using a large, sharp knife, cut away the crown and the thick skin from the pineapple, and then remove the small "eyes" with the tip of the knife. Quarter the pineapple lengthwise. Cut away and discard the thick core from each quarter, then cut crosswise into ¼-inch-thick slices.

Bring a large pot of lightly salted water to a boil over high heat. Add the sweet potatoes and cook until crisp-tender, about 5 minutes; do not overcook. Drain and rinse under cold running water.

Lightly butter a 9- by 13-inch baking dish. Layer the sweet potatoes in the dish in overlapping rows, slipping in a pineapple quarter every few potatoes, letting the curved edge of the pineapple peek out. (The dish can be prepared up to 8 hours ahead and kept, covered, in the refrigerator.)

Preheat the oven to 350°F. In a medium saucepan, melt the butter over medium heat. Add the pineapple juice, brown sugar, rum, and ginger and bring to a boil. Stir in the cornstarch and cook until thickened. Drizzle over the sweet potatoes and pineapple. Bake, basting the top often with the juices in the dish, until the sweet potatoes are tender and the cooking liquid is syrupy, about 35 minutes. Serve hot.

MASHED RUTABAGA WITH POTATOES

Rutabaga is a humble root vegetable in itself, but it can be very good when treated properly. Here, it is mashed together with potatoes, and enriched with the addition of a little cream.

BAKED NEW POTATOES WITH SAFFRON, CREAM, AND GARLIC

STUFFED TOMATOES

MAKES 4 SERVINGS

  1 pound rutabagas, peeled and cut into 1-inch chunks
  1 pound boiling potatoes, peeled and cut into
    1-inch chunks
  ¼ cup heavy cream
  2 tablespoons unsalted butter
  Salt and freshly ground pepper, to taste

Put the rutabaga and potatoes in a saucepan and add water to cover. Bring to a boil and cook until tender, 15 to 20 minutes. Drain, then return to the pan. Mash, adding the cream and butter and a seasoning of salt and pepper. If desired, beat until fluffy. Serve hot.

SPINACH AND CHICKPEA STEW

This is a fragrant vegetable stew with a sumptuous, deep flavor, substantial enough to make a whole meal. It is especially welcome on a cold day. Dried black-eyed peas could be substituted for the chickpeas.

MAKES 4 TO 6 SERVINGS

  4 tablespoons olive oil
  1 slice country-style bread
  1 medium onion, chopped
  4 ripe plum tomatoes, peeled, seeded, and chopped
  1 garlic clove, chopped
  1 tablespoon sweet Hungarian paprika
  1 pound fresh spinach leaves, tough stems discarded
  Salt, to taste
  1 generous cup dried chickpeas, cooked and drained

In a medium frying pan, heat 2 tablespoons of the oil over medium heat. Add the bread and fry, turning once, until golden-brown, about 3 minutes. Transfer the bread to paper towels to drain, leaving the oil in the pan, and let the bread cool. In the same pan, cook the onion until golden-brown, about 6 minutes. Stir in the tomatoes. Set aside.

  Using a mortar and pestle or a blender, crush the garlic. Crumble in the fried bread and crush to a paste. Set aside.

  In a large saucepan, heat the remaining 2 tablespoons of oil. Stir in the paprika. Immediately, in batches, add the spinach, waiting for the first batch to wilt before adding the next. Season with salt. Add the chickpeas, garlic and bread paste, and onion-tomato mixture. Add 1 cup of water. Cover and simmer very gently until the flavors are well blended, about 30 minutes, adding more water, if needed, to keep the mixture moist. Serve hot.

SESAME SPINACH

Grit has a tendency to hide in the crevices of spinach leaves, so be sure to rinse them thoroughly.

MAKES 4 SERVINGS

1 tablespoon Asian dark sesame oil
1 garlic clove, crushed under a knife and peeled
1 tablespoon sesame seeds
1½ pounds fresh spinach, tough stems discarded
Salt, to tase

Heat a large frying pan or wok, then add the oil and garlic and cook until the garlic begins to brown. Discard the garlic. Add the sesame seeds and fry until golden, about 30 seconds. Add the spinach. Increase the heat and cook, stirring and tossing, until the spinach is wilted, about 3 minutes. Season with salt.

Drain well in a sieve, pressing the spinach with the back of a spoon to remove excess moisture. Serve hot.

STUFFED TOMATOES

Serve these as a light lunch dish with salad.

MAKES 6 SERVINGS

6 large ripe but firm tomatoes
⅔ cup fresh bread crumbs
6 green Mediterranean olives, pitted and chopped
6 anchovy fillets packed in oil, drained and chopped
1 teaspoon chopped fresh basil or marjoram
1 large garlic clove, minced
4 tablespoons unsalted butter, melted
Salt and freshly ground pepper, to taste

Preheat the oven to 325°F. Lightly oil a baking dish. Cut the tomatoes in half horizontally. Over a bowl, scoop out the inside of each tomato half, leaving a ¼-inch-thick shell. Set the shells aside. If desired, remove the tomato seeds from the flesh. Add the bread crumbs, olives, anchovies, basil, and garlic to the tomato flesh. Moisten with the butter, and season. Stuff the mixture into the tomato shells. Bake until tender and browned on top, 30 to 40 minutes.

ZUCCHINI AND TOMATO GRATIN

This crusty gratin is a substantial side dish, or it could be served as a vegetarian main course.

MAKES 4 TO 6 SERVINGS

4 tablespoons olive oil
5 medium zucchini, cut into ½-inch-thick rounds
2 garlic cloves, minced
Salt and freshly ground pepper, to taste
¾ cup fresh bread crumbs
⅓ cup freshly grated Parmesan cheese
1 tablespoon chopped fresh basil
1 teaspoon chopped fresh rosemary
2 large ripe tomatoes, cut into ½-inch-thick rounds
    and lightly squeezed to remove seeds
1 cup shredded mozzarella cheese

Preheat the oven to 350°F. Lightly oil a 2½-quart baking dish. In a frying pan, heat 3 tablespoons of the oil. Add the zucchini and cook, stirring often, until lightly browned, about 10 minutes. Add the garlic and cook for 1 minute. Season, and set aside.

Mix the bread crumbs, Parmesan, basil, and rosemary. Sprinkle 2 tablespoons into the baking dish. Arrange half of the zucchini in the dish, then cover with half of the tomato slices. Sprinkle with half of the remaining crumbs, and all the mozzarella. Top with the remaining zucchini, tomatoes, and crumb mixture. Drizzle with the remaining 1 tablespoon oil. Bake until browned and bubbling, 30 minutes. Let stand for 5 minutes before serving.

RATATOUILLE

Here a rich and moist mélange of vegetables is just distinguishable in a smooth, aromatic tomato sauce.

MAKES 6 SERVINGS

⅔ cup olive oil
2 pounds ripe plum tomatoes, peeled, seeded, and
    chopped, or use drained canned tomatoes
Salt and freshly ground pepper, to taste
2 medium onions, sliced
3 garlic cloves, sliced
2 medium red or green bell peppers, seeded and cut
    into ¼-inch-wide strips
3 medium zucchini, cut into ¼-inch-thick rounds
1 eggplant, cut into ¼-inch slices, then quartered
½ cup black Mediterranean olives, pitted
2 tablespoon shredded fresh basil

In a saucepan, heat ⅓ cup of the oil. Add the tomatoes, and season with salt and pepper. Bring to a simmer, then cook, stirring, until the tomatoes form a thick sauce, 10 to 15 minutes.

Meanwhile, heat the remaining ⅓ cup olive oil over medium heat. Add the onions and garlic, and cook until translucent, about 5 minutes. Add the red peppers, zucchini, and eggplant. Season. Reduce the heat and cook, stirring, until the vegetables are almost tender, about 20 minutes. Stir in the tomato sauce and olives. Cook until the vegetables are tender, 5 to 10 minutes. Stir in the basil. Serve hot, warm, or cool.

Desserts and Candies

APPLE FRITTERS

Golden Delicious apples are the best choice of apples for making these fritters, as, unlike some others, they hold their shape well when cooked. The fritters are a nice dessert, but would also make a pleasant surprise to finish off brunch.

MAKES 4 TO 6 SERVINGS
¾ cup all-purpose flour
3 tablespoons unsalted butter, melted
⅓ cup granulated sugar
⅛ teaspoon ground cinnamon
A large pinch of ground cloves
A pinch of salt
8 Golden Delicious apples
Vegetable oil, for deep-frying
1 large egg white

About 1 hour before making the fritters, mix the flour and melted butter in a medium bowl. Gradually stir in 1 cup lukewarm water. Cover and let stand in a cool place, but not the refrigerator.

Just before serving, mix together the sugar, cinnamon, cloves, and salt in a small bowl. Peel and core the apples, and slice into ⅓-inch-thick rings. Toss the apple rings with about 2 tablespoons of the spiced sugar mixture.

Pour enough oil into a deep saucepan to come 2 or 3 inches up the sides, and heat to 350°F. Preheat the oven to 200°F.

In a small bowl, beat the egg white until it is stiff. Fold into the flour batter. In batches, dip the apple slices in the batter, gently shake off the excess batter, and add to the oil. Fry until golden-brown, turning once, about 3 minutes. Drain on paper towels and keep warm in the oven while making the remaining fritters. Serve hot, sprinkled with the remaining spiced sugar.

PEARS IN RED WINE

There are few desserts that are more appropriate as the finale to an autumn dinner than these beautiful pears in a deep ruby-colored syrup.

MAKES 4 SERVINGS
2½ cups hearty red wine
⅓ cup granulated sugar
½ vanilla bean (optional)
2 (3-inch) strips orange zest
1 cinnamon stick
6 whole cloves
4 large Bosc pears
1 lemon, halved

In a large saucepan, combine the wine, sugar, optional vanilla bean, orange zest, cinnamon stick, and cloves. Bring to a simmer over medium heat. Cook for 5 minutes.

Peel the pears, rubbing with the lemon halves to keep them from discoloring; leave the stems attached. Place the pears on their sides in the wine syrup. Cover and reduce the heat to low. Simmer gently, turning the pears occasionally in the syrup to ensure even coloring, until tender, about 1 hour. Using a slotted spoon, lift the pears onto a platter, standing them upright. Increase the heat to high and boil the wine syrup until it has reduced to about ⅔ cup, about 15 minutes. Pour over the pears. Serve warm or chilled, with cream.

FRENCH CHERRY CLAFOUTIS

This is a specialty of French country cooking, simple to make and delicious hot or cold.

MAKES 6 TO 8 SERVINGS
⅓ cup all-purpose flour
A pinch of salt
3 large eggs, beaten
2 cups milk
3 tablespoons granulated sugar, plus more
for serving
3 tablespoons kirsch
1½ pounds fresh sweet cherries, pitted
Sweetened whipped cream, for serving

Preheat the oven to 375°F. Lightly butter a 10-inch round pie plate or baking dish.

Place the flour and salt in a medium bowl. Make a well in the center and pour in the eggs. Gradually beat in the milk until smooth, then add the sugar and kirsch. Beat with a wooden spoon for about 3 minutes. (The batter can also be prepared in a blender, and blended until smooth, about 20 seconds.)

Spread the cherries in the prepared pie plate. Pour in the batter, straining it through a sieve to remove any lumps, if necessary. Bake until a toothpick inserted in the center comes out clean, about 1 hour.

Sprinkle with additional sugar and serve warm, with whipped cream.

SUMMER BERRY FOOL

Fools, those extremely simple desserts, are hard to beat when you want something sweet that requires little effort to make.

FRENCH CHERRY CLAFOUTIS

MAKES 4 SERVINGS
- 1½ pints strawberries or raspberries
- ¾ cup granulated sugar
- 1¼ cups heavy cream, chilled

Reserve a few whole berries, and chop the rest. In a medium bowl, mix the chopped strawberries with 6 tablespoons of the sugar. Cover and chill until the strawberries give off some juices, at least 1 hour. Crush the berries with a fork.

In a chilled large bowl, whip the cream with the remaining sugar just until it forms soft peaks—do not overwhip. Fold the berries into the cream. Spoon into individual glasses and garnish with the reserved berries, either whole or sliced. Serve cold.

JAMAICAN BAKED BANANAS

This dessert will appeal to everyone with a sweet tooth—the bananas are gorgeously sticky.

MAKES 4 SERVINGS
- 8 tablespoons (1 stick) unsalted butter
- 8 small ripe bananas, peeled
- ½ cup packed light brown sugar
- 2 tablespoons lime juice
- 3 tablespoons dark rum
- Coconut Ice Cream, for serving

Preheat the oven to 425°F. Place the butter in a flameproof baking dish (preferably enameled cast iron) large enough to hold the bananas in one layer. Melt the butter over medium heat. Add the bananas and turn to coat with butter. Sprinkle with the brown sugar, and turn the bananas until coated with the resulting sticky syrup. Sprinkle with the lime juice. Transfer to the oven and bake for 10 minutes.

Remove from the oven and place over medium heat again. Add the rum—be careful, as it may splatter. Bring to a simmer, holding the dish with a pot holder and swirling the liquids in the dish to mix them. Return to the oven and bake until nicely browned, about 5 minutes. (The bananas can also be browned in a preheated broiler.) Serve hot, with coconut ice cream.

RASPBERRY AND SHERRY TRIFLE

This delicious trifle is a holiday classic, and is simple to put together. The ingredients given here can easily be doubled to make a larger trifle when you have a bigger crowd to serve.

RASPBERRY AND SHERRY TRIFLE

MAKES 6 SERVINGS
- ½ (12-ounce) store-bought pound cake, cut into ⅓-inch-thick slices
- ½ cup sherry, preferably oloroso
- ⅓ cup seedless raspberry jam
- 1 cup fresh raspberries, plus more for garnish
- 1 cup slivered blanched almonds, plus more for garnish
- ⅔ cup heavy cream, chilled
- 2 tablespoons granulated sugar
- 1 teaspoon vanilla extract

Custard
- 2 cups milk
- ⅓ cup granulated sugar
- 2 large strips lemon zest
- 5 large egg yolks, at room temperature

For the custard, in a double boiler insert, heat the milk with the sugar and lemon zest over medium heat until bubbles form around the edge, stirring occasionally to dissolve the sugar. Remove from the heat and let stand for 10 minutes. Remove the lemon zest. In a large bowl, whisk the egg yolks until light and frothy. Gradually stir the hot milk into the eggs. Return to the double boiler insert and place over a saucepan of hot, not simmering, water over low heat. Cook, stirring constantly with a wooden spoon, until the custard is thick enough to coat the spoon (an instant-read thermometer will read 185°F), 5 to 10 minutes. Strain the custard through a sieve into a large bowl. Let cool to room temperature.

Place the cake slices in a 1½- to 2-quart glass bowl or trifle dish. Sprinkle with the sherry, then spread with the jam. Sprinkle with the raspberries and almonds. Pour in the cooled custard. (The trifle can be prepared up to 4 hours ahead, and kept, covered with plastic wrap, in the refrigerator.)

In a chilled medium bowl, whip the cream with the sugar and vanilla until soft peaks form. Spread over the trifle, and garnish with more raspberries and slivered almonds. Serve chilled.

CRÈME BRÛLÉE

For this version of the international favorite, the custard is cooked entirely on top of the stove, and not baked at all. Also, most of the sweetness comes from the caramelized sugar topping.

MAKES 4 SERVINGS
- 2 cups heavy cream
- 1 vanilla bean, split lengthwise
- 4 large egg yolks
- ¼ cup granulated sugar
- 3 tablespoons light brown sugar

In a medium heavy-bottomed saucepan, heat the cream with the vanilla bean over low heat until bubbles appear around the edge. Remove from the heat, and let stand for 10 minutes to infuse the cream with the vanilla flavor.

Whisk the egg yolks and sugar in a double boiler insert until the mixture is light and a little thickened. Gradually stir in the hot cream, adding the vanilla bean too. Place the insert over a saucepan of hot, not simmering, water over low heat. Do not let the base of the insert touch the water. Stir constantly until the custard is thick enough to coat a wooden spoon (about 185°F on an instant-read thermometer), 5 to 10 minutes. Discard the vanilla bean. Pour the custard into four ¾-cup ramekin cups. Let cool, then cover each and refrigerate until well chilled and set, at least 4 hours or overnight.

When ready to serve, preheat the boiler. Unwrap the custards. Place the brown sugar in a sieve, and rub it through the sieve to make an even layer about ¼ inch thick on the top of each custard. Place the ramekins on a baking sheet, and broil until the sugar melts and caramelizes, 1 to 2 minutes. Watch the sugar closely so it doesn't burn; don't worry if it colors unevenly. Let the caramel cool and harden before serving.

CHOCOLATE MOUSSE

Some things never go out of fashion. It's easy to see why chocolate mousse is a perennial favorite.

MAKES 4 TO 6 SERVINGS
    2 cups heavy cream
    3 egg yolks
    3½ ounces high-quality bittersweet chocolate, grated
    ¼ cup granulated sugar
    A tiny pinch of salt

In a double boiler insert, combine ⅔ cup of the cream, the egg yolks, chocolate, and sugar. Whisk until the mixture is light and foamy. Place the insert over a saucepan of hot, not simmering, water over low heat. Do not let the base of the insert touch the water. Cook, stirring occasionally, until the chocolate melts and the mixture is thick and creamy, 5 to 10 minutes. Remove from the heat and leave to cool to room temperature. Stir in the salt.

In a chilled medium bowl, whip the remaining 1⅓ cups cream until it forms soft peaks. Stir a spoonful of the whipped cream into the chocolate mixture to lighten it, then fold in the remaining cream. Spoon into individual ramekins, cover each, and refrigerate until well chilled and set, at least 4 hours or overnight. Serve chilled.

Orange Chocolate Mousse: Add the grated zest of ½ orange to the chocolate mixture just before folding in the whipped cream.

TIRAMISÙ

This little Italian sweet is popular the world over. Dry ladyfingers (*savoiardi*) are the ones to use if you can buy them, but if you can't find those you can use stale sponge-like ladyfingers.

MAKES 8 SERVINGS
    2 cups mascarpone, at room temperature
    ½ cup confectioners' sugar
    1 cup heavy cream, chilled
    1 teaspoon vanilla extract
    1½ cups cool, brewed espresso coffee, or 1 tablespoon
        instant espresso dissolved in 1½ cups boiling water
    ⅓ cup sweet marsala
    1 (7-ounce) package Italian dry ladyfingers (*savoiardi*)
    1 ounce bittersweet chocolate

In a medium bowl, gently work the mascarpone and confectioners' sugar together until smooth. In a chilled medium bowl, whip the cream together with the vanilla extract until soft peaks form. Fold the whipped cream into the mascarpone.

In a shallow dish, mix together the espresso and the marsala. One at a time, dip about half of the ladyfingers very briefly in the espresso mixture on both sides, just to moisten (do not soak them), then arrange in a single layer in an 7- by 11-inch serving dish. Spread with half of the mascarpone mixture. Moisten the remaining ladyfingers, and make a second layer, then spread with the remaining mascarpone mixture. Cover tightly with plastic wrap and refrigerate for at least 4 hours or overnight. When ready to serve, using the coarse holes of a cheese grater, grate the chocolate over the top.

MERINGUE CUPS WITH FRESH FRUIT

This is a sumptuous dessert, to be sure, but one that also enjoys the virtue of being low-fat. With the substitution of 1 cup sweetened whipped cream for the orange liqueur, it can be transformed into Pavlova, the beloved Australian sweet.

MAKES 6 SERVINGS
    3 cups mixed fresh fruit, such as sliced strawberries
        and chunks of mango
    2 tablespoons orange-flavored liqueur, such as
        Grand Marnier
    1 tablespoon granulated sugar

Meringue Cups
3 large egg whites, at room temperature
⅛ teaspoon cream of tartar
¾ cup granulated sugar
½ teaspoon vanilla extract

Preheat the oven to 250°F. Line a baking sheet with parchment paper or aluminum foil. Draw six 3-inch circles on the paper.

To make the meringue cups, in a large bowl, beat the egg whites at low speed until foamy. Add the cream of tartar and increase the speed to high. Beat until soft peaks form. Gradually beat in the sugar, and beat until very stiff, shiny peaks form. Beat in the vanilla. Transfer the meringue to a pastry bag fitted with a large plain tube (Number 5). Pipe a flat spiral of meringue inside each of the circles on the baking sheet, to form the bases. Pipe one or two rings, on top of each other, on the edge of each base, to make the wall of the cups. Or, simply drop six mounds of meringue onto the parchment paper, and form into cups with the back of a tablespoon dipped into water. Bake until the meringues are set but not browned, about 45 minutes. Let the meringues stand in the turned-off oven until crisp, at least 1 hour. (The meringue cups can be baked up to 1 day ahead, and kept, uncovered, at room temperature.)

In a bowl, toss the fruit with the liqueur and sugar. Fill the meringue cups with the fruit, and serve.

HOT RASPBERRY SOUFFLÉ

Here's a low-fat dessert that is no less delicious for its healthy profile. Soufflés are one of the most dramatic of all dishes, and always win praise for the cook.

MAKES 4 SERVINGS
Butter and granulated sugar, for the soufflé dish
3 cups fresh raspberries
½ cup granulated sugar
1 tablespoon lemon juice
5 large egg whites, at room temperature

Preheat the oven to 375°F. Lightly butter a 2-quart soufflé dish, then dust with sugar, tapping out the excess sugar. In a blender, purée the raspberries with the sugar and lemon juice. Strain through a fine sieve to remove the seeds. Pour the raspberry sauce into a medium saucepan and bring to a simmer over medium heat. Transfer ¾ cup of the sauce to a small saucepan and set aside.

In a large bowl, beat the egg whites at low speed until foamy. Increase the heat to high and beat until soft peaks form. Fold the beaten egg whites into the purée in the larger saucepan. Pour into the prepared dish. Bake until the top of the soufflé is browned and a long wooden skewer inserted in the center comes out clean, 20 to 25 minutes.

Reheat the raspberry sauce in the small saucepan. Present the soufflé at the table and serve, spooning some of the warm sauce over each portion.

BREAD AND BUTTER PUDDING

This is one of the best ways to use day-old bread.

MAKES 8 SERVINGS
6 slices day-old, firm white sandwich bread, crusts removed
3 tablespoons unsalted butter, at room temperature
⅓ cup raisins
3 large eggs
⅓ cup granulated sugar
⅛ teaspoon ground cinnamon
1 cup milk
1 cup light cream or half-and-half

Lightly butter a 1-quart baking dish. Butter the bread slices on one side. Buttered side up, layer the bread in the dish, sprinkling each layer with the raisins. In a medium bowl, whisk the eggs with 3 tablespoons of the sugar and the cinnamon. Gradually whisk in the milk and cream. Pour over the bread and let stand for 1 hour.

Preheat the oven to 275°F. Sprinkle the pudding with the remaining sugar. Bake until a knife inserted in the center comes out clean and the top is puffed and golden, 1 to 1¼ hours. Serve warm or chilled.

RICE PUDDING

The bay leaf adds an unusual, elusive flavor to this simple baked rice pudding.

MAKES 4 TO 6 SERVINGS
7 tablespoons short-grain rice, or use Arborio rice
2½ cups milk
2 tablespoons heavy cream
1 bay leaf
¼ cup vanilla sugar, or ¼ cup granulated sugar and 1 teaspoon vanilla extract

Preheat the oven to 300°F. Lightly butter a 1-quart baking dish. Put the rice in the dish. In a medium saucepan, heat the milk and cream with the bay leaf over medium heat until bubbles appear around the edge. Remove from the heat and let stand for 5 minutes. Pour the mixture over the rice, and stir in the sugar.

Bake until the pudding is thick and creamy and the rice is very tender, about 2 hours.

STRAWBERRY-CHOCOLATE TRUFFLES

Use mellow-flavored Dutch-processed cocoa for coating these melt-in-the-mouth truffles.

MAKES ABOUT 30 TRUFFLES

6 tablespoons unsalted butter, cut up
8 ounces good bittersweet chocolate, finely chopped
¼ cup strawberry preserves
2 tablespoons strawberry liqueur or Cognac
⅓ cup Dutch-processed cocoa powder

In a double boiler insert set over a saucepan of hot water, melt the butter. Add the chocolate and melt, stirring. Remove from the heat, and whisk in the strawberry preserves and liqueur. Cool, cover with plastic wrap, and chill until firm, at least 2 hours.

Using a melon baller, scoop out 1 tablespoon of the chocolate mixture for each truffle. (If the mixture is too firm, leave at room temperature to soften.) Roll between your palms into balls, and roll in the cocoa to coat. Keep refrigerated, in a covered container, until ready to serve. The truffles can be kept like this for up to 5 days or frozen for up to 1 month.

PINE NUT PRALINES

In New Orleans, pralines are made with pecans. This delicious Southwest version uses pine nuts instead.

MAKES ABOUT 2 DOZEN

3 cups packed light brown sugar
1 tablespoon unsalted butter
1 cup pine nuts
1 teaspoon vanilla extract

Line a work area with waxed paper. In a medium, heavy-bottomed saucepan, with a candy thermometer attached, combine the sugar, butter, and ¼ cup water. Bring to a boil and cook until the thermometer reads 238°F (soft-ball stage). Stir in the pine nuts and vanilla. Remove from the heat, and stir until the mixture is opaque and thickened, but still pourable. Drop from a heaping tablespoon onto the waxed paper to form small patties about 2½ inches wide. Let cool completely. Keep in an airtight container at room temperature for up to 5 days.

MACADAMIA-COCONUT CRUNCH

The texture of this golden candy is similar to toffee or brittle, but the flavor goes Hawaiian with macadamia nuts and coconut. If you can find it, substitute unsweetened coconut ribbons for the sweetened flaked coconut—it gives a better look and texture.

MAKES ABOUT 2 POUNDS

1 cup sweetened flaked coconut
2 cups granulated sugar
1 cup light corn syrup
1 cup (2 sticks) unsalted butter
2 teaspoons baking soda
1 teaspoon vanilla extract
2 cups salted macadamia nuts, coarsely chopped

Preheat the oven to 400°F. Spread the coconut on a baking sheet and bake, stirring often, until lightly toasted, about 5 minutes. Let cool completely.

Lightly butter two baking sheets. Butter a 3-quart saucepan and attach a candy thermometer. Put the sugar, corn syrup, butter, and ½ cup water in the saucepan, and bring to a boil over high heat, stirring constantly to dissolve the sugar. Stop stirring, and continue cooking until the thermometer reads 295°F (hard-crack stage). Remove from the heat and immediately sift the baking soda over the mixture. Add the vanilla and stir gently. (Be careful, because the mixture will froth up.) Stir in the toasted coconut and macadamia nuts. Quickly pour onto the prepared baking sheets and tilt them to spread the crunch into a layer about ½ inch thick. Let cool completely. Break into pieces of random size and shape. The crunch can be kept, in an airtight container at room temperature, for up to 1 week.

CASHEW ROCKY ROAD

This is one of the most popular of all American candies, and certainly one of the easiest to make. Other nuts, such as walnuts, peanuts, or pecans, can be used instead of the cashews.

MAKES ABOUT 2 POUNDS

1 pound milk chocolate, coarsely chopped
8 ounces large marshmallows, snipped with scissors into quarters
1 cup unsalted cashews, coarsely chopped

Lightly butter a baking sheet. In a double boiler insert set over a saucepan of hot, not simmering, water, heat the chocolate until almost completely melted. Remove from the heat, and stir until the chocolate is melted and smooth. Let cool until barely tepid (if the chocolate is too hot, the marshmallows will melt when added). Fold in the marshmallows and cashews. Spread out on the prepared baking sheet in a thick layer about 12 inches square. Refrigerate until completely chilled and firm. To serve, cut into squares with a sharp knife. The candy can be kept, in an airtight container stored at room temperature, for up to 1 week.

Frozen Desserts

SCENTED VANILLA ICE CREAM

This ice cream is a beautiful golden-yellow, and is scented deliciously with coriander and lemon zest along with the vanilla.

MAKES ABOUT 1½ QUARTS

6 large egg yolks
¾ cup plus 2 tablespoons granulated sugar
1¼ cups milk
1¼ cups light cream or half-and-half
1 vanilla bean, split lengthwise, or 1 teaspoon
   vanilla extract
1 (3-inch) strip lemon zest
1 teaspoon coriander seeds
⅔ cup heavy cream, chilled

In a double boiler insert, whisk the egg yolks with the sugar until the mixture is light in color and frothy. In a medium saucepan, heat the milk and light cream with the vanilla bean until bubbles form around the edge. Remove the vanilla bean and set aside. Gradually stir the hot liquid into the egg mixture. Return the vanilla bean, and add the lemon zest and coriander seeds. Set the insert over a saucepan of hot, not simmering, water. Stirring constantly with a wooden spoon, cook until the custard is thick enough to coat the spoon (an instant-read thermometer will read about 185°F), 5 to 10 minutes. If using vanilla extract, stir it in now. Strain into a medium bowl set in a larger bowl of ice water. Let stand until chilled, stirring often.

   In a chilled medium bowl, whip the heavy cream until it is stiff, then whisk the cream into the custard. Transfer to the container of an ice cream machine and freeze according to the manufacturer's instructions. Pack the ice cream into a container, cover, and let harden in the freezer for at least 4 hours before serving. Transfer the ice cream to the refrigerator about 20 minutes before serving, in order to allow it to soften slightly.

Scented Vanilla Gelato: An Italian-style ice cream, with a slightly less smooth texture but excellent flavor, this can be made without an ice cream machine. (This technique can be applied to any ice cream recipe.) Chill a 9- by 13-inch metal baking pan in the freezer until very cold. Pour the mixture into the chilled pan, and freeze until partially frozen, about 1½ hours. Whisk the mixture well to break up any ice crystals, or transfer to a food processor fitted with the metal blade and process. Repeat the freezing and whisking procedures two more times. After the third whisking, let the ice cream freeze until it can be scooped. The procedure will take about 6 hours.

STRAWBERRY ICE CREAM

Try to use the sweetest berries to make this summer treat. Taste the mixture before it goes into the ice cream machine—it should be sweeter than you want the finished ice cream to be.

MAKES ABOUT 1 QUART

3 large egg yolks
¾ cup granulated sugar, plus more as needed
⅔ cup milk
⅔ cup heavy or light cream
1½ pints fresh strawberries, hulled

In a double boiler insert, whisk the yolks with the sugar until light in color and frothy. In a medium saucepan, bring the milk and cream to a simmer. Gradually stir into the egg mixture. Set the insert over a saucepan of hot water. Stirring with a wooden spoon, cook until the custard is thick enough to coat it (an instant-read thermometer will read about 185°F), 5 to 10 minutes. Strain into a medium bowl set in a bowl of ice water. Leave until chilled, stirring often.

   In a food processor fitted with the metal blade or in a blender, purée the berries. Whisk into the chilled custard. Taste and whisk in more sugar, if needed. Transfer to the container of an ice cream machine and freeze according to the manufacturer's instructions. Pack the ice cream into a container, cover, and harden in the freezer for at least 4 hours. Or, make a strawberry gelato, freezing according to the directions for Scented Vanilla Gelato. Transfer the ice cream or gelato to the refrigerator about 20 minutes before serving.

Raspberry Ice Cream: Substitute raspberries for the strawberries, and, if you wish, add 2 teaspoons framboise *eau-de-vie* or other raspberry-flavored liqueur.

COCONUT ICE CREAM

This makes an exotic finale to a Caribbean or Indian meal. Desiccated coconut is available at health food stores. If necessary, use flaked coconut, rinsed under hot water to remove the sugar coating, and drained.

MAKES ABOUT 1 QUART

1¼ cups milk
½ vanilla bean, split lengthwise, or ½ teaspoon
   vanilla extract
Pared zest of ½ lime
½ cup unsweetened desiccated coconut
5 large egg yolks
½ cup granulated sugar
⅔ cup heavy cream
A pinch of salt

In a medium heavy-bottomed saucepan, heat the milk with the vanilla bean and lime zest over medium heat until bubbles form around the edge. Remove from the heat. Stir in the coconut, cover the pan, and let stand for 30 minutes. Strain through a fine sieve into a bowl. Discard the vanilla bean and lime zest, then press the coconut in the sieve to extract all the remaining milk; discard the coconut.

In a double boiler insert, whisk the yolks with the sugar until light in color and frothy. Gradually whisk in the flavored milk. Set the insert over a saucepan of hot water. Stirring with a wooden spoon, cook until the custard is thick enough to coat the spoon (an instant-read thermometer will read about 185°F), 5 to 10 minutes. Strain into a medium bowl, and stir in the cream, and salt. (If using vanilla extract, add it now.) Place the bowl in a larger bowl of ice water and let stand until chilled, stirring often.

Transfer to the container of an ice cream machine and freeze according to the manufacturer's instructions. Pack the ice cream into a container, cover, and let harden in the freezer for at least 4 hours before serving. Or, make a coconut gelato, freezing according to the directions for Scented Vanilla Gelato. Transfer the ice cream or gelato to the refrigerator about 20 minutes before serving, to allow it to soften slightly.

CASSATA

Many Sicilian desserts have their origins in Arabic cooking. For example, their ice cream specialty, cassata, is actually named for a certain type of Arabic bowl.

MAKES 6 TO 8 SERVINGS
    1 pint high-quality vanilla ice cream, slightly softened
    1 pint high-quality chocolate ice cream,
        slightly softened
    ⅔ cup heavy cream, chilled
    ½ cup confectioners' sugar
    ¾ cup chopped mixed candied fruit
    1 large egg white, at room temperature

Using a metal spoon dipped in hot water, spread the vanilla ice cream in a thick, even layer in a 1½-quart melon-shaped metal mold or bowl. Press a piece of plastic wrap onto the surface of the ice cream, and freeze until it is firm. Cover the vanilla ice cream with the chocolate ice cream in an even layer, leaving a well in the center for the filling. Cover and freeze again until firm.

In a chilled medium bowl, whip the cream with the confectioners' sugar until just before it reaches soft peak stage. Stir in the candied fruit. In a small bowl, beat the egg white until it forms soft peaks, and fold into the cream. Spoon into the well in the ice-cream-lined mold. Cover tightly and freeze until firm. To serve, dip the mold briefly in hot water, and invert the cassata onto a well-chilled serving plate. Refrigerate the cassata for about 20 minutes, to allow it to soften slightly, then cut into wedges.

RASPBERRY AND LIME SHERBET
Sherbets generally feature fruit juices frozen with milk. This combination of raspberry and lime is deliciously tangy.

MAKES ABOUT 1 QUART
    1½ cups fresh or frozen raspberries
    2 cups milk
    ½ cup granulated sugar
    Grated zest of 1 lime
    2 tablespoons lime juice

In a food processor fitted with the metal blade, or a blender, purée the raspberries. Strain through a fine sieve to remove the seeds. You should have 1 cup purée. In a large bowl, combine the raspberry purée with the milk, sugar, and lime zest and juice. Pour into the container of an ice cream machine and freeze according to the manufacturer's instructions. Pack into a container, cover, and let harden in the freezer for at least 4 hours before serving. Transfer the sherbet to the refrigerator about 30 minutes before serving, to allow it to soften slightly.

ORANGE SORBET
Be sure to make this with freshly squeezed juices. If you can find them during their short winter season, use garnet-hued blood oranges.

MAKES ABOUT 1 QUART
    2⅓ cups fresh orange juice
    3 tablespoons fresh lemon juice
    1 cup confectioners' sugar

Combine all of the ingredients, and whisk to dissolve the sugar. Strain into the container of an ice cream machine and freeze according to the manufacturer's instructions. Pack the sorbet into a container, cover, and let harden in the freezer for at least 4 hours before serving. Transfer the sorbet to the refrigerator about 30 minutes before serving, to allow it to soften slightly.

Or, make an orange granita, freezing according to the directions for Coffee Granita.

SORBETS

Frozen Desserts/Pastries

GRAPEFRUIT SORBET

One of the most refreshing, sophisticated ways to serve this sorbet for a dinner party is to put a scoop of the sorbet in a chilled martini glass, and then to drizzle Campari over it.

MAKES ABOUT 1 QUART
   ½ cup plus 1 tablespoon granulated sugar
   2 cups fresh grapefruit juice

In a saucepan, dissolve the sugar in 3 tablespoons water over high heat, and bring to a boil. Boil for 5 minutes. Transfer to a medium bowl and leave to cool completely. Whisk in the fresh grapefruit juice. Strain into the container of an ice cream machine and freeze according to the manufacturer's instructions. Pack the sorbet into a container, cover, and let harden in the freezer for at least 4 hours before serving. Transfer the sorbet to the refrigerator about 30 minutes before you wish to serve it, to allow it to soften slightly.

   Alternatively, make a grapefruit granita, freezing according to the directions for Coffee Granita.

MELON SORBET

Be sure the melons are sweet and full of juice—underripe melons won't do.

MAKES ABOUT 1 QUART
   2 (1-pound) ripe cantaloupe or
      honeydew melons
   2 cups confectioners' sugar
   ¼ cup lemon juice

Cut the melons in half and then discard the seeds. Using a large spoon, scoop out the flesh from both melons. In a food processor fitted with the metal blade, purée the melon flesh with the sugar and lemon juice. Transfer to the container of an ice cream machine and freeze according to the manufacturer's instructions. Pack the sorbet into a container, cover, and let harden in the freezer for at least 4 hours before serving. Transfer the sorbet to the refrigerator about 30 minutes before you wish to serve it, to allow it to soften slightly.

COFFEE GRANITA

This is the cooling late-morning favorite which many tourists (and of course the Italians) enjoy at the myriad pavement cafés in Rome and other big cities. The coffee must be really strong, preferably brewed from espresso or Viennese Roast.

MAKES ABOUT 1 QUART
   ½ cup plus 1 tablespoon granulated sugar
   2½ cups hot, very strong brewed coffee
   1¼ cups heavy cream
   2 tablespoons Tia Maria (optional)

Place a 9- by 13-inch metal baking dish in the freezer and chill while making the coffee mixture. In a bowl, dissolve the sugar in the coffee, stirring. Place the bowl in a larger bowl of ice water and leave to chill. Pour into the chilled pan. Freeze until the edges of the coffee mixture are icy and semi-solid, about 1 hour.

   Using a fork, mix the icy crystals at the edge into the still-liquid center. Do not use a whisk: you want to coax ice crystals into forming. Return to the freezer and freeze until the edges are icy again, about 30 minutes. Mix with a fork again. Continue freezing, mixing with a fork about every 30 minutes, until the mixture has frozen into a slush of separate, soft crystals of pale-brown coffee ice, about 2 hours.

   In a chilled medium bowl, whip the cream until it forms soft peaks. To serve, layer the granita and whipped cream in well-chilled goblets, drizzling the layers with the optional Tia Maria.

———————— • ————————

BASIC PIE DOUGH

This is a superlative pie dough, with a crispness and flavor provided by the butter and flakiness from the vegetable shortening.

MAKES ENOUGH FOR ONE 9-INCH PIE SHELL
   1½ cups all-purpose flour
   ¼ teaspoon salt
   6 tablespoons unsalted butter, cut into small
      pieces, chilled
   2 tablespoons vegetable shortening, cut into small
      pieces, chilled

Place the flour and salt in a medium bowl. Add the butter and shortening. Using a pastry blender or two knives, cut the fats into the flour until the mixture is crumbly with some pieces about the size of small peas. Stirring with a fork, gradually add about ⅓ cup ice water to moisten the dough—it should be just moist enough to hold together when pressed between your fingertips. Gather up the dough into a flat disk and wrap in plastic wrap. Chill for at least 20 minutes before rolling out.

Double Crust Pie Dough: Use 2 cups all-purpose flour, ¼ teaspoon salt, 7 tablespoons unsalted butter, and 3 tablespoons vegetable shortening. Moisten with a scant ½ cup ice water.

SWEET TART DOUGH

Use this for French-style dessert tarts.

MAKES ENOUGH FOR ONE 9-INCH TART SHELL

1¼ cups all-purpose flour
2 tablespoons granulated sugar
⅛ teaspoon salt
6 tablespoons unsalted butter, cut into small
    pieces, chilled
1 large egg yolk

Mix the flour, sugar, and salt in a medium bowl. Add the butter. Using a pastry blender or two knives, cut the fats into the flour until the mixture is crumbly with some pieces about the size of small peas. In a small bowl, mix the egg yolk and 3 tablespoons ice water. Stirring with a fork, gradually add enough of the yolk mixture to moisten the dough—it should be just moist enough to hold together when pressed between your fingertips. Gather up the dough into a flat disk and wrap in plastic wrap. Chill for at least 20 minutes before rolling out.

ROUGH PUFF PASTRY DOUGH

This is a variation of classic French puff pastry. It takes much less time to make than the French version, but you'll still end up with a light, flaky pastry that has 81 paper-thin layers!

MAKES ENOUGH FOR 2 DOUBLE-CRUST 9-INCH PIES

2 cups all-purpose flour
¼ teaspoon salt
6 tablespoons unsalted butter, cut into
    ½-inch cubes, chilled
6 tablespoons vegetable shortening, cut into
    ½-inch cubes, chilled

Mix the flour and salt in a large bowl. Add the butter and shortening. Using a pastry blender or two knives, cut in the fats until they are in pieces about ¼-inch square. Stirring with a fork, gradually add about ½ cup ice water, to make a lumpy dough. Cover with plastic wrap and refrigerate for 30 minutes.

Turn out the dough onto a well-floured work surface, and dust the top of the dough with flour. Roll out the dough into a ¼-inch-thick rectangle. Fold the dough into thirds, like a business letter, brushing off the excess flour as you do so. With the rolling pin, gently press the edges of the dough rectangle together to seal in the air. Wrap in plastic wrap and chill for 15 minutes.

Repeat the rolling, folding and chilling procedure three more times. Wrap and chill the dough for at least 15 minutes before using.

CREAM PUFF DOUGH

Cream puff dough is called *pâte au choux* ("cabbage dough") in French because baked cream puffs look like little cabbages. Use it for éclairs, profiteroles, and cream puffs, as well as puffs to be filled with savory mixtures such as herbed cream cheese.

MAKES ENOUGH FOR 10 TO 12 3-INCH CREAM PUFFS

8 tablespoons (1 stick) unsalted butter, cut into pieces
¼ teaspoon granulated sugar
¼ teaspoon salt, plus a pinch for the glazing mixture
1 cup plus all-purpose flour
4 large eggs, at room temperature

In a medium heavy-bottomed saucepan, combine 1 cup water, the butter, sugar, and ¼ teaspoon salt. Bring to a boil over medium heat, stirring occasionally to help the butter melt. Remove from the heat and let cool slightly, then sift the flour into the saucepan. Beat with a wooden spoon until smooth. Return to medium-low heat and continue beating until the mixture pulls away from the pan sides and forms a ball on the spoon, 1 to 2 minutes.

Remove from the heat and cool slightly. Break an egg into the saucepan and beat vigorously until the egg is absorbed. Beat in a second and third egg the same way. Beat the fourth egg in a small bowl. Beat in just enough of the fourth egg to make a soft dough that holds its shape—you may not need the whole egg. Mix the remaining beaten egg with a pinch of salt; cover and set aside for glazing the shaped dough before baking. Use the dough while still warm.

PRE-BAKING PASTRY SHELLS

To prevent the bottom of a pastry shell from becoming soggy, it is often suggested that the pastry is baked (either partially or fully) before the filling is added.

Roll out the pastry dough and use to line the pie or tart pan. Prick the bottom of the pastry shell a few times with a fork. Line the pastry shell with lightly buttered aluminum foil, buttered side down, or with parchment paper. (To discourage shrinkage, freeze the lined pan for about 30 minutes before baking.) Fill to the brim with about 2 cups of dried beans, rice, or ceramic pie weights, to weight down the dough and keep it from bubbling up or collapsing when heated in the oven. It is especially important to bank the beans against the sides of the pastry shell.

Bake in a preheated 400°F oven until the pastry looks set, 8 to 10 minutes. Lift off the foil or paper and beans. For a partially baked shell, continue baking until the pastry has lost its raw look but is not dry, 3 to 5 more minutes. For a completely baked shell, bake until lightly browned, about 10 more minutes.

1

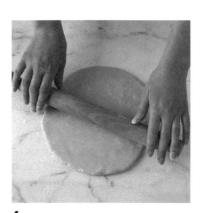

2

Making pie dough and lining a pie pan

1 Combine the flour and salt in a bowl. Using a pastry blender, cut in the butter and/or shortening.

2 Gradually add just enough ice water to moisten the mixture.

3 Gather the dough into a flat disk, wrap, and chill for 20 minutes.

4 On a floured surface, roll out the dough to a round about ⅛ inch thick.

5 Roll the dough around the rolling pin, then unroll it over the pan.

6 Lift the edges of the dough and gently press it over the bottom and up the sides of the pan.

7 For a single-crust pie, cut off the excess dough. For a double-crust pie, trim the dough after adding the top crust.

3

4

5

6

7

Pre-baking a pastry shell

1 Prick the bottom of the pastry shell all over with a fork.

2 Line the pastry shell with foil or parchment paper. Fill with dried beans, rice, or pie weights. Bake until the dough is set, then remove the foil or paper and weights and continue baking until the pastry is partially or completely baked, according to the recipe instructions.

1

2

Making a decorative edge
For a **forked edge**, trim the dough even with the edge of the pan. With the back of a fork, press firmly and evenly all around the edge. If the fork sticks, dip it in flour.

For a **crimped edge**, trim the dough to a ½-inch overhang. Put the tip of one index finger inside the dough edge. With the thumb and finger of your other hand, pinch the dough in a "V". Continue all around the edge.

For a **forked-fluted edge**, trim the dough to a ½-inch overhang. Put one thumb inside the dough edge, and use your other thumb and index finger to press the dough into a flute. Press a fork into each flute.

RHUBARB AND RAISIN PIE

This pie is at its best when served piping hot from the oven, accompanied by a bowl of whipped cream for guests to help themselves.

MAKES 6 SERVINGS
⅓ cup raisins
2 tablespoons tawny or ruby port or red wine
Double-Crust Pie Dough
2 pounds rhubarb, cut into 1-inch lengths
8 tablespoons granulated sugar
2 teaspoons all-purpose flour
1 tablespoon heavy cream or milk

In a small bowl, soak the raisins in the port or the red wine for 30 minutes.

Preheat the oven to 425°F. Divide the dough into two portions, one twice as large as the other. On a lightly floured surface, roll out the larger portion of dough into a ⅛-inch-thick round. Use to line a 9-inch pie pan, letting the excess dough hang over the edges. Fill with the rhubarb. Sprinkle with 7 tablespoons of the sugar and the flour, then add the raisins and their port. Roll out the smaller portion of dough into a ⅛-inch-thick round, and center over the pie. Seal and flute the edges. Make several cuts in the top crust. Lightly brush the top of the pie with the cream, then sprinkle with the remaining 1 tablespoon of sugar.

Bake for 15 minutes, then reduce the oven to 350°F. Continue baking until the filling is bubbling and the crust is nicely golden-brown in color, 20 to 25 more minutes. If the pastry browns too quickly, cover loosely with foil.

PUMPKIN "SOUFFLÉ" PIE

This light-textured version of pumpkin pie is a nice change from the usual, and seems less filling after a holiday meal. The recipe makes a good amount of filling, so try to get the pastry to stand a bit above the edge of the pie pan, to contain it all. If you still have a little too much filling for the pie, use what you need and pour the rest into a buttered ramekin, bake at 350°F until set, about 30 minutes, and enjoy it as the cook's treat.

MAKES 8 SERVINGS
Basic Pie Dough
1¾ cups canned pumpkin (15-ounce can)
¾ cup granulated sugar
½ cup packed light brown sugar
2 tablespoons all-purpose flour
2 teaspoons ground cinnamon
1 teaspoon ground ginger
1 teaspoon grated nutmeg
¼ teaspoon ground cloves
¼ teaspoon salt
1⅓ cups evaporated milk
3 large eggs, at room temperature
Sweetened whipped cream, for serving

Preheat the oven to 400°F. Roll out the dough to a ⅛-inch-thick round, and use to line a 10-inch deep-dish glass pie pan. Fold the excess dough over into the pan. Press the dough against the sides of the pan, pushing gently so that the dough rises to stand about ½ inch above the edge of the pan. Partially bake the pastry shell. Set aside; leave the oven on at 400°F.

In a medium bowl, whisk together all of the remaining ingredients, except the eggs and whipped cream, until smooth. In another medium bowl, beat the eggs at high speed until very light and tripled in volume, about 3 minutes. Fold the eggs into the pumpkin mixture. Pour into the pastry shell. Bake for 15 minutes, then reduce the heat to 350°F. Continue baking until a knife inserted into the filling 2 inches from the center comes out clean, 40 to 50 minutes. The center will seem slightly unset when shaken, but will firm upon standing. Let cool completely on a wire cake rack. Then cover with plastic wrap and refrigerate until chilled, at least 2 hours or overnight. Serve the pie chilled or at room temperature, with whipped cream.

SWEET POTATO AND ORANGE PIE

Sweet potato pie is to Southerners what pumpkin pie is to Yankees—an absolutely essential part of a holiday meal. This version gets a fillip from orange marmalade. Note that the recipe uses orange-fleshed sweet potatoes, which may be called yams, depending on where you live.

MAKES 6 TO 8 SERVINGS

Basic Pie Dough

2 medium orange-fleshed sweet potatoes
    (1 pound), unpeeled

2 tablespoons unsalted butter

½ cup orange marmalade

⅓ cup packed dark brown sugar

¼ teaspoon ground cinnamon

¼ teaspoon salt

2 large eggs plus 1 large yolk, beaten together

1 cup half-and-half

About 20 pecan halves

1 cup heavy cream, chilled

2 tablespoons granulated sugar

1 tablespoon orange-flavored liqueur (optional)

Preheat the oven to 400°F. Roll out the dough to a ⅛-inch-thick round, and use to line a 10-inch deep-dish glass pie dish. Partially bake the pastry shell. Leave the oven on at 400°F.

In a large saucepan of boiling salted water, cook the whole sweet potatoes until they are tender, about 30 minutes. Drain and rinse under cold water until easy to handle, then peel and place in a medium bowl. Add the butter and mash until smooth. Stir in the orange marmalade, brown sugar, cinnamon, and salt. Beat in the eggs and half-and-half. Pour into the pie shell and smooth the top. Arrange pecan halves around the edge of the pie.

Bake for 10 minutes, then reduce the oven temperature to 350°F. Continue baking until a knife inserted into the center of the filling comes out clean, about 45 more minutes. Leave to cool completely on a wire cake rack.

In a chilled medium bowl, whip the cream with the sugar and optional liqueur until soft peaks form. Serve the pie at room temperature or chilled, along with the whipped cream.

HONEY PECAN TART

Honey makes a nice change from corn syrup in this pecan pie. Serve it warm with vanilla ice cream. A delicious variation can be made by substituting walnuts for the pecans.

MAKES 6 SERVINGS

Sweet Tart Dough

6 tablespoons unsalted butter, at room temperature

⅓ cup packed light brown sugar

1 tablespoon granulated sugar

3 large eggs

¼ cup honey

1 teaspoon vanilla extract

A pinch of salt

2 cups pecan halves

Preheat the oven to 400°F. Roll out the dough and use to line a 9-inch pie pan. Partially bake the pastry shell. Increase the oven temperature to 425°F.

In a medium bowl, beat the butter, brown sugar, and granulated sugar together until smooth and fluffy, about 5 minutes. One at a time, beat in the eggs. Beat in the honey, vanilla, and salt.

Fill the pastry shell with the pecan halves. Pour in the honey mixture. Bake until a knife inserted in the center of the filling comes out clean, about 30 minutes. Let cool slightly, and serve warm.

TROPICAL CREAM PIE

Here's an irresistible combination—a banana and coconut pie with a crystallized ginger and whipped cream topping.

MAKES 8 SERVINGS

¾ cup plus 2 tablespoons granulated sugar

¼ cup cornstarch

3 cups milk

4 large egg yolks

1 cup unsweetened desiccated coconut

1 tablespoon unsalted butter

1 teaspoon vanilla extract

1 (9-inch) baked pie shell, made with Basic Pie Dough

2 ripe medium bananas, sliced

1 cup heavy cream

¼ cup finely chopped crystallized ginger

In a medium, heavy-bottomed saucepan, whisk ¾ cup of the sugar and the cornstarch to combine. Gradually whisk in the milk until the mixture is smooth. Bring to a boil over medium heat, stirring constantly, then reduce the heat to low and cook for 2 minutes. In a small bowl, beat the egg yolks. Gradually stir in about 1 cup of the hot milk mixture. Pour into the saucepan and cook, stirring, for 2 minutes. Stir in the coconut, butter, and vanilla. Transfer to a medium bowl and cover with plastic wrap, pressing the wrap directly on the surface of the filling. Pierce several holes in the wrap with a sharp knife. Cool to room temperature.

Cover the bottom of the baked pie shell with the banana slices. Spoon in the coconut filling and spread evenly (do not stir the filling, or it will thin out). Cover with plastic wrap and refrigerate until chilled, at least 2 hours. (The pie can be prepared up to 1 day ahead, and kept, covered, in the refrigerator.)

In a chilled medium bowl, whip the heavy cream with the remaining 2 tablespoons of sugar until soft peaks form. Spread over the top of the pie. Sprinkle with the chopped ginger. Serve the pie chilled.

DOUBLE-COOKED, TWO-APPLE PIE

Precooking the filling before baking gives you a plump pie full of apples. With two varieties of apples, you can have a blend of different textures and flavors.

MAKES 8 SERVINGS

4 tablespoons unsalted butter

5 Granny Smith apples, peeled, cored, and cut into ½-inch-thick wedges

5 Golden Delicious apples, peeled, cored, and cut into ½-inch-thick wedges

¼ cup granulated sugar

½ teaspoon ground cinnamon

2 tablespoons all-purpose flour

Double-Crust Pie Dough

In a large frying pan, heat the butter over medium heat. Add the apples, sugar, and cinnamon. Cook, stirring often, until the apples have reduced in volume by about half, 5 to 7 minutes. (If necessary, do this in batches.) Transfer to a large bowl and let cool completely. Stir in the flour.

Preheat the oven to 375°F. Divide the dough into two portions, one twice as large as the other. Roll out the larger portion of the dough into a round about ⅛ inch thick, and use to line a 10-inch pie pan. Fill the pastry shell with the cooled apples. Roll out the smaller portion of dough into a round about ⅛ inch thick, and center over the pie. Seal and flute the edges. Cut an "X" in the center of the top crust. Bake until the filling is bubbling and the crust is golden-brown, 35 to 45 minutes. If the pastry browns too quickly, cover loosely with foil.

STRAWBERRY GALETTE

A galette is a kind of free-form tart. The pastry base here can also be topped with raspberries.

MAKES 8 SERVINGS

Sweet Tart Dough

1 egg yolk beaten with 1 teaspoon milk

3 tablespoons raspberry or red-currant jelly

Grated zest of ½ orange

2 pints fresh strawberries, hulled

Preheat the oven to 400°F. Lightly butter a large baking sheet or metal pizza pan. On a lightly floured work surface, roll out the dough to a ⅛-inch-thick round. If you wish, trim the dough into a perfect circle, although part of a galette's charm is in its rustic look. Transfer to the prepared sheet. Prick the dough all over with a fork, and lightly brush with some of the egg mixture. Bake until crisp and golden-brown, about 20 minutes. If the dough bubbles up while baking, deflate it by piercing with a fork. Let cool slightly on the sheet. If you wish, slide the pastry base onto a flat serving dish.

In a small saucepan, warm the jelly with the orange zest over medium heat until melted, then bring just to a boil. Brush the pastry with the melted jelly. Arrange the strawberries, pointed ends up, on the pastry base in concentric circles. Serve warm or cool.

Lemon Galette: Spread the pastry base with about 1½ cups of warm, freshly made Lemon Curd.

LEMON MERINGUE TART

Here's a wonderful European-style reworking of an American specialty.

MAKES 6 TO 8 SERVINGS

1 (9-inch) baked tart shell, made with Sweet Tart Dough

Lemon Curd

3 large egg whites, at room temperature

½ teaspoon vanilla extract

¼ teaspoon cream of tartar

6 tablespoons granulated sugar

Preheat the oven to 350°F. Fill the tart shell with the lemon curd, spreading evenly. In a medium bowl, beat the egg whites on low speed until foamy. Add the vanilla and cream of tartar, increase the speed to high, and beat until soft peaks form. Gradually beat in the sugar until stiff, shiny peaks form. Transfer the meringue to a pastry bag fitted with a large open star tube. Randomly pipe large swirls of meringue over the lemon curd. (The lemon curd does not have to be completely covered.) Bake until the meringue is lightly browned, about 10 minutes. The lemon curd will melt slightly, but will firm again when chilled. Let cool, then refrigerate the tart until chilled, about 1 hour. Dip a sharp knife in hot water before each cutting each slice.

APRICOT TART

Make this with sweet, aromatic apricots in the summer, or with drained canned apricots at other times of the year. Thinly sliced apples can also be used.

MAKES 4 SERVINGS
Rough Puff Pastry Dough
1 pound apricots, halved and pitted
¼ cup granulated sugar
4 tablespoons unsalted butter, cut into small pieces

Preheat the oven to 425°F. Cut the pastry dough in half, and save one half for another use. On a lightly floured work surface, roll out the dough into an 8- by 12-inch rectangle about ⅛ inch thick. Using a very sharp knife, trim the edges neatly—they must be cut cleanly, or the pastry won't rise. Transfer the rectangle to a lightly dampened baking sheet. Top with the apricots, cut sides up, arranging them in neat rows and leaving a ½-inch margin around the edges. Press the apricots gently into the pastry. Sprinkle with the sugar, then dot with the butter.

Bake for 10 minutes. Reduce the heat to 400°F, and continue baking until the pastry is browned and the apricots are glazed and beginning to blacken around the edges, about 25 more minutes. Serve warm.

FRENCH ALMOND PIE

This shiny brown puff, called a Pithiviers, is often seen in French *pâtisseries*, decorated with geometric designs, and with the almond filling varying from a smooth honey-colored paste to a chocolate marzipan.

MAKES 8 SERVINGS
Rough Puff Pastry Dough
8 tablespoons (1 stick) unsalted butter, at room temperature

½ cup granulated sugar, plus extra for sprinkling
3 large egg yolks
2 cups ground almonds
⅓ cup heavy cream, chilled
2 teaspoons dark rum or ½ teaspoon grated lemon zest
1 large egg yolk beaten with 2 teaspoons milk, for glazing

Cut the pastry dough in half, and save one half for another use. In a medium bowl, beat the butter with the sugar at medium speed until light in color and texture, about 2 minutes. Add the yolks and beat for 2 more minutes. Stir in the almonds, heavy cream, and rum.

Preheat the oven to 400°F. Dampen a baking sheet or metal pizza pan. Cut the dough into two pieces, one slightly larger than the other. On a lightly floured work surface, roll out the smaller piece into an 8½-inch round about ⅛ inch thick. Transfer to the prepared baking sheet. Spread the almond mixture on the pastry base, leaving a 1-inch border around the edges.

Roll out the other piece of dough into a ⅛-inch-thick round, slightly larger than the first round. Moisten the edges of the first round, then center the second round on top and press the edges together lightly to seal. Trim the edges cleanly with a sharp knife to make a neat circle. With the back of the knife, notch the edge of the dough at 2-inch intervals. Brush the top of the pastry lightly with the egg glaze. Using the tip of a sharp knife, make a crisscross pattern of very shallow lines across the top of the pie. Bake until the pastry is puffed and golden-brown, 35 to 40 minutes. Sprinkle the the pastry with sugar. Let cool completely on the baking sheet before serving.

CHOCOLATE CREAM PUFFS

Light, golden puffs of *pâte au choux* are filled with sweetened cream and topped with a chocolate icing.

MAKES 10 TO 12 CREAM PUFFS
Cream Puff Dough
1 large egg beaten with a pinch of salt, for glazing
2 cups heavy cream
1 tablespoon vanilla sugar, or 1 tablespoon granulated sugar and ½ teaspoon vanilla extract
4 ounces high-quality bittersweet chocolate, finely chopped
2 teaspoons light rum
8 tablespoons (1 stick) unsalted butter, at room temperature

Preheat the oven to 400°F. Lightly dampen two baking sheets. Place heaping tablespoons of the warm dough on the sheets, spacing them well apart. (Or, pipe out

APRICOT TART

mounds of the dough about 1½ inches across and 1 inch high, using a pastry bag fitted with a ½-inch-wide plain tube.) Brush the tops with the leftover beaten egg from making the pastry (or, use freshly made egg glaze), flattening any peaks of dough with the pastry brush.

Bake until the puffs are firm and golden, about 20 minutes. Make a small hole in the bottom of each puff with the tip of a knife, to allow the steam to escape. Transfer to a wire cake rack to cool completely.

In a chilled medium bowl, whip the cream with the vanilla sugar until soft peaks form. Using a serrated knife, slice open the puffs a little, and fill with the whipped cream. (Or, put the cream into the pastry bag fitted with the tube, and pipe into the puffs through the holes in the bottoms.)

To make the icing, melt the chocolate with the rum in a double boiler insert set over a saucepan of hot, not simmering, water. Remove from the heat, and add the butter, 1 tablespoon at a time, stirring to incorporate each addition before adding another. Place the double boiler insert in a bowl of cold water,

and beat the icing with a wooden spoon until thick enough to spread. Spoon the icing over the tops of the puffs, and let cool and set before serving.

AUTUMN FRUIT CRISP

Here fruits are baked with a crumbled pastrylike topping to make an easy, warming dessert. All varieties of apples and pears are suitable, and you can combine them for different results.

MAKES 6 SERVINGS

2 medium apples, peeled, cored, and cut into
    ½-inch-thick wedges
2 medium pears, peeled, cored, and cut into
    ½-inch-thick wedges
½ cup granulated sugar
¼ teaspoon ground cinnamon
Grated zest of 1 lemon
8 tablespoons (1 stick) unsalted butter, in small pieces
⅔ cup all-purpose flour
A pinch of salt
Sweetened whipped cream or vanilla ice cream,
    for serving

Preheat the oven to 350°F. Lightly butter a 2-quart baking dish. Put the apples and pears in the baking dish. Add 2 tablespoons of the sugar, the ground cinnamon, and the grated lemon zest, and toss to mix with the fruit. Dot with 1 tablespoon of the butter.

Put the remaining sugar in a medium bowl with the flour and salt. Add the remaining butter. Using your fingertips, quickly and lightly rub together until the mixture resembles fine bread crumbs. Sprinkle the crumb topping evenly over the fruit.

Bake until the topping is nicely browned and the fruit is tender, about 40 minutes. Serve warm, with whipped cream.

PEACH MELBA COBBLER

Pastry chefs often name desserts made with peaches and raspberries "Melba," after the famous Australian soprano of the Victorian era.

MAKES 8 SERVINGS

3 pounds ripe peaches, peeled, pitted, and sliced into
½-inch-thick wedges
2 cups fresh raspberries
1 cup granulated sugar
4 tablespoons butter, cut into pieces
2 tablespoons cornstarch
Grated zest and juice of 1 lemon
Vanilla ice cream or sweetened whipped cream,
for serving
Cobbler Dough
1¾ cups all-purpose flour
⅓ cup granulated sugar
1 tablespoon baking powder
½ teaspoon salt
8 tablespoons (1 stick) unsalted butter, chilled,
cut into ¼-inch pieces
½ cup milk
1 large egg

Preheat the oven to 400°F. In a 9- by 13-inch baking dish, combine the peaches, raspberries, sugar, butter, cornstarch, and the grated lemon zest and juice. Toss gently together.

To make the dough, in a medium bowl, whisk the flour, sugar, baking powder, and salt to combine. Add the butter, and cut it into the flour with a pastry blender or two knives until the mixture resembles coarse crumbs with some pea-sized pieces of butter. In a small bowl, beat the milk with the egg. Stir enough of the milk and egg mixture into the dry ingredients to make a soft, sticky dough (you may not need all of the liquid, so add it gradually). Drop the dough by large tablespoons randomly over the top of the fruit. Bake until the cobbler topping is browned and the fruit juices are bubbling, about 45 minutes. (If the topping seems to be browning too quickly, cover the cobbler loosely with a sheet of aluminum foil.) Serve the cobbler warm, topped with ice cream.

MANGO SHORTCAKES WITH ORANGE CARAMEL SAUCE

Fresh mangoes make a lovely, refreshing filling for America's favorite shortcake.

MAKES 8 SERVINGS

4 ripe mangoes, peeled and sliced
2 tablespoons lime juice
2 cups heavy cream
3 tablespoons confectioners' sugar
1 teaspoon vanilla extract
2 cups Orange Caramel Sauce
Shortcakes
1 cup cake flour (not self-rising)
1 cup all-purpose flour
2 tablespoons granulated sugar
1 tablespoon baking powder
½ teaspoon salt
8 tablespoons (1 stick) unsalted butter, chilled,
cut into small pieces
¾ cup milk

Preheat the oven to 400°F. To make the shortcakes, in a medium bowl, whisk the cake flour, all-purpose flour, sugar, baking powder, and salt to combine. Add the butter, and cut into the flour mixture with a pastry blender or two knives until the mixture resembles coarse crumbs. Add the milk and stir until just combined. Knead lightly in the bowl just to form a soft, sticky dough. Turn out onto a lightly floured work surface and pat out until ½ inch thick. Using a 3½-inch cookie cutter, cut out rounds and transfer them to an ungreased baking sheet. When you have used up the dough, gather up the scraps, knead lightly, and cut out more rounds. Bake the shortcakes until golden-brown, about 15 minutes. Let cool slightly.

Meanwhile, in a medium bowl, combine the mangoes and the lime juice. In a chilled medium bowl, whip the cream with the confectioners' sugar and vanilla extract until soft peaks form.

Using a serrated knife, split the shortcakes horizontally. On each plate, pour ¼ cup of the caramel sauce. Place a shortcake bottom on each plate, top with mangoes and whipped cream, and then replace the shortcake top. Serve immediately.

Cakes and Cookies

YELLOW LAYER CAKE WITH LEMON BUTTER FROSTING

Here is the classic American layer cake that even beginning bakers can master. Instead of trying to decorate with fancy frosting flowers and swirls, just garnish simply with fresh flowers. However, be sure they are nontoxic and unsprayed—violets, nasturtiums, and roses are good choices.

MAKES 8 TO 12 SERVINGS

Cake

10 tablespoons (1 stick plus 2 tablespoons) unsalted butter, at room temperature

1¾ cups granulated sugar

2 large eggs, at room temperature

1 teaspoon vanilla extract

3 cups cake flour

2½ teaspoons baking powder

¼ teaspoon salt

1¼ cups milk

Lemon Butter Frosting

6 tablespoons unsalted butter, at room temperature

4 cups confectioners' sugar (1 pound), sifted

Grated zest of 1 lemon

1 tablespoon lemon juice

¼ cup milk, approximately

To make the cake, preheat the oven to 350°F. Lightly butter two 9-inch round cake pans and line the bottoms with waxed paper. Dust with flour and tap out the excess. In a large bowl, cream the butter with the sugar at medium speed until light in color and texture, about 2 minutes. One at a time, beat in the eggs, then the vanilla. Sift the flour, baking powder, and salt together. Alternately, one third at a time, beat the flour mixture and milk into the creamed mixture, beating on low speed just until smooth. Transfer the batter to the pans and smooth the tops. Bake until the tops spring back when pressed in the center, 25 to 30 minutes. Cool on a wire cake rack for 5 minutes. Invert and unmold the cakes, removing the waxed paper. Let cool completely, right sides up, on the rack.

To make the frosting, in a medium bowl, beat the butter at low speed until creamy. Gradually beat in the confectioners' sugar. Beat in the lemon zest and juice, then enough of the milk to make a spreadable frosting.

Put a small dab of frosting in the center of a serving platter. Place one cake layer, rounded side down, on the platter. Spread with about ½ cup of the frosting. Top with the remaining cake layer, rounded side up. Cover the top and then the sides of the cake with the remaining frosting. The cake can be kept, covered, in the refrigerator for up to 1 day. Remove it prior to serving, and serve at room temperature.

Orange Butter Frosting: Substitute the grated zest of 1 orange and 1 tablespoon orange juice for the lemon zest and juice.

Chocolate Butter Frosting: Omit the lemon zest and juice. When the frosting is thick, beat in 2 ounces melted, tepid unsweetened chocolate.

DEVIL'S FOOD CAKE WITH CHOCOLATE-CREAM FROSTING

This deep, dark chocolate layer cake gets its name from the tinge of red in the crumb, a phenomenon that results from the effect of baking soda on the chocolate. While the cake is all-American, the chocolate-cream frosting is a staple of European bakers, who call it ganache. A simple garnish would be chocolate shavings sprinkled over the top (make them from a block of bittersweet chocolate grated on the large holes of a box grater).

MAKES 8 SERVINGS

Cake

3 ounces unsweetened chocolate, finely chopped

8 tablespoons (1 stick) unsalted butter, at room temperature

1½ cups granulated sugar

2 large eggs, at room temperature

1 teaspoon vanilla extract

2 cups cake flour

1¼ teaspoons baking soda

½ teaspoon salt

1¼ cups buttermilk

Frosting

1½ cups heavy cream

12 ounces high-quality bittersweet or semisweet chocolate, finely chopped

To make the cake, preheat the oven to 350°F. Lightly butter two 9-inch round cake pans and line the bottoms with waxed paper. Dust with flour and tap out the excess. In a double boiler insert set over a saucepan of hot, not simmering, water, melt the chocolate. Remove from the heat and let stand until tepid. In a medium bowl, beat the butter with the sugar at medium speed until light in color and texture, about 2 minutes. One at a time, beat in the eggs, then the vanilla. Beat in the cooled chocolate. Sift together the flour, baking soda, and salt. Alternately, one third at a time, beat in the flour and buttermilk, beating well after each addition until smooth. Transfer the batter to the prepared pans and smooth the tops. Bake until the tops spring back when pressed in the center, about 25 minutes. Cool in the pans on a wire cake rack for 5 minutes. Invert and unmold onto the rack,

COFFEE-WALNUT CAKE WITH
WHITE FROSTING

then remove the waxed paper. Let cool completely, right sides up, on the rack.

To make the frosting, in a medium saucepan, bring the cream to a simmer over medium heat. Remove from the heat and add the chocolate. Let stand for 3 minutes to soften the chocolate, then whisk until smooth. Transfer to a medium bowl and let stand at room temperature until the mixture is as thick as pudding, about 3 hours. (To speed the cooling, place the bowl in a larger bowl of ice water, and let stand, folding often with a rubber spatula, until cooled but not set.) Whisk until soft peaks form and the frosting is spreadable. Do not overbeat, or the frosting will be grainy.

Put a small dab of frosting on a serving platter. Place one cake layer, upside down, on the platter. Spread with about ½ cup of the frosting. Top with the second cake layer, right side up. Cover the top and sides of the cake with the remaining frosting. Refrigerate until the frosting is firm, about 1 hour. The cake can be kept, covered loosely with plastic wrap, in the refrigerator for up to 1 day. Serve at room temperature.

COFFEE-WALNUT CAKE WITH WHITE FROSTING

Cakes like this are popular in the coffeehouses of Eastern Europe.

MAKES 6 TO 8 SERVINGS

Cake
   12 tablespoons (1½ sticks) unsalted butter, at
      room temperature
   1 cup granulated sugar
   3 large eggs, at room temperature
   1 teaspoon vanilla extract
   1¼ cups all-purpose flour
   1 teaspoon baking powder
   A pinch of salt
   ¾ cup coarsely chopped walnuts

Coffee Filling
   5 tablespoons unsalted butter, at room temperature
   1½ cups confectioners' sugar
   3 tablespoons strong brewed coffee, preferably
      espresso, cooled

White Frosting
   1 cup granulated sugar
   2 tablespoons vanilla sugar, or 2 tablespoons
      granulated sugar and 1 teaspoon vanilla extract

1 large egg white, at room temperature
8 walnut halves, for garnish

To make the cake, preheat the oven to 325°F. Lightly butter and 8-inch springform cake pan and line the bottom with waxed paper. In a large bowl, cream the butter with the sugar at medium speed until light in color and texture, about 2 minutes. One at a time, beat in the eggs, then the vanilla. Sift the flour, baking powder, and salt together. One third at a time, stir the flour mixture into the egg mixture using a rubber spatula. Fold in the walnuts. Transfer the batter to the prepared pan and smooth the top. Bake until a tester inserted into the center of the cake comes out clean, about 1 hour. Cool on a wire cake rack for 5 minutes. Invert and unmold the cake, and remove the waxed paper. Let cool completely, right sides up, on the rack.

To make the filling, in a small bowl, beat the butter with the confectioners' sugar at low speed until combined. Gradually beat in enough of the coffee to make a spreadable mixture. Slice the cake into two layers. Place one cake layer, upside down, on a serving platter. Spread with the filling. Place the second cake layer, right side up, on the filling.

To make the frosting, in a medium saucepan with a candy thermometer attached, dissolve the granulated sugar and vanilla sugar in 1/3 cup water over low heat. Increase the heat to high and bring to a boil. Boil, without stirring, until the thermometer reads 240°F (soft-ball stage). Remove from the heat. Immediately, using an electric mixer (a heavy-duty standing mixer works best), beat the egg white at medium speed until stiff. Reduce the mixer speed to low, and beat in the sugar syrup, pouring it in a thin stream and avoiding the beaters. Continue beating until the frosting is very thick. Beat in the vanilla extract, if using.

Pour the warm frosting over the top of the cake, and smooth out with a metal spatula; frost the sides of the cake too, if desired. Decorate with the walnut halves. Let cool until the frosting is completely set, about 2 hours.

ORANGE SPONGE CAKE WITH BUTTERCREAM FROSTING

Sponge cakes are butter-free, so a rich, luxurious buttercream frosting is the perfect finish. This elegant cake is an excellent choice for a celebration.

MAKES 8 SERVINGS
Cake
    4 large eggs, at room temperature
    1½ cups granulated sugar
    ½ cup boiling water

    2 cups cake flour
    2 teaspoons baking powder
    ¼ teaspoon salt
Frosting
    1½ cups granulated sugar
    3 large egg yolks
    1½ cups (3 sticks) unsalted butter, at cool room
        temperature so it is soft and malleable
    Grated zest of 1 large orange
To finish
    4 tablespoons orange-flavored liqueur or orange juice
    ½ cup orange marmalade
    ½ cup sliced blanched almonds, toasted (optional)

To make the cake, preheat the oven to 350°F. Lightly butter two 9-inch round cake pans and line the bottoms with waxed paper. Dust with flour and tap out the excess. In a medium bowl, beat the eggs with the sugar at high speed until very thick and fluffy, about 2 minutes. Beat in the boiling water. Sift the flour, baking powder, and salt together, and beat into the egg mixture at low speed. Transfer the batter to the prepared pans and smooth the tops. Bake until the tops of the cakes spring back when pressed in the center, 20 to 25 minutes. Cool in the pans on a wire cake rack for 5 minutes. Invert and unmold onto the rack, and remove the waxed paper. Let cool completely, right sides up, on the rack.

To make the frosting, combine the sugar and ¾ cup water in a medium saucepan. Fit a candy thermometer on the side. Bring to a boil over high heat. Boil, using a wet brush to wash down any sugar crystals that form on the sides, until the thermometer reads 240°F (hard-ball stage). Using an electric mixer (a heavy-duty standing mixer works best) set on high speed, gradually beat the hot syrup into the egg yolks, drizzling the syrup down the sides of the bowl and avoiding the beaters. Beat until the mixture is thick and completely cooled, about 10 minutes. (To speed up the cooling process, place the bowl on a wire cake rack so the bottom of the bowl is exposed to cool air.) Adding 1 tablespoon at a time, beat in the butter to make a thick frosting. Beat in the orange zest.

Put a dab of frosting in the center of a serving platter. Place one cake layer upside down on the platter. Sprinkle with 2 tablespoons of the liqueur. Spread with the orange marmalade. Top with the second cake layer, right side up, and sprinkle with the remaining liqueur. Transfer about ½ cup of the frosting to a pastry bag fitted with a large open star pastry tube (Number 5). Cover the top and sides of the cake with the remaining frosting. Pipe eight large rosettes of frosting around the edge of the cake. If desired, press the almonds onto the side of the cake. Refrigerate until the frosting is set, about 1 hour. The cake can be kept, loosely covered with plastic wrap (protect the frosting by first inserting toothpicks in the top of the cake), in the refrigerator for up to 1 day. The cake can be served either chilled or at room temperature.

ANGEL FOOD CAKE WITH BERRY FOOL

For the times when a light dessert is in order, look no further than angel food cake. One of the nicest ways to serve it is with an accompaniment of fresh berries, with (or without) whipped cream.

MAKES 10 SERVINGS

12 large egg whites, at room temperature
1½ teaspoons cream of tartar
¼ teaspoon salt
1 cup granulated sugar
1 teaspoon vanilla extract
1 cup cake flour
Summer Berry Fool, for serving

To make the cake, preheat the oven to 325°F. Using an electric mixer (a heavy-duty standing mixer will work best), beat the egg whites at low speed until they are foamy. Add the cream of tartar and salt, and continue to beat on high speed until soft peaks begin to form. Gradually beat in the sugar, and continue beating until stiff, shiny peaks form. Beat in the vanilla. One third at a time, sift the flour over the beaten egg whites and gently fold it in.

Transfer the batter to an ungreased 10-inch tube pan and smooth the top. Bake until the top springs back when pressed lightly with a finger, 50 to 60 minutes. Cool the cake in the pan upside-down, placing the edges of the pan on inverted coffee cups to hold it, if necessary. Using a long, thin serrated knife, cut the cake away from the pan, and gently pull it out. Cut the cake wedges with a serrated knife, and serve with spoonfuls of berry fool.

RICH CHOCOLATE CAKE

The recipe for this flourless cake may well have come about when someone decided to bake chocolate mousse just to see what would happen. The result is a rich though light-textured cake.

MAKES 8 TO 10 SERVINGS

12 tablespoons (1½ sticks) unsalted butter
12 ounces high-quality bittersweet chocolate, chopped
1 cup granulated sugar
6 large eggs, at room temperature
Whipped cream, for serving

Preheat the oven to 300°F. Lightly butter and flour a 9-inch round cake pan. Line the bottom with a round of parchment paper.

In a double boiler insert set over a saucepan of hot, not simmering, water, melt the butter and chocolate. Whisk until smooth. Remove from the heat, but keep warm over the hot water.

In a small saucepan, dissolve the sugar in ½ cup water. Bring to a boil over high heat, and boil without stirring for 3 minutes. While the syrup is boiling, using an electric mixer (a heavy-duty standing mixer works best), beat the eggs on medium-high speed until they are light in color and texture, about 2 minutes. With the mixer still running, pour in the hot sugar syrup in a thin stream, taking care to avoid the beaters. Beat until the egg mixture is very thick and cooled, 8 to 10 minutes. (You can also use a hand-held mixer for this, but it will take longer. Place the bowl on a wire cake rack to increase air circulation around the bowl and encourage cooling.) Using a large rubber spatula, fold the warm chocolate mixture into the beaten eggs until completely combined, trying not to deflate the batter too much.

Pour into the prepared pan, and set in a larger roasting pan. Place in the oven, and add enough hot water to the roasting pan to come three fourths up the sides of the cake pan. Bake until the top of the cake springs back when pressed lightly in the center with a finger, 40 to 45 minutes.

Remove from the oven and let the cake cool completely, still standing in the water. (If you prefer a firmer texture, lift out of the water, cover with plastic wrap, and refrigerate for 4 to 5 hours.)

Run a sharp knife around the inside of the pan, being careful not to tear the parchment paper on the bottom. Invert onto a serving plate to unmold, and peel off the parchment paper. Cut into wedges and serve chilled, with cream.

HAZELNUT MACAROONS

These are a rustic kind of macaroon, cut into squares, not shaped into mounds. They are have soft, chewy centers with crunchy edges. If you don't have superfine sugar, you can whirl granulated sugar in a blender until it has a finer texture.

MAKES ABOUT 16 COOKIES

3 large egg whites, at room temperature
2 cups ground hazelnuts
¾ cup plus 2 tablespoons superfine sugar

Preheat the oven to 350°F. Line a jellyroll pan with aluminum foil and dust with flour.

RICH CHOCOLATE CAKE

In a medium bowl, beat the egg whites at high speed until they form stiff, but not dry, peaks. With a rubber spatula, gently fold in the ground hazelnuts and sugar until they are evenly mixed. Pour the mixture onto the prepared pan, and spread into a rectangle about ½ inch thick.

Bake until lightly browned and crisp on top, about 20 minutes. Remove from the oven and cut into sixteen squares. Carefully slide a metal spatula under the macaroons to release them from the foil, then gently turn the macaroons over.

Reduce the oven temperature to 275°F. Return the macaroons to the oven and bake until the edges are beginning to crisp, about 10 minutes. Transfer to a wire cake rack and cool completely.

BLACK FOREST CHOCOLATE CHIP COOKIES

Butter drop cookies have long been very popular, appearing as far back as 1796 in Amelia Simmon's *American Cookery*, one of the first American cookbooks. However, they reached new heights when Mrs. Ruth Wakefield added chopped chocolate bars to the dough at her Toll House Inn in Massachusetts. This version includes dried cherries, too.

MAKES ABOUT 30 COOKIES

1 cup (2 sticks) unsalted butter,
   at room temperature
¾ cup granulated sugar
¾ cup packed light brown sugar
2 large eggs
1 teaspoon vanilla extract
2¼ cups all-purpose flour
1 teaspoon baking soda
1 teaspoon salt
2 (3-ounce) bars high-quality bittersweet chocolate,
   cut into ¼-inch pieces
1 cup dried cherries

Preheat the oven to 375°F. Lightly butter two baking sheets. In a medium bowl, beat the butter with the granulated sugar and brown sugar at medium speed until light in color and texture, about 2 minutes. One at a time, beat in the eggs, then the vanilla. Sift the flour, baking soda, and salt together. Using a wooden spoon, stir into the butter mixture. Stir in the chocolate and cherries.

Drop by tablespoons onto the prepared baking sheets, spacing the cookies 2 inches apart. Bake until golden-brown, 10 to 12 minutes. Cool on the baking sheets for 5 minutes, then transfer to wire cake racks to cool completely. The cookies can be kept in an airtight container for up to 5 days.

PEANUT BISCOTTI

Peanuts are hardly a traditional biscotti ingredient, but they work extremely well. Dunk these cookies into a cup of coffee or tea, or nibble them with a glass of sweet wine.

MAKES ABOUT 30 COOKIES

8 tablespoons (1 stick) unsalted butter,
 at room temperature
1 cup granulated sugar
2 large eggs
½ teaspoon almond extract
2 cups plus 2 tablespoons all-purpose flour
1 teaspoon baking powder
¼ teaspoon salt
1 cup coarsely chopped unsalted peanuts

Preheat the oven to 350°F. Lightly butter two baking sheets. In a medium bowl, beat the butter with the sugar at medium speed until light in color and texture, about 2 minutes. One at a time, beat in the eggs, then the almond extract. Sift together the flour, baking powder, and salt. Using a wooden spoon, stir the dry ingredients into the butter mixture. Stir in the peanuts. Turn the dough onto one of the baking sheets, and form the dough into two 10- by 2-inch logs, spacing them 2 inches apart. Bake until set and golden-brown,

ALMOND SHORTBREAD

about 30 minutes. Cool on the baking sheet for 20 minutes. Using a serrated knife, cut the logs on a slight diagonal into ½-inch-thick slices. Arrange the slices on the two baking sheets. Return to the oven and bake, turning once, until crisp, about 16 minutes. Let cool completely on wire cake racks. The cookies can be kept in an airtight container for up to 5 days.

MELT-IN-THE-MOUTH LEMON COOKIES

These are the tenderest, crumbliest cookies around.

MAKES ABOUT 2½ DOZEN LARGE COOKIES

8 tablespoons (1 stick) unsalted butter, at room
 temperature
½ cup vegetable oil
Grated zest of 2 lemons
½ cup granulated sugar, plus more for baking
½ cup confectioners' sugar
1 large egg
½ teaspoon vanilla extract
2¼ cups all-purpose flour
1 teaspoon baking powder
¼ teaspoon salt

In a medium bowl, beat the butter, oil, and lemon zest at low speed until combined. Add ½ cup of the granulated sugar and the confectioners' sugar, and beat at medium speed until light in color, about 2 minutes. Beat in the egg and vanilla. Sift together the flour, baking powder, and salt. Add to the butter mixture, and mix to form a soft dough. Cover tightly with plastic wrap and refrigerate until chilled, about 2 hours.

Preheat the oven to 375°F. Using a tablespoon of dough for each cookie, roll into balls. Place on ungreased baking sheets about 2 inches apart. Dip the flat bottom of a large glass in water, then in a shallow bowl of granulated sugar, and use to flatten the balls of dough. Bake until the edges of the cookies are golden, 10 to 12 minutes. Let cool on the sheets for 2 minutes, then transfer to a wire cake rack to cool completely. The cookies can be kept in an airtight container for up to 5 days.

COCOA BROWNIES

This is a nice and easy recipe for everyone's favorite, brownies. Optional additions are 1 cup chocolate or peanut butter chips, or chopped walnuts or pecans.

MAKES 9 BROWNIES
  6 tablespoons unsalted butter
  1 cup plus 2 tablespoons granulated sugar
  ½ cup unsweetened cocoa powder
  2 large eggs plus 1 egg yolk
  ⅓ cup plus 1 tablespoon all-purpose flour
  ½ teaspoon baking powder
  ¼ teaspoon salt
  1 teaspoon vanilla extract

Preheat the oven to 350°F. Lightly butter an 8-inch square pan. In a medium saucepan, melt the butter over low heat. Remove from the heat and stir in the sugar and cocoa. One at a time, add the eggs, beating in well with a spoon. Sift the flour, baking powder, and salt together, and stir into the chocolate mixture with the vanilla. Spread evenly in the prepared pan.

Bake until a toothpick inserted in the center comes out with a moist crumb, 25 to 30 minutes. Let cool in the pan on a wire cake rack, and cut into squares for serving.

ALMOND SHORTBREAD

Almonds and a quick dip of milk chocolate add distinction to buttery shortbread cookies.

MAKES 20 COOKIES
  1 cup (2 sticks) unsalted butter, at room temperature
  ½ cup granulated sugar
  2 cups all-purpose flour
  ½ cup ground almonds
  ¼ teaspoon salt
  5 ounces milk chocolate, finely chopped

Preheat the oven to 350°F. In a medium bowl, beat the butter with the sugar at medium speed until light in color and texture, about 2 minutes. Stir in the flour, ground almonds, and salt.

On a lightly floured surface, roll out the dough into a 6- by 12-inch rectangle. Cut the rectangle in half horizontally, then cut vertically into 20 rectangles. Use a spatula to transfer the cookies to an ungreased baking sheet, placing them about 1 inch apart. With a fork, prick each cookie once in the center. Bake until lightly browned around the edges, about 20 minutes. Let cool completely on a wire cake rack.

In a double boiler insert, or a medium heatproof bowl, set over a saucepan of hot, not simmering, water, heat the chocolate until almost melted. Remove from the heat and let stand until completely melted. Cool until slightly thickened, about 5 minutes. Tilt the boiler insert so the chocolate gathers in a pool (use a rubber spatula to clean off all the chocolate on the sides of the insert). One at a time, dip each cookie about 1 inch into the melted chocolate. Lift out and drag the underside of the cookie on the lip of the insert to remove excess chocolate. Place on a waxed-paper-lined baking sheet. Refrigerate until the chocolate is firm. The cookies can be kept in an airtight container for up to 5 days.

MAPLE-OAT BARS

Be sure to use pure maple syrup for these delicious, chewy bar cookies.

MAKES 16 TO 20 BARS
  9 tablespoons (1 stick plus 1 tablespoon) unsalted butter
  ½ cup plus 1 tablespoon granulated sugar
  ¼ cup maple syrup
  3 cups rolled oats
  1 cup raisins

Preheat the oven to 350°F. In a saucepan, warm the butter, sugar, and syrup until melted, 2 to 3 minutes. Remove from the heat, and add the oats and raisins. Stir to mix. Pour into a lightly buttered 9- by 13-inch shallow pan, and spread evenly into a layer about ½ inch thick. Bake until golden, 15 to 20 minutes. Let cool in the pan for 5 minutes, then mark into bars with a knife. Leave to cool completely in the pan, and break into bars for serving. The bars can be kept, in an airtight container, for up to 5 days.

Yeast and Quick Breads

Baking bread is one of the most enjoyable tasks the kitchen has to offer. While making bread at home requires tools no more complicated than a bowl, a spoon, and a strong pair of hands for kneading, you can make use of machines to help. For example, a food processor or a heavy-duty standing mixer both do an admirable job of mixing and kneading dough. Electric bread machines, which can do everything, make bread that is acceptable to many people. However, they rob the cook of the pleasure and feeling of accomplishment provided by handmade bread. **Using Yeast** There are four kinds of yeast available: active dry yeast, fresh compressed yeast, rapid-rise yeast, and instant yeast. You can use all of them interchangeably, following certain rules of substitution. No matter what kind you use, pay attention to the "use-by" dates printed on the package, as yeast will diminish in strength with age. Store yeast in a cool place, preferably the refrigerator. It can be frozen for convenience, but freezing won't extend its shelf life.

If you dissolve yeast in water before adding it to the dry ingredients, realize that not all yeasts will become foamy—some will just look creamy. The optimum water temperature for dissolving active dry yeast and fresh yeast is 100 to 110°F. Don't use liquid that is warmer than 110°F, as the heat will kill the yeast (it is a living organism). To test for water temperature, dip in your finger—the water should be comfortably warm, but not hot. Once mixed with the other ingredients, yeast will not make dough rise unless it has been "fed" with sugar in some form: as the yeast "eats" the sugar, carbon dioxide bubbles form.

Active dry yeast is the most common variety. A ¼-ounce package holds about 2¼ teaspoons. Fresh compressed yeast can be found in 0.6-ounce cakes in the refrigerated section of well-stocked supermarkets. Some bakers feel that fresh yeast gives bread better flavor than active dry. To substitute fresh yeast for dry, use twice as much—for example, 2 teaspoons (crumbled and packed) fresh yeast for 1 teaspoon active dry yeast.

Rapid-rise yeast is becoming popular with busy cooks, as it dramatically reduces the rising times. Many bread bakers report that they cannot taste the difference when breads are leavened with rapid-rise yeast. It is best to follow the instructions on the package if you are adjusting a recipe for rapid-rise yeast, but, in general, the yeast is mixed directly with the dry ingredients and then liquid (heated until quite hot, around 130°F) is added. Some specialty stores now carry instant yeast, which has a rising power

1

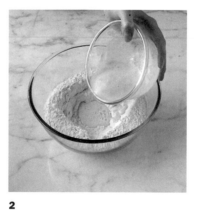

2

Making a yeast dough
1 Mix the yeast with the warm liquid, and then let it sit in a warm place until it is creamy or foamy.

2 Combine the flour and other dry ingredients in a large bowl, make a well in the center, and pour in the yeast mixture and the other liquids.

3 With your fingers, start mixing the flour into the liquid. Continue mixing in the flour in this way to make a rough dough.

3

1

2

3

Kneading and rising

1 Turn the dough out onto a lightly floured surface. Start kneading by pressing and pushing the dough firmly with the heel of your hand, stretching the dough away from you.

2 Turn the dough over on itself, rotate it slightly, and press and push it away again. Continue kneading, working with a rhythmic action.

3 After 8 to 10 minutes of kneading, the dough will be smooth and elastic. Shape it into a ball.

4 Put the dough in a greased bowl and turn the dough to coat on all sides. Cover the bowl with plastic wrap and let rise in a warm place.

5 During rising, the dough will double in size. When it has risen properly, a finger pressed down into the center of the dough will leave an indentation.

4

5

6

6 Punch down the ball of dough with your fist to knock out the air, then turn the dough out onto a work surface. Knead the dough briefly to return it to its original size and texture. The dough is now ready to be shaped.

1

2

Shaping a regular loaf

1 Pat and press out the dough into a flat rectangle or disk a little longer than the loaf pan. Roll up the dough like a jelly roll.

2 Turn the loaf seam-side down, tuck the ends under, and place in the pan. Cover and let rise again in a warm place before baking.

Shaping rolls

For **round rolls** (*top left*), on a lightly floured surface, roll each piece of dough under your cupped hand to make a neat, smooth ball.

For **knot rolls** (*top right*), roll each piece of dough under the palms of your hands into a 9-inch rope. Tie this loosely into a knot, with the knot in the center of the rope.

For **cloverleaf rolls** (*bottom left*), divide each piece of dough into three equal pieces and shape each one into a small ball. Put the three balls, side by side, in a buttered muffin pan.

Shaping pizza dough

(*bottom right*) Roll out the dough to a thin round to fit your baking sheet or pizza pan, stretching the dough with the rolling pin. Transfer to the floured baking sheet or pan. Push up the edge all around with your fingertips to make a rim.

similar to rapid-rise. Follow the package instructions if substituting instant yeast.

Kneading Kneading is important for distributing the yeast evenly and for developing the gluten contained in the flour. Put the dough on a lightly floured work surface, and fold the dough over toward you. Press with the heel of your hand, and push the dough away. Turn the dough slightly, and repeat the folding and pushing process. Keep turning and kneading the dough, with a rhythmic, regular action, until it is firm, supple, and elastic (that is, it retracts when pulled apart), 8 to 10 minutes. Resist the temptation to add too much flour during kneading—as long as the dough is not sticking to the board, there is enough flour. Some whole grain doughs will retain a slightly sticky texture, so it is especially important to hold back on adding too much flour to them, lest your bread bake up dry and crumbly.

Rising and Punching Down After kneading, form the dough into a smooth ball. Place it in a lightly buttered or oiled bowl, and turn the dough so that it is lightly coated with butter or oil all over (this will allow it to stretch and expand more easily as it rises). Cover the bowl tightly with plastic wrap. Let rise in a warm, draft-free place, such as a warm closet or an oven with a pilot light. When the dough has roughly doubled in volume, punch it in the center with your fist to expel the air. Turn the dough onto the work surface (it is not necessary to dust the surface with flour), and knead briefly until the dough is even in texture and has returned to its original volume. If the recipe requires a second kneading, shape the dough into a ball again, return to the bowl, cover, and let rise once more.

After shaping, most breads are given a final rising before baking. For loaf breads, cover loosely with plastic wrap, and let rise in a warm place until the dough almost reaches the top of the pan. For country-style bread, where the shaped dough is placed directly on a baker's peel or baking sheet, cover loosely with plastic wrap and let rise in a warm place until the dough has almost doubled in volume.

Baking To test whether a loaf is done, remove the bread from the pan (or turn a country-style loaf upside down), and rap on the underside with your knuckles—the bread should sound hollow, like a drum. If it doesn't sound hollow, return the bread to the oven (loaf breads can be placed on their sides directly on the oven rack) and bake for 5 to 10 more minutes or until they test done.

OLD-FASHIONED WHITE LOAF BREAD

There's nothing like good, old-fashioned homemade bread—slightly sweet, with a firm crumb and a thin, tender crust. This recipe makes two loaves, so you'll have one to freeze for another day, if you wish.

MAKES TWO 9-INCH LOAVES

1 (¼-ounce) package active dry yeast
4 tablespoons unsalted butter
2 cups milk
2 tablespoons granulated sugar
2½ teaspoons salt
6 cups bread flour or unbleached all-purpose flour, approximately

In a small bowl, dissolve the yeast in ¼ cup warm water, and let stand until creamy, about 5 minutes. In a small saucepan, heat the butter with ½ cup of the milk until the butter melts. Remove from the heat, and stir in the remaining 1½ cups milk to make a lukewarm mixture. Add the sugar and salt. Put the flour into a large bowl and make a well in the center. Pour the yeast mixture and milk mixture into the well. Gradually mix the flour into the liquid to make a stiff dough. Turn onto a lightly floured work surface. Knead, adding more flour as needed, until the dough is smooth and elastic, 8 to 10 minutes. Form into a ball and place in a buttered bowl. Cover with plastic wrap and let rise in a warm place until doubled in volume, about 1½ hours.

Lightly butter two 5- by 9-inch loaf pans. Punch down the dough, then divide it in half. Form each piece into a flat disk about 11 inches in diameter, then roll up loosely into a log shape. Tuck the ends under and place, seam sides down, in the prepared pans. Cover loosely with plastic wrap and let rise in a warm place until the dough has almost reached the top of the pans, about 45 minutes.

Preheat the oven to 400°F. Bake until the tops are golden-brown and the loaves sound hollow when tapped on the base, 25 to 30 minutes. Cool in the pans on a wire cake rack for 10 minutes, then unmold onto the rack and let cool completely.

Raisin-Cinnamon Loaf: Combine 1 cup dark raisins, 2 tablespoons granulated sugar, and 1 teaspoon ground cinnamon. After dividing the dough in half, roll out one portion into a 9-inch square. Brush with 1 tablespoon melted butter. Sprinkle with half of the raisin mixture, leaving a 1-inch border around the edges, and press the raisins lightly into the dough. Tightly roll up the dough, like a jelly roll. Pinch the seams closed. Place in a buttered loaf pan and cover loosely with plastic wrap. Repeat with the remaining ingredients. Let rise and bake as directed above.

WHOLE WHEAT BREAD

Breads made entirely with whole wheat flour are too firm in texture for most people, so this recipe combines whole wheat with white flour for a lighter texture. If possible, use stoneground flours (these are obtainable from health food stores) for the best flavor in this bread.

MAKES TWO 9-INCH LOAVES

2 (¼-ounce) packages active dry yeast
2 tablespoons unsulfured molasses
2½ teaspoons salt
2 cups whole wheat flour
4 cups bread flour or unbleached all-purpose flour, approximately

In a medium bowl, dissolve the active dry yeast in ½ cup warm water, and let stand until creamy, about 5 minutes. Add another 2 cups warm water, and stir in the molasses and salt. Put the whole wheat flour and 3 cups of the bread flour in a large bowl and make a well in the center. Pour the yeast mixture into the well. Gradually mix the flour into the liquid to make a stiff dough, adding more of the bread flour if necessary. Turn onto a lightly floured work surface. Knead, adding more bread flour as needed, until the dough is smooth and elastic, 8 to 10 minutes. Form into a ball and place in a buttered bowl. Cover with plastic wrap and let rise in a warm place until doubled in volume, about 1½ hours.

Lightly butter two 5- by 9-inch loaf pans. Punch down the dough, then divide it in half. Form each piece into a flat disk about 11 inches in diameter, then roll up loosely into a log shape. Tuck the ends under and place, seam sides down, in the prepared pans. Cover loosely with plastic wrap and let rise in a warm place until the dough has almost reached the top of the pans, about 45 minutes.

Preheat the oven to 400°F. Bake until the tops are golden-brown and the loaves sound hollow when tapped on the base, 25 to 30 minutes. Cool in the pans on a wire cake rack for 10 minutes, then unmold onto the rack and let cool completely.

Walnut Bread: For this variation on the bread, add ½ cup finely chopped walnuts to the well in the flour along with the liquid.

COUNTRY RYE BREAD

Rye bread—which is firm in texture, dark in color, and pleasantly sour to the taste—is especially delicious when served with sliced ham and assorted sharp cheeses.

MAKES 2 LARGE LOAVES

4½ cups rye flour

3 cups unbleached all-purpose flour

¼ cup whole wheat flour

2 (¼-ounce) packages active dry yeast

1 teaspoon granulated sugar

1 tablespoon plain yogurt

1 tablespoon salt

2 tablespoons caraway seeds (optional)

Cornmeal, for dusting baker's peel

In a large bowl, combine the rye, all-purpose, and whole wheat flours. In a small bowl, dissolve the yeast in ⅔ cup warm water, and let stand until creamy, about 5 minutes. Stir in ⅓ cup of the combined flours and a pinch of the sugar. Stir for one hundred strokes. Cover with plastic wrap and let the sponge stand in a warm place until risen and very bubbly, about 1 hour.

In another small bowl, mix 2 cups warm water with the remaining sugar, the yogurt, and salt. Stir in the caraway seeds, if using. Make a well in the flour in the large bowl and pour in the sponge and the yogurt mixture. Using a wooden spoon, mix to make a rough dough. Turn onto a lightly floured surface and knead, adding more flour as needed, until the dough is smooth and elastic, 8 to 10 minutes. (Rye doughs always retain a slight stickiness, so don't add too much flour.)

Form into a ball and place in a buttered bowl. Cover with plastic wrap, and let rise in a warm place until doubled in volume, about 2 to 3 hours. Or, even better, let rise in the refrigerator overnight. (If refrigerated, let the dough stand at room temperature for about 2 hours to warm up before proceeding.)

Punch down the dough, then cut in half. Form each portion into a ball and place on baking sheets or baker's peels sprinkled with cornmeal. Sprinkle the balls with flour. Cover with plastic wrap and let rise until almost doubled in volume, about 1 hour.

Place a baker's stone or a large heavy baking sheet on the center rack and preheat the oven to 425°F. Using a sharp knife, cut a shallow cross in the tops of the loaves, then slide onto the heated baking stone. Bake for 15 minutes. Reduce the heat to 350°F, and continue baking until the loaves sound hollow when tapped on the base, about 40 minutes. Place on a wire cake rack to cool.

BRIOCHE LOAF

This buttery, rich loaf is exquisite when toasted and served with the best jam or preserves. If you have a large fluted brioche tin, you can form the dough into the traditional brioche shape: divide the dough into a large ball and a much smaller ball. Put the large ball in the buttered brioche tin, brush with beaten egg, and set the small ball on top in the center; glaze this with egg too. Bake as for the loaf.

MAKES 2 LOAVES

2 (¼-ounce) packages active dry yeast

2 tablespoons granulated sugar

4 large eggs

⅓ cup milk, heated (100° to 110°F)

2 teaspoons salt

5 cups unbleached all-purpose flour

8 tablespoons (1 stick) unsalted butter, at room temperature

Beaten egg, for glazing

In a small bowl, dissolve the yeast and ½ teaspoon of the sugar in ⅓ cup warm water. Let stand until creamy, about 5 minutes. In a medium bowl, mix the remaining sugar with the eggs, milk, and salt.

Put the flour in a large bowl and make a well in the center. Pour the dissolved yeast and the egg mixture into the well. Gradually mix the flour into the liquid to make a rough dough. Turn onto a lightly floured work surface. Knead, adding more flour as needed, until the dough is smooth and elastic, 8 to 10 minutes. Cover the dough loosely with plastic wrap and let rest for 5 minutes.

Flatten the dough into a thick disk and dot with about 1 tablespoon of the butter. Fold the dough in half, then knead to work in the butter. Repeat the procedure, 1 tablespoon of butter at a time. It will be a little messy to do, but eventually all the butter will be incorporated and the dough will be satiny smooth. Cover and let rest for a couple of minutes, then form into a smooth ball. Place the ball in a buttered bowl. Cover with plastic wrap and let rise in a warm place until the dough has almost doubled in volume, about 1½ hours.

Punch down the dough, then knead briefly. Reform into a ball, return to the bowl, and cover again with plastic wrap. Let rise again until almost doubled in volume, about 1½ hours.

Lightly butter two 5- by 9-inch loaf pans. Punch down the dough again, then divide in half. Form each portion into a flat disk about 11 inches in diameter, then roll up loosely into a log shape. Tuck the ends under and place, seam sides down, in the loaf pans. Cover loosely with plastic wrap and let rise in a warm place until the dough almost reaches the top of the pan, about 45 minutes.

Preheat the oven to 400°F. Brush the top of the loaves lightly with beaten egg. Bake until the tops are glazed and golden-brown, and the loaves sound hollow when tapped on the base, 20 to 25 minutes. Cool in the pans on a wire cake rack for 10 minutes, then unmold onto the rack and let cool completely.

CRUSTY SOURDOUGH BREAD

Once you have a sourdough starter in the refrigerator, making a crusty, sourdough loaf is no more difficult than any other bread. However, you will need some special utensils that are essential to creating excellent rustic breads: a baking stone or heavy baking sheet, a baker's peel or a thin, rimless baking sheet, and a water-filled spray bottle. For superior results, use stoneground flours, preferably an organic variety.

MAKES 2 LARGE LOAVES
    6 cups unbleached all-purpose flour
    ½ cup rye flour
    ½ cup whole wheat flour
    1 tablespoon salt
    Yellow cornmeal or semolina, for dusting baker's peel
Sourdough Starter
    2½ cups unbleached all-purpose flour, preferably
        stoneground
    A scant ¹⁄₁₆ teaspoon active dry yeast

To make the starter, mix the flour and yeast with 1 cup water (at room temperature) to make a thick batter. Stir for 100 strokes. Transfer to a 1-quart jar and cover tightly. Let stand for 24 hours at warm room temperature; the starter will be bubbling and have a pleasantly sour aroma. The starter is now fermented and ready to use, but will be stronger in flavor and rising power if allowed to stand for up to 72 hours.

   The starter will keep for up to a week, refrigerated, (the initial batch makes 1½ cups, enough for two loaves, with ½ cup starter left over), or indefinitely if fed at least once a week. To feed the starter: after using 1 cup of starter to make two sourdough loaves, stir ½ cup water and ½ cup flour into the remaining starter in the jar. Let stand overnight at room temperature to ferment again, then refrigerate until the next use or feeding, within 1 week. If any clear liquid forms on the top of the starter, just stir it in. The sour flavor will develop as the starter ages.

   To make the bread, measure 1 cup sourdough starter using a rinsed metal cup measure. Put into a large bowl. Add 2 cups water (at room temperature) and stir to dissolve the starter. Stir in about 2½ cups unbleached flour to make a thick batter, and stir for 100 strokes. Cover tightly with plastic wrap and let the sponge stand in a warm spot until bubbling and approximately double in volume, about 2 hours.

   Stir in the rye flour, whole wheat flour, and salt. Gradually stir in enough of the remaining unbleached flour to make a stiff dough. Turn onto a lightly floured surface. Knead until the dough is smooth and elastic, 8 to 10 minutes. Form into a ball and place in a lightly oiled bowl. Tightly cover the bowl with plastic wrap,

and let rise in a warm place until doubled in volume, about 2 hours. Punch down the dough and knead briefly. Re-form into a ball, return to the bowl, and cover again. Let rise until almost doubled in volume, about 1 hour. Punch down the dough again, then cut in half. Form each portion into a taut ball. Place each ball on a large rimless baking sheet or baker's peel that has been sprinkled with cornmeal. Cover and let rise until doubled in size, about 1 hour.

   Place a baker's stone or a heavy baking sheet on the center rack and preheat the oven to 450°F. Using a sharp knife, cut a 3-inch crescent in the top of one loaf. Slide the loaf onto the heated baking stone. (Refrigerate the other loaf while the first is baking.) Spray the loaf with water. Start baking, spraying the loaf two more times at 3-minute intervals, then continue to bake until golden-brown and the loaf sounds hollow when tapped on the base, about 30 minutes in all. Let cool on a wire cake rack for at least 20 minutes before serving. Bake the other loaf in the same way.

BUTTERMILK DINNER ROLLS

These chewy rolls, with a thin, golden crust and wholesome, old-fashioned flavor, can be formed into a variety of shapes, so let your imagination go to work.

MAKES 18 ROLLS
    1 (¼-ounce) package active dry yeast
    5 cups bread flour or unbleached all-purpose flour,
        approximately
    1½ cups buttermilk, heated (100° to 110°F)
    6 tablespoons unsalted butter, melted
    2 large eggs
    3 tablespoons granulated sugar
    1½ teaspoons salt
    ¾ teaspoon baking soda
    Milk, for brushing

In a small bowl, dissolve the yeast in ¼ cup warm water, and let stand until creamy, about 5 minutes. Put the flour in a large bowl and make a well in the center. Pour the yeast mixture, buttermilk, melted butter, and eggs into the well, and add the sugar, salt, and baking soda. Gradually mix the flour into the liquid to make a stiff dough. Turn onto a lightly floured work surface. Knead, adding more flour as needed, until the dough is smooth and elastic, 8 to 10 minutes. Form into a ball and place in a buttered bowl. Cover with plastic wrap and let rise in a warm place until doubled in volume, about 1½ hours.

   Lightly butter two 9-inch round cake pans. Punch down the dough, then cut into 18 pieces. Form each into a taut ball and place in the pans. Cover with

plastic wrap and let rise in a warm place until almost doubled in volume, about 40 minutes.

Preheat the oven to 400°F. Brush the tops of the rolls lightly with a little milk. Bake until golden-brown, about 20 minutes. Remove from the pans and serve warm.

Buttermilk Knots: Form each piece of dough into a 9-inch-long rope. Tie each into an overhand knot, with the knot positioned in the center of the rope. Place on ungreased baking sheets. Cover loosely with plastic wrap and let rise until almost doubled in size. Bake as directed above.

Cloverleaf Rolls: Cut each piece of dough into thirds and form into small balls. Lightly butter 18 muffin tins. Place three balls side by side in each tin. Cover loosely with plastic wrap and let rise until almost doubled. Bake as directed.

SAFFRON BREAD

Golden saffron bread is especially good with fish soups and chowders, or with steamed shellfish such as moules à la marinière.

MAKES 1 LARGE ROUND LOAF
- 1 (¼-ounce) package active dry yeast
- ½ teaspoon granulated sugar
- 7 cups unbleached all-purpose flour, approximately
- ½ teaspoon crushed saffron threads
- 1 large egg, beaten
- 3 tablespoons olive oil
- 2½ teaspoons salt

In a medium bowl, dissolve the yeast and sugar in ⅔ cup warm water. Stir in ½ cup of the flour to make a batter. Cover tightly with plastic wrap and let the sponge stand in a warm place until bubbly and well risen, about 30 minutes. Meanwhile, soak the saffron in 1¼ cups warm water.

Put the remaining flour in a large bowl and make a well in the center. Pour the sponge mixture, saffron water, egg, and oil into the well, and add the salt. Gradually mix the flour into the liquid to make a rough dough. Turn onto a lightly floured work surface. Knead, adding more flour if needed, until the dough is smooth and elastic, 8 to 10 minutes. Form into a ball and place in a buttered bowl. Cover with plastic wrap and let rise in a warm place until doubled, about 1½ hours.

SAFFRON BREAD

Lightly butter a large baking sheet and dust with flour. Punch down the dough, then knead briefly. Form into a large ball and place on the baking sheet. Cover loosely with a lightly oiled sheet of plastic wrap, then with a clean dish towel. Let rise until the dough has doubled in volume, about 1 hour.

Preheat the oven to 425°F. Using a sharp knife, cut a shallow "X" in the top of the ball of dough. Bake for 15 minutes. Reduce the oven temperature to 350°F, and continue baking until the bread sounds hollow when tapped on the base, 30 to 40 minutes more. Let cool on a wire cake rack.

FLUFFY YEAST BISCUITS

These biscuits bake up incredibly light and fluffy, thanks to the addition of a bit of yeast. The dough can be refrigerated for up to 2 days, combining convenience with good flavor.

MAKES ABOUT 2 DOZEN
- 1 teaspoon active dry yeast
- 5 cups all-purpose flour
- 3 tablespoons granulated sugar
- 1 tablespoon baking powder
- 1 teaspoon baking soda
- 1 teaspoon salt
- 1 cup vegetable shortening, chilled, cut into small pieces
- 2 cups buttermilk, or 1½ cups plain low-fat yogurt mixed with ½ cup milk, approximately

In a small bowl, dissolve the yeast in 2 tablespoons warm water, and let stand until creamy, about 5 minutes. In a large bowl, combine the flour, sugar, baking powder, baking soda, and salt. Add the shortening, and cut into the flour with a pastry blender or two knives until the mixture resembles coarse crumbs. Mix in the dissolved yeast and the buttermilk. Knead in the bowl to make a soft, sticky dough. Cover tightly with plastic wrap, and refrigerate for at least 2 hours and up to 2 days.

Preheat the oven to 450°F. On a lightly floured work surface, knead the dough briefly. Roll out the dough into a ½-inch-thick rectangle. Using a 2½-inch biscuit cutter, cut out rounds and place on ungreased baking sheets. Knead the dough scraps together, reroll, and cut rounds until all the dough is used. Bake until the biscuits are lightly browned, 12 to 15 minutes. Serve warm.

EGGPLANT, TOMATO, AND PEPPER PIZZA

Pizza is fun to make at home. The dough can be shaped into six mini-pizzas if you prefer, and you can vary the toppings as you wish.

MAKES 6 SERVINGS

Pizza Dough

1 (¼-ounce) package active dry yeast

1½ tablespoons olive oil

1 teaspoon salt

3½ cups unbleached all-purpose flour

2 tablespoons semolina or cornmeal, approximately

Topping

1 large eggplant, sliced into ½-inch-thick rounds

3 medium ripe tomatoes, sliced into ½-inch-thick rounds

2 tablespoons chopped fresh thyme or ½ tablespoon dried thyme

5 tablespoons olive oil, plus more as needed

1 garlic clove, crushed with the side of a knife

2 medium bell peppers (1 red and 1 yellow), seeded and cut into ½-inch-thick strips

6 ounces mozzarella cheese, cut into thin strips

24 black Mediterranean olives, pitted

2 tablespoons drained capers

24 anchovy fillets packed in oil, drained (optional)

Salt, to taste

To make the pizza dough, in a small bowl, dissolve the yeast in 1½ cups warm water, and let stand until creamy, about 5 minutes. Stir in the olive oil and salt. Put the flour in a large bowl and make a well in the center. Pour the yeast mixture into the well. Gradually mix the flour into the liquid to make a soft dough. Turn onto a floured work surface. Knead, adding more flour as needed, until the dough is smooth and elastic, 8 to 10 minutes. Form into a ball and place in a lightly oiled bowl. Cover with plastic wrap and let rise in a warm place until tripled in volume, about 1½ hours.

To make the topping, sprinkle the eggplant and tomato slices with some of the thyme, and set aside. Heat 3 tablespoons of the oil in a large frying pan over medium heat. Add the garlic and cook until golden-brown; discard the garlic. In batches, cook the eggplant, turning once, until lightly browned and tender, about 5 minutes. Transfer to paper towels to drain. Heat the remaining 2 tablespoons oil in the pan. Cook the tomato slices, in batches, just until lightly browned, about 3 minutes; drain on paper towels. Add the pepper strips to the pan, and cook just until crisp-tender, about 5 minutes; drain on paper towels.

Preheat the oven to 400°F. Dust three baking sheets lightly with semolina. Punch down the dough and cut into thirds. Keep two pieces covered with plastic wrap, and put the third piece on a lightly floured work surface. Shape the dough into a ball, then flatten and roll out into a 10-inch round. Place the round on the baking sheet, and press all around the edge to make a rim. Top with one third each of the mozzarella, the cooked vegetables, olives, capers, and optional anchovies. Sprinkle with a little of the remaining thyme and a seasoning of salt. Repeat with the remaining dough and topping ingredients to make two more pizzas. Bake until the pizza crust is golden-brown and the cheese has melted, about 20 minutes. (If you can only fit two pizzas in your oven, cover the third pizza with plastic wrap, and refrigerate for up to 30 minutes, until ready to bake.) Serve hot.

FOCACCIA WITH CARAMELIZED ONIONS AND GARLIC

Focaccia can be served in any number of ways: as a snack, as a bread with meals, or even used to make sandwiches. This version uses the "sponge" method, where the dough is built upon a fermented batter to give extra flavor and moisture.

MAKES 8 TO 12 SERVINGS

1 (¼-ounce) package active dry yeast

3½ cups bread flour

7 tablespoons olive oil

¼ teaspoons salt

2 medium onions, sliced into ¼-inch-thick half-moons

2 garlic cloves, sliced

Coarse kosher salt, for sprinkling

In a medium bowl, dissolve ½ teaspoon of the yeast in ½ cup warm water. Stir in ¾ cup of the flour to make a thick batter. Beat for 100 strokes. Cover with plastic wrap and let the sponge stand until doubled in volume and bubbly, about 2 hours.

Scrape the sponge into a bowl. Add 4 tablespoons of the oil, the salt, the remaining 1½ teaspoons yeast, and ¾ cup warm water. Mix vigorously to break up and dissolve the sponge. Gradually stir in enough of the remaining 2¾ cups flour to make a stiff, sticky dough. Turn onto a lightly floured work surface. Knead, adding more flour as needed, until the dough is smooth and elastic, 8 to 10 minutes. Form into a ball and place in an oiled bowl. Cover with plastic wrap and let rise in a warm place until doubled in volume, about 1½ hours. Punch down the dough, and then cover again and let rise until doubled in volume, about 45 minutes.

Meanwhile, in a frying pan, heat 2 tablespoons of the remaining oil over medium heat. Add the onions and cook, stirring often, until golden-brown, about 10 minutes. Stir in the garlic and cook for 1 more minute. Set aside.

Preheat the oven to 400°F. Lightly oil a 10- by 15-inch jelly-roll pan. Punch down the dough, then turn it onto a lightly floured work surface. Roll out the dough into a 10- by 15-inch rectangle (if the dough seems too elastic,

FOCACCIA WITH CARAMELIZED ONIONS
AND GARLIC

cover and let stand for 10 minutes to relax, and roll
out again). Fit the dough into the pan, stretching it, if
necessary, to fit the corners. Spread the onion mixture
over the top, drizzle with the remaining 1 tablespoon
oil, and sprinkle with coarse salt. Bake until the
focaccia is puffed and golden, 18 to 22 minutes. Let
cool in the pan for at least 20 minutes. Cut into serving
portions and serve warm or at room temperature.

STICKY CARAMEL-NUT BUNS

These rolls have wonderful buttery caramel flavor
packed into every bite.

MAKES 15 BUNS
 ½ cup chopped pecans
 ¼ cup granulated sugar
 1 teaspoon ground cinnamon
 10 tablespoons (1 stick plus 2 tablespoons)
   unsalted butter
 ½ cup packed light brown sugar
 2 tablespoons corn syrup

Sweet Dough
 2 cups bread flour, approximately
 ¼ cup granulated sugar
 1 teaspoon active dry yeast
 ¼ teaspoon salt
 ½ cup milk
 4 tablespoons unsalted butter
 1 large egg

To make the sweet dough, in a medium bowl, mix
½ cup of the flour with the sugar, yeast, and salt. In a
small saucepan, heat the milk with the butter just until
the milk is warm (the butter doesn't have to melt
completely). Pour into the flour mixture, and add the
egg. Using an electric mixer at high speed, beat until
thick and elastic, about 3 minutes. Using a spoon,
work in enough of the remaining flour to make a soft
dough. Turn onto a lightly floured work surface.
Knead, adding more flour as needed, until the dough
is smooth and elastic, about 8 minutes. (The dough
should be soft and supple—do not add too much
flour.) Shape into a ball and place in a buttered bowl.
Cover with plastic wrap and let rise in a warm place
until doubled in volume, about 1½ hours.

Meanwhile, mix together the pecans, sugar,
and cinnamon in a small bowl. Set aside. Melt

2 tablespoons of the butter and set aside. In a medium saucepan, combine the remaining 8 tablespoons butter with the light brown sugar and corn syrup, and bring to a simmer. Pour the syrup mixture into a buttered 9- by 13-inch baking pan, tilting the pan to coat the bottom evenly with syrup.

Punch down the dough. On a lightly floured work surface, roll out the dough into a 9- by 15-inch rectangle. Brush the dough with the melted butter. Sprinkle with the pecan mixture, leaving a 1-inch border on the long sides. Starting at a long side, tightly roll up the dough. Cut the dough crosswise into 1-inch-thick rounds, and place, cut sides up, on the syrup in the pan. Cover loosely with plastic wrap and let rise until the buns have almost doubled in volume, about 45 minutes. (They will not fill the pan completely.)

Preheat the oven to 350°F. Bake until the buns are golden-brown, about 25 minutes. Cool for 5 minutes. Place a baking sheet over the pan, and invert with the pan to unmold the buns. Serve warm.

BLUEBERRY AND CORN MUFFINS

These muffins are chunky with corn and blueberries. For an optional crunchy topping, sprinkle them with amber, coarse-crystal raw sugar, which is available at health food stores.

MAKES 12 MUFFINS
    1½ cups all-purpose flour
    ¾ cup yellow cornmeal
    ½ cup granulated sugar
    1 tablespoon baking powder
    1 teaspoon salt
    1 cup milk
    ½ cup vegetable oil
    2 large eggs
    1½ cups fresh blueberries
    ½ cup fresh or defrosted frozen corn kernels
    1 tablespoon raw sugar crystals, for sprinkling (optional)

Preheat the oven to 350°F. Lightly oil 12 (2½-inch) muffin cups. In a medium bowl, combine the flour, cornmeal, sugar, baking powder, and salt. In another bowl, whisk together the milk, oil, and eggs. Stir into the dry ingredients, just until blended. Fold in the blueberries and corn. Spoon into the prepared muffin cups. Sprinkle the tops with the raw sugar, if desired. Bake until golden-brown, 25 to 30 minutes. Cool for 5 minutes on a wire cake rack, then unmold and serve warm.

BLUEBERRY AND CORN MUFFINS

SOUTHERN CORNBREAD

It's no trouble to serve warm bread with dinner (or breakfast or lunch) when it is as easy to make as this.

MAKES 6 TO 8 SERVINGS
    1¼ cups all-purpose flour
    1 cup yellow cornmeal, preferably stoneground
    2 teaspoons granulated sugar (optional)
    1 teaspoon baking powder
    1 teaspoon salt
    1½ cups milk
    ¼ cup unsalted butter, melted
    1 large egg

Preheat the oven to 425°F. Lightly butter an 8-inch square baking dish. In a medium bowl, whisk the flour, cornmeal, optional sugar, baking powder, and salt to mix. Make a well in the center, and pour in the milk, melted butter, and egg. Mix just until smoothly blended, and spread in the prepared dish.

Bake until golden-brown and a tester inserted in the center comes out clean, about 35 minutes. Leave to cool on a wire cake rack. Serve either warm or at room temperature, with plenty of butter.

BUTTERMILK SCONES

Britain used to be the only place where you could get a good scone, but as muffins increased in popularity in America, scones became better known. Buttermilk makes the lightest scones. If you like sweet scones, add 3 tablespoons granulated sugar to the flour.

MAKES 15 (2-INCH) SCONES
    1¾ cups all-purpose flour
    2 teaspoons baking powder
    ¼ teaspoon baking soda
    ⅛ teaspoon salt
    3 tablespoons unsalted butter, chilled
    ⅔ cup buttermilk

Preheat the oven to 375°F. Sift the flour, baking powder, baking soda, and salt into a bowl. Using a pastry blender or two knives, cut the butter into the flour until the mixture is in coarse crumbs. Add the buttermilk and mix to a soft dough.

Turn the dough onto a lightly floured work surface. Lightly roll out the dough to ½ inch thick. Using a 2-inch round biscuit cutter, cut out the scones. Gather up the scraps and knead briefly, then roll and cut more scones until the dough is used. Dust each scone with flour, and put on an ungreased baking sheet. Bake until puffed and golden, 10 to 15 minutes. Cool on a wire cake rack. Serve warm or at room temperature.

CINNAMON CRUMB COFFEE CAKE

Every cook needs a fast coffee cake recipe. Make this on a Saturday morning, and there will certainly be nothing but crumbs left by Sunday evening.

MAKES 12 SERVINGS

2½ cups all-purpose flour

1 cup granulated sugar

1 cup packed light brown sugar

10 tablespoons (1 stick plus 2 tablespoons) unsalted butter, chilled, cut into small pieces

½ cup chopped pecans

¾ teaspoon ground cinnamon

2 teaspoons baking powder

½ teaspoon baking soda

½ teaspoon grated nutmeg

¼ teaspoon salt

¾ cup plain low-fat yogurt

¼ cup milk

2 large eggs, beaten

Preheat the oven to 375°F. Lightly butter a 9- by 13-inch baking dish. In a bowl, combine the flour, sugar, brown sugar, and butter, and use your fingertips to blend until crumbly. In a small bowl, stir ½ cup of the crumb mixture with the pecans and ¼ teaspoon of the cinnamon; set aside. To the remaining crumb mixture, add the remaining ½ teaspoon cinnamon, the baking powder, baking soda, nutmeg, and salt. Add the yogurt, milk, and eggs, and mix.

Pour into the dish and smooth the top. Sprinkle with the crumb mixture. Bake until a tester inserted in the center of the cake comes out clean, about 25 minutes. Leave to cool on a wire cake rack, and serve warm or at room temperature.

HERBED BREAD STUFFING WITH ONIONS AND APPLES

Fresh herbs and a good, firm bread from your favorite bakery will make all the difference in this stuffing for the holiday bird. Allow about ¾ cup stuffing for each pound of turkey. The recipe is easy to double, or even triple, when serving a crowd.

MAKES ABOUT 8 CUPS STUFFING (ENOUGH FOR A 12-POUND TURKEY)

8 tablespoons (1 stick) unsalted butter

1 large onion, chopped

1 medium tart apple (such as Granny Smith), peeled, cored, and chopped

2 medium celery ribs, chopped

8 cups (½-inch cubes) day-old, firm white bread

¼ cup chopped fresh parsley

2 teaspoons chopped fresh rosemary or 1 teaspoon dried rosemary

2 teaspoons chopped fresh sage or 1 teaspoon dried sage

1 teaspoon chopped fresh marjoram or ½ teaspoon dried marjoram or oregano

1 teaspoon salt

½ teaspoon freshly ground pepper

1 cup chicken stock, approximately

In a frying pan, melt the butter over medium-high heat. Add the onion, apple, and celery, and cook until the onion is golden, about 10 minutes. Transfer to a large bowl. Add the remaining ingredients, and stir in enough stock to moisten. Use as a poultry stuffing, stuffing the neck and body cavities loosely. Or, place the stuffing in a buttered baking dish, cover with foil, and bake in a 325°F oven for 30 to 40 minutes.

Herb Bread Stuffing with Sausage: In a large frying pan, heat 2 tablespoons vegetable oil over medium heat. Add 1 pound bulk pork sausage and cook, breaking up the meat with spoon, until browned, about 10 minutes. Drain well. Stir into the stuffing mixture.

CORNBREAD STUFFING WITH HAM AND PECANS

Bake the cornbread the day before, crumble, and let stand, uncovered, overnight, to dry out.

MAKES ABOUT 12 CUPS STUFFING (ENOUGH FOR A 16-POUND TURKEY)

4 tablespoons unsalted butter

8 ounces smoked ham, cut into ¼-inch dice

2 celery ribs, chopped

1 cup chopped scallions

1 recipe Southern Cornbread, crumbled

3 cups (½-inch cubes) day-old, firm white bread

½ cup coarsely chopped pecans

2 teaspoons chopped fresh rosemary or 1 teaspoon dried rosemary

1 teaspoon chopped fresh thyme or ½ teaspoon dried thyme

½ cup half-and-half

1 cup chicken stock, approximately

Salt and freshly ground pepper, to taste

In a medium frying pan, melt the butter over medium heat. Add the ham and celery, and cook until the celery is soft, about 5 minutes. Stir in the scallions and cook until wilted, about 3 minutes. Transfer to a bowl. Add the cornbread, bread, pecans, rosemary, thyme, and half-and-half. Mix in enough stock to moisten, and season to taste. Use as a poultry stuffing, filling the neck and body cavities loosely. Or, place the stuffing in a buttered baking dish, cover with foil, and bake in a 350°F oven until heated through, 30 to 40 minutes.

Oyster, Ham, and Cornbread Stuffing: Omit the pecans. Shuck 1 dozen oysters, reserving their juices, and coarsely chop into bite-sized pieces. Add the oysters with the cornbread. Use the oyster juices to moisten the stuffing, adding chicken stock, if needed.

SPICED APPLE PANCAKES

Adding grated apples and spices to the batter puts these pancakes in their own special class.

MAKES ABOUT 12 PANCAKES
2 cups all-purpose flour
¼ cup granulated sugar
1 teaspoon baking powder
1 teaspoon baking soda
1 teaspoon ground cinnamon
¼ teaspoon ground allspice
¼ teaspoon salt
1 cup plain yogurt
¾ cup milk
¾ cup vegetable oil
3 large eggs
1 cup grated tart apple, peeled, cored, and grated
Butter and maple syrup, for serving

In a large bowl, combine the flour, sugar, baking powder, baking soda, cinnamon, allspice, and salt. In a small bowl, whisk together the yogurt, milk, oil, and eggs. Pour into the dry ingredients and mix just until moistened. Fold in the apple. Do not overbeat.

Preheat a greased griddle until a splash of water flicked on it sizzles and forms tiny balls. In batches, using about ⅓ cup batter for each pancake, pour the batter onto the griddle, and cook until tiny bubbles appear on the surface and the edges look dry, about 2 minutes. Turn and cook until the other sides are golden. Serve hot, with butter and maple syrup.

PECAN WAFFLES

Finely ground pecans provide a nutty flavor.

MAKES 6 (8-INCH-SQUARE) WAFFLES
Vegetable oil or nonstick vegetable oil spray, for waffle iron
2 cups pecans
2 cups all-purpose flour
½ cup granulated sugar
1 tablespoon baking powder
½ teaspoon baking soda
½ teaspoon salt
1½ cups plain low-fat yogurt
1 cup milk
4 large eggs
⅔ cup vegetable oil
Maple syrup and butter, for serving

Preheat a waffle iron. Lightly oil the waffle grids. Preheat the oven to 200°F. In a food processor fitted with the metal blade, pulse the pecans with 1 cup of the flour until the nuts are very finely chopped—the consistency should be just short of a flour. Transfer to a large bowl, and stir in the remaining 1 cup flour, the sugar, baking powder, baking soda, and salt. In a medium bowl, whisk the yogurt, milk, eggs, and oil. Add to the flour mixture and mix just until blended. Do not overbeat. Pour ¼ cup of the batter into the center of the waffle iron and close it. Bake for about 2 minutes—the waffle is done when no steam comes from the sides of the waffle iron. Transfer to a baking sheet and keep warm while making the remaining waffles. If the batter thickens on standing, thin with a little milk. Serve warm, with maple syrup and butter.

CRUMBS, CROUTONS, AND TOASTS

Fresh Bread Crumbs: Remove crusts from thick slices of day-old white bread, and cut the slices into large cubes. In a food processor fitted with the metal blade, or a blender, reduce the bread to crumbs.

Dry Bread Crumbs: Preheat the oven to 300°F. Spread out slices of bread on baking sheets and bake until golden-brown, 15 to 20 minutes. Cool. Wrap in a dish towel, and pound and roll with a rolling pin to crush into crumbs. Sift the crumbs through a sieve so they are uniform in size (pound any remaining large bits). Or, reduce the dried bread to crumbs in a food processor fitted with the metal blade, or a blender.

Croutons: Remove crusts from ½-inch-thick slices of bread, then cut the bread into ¼- or ½-inch dice. In a frying pan, heat equal quantities of unsalted butter and vegetable oil (about ¼ inch deep) over medium heat. Add the bread dice and cook, stirring and tossing, until golden-brown all over. Remove with a slotted spoon and drain on paper towels. Or, spread out the bread dice on a baking sheet and bake in a preheated 350°F oven until crisp and lightly browned, 10 to 15 minutes.

Melba Toast: Preheat the oven to 350°F. Toast medium slices of white bread. With a serrated knife, cut each slice horizontally in half. Scrape away the untoasted side, and cut off the crusts. Spread out the wafer-thin slices, untoasted side up, on baking sheets and bake until crisp and lightly browned, about 5 minutes.

Planning menus

Memorable meals come in all shapes and sizes. From a casual picnic on a perfect summer's day to a celebratory dinner party, from a quiet night at home without the children to a classic Sunday lunch with all the family. Good company, a comfortable and attractive environment, and a relaxed and happy atmosphere will all shape our experience of a meal, but generally the cornerstone will be the food itself.

The emphasis of this book, quite deliberately, is on the quality and availability of ingredients. If you know what to look for when you are shopping; if you select from produce in season that is at its best and full of flavor; and if you know how to identify the good from the average—and from the bad— then you have already won half the battle. If you are like me, you will take great pleasure in going shopping and planning a meal around just what happens to be available: you might see some wonderful cod at the fish market, and this might inspire you to buy some ginger and scallions so that you can cook it in a slightly different and more interesting way than usual.

Of course, some people prefer to go shopping armed with a list of ingredients for the dishes they have decided to cook, and here the season should give you a good idea of what to expect: asparagus and lamb in spring, for example. But whichever method you adopt, you have to consider how the various ingredients will combine in a dish, and how the various dishes will complement each other. Garlic, for example, has a capacity to overwhelm other flavors, and, indeed, it's the garlic we taste first and foremost when it is served with mushrooms or shrimp or perhaps escargots; but when you think about it, the subtlety of the mushrooms or shrimp or escargots remains and produces something quite different in each case.

Still other foods act as a vehicle for the ingredients with which they are combined. Chicken is a fine example: depending on how it's cooked, you get amazingly diverse results—Coq au Vin is vastly different from roast chicken, and neither is remotely similar to chicken that has been used as the base for a curry or one that has been cooked with soy sauce and sesame for a Sichuan Chicken Salad.

This confidence in handling and balancing ingredients is something that comes with experience, not just in cooking but in eating out at restaurants or at other people's houses. The true cook develops an instinct for combining ingredients in the right quantities to produce something exceptional: I don't know who it was who first thought of combining poultry and chocolate in a *mole* sauce—it sounds so unpromising, and yet it works wonderfully well. As culinary influences circle the world in search of new and exciting ingredients and recipes, the repertoire of combinations at our disposal becomes ever more eclectic.

The care we apply to the combination of ingredients in a single dish applies equally to the balance of dishes that makes up a meal. Only a greedy child, I suspect, would want to follow up a rich first course with an equally rich entrée, finishing the meal with a rich chocolate pudding and whipped cream. Most of us prefer to balance flavors and courses according to the time of year and the type of occasion—even, perhaps, the day of the week.

When it comes to presentation of the food on the plate, balance is equally important. Most of us, from time to time, succumb to the temptations of "comfort food," filling the plate with a favorite dish. Yet I sigh when confronted by the classic Sunday roast with its many elements on one cluttered plate. Each item on its own is often quite delicious, but they lose their individual flavors and qualities when indiscriminately heaped together. Although the faddish precision of nouvelle cuisine (the opposite extreme) is now, largely, a thing of the past, we have undoubtedly taken from it some important lessons about presentation. A good-looking dish excites the eyes and gets the tastebuds going just as surely as tempting smells from the kitchen do.

The recipes in this book cover food for every occasion, from hearty winter soups to light summer salads, from pasta dishes that can be brought to the table within minutes, to stews and roasts that repay the preparation time in their wonderful combination of textures and flavors.

Above all, food is for pleasure. In the last twenty years, we have thankfully become less concerned with pretentious social niceties: pressures of space at home and pressures on time at work mean that a dinner party is just as likely to take place around the kitchen table as it is in a separate diningroom. A sense of pleasure in the rituals of serving dinner is simply and easily suggested: homemade food, large white cloth napkins, plain knives and forks, a couple of well-shaped wine glasses each, good wine, and perhaps a bunch of fresh flowers are, for me, all the accompaniments you need.

SPRING

Squash Fritters with
Garlicky Yogurt Dip

Bouillabaisse

Strawberry Galette

***

Spring Greens Soup

Shrimp Brochettes with
Mint Butter
Spiced Basmati Rice
Peas in the Indian Fashion

Orange Sorbet

***

Apple, Cheddar, and
Pecan Quesadillas

New Mexican Pork and
Vegetable Chili
Southern Cornbread

Tropical Cream Pie

***

Artichokes Roman-Style

Garlic-Braised Lamb
Shanks with Sweet
Peppers
Soft Polenta Veneto-Style

Meringue Cups with
Fresh Fruit

***

Hot and Sour Shellfish
Soup

Glazed Cornish Game
Hens with Rice and Pine
Nut Stuffing
Stir-Fried Asparagus with
Ginger

Melon Sorbet

SUMMER

Cauliflower Vichysoisse

Baked Bluefish with
Sweet Mustard Glaze
Roasted Sweet Pepper
Salad

Apricot Tart

***

Pan Catalan

Grilled Butterflied Leg
of Lamb with Dijon
and Herbs
Green Bean Salad with
Anchovy-Cream Dressing
Rice Salad with Oranges
and Olives

Angel Food Cake
Summer Berry Fool

Pink Raspberry Lemonade

***

Olivada with grilled
baguette slices

Salade Niçoise

Raspberry and Lime Sherbert

***

Cool Cucumber and Mint
Soup

Indian Chicken Kebabs
Lentils with Rice and
Fried Onions
Indian Potato Salad with
Yogurt and Scallion
Dressing

Coconut Ice Cream

***

Ratatouille

Moules à la Marinière
Saffron Bread

French Cherry Clafoutis

AUTUMN

Bibb Lettuce with Lemon-
Poppy Seed Dressing

Sausage and Beer Gumbo
Fluffy Yeast Biscuits

Pine Nut Pralines

***

Creamy Wild Mushroom
Soup

Roast Loin of Pork
Orange-Glazed Acorn
Squash
Cajun Smothered Corn

Double-Cooked, Two-
Apple Pie

***

Arugula and Bacon Salad

Eggplant, Tomato, and
Pepper Pizza

Coffee Granita

***

Spinach and Walnut Salad

Braised Rabbit with
Prunes
Pan-Roasted New
Potatoes
Glazed Baby Carrots

Autumn Fruit Crisp

A Thanksgiving Menu

Shrimp and Corn
Chowder

Roast Turkey with Herb
and Apple Bread Stuffing
or Cornbread Stuffing
with Ham and Pecans
Green Beans with
Portobello Mushrooms
and Prosciutto
Gratinéed Onions in
Gorgonzola Sauce
Parsley Mashed Potatoes
Baked Sweet Potatoes
with Pineapple
Cranberry-Orange Sauce
Cranberry and Raspberry
Mold
Buttermilk Dinner Rolls

Pumpkin "Soufflé" Pie
Sweet Potato and Orange Pie

WINTER

Romaine Salad with
Balsamic Herb
Vinaigrette

Lasagne with Portobello
Mushrooms, Artichokes,
and Pancetta

Grapefruit Sorbet

***

Zucchini and Goat Cheese
Filo Tart

Pomegranate-Marinated
Leg of Lamb
Pan-Roasted New
Potatoes
Fennel Parmigiano

Pears in Red Wine

***

Crab Chile con Queso

Jambalaya Classique

Bread and Butter Pudding

A Holiday Buffet

Crudités with Garlic
Mayonnaise
Bistro Pâté de Campagne
with baguette slices
Herbed Carrot Pâté with
crackers
Eggplant Caviar with
pita bread

Baked Chicken with
Lemon and Olives
Sherry-Glazed Ham with
Sweet Pepper Chutney
Italian Seafood Salad
Lido Pasta Salad

Cocoa Brownies
Chocolate-Hazelnut
Shortbread
Macadamia-Coconut
Crunch

Glögg

A Holiday Dinner

Oyster Chowder

Celery and Parmesan
Salad

Roast Beef Tenderloin
Baked Stuffed Potatoes
Glazed Baby Carrots
Buttermilk Dinner Rolls

Crème Brûlée

Glossary

Cooking terms

acidulated water: water to which lemon juice or vinegar, preferably white wine vinegar, is added, and in which certain vegetables, such as celeriac, salsify, and globe artichokes, are immersed to prevent discoloration.

à la grecque: refers to a preparation of vegetables, particularly mushrooms, onions, and artichoke bottoms, cooked in olive oil with coriander seeds and other seasonings and served cold.

à la meunière: refers to a mixture of browned butter, lemon juice, and parsley served with food such as fish.

al dente: Italian term (literally "to the tooth") used to describe the texture of food, mainly pasta, when it is properly cooked and just firm to the bite.

antipasto: literally meaning "before the pasta," this is the Italian equivalent of hors d'oeuvres and may consist of slices of salami and other cured meats, vegetables grilled or marinated in oil, seafood salads, and other hot and cold dishes.

au gratin: refers to dishes that are sprinkled with cheese and/or bread crumbs, then broiled or cooked in the oven just long enough to brown the top.

baker's peel and stone: the pizza or bread dough is shaped on the large, flat, wooden peel, then slid directly onto the hot baking stone in the oven; the baking stone duplicates the baking properties of commercial brick-floored pizza ovens.

bard: originating from the old French word *barde*, which was a horse's iron armor, this means to wrap thin sheets of fat, usually pork fat, around meat, poultry, or game to prevent the flesh from drying out while roasting.

baste: to spoon cooking juices or another liquid over food while it cooks to keep it moist.

battuto: Italian term for a mixture of very finely chopped vegetables and pancetta or pork fat, which is cooked and then used for flavoring sauces, stews, and soups.

beurre manié: flour and softened butter worked together to a paste, used to thicken soups, sauces, and stews.

beurre noir: literally, in French, black butter, this usually refers to a sauce for skate and other fish, made by cooking butter until nut brown (not black, despite the name) and mixing in vinegar, parsley, and capers.

beurre noisette: butter cooked until just brown; lemon juice and seasoning may be added when used as a sauce.

bind: to add egg, liquid, or a thickening agent to a mixture to hold it together. Foods such as pâtés and stuffings sometimes require binding.

bisque: thick creamy soup based usually on seafood—especially lobster, crayfish, or shrimp—but sometimes game or poultry.

blanch: to immerse food briefly in boiling water to soften it, to keep it white, to make it easy to remove its skin (as for almonds and some fruits and vegetables), or to remove excess salt or bitterness.

braise: to cook food slowly, after it has been browned, in a minimum of liquid in a tightly covered pan or casserole.

brine: saltwater solution used to preserve or flavor meat, fish, or vegetables.

canapés: small appetizers made of bread—fresh or toasted—topped with various savory mixtures, or other small foods that can be eaten with the fingers, to be served with cocktails.

charcuterie: French term that refers to the wide assortment of pork products—sausages, pâtés, hams, etc.—sold in the specialty shops called *charcuteries*. The Italian equivalent is *salumi*, sold at *salumerie*.

chine: the backbone of an animal; this is often loosened or severed from the ribs in a roast, to allow easier carving.

choucroute garnie: classic dish from the Alsace region in France of sauerkraut garnished with sausages, pig's ears or feet, ham, pickled pork knuckles, and similar meats.

chowder: thick soup, most often of seafood, notably clams, that takes its name from the French word for pot or cauldron, *chaudière*.

chutney: From the Indian word *chatni*, a relish, cooked or uncooked, of fruits or vegetables and spices, served with curries, cold meats, and other dishes.

clarify: to remove impurities from fats—particularly from butter, for cooking—and from stocks, and consommés.

compote: fruit cooked in a sugar syrup.

confits: meat or poultry preserved in its own fat, such as *confit d'oie* (goose) and *confit de canard* (duck); or fruits candied in sugar, often with brandy added.

cream: to beat butter or butter and sugar to a light consistency.

croquette: cylindrical- or oval-shaped mixtures of chopped meat, fish, eggs, or vegetables, coated in beaten eggs and bread crumbs and deepfried.

curd: coagulated substance that is produced in milk when it is soured; cheese is made from curds.

cut in: to mix fat, usually butter or lard, with flour or other dry ingredients using a pastry cutter to give a crumbly rather than a smooth result. This technique is especially important in the making of pie crusts and biscuits.

daube: French stew of braised meat and vegetables.

deglaze: to scrape browned solidified cooking juices from the bottom of a roasting pan, frying pan, or saucepan, loosening them with the help of a liquid such as wine, brandy, or stock.

devil: to season foods with spicy ingredients, usually mustard, cayenne, and Tabasco sauce.

disgorge: to salt vegetables such as egg plant and cucumber to draw out their bitter juices; also to soak certain foods, such as sweetbreads, in water to remove a strong flavor and blood or to improve color.

dredge: to coat foods lightly with flour, confectioners' sugar, or other fine powder.

duxelles: finely chopped mushrooms, often mixed with chopped shallots or onions, sautéed in butter, and used for stuffings and garnishes.

emulsion: mixture, such as mayonnaise or vinaigrette, in which fat or oil is held in suspension in another liquid.

en croûte: refers to cooking food, particularly pâté and meat, entirely encased in pastry.

en papillote: refers to cooking food, and often serving it, wrapped in parchment paper; today, foil is often used instead.

escabèche: Portuguese, Spanish, and Latin American way of preparing fish, poultry, and game by cooking it, often by frying it, and then marinating it and serving cold.

filo, phyllo pastry: paper-thin pastry dough sheets, very similar to strudel dough. Filo is usually brushed with butter and then layered; sweet or savory fillings may be layered with the pastry or wrapped in it, before baking.

flan: open-faced pie or tart, normally cooked in a metal flan ring. In Spain and Mexico, flan is a baked caramel custard.

fumet: reduced stock, usually made with fish, used to give flavor to other stocks and sauces.

galantine: boned and stuffed poultry, game, or meat, often glazed with aspic, decorated and served cold.

glaze: to make food shiny by coating it with a sugar syrup, aspic, beaten egg, milk, melted chocolate, etc.

gluten: elastic protein found in some grains, such as hard or strong wheat; it develops with kneading and in the presence of water, and helps to trap the air bubbles produced by fermenting yeast, resulting in a light, well-risen bread.

granita: sweet Italian ice with a granular texture, flavored with fruit, coffee, etc.

infuse: to extract flavor from food by steeping in a hot liquid—the resulting liquid is an infusion. This technique is usually applied when making coffee and tea, including herbal tea. Milk is infused with onion and other flavorings for béchamel sauce or with vanilla for custard.

julienne: thin matchstick-like strips of vegetables, ham, etc., often used as a garnish.

lard: to insert strips of fat (lardons), usually pork fat, or bacon, into meat to be roasted, using a special needle, to make the meat more succulent.

lardons, lardoons: strips of pork fat or bacon.

liaison: thickening for a sauce or soup, which may be a starch such as flour or cornstarch, a mixture of egg yolk and cream, or a combination of flour and butter; in mayonnaise, the liaison is oil and egg yolk.

macedoine: mixture, cooked or uncooked, of fruits, usually, or vegetables cut into small cubes.

macerate: to steep in liquid, often liquor or liqueurs, so that the food (usually fruit) becomes infused with the liquid's flavor.

marinate: to soak raw meat, fish, or vegetables in a seasoned liquid (a marinade) to make it more tender and/or flavorful.

mezze: Middle Eastern hors d'oeuvres, often including olives, baked or broiled cheese, small spiced meatballs, cooked vegetable salads and purées, and nuts such as pistachios and almonds.

mirepoix: diced vegetables such as carrots, onions, and leeks used as a base for a sauce, soup, or stew, or, cooked in butter, as a garnish for some meat or fish dishes.

navarin: French lamb or mutton stew made with turnips, carrots, onions, and potatoes, and, in spring, with peas and young vegetables—when it becomes *navarin printemps*.

pâté: savory mixture of chopped meat or game, usually containing some pork and pork fat, which is baked, either with or without a casing of pastry, and served cold. The word is also used to cover similar mixtures that are not baked, such as smoked fish pâtés.

poach: to cook food immersed in gently simmering liquid.

purée: raw or cooked food, usually vegetables or fruit, that is finely mashed and then strained, or processed in a food processor or blender (or put through a food mill) until smooth.

quenelles: lightly cooked dumplings made of finely chopped fish or meat; a French delicacy.

quiche: a savory custard tart, originally from France's Lorraine.

ragout: French stew of meat and vegetables.

ragù: Italian term for a meat stew or sauce.

ramekin: small round baking dish for individual servings.

reduce: to concentrate or thicken a liquid by evaporation through rapid boiling.

refresh: to rinse or immerse hot food (usually green vegetables) in very cold or ice water to stop further cooking and to set the color of the food.

render: to melt animal fat, such as duck, slowly so that it separates into, mostly, liquid and particles usually called cracklings.

risotto: Italian rice dish, usually with a creamy consistency; it should be made with round Italian long-grain rice.

roux: cooked mixture of flour and fat, usually butter, used as the basis for savory sauces and soups.

sauté: to cook briskly in a small amount of fat in a shallow pan, shaking the pan to make sure that the pieces being cooked are evenly browned.

scald: to heat liquid, usually milk, to just below boiling point, until bubbles form around the edge of the pan.

score: to make shallow cuts in the surface of food. Steaks may be scored before they are grilled, broiled, or panfried to tenderize them (by cutting through the fine connective tissues), and some whole fish or skin-on fillets are scored before broiling or grilling so that they will cook through quickly and evenly.

seviche: a dish of raw fish marinated in lemon or lime juice, the acidity of which "cooks" the fish.

simmer: to keep a liquid at just below boiling point so that it remains gently "shivering."

steam: to cook food in steam, usually in a perforated container set above boiling water.

stir-fry: to cook food quickly in a little oil over high heat, stirring and tossing it constantly. A wok is the best pan for this as the rounded shape distributes the heat evenly and a lot of food can be cooked in a very little fat.

stock: well-flavored broth in which meat, poultry, or vegetables or a combination of these have been cooked. It is used instead of water in many dishes, particularly soups and sauces, to enhance their flavor.

sweat: to soften vegetables, particularly onions, by cooking them gently so that they release their juices but do not brown.

tapas: snacks or appetizers traditionally served in Spanish bars, consisting of marinated vegetables, olives, meats, slices of cold Spanish omelet, and the like.

tart: basically an open-faced pie, usually no more than an inch high, made with fruit or other sweet fillings or with savory custard mixtures.

terrine: both a deep rectangular or oval mold used for cooking a pâté, and the pâté itself. Terrines are traditionally made of earthenware, but may also be enameled cast iron.

timbale: both a cup-shaped earthenware or metal mold and the food cooked in such a mold, often rice or pasta.

water bath: also known as a bain marie, this consists of a large saucepan or a roasting pan filled with water in which baking dishes or ramekins, or saucepans or bowls, containing food are set (ideally on a special trivet). The water bath may be used to keep prepared foods hot and moist, but its most useful purpose is to ensure that certain delicate foods, such as custards and sauces, cook at a constant low temperature without drying out, curdling, or scorching. The advantage of a water bath over a double boiler is that the former ensures that the food remains moist while cooking and cooks evenly, due to the surrounding steam caused by evaporation.

whey: watery liquid that separates out when milk or cream curdles; unlike most cheeses, which are made from the curds left behind, ricotta is usually made from whey.

zest: oily, colored part of citrus peel, used as a flavoring agent or garnish.

Basic cooking techniques

making beurre manié: mash together equal parts of softened butter and flour to make a paste. Add it in small pieces to a hot sauce, soup, etc., at the end of cooking, whisking in enough of the beurre manié to thicken the liquid to the desired consistency.

clarifying butter: melt butter over low heat, then continue to heat gently, without allowing the butter to color, until the milk solids separate and sink to the bottom of the pan. Remove from the heat and allow to settle for 10 minutes, then strain through a strainer lined with moist paper towels. Clarified butter can be refrigerated, tightly covered, for weeks or frozen for months.

whipping cream: pour chilled cream into a chilled bowl. Use a whisk, a rotary beater, or electric mixer to whip the cream until it is thickened or stiff enough to pipe, according to the recipe instructions. A tablespoon or two of ice water can be added to lighten the cream. For sweetened whipped cream, add 2 tablespoons granulated sugar to each cup of cream before whipping.

making crème fraîche: stir 2 tablespoons buttermilk into 1 cup whipping or heavy cream and keep in a warm place (75 to 85°F) for about 8 hours or until thickened and slightly soured in flavor. Store in the refrigerator.

draining yogurt: put plain yogurt into a sieve lined with a paper towel (or a coffee filter) set over a bowl, or put it in a cheesecloth bag hung over the sink. Let drain at room temperature for about 2 hours, and use the thick yogurt for dishes such as the Indian raita; or let drain overnight to make a yogurt cheese.

beating egg whites: if using an electric mixer, start at low speed; or beat slowly with a whisk. When the egg whites are foamy, increase the speed (to high for an electric mixer) and beat until stiff peaks form. If adding sugar, beat the whites just until soft peaks form, then beat in the sugar gradually and continue beating until the mixture holds stiff, shiny peaks.

coating with egg and crumbs: first dip the food to be coated into seasoned flour, turning to coat both sides, and shake off excess flour; then dip into beaten egg, moistening both sides; and finally, dip into fine bread crumbs, coating both sides and pressing lightly so the crumbs adhere.

dissolving gelatin: sprinkle the gelatin over liquid as specified in the recipe and let soften for about 5 minutes, then heat gently, without stirring, until the gelatin has completely dissolved.

peeling and seeding tomatoes: cut a small cross in the bottom of each tomato, then plunge into boiling water. Leave for about 10 seconds, or until the skin begins to peel away from the cuts, then lift out the tomatoes and immerse in cold water. As soon as the tomatoes are cool enough to handle, drain them and slip off the skin. To remove the seeds, cut each tomato in half crosswise. Gently squeeze each half and shake out the seeds; remove any remaining seeds with the tip of a teaspoon or your fingers.

roasting and peeling peppers: roast, grill, or broil the peppers until the skin is blistered and blackened all over, turning the peppers as necessary. Put the peppers in a plastic bag and let cool. Peel off the skins with the help of a small knife, then core and seed.

seeding chile peppers: cut each chile lengthwise in half, then scrape out the seeds and cut away the white ribs with a small knife. Take care not to touch your eyes or any other sensitive area when handling chiles, and be sure to wash your hands thoroughly in hot soapy water when you have finished.

crushing and chopping garlic: put a cook's knife flat on top of the garlic clove and bang the knife with the side of your fist to crush the garlic slightly. This will loosen the skin, which can then easily be peeled off. Crush the garlic further under the side of the knife, to flatten it completely. Then, according to the recipe instructions, coarsely or finely chop the garlic with the knife blade.

cooking dried beans: most dried beans need to be soaked for at least 8 hours, or overnight, in cold water before cooking (lentils and split peas are exceptions). Drain off the soaking water and replace with fresh water. To cook all dried beans, simmer in plenty of unsalted water until they are tender. The cooking time will vary according to the age and dryness of the bean, but in general most need 1½ to 2 hours; split peas and lentils require less time. Add salt just before they're tender.

peeling peaches: as for tomatoes.

zesting citrus fruits: for large strips of zest, use a vegetable peeler to shave off just the colored part (the strips can then be cut into very thin shreds with a knife); for small, curled strips, use a canelle knife; for very fine filaments use a citrus zester. Zest can be grated using the fine holes of a box or other grater.

toasting and grinding nuts: spread the nuts on a baking sheet and toast in a preheated 350°F oven, stirring occasionally, until golden brown; or toast in a dry frying pan over moderate heat, stirring frequently. Grind nuts in a nut mill, clean coffee grinder or a food processor, taking care not to overgrind the nuts to an oily paste (adding a little sugar or flour will help prevent this).

making coconut milk: mix equal parts grated fresh or dried (desiccated) coconut and boiling water, then let cool; strain through cheesecloth, squeezing to extract all the liquid. Canned coconut milk will normally separate into thin milk with a thick layer at the top (which can be spooned off to use as coconut cream). For a thicker coconut milk, shake the can well before opening.

Index

ACKNOWLEDGMENTS

The Authors would like to thank the following:
Sophie Grigson, Dee MacQuillan and Robert Neild

The Publisher would like to thank the following for their invaluable assistance
in preparing this book:

Lewis Esson, for first suggesting a new edition of *The Cook Book*

Editorial
Tessa Clayton, Indexing Specialists, Jenny Linford, Kate Quarry, Jane Royston, Susanna Tee,
Kate Whiteman, Sarah Widdecombe, Simon Willis, Jeni Wright.

Photography and illustration
Meg Jansz (recipe home economist), Róisín Neild (recipe stylist), Amanda Hills (ingredients buyer and stylist),
Dave King and Allison Tyler (additional ingredients photography), Nato Welton (equipment stylist),
Denys Ovenden (new fish artworks), Susan Campbell/King and King (meat cut artworks).

Ingredients
City Herbs, New Spitalfields Market; C. Lidgates, London W11; Jarvis & Co., Kingston; R.A. Bevan & Son, Kingston;
Harrods Food Halls; Brogdale Horticultural Trust; Wild Harvest Mushrooms, London; Henry Doubleday Research Association;
Harvey Nichols Food Halls; Selfridges Food Halls; Idencroft Herb Nursery, Staplehurst; Yaohan Oriental Supermarket,
Colindale; G.M. & E.A. Innes, Newmachar, Aberdeen; Winterwood Soft Fruit Farm, Nr Maidstone; Remfresh, Colchester;
E.W. King's, Chertsey; Garson Farm, Esher; Potato Marketing Board; Vivians, Richmond; Mrs Tee's Wild Mushrooms,
Haslemere; C.R. Upton Pumpkins & Squashes, Arundel; Tawana Supermarket, London; Syon Park Garden Centre.

Equipment and props
Braun, The Conran Shop, Le Creuset, Divertimenti, Kenwood, Krups, Petra (Beam Group Ltd), Sabatier, Salter.

Contributors to the original edition of the book
Maria Kroll, Ann Sayer (contributors), Clive Corless (photography), Ingrid Jacob, Andrew Davidson, Paul Brooks (illustrators).